interchange

THIRD EDITION

TEACHER'S EDITION

Jack C. Richards

with Jonathan Hull and Susan Proctor

Interchange Third Edition Teacher's Edition revision prepared by Kate Cory–Wright

CAMBRIDGE UNIVERSITY PRESS
Cambridge, New York, Melbourne, Madrid, Cape Town, Singapore, São Paulo, Delhi

Cambridge University Press
32 Avenue of the Americas, New York, NY 10013–2473, USA

www.cambridge.org
Information on this title: www.cambridge.org/9780521602037

First published 2005
8th printing 2008

Interchange Third Edition Teacher's Edition 2 has been developed from *New Interchange* Teacher's Edition 2, first published by Cambridge University Press in 1998

Printed in Hong Kong, China, by Golden Cup Printing Company Limited

A catalog record for this publication is available from the British Library

ISBN 978-0-521-60203-7 Teacher's Edition

Art direction, book design, photo research, and layout services: Adventure House, NYC
Audio production: Richard LePage & Associates

Contents

Plan of Book 2

Titles/Topics	Speaking	Grammar
UNIT 1 PAGES 2-7		
A time to remember People; childhood; memories	Introducing yourself; talking about yourself; exchanging personal information; remembering your childhood; asking about someone's childhood	Past tense; *used to* for habitual actions
UNIT 2 PAGES 8-13		
Caught in the rush Transportation; transportation problems; city services	Talking about transportation and transportation problems; evaluating city services; asking for and giving information	Adverbs of quantity with count and noncount nouns: *too many*, *too much*, *fewer*, *less*, *more*, *not enough*; indirect questions from Wh-questions
PROGRESS CHECK PAGES 14-15		
UNIT 3 PAGES 16-21		
Time for a change! Houses and apartments; lifestyle changes; wishes	Describing positive and negative features; making comparisons; talking about lifestyle changes; expressing wishes	Evaluations and comparisons with adjectives: *not . . . enough*, *too*, *(not) as . . . as*; evaluations and comparisons with nouns: *not enough . . .* , *too much/many . . .* , *(not) as much/many . . . as*; *wish*
UNIT 4 PAGES 22-27		
I've never heard of that! Food; recipes; instructions; cooking methods	Talking about food; expressing likes and dislikes; describing a favorite snack; giving instructions	Simple past vs. present perfect; sequence adverbs: *first*, *then*, *next*, *after that*, *finally*
PROGRESS CHECK PAGES 28-29		
UNIT 5 PAGES 30-35		
Going places Travel; vacations; plans	Describing vacation plans; giving travel advice; planning a vacation	Future with *be going to* and *will*; modals for necessity and suggestion: *must*, *need to*, *(don't) have to*, *better*, *ought to*, *should (not)*
UNIT 6 PAGES 36-41		
OK. No problem! Complaints; household chores; requests; excuses; apologies	Making requests; accepting and refusing requests; complaining; apologizing; giving excuses	Two-part verbs; *will* for responding to requests; requests with modals and *Would you mind . . . ?*
PROGRESS CHECK PAGES 42-43		
UNIT 7 PAGES 44-49		
What's this for? Technology; instructions	Describing technology; giving instructions; giving suggestions	Infinitives and gerunds for uses and purposes; imperatives and infinitives for giving suggestions
UNIT 8 PAGES 50-55		
Let's celebrate! Holidays; festivals; customs; celebrations	Describing holidays, festivals, customs, and special events	Relative clauses of time; adverbial clauses of time: *when*, *after*, *before*
PROGRESS CHECK PAGES 56-57		

Pronunciation/Listening	Writing/Reading	Interchange Activity
Reduced form of *used to* Listening to people talk about their past *Self-study*: Listening to people discuss their favorite childhood memories	Writing a paragraph about your childhood "Nicole Kidman: New Hollywood Royalty": Reading about an actress's career	"Class profile": Finding out about a classmate's childhood
Syllable stress Listening to a description of a transportation system *Self-study*: Listening to people ask for information	Writing a letter to the editor "New Ways of Getting Around": Reading about new transportation inventions	"Tourism campaign": Suggesting ways to attract tourists to a city
Unpronounced vowels Listening to people talk about capsule hotels *Self-study*: Listening to people ask and answer questions about apartments for rent	Writing an e-mail describing an apartment "Break Those Bad Habits": Reading about ways to end bad habits	"Wishful thinking": Finding out about a classmate's wishes
Consonant clusters Listening to descriptions of foods *Self-study*: Listening to people talk about food	Writing a recipe "Food and Mood": Reading about how food affects the way we feel	"Risky business": Collecting personal information from classmates
Linked sounds with /w/ and /y/ Listening to travel advice *Self-study*: Listening to people discuss vacation plans	Writing travel suggestions "Getting Away From It All": Reading tips from an expert backpacker	"Fun vacations": Deciding on a trip
Stress in two-part verbs Listening to results of a survey *Self-study*: Listening to people make requests	Writing a set of guidelines "Neighbor vs. Neighbor": Reading about ways to deal with neighbors	"That's no excuse!": Apologizing and making excuses
Syllable stress Listening to a radio program; listening to people give advice *Self-study*: Listening to people discuss computers	Writing a note giving instructions "A Day in Your Life – In the Year 2020": Reading about life in the future	"Talk radio": Giving advice to classmates
Stress and rhythm Listening to a description of Carnaval *Self-study*: Listening to someone talk about Halloween	Writing a travel guide "Unique Customs": Reading about holidays and unusual customs	"Once in a blue moon": Finding out how classmates celebrate special events

Titles/Topics	Speaking	Grammar
UNIT 9 PAGES 58-63		
Back to the future Life in the past, present, and future; changes and contrasts; consequences	Talking about change; comparing time periods; describing possibilities	Time contrasts; conditional sentences with *if* clauses
UNIT 10 PAGES 64-69		
I don't like working on weekends! Abilities and skills; job preferences; personality traits; careers	Describing abilities and skills; talking about job preferences; describing personality traits	Gerunds; short responses; clauses with *because*
PROGRESS CHECK PAGES 70-71		
UNIT 11 PAGES 72-77		
It's really worth seeing! Landmarks and monuments; world knowledge	Talking about landmarks and monuments; describing countries; discussing facts	Passive with *by* (simple past); passive without *by* (simple present)
UNIT 12 PAGES 78-83		
It could happen to you! Information about someone's past; recent past events	Asking about someone's past; describing recent experiences	Past continuous vs. simple past; present perfect continuous
PROGRESS CHECK PAGES 84-85		
UNIT 13 PAGES 86-91		
Good book, terrible movie! Entertainment; movies and books; reactions and opinions	Describing movies and books; talking about actors and actresses; asking for and giving reactions and opinions	Participles as adjectives; relative clauses
UNIT 14 PAGES 92-97		
So that's what it means! Nonverbal communication; gestures and meanings; signs; drawing conclusions	Interpreting body language; explaining gestures and meanings; describing emotions; asking about signs and meanings	Modals and adverbs: *might*, *may*, *could*, *must*, *maybe*, *perhaps*, *possibly*, *probably*, *definitely*; permission, obligation, and prohibition
PROGRESS CHECK PAGES 98-99		
UNIT 15 PAGES 100-105		
What would you do? Money; hopes; predicaments; speculations	Speculating about past and future events; describing a predicament; giving advice and suggestions	Unreal conditional sentences with *if* clauses; past modals
UNIT 16 PAGES 106-111		
What's your excuse? Requests; excuses; invitations	Reporting what people say; making requests; making invitations and excuses	Reported speech: requests; reported speech: statements
PROGRESS CHECK PAGES 112-113		
SELF-STUDY		

Pronunciation/Listening	Writing/Reading	Interchange Activity
Intonation in statements with time phrases Listening to people talk about changes *Self-study*: Listening to people discuss technology	Writing a description of a person "Are You in Love?": Reading about the signs of being in love	"Consider the consequences": Agreeing and disagreeing with classmates
Unreleased and released /t/ and /d/ Listening to people talk about their job preferences *Self-study*: Listening to a student election debate	Writing a cover letter for a job application "Find the Job That's Right for You!": Reading about how to find the perfect job	"Dream job": Deciding which job to apply for
The letter *o* Listening to descriptions of monuments; listening for information about a country *Self-study*: Listening for information about the Statue of Liberty	Writing a guidebook introduction "A Guide to Unusual Museums": Reading about interesting museums	"Who is this by?": Sharing information about famous works
Contrastive stress in responses Listening to people talk about recent experiences *Self-study*: Listening to people talk about events in their careers	Writing a short story "Child Prodigies": Reading about gifted children	"Life is like a game!": Playing a board game
Emphatic stress Listening for opinions; listening to a movie review *Self-study*: Listening to people talk about a book	Writing a movie review "The Magic of Potter": Reading about an author's career	"Famous faces": Asking classmates' opinions about movies and TV shows
Pitch Listening to people talk about the meanings of signs *Self-study*: Listening to people discuss street signs	Writing a list of rules "Pearls of Wisdom": Reading about proverbs	"What's going on?": Interpreting body language
Reduction of *have* Listening to people talk about predicaments; listening to a radio talk show *Self-study*: Listening to people describe situations	Writing a letter to an advice columnist "Ask Amy": Reading an advice column	"Do the right thing!": Deciding what to do in a difficult situation
Reduction of *had* and *would* Listening for excuses; listening to voice mail messages *Self-study*: Listening to a telephone conversation	Writing a voice mail message "The Truth About Lying": Reading about "white lies"	"Excuses, excuses": Making up excuses

The new edition

Interchange Third Edition is a fully revised edition of ***New Interchange***, the world's most successful series for adult and young adult learners of English. Written in American English, the course reflects the fact that English is the major language of international communication and is not limited to any one country, region, or culture.

The course has been thoroughly revised to reflect the most recent approaches to language teaching and learning. It remains the innovative series teachers and students have grown to love, while incorporating suggestions from teachers and students all over the world. This edition offers updated content in every unit, additional grammar practice, and more opportunities to develop speaking and listening skills.

SYLLABUS AND APPROACH

Interchange Third Edition uses high-interest themes to integrate speaking, grammar, vocabulary, pronunciation, listening, reading, and writing. There is a strong focus on both accuracy and fluency. The underlying philosophy of the course remains that language is best learned when it is used for meaningful communication.

Topics

The course covers contemporary, real-world topics that are relevant to students' lives (e.g., free time, entertainment). Students have background knowledge and experience with these topics, so they can share opinions and information productively. In addition, cultural information stimulates cross-cultural comparison and discussion.

Functions

A functional syllabus parallels the grammar syllabus in the course. For example, at the same time students learn *Do you . . . ?* questions in Level 1 (e.g., *Do you like jazz?*), they learn how to express likes and dislikes (e.g., *I love it. I can't stand it.*). Throughout the course, students learn useful functions, such as how to introduce themselves, or agree and disagree. Each level presents 50 to 65 functions.

Grammar

Interchange Third Edition has a graded grammar syllabus. Intro Level presents the basic structures for complete beginners, and Level 1 reviews and expands on them. Levels 2 and 3 present more advanced structures, such as passives and conditionals. The course views meaning, form, and use as the three interacting dimensions of language. First, students notice the new grammar in context in the *Conversations* or *Perspectives*. Then they learn and practice using the grammar forms in the *Grammar Focuses*. While they initially practice grammar in a controlled way, students soon move on to freer tasks that lead toward fluency. In other words, students acquire new grammar by using it, and grammar is a means to an end – communicative competence.

Vocabulary

Vocabulary development plays a key role in ***Interchange Third Edition***. Productive vocabulary (vocabulary students are encouraged to use) is presented mainly in *Word Powers* and *Snapshots*. Receptive vocabulary is introduced primarily in *Readings* and *Listenings*. In *Word Powers*, students typically categorize new vocabulary, to reflect how the mind organizes new words. Then they internalize the new vocabulary by using it in a personalized way. Photocopiable *Language summaries* in the Teacher's Edition provide lists of productive vocabulary and expressions for each unit. Each level teaches a productive vocabulary of about 1,000 to 1,300 words.

Speaking

Speaking skills are a central focus of ***Interchange Third Edition***, with an emphasis on natural, conversational language. The *Discussion*, *Role Play*, and *Speaking* exercises, as well as the *Interchange activities*, provide speaking opportunities that systematically build oral fluency. In addition, the *Conversations* illustrate different speaking strategies, such as how to open and close conversations, ask follow-up questions, take turns, and use filler words (e.g., *well*, *you know*, *so*). Moreover, almost all other exercises offer fun, personalized speaking practice and opportunities to share opinions.

Listening

The listening syllabus emphasizes task-based listening activities and incorporates both top-down processing skills (e.g., making predictions) and bottom-up processing skills (e.g., decoding individual words). The *Listening* exercises for all levels provide focus questions or tasks that give students a purpose for listening, while graphic organizers such as charts provide note-taking support. Moreover, most *Conversations* in Levels 1 to 3 provide follow-up listening tasks (e.g., *Listen to the rest of the conversation. What happened?*). Additional listening practice is provided in the Self-study section at the back of the Student's Book.

Reading

In the *Reading* exercises, students read a variety of text types (e.g., newspaper and magazine articles, surveys, letters) for different purposes. For example, they skim the texts for main ideas, scan them for specific information, or read them carefully for details. Then they complete exercises that help develop reading strategies and skills, such as inferencing and guessing meaning from context. They also discuss their opinions about the readings.

Writing

Levels 1 to 3 include a writing syllabus. In the *Writing* exercises, students write a variety of real-world text types (e.g., e-mail messages, postcards, memos). These exercises recycle and review the themes, vocabulary, and grammar in the unit. Students typically look at writing models before they begin writing. They use their experiences and ideas in their writing, and then share their writing with their classmates.

Pronunciation

The pronunciation syllabus focuses on important features of spoken English, such as word stress, intonation, and linked sounds. Every unit includes a *Pronunciation* exercise, the approach being that students benefit most from practicing a little pronunciation on a regular basis. In each unit, students typically notice and then practice a pronunciation feature linked to the new grammar or vocabulary.

CUSTOMIZATION

It's important for teachers to adapt the course materials to the needs, interests, ages, and learning styles of their students. The Teacher's Edition provides numerous additional resources that help teachers tailor their classes for maximum learning and enjoyment. For example, *Games* provide stimulating and fun ways to review or practice skills. In addition, *Fresh ideas* provide stimulating and fun techniques for presenting and reviewing the exercises. Moreover, there are *Photocopiables* for one exercise in every unit, or handouts for innovative supplementary activities.

ASSESSMENT

Interchange Third Edition has a complete and flexible assessment program. The *Progress checks* in the Student's Book encourage students to self-assess their progress in key skill areas after every two units. *Oral quizzes* and *Written quizzes* in the Teacher's Edition provide more formal assessment. In addition, the *Placement and Evaluation Package* is an indispensable tool for placing students at the correct level and regularly evaluating progress.

Student's Book overview

Every unit in ***Interchange Third Edition*** contains two cycles, each of which has a specific topic, grammar point, and function. The units in Level 2 contain a variety of exercises, including a Snapshot, Conversation, Pronunciation, Grammar Focus, Listening, Speaking (or Discussion/Role Play), Interchange Activity, Word Power, Perspectives, Writing, and Reading. The sequence of these exercises differs from unit to unit. Here is a sample unit from Level 2.

CYCLE 1 (Exercises 1–8)

Topic: *food*
Grammar: *simple past vs. present perfect*
Function: *express preferences*

4 I've never heard of that!

1 *SNAPSHOT*

Favorite Ethnic Dishes

KOREA	BRAZIL	SINGAPORE	LATIN AMERICA
Bulgogi	Feijoada	Fish Head Curry	Ceviche
Beef marinated with soy sauce and other spices	A dish made of black beans, garlic, spices, and pork	A dish made from a fish head cooked in a rich curry sauce	Raw seafood marinated in lime juice and chili peppers

Sources: Fodor's South America; Fodor's Southeast Asia; www.globalgourmet.com

Which dishes are made with meat? with fish or seafood?
Have you ever tried any of these dishes? Which ones would you like to try?
What ethnic foods are popular in your country?

2 *CONVERSATION* Have you ever . . . ?

A Listen and practice.

Steve: Hey, this sounds strange – snails with garlic. Have you ever eaten snails?
Kathy: Yes, I have. I had them here just last week.
Steve: Did you like them?
Kathy: Yes, I did. They were delicious! Why don't you try some?
Steve: No, I don't think so.
Waiter: Have you decided on an appetizer yet?
Kathy: Yes. I'll have a small order of the snails, please.
Waiter: And you, sir?
Steve: I think I'll have the fried brains.
Kathy: Fried brains? I've never heard of that! It sounds scary.

B Listen to the rest of the conversation. How did Steve like the fried brains? What else did he order?

22

SNAPSHOT

- Introduces the unit or cycle topic
- Presents vocabulary for discussing the topic
- Uses real-world information
- Provides personalized guided discussion questions

CONVERSATION

- Provides structured listening and speaking practice
- Introduces the meaning and use of the Cycle 1 grammar in context
- Uses pictures to set the scene and illustrate new vocabulary
- Provides follow-up listening tasks

PRONUNCIATION

- Provides controlled practice in recognizing and producing sounds linked to the cycle grammar
- Promotes extended or personalized pronunciation practice

GRAMMAR FOCUS

- Summarizes the Cycle 1 grammar
- Includes audio recordings of the grammar
- Provides controlled grammar practice in realistic contexts, such as short conversations
- Promotes freer, more personalized speaking practice

LISTENING

- Provides pre-listening focus tasks or questions
- Develops a variety of listening skills, such as listening for main ideas and details

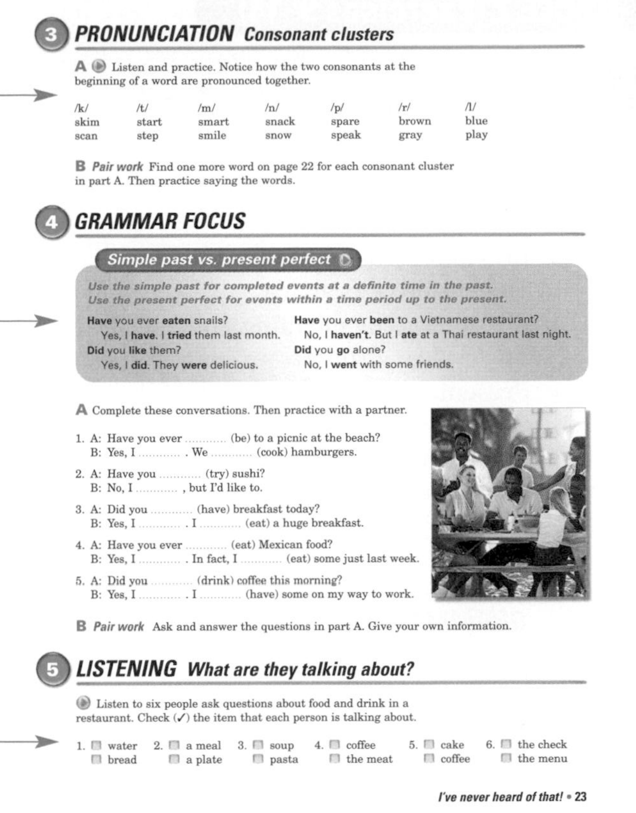

3 PRONUNCIATION Consonant clusters

A Listen and practice. Notice how the two consonants at the beginning of a word are pronounced together.

/k/	/t/	/m/	/n/	/p/	/r/	/l/
skim	start	smart	snack	spare	brown	blue
scan	step	smile	snow	speak	gray	play

B *Pair work* Find one more word on page 22 for each consonant cluster in part A. Then practice saying the words.

4 GRAMMAR FOCUS

Simple past vs. present perfect

Use the simple past for completed events at a definite time in the past.
Use the present perfect for events within a time period up to the present.

Have you ever **eaten** snails?
Yes, I **have.** I **tried** them last month.
Did you **like** them?
Yes, I **did.** They **were** delicious.

Have you ever **been** to a Vietnamese restaurant?
No, I **haven't.** But I **ate** at a Thai restaurant last night.
Did you **go** alone?
No, I **went** with some friends.

A Complete these conversations. Then practice with a partner.

1. A: Have you ever .... (be) to a picnic at the beach?
   B: Yes, I .... We .... (cook) hamburgers.
2. A: Have you .... (try) sushi?
   B: No, I .... , but I'd like to.
3. A: Did you .... (have) breakfast today?
   B: Yes, I .... I .... (eat) a huge breakfast.
4. A: Have you ever .... (eat) Mexican food?
   B: Yes, I .... In fact, I .... (eat) some just last week.
5. A: Did you .... (drink) coffee this morning?
   B: Yes, I .... I .... (have) some on my way to work.

B *Pair work* Ask and answer the questions in part A. Give your own information.

5 LISTENING What are they talking about?

Listen to six people ask questions about food and drink in a restaurant. Check (✓) the item that each person is talking about.

1. ☐ water ☐ bread
2. ☐ a meal ☐ a plate
3. ☐ soup ☐ pasta
4. ☐ coffee ☐ the meat
5. ☐ cake ☐ coffee
6. ☐ the check ☐ the menu

I've never heard of that! • 23

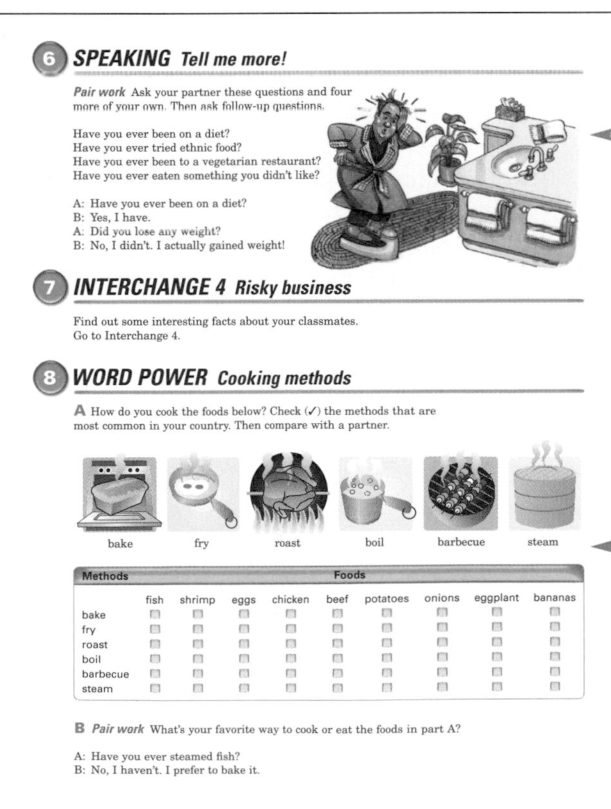

6 SPEAKING Tell me more!

Pair work Ask your partner these questions and four more of your own. Then ask follow-up questions.

Have you ever been on a diet?
Have you ever tried ethnic food?
Have you ever been to a vegetarian restaurant?
Have you ever eaten something you didn't like?

A: Have you ever been on a diet?
B: Yes, I have.
A: Did you lose any weight?
B: No, I didn't. I actually gained weight!

7 INTERCHANGE 4 Risky business

Find out some interesting facts about your classmates. Go to Interchange 4.

8 WORD POWER Cooking methods

A How do you cook the foods below? Check (✓) the methods that are most common in your country. Then compare with a partner.

bake fry roast boil barbecue steam

Methods	fish	shrimp	eggs	chicken	beef	potatoes	onions	eggplant	bananas
bake	☐	☐	☐	☐	☐	☐	☐	☐	☐
fry	☐	☐	☐	☐	☐	☐	☐	☐	☐
roast	☐	☐	☐	☐	☐	☐	☐	☐	☐
boil	☐	☐	☐	☐	☐	☐	☐	☐	☐
barbecue	☐	☐	☐	☐	☐	☐	☐	☐	☐
steam	☐	☐	☐	☐	☐	☐	☐	☐	☐

(Foods)

B *Pair work* What's your favorite way to cook or eat the foods in part A?

A: Have you ever steamed fish?
B: No, I haven't. I prefer to bake it.

24 • *Unit 4*

SPEAKING

- Provides communicative tasks that help develop oral fluency
- Recycles grammar and vocabulary in the cycle
- Includes pair work, group work, and class activities

WORD POWER

- Presents vocabulary related to the unit topic
- Provides practice categorizing vocabulary
- Promotes freer, more personalized practice

CYCLE 2 (Exercises 9–14)

Topic: *recipes*
Grammar: *sequence adverbs*
Function: *give instructions*

PERSPECTIVES

- Provides structured listening and speaking practice
- Introduces the meaning and use of the Cycle 2 grammar in context
- Presents people's opinions and experiences about a topic
- Introduces useful expressions and discourse features

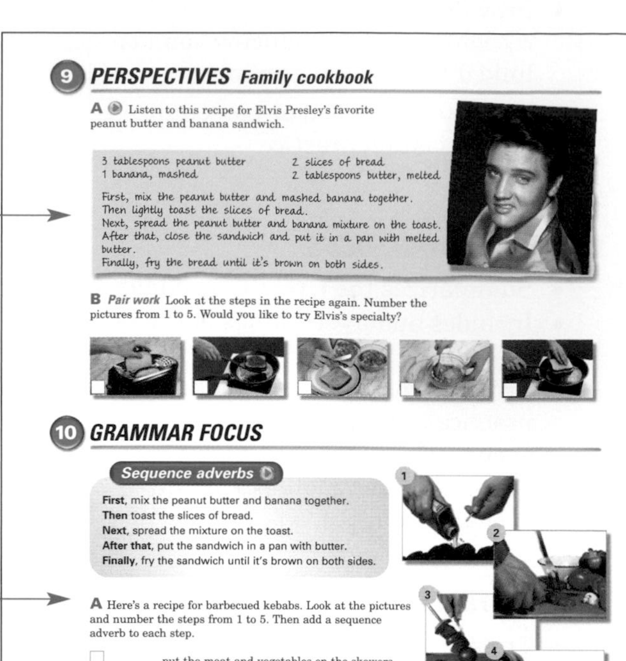

GRAMMAR FOCUS

- Summarizes the Cycle 2 grammar
- Presents examples from the previous Conversation or Perspectives
- Provides controlled grammar practice in realistic contexts

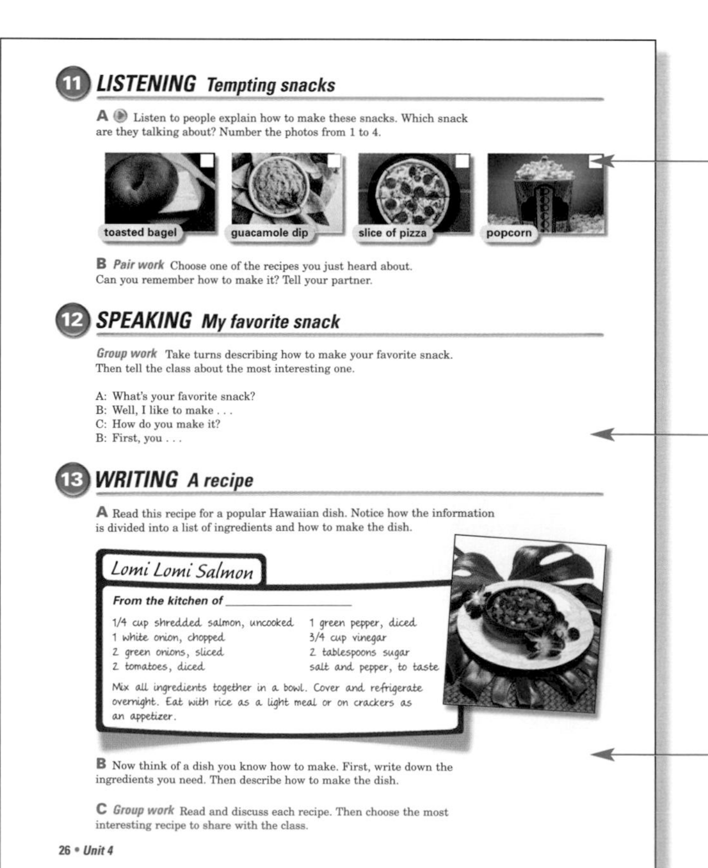

LISTENING

- Provides pre-listening focus tasks or questions
- Develops a variety of listening skills, such as listening for main ideas and details
- Includes post-listening speaking tasks

SPEAKING

- Provides communicative tasks that help develop oral fluency
- Recycles grammar and vocabulary in the cycle
- Includes pair work, group work, and class activities

WRITING

- Provides a model writing sample
- Develops skills in writing different texts, such as postcards and e-mail messages
- Reinforces the vocabulary and grammar in the cycle or unit

READING

- Presents a variety of text types
- Introduces the text with a pre-reading task
- Develops a variety of reading skills, such as reading for main ideas, reading for details, and inferencing
- Promotes discussion that involves personalization and analysis

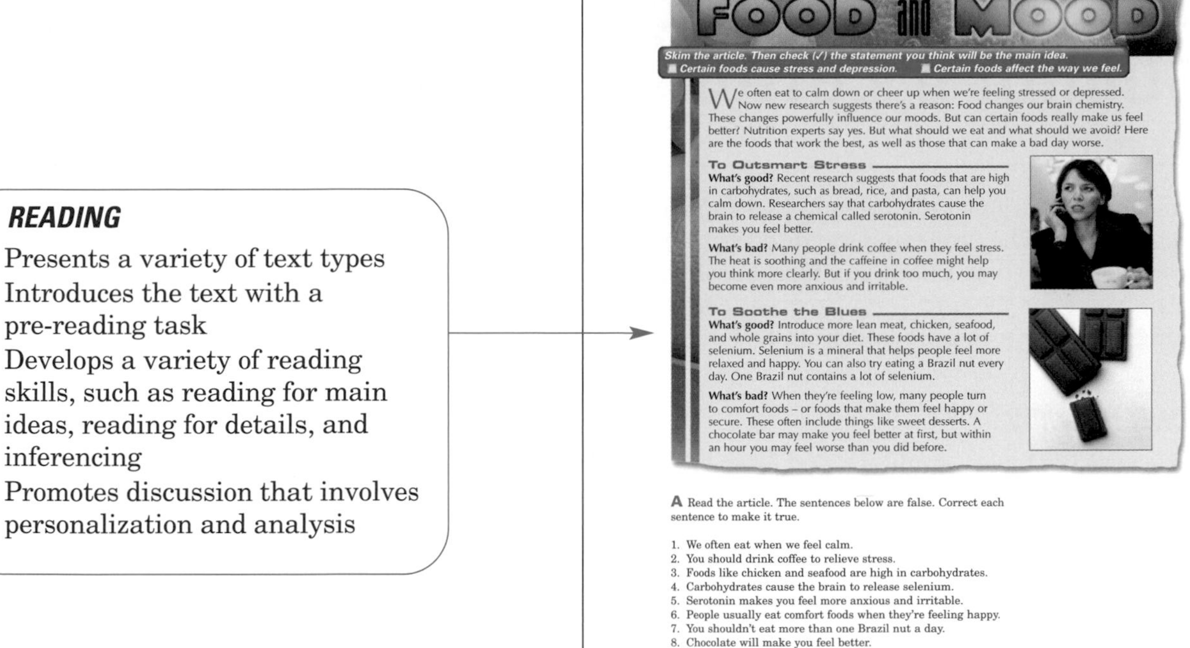

14 READING

FOOD and MOOD

Skim the article. Then check (✓) the statement you think will be the main idea.
■ *Certain foods cause stress and depression.* ■ *Certain foods affect the way we feel.*

We often eat to calm down or cheer up when we're feeling stressed or depressed. Now new research suggests there's a reason: Food changes our brain chemistry. These changes powerfully influence our moods. But can certain foods really make us feel better? Nutrition experts say yes. But what should we eat and what should we avoid? Here are the foods that work the best, as well as those that can make a bad day worse.

To Outsmart Stress

What's good? Recent research suggests that foods that are high in carbohydrates, such as bread, rice, and pasta, can help you calm down. Researchers say that carbohydrates cause the brain to release a chemical called serotonin. Serotonin makes you feel better.

What's bad? Many people drink coffee when they feel stress. The heat is soothing and the caffeine in coffee might help you think more clearly. But if you drink too much, you may become even more anxious and irritable.

To Soothe the Blues

What's good? Introduce more lean meat, chicken, seafood, and whole grains into your diet. These foods have a lot of selenium. Selenium is a mineral that helps people feel more relaxed and happy. You can also try eating a Brazil nut every day. One Brazil nut contains a lot of selenium.

What's bad? When they're feeling low, many people turn to comfort foods – or foods that make them feel happy or secure. These often include things like sweet desserts. A chocolate bar may make you feel better at first, but within an hour you may feel worse than you did before.

A Read the article. The sentences below are false. Correct each sentence to make it true.

1. We often eat when we feel calm.
2. You should drink coffee to relieve stress.
3. Foods like chicken and seafood are high in carbohydrates.
4. Carbohydrates cause the brain to release selenium.
5. Serotonin makes you feel more anxious and irritable.
6. People usually eat comfort foods when they're feeling happy.
7. You shouldn't eat more than one Brazil nut a day.
8. Chocolate will make you feel better.

B *Pair work* What foods do you eat to feel better? After reading the article, which of the advice will you follow?

I've never heard of that! • 27

interchange 4 RISKY BUSINESS

A How much do you really know about your classmates? Look at the survey and add two more situations to items 1 and 2.

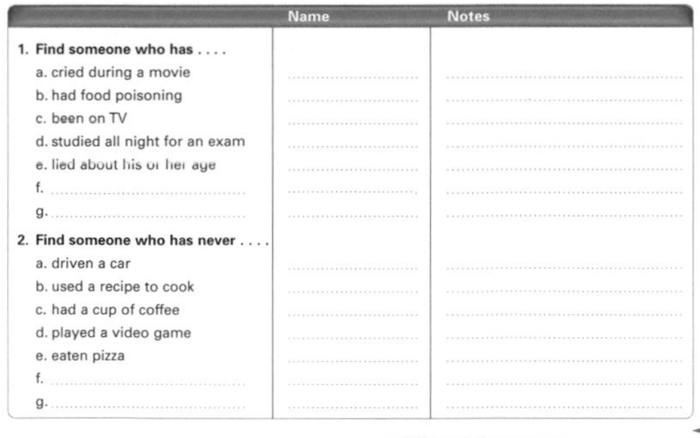

	Name	Notes
1. Find someone who has		
a. cried during a movie		
b. had food poisoning		
c. been on TV		
d. studied all night for an exam		
e. lied about his or her age		
f.		
g.		
2. Find someone who has never		
a. driven a car		
b. used a recipe to cook		
c. had a cup of coffee		
d. played a video game		
e. eaten pizza		
f.		
g.		

B *Class activity* Go around the class and ask the questions in the survey. Write down the names of classmates who answer "yes" for item 1 and "no" for item 2. Then ask follow-up questions and take notes.

A: Have you ever cried during a movie?
B: Yes. I've cried during a lot of movies.
A: What kinds of movies?
B: Well, sad ones like *Casablanca* and . . .

A: Have you ever driven a car?
C: No, I haven't.
A: Why not?
C: Well, I'm too young. I don't have a driver's license.

C *Group work* Compare the information in your surveys.

Interchange 4

INTERCHANGE ACTIVITY

- Expands on the unit topic, vocabulary, and grammar
- Provides opportunities to consolidate new language in a creative or fun way
- Promotes fluency with communicative activities, such as discussions, information gaps, and games

Teacher's Edition overview

The Teacher's Editions provide complete support for teachers who are using ***Interchange Third Edition***. They contain Oral and Written quizzes, Language summaries, and Workbook answer keys as well as Photocopiables, Fresh ideas, and Games. They also include detailed teaching notes for the units and Progress checks in the Student's Book. Here are selected teaching notes for a sample unit from Level 2.

UNIT PREVIEW

- Previews the topics, grammar, and functions in each unit

TEACHING NOTES

- Includes the ***Learning objectives*** for each exercise
- Provides step-by-step lesson plans
- Suggests ***Options*** for alternative presentations or expansions
- Includes ***Answers*** and ***Vocabulary*** definitions
- Provides ***TIPs*** that promote teacher training and development

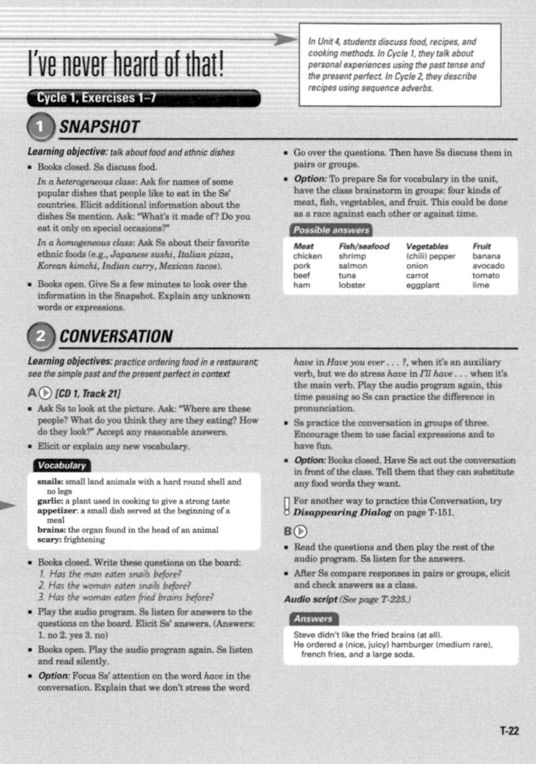

I've never heard of that!

In Unit 4, students discuss food, recipes, and cooking methods. In Cycle 1, they talk about personal experiences using the past tense and the present perfect. In Cycle 2, they describe recipes using sequence adverbs.

Cycle 1, Exercises 1–7

1 SNAPSHOT

Learning objective: *talk about food and ethnic dishes*

- Books closed. Ss discuss food.

  In a heterogeneous class: Ask for names of some popular dishes that people like to eat in the Ss' countries. Elicit additional information about the dishes Ss mention. Ask: "What's it made of? Do you eat it only on special occasions?"

  In a homogeneous class: Ask Ss about their favorite ethnic foods (e.g., *Japanese sushi*, *Italian pizza*, *Korean kimchi*, *Indian curry*, *Mexican tacos*).
- Books open. Give Ss a few minutes to look over the information in the Snapshot. Explain any unknown words or expressions.
- Go over the questions. Then have Ss discuss them in pairs or groups.
- ***Option:*** To prepare Ss for vocabulary in the unit, have the class brainstorm in groups: four kinds of meat, fish, vegetables, and fruit. This could be done as a race against each other or against time.

Possible answers

Meat	Fish/seafood	Vegetables	Fruit
chicken	shrimp	(chili) pepper	banana
pork	salmon	onion	avocado
beef	tuna	carrot	tomato
ham	lobster	eggplant	lime

2 CONVERSATION

Learning objectives: *practice ordering food in a restaurant; see the simple past and the present perfect in context*

A *[CD 1, Track 21]*

- Ask Ss to look at the picture. Ask: "Where are these people? What do you think they are they eating? How do they look?" Accept any reasonable answers.
- Elicit or explain any new vocabulary.

Vocabulary

snails: small land animals with a hard round shell and no legs
garlic: a plant used in cooking to give a strong taste
appetizer: a small dish served at the beginning of a meal
brains: the organ found in the head of an animal
scary: frightening

- Books closed. Write these questions on the board:
  1. *Has the man eaten snails before?*
  2. *Has the woman eaten snails before?*
  3. *Has the woman eaten fried brains before?*
- Play the audio program. Ss listen for answers to the questions on the board. Elicit Ss' answers. (Answers: 1. no 2. yes 3. no)
- Books open. Play the audio program again. Ss listen and read silently.
- ***Option:*** Focus Ss' attention on the word *have* in the conversation. Explain that we don't stress the word *have* in *Have you ever . . . ?*, when it's an auxiliary verb, but we do stress *have* in *I'll have . . .* when it's the main verb. Play the audio program again, this time pausing so Ss can practice the difference in pronunciation.
- Ss practice the conversation in groups of three. Encourage them to use facial expressions and to have fun.
- ***Option:*** Books closed. Have Ss act out the conversation in front of the class. Tell them that they can substitute any food words they want.

For another way to practice this Conversation, try ***Disappearing Dialog*** on page T-151.

B

- Read the questions and then play the rest of the audio program. Ss listen for the answers.
- After Ss compare responses in pairs or groups, elicit and check answers as a class.

Audio script *(See page T-225.)*

Answers

Steve didn't like the fried brains (at all).
He ordered a (nice, juicy) hamburger (medium rare), french fries, and a large soda.

T-22

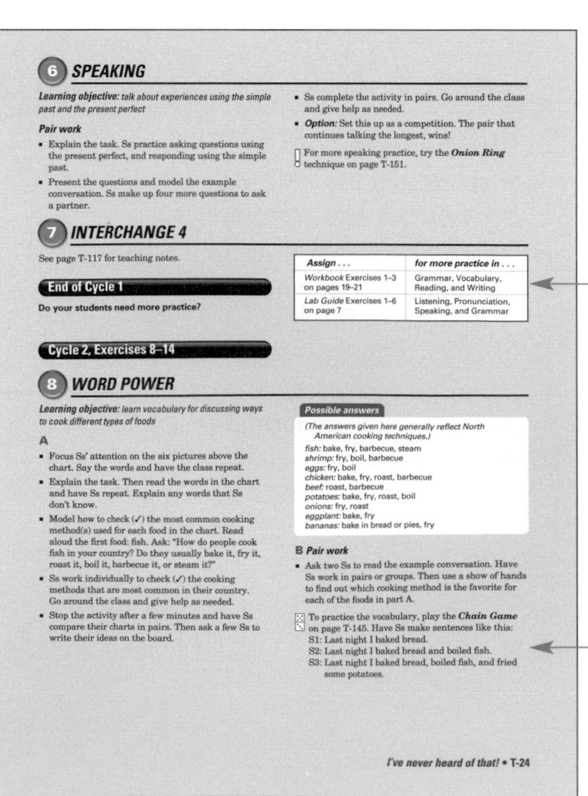

6 SPEAKING

Learning objective: *talk about experiences using the simple past and the present perfect*

Pair work

- Explain the task. Ss practice asking questions using the present perfect, and responding using the simple past.
- Present the questions and model the example conversation. Ss make up four more questions to ask a partner.
- Ss complete the activity in pairs. Go around the class and give help as needed.
- ***Option:*** Set this up as a competition. The pair that continues talking the longest, wins!

For more speaking practice, try the ***Onion Ring*** technique on page T-151.

7 INTERCHANGE 4

See page T-117 for teaching notes.

End of Cycle 1

Do your students need more practice?

Assign . . .	for more practice in . . .
Workbook Exercises 1–3 on pages 19–21	Grammar, Vocabulary, Reading, and Writing
Lab Guide Exercises 1–6 on page 7	Listening, Pronunciation, Speaking, and Grammar

Cycle 2, Exercises 8–14

8 WORD POWER

Learning objective: *learn vocabulary for discussing ways to cook different types of foods*

A

- Focus Ss' attention on the six pictures above the chart. Say the words and have the class repeat.
- Explain the task. Then read the words in the chart and have Ss repeat. Explain any words that Ss don't know.
- Model how to check (✓) the most common cooking method(s) used for each food in the chart. Read aloud the first food: fish. Ask: "How do people cook fish in your country? Do they usually bake it, fry it, roast it, boil it, barbecue it, or steam it?"
- Ss work individually to check (✓) the cooking methods that are most common in their country. Go around the class and give help as needed.
- Stop the activity after a few minutes and have Ss compare their charts in pairs. Then ask a few Ss to write their ideas on the board.

Possible answers

(The answers given here generally reflect North American cooking techniques.)
fish: bake, fry, barbecue, steam
shrimp: fry, boil, barbecue
eggs: fry, boil
chicken: bake, fry, roast, barbecue
beef: roast, barbecue
potatoes: bake, fry, roast, boil
onions: fry, roast
eggplant: bake, fry
bananas: bake in bread or pies, fry

B ***Pair work***

- Ask two Ss to read the example conversation. Have Ss work in pairs or groups. Then use a show of hands to find out which cooking method is the favorite for each of the foods in part A.

To practice the vocabulary, play the ***Chain Game*** on page T-145. Have Ss make sentences like this:
S1: Last night I baked bread.
S2: Last night I baked bread and boiled fish.
S3: Last night I baked bread, boiled fish, and fried some potatoes.

I've never heard of that! • T-24

END-OF-CYCLE

- Provides suggestions for further practice in the Workbook, Lab Guide, Video Activity Book, and CD-ROM
- Provides suggestions for regular assessment using quizzes and achievement tests

SUPPLEMENTARY ACTIVITIES

Photocopiables include handouts for innovative supplementary activities.

Fresh ideas provide alternative ways to present and review the exercises.

Games provide stimulating and fun ways to review or practice skills such as grammar and vocabulary.

Course components

Interchange Third Edition is the most complete English language course for adult and young adult learners of English. Here is a list of the core components.

Component	*Description*
Student's Book with Self-study Audio CD	The Student's Book is intended for classroom use, and contains 16 six-page units. (See the Student's Book overview for a sample unit on pages x-xiii.) Progress checks are provided after every two units, and a Self-study section is included at the back of the book.
Class Audio Program	The Class Audio Cassettes/CDs are intended for classroom use. The program consists of cassettes/CDs with all the audio sections in the Student's Book, such as Conversations, Listenings, Grammar Focuses, and Pronunciations. The program also includes the Student Self-study Audio Cassette/CD.
Teacher's Edition	The interleaved Teacher's Edition includes: • page-by-page notes, with detailed lesson plans, learning objectives, vocabulary glosses, optional activities, and teaching tips • alternative ways to teach the exercises, using Games, Fresh ideas, and Photocopiables • Language summaries of the new vocabulary and expressions in each unit • a complete assessment program, including Oral and Written quizzes • Audio scripts and answer keys for the Student's Book, Workbook, and Quizzes (See the Teacher's Edition overview for sample pages on page xiv.)
Workbook	The six-page units in the Workbook can be used in class or for homework. They follow the same sequence as the Student's Book, and provide students with more practice in grammar, vocabulary, and writing. In addition, Levels 1–3 provide more reading practice.
Placement and Evaluation Package	The package provides three versions of a placement test and four achievement tests for each level of the Student's Book, as well as for *Passages 1* and *2*. The package is composed of a photocopiable testing booklet and two audio CDs.
Video Program	Videos for each level offer dramatized and documentary sequences that reinforce and extend the language presented in the Student's Book. Video Activity Books include step-by-step comprehension and conversation activities, and the Video Teacher's Guides include detailed teaching suggestions.
CD-ROM	Available in PC format, CD-ROMs for Levels Intro, 1, and 2 provide engaging activities for students to do at home or in self-study centers. They include sequences from the Video Program, with over 100 interactive reading, listening, speaking, vocabulary, and grammar activities. They also include progress tests.

For a complete list of components, see the Web site (www.cambridge.org/interchange) or contact your local Cambridge University Press representative.

Frequently asked questions

SNAPSHOT

Q: How long should it take to present and teach the Snapshot?

A: You probably don't need to spend more than 15 minutes. Remember that it's just a warm-up activity.

Q: Should I expect students to learn all the new words in the Snapshot?

A: It's not necessary for students to learn the passive vocabulary in the Snapshots. However, it's a good idea to encourage them to use the productive vocabulary. The productive vocabulary is recycled throughout the unit and listed in the Language summaries at the back of the Teacher's Edition.

CONVERSATION

Q: Is it OK to present the Grammar Focus before the Conversation?

A: Remember that the Conversation is placed first because it introduces the new grammar in context. Also, it illustrates the meaning of the new grammar before the grammar rules are presented. However, you can change the order for variety or if it's more appropriate for your students' learning style.

Q: How helpful is it for students to memorize the Conversation?

A: Students generally benefit more from practicing and expanding on the Conversation than from memorizing it.

PERSPECTIVES

Q: What are Perspectives?

A: Like Conversations, Perspectives introduce the new grammar in context. However, they present the grammar in different ways, such as quotes, surveys, and television or radio shows.

Q: Why aren't there any Perspectives in Levels Intro and 1?

A: The Perspectives typically contain ideas and opinions that serve as starting points for more advanced discussions and debates. Therefore, they are more appropriate for higher levels.

GRAMMAR FOCUS

Q: Should I teach my students more grammar than that in the Grammar Focus box?

A: To avoid overloading students, it's preferable to teach only the grammar in the Grammar Focus box. Then progress to the speaking activities, so that they can apply the rules in communication.

Q: What should I do if my students need more controlled grammar practice?

A: You can assign practice exercises in the Workbook, Lab Guide, Video Activity Book, or CD-ROM for homework. The teaching notes in the Teacher's Edition suggest appropriate assignments for each cycle.

Q: Should I explain the rules to my students or encourage them to guess the rules?

A: Students have different learning styles, so you may want to use different techniques. First, try to involve them in guessing the rules. If they can't guess the rules, then you can explain them.

WORD POWER

Q: How can I help students remember recently taught vocabulary?

A: One way is to spend five minutes of each class reviewing new words. You can also try different vocabulary review techniques from the Fresh ideas and Games in the Teacher's Edition.

LISTENING

Q: What should I do if my students have difficulty understanding the audio program?

A: You can ask students to make predictions before you play the audio program. Then play the audio program a few times, asking students to listen for something different each time. Alternatively, divide the audio program into short sections (e.g., short conversations), stopping the audio program after each section.

Q: My students get very nervous during listening practice. What's the solution?

A: One way is to assure students that they don't need to understand every word. Tell them that they will hear the audio program again. Another option is to have students work collaboratively in pairs or small groups.

SPEAKING ACTIVITIES

Q: My students often have problems understanding my instructions. What am I doing wrong?

A: It is often more helpful to model the activity than to give instructions, especially at lower levels. Model the activity with several students, preferably of different abilities and in different parts of the room.

Q: My students make a lot of errors during pair work and group work. What can I do?

A: Remember that errors are an important part of learning. During fluency-building activities, allow students to practice speaking without interruption and make a list of any errors you hear. Then have the class correct the most common errors at the end of the activity.

READING

Q: How can I teach the Reading sections most effectively?

A: Encourage students to read silently and quickly. When they are skimming or scanning, discourage them from reading aloud, following each sentence with a pencil, or looking up each new word in a dictionary. Also, encourage them to use the discussion questions to share ideas.

PROGRESS CHECKS

Q: The Progress checks are helpful, but I don't have enough time to use them. What can I do?

A: You can use the Progress checks in a variety of ways. For example, you can assign some of the exercises for homework. Alternatively, you can assign students to complete only the Self-assessment section for homework, and then choose exercises related to areas they need to improve.

FLEXIBILITY

Q: The Student's Book doesn't have enough material for my classes. What can I do?

A: Supplement the Student's Book exercises with Photocopiables, Games, and Fresh ideas from the Teacher's Edition or activities from the Web site.

Q: I don't have enough time to complete every exercise. How can I finish them more quickly?

A: Remember that you don't have to complete every exercise in the Student's Book. You can omit selected exercises, such as the Writings, Readings, and Interchange activities.

Authors' acknowledgments

A great number of people contributed to the development of *Interchange Third Edition*. Particular thanks are owed to the following:

The **reviewers** using *New Interchange* in the following schools and institutes – their insights and suggestions have helped define the content and format of the third edition: Gino Pumadera, **American School**, Guayaquil, Ecuador; Don Ahn, **APEX**, Seoul, Korea; teachers at **AUA Language Center**, Bangkok, Thailand; Linda Martinez, **Canada College**, Redwood City, California, USA; Rosa Maria Valencia Rodriguez, **CEMARC**, Mexico City, Mexico; Wendel Mendes Dantas, **Central Universitária**, São Paulo, Brazil; Lee Altschuler, **Cheng Kung University**, Tainan, Taiwan; Chun Mao Le, **Cheng Siu Institute of Technology**, Kaohsiung, Taiwan; Selma Alfonso, **Colégio Arquidiocesano**, São Paulo, Brazil; Daniel de Mello Ferraz, **Colégio Camargo Aranha**, São Paulo, Brazil; Paula dos Santos Dames, **Colegio Militar do Rio de Janeiro**, Rio de Janeiro, Brazil; Elizabeth Ortiz, **COPOL-COPEI**, Guayaquil, Ecuador; Alexandre de Oliveira, **First Idiomas**, São Paulo, Brazil; João Franco Júnior, **2B Idiomas**, São Paulo, Brazil; Jo Ellen Kaiser and David Martin, **Fort Lauderdale High School**, Fort Lauderdale, Florida, USA; Azusa Okada, **Hiroshima Shudo University**, Hiroshima, Japan; Sandra Herrera and Rosario Valdiria, **INACAP**, Santiago, Chile; Samara Camilo Tome Costa, **Instituto Brasil-Estados Unidos**, Rio de Janeiro, Brazil; Eric Hamilton, **Instituto Chileno Norteamericano de Cultura**, Santiago, Chile; **ICNA**, Santiago, Chile; Pedro Benites, Carolina Chenett, Elena Montero Hurtado, Patricia Nieto, and Antonio Rios, **Instituto Cultural Peruano Norteamericano (ICPNA)**, Lima, Peru; Vanclei Nascimento, **Instituto Pentágono**, São Paulo, Brazil; Michael T. Thornton, **Interactive College of Technology**, Chamblee, Georgia, USA; Norma Aguilera Celis, **IPN ESCA Santo Tomas**, Mexico City, Mexico; Lewis Barksdale, **Kanazawa Institute of Technology**, Ishikawa, Japan; Clare St. Lawrence, Gill Christie, and Sandra Forrester, **Key Language Services**, Quito, Ecuador; Érik Mesquita, **King's Cross**, São Paulo, Brazil; Robert S. Dobie, **Kojen English Language Schools**, Taipei, Taiwan; Shoko Miyagi, **Madison Area Technical College**, Madison, Wisconsin, USA; Atsuko K. Yamazaki, **Institute of Technologists**, Saitama, Japan; teachers and students at **Institute of Technologists**, Saitama, Japan; Gregory Hadley, **Niigata University of International and Information Studies**, Niigata, Japan; Tony Brewer and Frank Claypool, **Osaka College of Foreign Languages and International Business**, Osaka, Japan; Chris Kerr, **Osaka University of Economics and Law**, Osaka, Japan; Angela Suzete Zumpano, **Personal Language Center**, São Paulo, Brazil; Simon Banha Jr. and Tomas S. Martins, **Phil Young's English School**, Curitiba, Brazil; Mehran Sabet and Bob Diem, **Seigakuin University**, Saitama, Japan; Lily Beam, **Shie Jen University**, Kaohsiung, Taiwan; Ray Sullivan, **Shibuya Kyoiku Gakuen Makuhari Senior and Junior High School**, Chiba, Japan; Robert Gee, **Sugiyama Jogakuen University**, Nagoya, Japan; Arthur Tu, **Taipei YMCA**, Taipei, Taiwan; Hiroko Nishikage, Alan Hawk, Peter Riley, and Peter Anyon, **Taisho University**, Tokyo, Japan; Vera Berk, **Talkative Idiomas**, São Paulo, Brazil; Patrick D. McCoy, **Toyo University**, Saitama, Japan; Kathleen Krokar and Ellen D. Sellergren, **Truman College**, Chicago, Illinois, USA; Gabriela Cortes Sanchez, **UAM-A**, Mexico City, Mexico; Marco A. Mora Piedra, **Universidad de Costa Rica**, San Jose, Costa Rica; Janette Carvalhinho de Oliveira, **Universidade Federal do Espirito Santo**, Vitoria, Brazil; Belem Saint Martin Lozada, **Universidad ISEC**, Colegio del Valle, Mexico City, Mexico; Robert Sanchez Flores, **Universidad Nacional Autonoma de Mexico**, Centro de Lenguas Campus Aragon, Mexico City, Mexico; Bertha Chela de Rodriguez, **Universidad Simòn Bolìvar**, Caracas, Venezuela; Marilyn Johnson, **Washoe High School**, Reno, Nevada, USA; Monika Soens, **Yen Ping Senior High School**, Taipei, Taiwan; Kim Yoon Gyong, **Yonsei University**, Seoul, Korea; and Tania Borges Lobao, **York Language Institute**, Rio de Janeiro, Brazil.

The **editorial** and **production** team:
David Bohlke, Jeff Chen, Yuri Hara, Pam Harris, Paul Heacock, Louisa Hellegers, Lise R. Minovitz, Pat Nelson, Bill Paulk, Danielle Power, Mary Sandre, Tami Savir, Kayo Taguchi, Louisa van Houten, Mary Vaughn, Jennifer Wilkin, and Dorothy Zemach.

And Cambridge University Press **staff** and **advisors**:
Jim Anderson, Angela Andrade, Mary Louise Baez, Carlos Barbisan, Kathleen Corley, Kate Cory-Wright, Elizabeth Fuzikava, Steve Golden, Cecilia Gomez, Heather Gray, Bob Hands, Pauline Ireland, Ken Kingery, Gareth Knight, Nigel McQuitty, João Madureira, Andy Martin, Alejandro Martinez, Carine Mitchell, Mark O'Neil, Tom Price, Dan Schulte, Catherine Shih, Howard Siegelman, Ivan Sorrentino, Alcione Tavares, Koen Van Landeghem, and Ellen Zlotnick.

CLASSROOM LANGUAGE Working together

1 A time to remember

1 SNAPSHOT

Getting to Know You

Many people use the Internet to meet people. Here is some typical information found in online personal ads.

Tell us about yourself!

Background
Born: Dallas
Grew up: Los Angeles

Professional information
Education: college degree
Occupation: computer specialist

Interests and hobbies
I love to be outdoors. I enjoy skiing and swimming. And I'm a good cook.

Background
Born: Buenos Aires
Grew up: Los Angeles

Professional information
Education: high school diploma
Occupation: college student

Interests and hobbies
I like to go to the movies and take long walks. And I'm learning to in-line skate!

Source: *http://personals.yahoo.com*

Do you think Ana and Ted could be friends?
Do people in your country use personal ads? How else can people meet?
Create your own personal profile and compare it with a partner.
How are you the same? different?

2 CONVERSATION Where did you learn to skate?

A Listen and practice.

Ted: Oh, I'm really sorry. Are you OK?
Ana: I'm fine. But I'm not very good at this.
Ted: Neither am I. . . . Say, are you from South America?
Ana: Yes, I am, originally. I was born in Argentina.
Ted: Did you grow up there?
Ana: Yes, I did, but my family moved here ten years ago, when I was in junior high school.
Ted: And where did you learn to skate?
Ana: Here in the park. This is only my third time.
Ted: Well, it's my *first* time. Can you give me some lessons?
Ana: Sure. Just follow me.
Ted: By the way, my name is Ted.
Ana: And I'm Ana. Nice to meet you.

B Listen to the rest of the conversation. What are two more things you learn about Ted?

A time to remember

In Unit 1, students discuss the past. In Cycle 1, they get to know people using past tense questions with did and was/were to ask them about their past. In Cycle 2, they talk about their childhoods using used to.

Cycle 1, Exercises 1–5

1 SNAPSHOT

Learning objectives: *read personal ads on the Internet; discuss how people meet*

- Books closed. Introduce the topic of meeting people. Ask: "Do people use the Internet to make new friends in your country? What do you think about chat rooms? What do you think about online personal ads?"
- Books open. Ss look at two examples of personal ads on the Internet. Ask: "What kind of information did these people include in their ads?" (Answer: background, professional information, and personal information)
- ***Option:*** Ss work in pairs. Student A reads the ad on the left, and Student B reads the ad on the right. Then partners exchange information about the ads.
- Ss work in pairs or groups to discuss the questions. Go around the class and give help as needed.
- If necessary, review the structures "they both . . . " and "so does (s)he."
- ***Option:*** The third task, creating a personal profile, could be assigned as homework or turned into a project.
- Ss compare their profile with a partner. They discuss how they are similar and different.

2 CONVERSATION

Learning objectives: *practice a conversation between two people meeting each other for the first time; see past simple questions in context*

A [CD 1, Track 1]

- Ss cover the text with a "Don't Look" card and look at the picture. Ask Ss to guess some information (e.g., "Where are these people? What are they doing? What has just happened? Do they know each other?"). Don't give the answers yet.

TIP To help focus Ss' attention on the picture rather than the text, ask Ss to bring a small card to class. Then have Ss cover the text with their "Don't Look" card.

- Play the audio program. Ss listen and check their predictions. (Answer: Two strangers were skating in the park and crashed into each other.)
- Ask Ss to listen for three facts about Ana's background. Play the audio program again. Ss listen and take notes.
- Check Ss' answers. (Answers: She's from South America. She was born and grew up in Argentina. Her family moved ten years ago, when she was in junior high school.)
- Point out how Ana gives additional information (e.g., *Yes, I am, . . . I was born . . . , Yes, I did, but . . .*). Tell Ss they will practice this.
- Play the audio program again. Ss listen and read silently. Go over any vocabulary that Ss find difficult.
- Ss practice the conversation in pairs. Go around the class and encourage Ss to be enthusiastic and to have fun.

For more practice exchanging personal information, try ***Say It With Feeling!*** on page T-150. Gestures and emotions Ss could use here include surprise when bumping into each other, hand gestures when saying "Here in the park," and a handshake when introducing themselves.

- ***Option:*** Books closed. Ask pairs to stand up and act out the conversation. For a challenge, have Ss substitute their own personal information.

TIP In order not to take up too much time, ask only one or two pairs to act out the Conversation for the class.

B

- Read the instructions and the question. Tell Ss not to worry about understanding every word. Then play the rest of the audio program. Ss listen to find the answers.

Audio script *(See page T-224.)*

(Note: Because *Interchange Third Edition* Student's Book 2 contains longer listening materials than Student's Book 1, the audio scripts appear at the back of this Teacher's Edition.)

Answers

Ted works in a travel agency. He's a computer specialist.

3 GRAMMAR FOCUS

Learning objectives: *practice talking about the past; ask and answer questions using Wh-questions with* was/were *and* did

[CD 1, Track 2]

Past tense questions

- Books closed. Write these questions on the board. Ask Ss to complete them:
  1. Where ____________ you born?
  2. When ____________ you move to Los Angeles?
- Focus Ss' attention on the Grammar Focus box. Then ask them to check their answers.
- Ask: "What is the difference between column 1 and column 2?" (Answer: Column 1 contains questions with *be*; column 2 contains questions with *did*.)
- Point out that we say "to *be* born" (not "to born") and "to die" (not "to be died").
- Elicit the rule for the two types of questions:
  To be: Wh- + ***was/were*** + subject + (rest)?
  Other verbs: Wh- + ***did*** + subject + verb + (rest)?
- Books open. Focus Ss' attention on the Grammar Focus box. Play the audio program to present the questions and statements.
- ***Option:*** Play the audio program again. Divide the class into two groups: One group repeats the questions and the other repeats the responses. For additional practice, switch roles.

A

- Read the instructions and model the task with the first question. Ss complete the exercise individually and then go over answers in pairs.
- Elicit Ss' responses to check answers.

Answers

1. A: Could you tell me a little about yourself? Where **were** you born?
   B: I **was** born in Korea.
   A: **Did** you grow up there?
   B: No I **didn't**. I **grew** up in Canada.
2. A: Where **did** you go to high school?
   B: I **went** to high school in Ecuador.
   A: And when **did** you graduate?
   B: I **graduated** last year. Now I work as a salesperson.
3. A: **Did** you have a favorite teacher when you **were** a child?
   B: Yes, I **did**. I **had** an excellent teacher named Mr. Woods.
   A: What **did** he teach?
   B: He **taught** English.

- Ss practice the conversations in pairs, then change roles and practice again.

For another way to practice this Conversation, try ***Look Up and Speak!*** on page T-150.

B *Pair work*

- Read the instructions. Model the task with one or two Ss by asking them these questions in part A: "Where were you born? Did you grow up there?"
- Ss work in pairs to take turns asking the questions and responding with their own information.
- Go around the class and give help as needed. Note any common grammatical problems. After pairs finish, go over the errors you noticed.

LISTENING

Learning objectives: *learn about immigrants' difficulties; develop skills in listening for detail*

A ***[CD 1, Track 3]***

- As a topic warm-up, ask Ss questions about immigrants (e.g., "Are there many immigrants where you live? Where are they from? What do you think they miss? What do you think they find difficult?").
- Set the scene. Ss are going to hear interviews with two immigrants. Play the audio program. Ss listen to find out where they come from. (Answer: China and India)

Audio script *(See page T-224.)*

B

- Present the questions in the chart. Point out that Ss need to write only key words and phrases – not full sentences. Play the audio program again. Ss listen and complete the chart.
- After Ss compare answers in pairs, check answers by asking some Ss to write their responses on the board.

Answers

Yu Hong	*Ajay*
1. in 1992	in 1991
2. no relatives in the U.S.	different educational system
3. mom's soup	weather, family, quality of life

- ***Option:*** Have Ss discuss other difficulties that immigrants face.

3 GRAMMAR FOCUS

Past tense

Where **were** you born?
I **was** born in Argentina.

Were you born in Buenos Aires?
Yes, I **was**.
No, I **wasn't**. I **was** born in Córdoba.

When **did** you **move** to Los Angeles?
I **moved** here ten years ago. I **didn't speak** English.

Did you **take** English classes in Argentina?
Yes, I **did**. I **took** classes for a year.
No, I **didn't**. My aunt **taught** me at home.

A Complete these conversations. Then practice with a partner.

1. A: Could you tell me a little about yourself? Where .... you born?
   B: I .... born in Korea.
   A: .... you grow up there?
   B: No, I .... I .... up in Canada.
2. A: Where .... you go to high school?
   B: I .... to high school in Ecuador.
   A: And when .... you graduate?
   B: I .... last year. Now I work as a salesperson.
3. A: .... you have a favorite teacher when you .... a child?
   B: Yes, I .... I .... an excellent teacher named Mr. Woods.
   A: What .... he teach?
   B: He .... English.

B *Pair work* Take turns asking the questions in part A. Give your own information when answering.

4 LISTENING *Life as an immigrant*

A Listen to interviews with two immigrants to the United States. Where are they from?

B Listen again and complete the chart.

	Yu Hong	Ajay
1. When did he/she move to the United States?	....	....
2. What is difficult about being an immigrant?	....	....
3. What does he/she miss the most?	....	....

5 SPEAKING *Tell me about yourself.*

A ***Pair work*** Check (✓) six questions below. Then interview a classmate you don't know very well.

- ☐ Where did you go to elementary school?
- ☐ Were you a good student in elementary school?
- ☐ What were your best subjects?
- ☐ What subjects didn't you like?
- ☐ When did you first study English?
- ☐ What other languages can you speak?
- ☐ Do you have a big family?
- ☐ Did you enjoy your childhood?
- ☐ Who was your hero when you were a child?
- ☐ Did you ever have a part-time job?

B ***Group work*** Tell the group what you learned about your partner. Then answer any questions.

A: Carlos went to elementary school in Mexico City.
B: Pam first studied English when she was 10.
C: Really? Where did she study English?

useful expressions

Really? Me, too!
Wow! What was it like?
Can you tell us more?

6 WORD POWER

A Complete the word map. Add two more words to each category. Then compare with a partner.

✓ beach
bicycle
cat
collect comic books
paint
play chess
rabbit
scrapbook
snake
soccer ball
summer camp
tree house

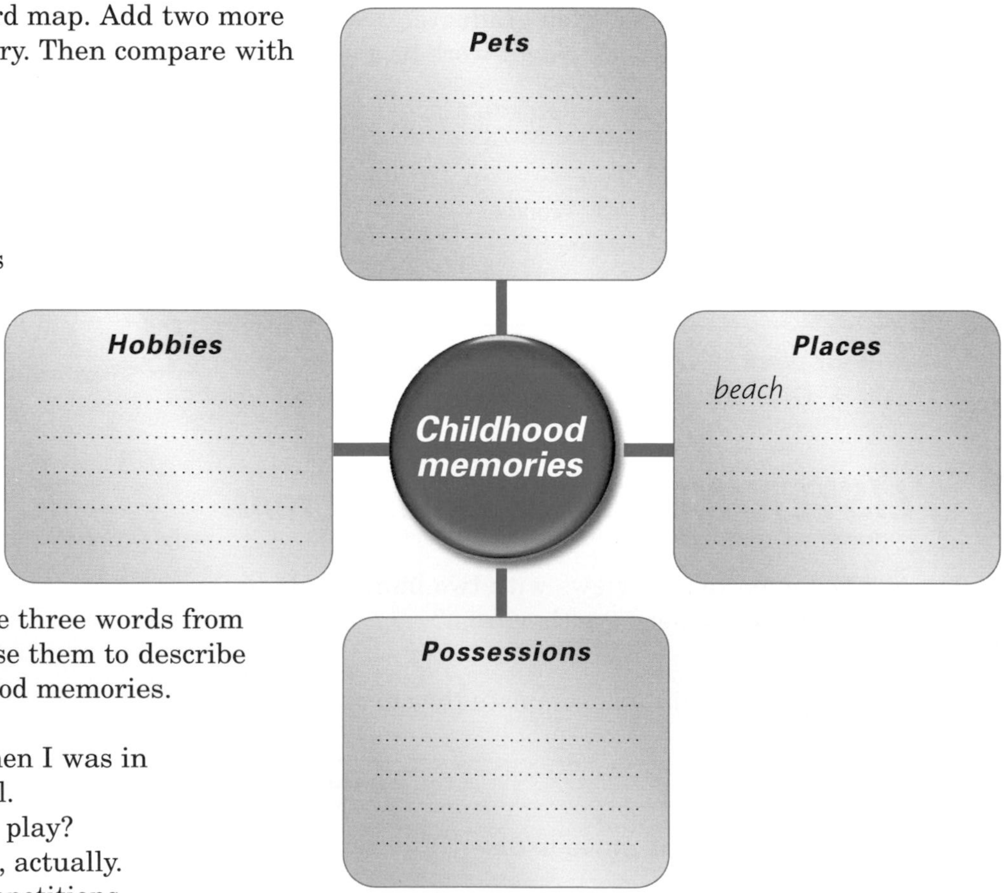

Childhood memories

Pets
....
....
....
....
....

Hobbies
....
....
....
....
....

Places
beach
....
....
....
....

Possessions
....
....
....
....
....

B ***Pair work*** Choose three words from the word map and use them to describe some of your childhood memories.

A: I played chess when I was in elementary school.
B: How well did you play?
A: I was pretty good, actually. I won several competitions.

5 SPEAKING

Learning objectives: *talk about the past using Wh-questions with* was/were *and* did*; practice giving additional information*

A Pair work

- Have Ss silently read the instructions and questions. Then let them choose six questions to ask a classmate.
- Model the task with a S.
  T: Hi, my name's . . .
  S: Hello. I'm . . . . Nice to meet you.
  T: Nice to meet you, too. So, where did you go to elementary school?
  S: In Peru. In Lima, actually.
- Ss work in pairs, preferably with a partner they don't know very well. Remind Ss to ask follow-up questions and give additional information. Point out the *useful expressions* box.
- While Ss are interviewing each other, go around the class and give help as needed.

For a new way to practice exchanging personal information, try the ***Onion Ring*** technique on page T-151.

B Group work

- Read the instructions and the example conversation. Have Ss form groups.
- Ss take turns telling the group three interesting things they learned about their partner and answering any questions.
- ***Option:*** Ss introduce their partner from part A to the class.

For more practice asking and answering past tense questions, try ***Ask the Right Questions*** on page T-156.

End of Cycle 1

Do your students need more practice?

Assign . . .	*for more practice in . . .*
Workbook Exercises 1–4 on pages 1–3	Grammar, Vocabulary, Reading, and Writing
Lab Guide Exercises 1–5 and 9 on pages 1–2	Listening, Pronunciation, Speaking, and Grammar

Cycle 2, Exercises 6–13

6 WORD POWER

Learning objective: *learn vocabulary for discussing childhood*

A

- Read the instructions and focus Ss' attention on the word map. Then ask Ss to look at the vocabulary list and help them with the first word. Ask the class: "Is *beach* an example of a pet, hobby, possession, or place?" (Answer: place)
- Ss complete the word map individually. Remind them to add two more words to each category. Let Ss use their dictionaries if they want.
- Elicit answers from the class. Write additional words on the board and encourage Ss to add them to their own maps. Explain the meaning and pronunciation of any new vocabulary.

Answers

Hobbies	***Places***	***Pets***	***Possessions***
collect comic books	beach	cat	bicycle
paint	summer camp	rabbit	scrapbook
play chess	tree house	snake	soccer ball
play computer games	*amusement park*	*bird*	*teddy bear*
go camping	*swimming pool*	*dog*	*posters*

(Note: Additional examples are italicized.)

B Pair work

- Go over the task and the example conversation. Model the task with one or two Ss.
- After Ss choose three words from the word map, they form pairs and take turns talking about some of their childhood memories. Go around the class and give help as needed.
- ***Option:*** If possible, have Ss bring photos or mementos from their childhood to share with the class.

For more practice with childhood vocabulary and past tense verbs, play the ***Chain Game*** on page T-145. Start like this:
S1: Many years ago, I played chess.
S2: Many years ago, S1 played chess and I had a cat.

7 PERSPECTIVES

Learning objectives: *discuss childhood habits; see past habitual actions with* used to *in context*

TIP The objective of the Perspectives section is to show Ss how a new structure is used. Don't expect Ss to produce the new language until it is presented in the Grammar Focus section.

A [CD 1, Track 4]

- Books closed. Write this sentence on the board: *When I was a kid, I used to be very messy, but now I'm very neat.*
- Explain that *used to* refers to something that you regularly did in the past but don't do anymore.
- Elicit examples of activities that Ss regularly did in the past but don't do anymore (e.g., *be afraid of the dark, talk in class, play with dolls*).
- Books open. Explain the task. Ss silently read the statements and check (✓) those that are true about them.
- Ss work individually. Go around the class and give help as needed. Explain any new vocabulary.

Vocabulary

messy: untidy; not neat
be into something: be very interested in or involved with something (e.g., a kind of music or fashion)

- Play the audio program. Ss listen and raise their hand every time they hear a statement that is true about them. Find out which changes are most common in your Ss' lives.
- ***Option:*** Have Ss study some of the verbs and their collocations (e.g., *be into fashion, keep fit, worry about money, follow politics, care about appearance*).

B Pair work

- Read the instructions and the example sentence. Then have Ss work in pairs to discuss the changes. Point out that there are no right or wrong answers.

8 GRAMMAR FOCUS

Learning objective: *practice forming questions, statements, negatives, and short answers with* used to

[CD 1, Track 5]

- Focus Ss' attention on the statements in the Perspectives section. Check that Ss understand the meaning of *used to*. If helpful, point out that *used to* refers to an activity that takes place over an extended period of time. We can't say, "I used to go to the movies last Saturday."
- Have Ss find some examples in the Perspectives section of positive statements with *used to* (Answers: 1, 3, 5, 7), and negative statements with *used to* (Answers: 2, 4, 6, 8). Then elicit the rules for forming positive and negative structures with *used to*:
  Positive: subject + *used to* + verb + (rest)
  I used to be (messy . . .)
  Negative: subject + *didn't* + *use to* + verb + (rest)
  I didn't use to collect . . .
- Point out that while *never* is used in negative statements, it follows the rule for the positive structure.
  subject + *never* + *used to* + verb + (rest)
  I never used to play . . .
- Play the audio program. Ss listen and silently read the Grammar Focus box. Then point out how questions are formed (*did* + *use to*) and elicit examples from the class.

A

- Before Ss begin the task, use the picture in Exercise 7 or your own information to model how the first sentence could be completed. Possible responses:
  In elementary school, I used to **play with toys**.
  In elementary school, I used to **like homework**.
- Ss work individually. When they finish, have them compare answers with a partner.

TIP To encourage Ss to use English as they work in pairs, have them look at the Classroom Language on page v. If possible, write the phrases on posters, and display them on the classroom walls.

- Go over answers with the class. Accept any answer that is logical and grammatically correct.

B Pair work

- Explain the task. Ss first work individually to write five sentences about themselves with *used to*. Then Ss work in pairs, taking turns reading their sentences to each other.
- Encourage pairs to share their similarities and differences with the class.
- ***Option:*** Read some sentences written by Ss. Ask the class to guess who wrote the sentences.

For more practice with new vocabulary and *used to*, play ***Mime*** on page T-148. Ss act out statements from the Perspectives section or make up their own.

7 PERSPECTIVES How have you changed?

A Listen to these statements about changes. Check (✓) those that are true about you.

- ☐ 1. "When I was a kid, I used to be very messy, but now I'm very neat."
- ☐ 2. "I used to have a lot of hobbies, but now I don't have any free time."
- ☐ 3. "I didn't use to collect anything, but now I do."
- ☐ 4. "I used to be really into fashion, but these days I'm not interested anymore."
- ☐ 5. "I never used to play sports, but now I like to keep fit."
- ☐ 6. "I never used to worry about money, but now I do."
- ☐ 7. "I didn't use to follow politics, but now I read the newspaper every day."
- ☐ 8. "When I was younger, I used to care a lot about my appearance. Now, I'm too busy to care how I look."

B ***Pair work*** Look at the statements again. Which changes are positive? Which are negative?

"I think the first one is a positive change. It's good to be neat."

8 GRAMMAR FOCUS

Used to

Used to refers to something that you regularly did in the past but don't do anymore.

I **used to** be very messy, but now I'm very neat.
Did you **use to** collect things?
Yes, I **used to** collect comic books.
No, I **didn't use to** collect anything, but now I collect art.
What sports **did** you **use to** play?
I **never used to** play sports, but now I play tennis.

A Complete these sentences. Then compare with a partner.

1. In elementary school, I used to . . .
2. I used to be . . . , but I'm not anymore.
3. When I was a kid, I used to play . . .
4. I didn't use to . . .
5. After school, my best friend and I used to . . .
6. My parents never used to . . .

B ***Pair work*** How have you changed these things? Write five more sentences about yourself using *used to*.

your hairstyle the way you dress your hobbies and interests

"I used to wear my hair much longer. Now I wear it short."

9 PRONUNCIATION Used to

A Listen and practice. Notice that the pronunciation of **used to** and **use to** is the same.

When I was a child, I **used to** play the trumpet.
I **used to** have a nickname.
I didn't **use to** have a bicycle.
I didn't **use to** study very hard at school.

B *Pair work* Practice the sentences you wrote in Exercise 8 again. Pay attention to the pronunciation of **used to** and **use to**.

10 SPEAKING Memories

A *Pair work* Add three questions to this list. Then take turns asking and answering the questions.

1. What's your favorite childhood memory?
2. What kinds of sports or games did you use to play when you were younger?
3. Did you use to have a nickname?
4. Where did you use to spend your vacations?
5. How has your taste in music changed?
6. ....
7. ....
8. ....

B *Class activity* Tell the class two interesting things about your partner.

11 WRITING About yourself

A Write a paragraph about things you used to do as a child. Use some of your ideas from Exercise 10. Just for fun, include one false statement.

When I was four years old, my family moved to Australia. We had an old two-story house and a big yard. My older brother and I used to play lots of games together. In the summer, my favorite outdoor game was . . .

B *Group work* Share your paragraphs and answer any questions. Can you find the false statements?

12 INTERCHANGE 1 Class profile

Find out more about your classmates. Go to Interchange 1 at the back of the book.

9 PRONUNCIATION

Learning objective: *notice the similar pronunciation of* used to *and* use to

A [CD 1, Track 6]

- Play the audio program. Point out the reduction of *used to* /ju:s•tu/: The *d* in *used* is silent, so the pronunciation of *used to* and *use to* is the same. *To* sounds like "tuh."
- Play the audio program again. This time, Ss listen and repeat each sentence using the reduced pronunciation of *used to*.

B *Pair work*

- Explain the task. Focus Ss' attention on their sentences from Exercise 8. Ss work in pairs, taking turns reading the sentences and paying close attention to the pronunciation of *used to*. If possible, have Ss work with a different partner from the one they had in Exercise 8.
- Go around the class and listen to Ss' pronunciation. If Ss are having any difficulty, model the correct reduced sounds again.
- ***Option:*** For more practice, have Ss pronounce the statements from Exercise 7.

10 SPEAKING

Learning objective: *talk about childhood memories*

A *Pair work*

- Explain the task. Ss write three more questions to ask each other. Tell Ss that they may work individually or in pairs on this initial task.
- Pairs take turns asking and answering the questions. Go around the class and give help as needed. If Ss feel a question is too personal, tell them to make up an answer or say "I'm sorry, but I'd rather not answer that."

B *Class activity*

- Ss take turns telling the class two interesting things they learned about their partner.

For more speaking practice, play ***Just One Minute*** on page T-146.

11 WRITING

Learning objective: *write a paragraph about childhood with* used to

(Note: Writing exercises can be done in class or assigned as homework.)

A

- Have Ss silently read the example paragraph. Elicit some topics in the model that Ss may wish to include in their own paragraphs (e.g., *family*, *moving*, *houses*, *games and hobbies*, *summer*). Write the topics on the board.
- Tell the class to use their questions, notes, and ideas from Exercise 10 as additional topics (e.g., *sports* and *vacations*). Add these to the list on the board.
- Explain the task. Ss write a draft paragraph about their childhood. Encourage them to start by brainstorming ideas for each topic they choose to include. Then they should use that information to write a first draft. Remind Ss to include one false statement.
- While Ss are writing their first drafts, go around the class and give individual feedback on the content and organization of each S's draft. Alternatively, have Ss work in pairs to give each other helpful comments on what is good and what could be improved.
- Have Ss revise their paragraphs in class or for homework.

For another way to help Ss plan their paragraphs, try ***Mind Mapping*** on page T-154.

B *Group work*

- Read the instructions. Ss take turns reading their paragraphs in small groups and answering any questions. Then the group guesses which statement is false.
- ***Option:*** Collect the paragraphs and give Ss written comments. You could also post Ss' paragraphs on a wall or bulletin board for others to read.
- ***Option:*** Turn this into a project. Have Ss include photos of their childhood, write poems or songs, or find out what else happened the year they were born.

12 INTERCHANGE 1

See page T-114 for teaching notes.

13 READING

Learning objectives: *read an article about Nicole Kidman; develop skills in scanning for key facts and guessing meaning from context*

- Books closed. Ask Ss to work in pairs to brainstorm what they know about actress Nicole Kidman.

To help activate Ss' schema, play ***Prediction Bingo*** on page T-146.

- Books open. Focus Ss' attention on the title of the reading. Ask: "Why do you think Nicole Kidman is considered 'New Hollywood Royalty'?" Elicit answers.
- Ss scan the text quickly, ignoring words they don't know. They should simply look for the answers to the pre-reading questions. (Answers: She was born in Hawaii. She was married in Colorado. She won an Academy Award in 2003.)

TIP To encourage Ss to read quickly and focus on the task, give them a time limit.

A

- Ss read the article individually. Tell them not to use their dictionaries. Instead, encourage them to circle or highlight any words they can't guess from the context of the article.
- Explain the task. Ss find each italicized word or phrase in the text and guess its meaning from context.
- Ss circle the meaning of each word or phrase. Go over answers with the class.

Answers

1. advance
2. fear and disgust
3. quickly
4. worked very hard
5. short

- Elicit or explain any new vocabulary.

Vocabulary

early on: in the beginning
sheep: a farm animal that is kept for wool, skin, and meat
pageant: a play or show
lead role: the most important part
costar: an actor who appears in a movie with other actors
following: after
high-profile: very important

B

- Explain the task and use the example answer to model the task. Point out that Ss should order the events as they happened in time, not as they were mentioned in the article. Ss work individually to sequence the events. Go around the class and give help as needed.
- Check answers as a class. Ask: "What happened first/second/etc.?"

Answers

1. h. She was born in Hawaii.
2. d. She moved to Australia.
3. b. She had her first acting experience.
4. i. She studied drama and dance.
5. f. She won her first award.
6. e. She made her first American movie.
7. j. She married Tom Cruise.
8. g. She adopted two children.
9. a. She divorced Tom Cruise.
10. c. She won an Academy Award.

- ***Option:*** Write each answer on a card. Ask ten Ss to come to the front of the class and give each S a card. Then tell them to stand in line, in order of the events.

C Pair work

- Ss discuss their favorite actors in pairs. Encourage Ss to ask follow-up questions.
- ***Option:*** Ss summarize the facts they learned from their partner and tell the class.

For more practice with past tense questions, play ***Twenty Questions*** on page T-145. Have Ss use famous people to play the game.

End of Cycle 2

Do your students need more practice?

Assign . . .	*for more practice in . . .*
Workbook Exercises 5–10 on pages 4–6	Grammar, Vocabulary, Reading, and Writing
Lab Guide Exercises 6–8 on page 2	Listening, Pronunciation, Speaking, and Grammar
Video Activity Book Unit 1	Listening, Speaking, and Cultural Awareness
CD-ROM Unit 1	Grammar, Vocabulary, Reading, Listening, and Speaking

13 READING

Nicole Kidman: *New Hollywood Royalty*

Scan the article. Where was Nicole Kidman born? Where was she married? When did she win an Academy Award?

Actress Nicole Kidman was born in Honolulu, Hawaii, in 1967. Her father, an Australian, was a student in Hawaii at the time. When she was 4, the family returned to Australia, and Kidman grew up in a suburb of Sydney.

Kidman became interested in acting early on. Her first experience came when she was 6 years old and she played a sheep in her school's Christmas pageant. She trained in drama and dance through her teen years. She got a couple of TV parts before she made her breakthrough: In 1985, the Australian Film Institute named her Actress of the Year for her role in the TV miniseries *Vietnam.* She was only 17.

In 1989, Kidman appeared in the creepy thriller *Dead Calm.* This performance earned her the lead role in her first American movie, *Days of Thunder.* Her costar was Tom Cruise. Following a whirlwind romance, Kidman and Cruise were married in Colorado on Christmas Eve, 1990.

During the marriage, Kidman's career continued to grow. She and Cruise adopted two children, and they worked hard to balance their careers and family life.

One of the most fascinating actresses of our time

Unfortunately, the marriage didn't last. Kidman and Cruise divorced in 2001. After the divorce, Kidman threw herself into her work. She starred in a number of high-profile movies, including the musical *Moulin Rouge.* Then, in 2003, she won both an Academy Award and a Golden Globe for her role as Virginia Woolf in the film *The Hours.*

And what does she think of her fame? "It's a fleeting moment," she has said. "How long will it last? Who knows? But it's here and it's now."

A Read the article. Find the words in *italics* in the article. Then circle the meaning of each word or phrase.

1. When you make a *breakthrough*, you experience a sudden **advance** / **accident**.
2. When something is *creepy*, it gives you a feeling of **joy and excitement** / **fear and disgust**.
3. A *whirlwind* describes something that happens **slowly** / **quickly**.
4. When Kidman *threw herself into* her work, she **worked very hard** / **stopped working**.
5. When something is *fleeting*, it lasts a **short** / **long** time.

B Number these sentences from 1 (first event) to 10 (last event).

.... a. She divorced Tom Cruise.
.... b. She had her first acting experience.
.... c. She won an Academy Award.
.... d. She moved to Australia.
.... e. She made her first American movie.
.... f. She won her first award.
.... g. She adopted two children.
...*1*... h. She was born in Hawaii.
.... i. She studied drama and dance.
.... j. She married Tom Cruise.

C ***Pair work*** Who is your favorite actor or actress? What interesting details do you know about his or her life and career?

2 Caught in the rush

1 WORD POWER Compound nouns

A Match the words in columns A and B to make compound nouns. (More than one answer may be possible.)

subway + station = subway station

A	*B*
bicycle	garage
bus	jam
news	lane
parking	light
street	space
subway	stand
taxi	station
traffic	stop
train	system

a taxi stand

a bicycle lane

B ***Pair work*** Which of these things can you find where you live?

A: There is a bus system here.
B: Yes. There are also a lot of traffic jams.

2 PERSPECTIVES Transportation services

A Listen to these comments about transportation services.

"I think there are too many cars on the road. All the cars, taxis, and buses make it really dangerous for bicycles. There is too much traffic!"

"What about the buses? They are old, slow, and cause too much pollution. I think there should be less pollution in the city."

"There should be fewer cars, but I think that the biggest problem is parking. There just isn't enough parking."

B ***Pair work*** Look at the comments again. Which statements do you agree with?

Caught in the rush

In Unit 2, students discuss city life. In Cycle 1, they talk about transportation and other public services using adverbs of quantity and compound nouns. In Cycle 2, they practice asking indirect questions.

Cycle 1, Exercises 1–6

WORD POWER

Learning objectives: *learn compound nouns; talk about transportation*

- ***Option:*** To introduce the topic of this cycle (transportation and other public services in a city), ask: "How many hours do you spend traveling each day? How do you get around the city? Do you ever get stuck in traffic? What do you do to keep calm?"

A

- Ask Ss: "What do we call a police officer who is a man? What do we call the car he drives? What do we call his dog?" (Answers: a policeman, a police car, a police dog)
- Write these words on the board and explain that they are compound nouns, or nouns that consist of two or more words. Point out that some compound nouns are written as one word while others are written as two separate words.
- Use the example answer to model the task. Help Ss make a compound noun using the first word in column A (*bicycle*). Point out that more than one answer is sometimes possible.
- Ss work individually or in pairs to complete the task before looking at a dictionary.
- Elicit answers and ask Ss to write them on the board.

Possible answers

bicycle: bicycle lane, bicycle stand
bus: bus lane, bus station, bus stop, bus system
news: newsstand
parking: parking garage, parking space
street: streetlight
subway: subway station, subway stop, subway system
taxi: taxi lane, taxi stand
traffic: traffic jam, traffic light
train: train station, train stop, train system

To develop Ss' ability to use a dictionary, try ***Dictionary Skills*** on page T-156.

TIP Encourage Ss to keep a vocabulary notebook.

B *Pair work*

- Ss work in pairs to discuss which things in part A can be found where they live. Go around the class and give help as needed.

TIP To help Ss remember the new vocabulary, make a vocabulary box. Ask them to write the new words on slips of paper and put the slips into a shoebox or container. Review a few of these words during each class. Write a check (✓) on the slip if Ss were able to recall the word. When a slip has three checkmarks, remove it from the box.

To review the new vocabulary, play ***Picture It!*** on page T-147.

PERSPECTIVES

Learning objectives: *read about transportation services; see expressions with adverbs of quantity in context*

A [CD 1, Track 7]

- Books closed. Write these questions on the board:
  1. Which speaker says the biggest problem is parking?
  2. Which speaker says it's dangerous for bicycles?
  3. Which speaker says the buses are old and slow?
- Play the audio program. Ss listen and decide which speaker made each statement.
- Books open. Have Ss look at the comments made by each speaker and check their answers to the questions on the board. (Answers: 1. the third 2. the first 3. the second)
- Explain that *too many/too much* means "more than we want." Ask: "Which things do the speakers think there are *too many* or *too much* of?" (Answers: cars, taxis, buses, traffic, pollution) Then ask: "What thing do the speakers think there is *not enough* of?" (Answer: parking)

For another way to teach this Perspectives, try ***Running Dictation*** on page T-153.

B *Pair work*

- Explain the task. Ss work in pairs to underline the statements they agree with. Then elicit answers from the class.
- ***Option:*** Play the audio program again. Ask Ss to raise their hand when they agree.

3 GRAMMAR FOCUS

Learning objectives: *practice using adverbs of quantity with count and noncount nouns; use comparatives with* more *and* -er

[CD 1, Track 8]

Count/noncount nouns

- Elicit or explain the differences between count and noncount nouns:
  1. Count nouns have a plural form – usually with *-s* – because they are considered separate and countable things (e.g., *a car, two cars*).
  2. Noncount nouns do not have a plural form because they are impossible to separate and count (e.g., *traffic*, but not *one traffic, two traffics*).
- Draw two columns on the board with the headings: *Count nouns* and *Noncount nouns*. Ask Ss to find examples of each in the Perspectives section. Then elicit answers and write them on the board.

For more practice with count and noncount nouns, play ***Run For It!*** on page T-148. Prepare a list of sentences with missing nouns. Then write each missing noun on a sign and post the signs on the classroom walls.

Too much/many; less/fewer

- Write this on the board:
  Count nouns: *there are + too many/few, fewer*
  Noncount nouns: *there is + too much/little, less*
- Refer Ss to Exercise 2. Ask them to underline all examples of *too much/too many*. Then ask them to circle all examples of *fewer/less*.
- ***Option:*** Do a quick substitution drill. Ask Ss to use information about their city.
  T: Streetlights.
  S1: There are too few streetlights.
  T: Pollution.
  S2: There is too much pollution.
- Point out the first two sentences in the Grammar Focus box. Elicit sentences that mean the same:
  There are too many cars. (Answer: There should be fewer cars.)
  There is too much traffic. (Answer: There should be less traffic.)
- ***Option:*** Ask Ss to change the other sentences so that they mean the same.

More/(not) enough

- Ss read the *more/(not) enough* examples in the Grammar Focus box. Answer any questions they have.
- Play the audio program to present the information in the box.

A

- Read the instructions and model the task with the first two sentences. Ss work individually then compare answers in pairs. Elicit answers.

Answers

1. There are**n't enough/too few** police officers.
2. There should be **fewer** cars in the city.
3. There is**n't enough/too little** public transportation.
4. The government needs to build **more** highways.
5. There should be **less** noise.
6. We should have **more** public parking garages.
7. There is **too much** air pollution in the city.
8. There are **too many** cars parked on the streets.

B *Group work*

- Read the instructions and elicit some answers for the first item. Ss work in small groups to write sentences. Ss will use their sentences again in Exercise 6.

4 LISTENING

Learning objectives: *listen to solutions to traffic problems; develop skills in listening for detail*

A *[CD 1, Track 9]*

- Books closed. Ask: "Do you know anything about Singapore?" Elicit responses.
- Set the scene. An engineer is talking about what Singapore has done to solve its traffic problems. Play the audio program. Ss listen and mark statements true or false.

Audio script *(See page T-224.)*

Answers

1. False 2. True 3. True 4. False

B

- Read the instructions and play the audio program again. Ss listen and correct statements 1 and 4 in the chart. Go over answers with the class.

Possible answers

1. Motorists are allowed to drive into the business district if they have a special pass.
4. Public transportation in Singapore is excellent.

C *Class activity*

- Read the questions and elicit Ss' comments.

3 GRAMMAR FOCUS

Adverbs of quantity

With count nouns	*With noncount nouns*
There are **too many** cars.	There is **too much** traffic.
There should be **fewer** cars.	There should be **less** pollution.
We need **more** subway lines.	We need **more** public transportation.
There are**n't enough** buses.	There is**n't enough** parking.

A Complete these statements about transportation problems. Then compare with a partner. (More than one answer may be possible.)

1. There are .... police officers.
2. There should be .... cars in the city.
3. There is .... public transportation.
4. The government needs to build .... highways.
5. There should be .... noise.
6. We should have .... public parking garages.
7. There is .... air pollution in the city.
8. There are .... cars parked on the streets.

B ***Group work*** Write sentences about the city or town you are living in. Then compare with others.

1. The city should provide more . . .
2. We have too many . . .
3. There's too much . . .
4. There isn't enough . . .
5. There should be fewer . . .
6. We don't have enough . . .
7. There should be less . . .
8. We need more . . .

4 LISTENING Singapore solves it.

A Listen to someone talk about how Singapore has tried to solve its traffic problems. Check (✓) True or False for each statement.

	True	False
1. Motorists are never allowed to drive into the business district.	☐	☐
2. People need a special certificate to buy a car.	☐	☐
3. Cars cost more than in the United States or Canada.	☐	☐
4. Public transportation still needs to be improved.	☐	☐

B Listen again. For the false statements, write the correct information.

C ***Class activity*** Could the solutions adopted in Singapore work in your city or town? Why or why not?

5 DISCUSSION *You be the judge!*

A ***Group work*** Which of these transportation services are available in your city or town? Discuss what is good and bad about each one.

.... taxi service .... the subway system .... facilities for pedestrians
.... the bus system .... the train system .... parking

B ***Group work*** How would you rate the transportation services where you live? Give each item a rating from 1 to 5.

5 = excellent 4 = good 3 = average 2 = needs improvement 1 = terrible

A: I'd give the taxi service a rating of 4. There are enough taxis, but there are too many bad drivers.
B: I think a rating of 4 is too high. There should be more taxi stands and . . .

6 WRITING *A letter to the editor*

A Read this letter to a newspaper editor about traffic problems in the city.

B Use your statements from Exercise 3 and any new ideas to write a letter to your local newspaper.

C ***Pair work*** Take turns reading your letters. Give your partner suggestions for revision.

To whom it may concern:

There's too much traffic in this city, and it's getting worse! A few years ago, it took me ten minutes to get downtown. Now it takes more than *thirty* minutes during the rush hour! Here are my suggestions to solve some of our traffic problems. First of all, there should be more subway lines. I think people want to use public transportation, but we need more . . .

7 SNAPSHOT

Common Questions
Asked by Visitors to a City

- ☐ How much do cabs cost?
- ☐ Where can I get a map?
- ☐ Where can I rent a cell phone?
- ☐ Where can I walk my dog?
- ☐ Which hotel is closest to the airport?
- ☐ Where is the best place to meet friends?
- ☐ What's an inexpensive way to sightsee?
- ☐ Where should I go shopping?
- ☐ What are some interesting stores?
- ☐ What museums should I see?

Sources: *www.choosechicago.com*; *www.orlandoairports.net*

Check (✓) the questions you can answer about your city.
What other questions could a visitor ask about your city?
Talk to your classmates. Find answers to the questions you didn't check.

5 DISCUSSION

Learning objectives: *discuss transportation services using adverbs of quantity; develop the skill of giving opinions and reasons*

A Group work

- Write these expressions on the board:
  It's terrible/not bad/OK/pretty good/excellent.
  I think it's better/worse than it used to be.
  In my opinion, it's getting better/worse.
  On the positive side . . . ; On the other hand . . .
  The problem is that . . .
- Model the task with the first item (*taxi service*). Ask Ss to think about things like quantity, quality, cost, safety, frequency, comfort, and cleanliness. Remind Ss to use the new language from the Grammar Focus.
- Ss discuss the other services in groups.

B Group work

- Read the instructions. Then explain the rating system and any unknown vocabulary.
- Ss work in groups with classmates who live, work, or go to school in the same city or town.
- Go around the class and give help as needed. Then have groups take turns explaining their ratings to the rest of the class.
- ***Option:*** Take a poll. Ask each group to announce how many points they gave each service. Add up the total points to see which services are best and worst.

6 WRITING

Learning objective: *write a letter of complaint*

A

- Ask: "Have you ever written a letter to a magazine or a newspaper?" If someone has, tell the others to ask that S questions.
- Ss silently read the example paragraph. Explain any new vocabulary and stylistic issues (e.g., *The writer begins with a story and then gives suggestions.*). Focus Ss' attention on useful expressions (e.g., *First of all*) and how to begin the paragraph (*To whom it may concern, Dear editor*).

B

- Ss brainstorm ideas for a letter. They can work individually, or, if they are going to write about the same city's traffic problems, in pairs or small groups.
- Ss use their brainstorming ideas and notes from Exercise 3 to write a first draft. Go around the class and make general comments about content or organization. Give individual feedback or words of encouragement as needed. Alternatively, sit in one place and encourage Ss to come to you to get help or ask questions.

C Pair work

- Ss work in pairs to give each other suggestions on ways to improve their letters. Then Ss revise their letters into a final draft.
- ***Option:*** Collect the letters and display them on a wall or bulletin board for others to read. If an English-language newspaper is available, encourage Ss to send their letters to the editor.

End of Cycle 1

Do your students need more practice?

Assign . . .	*for more practice in . . .*
Workbook Exercises 1–4 on pages 7–10	Grammar, Vocabulary, Reading, and Writing
Lab Guide Exercises 1–4 on page 3	Listening, Pronunciation, Speaking, and Grammar

Cycle 2, Exercises 7–13

7 SNAPSHOT

Learning objectives: *read common questions about cities; ask and answer questions about cities*

- Books closed. Ask Ss to brainstorm information about tourists who visit the city where Ss live. Ask: "Where are they from? Where do they stay? What places do they visit? Where do they eat?"
- Books open. Ss silently read the questions in the Snapshot. Go over any new vocabulary.
- Ss check the questions they can answer about their city. Then they brainstorm additional questions that visitors ask and discuss possible answers to these questions.
- ***Option:*** Have Ss work in small groups to find answers to all the questions.

8 CONVERSATION

Learning objectives: *practice asking questions about schedules and locations; see indirect questions in context*

A [CD 1, Track 10]

- Books closed. Write these focus questions on the board:
  ____ *Where are the rest rooms?*
  ____ *Where is the bank?*
  ____ *What time does the bank open?*
  ____ *How often do the buses leave for the city?*
- Ask: "In what order does the woman want to know these things?"
- Play the audio program. Ss listen and order the questions. Elicit answers. (Answers: 4, 1, 2, 3)
- Books open. Play the audio program again. Ss listen for the answers to Erica's questions. Go over answers with the class. (Answers: 1. upstairs, across from the duty-free shop 2. at 8:00 A.M. 3. check at the transportation counter down the hall 4. right behind her)
- Elicit or explain any new vocabulary.

Vocabulary

duty-free shop: a store selling goods on which tax doesn't have to be paid
counter: a table or flat surface in a store, bank, restaurant, etc., at which people are served
rest room: a public toilet

- Ss practice the conversation in pairs. Ask them to act it out, standing up as if at a counter.

B

- Play the second part of the audio program. Ss listen and check (✓) the information that Erica asks for. Then have Ss compare answers in pairs.

Audio script *(See page T-224.)*

Answers

the cost of a taxi to the city; the location of a restaurant

9 GRAMMAR FOCUS

Learning objectives: *practice changing Wh-questions into indirect questions; ask and answer indirect questions*

[CD 1, Track 11]

***Indirect questions with* be *and* do**

- Write one of these words and phrases on nine cards:
  Do you know *Could you tell me* *Where* *is*
  the bank *What time* *does* *open* *s*
- Ask a S to read Erica's first question from the board (*Where is the bank?*). Then ask three Ss to come to the front of the class. Give Ss the relevant cards (e.g., *Where, is, the bank*). Have Ss stand in order and hold the cards for the rest of the class to see:
  S1: *Where* S2: *is* S3: *the bank*
- Now focus Ss' attention on the Conversation and ask them to find her exact question (*Could you tell me where the bank is?*). Point out that *Could you tell me* is a polite way to ask the same thing. Give another S the *Could you tell me* card and ask the S to stand with the others to form Erica's original question:
  S1: *Could you tell me* S2: *where* S3: *the bank* S4: *is*
- Ask: "What happened to the question?" (Answer: The word order changed.)
- Repeat the activity for Wh-questions with *do*. Ask four volunteers to stand in line holding up these cards:
  S1: *What time* S2: *does* S3: *the bank* S4: *open*
- Give another S the *Do you know* card and ask the Ss to form Erica's original question. Make sure that S2 puts down the *does* card and takes the *s*.
- Play the audio program. Ss listen and read the Grammar Focus box.
- ***Option:*** For extra practice, have Ss turn the questions in the Snapshot into indirect questions.

A

- Read the instructions. Use the first item to model the task. Then have Ss work individually to complete the task. After Ss go over their answers in pairs, elicit answers from the class.

Possible answers

Answers begin with:
Could/Can you tell me . . . or *Do you know . . .*
1. . . . how much a newspaper costs?
2. . . . where the nearest cash machine is?
3. . . . what time the banks open?
4. . . . how often the buses come?
5. . . . where you can get a good meal?
6. . . . how late the nightclubs stay open?
7. . . . how early the trains run?
8. . . . what the best hotel in the area is?

B *Pair work*

- Ss work in pairs to discuss the answers to the questions they wrote in part A.

8 CONVERSATION Could you tell me . . . ?

A Listen and practice.

Erica: Excuse me. Could you tell me where the bank is?
Clerk: There's one upstairs, across from the duty-free shop.
Erica: Do you know what time it opens?
Clerk: It should be open now. It opens at 8:00 A.M.
Erica: Oh, good. And can you tell me how often the buses leave for the city?
Clerk: You need to check at the transportation counter. It's right down the hall.
Erica: OK. And just one more thing. Do you know where the rest rooms are?
Clerk: Right behind you. Do you see where that sign is?
Erica: Oh. Thanks a lot.

B Listen to the rest of the conversation. Check (✓) the information that Erica asks for.

- ☐ the cost of a taxi to the city
- ☐ the location of the taxi stand
- ☐ the cost of a bus to the city
- ☐ the location of a restaurant

GRAMMAR FOCUS

Indirect questions from Wh-questions

***Wh*-questions with be**	***Indirect questions***
Where is the bank?	Could you tell me **where the bank is**?
Where are the rest rooms?	Do you know **where the rest rooms are**?
***Wh*-questions with do or did**	***Indirect questions***
How often do the buses leave?	Can you tell me **how often the buses leave**?
What time does the bank open?	Do you know **what time the bank opens**?
When did Flight 566 arrive?	Do you know **when Flight 566 arrived**?

A Write indirect questions using these Wh-questions. Then compare with a partner.

1. How much does a newspaper cost?
2. Where is the nearest cash machine?
3. What time do the banks open?
4. How often do the buses come?
5. Where can you get a good meal?
6. How late do the nightclubs stay open?
7. How early do the trains run?
8. What is the best hotel in the area?

B ***Pair work*** Take turns asking the questions you wrote in part A. Give your own information when answering.

"Do you know how much a newspaper costs?"

10 PRONUNCIATION Syllable stress

A Listen and practice. Notice which syllable has the main stress in these two-syllable words.

● •	• ●
subway	garage
traffic	police

B Listen to the stress in these words. Write them in the correct column. Then compare with a partner.

		● •	• ●
buses	improve	....	....
newsstand	provide	....	....
hotel	public	....	....
taxis	machine	....	....

11 SPEAKING What do you know?

A Complete the chart with indirect questions.

	Name:	Name: ....
1. Where is the tourist information center? "*Can you tell me where*................................?"	....	....
2. What time do the stores close? "..?"	....	....
3. Where is the nearest hospital? "..?"	....	....
4. How much does a taxi to the airport cost? "..?"	....	....
5. Where can I find a good shopping mall? "..?"	....	....
6. Where is the nearest drugstore? "..?"	....	....
7. What is a good place for families with children? "..?"	....	....

B *Group work* Use the indirect questions in the chart to interview two classmates about the city or town where you live. Take notes.

A: Can you tell me where the tourist information center is?
B: I'm not really sure, but I think . . .

C *Class activity* Share your answers with the class. Who knows the most about your city or town?

12 INTERCHANGE 2 Tourism campaign

Discuss ways to attract tourists to a city. Go to Interchange 2 at the back of the book.

10 PRONUNCIATION

Learning objective: *notice and practice syllable stress*

A [CD 1, Track 12]

- Point out that the bubbles over words show the different stress patterns in two-syllable words. The larger bubble means a syllable has the main stress.
- Play the audio program. Ss listen and practice.

B

- Model the task with first word. Have Ss write *buses* in the first column.
- Ss listen to the audio program and write the words in the correct column.
- ***Option:*** Change the order of the task above. First Ss guess in which column each word belongs, then they listen to the audio program and check their answers.
- Ss compare answers in pairs. Then elicit answers from the class.

Answers

● •	• ●
buses	hotel
newsstand	improve
taxis	provide
public	machine

For more practice with syllable stress, play ***Tic-Tac-Toe*** on page T-148.

- ***Option:*** To prepare Ss for the next activity, have them find the syllable pattern for these words: tourist, center, nearest, airport, shopping, drugstore, children. (Answer: All belong in the first column.)

11 SPEAKING

Learning objectives: *practice asking indirect questions; talk about your city or town*

A

- Explain the task. Ss find out how much they know about their city or town by asking and answering questions about it.
- Ask Ss to give you the indirect question for each direct question in the chart. Then have Ss write the questions in the chart. Check answers by asking individual Ss to read their questions.

TIP To make sure you include everyone, write each S's name on a slip of paper. Put the slips in a pile on your desk. After asking a S a question, remove the slip with that S's name. Continue until you have asked each S a question. Alternatively, keep track of participation by checking names off a class list.

B *Group work*

- Model the task with a few Ss. Write these useful expressions on the board:
  Let me think. . . .
  That's an easy/a difficult question!
  I know this one.
  Sorry. I have no idea.
  I'm not sure, but I think . . .
- Ss complete the task in small groups. Remind Ss to give additional information when possible.
- Go around the class and listen for correct questions and good intonation. Take notes on any difficulties Ss have. After the groups finish, go over errors with the class.

C *Class activity*

- Elicit answers from the class. Who knows the most about their city?
- ***Option:*** Ss work in pairs to ask questions about places their partner has visited on vacation. Ss can use the questions from Exercise A or their own ideas.

For a new way to practice indirect questions, try ***Question Exchange*** on page T-152.

12 INTERCHANGE 2

See page T-115 for teaching notes.

13 READING

Learning objectives: *read an article about new types of transportation; develop skills in skimming and reading for detail; develop discussion skills*

- Books closed. As a class, brainstorm ways to get around on land and on sea (e.g., *land – car, motorcycle, skis, camel, truck; sea – boat, ferry, canoe, ship*). Write Ss' ideas on the board. Then tell Ss they are going to learn about some new ways to get around.
- Books open. Go over the pre-reading task. Ss skim the article quickly and write the name of each invention under its picture. Then elicit answers. (Answers: 1. OutRider, 2. PowerSki Jetboard, 3. Trikke Scooter, 4. Wheelman)

A

- Ss silently read the article and decide where it is from. Ask Ss to explain their answers.

Answer

a newsmagazine

- To carry out the next task, Ss need to know the meaning of certain words. List vocabulary words on the board and go over them with the class.

Vocabulary

steer: control the direction
stable: secure
aluminum: a type of lightweight metal
turn back and forth: move left and right
attached to: connected to
smoothly: evenly
former surfer: someone who used to surf
pro: a professional
combine: join together

- ***Option:*** Have Ss work in groups to share the meanings of the words they know. They can use synonyms, antonyms, mime, examples, or pictures to define the words. If Ss can't provide a definition, let them check their dictionaries.

B

- Go over the questions to make sure Ss understand them. Ss work individually to answer the questions.
- ***Option:*** For more speaking practice, divide the class into two groups. Assign questions 1–4 to Group A, and questions 5–8 to Group B. Have Ss work individually to find the answers to their questions. Then Ss work with someone from the other group to share answers.

Answers

1. the Wheelman, the OutRider, and the PowerSki Jetboard
2. in the wheels
3. you use your body weight
4. it has three wheels
5. by turning back and forth
6. it's attached to a ski
7. surfing and waterskiing
8. a former pro surfer

C *Pair work*

- Ss work in pairs to discuss the questions in part C.
- ***Option:*** Have pairs share some of their ideas with the rest of the class.

End of Cycle 2

Do your students need more practice?

Assign . . .	*for more practice in . . .*
Workbook Exercises 5–8 on pages 11–12	Grammar, Vocabulary, Reading, and Writing
Lab Guide Exercises 5–9 on page 4	Listening, Pronunciation, Speaking, and Grammar
Video Activity Book Unit 2	Listening, Speaking, and Cultural Awareness
CD-ROM Unit 2	Grammar, Vocabulary, Reading, Listening, and Speaking

Evaluation

Assess Ss' understanding of Units 1 and 2 with the quiz on pages T-200 and T-201.

13 READING

NEW WAYS OF *Getting Around*

Look at the pictures and skim the article. Then write the name of the invention below each picture.

....

....

....

....

Here are some of the best new inventions for getting around on land and sea.

On land

If you love to take risks when you travel, this is for you: the **Wheelman**. The design is simple: two wheels and a motor. You put your feet in the wheels. It's very similar to skateboarding or surfing. You use your weight to steer and control the speed with a ball you hold in your hand.

Why use two wheels when you can use three? The **Trikke Scooter** looks a little silly, but it's serious transportation. The three wheels make it very stable. And because it's made of aluminum, it's very light. It moves by turning back and forth – just like skiing on the street.

On sea

If you're the kind of person who enjoys being out at sea, but suffers from motion sickness, the **OutRider** will interest you. The boat is attached to a strange-looking ski, allowing it to move smoothly over the water, even at high speeds. It's perfect for those who refuse to give up their love of boating over an upset stomach.

Do you ever feel like surfing when the sea is too flat? Then you need the **PowerSki Jetboard**, a board that makes its own waves. This creation brings together the ease of waterskiing and the freedom of surfing. A former pro surfer designed the lightweight engine to be able to stir up even the calmest water.

A Read the article. Where do you think it is from? Check (✓) the correct answer.

☐ an instruction manual ☐ a catalog ☐ a newsmagazine ☐ an encyclopedia

B Answer these questions.

1. Which inventions have motors? ....
2. Where do you put your feet in the Wheelman? ....
3. How do you steer the Wheelman? ....
4. What makes the Trikke Scooter stable? ....
5. How does the Trikke Scooter move? ....
6. What makes the OutRider move smoothly on the water? ....
7. What two sports does the PowerSki Jetboard combine? ....
8. Who designed the engine for the PowerSki Jetboard? ....

C ***Pair work*** Which of the above inventions is the most useful? the least useful? Would you like to try any of them?

Units 1–2 Progress check

SELF-ASSESSMENT

How well can you do these things? Check (✓) the boxes.

I can	Very well	OK	A little
Listen to and understand the past tense and *used to* (Ex. 1)	☐	☐	☐
Ask and answer questions using the past tense and *used to* (Ex. 1, 2)	☐	☐	☐
Talk about city services using adverbs of quantity (Ex. 3)	☐	☐	☐
Ask for and give information using indirect questions (Ex. 4)	☐	☐	☐

1 LISTENING Celebrity interview

A Listen to an interview with Jeri, a fashion model. Answer the questions.

1. Where did she grow up? ....
2. What did she want to do when she grew up? ....
3. Did she have a hobby? ....
4. Did she have a favorite game? ....
5. What was her favorite place? ....

B ***Pair work*** Use the questions in part A to interview a partner about his or her childhood. Ask additional questions to get more information.

2 DISCUSSION How times have changed!

A ***Pair work*** Talk about how life in your country has changed in the last 50 years. Ask questions like these:

How big were families 50 years ago?
What kinds of homes did people live in?
How did people use to dress?
How were schools different?
What kinds of jobs did men have? women?
How much did people use to earn?

B ***Group work*** Compare your answers. Do you think life was better in the old days? Why or why not?

Units 1–2 Progress check

SELF-ASSESSMENT

Learning objectives: *reflect on one's learning; identify areas that need improvement*

- Ask: "What did you learn in Units 1 and 2?" Elicit Ss' answers.
- Ss complete the Self-assessment. Encourage them to be honest, and point out they will not get a bad grade if they check (✓) "a little."
- Ss move on to the Progress check exercises. You can have Ss complete them in class or for homework, using one of these techniques:

1. Ask Ss to complete all the exercises.
2. Ask Ss: "What do you need to practice?" Then assign exercises based on their answers.
3. Ask Ss to choose and complete exercises based on their Self-assessment.

TIP In a large class, Ss will inevitably identify different weak and strong areas. Remind Ss that even if they have no difficulty with one of the review exercises below, they can still work on fluency and pronunciation. Ss who need more practice can practice with a partner outside class.

1 LISTENING

Learning objectives: *assess one's ability to listen to and understand the past tense and* used to*; assess one's ability to ask and answer questions using the past tense and* used to

A [CD 1, Track 13]

- Set the scene. Jeri is a fashion model who is being interviewed about her childhood.
- Read the interview questions aloud. Remind Ss to take notes, writing down key words and phrases only.
- Play the audio program once or twice. Ss listen and complete the chart. Then check answers.

Audio script *(See page T-225.)*

Answers

1. She grew up in Brighton, England.
2. She wanted to be a doctor or a writer.
3. She used to paint./She (still) paints.
4. Her favorite game was chess.
5. Her favorite place was a summer camp in Ireland.

B *Pair work*

- Explain the task. Then model the first question with a S to show how to respond and add follow-up questions.
  T: Where did you grow up, Maria?
  S: I grew up in Brasília.
  T: Really? That's interesting. How did you like it?
  S: I liked it. There were a lot of things to do.
- In pairs, Ss take turns interviewing each other about their childhoods. Have them add at least two follow-up questions for each topic.

2 DISCUSSION

Learning objective: *assess one's ability to ask and answer questions using the past tense and* used to

A *Pair work*

- Focus Ss' attention on the picture. Ask: "Where is the man going? What did women use to do in those days?" (Answers: He's going to work. They used to stay at home.)
- Ss form pairs. Remind them to give as much information as possible and to ask follow-up questions. Set a time limit of about ten minutes.

B *Group work*

- Each pair joins another pair to compare information.
- Read the questions. Then have Ss discuss their points of view, giving reasons and explanations. Go around the class and listen in.
- ***Option:*** Ask groups to share some of their ideas with the class.

TIP If you don't have enough class time for the speaking activities, assign each S a speaking partner. Then have Ss complete the activities with their partners for homework.

3 SURVEY

Learning objective: *assess one's ability to talk about city services using adverbs of quantity*

A

- Ask a S to read the survey topics aloud. Then Ss complete the survey by checking (✓) the appropriate boxes. Point out that answers are the Ss' opinions.
- Ss complete the task individually.

B *Group work*

- Explain the task and have three Ss read the example conversation. Remind Ss to choose three ways to improve the city.
- Divide the class into small groups. Set a time limit of about ten minutes. Go around the class and make notes on common errors, especially adverbs of quantity. When time is up, write the errors on the board and elicit corrections.
- ***Option:*** Ask one S from each group to write the group's suggestions on the board. Then have the class vote on which three ideas are the best.

ROLE PLAY

Learning objective: *assess one's ability to ask for and give information using indirect questions*

- Divide the class into two groups, A and B. Explain that Student A is a visitor to his or her city or town and Student B is a hotel receptionist. Based on the topics given, each Student A should write some indirect questions to ask about the city.
- While each Student A is writing questions, go over the useful expressions with students in group B. Remind them how a receptionist might begin and end the conversation (e.g., *Can I help you? Have a nice day!*).
- Ss A and B form pairs. If possible, have them stand on either side of a desk, which will represent the reception counter. Set a time limit of about ten minutes.
- During the role play, go around the class and listen. When time is up, suggest ways the conversations could be improved, such as giving more information or asking follow-up questions. Give examples of good communication that you heard.
- Ss change roles and try the role play again.

WHAT'S NEXT?

Learning objective: *become more involved in one's learning*

- Focus Ss' attention on the Self-assessment again. Ask: "How well can you do these things now?"
- Ask Ss to underline one thing they need to review. Ask: "What did you underline? How can you review it?"
- If needed, plan additional activities or reviews based on Ss' answers.

3 SURVEY City planner

A What do you think about these things in your city or town? Complete the survey.

	Not enough	OK	Too many/Too much
places to go dancing	☐	☐	☐
places to listen to music	☐	☐	☐
noise	☐	☐	☐
places to sit and have coffee	☐	☐	☐
places to go shopping	☐	☐	☐
parking	☐	☐	☐
public transportation	☐	☐	☐
places to meet new people	☐	☐	☐

B ***Group work*** Compare your opinions and suggest ways to make your city or town better. Then agree on three improvements.

A: How would you make the city better?
B: There aren't enough places to go dancing. We need more nightclubs.
C: I disagree. There should be fewer clubs. There's too much noise downtown!

4 ROLE PLAY Could you tell me . . . ?

Student A: Imagine you are a visitor in your city or town. Write five indirect questions about these categories. Then ask your questions to the hotel receptionist.

Transportation
Sightseeing
Shopping
Restaurants
Entertainment

Student B: You are a hotel receptionist. Answer the guest's questions. Start like this: *Can I help you?*

Change roles and try the role play again.

useful expressions

Let me think. Oh, yes, . . .
I'm not really sure, but I think . . .
Sorry, I don't know.

WHAT'S NEXT?

Look at your Self-assessment again. Do you need to review anything?

3 Time for a change!

1 WORD POWER Houses and apartments

A These words are used to describe houses and apartments. Which are positive (**P**)? Which are negative (**N**)?

bright	...P...	dingy	....	private	....
comfortable	....	expensive	....	quiet	....
convenient	....	huge	....	safe	....
cramped	....	inconvenient	....	shabby	....
dangerous	....	modern	....	small	....
dark	....	noisy	....	spacious	....

B ***Pair work*** Tell your partner two positive and two negative features about your house or apartment.

"My apartment is very dark and a little cramped. However, it's in a safe neighborhood and it's very private."

2 PERSPECTIVES Which would you prefer?

A Listen to these opinions about houses and apartments.

Apartments are too small for pets.
Apartments aren't big enough for families.
Apartments don't have as many rooms as houses.
Apartments have just as many expenses as houses.
Apartments don't have enough parking spaces.

Houses cost too much money.
Houses aren't as safe as apartments.
Houses aren't as convenient as apartments.
Houses don't have enough closet space.
Houses don't have as much privacy as apartments.

B ***Pair work*** Look at the opinions again. Which statements do you agree with?

A: I agree that apartments are too small for pets.
B: And they don't have enough parking spaces!

Time for a change!

In Unit 3, students discuss homes and making changes. In Cycle 1, they evaluate and compare houses and apartments, using too *and comparatives. In Cycle 2, they talk about changes in their lives, using* I wish.

Cycle 1, Exercises 1–6

WORD POWER

TIP To show the purpose of activities, write the objectives on the board. As you complete each activity, check (✓) that objective, so Ss know what they've learned.

Learning objective: *learn positive and negative adjectives to describe houses and apartments*

- Have Ss discuss their ideal home in pairs. Tell them to think about location, size, view, facilities, and features (e.g., *I'd like a really big house next to the sea. I'd like to have three bedrooms and . . .*).
- ***Option:*** Divide Ss into three groups and assign each group a column of vocabulary words. Ss look up the assigned words in a dictionary. Then Ss re-group and explain the meanings.

A

- Go over the instructions and use the example sentence to model the task.
- Ss work individually to complete the task. Tell them to guess about any words they don't know.
- When Ss finish, let them check their dictionaries.
- ***Option:*** Model the pronunciation of the adjectives in the list and have Ss repeat each word.

Vocabulary

cramped: having very little space; too small
dingy: dark and unattractive
shabby: old and in poor condition
spacious: large; with lots of extra room

- After Ss compare answers in pairs, go over answers as a class.

Answers

bright	P	inconvenient	N
comfortable	P	modern	P
convenient	P	noisy	N
cramped	N	private	P
dangerous	N	quiet	P
dark	N	safe	P
dingy	N	shabby	N
expensive	N	small	N
huge	P	spacious	P

For a new way to practice the vocabulary, try ***Vocabulary Steps*** on page T-154. Choose six positive words. Ss order the words according to what is most important to them.

To review vocabulary, play ***Picture It!*** on page T-147.

B *Pair work*

- Go over the instructions and read the example sentence aloud. Remind Ss that *however, though,* and *but* are all used to show contrast.
- Ss do the activity in pairs. Go around the class and give help as needed.

PERSPECTIVES

Learning objectives: *listen to opinions about houses and apartments; see evaluations and comparisons in context*

A *[CD 1, Track 15]*

- Books closed. Ask: "Do you prefer houses or apartments? Why?" Ss discuss the question in pairs.
- Divide Ss into two groups: houses and apartments. One group writes down three disadvantages of apartments; the other does the same for houses. After three minutes, have the groups exchange papers and add to the list. Go around the class and monitor Ss' comparisons and evaluations. Don't correct their language yet.
- Books open. Ss look at the statements to see which ones they also listed. Explain the meaning of any new words.
- Play the audio program. Ss listen and read silently.

For a new way to teach this Perspectives, try ***Hear the Differences*** on page T-156.

For another way to teach this Perspectives, try ***Running Dictation*** on page T-153.

B *Pair work*

- Explain the task. Ss go over the list and decide which opinions they agree with. Give help as needed.
- ***Option:*** Play the audio program. Pause after each sentence and have Ss put up their hand if they agree. Determine which opinions are most common.

3 GRAMMAR FOCUS

Learning objective: *practice ways to evaluate and compare using adjectives and nouns*

[CD 1, Track 16]

Evaluations with adjectives and nouns

- Explain the difference between *evaluations* and *comparisons*: Both are judgments, but a comparison evaluates one thing against another.
- Have Ss circle the examples of *enough* and *too* in Exercise 2. Ask: "Is the adjective before or after *enough*/*too*?" (Answer: before *enough*, after *too*) Then write this on the board:
  1. *Enough goes after the adjective (big + enough)*
     The apartment isn't big enough.
     Enough goes before the noun (enough + closets)
     Houses don't have enough closets.
  2. *Too always goes before the adjective (too + small)*
     Apartments are too small for pets.

TIP Use a different color for each structure. This helps visual Ss remember them.

- Do a quick substitution drill to practice these structures. Start with *evaluations with adjectives* and then switch to *evaluations with nouns*:
  T: The kitchen isn't big enough. Bedroom.
  S: The bedroom isn't big enough.
  T: There aren't enough closets. Windows.
  S: There aren't enough windows.
- ***Option:*** Begin part A at this point.

Comparisons with adjectives and nouns

- Point out the new structures and have Ss find examples in Exercise 2. For a challenge, have Ss determine the rules. Then write this on the board:
  1. *as + adjective (+ as)*
     Houses are as convenient as apartments.
     Houses aren't as safe as apartments.
  2. *as many + count noun (+ as)*
     Apartments have as many expenses as houses.
     Apartments don't have as many rooms as houses.
  3. *as much + noncount noun (+ as)*
     Houses don't have as much privacy as apartments.
- Do another substitution drill using the information on the board and the sentences in the boxes.
- Play the audio program.
- ***Option:*** Begin part B at this point.

A

- Go over the instructions. Ss look at the two pictures and the ads. Model the first two sentences using *not enough* and *too*.
- Ss work individually to complete the task. Remind them to use words from Exercise 1. Go around the class and give help as needed. Then check answers.

Possible answers

1. There aren't enough windows.
2. It's too dark.
3. It doesn't have enough bathrooms.
4. It's too inconvenient.
5. It's too small./It's too cramped.
6. It's not modern enough./It's not new enough.
7. It's too unsafe./It's too dangerous.
8. There aren't enough parking spaces./There isn't enough parking.

B

- Read the task and example sentences. Remind Ss that all answers must follow one of these three patterns: *as* + adjective + *as*, *as many* + count noun + *as*, *as much* + noncount noun + *as*.
- Ss work individually to complete the task. Have Ss who finish early write their sentences on the board.

Answers

The house isn't as noisy as the apartment.
The apartment doesn't have as many bedrooms as the house.
The house has (just) as many bathrooms as the apartment.
The apartment isn't as spacious as the house.
The apartment isn't as private as the house.
The apartment isn't as big as the house.
The apartment isn't as expensive as the house.
The apartment isn't as modern as the house.
The house isn't as convenient as the apartment.
The apartment doesn't have as many parking spaces as the house.

C *Group work*

- Go over the instructions and the example conversation. Then model the task with one or two Ss.
- As Ss work in pairs, go around the class and give help as needed.
- Elicit opinions and reasons from the class.

For more practice with evaluations and comparisons, play ***Concentration*** on page T-144. Ss match cards with the same meaning (e.g., *It's too small.* and *It's not big enough.*).

3 GRAMMAR FOCUS

Evaluations and comparisons

Evaluations with adjectives
Apartments are**n't** big **enough** for families.
Apartments are **too** small for pets.

Comparisons with adjectives
Houses are**n't as** convenient **as** apartments.
Houses are **just as** convenient **as** apartments.

Evaluations with nouns
Apartments do**n't** have **enough** parking spaces.
Houses cost **too much** money.

Comparisons with nouns
Apartments have **just as many** rooms **as** houses.
Apartments don't have **as much** privacy **as** houses.

A Imagine you are looking for a house or apartment to rent. Read the two ads. Then rewrite the opinions below using the words in parentheses.

Spacious, modern house
3 bedrooms, 1 bathroom; very private; located in quiet suburb; 2-car garage; $950 per month.

Small, older apartment
2 bedrooms, 1 bathroom; located downtown, convenient to the subway; 1 parking space; $500 per month.

1. There are only a few windows. (not enough)
2. It's not bright enough. (too)
3. It has only one bathroom. (not enough)
4. It's not convenient enough. (too)
5. It's not spacious enough. (too)
6. It's too old. (not enough)
7. It isn't safe enough. (too)
8. There's only one parking space. (not enough)

There aren't enough windows.

B Write comparisons of the house and apartment using these words and *as . . . as*. Then compare with a partner.

noisy	big
bedrooms	expensive
bathrooms	modern
space	convenient
private	parking spaces

The house isn't as noisy as the apartment.
The apartment doesn't have as many bedrooms as the house.

C ***Group work*** Which would you prefer to rent, the house or the apartment? Explain your reasons.

A: I'd rent the apartment because the house costs too much.
B: I'd choose the house. The apartment isn't big enough for my dogs!

4 PRONUNCIATION Unpronounced vowels

A Listen and practice. The vowel immediately after a stressed syllable is frequently not pronounced.

avørage	comførtable
difførent	intøresting
sepårate	vegøtable

B Write four sentences using some of the words in part A. Then practice reading them with a partner. Pay attention to unpronounced vowels.

In my hometown, the average apartment has two bedrooms.

5 LISTENING Capsule hotels

A Listen to Brad describe a "capsule hotel." Check (✓) the words that best describe it.

- [ ] busy
- [ ] comfortable
- [ ] convenient
- [ ] cramped
- [ ] dangerous
- [ ] expensive

B Listen again. In addition to a bed, what else does the hotel provide? Write four things.

....

....

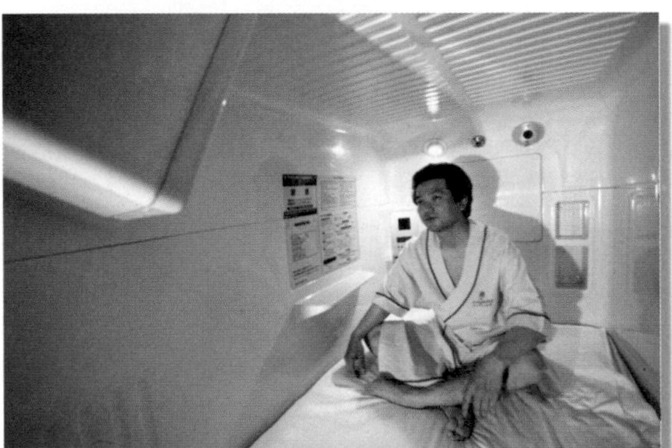

C ***Pair work*** Would you like to stay in a capsule hotel? Why or why not?

6 WRITING A descriptive e-mail

A Imagine you've just moved to a new apartment. Write an e-mail to a friend comparing your old apartment to your new one.

Dear Emma

Dear Emma,

How are things with you? My big news is that Mike and I just moved to a new apartment! Do you remember our old apartment? It didn't have enough bedrooms for us. Well, the new apartment has three bedrooms. Also, the old apartment was too cramped, but the new one . . .

B ***Pair work*** Take turns reading each other's e-mails. Is there anything else you'd like to know about your partner's new apartment?

4 PRONUNCIATION

Learning objective: *practice stress and unpronounced vowels*

A [CD 1, Track 17]

- Books closed. Write the words *average* and *different* on the board. Ask: "How many syllables do these words have?" Elicit answers, but don't say if they are right or wrong.
- Explain that although they are written with three syllables, we only hear two. Play the first two words on the audio program.
- Books open. Give Ss a minute to read part A. Then play the rest of the audio program.

B

- Explain the task and model the example sentence. Ss write their own sentences.
- Ss practice their sentences in pairs. Go around the class and listen in. If necessary, model the words and let Ss repeat.
- ***Option:*** Have pairs exchange sentences with another pair, or have Ss pass their sentences around the class. Ss take turns reading a new sentence aloud to the class. Correct pronunciation if necessary.

5 LISTENING

Learning objective: *develop skills in listening for main ideas and details*

A [CD 1, Track 18]

- Ask the class if anyone knows what a capsule hotel is. If not, explain the meaning of the word capsule (a small container). Have them predict which adjectives describe a capsule hotel.

> **TIP** To develop Ss' top-down listening skills, encourage them to make predictions before playing the audio program.

- Explain the task and read the six adjectives. Then play the audio program. Ss check (✓) the words that best describe a capsule hotel.

Answers

busy, convenient, cramped

Audio script *(See page T-225.)*

B

- Play the audio program again. This time Ss listen for details. Let Ss compare their answers in pairs before you go over them as a class.

Possible answers

The capsule hotel provides a TV, a reading light, a radio, an alarm clock, and lockers.

C *Pair work*

- Ss form pairs and discuss the questions. Encourage them to explain their opinions.

6 WRITING

Learning objectives: *learn e-mail writing skills; practice comparing two apartments*

A

- Have Ss read the instructions and the example e-mail silently.
- Write this on the board:

Old apartment	New apartment
not enough bedrooms	three bedrooms
too cramped	spacious

- As a class, Ss brainstorm other ways to compare the two apartments (e.g., *dangerous – safe, only one parking space – two parking spaces*).
- Have Ss select at least three comparisons for their e-mail. Then Ss write an e-mail.

> **TIP** If you are going to grade Ss' writing, be sure to let them know what you expect of them.

B *Pair work*

- Ss exchange papers with another classmate. Then they read each other's e-mails and ask questions.

End of Cycle 1

Do your students need more practice?

Assign . . .	*for more practice in . . .*
Workbook Exercises 1–4 on pages 13–15	Grammar, Vocabulary, Reading, and Writing
Lab Guide Exercises 1 and 3–5 on page 5	Listening, Pronunciation, Speaking, and Grammar

7 SNAPSHOT

Learning objective: *learn vocabulary for talking about wishes*

- Books closed. Ask Ss to brainstorm some common wishes people have about their lives (e.g., *earn more money*).
- Books open. Ss read the Snapshot and compare the wishes with their predictions.
- Explain the task. Ss discuss the questions in pairs or groups.
- Go around the class and give help as needed. Then ask pairs or groups if they discovered anything interesting. Don't expect Ss to produce expressions with *wish* correctly. Instead, notice how they express their ideas.

8 CONVERSATION

Learning objectives: *practice a conversation about wishes; see examples of the verb* wish *in context*

A [CD 1, Track 19]

- Ss cover the text and look at the picture. Ask: "Do you think they are friends? Strangers? Where are they? How old do you think they are? What do you think they are talking about?" Accept any reasonable answers.
- Books closed. Play the audio program. Ss listen to find out if the two men are friends or strangers and what they are talking about. (Answers: friends; Terry is complaining about living with his parents.)
- Write these focus questions on the board:
  True or false?
  1. Terry hates living at home.
  2. Terry's parents are always asking him to be home before midnight.
  3. Terry thinks his life is difficult.
  4. Terry is going to move out of his parents' house soon.
- Play the audio program again. Ss listen and answer the questions on the board. Then check answers. (Answers: 1. F 2. T 3. T 4. F)
- ***Option:*** Ask Ss to listen for examples of additional information that Terry gives.
- Elicit or explain any new vocabulary.

Vocabulary

I'm afraid so.: unfortunately
room and board: accommodation and food

- Ask Ss to think about the two men's personalities and the kinds of gestures and facial expressions they would use. Then play the audio program and have Ss listen for the emotions expressed by the speakers.
- Books open. Ss practice the conversation in pairs.

> **TIP** To find out how your Ss learn best, try different methods (e.g., *listen and repeat, listen and read silently, listen and mouth the words*). Then ask your Ss which method(s) they find most useful.

! For another way to practice this Conversation, try ***Say It With Feeling!*** on page T-150.

- ***Option:*** Have a class discussion about living with parents. Is Terry's life easy or difficult? Should a son help his parents around the house? Should parents worry about an adult son? Should Terry pay for his room and board?

B

- Read the instructions aloud. Then play the second part of the audio program. Have Ss listen to Brian's wishes. Then elicit Ss' responses from the class.

Audio script *(See page T-225.)*

Answers

Brian would like to change jobs and live somewhere more exciting.

! For another way to practice *wish* and other expressions, try ***Substitution Dialog*** on page T-151. Use only the first half of the dialog, until ". . . parents are like that!" Ss replace these underlined expressions with:

1. living with your parents? / working at the bank? / studying? / . . .
2. my own apartment / a different job / a career / . . .
3. parents / co-workers / teachers / . . .
4. be home before midnight / make photocopies / write long compositions / . . .
5. worrying about me / nagging me / giving me so much homework / . . .

7 SNAPSHOT

Common Wishes People Have About Their Lives
☐ add more hours to the day
☐ change my appearance
☐ improve my personality
☐ move to a new home
☐ enjoy life more
☐ go back to school
☐ become healthier
☐ find a better job
☐ make new friends

Based on interviews with adults between the ages of 18 and 50

Which of these wishes would be easy to do? Which would be difficult or impossible?
Check (✓) some of the things you would like to do. Then tell a partner why.
What other things would you like to change about your life? Why?

8 CONVERSATION Making changes

A Listen and practice.

Brian: So, are you still living with your parents, Terry?
Terry: I'm afraid so. I wish I had my own apartment.
Brian: Why? Don't you like living at home?
Terry: It's OK, but my parents are always asking me to be home before midnight. I wish they'd stop worrying about me.
Brian: Yeah, parents are like that!
Terry: And they expect me to help around the house. I hate housework. I wish life weren't so difficult.
Brian: So, why don't you move out?
Terry: Hey, I wish I could, but where else can I get free room and board?

B Listen to the rest of the conversation. What changes would Brian like to make in his life?

9 GRAMMAR FOCUS

Wish

Use wish + past tense to refer to present wishes.

I **live** with my parents.
I wish I **didn't live** with my parents.
I wish I **had** my own apartment.

I **can't move** out.
I wish I **could move** out.

Life **is** difficult.
I wish it **were*** easier.
I wish it **weren't** so difficult.

My parents **won't stop** worrying about me.
I wish they **would stop** worrying about me.

**After* wish, were *is used with all pronouns.*

A Read these facts about people's lives. Then rewrite the sentences using *wish*. (More than one answer is possible.)

1. Diane can't wear contact lenses. *She wishes she could wear contact lenses.*
2. Beth's class is so boring. ....
3. My parents can't afford a new car. ....
4. Dan can't fit into his old jeans. ....
5. I can't remember my PIN number. ....
6. Laura doesn't have any free time. ....

B ***Pair work*** Think of five things you wish you could change. Then discuss them with your partner.

A: What do you wish you could change?
B: Well, I'm not in very good shape. I wish I were more fit.

10 SPEAKING Wish list

A What do you wish were different about these things? Write down your wishes.

my bedroom	my appearance	my possessions
my school or job	my family	my skills

B ***Group work*** Compare your wishes. Does anyone have the same wish?

A: I wish my bedroom were a different color. It's not bright enough.
B: Me, too! I wish I could paint my bedroom bright orange.
C: I like the color of my bedroom, but my bed is too small.

11 INTERCHANGE 3 Wishful thinking

Find out more about your classmates' wishes. Go to Interchange 3.

9 GRAMMAR FOCUS

Learning objective: *practice using* wish

[CD 1, Track 20]

- Explain that we use *wish* when we would like reality to be different. Refer Ss to the Conversation on page 19 and have Ss underline the four examples of *wish* that Terry uses.
- Draw the chart below on the board. Write the four sentences about Terry in the left-hand column. Ask Ss to complete the right-hand column with examples of Terry's wishes from the dialog:

Terry's reality	Terry's wishes
1. I live with my parents.	I wish I had my own apartment.
2. I can't move out.	
3. My parents won't stop worrying about me.	
4. Life is so difficult.	

- Focus Ss' attention on the Grammar Focus box on page 20. Explain that if we want the present situation to change, we use the past tense with *wish*.
- Go over the six wishes in the Grammar Focus box and ask Ss to underline the past tense verbs. (Answers: *didn't live, had, could, were, weren't, would*)
- Point out that the *wish* sentence must be the opposite of the reality. For example:
  I am poor. I wish I were rich. or *I wish I weren't poor.*
- Point out that with the verb *be*, we use *were/weren't* with all pronouns, even *it*. Some native speakers also use *was/wasn't* in informal situations (e.g., *I wish I was . . .*).
- Practice this drill with the class. Give the real situation and have Ss say a sentence using *wish*.
  For example:
  T: I don't have a car.
  S: I wish I had a car.
  T: I can't fly.
  S: I wish I could fly.
  T: I'm tired.
  S: I wish I weren't tired.
  T: It won't stop raining.
  S: I wish it would stop raining.

For more practice, play the ***Chain Game*** on page T-145. Ss make one wish each, then play the game.
S1: I wish I could fly.
S2: S1 wishes he could fly and I wish I were . . .
S3: S1 wishes he could fly, S2 wishes she were . . . , and I wish . . .

- Play the audio program to present the statements in the box.

A

- Explain the task and any new vocabulary (**PIN number:** Personal Identification Number, or the number you need to get money from a cash machine).
- Ss complete the task individually before comparing answers in pairs. Elicit Ss' responses.

Possible answers

1. Diane/She wishes she could wear contact lenses.
2. Beth wishes her class were more interesting./She wishes her class weren't so boring.
3. My parents/They wish they could afford a new car.
4. Dan/He wishes he could fit into his old jeans.
5. I wish I could remember my PIN number.
6. Laura/She wishes she had some free time.

B *Pair work*

- Go over the instructions and give Ss time to think of five wishes. Ask two Ss to model the example conversation. Then have Ss discuss their wishes in pairs.

10 SPEAKING

Learning objectives: *practice talking about wishes; develop discussion skills*

A

- Explain the task and remind Ss to use language from the unit. Ss write at least one wish for each topic. Ss who finish early can write down more wishes for some topics.

B *Group work*

- Have Ss compare their wishes in small groups. Tell them to check (✓) the topic in part A each time they find something in common with a classmate.
- Ask Ss to share with the class some things they have in common.

11 INTERCHANGE 3

See page T-116 for teaching notes.

12 READING

Learning objectives: *read an article about bad habits; develop skills in skimming, summarizing, and organizing text*

- Books closed. Ask: "Do you know people who like to gossip? What kinds of things do they gossip about? What's the most interesting piece of gossip you heard recently? How harmful is gossip?"
- Books open. Explain that the article is about bad habits, including gossiping. Ask: "What are the other two bad habits mentioned in the article?" Have Ss skim the text quickly to find the answers. (Answers: leaving things until the last minute, being late)
- ***Option:*** Point out that the answers are in the first sentence. Explain that it's common to write the main points at the beginning of an article. We call this the *topic sentence*.
- Ask Ss if they are guilty of any of these habits. Have a brief discussion. Did anyone *use to* have one of these habits, but changed? Which habit do they think is the worst?

A

- Explain the task. Have Ss read the article. Then elicit the answer.

Answer

1. The article starts with a description and then gives advice.

- Encourage Ss to look at the organization of the text: The opening paragraph is a description and the three other paragraphs give advice on how to break each habit. This will help Ss see how they should organize their own compositions.

B

- Have Ss read the article again silently and at their own pace, without using their dictionaries. Ask them to underline, circle, or highlight any words they can't guess from context.
- Elicit or explain any new vocabulary.

Vocabulary

gossip: tell other people rumors, without knowing the facts
trouble: problems
for good: forever; permanently
put things off: delay doing some tasks or jobs
overwhelming: too difficult or complicated
project: task
reward yourself: give yourself a little present after you have done something good
secret: a piece of information that is private
set an alarm clock: put the alarm on for a specific time

For a new way to practice this vocabulary, try ***Vocabulary Mingle*** on page T-153.

- Explain the task. Ss read the sentences and decide where each sentence could go in the article. Read the first sentence aloud and ask the class to which bad habits it refers. (Answer: Never On Time) Next, ask Ss if this is a problem or a solution. (Answer: Solution) So, the sentence could go in paragraph 6. Write 6 next to the sentence.
- Ss complete the task individually then compare answers in pairs.
- Write the answers on the board and then go over them with the class.

Answers

a. 6 b. 4 c. 1 d. 5 e. 2 f. 3

C Pair work

- Write the three bad habits on the board:
  I Can Do It Tomorrow *Guess What I Just Heard*
  Never On Time
- In pairs, Ss think of at least one other way to break each habit. Ss write their ideas on the board under the appropriate heading. Elicit ideas and keep the activity moving by having several pens or chalk available.

Possible answers

I Can Do It Tomorrow: Move your deadline forward and plan something nice for the free time you will have.
Guess What I Just Heard: Politely tell the person who is gossiping that you don't want to hear it.
Never On Time: Set your watch ahead by ten minutes.

- Ss choose the two best ideas from each column.

For more speaking practice, play ***Just One Minute*** on page T-146. Give Ss topics (e.g., *my ideal home, houses and apartments, common wishes, bad habits*).

End of Cycle 2

Do your students need more practice?

Assign . . .	*for more practice in . . .*
Workbook Exercises 5–8 on pages 16–18	Grammar, Vocabulary, Reading, and Writing
Lab Guide Exercises 2 and 6–9 on pages 5–6	Listening, Pronunciation, Speaking, and Grammar
Video Activity Book Unit 3	Listening, Speaking, and Cultural Awareness
CD-ROM Unit 3	Grammar, Vocabulary, Reading, Listening, and Speaking

12 READING

Break Those Bad Habits

Skim the article. What three bad habits does the article mention?

Some people leave work until the last minute, a lot of us can't stop gossiping, and others always arrive to events late. These aren't serious problems, but they are bad habits that can cause trouble. Habits like these waste your time and, in some cases, might even affect your relationships. What can you do about them? Read this advice to end your bad habits for good!

I Can Do It Tomorrow

1 PROBLEM: Do you leave projects until the very last minute and then stay up all night to finish them?

2 SOLUTION: People often put things off because they seem overwhelming. Try dividing the project into smaller steps. After you finish each task, reward yourself with a snack or a call to a friend.

Guess What I Just Heard

3 PROBLEM: Do you try not to talk about other people, but can't help yourself? Do you often feel bad after you've done it?

4 SOLUTION: First, don't listen to gossip. If someone tells you a secret, just say, "Really? I haven't heard that." Then think of some other news to offer – about yourself.

Never On Time

5 PROBLEM: Are you always late? Do your friends invite you to events a half hour early?

6 SOLUTION: Set an alarm clock. For example, if a movie starts at 8:00 and it takes 20 minutes to get to the theater, you have to leave at 7:40. Set the alarm to go off at the time you need to leave.

A Read the article. Then check (✓) the best description of the article.

- ☐ 1. The article starts with a description and then gives advice.
- ☐ 2. The article starts with a description and then gives facts.
- ☐ 3. The article gives the writer's opinion.

B Where do these sentences belong? Write the number of the paragraph where each sentence could go.

.... a. You can also ask a friend to come to your home before the event.
.... b. Ask yourself: "How would I feel if someone told my secrets?"
.... c. Do you ever make up excuses to explain your unfinished work?
.... d. Are you ever so late that the people you're meeting leave?
.... e. You can also ask a friend to call you to ask about your progress.
.... f. Are people afraid to tell you things about themselves?

C ***Pair work*** Can you think of another way to break each of these bad habits?

4 I've never heard of that!

1 SNAPSHOT

Favorite Ethnic Dishes
KOREA
BRAZIL
SINGAPORE
LATIN AMERICA
Bulgogi
Beef marinated with soy sauce and other spices
Feijoada
A dish made of black beans, garlic, spices, and pork
Fish Head Curry
A dish made from a fish head cooked in a rich curry sauce
Ceviche
Raw seafood marinated in lime juice and chili peppers

Sources: *Fodor's South America*; *Fodor's Southeast Asia*; *www.globalgourmet.com*

Which dishes are made with meat? with fish or seafood?
Have you ever tried any of these dishes? Which ones would you like to try?
What ethnic foods are popular in your country?

2 CONVERSATION Have you ever . . . ?

A Listen and practice.

Steve: Hey, this sounds strange – snails with garlic. Have you ever eaten snails?
Kathy: Yes, I have. I had them here just last week.
Steve: Did you like them?
Kathy: Yes, I did. They were delicious! Why don't you try some?
Steve: No, I don't think so.
Waiter: Have you decided on an appetizer yet?
Kathy: Yes. I'll have a small order of the snails, please.
Waiter: And you, sir?
Steve: I think I'll have the fried brains.
Kathy: Fried brains? I've never heard of that! It sounds scary.

B Listen to the rest of the conversation. How did Steve like the fried brains? What else did he order?

I've never heard of that!

In Unit 4, students discuss food, recipes, and cooking methods. In Cycle 1, they talk about personal experiences using the past tense and the present perfect. In Cycle 2, they describe recipes using sequence adverbs.

Cycle 1, Exercises 1–7

1 SNAPSHOT

Learning objective: *talk about food and ethnic dishes*

- Books closed. Ss discuss food.

  In a heterogeneous class: Ask for names of some popular dishes that people like to eat in the Ss' countries. Elicit additional information about the dishes Ss mention. Ask: "What's it made of? Do you eat it only on special occasions?"

  In a homogeneous class: Ask Ss about their favorite ethnic foods (e.g., *Japanese sushi*, *Italian pizza*, *Korean kimchi*, *Indian curry*, *Mexican tacos*).

- Books open. Give Ss a few minutes to look over the information in the Snapshot. Explain any unknown words or expressions.
- Go over the questions. Then have Ss discuss them in pairs or groups.
- ***Option:*** To prepare Ss for vocabulary in the unit, have the class brainstorm in groups: four kinds of meat, fish, vegetables, and fruit. This could be done as a race against each other or against time.

Possible answers

Meat	*Fish/seafood*	*Vegetables*	*Fruit*
chicken	shrimp	(chili) pepper	banana
pork	salmon	onion	avocado
beef	tuna	carrot	tomato
ham	lobster	eggplant	lime

2 CONVERSATION

Learning objectives: *practice ordering food in a restaurant; see the simple past and the present perfect in context*

A [CD 1, Track 21]

- Ask Ss to look at the picture. Ask: "Where are these people? What do you think they are they eating? How do they look?" Accept any reasonable answers.
- Elicit or explain any new vocabulary.

Vocabulary

snails: small land animals with a hard round shell and no legs
garlic: a plant used in cooking to give a strong taste
appetizer: a small dish served at the beginning of a meal
brains: the organ found in the head of an animal
scary: frightening

- Books closed. Write these questions on the board:
  1. *Has the man eaten snails before?*
  2. *Has the woman eaten snails before?*
  3. *Has the woman eaten fried brains before?*
- Play the audio program. Ss listen for answers to the questions on the board. Elicit Ss' answers. (Answers: 1. no 2. yes 3. no)
- Books open. Play the audio program again. Ss listen and read silently.
- ***Option:*** Focus Ss' attention on the word *have* in the conversation. Explain that we don't stress the word *have* in *Have you ever . . . ?*, when it's an auxiliary verb, but we do stress *have* in *I'll have . . .* when it's the main verb. Play the audio program again, this time pausing so Ss can practice the difference in pronunciation.
- Ss practice the conversation in groups of three. Encourage them to use facial expressions and to have fun.
- ***Option:*** Books closed. Have Ss act out the conversation in front of the class. Tell them that they can substitute any food words they want.

! For another way to practice this Conversation, try ***Disappearing Dialog*** on page T-151.

B

- Read the questions and then play the rest of the audio program. Ss listen for the answers.
- After Ss compare responses in pairs or groups, elicit and check answers as a class.

Audio script *(See page T-225.)*

Answers

Steve didn't like the fried brains (at all).
He ordered a (nice, juicy) hamburger (medium rare), french fries, and a large soda.

3 PRONUNCIATION

Learning objective: *notice and practice saying common consonant clusters*

A  ***[CD 1, Track 22]***

- Play the audio program. Ss listen and notice how two consonants at the beginning of a word, called *consonant clusters*, are pronounced.
- Play the audio program again, pausing after each word.

B *Pair work*

- Refer Ss to page 22 and have them find examples of each consonant cluster. Check answers as a class.

Possible answers

scary, strange, small, snails, spices, brains/fried, black

4 GRAMMAR FOCUS

Learning objective: *ask and answer questions using the simple past and the present perfect*

[CD 1, Track 23]

Simple past and present perfect

- As a review, write these sentences on the board:
  1. *We use the ________ for completed events at a definite time in the past.*
  2. *We use the ________ for events that happened at an indefinite time in the past.*
  3. *We use the ________ for events that began in the past and continue up to the present.*
  4. *We usually use the ________ with ever and never.*
- Ask Ss to complete the sentences with either *simple past* or *present perfect*. Then elicit answers from the class. (Answers: 1. simple past 2. present perfect 3. present perfect 4. present perfect)
- Draw the following time line on the board to show how we use the present perfect to describe events that occur any time between birth and now.

Birth *(from birth until now)* *Now*

Have you (ever) eaten snails?

Present perfect

- Have Ss circle the past participles in the Conversation on page 22. (Answers: eaten, decided, heard) If necessary, refer Ss to the list of participles in the appendix at the back of the book.
- Explain that when the present perfect is used to introduce a topic, it becomes a definite event and the simple past is used.
- Play the audio program. Ss read the Grammar Focus box as they listen and repeat.

A

- Read the instructions and model the first dialog with a S. Ss complete the task individually. Check responses before pairs practice together.

Answers

1. A: Have you ever **been** to a picnic at the beach?
   B: Yes, I **have**. We **cooked** hamburgers.
2. A: Have you **tried** sushi?
   B: No, I **haven't**, but I'd like to.
3. A: Did you **have** breakfast today?
   B: Yes, I **did**. I **ate** a huge breakfast.
4. A: Have you ever **eaten** Mexican food?
   B: Yes, I **have**. In fact, I **ate** some just last week.
5. A: Did you **drink** coffee this morning?
   B: Yes, I **did**. I **had** some on my way to work.

B *Pair work*

- Explain the task. Encourage Ss to give their own information. Then model the task with a S.
  T: Have you ever been to a picnic at the beach?
  S: Yes, I have. We ate chicken and . . .
- Ss work in pairs. Go around the class and give help as needed. Go over problems when Ss finish the task.

For a new way to practice past participles, try ***Participle Concentration*** on page T-156.

5 LISTENING

Learning objective: *develop skills in listening for specific information and making inferences*

 ***[CD 1, Track 24]***

- Set the scene. People are talking in a restaurant. Explain the task and the listed items.
- Ss work in pairs to guess what words they might hear for each item. For example, for *water*, the speakers might mention *glass*, *thirsty*, *drink*, or *ice*. For *bread*, they might mention *hungry*, *sandwich*, *slice*, *butter*, or *jam*.
- Play the audio program. Ss listen and then compare answers with a partner. Check answers as a class.

Audio script *(See page T-226.)*

Answers

1. water	3. pasta	5. coffee
2. a meal	4. the meat	6. the check

3 PRONUNCIATION Consonant clusters

A Listen and practice. Notice how the two consonants at the beginning of a word are pronounced together.

/k/	/t/	/m/	/n/	/p/	/r/	/l/
skim	start	smart	snack	spare	brown	blue
scan	step	smile	snow	speak	gray	play

B ***Pair work*** Find one more word on page 22 for each consonant cluster in part A. Then practice saying the words.

4 GRAMMAR FOCUS

Simple past vs. present perfect

Use the simple past for completed events at a definite time in the past.
Use the present perfect for events within a time period up to the present.

Have you ever **eaten** snails?
Yes, I **have**. I **tried** them last month.
Did you **like** them?
Yes, I **did**. They **were** delicious.

Have you ever **been** to a Vietnamese restaurant?
No, I **haven't**. But I **ate** at a Thai restaurant last night.
Did you **go** alone?
No, I **went** with some friends.

A Complete these conversations. Then practice with a partner.

1. A: Have you ever .... (be) to a picnic at the beach?
   B: Yes, I .... We .... (cook) hamburgers.
2. A: Have you .... (try) sushi?
   B: No, I .... , but I'd like to.
3. A: Did you .... (have) breakfast today?
   B: Yes, I .... I .... (eat) a huge breakfast.
4. A: Have you ever .... (eat) Mexican food?
   B: Yes, I .... In fact, I .... (eat) some just last week.
5. A: Did you .... (drink) coffee this morning?
   B: Yes, I .... I .... (have) some on my way to work.

B ***Pair work*** Ask and answer the questions in part A. Give your own information.

5 LISTENING What are they talking about?

Listen to six people ask questions about food and drink in a restaurant. Check (✓) the item that each person is talking about.

1. ☐ water ☐ bread
2. ☐ a meal ☐ a plate
3. ☐ soup ☐ pasta
4. ☐ coffee ☐ the meat
5. ☐ cake ☐ coffee
6. ☐ the check ☐ the menu

6 SPEAKING *Tell me more!*

Pair work Ask your partner these questions and four more of your own. Then ask follow-up questions.

Have you ever been on a diet?
Have you ever tried ethnic food?
Have you ever been to a vegetarian restaurant?
Have you ever eaten something you didn't like?

A: Have you ever been on a diet?
B: Yes, I have.
A: Did you lose any weight?
B: No, I didn't. I actually gained weight!

7 INTERCHANGE 4 *Risky business*

Find out some interesting facts about your classmates.
Go to Interchange 4.

8 WORD POWER *Cooking methods*

A How do you cook the foods below? Check (✓) the methods that are most common in your country. Then compare with a partner.

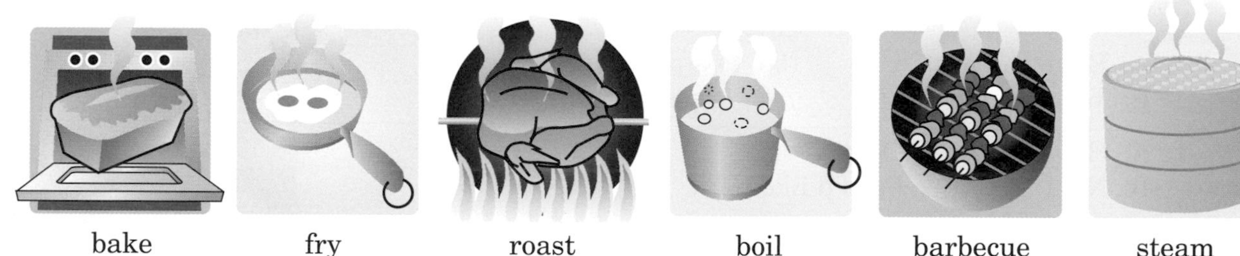

Methods	Foods								
	fish	shrimp	eggs	chicken	beef	potatoes	onions	eggplant	bananas
bake	☐	☐	☐	☐	☐	☐	☐	☐	☐
fry	☐	☐	☐	☐	☐	☐	☐	☐	☐
roast	☐	☐	☐	☐	☐	☐	☐	☐	☐
boil	☐	☐	☐	☐	☐	☐	☐	☐	☐
barbecue	☐	☐	☐	☐	☐	☐	☐	☐	☐
steam	☐	☐	☐	☐	☐	☐	☐	☐	☐

B ***Pair work*** What's your favorite way to cook or eat the foods in part A?

A: Have you ever steamed fish?
B: No, I haven't. I prefer to bake it.

6 SPEAKING

Learning objective: *talk about experiences using the simple past and the present perfect*

Pair work

- Explain the task. Ss practice asking questions using the present perfect, and responding using the simple past.
- Present the questions and model the example conversation. Ss make up four more questions to ask a partner.
- Ss complete the activity in pairs. Go around the class and give help as needed.
- ***Option:*** Set this up as a competition. The pair that continues talking the longest, wins!

For more speaking practice, try the ***Onion Ring*** technique on page T-151.

7 INTERCHANGE 4

See page T-117 for teaching notes.

End of Cycle 1

Do your students need more practice?

Assign . . .	***for more practice in . . .***
Workbook Exercises 1–3 on pages 19–21	Grammar, Vocabulary, Reading, and Writing
Lab Guide Exercises 1–6 on page 7	Listening, Pronunciation, Speaking, and Grammar

Cycle 2, Exercises 8–14

8 WORD POWER

Learning objective: *learn vocabulary for discussing ways to cook different types of foods*

A

- Focus Ss' attention on the six pictures above the chart. Say the words and have the class repeat.
- Explain the task. Then read the words in the chart and have Ss repeat. Explain any words that Ss don't know.
- Model how to check (✓) the most common cooking method(s) used for each food in the chart. Read aloud the first food: fish. Ask: "How do people cook fish in your country? Do they usually bake it, fry it, roast it, boil it, barbecue it, or steam it?"
- Ss work individually to check (✓) the cooking methods that are most common in their country. Go around the class and give help as needed.
- Stop the activity after a few minutes and have Ss compare their charts in pairs. Then ask a few Ss to write their ideas on the board.

Possible answers

(The answers given here generally reflect North American cooking techniques.)

fish: bake, fry, barbecue, steam
shrimp: fry, boil, barbecue
eggs: fry, boil
chicken: bake, fry, roast, barbecue
beef: roast, barbecue
potatoes: bake, fry, roast, boil
onions: fry, roast
eggplant: bake, fry
bananas: bake in bread or pies, fry

B *Pair work*

- Ask two Ss to read the example conversation. Have Ss work in pairs or groups. Then use a show of hands to find out which cooking method is the favorite for each of the foods in part A.

To practice the vocabulary, play the ***Chain Game*** on page T-145. Have Ss make sentences like this:
S1: Last night I baked bread.
S2: Last night I baked bread and boiled fish.
S3: Last night I baked bread, boiled fish, and fried some potatoes.

9 PERSPECTIVES

Learning objectives: *read about Elvis Presley's favorite recipe; see sequence adverbs in context*

- Books closed. Ask: "What do you know about Elvis Presley?" Elicit ideas. Then tell Ss that his favorite sandwich was peanut butter and banana!

A [CD 1, Track 25]

- Set the scene. Someone is describing how to make Elvis's favorite sandwich. Write these questions on the board:
  1. What food do you need to make the sandwich?
  2. How many steps are there?
  (Answers: 1. peanut butter, banana, bread, and butter 2. five)
- Play the audio program. Then check Ss' answers to the questions on the board. Ask: "What do you think of the sandwich? Is it easy or difficult to make? Does it sound delicious, OK, or scary?"
- Books open. Play the audio program again. Ss listen and read along silently.
- ***Option:*** Ss list the kitchen tools that a person needs to make the sandwich (e.g., *plate, tablespoon, toaster, fork, bowl, frying pan*). This could be done as a race.

B Pair work

- Explain the task. Ss number the pictures from 1 to 5. Elicit answers.

Answers

2, 5, 3, 1, 4

- ***Option:*** Have Ss describe how to make the sandwich from memory. Don't expect Ss to use sequence adverbs at this point.
- Ask Ss: "Would you like to try the sandwich? Why or why not?" Elicit responses.

10 GRAMMAR FOCUS

Learning objective: *describe how to prepare food using sequence adverbs*

[CD 1, Track 26]

- Play the audio program to present the sentences in the box. Ss listen and repeat. Explain that these sequence adverbs – *first*, *then*, *next*, *after that*, and *finally* – are connecting words that show the order of steps in a process or events in a story.
- Point out that *then*, *next*, and *after that* are interchangeable. In other words, after *first* and before *finally*, they can be used in any order.

A

- Go over the task. If necessary, use the pictures to explain new vocabulary. Then model the first part of the task by using the first picture.
  T: In the first picture, someone is lighting charcoal for a barbecue. Look at the mixed-up sentences in the list for the one that matches it. Can anyone find it?
  S: Yes, it's the second sentence, *put charcoal in the barbecue and light it.*
  T: That's right. So write *1* in the box to the left of that sentence.

> **TIP** To get Ss' attention while you explain the instructions, vary your technique and position (e.g., give the instructions from the back of the classroom sometimes).

- Ss complete the first part of the task individually. Check answers before Ss begin the second part.

Answers

(Answers here are for both parts of the task.)

1. **First**, put charcoal in the barbecue and light it.
2. **Then** cut up some meat and vegetables. Marinate them for 20 minutes in your favorite barbecue sauce.
3. **Next**, put the meat and vegetables on the skewers.
4. **After that**, put the kebabs on the barbecue and cook for 10 to 15 minutes, turning them over from time to time.
5. **Finally**, take the kebabs off the barbecue and enjoy!

- Ss complete the second part of the task. When they finish, go over answers (see above).

B Pair work

- Explain the task. Ss cover the recipe in part A and look only at the five pictures showing how to barbecue kebabs. Ss take turns explaining each step to a partner. They do not need to use exactly the same words. Remind Ss to use sequence adverbs.

For more practice with sequence adverbs, play ***Mime*** on page T-148. Ask Ss to act out a sequence of actions, such as changing a flat tire.

PERSPECTIVES Family cookbook

A Listen to this recipe for Elvis Presley's favorite peanut butter and banana sandwich.

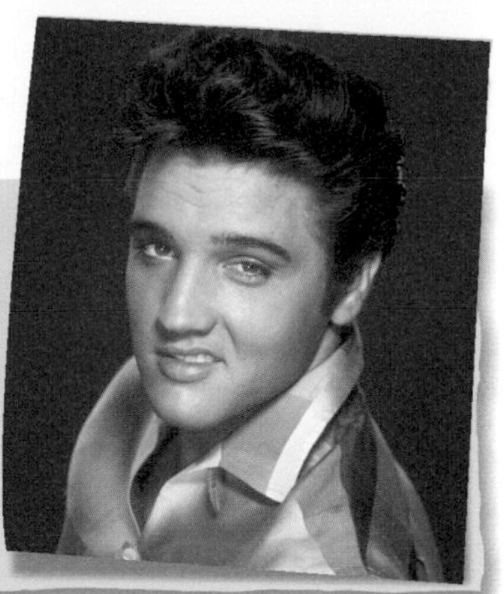

3 tablespoons peanut butter
1 banana, mashed
2 slices of bread
2 tablespoons butter, melted

First, mix the peanut butter and mashed banana together.
Then lightly toast the slices of bread.
Next, spread the peanut butter and banana mixture on the toast.
After that, close the sandwich and put it in a pan with melted butter.
Finally, fry the bread until it's brown on both sides.

B ***Pair work*** Look at the steps in the recipe again. Number the pictures from 1 to 5. Would you like to try Elvis's specialty?

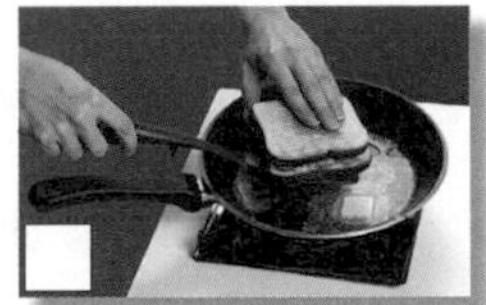

10 GRAMMAR FOCUS

Sequence adverbs

First, mix the peanut butter and banana together.
Then toast the slices of bread.
Next, spread the mixture on the toast.
After that, put the sandwich in a pan with butter.
Finally, fry the sandwich until it's brown on both sides.

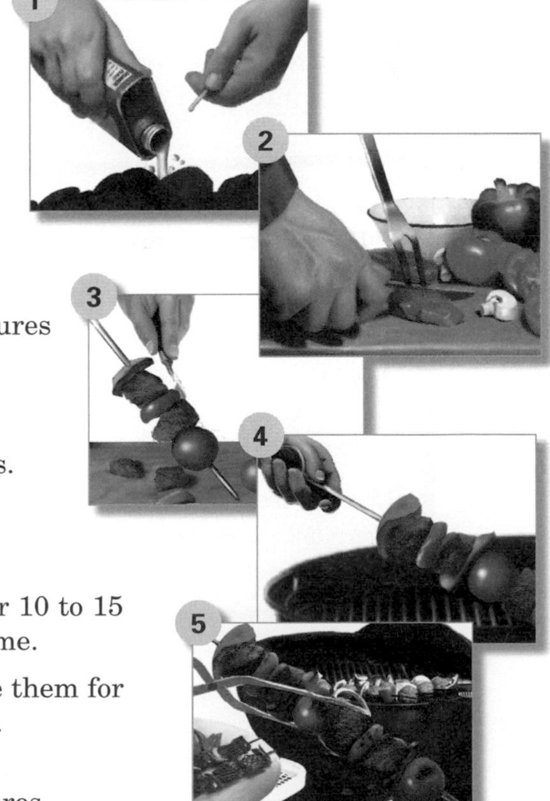

A Here's a recipe for barbecued kebabs. Look at the pictures and number the steps from 1 to 5. Then add a sequence adverb to each step.

☐ .... put the meat and vegetables on the skewers.
☐ .... put charcoal in the barbecue and light it.
☐ .... take the kebabs off the barbecue and enjoy!
☐ .... put the kebabs on the barbecue and cook for 10 to 15 minutes, turning them over from time to time.
☐ .... cut up some meat and vegetables. Marinate them for 20 minutes in your favorite barbecue sauce.

B ***Pair work*** Cover the recipe and look only at the pictures. Explain each step of the recipe to your partner.

11 LISTENING *Tempting snacks*

A Listen to people explain how to make these snacks. Which snack are they talking about? Number the photos from 1 to 4.

toasted bagel

guacamole dip

slice of pizza

popcorn

B ***Pair work*** Choose one of the recipes you just heard about. Can you remember how to make it? Tell your partner.

12 SPEAKING *My favorite snack*

Group work Take turns describing how to make your favorite snack. Then tell the class about the most interesting one.

A: What's your favorite snack?
B: Well, I like to make . . .
C: How do you make it?
B: First, you . . .

13 WRITING *A recipe*

A Read this recipe for a popular Hawaiian dish. Notice how the information is divided into a list of ingredients and how to make the dish.

Lomi Lomi Salmon

From the kitchen of ____________________

1/4 cup shredded salmon, uncooked	1 green pepper, diced
1 white onion, chopped	3/4 cup vinegar
2 green onions, sliced	2 tablespoons sugar
2 tomatoes, diced	salt and pepper, to taste

Mix all ingredients together in a bowl. Cover and refrigerate overnight. Eat with rice as a light meal or on crackers as an appetizer.

B Now think of a dish you know how to make. First, write down the ingredients you need. Then describe how to make the dish.

C ***Group work*** Read and discuss each recipe. Then choose the most interesting recipe to share with the class.

LISTENING

Learning objective: *develop skills in listening for details*

- Ask: "Does anyone know what *tempting* in the exercise title means?" (Answer: A *tempting* snack looks or sounds so delicious that it's hard to refuse.)
- Set the scene. Four people are describing their favorite snacks. In pairs, Ss look at the pictures and predict some of the words they are going to hear (e.g., *toasted bagel – spread, cheese, cut*).

A ▶ *[CD 1, Track 27]*

- Explain the task. Read the names of the four snacks (guacamole: /gwak•e'mou•li/) and have Ss repeat.
- Play the audio program, pausing after each speaker. Ss listen and match the picture of each snack with the number of the speaker who described it. Then go over answers with the class.

Audio script *(See page T-226.)*

Answers

3, 2, 4, 1

B *Pair work*

- Read the instructions. In pairs, Ss decide which recipe each is going to describe. They should choose different snacks. If any Ss want to hear the audio program again, play it for the whole class. Ss can take notes if they wish.
- Ss take turns explaining how to make one of the snacks from part A. Go around the class and give help as needed.

SPEAKING

Learning objective: *describe how to make snacks using sequence adverbs*

Group work

- Model the activity by having three students read the example conversation.
- Give Ss time to think about their favorite snacks. Some Ss may need to check a dictionary or ask you for specialized vocabulary.
- Ss form groups and take turns describing how to make their favorite snacks. Set a time limit of about ten minutes for this. Encourage group members to ask follow-up questions. Go around the class and give help as needed.

> **TIP** To stop an activity, silently raise your right hand and keep it there. When Ss see your hand up, they should also put their right hand up and stop talking. Alternatively, count down from five to zero, giving Ss a chance to finish their sentences.

- Finally, groups take turns telling the class about the most tempting or unusual snack they discussed.
- ***Option:*** Regroup Ss and have them share ideas.

> **TIP** It's important to give Ss feedback on their speaking. If possible, try to include both praise and correction.

13 WRITING

Learning objective: *write a recipe using cooking methods and sequence adverbs*

A

- Go over the instructions and example recipe. If necessary, explain how to read fractions used in recipes. Answer any vocabulary questions.
- Point out that recipes usually have two separate parts: a list of ingredients and a series of steps, usually written as imperatives.

B

- Ss work individually to write a first draft. Go around the class and give help as needed. Alternatively, let Ss come to you with their questions and drafts.
- ***Option:*** If Ss need more time to prepare, this part can be assigned as homework.
- When Ss are finished, have them read their drafts to check their grammar and spelling, and to make sure they didn't leave out any important ingredients or directions.

C *Group work*

- Explain the task. Ss take turns discussing their recipes in groups.
- Have each group share one recipe with the class.
- ***Option:*** Post the recipes on the walls for the whole class to read. Alternatively, turn this into a project. Put Ss' favorite recipes together in a class cookbook.

14 READING

***Learning objectives:** read an article about how food affects the way we feel; develop skills in reading for details*

- Books closed. Ask: "What foods do people eat to make themselves feel happy? relaxed? energized? Are these foods healthy?" Ss discuss in small groups.
- Books open. Set a time limit of one to two minutes. Ss skim the article and check (✓) the main idea of the text. (Answer: Certain foods affect the way we feel.)
- ***Option:*** Pre-teach some vocabulary in the article with the game "Odd Man Out." Write this on the board:

1. depressed	*low*	*have the blues*	*calm*
2. stressed	*angry*	*anxious*	*nervous*
3. relaxed	*happy*	*secure*	*tired*

- Ask Ss to find the word that does not mean the same as the others in the list. (Answers: 1. calm 2. angry 3. tired)

A

- Ss read the article silently. Encourage Ss to guess the meaning of words they don't know before checking their dictionaries.
- Go over any new vocabulary.

Vocabulary

calm down: relax
cheer up: feel happier
powerfully: strongly
influence: have an effect on
as well as: in addition to
soothing: gentle
irritable: angry
the blues: a feeling of sadness or depression
lean meat: meat without fat on it
turn to: try
comfort foods: foods that make you feel happier

- Go over the instructions and point out that all the sentences are false. Ss reread the article to correct the statements.
- Have Ss compare answers in pairs or small groups. Then go over answers with the class.

Possible answers

1. We often eat when we feel stressed or depressed.
2. You shouldn't drink coffee to relieve stress.
3. Foods like chicken and seafood are high in selenium.
4. Carbohydrates cause the brain to release serotonin.
5. Serotonin makes you feel better.
6. People usually eat comfort foods when they're feeling low.
7. You should eat one Brazil nut a day.
8. Chocolate will make you feel better at first, but later you may feel worse.

- ***Option:*** To review the main ideas of the article, divide the class into two groups: stress and depression. Have Ss read the article again and find out what is good and bad for each. Then go over answers with the class. (Answers: **Stress(+):** bread, rice, pasta **(–):** coffee; **Depression(+):** lean meat, chicken, seafood, whole grains, Brazil nuts **(–):** sweet desserts, chocolate)

B *Pair work*

- Go over the questions. Then Ss discuss the questions in pairs.
- ***Option:*** As a class, Ss take turns sharing some interesting ideas they discussed in pairs.

End of Cycle 2

Do your students need more practice?

Assign . . .	***for more practice in . . .***
Workbook Exercises 4–8 on pages 22–24	Grammar, Vocabulary, Reading, and Writing
Lab Guide Exercise 7 on page 7	Listening, Pronunciation, Speaking, and Grammar
Video Activity Book Unit 4	Listening, Speaking, and Cultural Awareness
CD-ROM Unit 4	Grammar, Vocabulary, Reading, Listening, and Speaking

Evaluation

Assess Ss' understanding of Units 3 and 4 with the quiz on pages T-202 and T-203.

14 READING

FOOD and MOOD

Skim the article. Then check (✓) the statement you think will be the main idea.
■ Certain foods cause stress and depression. ■ Certain foods affect the way we feel.

We often eat to calm down or cheer up when we're feeling stressed or depressed. Now new research suggests there's a reason: Food changes our brain chemistry. These changes powerfully influence our moods. But can certain foods really make us feel better? Nutrition experts say yes. But what should we eat and what should we avoid? Here are the foods that work the best, as well as those that can make a bad day worse.

To Outsmart Stress

What's good? Recent research suggests that foods that are high in carbohydrates, such as bread, rice, and pasta, can help you calm down. Researchers say that carbohydrates cause the brain to release a chemical called serotonin. Serotonin makes you feel better.

What's bad? Many people drink coffee when they feel stress. The heat is soothing and the caffeine in coffee might help you think more clearly. But if you drink too much, you may become even more anxious and irritable.

To Soothe the Blues

What's good? Introduce more lean meat, chicken, seafood, and whole grains into your diet. These foods have a lot of selenium. Selenium is a mineral that helps people feel more relaxed and happy. You can also try eating a Brazil nut every day. One Brazil nut contains a lot of selenium.

What's bad? When they're feeling low, many people turn to comfort foods – or foods that make them feel happy or secure. These often include things like sweet desserts. A chocolate bar may make you feel better at first, but within an hour you may feel worse than you did before.

A Read the article. The sentences below are false. Correct each sentence to make it true.

1. We often eat when we feel calm.
2. You should drink coffee to relieve stress.
3. Foods like chicken and seafood are high in carbohydrates.
4. Carbohydrates cause the brain to release selenium.
5. Serotonin makes you feel more anxious and irritable.
6. People usually eat comfort foods when they're feeling happy.
7. You shouldn't eat more than one Brazil nut a day.
8. Chocolate will make you feel better.

B ***Pair work*** What foods do you eat to feel better? After reading the article, which of the advice will you follow?

Units 3–4 Progress check

SELF-ASSESSMENT

How well can you do these things? Check (✓) the boxes.

I can	Very well	OK	A little
Make evaluations and comparisons using nouns and adjectives (Ex. 1)	☐	☐	☐
Listen to, understand, and express wishes (Ex. 2)	☐	☐	☐
Talk about food using the simple past and the present perfect (Ex. 3)	☐	☐	☐
Describe recipes using cooking methods and sequence adverbs (Ex. 4)	☐	☐	☐

1 SPEAKING *Apartment ads*

A ***Pair work*** Use the ad and the topics in the box to write an ad for an apartment. Make the apartment sound as good as possible.

Quiet, Private Apartment
Small, but very comfortable, with many windows; located downtown; convenient to stores; 1 bedroom, 1 bathroom, 1-car garage; $300 a month!

age	windows	parking
size	bathroom(s)	cost
location	bedroom(s)	noise

B ***Group work*** Join another pair. Evaluate and compare the apartments. Which would you prefer to rent? Why?

A: There aren't enough bedrooms in your apartment.
B: But it's convenient.
C: Yes, but our apartment is just as convenient!

2 LISTENING *I really need a change!*

A Listen to three people talk about things they wish they could change. Check (✓) the topic each person is talking about.

1. ☐ leisure time ☐ school ....
2. ☐ skills ☐ hobbies ....
3. ☐ opportunities ☐ appearance ....

B Listen again. Write one change each person would like to make.

C ***Group work*** Use the topics in part A to express some wishes. How can you make the wishes come true? Offer suggestions.

Units 3–4 Progress check

SELF-ASSESSMENT

Learning objectives: *reflect on one's learning; identify areas that need improvement*

- Ask: "What did you learn in Units 3 and 4?" Elicit Ss' answers.
- Ss complete the Self-assessment. Encourage them to be honest, and point out they will not get a bad grade if they check (✓) "a little."
- Ss move on to the Progress check exercises. You can have Ss complete them in class or for homework, using one of these techniques:
  1. Ask Ss to complete all the exercises.
  2. Ask Ss: "What do you need to practice?" Then assign exercises based on their answers.
  3. Ask Ss to choose and complete exercises based on their Self-assessment.

SPEAKING

Learning objective: *assess one's ability to make evaluations and comparisons using nouns and adjectives*

A Pair work

- Explain the task. Ss write a short ad for an apartment. Read the example ad and the topics in the box.
- Ss form pairs. Remind them to make the apartment sound as good as possible. Set a time limit of about ten minutes. Go around the class and give help as needed.

B Group work

- Each pair joins another pair to evaluate and compare the apartments. Remind Ss that an evaluation is a statement based on an opinion (e.g., *It's very cheap.*), while a comparison measures one thing against another (e.g., *It's not as cheap as the other apartment.*). Ask three Ss to read the example conversation aloud. Point out that after making their evaluations and comparisons, Ss should say which they would prefer to rent and why.
- Ss complete the task. Go around the class, paying particular attention to Ss' use of comparisons with nouns and adjectives.
- Write a list on the board of some comparisons you heard. Include some incorrect comparisons for the class to correct.

LISTENING

Learning objective: *assess one's ability to listen to, understand, and express wishes*

A [CD 1, Track 28]

- Set the scene. Three people are talking about things they wish they could change.
- Play the audio program. Ss listen and check (✓) the topic each person is talking about. Then go over answers with the class.

Audio script *(See page T-226.)*

Answers

1. leisure time 2. skills 3. appearance

B

- Read the instructions. Then play the audio program again. Ss listen and write the changes.
- Go over answers with the class.

Possible answers

1. She wishes she belonged to a club or sports team.
2. He wishes he could type better.
3. She wishes she didn't like desserts so much.

C Group work

- Ss form groups and use the topics in part A to express at least three wishes each. The rest of the group offers suggestions on how to make the wishes come true.
- Ss take turns talking about their wishes. Go around the class and listen to Ss' use of *wish*.
- ***Option:*** Ss write their wishes on slips of paper and give them to you. Distribute the wishes so that Ss don't have their own slip. Ss write a suggestion about how to make the wish come true. Then Ss take turns standing up and reading the wish and their suggestion. The S who wrote the wish goes next.

3 SURVEY

Learning objective: *assess one's ability to talk about food using the simple past and the present perfect*

A

- Explain the task. First, Ss complete sentences with their own opinions and experiences. Read the five sentences aloud. Then Ss complete them individually.
- Now explain the second task. Ss use the information from the sentences they wrote to make questions. Model the first question with a few Ss:
  T: What's your first sentence, Sonia?
  S: "I've tried octopus, but I didn't really like it."
  T: OK. Can you turn that into a question to ask someone else?
  S: Have you ever tried octopus? What did you think of it?
- Ss work individually to write five questions. Go around the class to check Ss' questions, or ask Ss to read their questions aloud. Make sure Ss check their questions before moving on to part B.

B Class activity

- Explain the task and go over the example conversation with the class. If necessary, have two Ss model the second question in front of the class.
- Point out that Ss write a classmate's name only if they share the experience or opinion (e.g., *Student A didn't like peanut butter and Student B didn't either.*). If the experience or opinion is different, Student A asks another S the same question. Remind Ss to write a classmate's name only once.
- Encourage Ss to stand up and move around the room. They continue to ask and answer questions until they complete the list of classmate's names in the Name column.
- ***Option:*** Ask a few Ss to tell the class some interesting things they found out about their classmates.

ROLE PLAY

Learning objective: *assess one's ability to describe recipes using cooking methods and sequence adverbs*

Group work

- Explain the meaning of the title. Tell Ss that *Iron Chef* is the name of a TV program in which celebrity chefs use the same ingredients to compete against each other and race against the clock.
- Divide the class into groups of four. Assign roles. In each group two Ss are judges and two Ss are chefs.
- Tell the judges to write down three ingredients for the chefs to use. While the judges are making their lists, go over the task with the chefs. Explain that they will have to make a recipe using the three basic ingredients (from the judges) and others of their own. Use the example sentences to model how to explain the recipe.
- Tell the judges to give their lists to the chefs. Then the chefs have a few minutes to think of a recipe and name it.
- Chefs take turns telling the judges about their recipes, using sequence markers. Go around the class and listen to the descriptions without interrupting. Make a note of common errors or ways that the role plays could be improved.
- When both chefs have explained their recipes, the judges decide the winner.
- Give feedback to the class on their performance and language. Make suggestions on how they could improve their role plays. Give examples of good communication that you heard.
- Ss change roles and try the role play again.

WHAT'S NEXT?

Learning objective: *become more involved in one's learning*

- Focus Ss' attention on the Self-assessment again. Ask: "How well can you do these things now?"
- Ask Ss to underline one thing they need to review. Ask: "What did you underline? How can you review it?"
- If needed, plan additional activities or reviews based on Ss' answers.

3 SURVEY Food experiences

A Complete the survey with your food opinions and experiences. Then use your information to write questions.

Me	Name
1. I've tried .... , but I didn't really like it. *Have you ever tried .... ? What did you think of it?*	....
2. One of the best foods I've ever eaten is .... *Is .... one of the best foods you've ever eaten?*	....
3. One of the worst foods I've ever eaten is	....
4. I've never tried .... , but I'd like to.	....
5. I've made .... for my friends and family.	....

B ***Class activity*** Go around the class and ask your questions. Find people who have the same opinions and experiences. Write a classmate's name only once.

A: Have you ever tried peanut butter?
B: Yes, I have.
A: What did you think of it?
B: I didn't really like it.

4 ROLE PLAY Iron Chef

Group work Work in groups of four. Two students are the judges. Two students are the chefs.

Judges: Think of a list of three ingredients for the chefs to use. You will decide which chef creates the best recipe.

Chefs: Think of a recipe using the three ingredients the judges give you and other basic ingredients. Name the recipe and describe how to make it.

"My recipe is called . . . . To make it, first you . . . . Then . . . . Next, ..."

Change roles and try the role play again.

***Iron Chef*, a TV cooking competition**

WHAT'S NEXT?

Look at your Self-assessment again. Do you need to review anything?

5 Going places

1 SNAPSHOT

What do you like to do on vacation?
Take an exciting trip
visit a foreign country
travel through my own country
Discover something new
take language or cooking lessons
visit museums and art galleries
Stay home
catch up on reading
fix up the house
Enjoy nature
go camping, hiking, or fishing
relax at the beach

Based on information from *U.S. News and World Report*; *American Demographics*

Which activities do you like to do on vacation? Check (✓) the activities.
Which activities did you do on your last vacation?
Make a list of other activities you like to do on vacation. Then compare with a partner.

2 CONVERSATION What are you going to do?

A Listen and practice.

Julia: I'm so excited! We have two weeks off! What are you going to do?
Nancy: I'm not sure. I guess I'll just stay home. Maybe I'll watch a few DVDs. What about you? Any plans?
Julia: Yeah, I'm going to relax at the beach with my cousin for a couple of weeks. We're going to go surfing every day.
Nancy: Sounds like fun.
Julia: Say, why don't you come with us?
Nancy: Do you mean it? I'd love to! I'll bring my surfboard!

B Listen to the rest of the conversation. Where are they going to stay? How will they get there?

Going places

Cycle 1, Exercises 1–5

In Unit 5, students discuss vacations and travel plans. In Cycle 1, they describe plans using the future with be going to *and* will. *In Cycle 2, they give travel advice using modals for necessity and suggestion.*

SNAPSHOT

Learning objective: *learn vocabulary for talking about vacation activities*

- Books closed. Write on the board while the class brainstorms types of vacations.

Types of Vacations

go abroad	*visit relatives*	*go skiing*
travel around the world	*relax*	*have fun*
take a bicycle tour	*go on a cruise*	

- Books open. Ss read the Snapshot individually. Ask: "Which categories (*Take an exciting trip, Discover something new, etc.*) describe the ideas on the board? Do we need to add any new categories?"
- Elicit or explain any new vocabulary.
- Read the discussion questions. Ss discuss the topics in small groups.
- ***Option:*** Ask Ss to bring vacation photos to class. Encourage them to share and explain their photos.

TIP Tell Ss to make a "time-out" signal (by forming a T shape with their hands) or stand up if they want to use their first language.

- Use a show of hands to find out which activities are their favorites.
- ***Option:*** To review the verb *wish* from Unit 3, have Ss express some wishes about vacations (e.g., *I wish I had more vacation time. I wish I could go on a cruise.*).

CONVERSATION

Learning objectives: *practice a conversation about vacation plans; see* be going to *and* will *in context*

A [CD 1, Track 30]

- Focus Ss' attention on the picture. Tell them to cover the text. Ask: "Are these people friends? How old are they? What do they do? What time of year is it? How do they feel?" Ss predict the answers.
- Play the first two lines of the audio program. Ask: "Why are they so happy?" (Answer: They have two weeks off.)
- Set the scene. Two friends are talking about vacation plans.
- Write these focus questions on the board:
  1. What is Nancy going to do?
  2. What is Julia going to do?
  3. What sport is Julia going to practice?
  4. What does Julia do to help Nancy?
- Point out that Julia is the first speaker and Nancy is the second. Ask Ss to listen for the answers to the questions on the board. Play the audio program. Then elicit responses. (Answers: 1. She isn't sure. 2. relax at the beach 3. surfing 4. Julia invites Nancy to the beach.)
- With Ss now looking at the text, play the audio program again. Explain any new vocabulary.
- Focus Ss' attention on the follow-up questions used by Nancy and Julia to keep the conversation going (e.g., *What are you going to do? What about you? Any plans?*). Explain that Ss will practice this in the next few units.
- Ss practice this Conversation in pairs.

! To practice this Conversation several times, try ***Moving Dialog*** on page T-150.

- ***Option:*** Discuss the situation with the class. Ask: "Have you ever been on vacation to the beach? Have you ever spent a vacation with your cousin? Have you ever invited a classmate or friend to go on vacation with you?"

B

- Read the two questions. Then play the rest of the audio program and elicit answers from the class.

Audio script *(See page T-226.)*

Answers

They are going to stay at Julia's aunt and uncle's beach house.
They will get there by bus.

- ***Option:*** Ss write a conversation between Nancy (or Julia) and a friend describing what happened on the vacation. Then Ss practice the conversation in pairs.

3 GRAMMAR FOCUS

Learning objective: *practice using* be going to *and* will *to talk about future plans*

[CD 1, Track 31]

- Have Ss read the Conversation on page 30 again silently. Then write this on the board:
  be going to   will
- Ask Ss to find examples of *be going to* and *will* in the Conversation and write them in the correct column on the board. (Answers: **be going to:** What are you going to do? I'm going to relax . . . We're going to go surfing . . . ; **will:** I guess I'll just stay home. Maybe I'll watch . . . I'll bring my surfboard!)
- Elicit or explain the difference between *be going to* and *will*. Ask: "Who has definite plans, Julia or Nancy?" (Answer: Julia) "Does Julia use *be going to* or *will*?" (Answer: be going to) "Nancy is not sure of her plans. What does she use?" (Answer: will) "What other words does Nancy use to show she is not certain?" (Answer: maybe, I guess)

Be going to + *verb*

Explain that we use *be going to + verb* for plans we have decided on. Julia is 100 percent sure, so she uses *be going to*.

Will + *verb + I guess/maybe/I think/probably*

- We use *will + verb* for possible plans. *Will* is often accompanied by other words to show possibility or probability (e.g., *I guess*, *maybe*, *I think*, *probably*, *I suppose*, *I expect*). We also use *will* for spontaneous offers and sudden decisions (e.g., *I'll bring my surfboard! I'll help you! I'll get the phone.*).
- Refer Ss to the Grammar Focus box. Point out that *be* in *be going to* is normally contracted in conversation. Ask Ss to find examples in the left-hand column (e.g., *I'm, we're*). Move to the right-hand column. Show *will* and *will not* in contracted forms (*I'll, I won't*).
- Practice *be going to* by asking questions (e.g., *What are you going to do . . . tonight/on Friday/this weekend/etc.?*). Ss give real responses with *be going to* + verb. Repeat the activity with *What will you probably do (this summer/next year/etc.?)*.
- Play the audio program to present information in the box. Ss listen and repeat.

A

- ***Option:*** To introduce Ss to the topic of camping, have Ss label things in the picture (i.e., tent, fishing pole, net).
- Go over the instructions. Model the first one or two blanks with a S. Then Ss complete the task individually. As this is a conversation, tell Ss to use contractions where they can. Go around the class and give help as needed.
- Ss compare answers in pairs. Then elicit Ss' answers.

Answers

A: Have you made any vacation plans?
B: Well, I've decided on one thing – I**'m going to** go camping.
A: That's great! For how long?
B: I**'m going to** be away for a week. I only have five days of vacation.
A: So, when are you leaving?
B: I'm not sure. I**'ll** probably leave around the end of May.
A: And where **are** you **going to** go?
B: I haven't thought about that yet. I guess I**'ll** go to one of the national parks.
A: That sounds like fun.
B: Yeah. Maybe I**'ll** go hiking and do some fishing.
A: **Are** you **going to** rent a camper?
B: I'm not sure. Actually, I probably **won't** rent a camper – it's too expensive.
A: **Are** you **going to** go with anyone?
B: No, I need some time alone. I**'m going to** travel by myself.

For another way to practice this Conversation, try the ***Onion Ring*** technique on page T-151.

B

- Explain the task. Then read the questions and have Ss repeat.
- Ask a few Ss to answer the first question.
- Ss work individually to complete the task on a separate piece of paper. While Ss work, go around the room and check their use of *be going to* and *will*.

C *Group work*

- Explain the task. Ss look over their notes and then talk about their vacation plans in groups. Encourage them to ask questions and give additional information.
- ***Option:*** Each group shares their most interesting or unusual vacation plans with the rest of the class.

3 GRAMMAR FOCUS

Future with be going to *and* will

Use be going to *+ verb for plans you've decided on.*	*Use* will *+ verb for possible plans before you've made a decision.*
What **are** you **going to do**?	What **are** you **going to do**?
I'**m going to relax** at the beach.	I'm not sure. I **guess** I'**ll** just **stay** home.
We'**re going to go** surfing every day.	**Maybe** I'**ll watch** a few DVDs.
I'**m** not **going to do** anything special.	I don't know. I **think** I'**ll go** camping.
	I **probably won't go** anywhere.

A Complete the conversation with appropriate forms of *be going to* or *will*. Then compare with a partner.

A: Have you made any vacation plans?
B: Well, I've decided on one thing –
I .... go camping.
A: That's great! For how long?
B: I .... be away for a week.
I only have five days of vacation.
A: So, when are you leaving?
B: I'm not sure. I .... probably leave around the end of May.
A: And where .... you .... go?
B: I haven't thought about that yet. I guess
I .... go to one of the national parks.
A: That sounds like fun.
B: Yeah. Maybe I .... go hiking and do some fishing.
A: .... you .... rent a camper?
B: I'm not sure. Actually, I probably .... rent a camper – it's too expensive.
A: .... you .... go with anyone?
B: No. I need some time alone.
I .... travel by myself.

B Have you thought about your next vacation? Write answers to these questions. (If you already have plans, use *be going to*. If you don't have fixed plans, use *will*.)

1. How are you going to spend your next vacation?
2. Where are you going to go?
3. When are you going to take your vacation?
4. How long are you going to be on vacation?
5. Is anyone going to travel with you?

I'm going to take my next vacation . . .
OR
I'm not sure. Maybe I'll . . .

C ***Group work*** Take turns telling the group about your vacation plans. Use your information from part B.

WORD POWER *Travel planning*

A Complete the chart. Then add one more word to each category.

backpack
cash
credit card
first-aid kit
hiking boots
medication
overnight bag
passport
plane ticket
shorts
suitcase
traveler's checks
vaccination
visa
windbreaker

Clothing	Money	Health	Documents	Luggage
....	....	....	....	....
....	....	....	....	....
....	....	....	....	....

B ***Pair work*** What are the five most important items you need for these vacations: a trip to a foreign country? a rafting trip? a mountain-climbing expedition?

5 INTERCHANGE 5 *Fun vacations*

Decide between two vacations. Go to the back of the book. Student A find Interchange 5A; Student B find Interchange 5B.

6 PERSPECTIVES *Travel advice*

A Listen to these pieces of advice from experienced travelers.

"You should tell the driver where you're going before you get on. And you have to have exact change for the fare." – Patrick

"In most countries, you don't have to have an international driver's license, but you must have a license from your own country. You also need to be over 21." – Jackie

"You should try some of the local specialties, but you'd better avoid the stalls on the street." – Paul

"You ought to pack a first-aid kit and any medication you need. You shouldn't drink water from the tap." – Susan

"You ought to keep a copy of your credit card numbers at the hotel. And you shouldn't carry a lot of cash when you go out." – Luis

B ***Pair work*** Look at the advice again. What topic is each person talking about?

A: Paul is probably talking about food, because he mentions "specialties."
B: And I think Jackie is giving advice about . . .

4 WORD POWER

Learning objective: *learn vocabulary for discussing travel*

A

- Model the pronunciation of the words in the list and the category headings in the chart. Answer any vocabulary questions.
- Ss work individually or in pairs to complete the task, using dictionaries if necessary. Remind them to add one more word to each category. Then go over answers with the class.

Answers

Clothing	hiking boots, shorts, windbreaker, *T-shirt*
Money	cash, credit card, traveler's checks, *ATM card*
Health	first-aid kit, medication, vaccination, *vitamins*
Documents	passport, plane ticket, visa, *driver's license*
Luggage	backpack, overnight bag, suitcase, *briefcase*

(Note: Additional examples are italicized.)

B *Pair work*

- Explain the three types of vacations. In pairs, Ss discuss the five most important things needed for each vacation. Encourage them to use words from part A and some of their own.
- Elicit answers by asking Ss to use *be going to* (e.g., *We're going to take our passports to a foreign country.*).

 To review the vocabulary, play ***Bingo*** on page T-147. Give definitions if possible.

TIP To help Ss remember the new vocabulary, always review it during the next class. Ss forget new words quickly (80 percent is lost after 24 hours).

5 INTERCHANGE 5

See pages T-118 and T-119 for teaching notes.

End of Cycle 1

Do your students need more practice?

Assign . . .	*for more practice in . . .*
Workbook Exercises 1–4 on pages 25–27	Grammar, Vocabulary, Reading, and Writing
Lab Guide Exercises 1–3 and 8 on page 8	Listening, Pronunciation, Speaking, and Grammar

Cycle 2, Exercises 6–12

6 PERSPECTIVES

Learning objectives: *discuss travel advice; see modals for necessity and suggestion in context*

A  ***[CD 1, Track 32]***

- Books closed. Ask Ss to imagine that someone is going to visit them in their city. Ask: "What advice would you give about the climate?" (E.g., *Bring a warm sweater and . . .*)
- Write these sentences on the board:
  1. *It's necessary to have the exact change for a bus.*
  2. *You must be 21 or older to rent a car.*
  3. *Travelers should try eating at stalls on the street.*
  4. *It's OK to drink water from the tap.*
  5. *You should keep a copy of your credit card numbers.*
- Explain the task. Ss will hear five pieces of advice from travelers and decide if the sentences on the board are true or false.
- Play the audio program. Then elicit answers. (Answers: 1. T 2. T 3. F 4. F 5. T)
- Books open. Play the audio program again. Ss listen and read along silently.

TIP If Ss are worried about a new structure they see in the Perspectives section, tell them that they only need to understand the *meaning*. They will learn how to form the structure in the next exercise.

B *Pair work*

- Explain the task and model the example conversation. In pairs, Ss decide what topic each person is talking about. Elicit answers and ask which words helped them with each answer.

Possible answers

transportation/buses, driving/renting a car, food, health/safety, money

- ***Option:*** Ask Ss to suggest one more piece of advice for each topic.

7 GRAMMAR FOCUS

***Learning objective:** practice using modal verbs to express necessity and suggestion*

[CD 1, Track 33]

Modals for necessity

- Focus Ss' attention on the Grammar Focus box. Point out that there are many ways to express necessity. Explain that *must*, *need to*, and *have to* have similar meanings and are therefore interchangeable.
- Refer Ss to the traveler's advice in Exercise 6. Have Ss underline the modals for necessity.

Modals for suggestion

- Point out that *had better*, *ought to*, and *should* have similar meanings, but differ in strength. They are listed in the chart with the strongest (*had better*) first. Refer Ss to the traveler's advice in Exercise 6. Have Ss circle the modals for suggestion.
- Play the audio program to present the sentences in the box. Ss listen and repeat.

A

- Explain the task. Elicit or explain any new vocabulary.
- Model the first item for the class. Ss work individually to complete the task then compare answers in pairs. Go over answers with the class.

Answers

1. 'd better
2. must
3. should
4. shouldn't
5. need to
6. ought to

B *Pair work*

- Explain the task and read the example sentence. Ss take turns giving each other the advice in pairs. Go around the class and give help as needed. Then check answers.

Culture note: An ATM (Automated Teller Machine) card allows people to withdraw money from their bank accounts using an automated machine. In North America, ATMs can be found outside banks and inside many stores, hotels, and restaurants.

Possible answers

1. must/have to/need to
2. ought to/should/'d better
3. must/have to/need to
4. shouldn't
5. must/have to/need to
6. don't have to

- ***Option:*** Pairs add four more pieces of advice.

C *Group work*

- Read the instructions. In small groups, Ss discuss at least six pieces of advice. Ask each group to choose someone to write the ideas on a piece of paper. Remind Ss to use structures from the Grammar Focus during their discussion.
- Elicit ideas and write them on the board.
- ***Option:*** Groups exchange papers and read the ideas. Then they choose the best ideas and report them to the class.

8 PRONUNCIATION

***Learning objective:** notice and practice words linked together with a /w/ or /y/ sound*

[CD 1, Track 34]

- Explain that some words are linked together by a /w/ or /y/ sound. This happens when words end in a *w* or *y* sound and are followed by a vowel (e.g., *know about*, *carry a*). When a word ends with a /oo/ or /o/ and is followed by a word that begins with a vowel sound, the words are linked with a /w/ sound. When a word ends with an /a/, /ee/, or /i/ sound and is followed by a word beginning with a vowel sound, the words are linked with a /y/ sound.
- Play the audio program. Ss listen and notice how the words are linked. Then play the audio program again while Ss listen and repeat.

TIP To practice linking, use the *Back Chaining* technique. Ss practice the last word, then the last two words, then the last three words, etc., until they can say the whole line.

- ***Option:*** Refer Ss to the Perspectives section on page 32. Ask them to listen again and find examples of words linked with /w/ or /y/ (e.g., *when you go out*, *copy of your credit card numbers*).

7 GRAMMAR FOCUS

Modals for necessity and suggestion

Describing necessity	*Giving suggestions*
You **must** have a driver's license.	You**'d better** avoid the stalls on the street.
You **need to** make a reservation.	You **ought to** pack a first-aid kit.
You **have to** get a passport.	You **should** try some local specialties.
You **don't have to** get a visa.	You **shouldn't** carry a lot of cash.

A Choose the best advice for someone who is going on vacation. Then compare with a partner.

1. You .... make hotel reservations in advance. It might be difficult to find a room after you get there. (have to / 'd better)
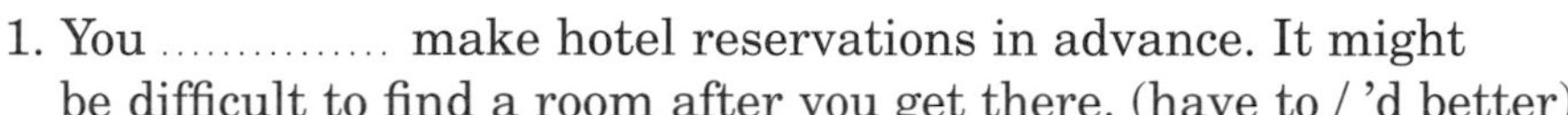
2. You .... carry identification with you. It's the law! (must / should)
3. You .... buy a round-trip plane ticket because it's cheaper. (must / should)
4. You .... pack too many clothes. You won't have room to bring back any gifts. (don't have to / shouldn't)
5. You .... check out of most hotel rooms by noon if you don't want to pay for another night. (need to / ought to)
6. You .... buy a new suitcase because your old one is getting shabby. (have to / ought to)

B ***Pair work*** Imagine you're going to travel abroad. Take turns giving each other advice.

"You must get the necessary vaccinations."

1. You . . . get the necessary vaccinations.
2. You . . . take your ATM card with you.
3. You . . . get the visa required for each country.
4. You . . . forget to pack your camera.
5. You . . . have a passport to enter a foreign country.
6. You . . . change money before you go. You can do it when you arrive.

C ***Group work*** What advice would you give someone who is going to study English abroad? Report your best ideas to the class.

8 PRONUNCIATION Linked sounds with /w/ and /y/

Listen and practice. Notice how some words are linked by a /w/ sound, and other words are linked by a /y/ sound.

You should know /w/ about local conditions.

You ought to do /w/ it right away.

You shouldn't carry /y/ a lot of cash.

You must be /y/ over 18 years old.

9 LISTENING Tourist tips

A Listen to an interview with a spokeswoman from the New York City Visitor's Center. Check (✓) the four topics she discusses.

☐ planning a trip ☐ safety ☐ money ☐ eating out ☐ tours ☐ history

B Listen again. For each topic, write one piece of advice she gives.

10 WRITING Travel suggestions

A Imagine someone is going to visit your town, city, or country. Write a letter giving some suggestions for sightseeing activities.

Dear Rosa,

I'm so glad you're going to visit Prague! As you know, Prague is the capital of the Czech Republic. It's a very beautiful city, so you should bring your camera. Also, you ought to bring some good shoes, because we're going to walk a lot. It will be warm, so you don't have to pack . . .

B ***Pair work*** Exchange letters. Is there anything else the visitor needs to know about (food, money, business hours, etc.)?

11 DISCUSSION Dream vacation

A ***Pair work*** You just won a free 30-day trip around the world. Discuss the following questions.

When will you leave and return?
Which route will you take?
Where will you choose to stop? Why?
How many days will you spend in each place?

B ***Pair work*** What do you need to do before you go? Discuss these issues.

visas	hotel reservations	vaccinations
money	what to buy and pack	

A: We'd better find out if we need to get any visas.
B: Yes, and I think we ought to buy some guidebooks.

9 LISTENING

Learning objectives: *develop skills in listening for main ideas and details; develop summarizing skills*

A ▶ ***[CD 1, Track 35]***

- Books closed. Explain the situation. A woman is giving some advice to people who visit New York City. Ask: "What do you already know about New York City? Do you know any famous places to visit?" Elicit answers from the class.
- Books open. Explain the task. Play the audio program while Ss listen and complete the chart.

Audio script *(See page T-226–227.)*

- Have Ss compare answers in pairs. Then elicit Ss' responses.

Answers

planning a trip, tours, safety, money

B ▶

- Explain the task. For each topic, Ss write one piece of advice. Ss should write only key words and phrases to summarize each piece of advice.
- Play the audio program. Pause to give Ss a chance to take notes.
- Encourage Ss to use their notes to write complete sentences using modals. Then go over answers. Ask the S with the best or most correct piece of advice for each topic to write it on the board.

Possible answers

1. You should start planning before you get there.
2. It's a good idea to buy a bus pass. You should visit the Web site to find out about tours and special events.
3. You shouldn't go off on your own, especially at night. You shouldn't be afraid to ask questions.
4. If you're a student, you should bring your student ID card with you. You should never carry much money on you.

- ***Option:*** In pairs, Ss role-play an interview with an official from their city. Student A asks questions. Student B gives advice. Then they switch roles.

For another way to practice modals, play ***Just One Minute*** on page T-146.

10 WRITING

Learning objective: *write a letter of advice using modals and* be going to

A

- Ask Ss to read the example letter. Explain any vocabulary that Ss don't understand.
- Point out features of a written letter to a friend (e.g., use *Dear + first name* to open the letter; include an introductory sentence; close the letter with a phrase like *Can't wait to see you!* and a final good-bye, such as *Best wishes*, *Love*, *All the best*, *Your friend*; and their own name).
- Ss write their first draft individually. Go around the class and give help as needed.

B *Pair work*

- Ss exchange letters and read their partner's letter to see what else the writer should include (e.g., *information about money, climate, visas*). Encourage Ss to focus on content rather than grammar or spelling.
- Pairs give each other feedback. Then Ss write a second draft, using correct grammar and spelling.
- ***Option:*** Collect final drafts to either mark or post around the classroom for everyone to read.

11 DISCUSSION

Learning objective: *discuss vacation plans using* be going to *and* will, *modals for necessity and suggestion, and travel vocabulary*

A *Pair work*

- Focus Ss' attention on the title of the exercise. Ask: "What do you think the title *Dream vacation* means?" (Answer: a wonderful trip that a person would love to take.)
- Explain the task. Have a S read the questions aloud and check pronunciation. Then Ss discuss the questions in pairs.

B *Pair work*

- Go over the topics and the example conversation. With the same partner, Ss take turns discussing the things they need to take on their trip. Encourage Ss to ask follow-up questions.

For more speaking practice, try ***Role Cards*** on page T-157.

12 READING

Learning objectives: *read an article about an expert backpacker; develop skills in organizing information and summarizing*

- Books closed. Write these words on the board: *camping, clothes, wind, equipment, backpack, fun*
- Tell Ss the words are all related to the topic. Ss guess what the article is about.
- Books open. Have Ss read the title. Elicit the meaning of *Getting Away from It All*. (Answer: going far away from the city/busy life to have some peace and quiet)
- Tell Ss to check (✓) the pre-reading statements that they think are true. Then ask them to scan the article quickly to find the answer. Remind Ss to look for the information quickly, and not to worry about words they don't know. Give them a time limit of two minutes. Then elicit the answer. (Answer: Wear layers of clothing to go backpacking.)
- Ss read the article silently. Tell them not to worry about the missing questions for now.
- Tell Ss they may look up three new words in their dictionaries or with a partner, but must underline those words.
- When the class finishes reading, ask Ss to tell which three words they underlined. Write them on the board and go over the definitions. Look at the sentences and point out any contextual clues. These clues can sometimes help Ss guess the meaning of unfamiliar words.
- Elicit or explain any other new vocabulary.

Vocabulary

outdoors: in the open air; not in a building
tip: a useful piece of information; a recommendation
pack: put things into a backpack or suitcase
light: having little weight; the opposite of *heavy*
layers (of clothing): clothes that are worn on top of or underneath other clothes
access: ability to find something easily
bury: put one thing under another

A

- Make sure Ss know that OM and MO in the article refer to *Outdoor Magazine* and Mike O'Brien.
- Explain the task. Ss write the questions OM asks in the appropriate spaces. Model one example with the class.
- Ss work individually. Then go over answers.

Answers

5, 1, 4, 2, 3

- ***Option:*** Ss read the interview in pairs.

B

- Explain the task and complete the first space with the Ss. Ss read the text again to find the answers and then write a word or phrase in each space.
- Ss work individually and then check their answers in pairs. Remind Ss that some answers can be phrased in more than one way. Check answers with the class and write all possible answers on the board.

Possible answers

backpacker
two
how to dress comfortably
how to pack your equipment well
the weather/the temperature
(light) layers (of clothing)
access
balance
bury things you need
too heavy at the top or bottom

For more speaking practice, play ***Hot Potato*** on page T-147. The first S begins by saying something about the text from memory. Then he or she throws an object to another S, who says another fact from the text. Ss continue to throw the object and say things about the text.

C *Group work*

- Ask Ss to choose an activity they know well. If necessary, suggest some ideas (e.g., *using a cell phone, cooking, using a computer, putting on makeup*).
- In small groups, Ss take turns giving tips on how to do the activity. Other Ss play the role of beginners and ask questions.

End of Cycle 2

Do your students need more practice?

Assign . . .	*for more practice in . . .*
Workbook Exercises 5–9 on pages 28–30	Grammar, Vocabulary, Reading, and Writing
Lab Guide Exercises 4–7 on page 8	Listening, Pronunciation, Speaking, and Grammar
Video Activity Book Unit 5	Listening, Speaking, and Cultural Awareness
CD-ROM Unit 5	Grammar, Vocabulary, Reading, Listening, and Speaking

12 READING

Getting Away From It All

Check (✓) the statements you think are true. Then scan the article to check your answers.
- ☐ Wear layers of clothing to go backpacking.
- ☐ Put heavy items at the top of your backpack.

Mike O'Brien has been backpacking for over 20 years. He often spends up to 30 days at a time outdoors. In a recent interview with *Outdoor Magazine*, he offered some expert tips for new backpackers.

OM: ....

MO: Backpacking and camping are my favorite things to do. It can get difficult at times, but I just love getting away from it all.

OM: ....

MO: The two most important things to know are how to dress comfortably and how to pack your equipment well.

OM: ....

MO: They need to understand the purpose of outdoor clothing. Clothes need to keep you warm in the cold, block the wind, and keep you dry in the rain. In hot environments, clothes should also protect you from the sun. You don't have control over the weather or the temperature. So you should dress in light layers of clothing. That way, if you are hot, you can take off clothes. And if you are cold, you can add clothes.

OM: ....

MO: Access and balance are the keys to packing well. First, access: Don't bury things you need – such as extra clothes, food, or water – at the bottom of your backpack. Second, balance: Remember, you're going to wear your backpack. It has to be balanced or you could fall over! Don't make your pack too heavy at the top or bottom. It's best to keep the heaviest items close to your back.

OM: ....

MO: Yes. Have fun! That's the only reason to do it!

A Read the article. Then write these questions in the appropriate place.

1. What do all beginners need to know?
2. And how should they pack for a trip?
3. Any final words?
4. How should people dress for backpacking?
5. Why do you spend so much time in the wilderness?

B Complete the summary with information from the article.

Mike O'Brien is an expert .... For beginners, he says that there are .... important things to remember: .... and .... Because you don't have control over .... , you should dress in .... The keys to packing are .... and .... Don't .... at the bottom of your backpack. And don't make your pack ....

C ***Group work*** Choose a sport or activity you know well. What "expert" tips would you offer beginners?

6 OK. No problem!

1 SNAPSHOT

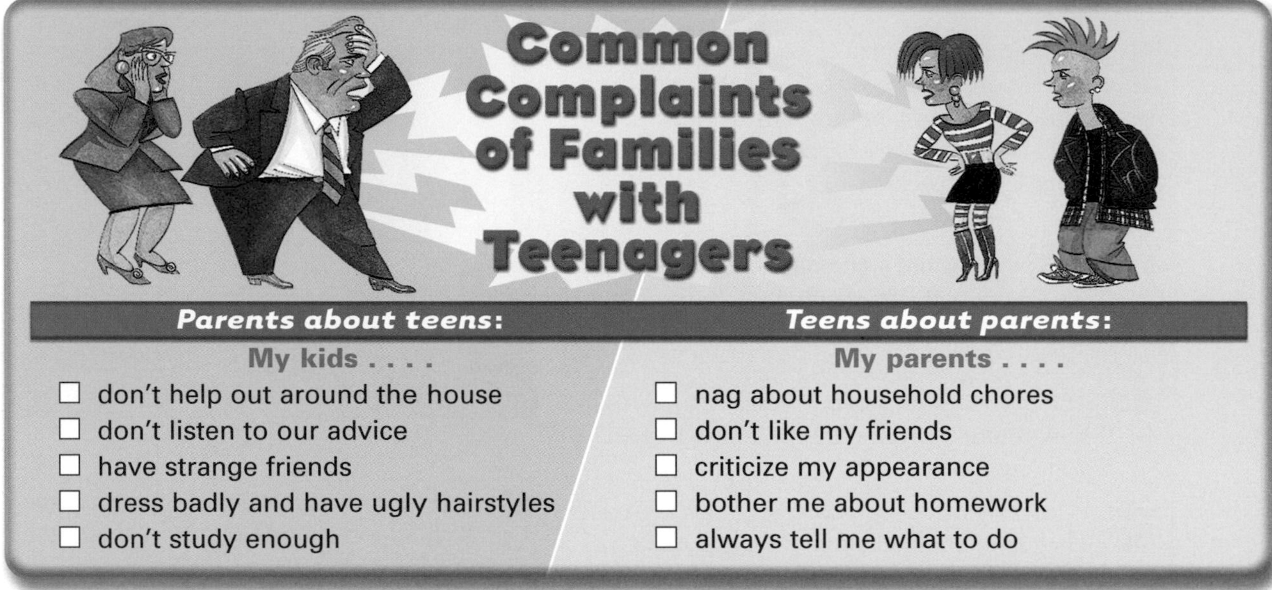

Parents about teens:	Teens about parents:
My kids	My parents . . . .
☐ don't help out around the house	☐ nag about household chores
☐ don't listen to our advice	☐ don't like my friends
☐ have strange friends	☐ criticize my appearance
☐ dress badly and have ugly hairstyles	☐ bother me about homework
☐ don't study enough	☐ always tell me what to do

Based on information from *America Online's Parent Resource Site*

Which complaints seem reasonable? Which ones seem unreasonable? Why?
Check (✓) a complaint you have about a family member.
What other complaints do people sometimes have about family members?

2 CONVERSATION Turn down the TV!

A Listen and practice.

Mr. Field: Jason . . . Jason! Turn down the TV, please.
Jason: Oh, but this is my favorite program!
Mr. Field: I know. But it's very loud.
Jason: OK. I'll turn it down.
Mr. Field: That's better. Thanks.
Mrs. Field: Lisa, please pick up your things. They're all over the floor.
Lisa: In a minute, Mom. I'm on the phone.
Mrs. Field: All right. But do it as soon as you hang up.
Lisa: OK. No problem!
Mrs. Field: Goodness! Were we like this when we were kids?
Mr. Field: Definitely!

B Listen to the rest of the conversation. What complaints do Jason and Lisa have about their parents?

OK. No problem!

Cycle 1, Exercises 1–6

In Unit 6, students talk about common complaints. In Cycle 1, they use two-part verbs to make and respond to requests. In Cycle 2, they make and respond to requests using modals and Would you mind?

SNAPSHOT

Learning objective: *learn vocabulary for talking about common complaints*

- Books closed. Write these questions on the board and have Ss discuss them in pairs:
  1. Do your parents, children, or siblings ever bother you?
  2. What do they do to bother you?
  3. What do you do or say about it, if anything?
- Books open. Read the headings aloud. Have Ss skim the two lists of common complaints. Elicit or explain any new vocabulary.

Vocabulary

nag: complain continuously to someone in order to get him or her to do something
criticize: say bad things about

- Read the questions aloud. Then Ss discuss them in groups or pairs. Remind Ss to ask follow-up questions to keep the discussion going.
- Have Ss vote on their biggest complaint to find out which is the most common. For the third question, ask Ss to suggest some other complaints (e.g., *parents don't lend the car, teens stay out too late, sisters spend too long on the phone or computer*).

CONVERSATION

Learning objectives: *practice a conversation between family members; see two-part verbs and* will *for responding to requests in context*

A ***[CD 1, Track 36]***

- Focus Ss' attention on the picture. Tell them to cover the text. Ask: "What is the son/daughter doing? What are the parents going to nag them about?" Ss predict the answers.
- Books closed. Play the first eight lines of the audio program (until *In a minute, Mom.*). Then check answers. (Answers: Jason is watching TV. Lisa is on the phone. The dad asks Jason to turn down the TV. The mom asks Lisa to pick up her things.)
- Ask these focus questions: "Does Jason turn the TV down? Does Lisa pick up her things right away? Were the parents like this when they were kids?"
- Play the audio program. Elicit answers. (Answers: yes, no, yes)
- Books open. Play the audio program again while Ss read silently. Explain any new vocabulary words or expressions.

Vocabulary

loud: making a lot of noise
hang up: finish your telephone conversation
Goodness!: an exclamation showing surprise or annoyance
Definitely!: Certainly!; Yes!

- Ss practice the conversation in groups of four.

! For another way to practice this Conversation, try ***Say It With Feeling!*** on page T-150.

- ***Option:*** Ask a few Ss to act out the conversation in front of the class, using props and actions. Encourage them to use their own words.

B

- Read the instructions and focus question Ss need to listen for. Tell Ss to take notes. Then play the second part of the audio program.

Audio script *(See page T-227.)*

- After pairs compare answers, go over answers with the class.

Answers

Jason complains about how forgetful his dad is getting: He's always forgetting where his car keys are. Lisa complains that he can never find his glasses.
Lisa complains that her mom watches awful talk shows on TV.

3 GRAMMAR FOCUS

Learning objectives: *practice using two-part verbs to make requests; practice using* will *for responding to requests*

[CD 1, Track 37]

Two-part verbs

- Refer Ss to the Conversation on page 36. Elicit the parents' requests and have Ss underline them. (Answers: Turn down the TV, please. Please pick up your things.)
- Explain that *turn down* and *pick up* are examples of two-part verbs. They are made up of a verb and another word called a particle, which changes the meaning of the verb.
- ***Option:*** Show Ss how to store two-part verbs in a logical way, by drawing a "Ripple Diagram" on the board:

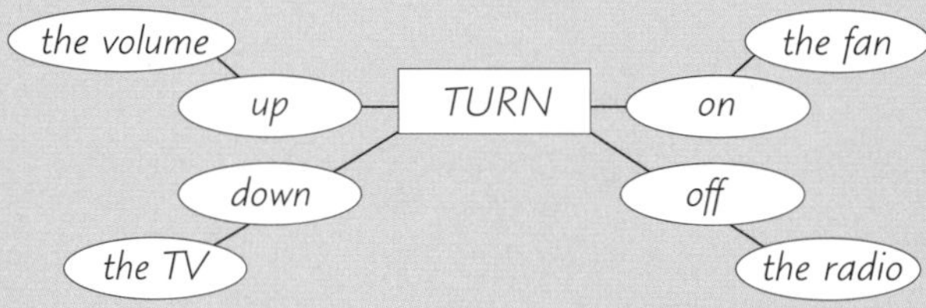

TIP To help Ss find out how they learn best, have them try different ways to store vocabulary in their notebooks. Then ask Ss which method(s) work best for them.

- Point out that the object noun (e.g., *TV*, *things*) can come before or after the particle:
  Turn *the TV* down. Pick *your things* up.
  Turn down *the TV*. Pick up *your things*.
- When the object of the two-part verb is a pronoun, it can only come between the verb and the particle:
  Turn *it* down. Pick *them* up.

Making requests

- It is polite to use *please* to make a request. *Please* can go at the beginning or the end of a sentence.
  Please turn down the music. Turn it down, *please*.

***Responding with* will**

- The modal *will* is used to respond to a request.
  OK. I'*ll* turn it down.
  All right. I'*ll* pick them up.
- Play the audio program to present the sentences in the Grammar Focus box. Ss listen and repeat.

A

- Before Ss begin the task, focus their attention on the pictures and captions below. Model the first item for the class. Then elicit suggestions for the second item.
- Ss complete the task individually and then compare answers in pairs. Elicit responses.

Answers

1. Pick up **the toys**, please.
2. Turn **the radio/the TV/the lights** off, please.
3. Clean **the yard** up, please.
4. Please put **the books/the toys/your jacket** away.
5. Please turn down **the radio/the TV**.
6. Please take off **your boots**.
7. Hang **your jacket** up, please.
8. Please take out **the trash**.
9. Please let **the dog** out.
10. Turn on **the radio/the TV/the lights**, please.

B *Pair work*

- Model the example conversation and ask one or two Ss to give their own responses. Remind Ss to use expressions like *sure, OK, no problem,* and *all right.*
- In pairs, Ss take turns making and responding to each other's requests from part A. Go around and make sure Ss use pronouns in their responses.

For more practice with two-part verbs, play ***Simon Says*** on page T-145.

4 PRONUNCIATION

Learning objective: *notice the stress patterns in requests with two-part verbs*

A [CD 1, Track 38]

- Play the audio program to present the sentences. Ss tap the desk or clap in time to the stress. Then they repeat.

For another way to practice stress patterns, try ***Walking Stress*** on page T-152.

B

- Explain and model the task by eliciting several examples and writing them on the board. Then have Ss work individually to write four more requests.
- Have Ss form pairs and take turns making their requests and giving appropriate responses.

3 GRAMMAR FOCUS

Two-part verbs; *will* for responding to requests

With nouns	*With pronouns*	*Requests and responses*
Turn down the TV.	**Turn** it **down**.	Please turn down the music.
Turn the TV **down**.		OK. I'**ll** turn it down.
Pick up your things.	**Pick** them **up**.	Pick up your clothes, please.
Pick your things **up**.		All right. I'**ll** pick them up.

A Complete the requests with these words. Then compare with a partner.

the books

the toys

the radio

your jacket

the TV

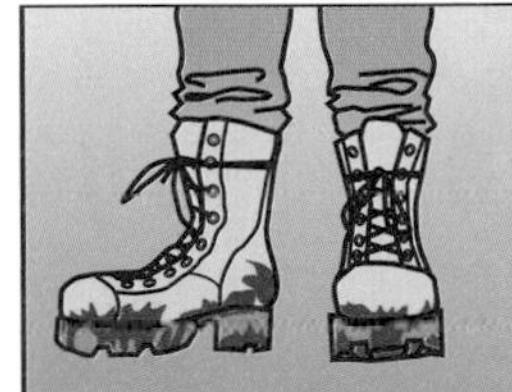
your boots

the yard

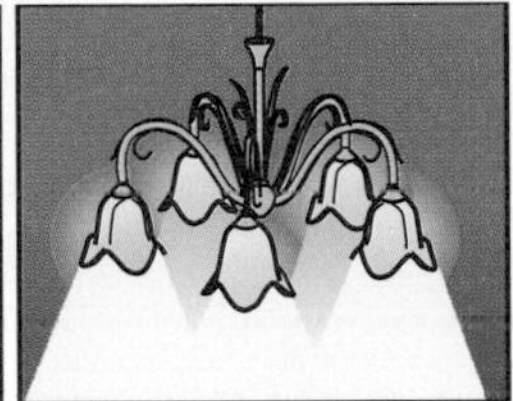
the lights

the trash

the dog

1. Pick up ....*the toys*......... , please.
2. Turn .... off, please.
3. Clean .... up, please.
4. Please put .... away.
5. Please turn down ....
6. Please take off ....
7. Hang .... up, please.
8. Please take out ....
9. Please let .... out.
10. Turn on .... , please.

B ***Pair work*** Take turns making the requests above. Respond with pronouns.

A: Pick up the toys, please.
B: No problem. I'll pick them up.

4 PRONUNCIATION Stress in two-part verbs

A Listen and practice. Both words in a two-part verb receive equal stress.

●	●	•	●
Pick	up	the	toys.
Turn	off	the	light.

●	•	●	●
Pick	the	toys	up.
Turn	the	light	off.

●	•	●
Pick	them	up.
Turn	it	off.

B Write four more requests using the verbs in Exercise 3. Then practice with a partner. Pay attention to stress.

5 WORD POWER Household chores

A Find a phrase that is usually paired with each two-part verb. (Some phrases go with more than one verb.) Then add one more phrase for each verb.

the garbage	the mess	the newspapers	your coat
the groceries	the microwave	the towels	your laptop

clean up	....	....	take out	....	....
hang up	....	....	throw out	....	....
pick up	....	....	turn off	....	....
put away	....	....	turn on	....	....

B What requests can you make in each of these rooms? Write four requests and four unusual excuses. Use two-part verbs.

the kitchen	the living room
the bathroom	the bedroom

C ***Pair work*** Take turns making the requests you wrote in part B. Respond by giving an unusual excuse.

A: Kim, please clean up your mess in the kitchen.
B: Sorry, I can't clean it up right now. I have to take the cat out for a walk.

6 LISTENING Family life

A Listen to the results of a survey about family life. For each question, write men (**M**), women (**W**), boys (**B**), or girls (**G**).

Who is the messiest in the house? ....
Who does most of the work in the kitchen? ....
Who usually takes out the garbage? ....
Who worries most about expenses? ....

B Listen again. According to the survey, what specific chores do men, women, boys, and girls usually do? Take notes.

C ***Group work*** Discuss the questions in parts A and B. Who does these things in your family?

5 WORD POWER

Learning objective: *learn more two-part verbs and common household chores*

A

- Explain the task. Then read the nouns and the two-part verbs while Ss repeat. Use the first two-part verb to elicit Ss' responses. Model how to complete the chart.
- Tell Ss not to use their dictionaries until they have matched all eight two-part verbs with nouns. Alternatively, have Ss work in pairs.
- Check Ss' answers. Explain any new vocabulary.

Answers

clean up	the mess, *the kitchen*
hang up	the towels, your coat, *the phone*
pick up	the mess, your coat, the newspapers, the towels, *the toys*
put away	the newspapers, the groceries, the towels, *your things*
take out	the garbage, the newspapers, *the dog*
throw out	the garbage, the newspapers, *the old food*
turn off/on	your laptop, the microwave, *the light*

(Note: Additional phrases are italicized.)

B

- Explain the task. Ss use the words from page 37 or the chart in part A.
- Model the task by reading the example conversation in part C. Then Ss work individually to write their requests and excuses. To keep an element of surprise in the next task, go around the class to check Ss' answers.

C *Pair work*

- Read the example conversation again. Tell Ss to listen carefully to each request so they can match it to one of their unusual excuses.
- Ss form pairs and take turns making their requests and giving excuses. Go around the class and listen in. If a pair's request and excuse don't match, help them find a better match.

To practice two-part verbs with requests and excuses, try the ***Requests Picture Game*** on page T-157.

To review two-part verbs, play ***Mime*** on page T-148.

LISTENING

Learning objectives: *listen to the results of a survey; develop skills in listening for main ideas and details*

A *[CD 1, Track 39]*

- Ask: "Do you think men and women share housework equally? Who does more? What about boys and girls? What do they have to do?"
- Explain that Ss will listen to the results of a survey about family life. Go over the four questions and have Ss predict the answers. Explain that Ss need to write the letters *M, W, B,* or *G.*
- Play the audio program. Ss listen and write the answers. Then go over answers with the class.

Audio script *(See page T-227.)*

Answers

B, W, B and M, W

B

- Read the question. Encourage Ss to take notes. Then play the audio program again, repeating if necessary.
- Ss compare answers in pairs or groups. If they disagree, play the audio program again, pausing after each section. Then elicit Ss' responses.

Answers

Men: take out the garbage
Women: cook, do the dishes, clean up
Boys: take out the garbage, put the groceries away
Girls: cook, do the dishes, clean up, put the groceries away

C *Group work*

- Explain the task. Remind Ss to ask follow-up questions and give additional information.
- In small groups, Ss use the questions from parts A and B to discuss who does these things in their family.

End of Cycle 1

Do your students need more practice?

Assign . . .	*for more practice in . . .*
Workbook Exercises 1–5 on pages 31–33	Grammar, Vocabulary, Reading, and Writing
Lab Guide Exercises 1–2 on page 9	Listening, Pronunciation, Speaking, and Grammar

7 PERSPECTIVES

Learning objectives: *discuss common requests; see requests with modals and* Would you mind . . . ? *in context*

A [CD 1, Track 40]

- Books closed. Set the scene. Ss will hear five requests neighbors sometimes make. Write these questions on the board:
  Which speaker is bothered by:
  Safety? Noise? Parties? Garbage? Parking?
- Explain that Ss need to write the number of the speaker next to the concern. Play the audio program. Ss listen for answers to the questions on the board. Then elicit answers. (Answers: 3, 1 and 2, 1, 5, 4)
- Books open. Play the audio program again while Ss read silently. Explain any new vocabulary.

Vocabulary

thin: not thick or strong
guests: visitors
Would you mind (doing something)?: Please (do something).
make sure: be certain that something will happen
lock: close with a key

- Point out that *can, could, would,* and *Would you mind . . . ?* mean the same thing. Differences in feeling will be discussed in Exercise 8.
- Ss discuss the two questions in pairs.
- ***Option:*** Play the audio program again. Ss listen to the intonation of the speakers. Then Ss take turns reading the requests in pairs.

B

- Explain the task. In pairs, Ss discuss which requests are reasonable and which are not. Encourage them to give a reason.
- ***Option:*** Ss share their ideas with another pair.

8 GRAMMAR FOCUS

Learning objective: *practice making requests using modals* can, could, would, *and* Would you mind . . . ? *+ gerund*

[CD 1, Track 41]

- Play the audio program to present the questions in the box. Ss listen and repeat.

***Modals* can, could, *and* would**

- Explain that it is OK to say, "Please turn the stereo off." to people we know well. We should use a more polite request, however, for neighbors and strangers. Modals become more formal and more polite from *can* to *could* to *would*. Tone of voice is also important.

Would you mind . . . ? + *gerund*

- Point out the structure *Would you mind . . . ?* + gerund in the Perspectives section. Explain that the verb *mind* must be followed by a gerund (or verb + *-ing*). Elicit examples from Ss and write them on the board.
- Go over the negative request with *not* in the Perspectives section. Elicit other examples for the class to practice (e.g., *Would you mind* not *talking while I'm speaking? Would you mind* not *coming late to class, please?*).

A

- Explain the task. Ss work individually to match each request with a response. Then pairs compare answers. Have the first S to finish write the answers on the board.

Possible answers

1. d, f	3. e, f	5. b, e, f
2. d, e, f	4. c	6. a

- Ss practice the requests and responses in pairs.

B *Pair work*

- Model the task with one or two Ss.
  T: Could you lend me twenty dollars?
  S: Sorry! I was just going to ask *you* for a loan!
- In pairs, Ss take turns making the requests and giving their own responses.

For another way to practice requests, try ***Moving Dialog*** on page T-150.

C *Class activity*

- Explain the task. Encourage Ss to think of unusual requests. Then Ss move around the classroom and make their requests.
- Find out who had the most unusual requests.

7 PERSPECTIVES Would you mind . . . ?

A Listen to the requests people make of their neighbors. Have you ever made a similar request? Has anyone ever asked you to do these things?

"Could you please tell me the next time you have a party? I'd like to make sure I'm not at home."

"Can you turn the stereo off, please? The walls are really thin, so the sound goes through to my apartment."

"Would you mind closing the door behind you and making sure it locks? We don't want any strangers to enter the building."

"Would you please tell your guests to use the visitor parking spaces? A lot of cars have been using my space recently."

"Would you mind not putting your garbage in front of your door? It's not very pleasant to see it in the hallway."

B Look at the requests again. Which are reasonable? Which are unreasonable?

8 GRAMMAR FOCUS

Requests with modals and Would you mind . . . ?

Modal + simple form of verb	*Would you mind . . . + gerund*
Can you **turn** the stereo **off**?	**Would** you **mind turning** the stereo **down**?
Could you **close** the door, please?	**Would** you **mind closing** the door, please?
Would you please **take** your garbage **out**?	**Would** you **mind not putting** your garbage here?

A Match the requests with the appropriate responses. Then compare with a partner and practice them. (More than one answer may be possible.)

1. Could you lend me twenty dollars? ....
2. Can you get me a sandwich? ....
3. Can you help me move to my new house? ....
4. Would you mind not sitting here? ....
5. Could you move your car from my space? ....
6. Would you mind not talking so loudly? ....

a. We're sorry. We'll talk more quietly.
b. I'm sorry. I'll do it right away.
c. Sorry. I didn't realize this seat was taken.
d. Are you kidding? I don't have any cash.
e. I'm really sorry, but I'm busy.
f. Sure, no problem. I'd be glad to.

B ***Pair work*** Take turns making the requests in part A. Give your own responses.

C ***Class activity*** Think of five unusual requests. Go around the class and make your requests. How many people accept? How many refuse?

A: Could you lend me your toothbrush?
B: Oh, I'm sorry. I don't have it with me.

9 SPEAKING Apologies

A Think of three complaints you have about your neighbors. Write three requests you want to make. Choose from these topics or use ideas of your own.

garbage guests noise parking pets security

B ***Pair work*** Take turns making your requests. The "neighbor" should apologize by giving an excuse, admitting a mistake, or making an offer or promise.

A: Would you mind not putting your garbage in the hallway?
B: Oh, I'm sorry. I didn't realize it bothered you.

different ways to apologize	
give an excuse	"I'm sorry. I didn't realize . . ."
admit a mistake	"I forgot I left it there."
make an offer	"I'll take it out right now."
make a promise	"I promise I'll . . . / I'll make sure to . . ."

10 INTERCHANGE 6 That's no excuse!

How good are you at apologizing? Go to Interchange 6.

11 WRITING A set of guidelines

A ***Pair work*** Imagine that you live in a large apartment building. Use complaints from Exercise 9 and your own ideas to write a set of eight guidelines.

The Riverview Apartments

Please read the following tenant association guidelines. Feel free to contact Joseph (#205) or Tina (#634) if you have any questions.

1. *The pool summer hours are 8 A.M. to 9 P.M. Please clear the area by 9 P.M.*
2. *Can everyone make an effort to keep the laundry room clean? Please pick up after yourself!*
3. *Would you mind not picking the flowers in the garden? They're for everyone's enjoyment.*

B ***Group work*** Take turns reading your guidelines aloud. What is the best new guideline? the worst one?

9 SPEAKING

Learning objective: *practice making requests and apologizing*

A

- Explain the task. Then give Ss time to write three complaints. They can choose from the list of topics or use their own ideas. Remind them to use the polite form of requests.

B *Pair work*

- Ask: "What reasons do students give when they come late to class? When they forget to bring their books?" Accept any reasonable answers.
- Explain that an *apology* is a statement that a person makes to show that he or she is sorry. Point out that there are different ways to apologize.
- Have Ss read the information in the chart. Explain any new vocabulary.

Vocabulary

admit a mistake: say that you did something wrong
make an offer: say you are willing to do something for someone
make a promise: say that you definitely will (or won't) do something

- Explain and model the task with a few Ss. Make complaints and give direction on how Ss should apologize.

T: You're late again! Give an excuse.
S1: Oh, I'm sorry. I had to visit my aunt and . . .
T: You forgot to do your homework. Make an offer.
S2: I'm sorry. I'll do it tonight.

- In pairs, Ss take turns complaining and apologizing. Go around the class and listen.

TIP To let Ss concentrate on what they are saying during a speaking activity, it is best not to interrupt. Listen and take note of any errors you hear. Then go over the errors at the end of the activity.

- Go over errors by writing the most common ones on the board and asking Ss to correct them. Give help as needed.

For another way to practice complaints and apologies, try ***Question Exchange*** on page T-152. Ss put their own requests in the bag.

- ***Option:*** Discuss ways to apologize in other cultures.

In a heterogeneous class: Ask: "How and why do people in other countries apologize? What are some differences you know about?"

In a homogeneous class: Ask: "How and why do people in your country usually apologize?"

10 INTERCHANGE 6

See page T-120 for teaching notes.

11 WRITING

Learning objective: *write a set of guidelines using requests with modals and* Would you mind . . . ?

A *Pair work*

- Ask if any Ss live in an apartment building. If so, ask: "Is there a committee made up of people who live there? Does someone write notices about issues, like safety, what to do with your garbage, etc.?"
- Have Ss read the instructions and the example letter silently. Explain any new vocabulary.
- Point out the features of the notice (e.g., *a general introduction to the guidelines, contact information, individual points*). Each point contains one piece of information and a request.
- In pairs, Ss brainstorm things they would like to include in their guidelines. Remind Ss to use the list of topics in Exercise 9 or their own ideas.
- In pairs, Ss write their own set of guidelines. Encourage them to use a variety of requests (e.g., *Could you, Would you, Please, Would you mind?*).

B *Group work*

- Ss take turns reading their guidelines aloud in small groups.
- Ss discuss their guidelines. Then ask them to choose the best and worst one. The best guideline could be the easiest to obey; the worst might be the hardest to obey.
- ***Option:*** Ss tell the class which guidelines they chose.
- ***Option:*** Follow up with a role play where neighbors are at a condominium meeting. In small groups, Ss use the complaints they wrote in Exercise 9.

12 READING

***Learning objective:** develop skills in guessing meaning from context and reading for specific information*

- Books closed. Ask: "Do you know your neighbors? Do you like them? What kinds of problems have you had with them?" Ss discuss the questions in small groups or as a class.
- Books open. Have Ss read the three situations in the article. Elicit or explain any new vocabulary.

Vocabulary

yard: a piece of land surrounding a house
blow: be carried by the wind
driveway: a paved area for your car in front of your house or garage

- In pairs or small groups, Ss discuss what they would do. Elicit suggestions. Accept any reasonable answers.
- Ss read the article silently. Tell Ss not to use their dictionaries because guessing meaning from context is the skill practiced in part A.

A

- Explain the task. Ss work individually to complete the exercise.
- Elicit answers.

Answers

1. b   2. d   3. f   4. e   5. a   6. c

- Elicit any words that Ss still don't know. Then explain the words or have Ss check their dictionaries.

Vocabulary

share: enjoy an experience with others
wave: a movement of the hand or arm to say hello or good-bye
frustration: a negative feeling of disappointment or inability to do something
get on your nerves: irritate; make very angry
approach: start communication with
compliment: express admiration or approval
avoid: stay away from
issue: problem or subject

B

- Explain the task. Point out that not all the questions are answered in the text. Read the first question and ask Ss if it is answered in the text. (Answer: No) Ss complete the first part of the task individually. Then go over answers with the class.

Answers

Questions that the article answers:
2 4 5

- Explain the second part of the task. Ss underline the sentences in the text that answer questions 2, 4, and 5.
- Have Ss check their answers in pairs. Then go over answers with the class.

Answers

2 When you don't know someone, it's easy to build up frustration and resentment.
4 You should talk to them in a friendly manner . . . suggest it.
5 If talking doesn't work, . . . sometimes it's a good idea to avoid the problem.

C *Pair work*

- Ss discuss the questions in pairs.
- Pairs share some interesting ideas that they discussed with the rest of the class.
- ***Option:*** Pairs act out one of these situations in front of the class.

For more speaking practice, play ***Just One Minute*** on page T-146.

End of Cycle 2

Do your students need more practice?

Assign . . .	***for more practice in . . .***
Workbook Exercises 6–11 on pages 34–36	Grammar, Vocabulary, Reading, and Writing
Lab Guide Exercises 3–8 on page 9	Listening, Pronunciation, Speaking, and Grammar
Video Activity Book Unit 6	Listening, Speaking, and Cultural Awareness
CD-ROM Unit 6	Grammar, Vocabulary, Reading, Listening, and Speaking

Evaluation

Assess Ss' understanding of Units 5 and 6 with the quiz on pages T-204 and T-205.

12 READING

Neighbor vs. Neighbor

Read the situations in the list below. What would you do in each situation?

- **The woman in the apartment upstairs plays her piano after midnight.**
- **The family across the street never cleans up their yard. The garbage blows into your yard.**
- **The guy next door always parks his car in front of your driveway.**

Have things like this ever happened to you? If so, you may ask yourself, "Who are these people? Why are they doing these things to me?"

These days, many people don't know their neighbors. Sometimes we share a friendly wave or say hello, but a lot of people don't even know their neighbors' names! When you don't know someone, it's easy to build up frustration and resentment. You think, "Maybe they like to annoy me," or "Maybe they do it deliberately."

Believe it or not, your neighbors probably don't mean to irritate you. Often, they don't even know that they're getting on your nerves. So before you take extreme measures to fix the problem, you should discuss it with them first.

When you approach your neighbors, you should talk to them in a friendly manner. Compliment their children or do something else to make them feel good. Then explain the situation. And if you can think of a simple solution, suggest it.

If talking doesn't work, ask another person to help. This person can listen to both sides of the story and help you and your neighbor resolve the situation.

Finally, sometimes it's a good idea to avoid the problem. Depending on the issue, it might be best to just stay out of your neighbor's way.

A Read the article. Find the words in *italics* in the article. Then match each word with its meaning.

.... 1. *resentment*	a. a way of behaving
.... 2. *deliberately*	b. anger that grows over time
.... 3. *irritate*	c. end a problem or difficulty
.... 4. *measure*	d. on purpose
.... 5. *manner*	e. a step taken in order to achieve something
.... 6. *resolve*	f. bother or annoy

B Check (✓) the questions that the article answers. Then find sentences in the article that support your answers.

- ☐ 1. Why don't many people know their neighbors?
- ☐ 2. Why do we become angry at neighbors?
- ☐ 3. What are some extreme measures you can take to solve a problem?
- ☐ 4. How should you approach a neighbor about a problem?
- ☐ 5. What can you do when discussion doesn't work?

C ***Pair work*** Have you ever had a problem with a neighbor, classmate, or co-worker? How did you resolve it?

Units 5–6 Progress check

SELF-ASSESSMENT

How well can you do these things? Check (✓) the boxes.

I can	Very well	OK	A little
Listen to and understand plans using *be going to* and *will* (Ex. 1)	☐	☐	☐
Ask and answer questions about plans using *be going to* and *will* (Ex. 2)	☐	☐	☐
Give travel advice using modals for necessity and suggestion (Ex. 2)	☐	☐	☐
Make requests using two-part verbs (Ex. 3)	☐	☐	☐
Apologize, give excuses, and accept or refuse requests using *will* (Ex. 3, 4)	☐	☐	☐
Make requests using modals and *Would you mind . . . ?* (Ex. 4)	☐	☐	☐

1 LISTENING Summer plans

A Listen to Judy, Paul, and Brenda describe their summer plans. What is each person going to do?

	Summer plans	Reason
1. Judy	....	....
2. Paul	....	....
3. Brenda	....	....

B Listen again. What is the reason for each person's choice?

2 DISCUSSION Planning a vacation

A *Group work* Imagine you are going to go on vacation. Take turns asking and answering these questions.

A: **Where are you going to go on your next vacation?**
B: I'm going to go to Hawaii.
C: **What are you going to do?**
B: I'm going to go camping and hiking. Maybe I'll try rock climbing.
A: **Why did you choose that?**
B: Well, I really enjoy nature. And I want to do something different!

B *Group work* What should each person do to prepare for his or her vacation? Give each other advice.

Units 5–6 Progress check

SELF-ASSESSMENT

Learning objectives: *reflect on one's learning; identify areas that need improvement*

- Ask: "What did you learn in Units 5 and 6?" Elicit Ss' answers.
- Ss complete the Self-assessment. Encourage them to be honest, and point out they will not get a bad grade if they check (✓) "a little."
- Ss move on to the Progress check exercises. You can have Ss complete them in class or for homework, using one of these techniques:
  1. Ask Ss to complete all the exercises.
  2. Ask Ss: "What do you need to practice?" Then assign exercises based on their answers.
  3. Ask Ss to choose and complete exercises based on their Self-assessment.

1 LISTENING

Learning objective: *assess one's ability to listen to and understand plans using* be going to *and* will

A [CD 1, Track 42]

- Set the scene. Three people are talking about their summer plans. Go over the chart and explain that Ss should complete only the first column.
- Play the audio program. Ss listen and write what each person is going to do. Check answers with the class.

Audio script *(See page T-227.)*

Answers

Summer plans
1. go white-water rafting
2. stay home and get a job
3. work the first month; visit sister in Mexico

B

- Explain the task. Ss listen for each person's reasons.
- Play the audio program again. Ss listen and complete the second column.
- Check answers with the class.

Answers

Reason
1. wants to do something different this year
2. needs to save some money for school
3. wants to save some money; wants to see what Mexico (Guadalajara) is like

2 DISCUSSION

Learning objectives: *assess one's ability to ask and answer questions about plans using* be going to *and* will; *assess one's ability to give travel advice using modals for necessity and suggestion*

A Group work

- Explain the task. Ss imagine they are going on vacation. Then they ask and answer questions about each other's vacation plans.
- Call on three Ss to read the example conversation. Remind Ss to add additional information and ask follow-up questions to keep the conversation going.
- Give Ss a few minutes to plan their vacation and prepare some questions to ask others in the group.
- In small groups, Ss take turns asking and answering questions about their vacations. Go around the class, paying attention to Ss' use of *be going to* and *will*, and their ability to keep a conversation going.
- Give the class feedback on their discussions. What went well? What problems did you hear?

B Group work

- Explain the task. Then ask Ss about their vacation plans to model how to give advice.
  T: What are you going to do on your vacation?
  S1: I'm going to go skiing with my friends.
  T: I think you should take warm clothing with you.
  S2: I agree. I think you also need to take money.
- Ss complete the task. Go around the class, paying particular attention to their use of modals for necessity and suggestion.
- ***Option:*** Ask groups to tell the class about one vacation and how someone should prepare for it.

3 ROLE PLAY

Learning objectives: *assess one's ability to make requests using two-part verbs; assess one's ability to apologize, give excuses, and accept or refuse requests using* will

- Explain the task and focus Ss' attention on the pictures. Elicit useful vocabulary from Ss.
- Divide the class into pairs and assign roles. Student A makes a request about each picture, while Student B apologizes and either accepts or refuses the request.
- Call on two Ss to read the example conversation. Explain that Student B accepts the request, but can also refuse the request by giving an excuse. Ask: "How could Student B politely refuse the request? What excuse could he or she make?" Elicit ideas (e.g., *I'm sorry. I forgot about them. But I can't pick them up, because I have a bad back / am late for an appointment.*). Encourage Ss to be creative when they make excuses.
- Student A begins by using the picture to make a request. Student B replies with an apology and then accepts or refuses the request.
- Go around the class and listen to the role plays without interrupting. Make a note of common errors or ways in which the role plays could be better.
- Make suggestions on how Ss could improve their role plays. Give examples of good communication that you heard.
- Ss change roles and try the role play again.

GAME

Learning objectives: *assess one's ability to apologize, give excuses, and accept or refuse requests using* will; *assess one's ability to make requests using modals and* Would you mind . . . ?

A

- Give three cards or slips of paper to each S. Explain the task. Ss write one request on each card. Read the examples and elicit more suggestions. Ask Ss to try to write one request with *Can*, one with *Could*, and one with *Would you mind . . . ?*
- Individually, Ss write one request on each card. Then tell them to write an *X* on the back of two cards.
- Collect the cards and shuffle them all together.

B *Class activity*

- Give each S three cards. Ss should make sure they did not get any of their own cards.
- Explain the task. Ss get up and move around the room, making the requests written on their cards. As they make the request, they should hold up the card so the other S can see the back of the card. If the card has an *X* on the back, the person should refuse the request. If the card does not have an *X*, the person must accept the request.
- Model the task several times with cards and different Ss.
- Ss stand up and complete the activity. Go around the class and listen to the requests and responses, paying attention to the Ss' use of modals and *will* for acceptance.

WHAT'S NEXT?

Learning objective: *become more involved in one's learning*

- Focus Ss' attention on the Self-assessment again. Ask: "How well can you do these things now?"
- Ask Ss to underline one thing they need to review. Ask: "What did you underline? How can you review it?"
- If needed, plan additional activities or reviews based on Ss' answers.

3 ROLE PLAY Excuses, excuses!

Student A: Your partner was supposed to do some things, but didn't. Look at the pictures, and make a request about each one.

Student B: You were supposed to do some things, but didn't. Listen to your partner's requests. Apologize and either accept the request or give an excuse.

A: You left the towels on the floor. Please hang them up.
B: I'm sorry. I forgot about them. I'll hang them up right now.

Change roles and try the role play again.

4 GAME Could you do me a favor?

A Write three requests on separate cards. Put an *X* on the back of two of the cards.

Can you cook dinner tonight?

Could you get me a cup of coffee?

Would you mind closing the window?

B ***Class activity*** Shuffle all the cards together. Take three new cards.

Go around the class and take turns making requests with the cards. Hold up each card so your classmate can see the back.

When answering:
X on the back = refuse the request and give an excuse
No *X* = accept the request

Can you cook dinner tonight?
X

I'm sorry, I can't. I'm . . .

WHAT'S NEXT?

Look at your Self-assessment again. Do you need to review anything?

7 What's this for?

1 SNAPSHOT

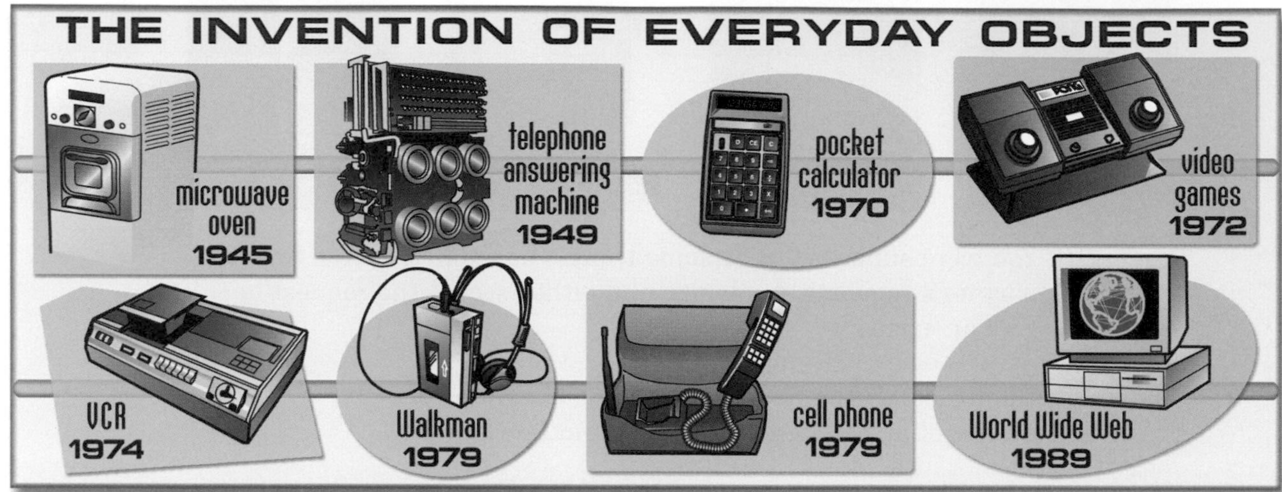

Sources: *The People's Almanac Presents the 20th Century*; *www.about.com*

Circle the things that you use every day or almost every day.
Which invention do you think is the most important? the least important?
What are some other things you use every day?

2 PERSPECTIVES Computer usage

A How do you use your computer, or how would you use a computer if you had one? Listen and respond to the statements.

Rate Your Computer Usage

I use/would use a computer	Often	Sometimes	Hardly ever	Never
to send and receive e-mails	☐	☐	☐	☐
for paying bills	☐	☐	☐	☐
to play games	☐	☐	☐	☐
to find information on the Web	☐	☐	☐	☐
for doing school assignments	☐	☐	☐	☐
to learn languages	☐	☐	☐	☐
for writing letters	☐	☐	☐	☐
to check the weather	☐	☐	☐	☐
to read the news	☐	☐	☐	☐
for downloading music	☐	☐	☐	☐

B ***Pair work*** Compare your answers. Are your answers similar or different?

What's this for?

In Unit 7, students discuss modern technology and inventions. In Cycle 1, they use infinitives and gerunds to describe uses and purposes. In Cycle 2, they use imperatives and infinitives to give suggestions.

Cycle 1, Exercises 1–6

1 SNAPSHOT

Learning objective: *read about some important scientific and technological inventions*

- ***Option:*** Have Ss brainstorm machines and modern inventions they use every day (e.g., *telephone, credit cards, TV, CDs, computer, video games*).

TIP To help Ss get ready to speak English, start each class with a quick warm-up activity. This will also help deal with Ss who arrive late!

- Books closed. Write this on the board:

cell phone	*1945*
pocket calculator	*1949*
microwave oven	*1970*
World Wide Web	*1979*
telephone answering machine	*1989*

- Tell Ss to match the invention with the year it was invented. Elicit answers.
- Books open. Ss check their answers. Did anything surprise them?
- Ss look at the pictures and the information. Model the pronunciation of the items while Ss repeat. If necessary, review the pronunciation of years (e.g., *nineteen forty-five*).
- Read the questions. Ss answer them in pairs or groups. Go around the class and give help as needed.
- ***Option:*** Ask Ss to describe how the inventions have changed (e.g., *Cell phones are much smaller now.*).

2 PERSPECTIVES

Learning objectives: *discuss your computer use; see infinitives and gerunds for uses and purposes in context*

A [CD 2, Track 1]

- Books closed. Ask Ss to raise their hands if they have a computer. Ask those Ss what they use their computers for (e.g., *play games, buy things, do research*). Write Ss' ideas on the board. If none of the Ss have computers, ask: "How often do you use a computer? How do you use it? Where do you go to use it?" Write some common uses on the board.

TIP To give Ss more incentive to listen to the Perspectives section, give focus questions before playing the audio program.

- Play the audio program. Ask Ss to name some of the uses they heard. Check to see if they heard any of the uses on the board.
- Books open. Explain the task. Point out that Ss can check (✓) *Often, Sometimes, Hardly ever,* or *Never*. Model the first sentence.
- Give Ss time to check (✓) the appropriate box.
- ***Option:*** Ss count the boxes to find out who uses the computer for the most purposes.
- Elicit any new vocabulary. Ask the class to give definitions or examples. Then explain any scientific or technical terms that Ss can't find in their dictionaries.

Vocabulary

e-mail: a letter which is sent electronically
bill: a note listing how much money you owe for something, e.g., water or electricity
school assignment: projects or homework
download music: transfer music files from the Web to a personal computer

B *Pair work*

- Write these expressions on the board:
  both . . . and I . . .
  neither . . . nor I . . .
  he/she does, but I don't.
- Ss compare answers in pairs. Ask: "How different or similar are you?" Elicit responses.
- ***Option:*** Have a brief class discussion about some controversial issues concerning computers (e.g., *How safe are chat rooms? How can you stop young people from finding bad material? Is it all right to download music?*).

3 GRAMMAR FOCUS

Learning objective: *practice using infinitives and gerunds for uses and purposes*

[CD 2, Track 2]

Infinitives and gerunds

- Explain that we can describe how something is used with either an infinitive or a gerund. The meaning is the same.
- Refer Ss to the Perspectives section. Point out that the chart contains ten uses of the computer. The examples use both infinitives and gerunds. Elicit or explain the difference between the two forms:
  With an infinitive (to + verb)
  I use my computer *to send e-mails.*
  With a gerund (for + verb + *-ing*)
  I use my computer *for sending e-mails.*
- Have Ss underline the examples of infinitives and circle the examples of gerunds.
- ***Option:*** You might want to mention that passives (*computers are often used . . .*) are found in the Grammar Focus box. Passives will be taught in Unit 11.
- Play the audio program to present the statements in the Grammar Focus box. For pronunciation practice, point out that the prepositions *to* and *for* are unstressed.
- Play the audio program again. Ss listen and repeat.

A

- Ask Ss to skim the phrases in part A. Then elicit or explain any new vocabulary.

Vocabulary

satellite: an unmanned manufactured object sent into orbit around the earth
robot: a computer-controlled factory machine
DNA fingerprinting: a way to identify people using information from their cells
CD-ROM: abbreviation for "compact disc read-only memory" – a compact disc on which information is stored for use by a computer
transmit: send
text message: a message that you can type and send on your cell phone
criminal: a person who has done something illegal

- Explain the task. Point out that *You* in the third item is an impersonal pronoun. It refers to people in general.
- Model the task by eliciting three possible answers for the first item. Then Ss complete the task individually.
- Ss compare answers. Then go over answers with both infinitives and gerunds.

Possible answers

1. Satellites are used **to study/for studying** the world's weather / **to transmit/for transmitting** telephone calls / **to transmit/for transmitting** television programs.
2. Robots are sometimes used **to perform/for performing** dangerous tasks.
3. You can use a cell phone **to transmit/for transmitting** telephone calls / **to send/for sending** text messages.
4. People use the Internet **to read/for reading** the latest weather report / **to make/for making** travel reservations.
5. DNA fingerprinting is used **to identify/for identifying** criminals.
6. CD-ROMs are used **to store/for storing** an encyclopedia.

B *Group work*

- In groups, Ss brainstorm new items and uses. Encourage them to think of interesting and creative uses for each item. Ask one S in each group to write down the group's sentences. Go around and give help as needed.
- Call on one S from each group to read some of the group's sentences to the class.

For more practice with vocabulary from this unit, try ***Information Gap Crossword*** on page T-157.

For more practice with infinitives and gerunds, play ***Twenty Questions*** on page T-145. Ss guess what object someone is thinking of.

4 PRONUNCIATION

Learning objective: *notice and practice stress in words with more than two syllables*

A ***[CD 2, Track 3]***

- Model how to pronounce the main stress in the words ***sat****ellite*, *in****ven****tion*, and *CD-****ROM***. Ss tap the desk or clap in time to the stress.
- Play the audio program while Ss pay attention to the syllable stress. Then play the audio program again. Ss listen and repeat.

B

- Ss mark the syllable stress in the words and write them in the correct column.
- Play the audio program. Ss listen and check their answers.

Answers

● • • languages, telephone
• ● • transmission, robotics
• • ● understand, VCR

3 GRAMMAR FOCUS

Infinitives and gerunds for uses and purposes

Infinitives	*Gerunds*
I use my computer **to send** e-mails.	I use my computer **for sending** e-mails.
Computers are often used **to pay** bills.	Computers are often used **for paying** bills.

A What do you know about this technology? Complete the phrases in column A with information from column B. Then compare with a partner. (More than one answer is possible.)

A	*B*
1. Satellites are used . . .	study the world's weather
2. Robots are sometimes used . . .	perform dangerous tasks
3. You can use a cell phone . . .	read the latest weather report
4. People use the Internet . . .	transmit telephone calls
5. DNA fingerprinting is used . . .	send text messages
6. CD-ROMs are used . . .	identify criminals
	make travel reservations
	transmit television programs
	store an encyclopedia

Satellites are used to study the world's weather.
Satellites are used for studying the world's weather.

B ***Group work*** Think of three more items of technology. Then talk about possible uses for each one.

"You can use DVD players to watch movies and to play CDs."

4 PRONUNCIATION Syllable stress

A Listen and practice. Notice which syllable has the main stress.

● • •	• ● •	• • ●
satellite	invention	CD-ROM
Internet	assignment	engineer
photograph	computer	entertain
....	....	....
....	....	....

B Where is the stress in these words? Add them to the columns in part A. Then listen and check.

languages understand telephone transmission robotics VCR

WORD POWER The world of computers

A Complete the chart with words and phrases from the list. Add one more to each category. Then compare with a partner.

✓ browse Web sites	drag and drop	keyboard	scan photographs
cut and paste	geek	monitor	surf the net
disk drive	hacker	mouse	technophile
double-click (on)	highlight text	play games	whiz

People who are "into" computers	Types of computer hardware	Fun things to do with a computer	Things to do with a mouse
....	....	browse Web sites	....
....	....	....	....
....	....	....	....
....	....	....	....
....	....	....	....

B ***Group work*** Discuss how computers have changed our lives. Ask and answer questions like these:

How do computers make your life easier? more difficult?
How do computers affect the way you spend your free time?
How do computers influence the kinds of jobs people have?
What kinds of problems do computers cause?
Do you know anyone who is a computer whiz?
Are hackers a problem where you live?

LISTENING Off-line – and proud!

A Guess the answers to the questions below. Then listen to a radio program about the Internet and check your answers.

What percentage of the population never uses the Internet? What kinds of people don't use the Internet?

B Listen to the rest of the program. Then answer these questions.

What does the term "net evaders" mean?
What are "Internet dropouts"?
Why do some people become Internet dropouts?

5 WORD POWER

Learning objective: *learn vocabulary for discussing computers*

A

TIP To avoid spending a long time teaching words in class, have Ss look up the vocabulary for homework before class.

- ***Option:*** Assign each S four words to look up in a dictionary. Then put Ss in groups of four and have them teach each other their words.

Vocabulary

disk drive: a piece of computer equipment that allows information to be stored and read
geek, technophile: someone who is very interested in computers (*Geek* is a somewhat insulting term.)
hacker: someone who illegally goes into other people's computer systems
monitor: a computer screen
mouse: a small hand-operated device that connects the keyboard to the monitor
surf the net: look at different Web sites online
be into: be very interested in
hardware: parts of a computer or machine

- Read the instructions. Then use the example (*browse Web sites*) to model the task. Remind Ss to try to add one more word to each category. Ss work individually to complete the chart.
- Draw the chart on the board. Elicit answers and write them on the board.

Answers

People who are "into" computers	***Types of hardware***
geek	disk drive
hacker	keyboard
technophile	monitor
whiz	mouse
nerd	*printer*
Fun things to do with a computer	***Things to do with a a mouse***
browse Web sites	cut and paste
play games	double-click
scan photos	drag and drop
surf the net	highlight text
send birthday cards	*change fonts*

(Note: Additional examples are italicized.)

B Group work

- Explain the task. Ss read the questions silently and ask any vocabulary questions. Pre-teach the words *spam* (unwanted e-mail) and *virus* (a damaging program that disrupts normal computer operations).
- Ss discuss the questions in small groups. Encourage them to use the vocabulary they learned in part A. Go around the class and give help as needed.

To review this vocabulary, play ***Tic-Tac-Toe*** on page T-148.

LISTENING

Learning objective: *develop skills in listening for details*

A *[CD 2, Track 4]*

- Focus Ss' attention on the picture and the title of the exercise. Ask: "What do you think *Off-line – and proud!* means?" (Answer: Some people don't use computers and they're happy about it.)
- Read the questions and have Ss predict answers.
- Play the audio program. Ss listen to check their predictions and make corrections. Elicit answers.

Audio script *(See page T-228.)*

Answers

Forty-two percent of the population never uses the Internet.
Older people, people living in rural areas, those who are worried about privacy, or who think the Internet isn't necessary in their life don't use the Internet.

B

- Ss read the questions silently. Then play the audio program again. Ss listen and answer the questions.
- Have Ss compare their answers in small groups.

Answers

"Net evaders" are people who ask others to send e-mails or browse Web sites for them.
"Internet dropouts" are people who once used the Internet, but don't any more.
People may become Internet dropouts because they don't have a computer anymore, don't have enough time, or aren't interested.

End of Cycle 1

Do your students need more practice?

Assign . . .	***for more practice in . . .***
Workbook Exercises 1–6 on pages 37–40	Grammar, Vocabulary, Reading, and Writing
Lab Guide Exercises 1–4 on page 10	Listening, Pronunciation, Speaking, and Grammar

7 CONVERSATION

Learning objectives: *practice a conversation about using a cell phone; see imperatives and infinitives for giving suggestions in context*

- ***Option:*** Introduce the topic by bringing a cell phone to class. Tell Ss to imagine that you don't know how to use it. Ask the class for instructions. For fun and challenge, pretend you don't understand!

A *[CD 2, Track 5]*

- Books closed. Set the scene. Someone is giving advice on how to use a cell phone. Write these questions on the board:
  1. Who owns the cell phone?
  2. Who are they calling?
  3. What's the first thing to do?
  4. What should the woman press?
- Play the audio program. Then elicit Ss' answers. (Answers: 1. the man 2. the woman's boss 3. turn the phone on 4. the "call" button)
- Books open. Play the audio program again as Ss look at the picture and read silently. Explain any new vocabulary. If necessary, explain the difference between *borrow* and *lend*.
- Write these instructions on the board:
  ___ *Hit the "end" button.*
  ___ *Turn the cell phone on.*
  ___ *Leave a message.*
  ___ *Press the "call" button.*
  ___ *Dial the area code and number.*
- Have Ss put the instructions in the correct order. (Answers: 5, 1, 4, 3, 2)
- ***Option:*** Find out who has a cell phone. Ask if the instructions for their phones are the same. If not, ask a S to describe how his or her cell phone works.
- Ss practice the conversation in pairs.

! For another way to practice this Conversation, try ***Look Up and Speak!*** on page T-150.

B

- Play the rest of the audio program. Ss listen to find out who Jenny wants to call next. Elicit answers.

Audio script *(See page T-228.)*

Answer

Jenny wants to call her own answering machine.

- ***Option:*** Have a class discussion on the advantages of having a cell phone. Then vote on the three best reasons to own a cell phone.

8 GRAMMAR FOCUS

Learning objective: *practice using imperatives and infinitives to give suggestions*

[CD 2, Track 6]

- Play the audio program to present the sentences in the box. Ss listen and repeat.
- Ask Ss to look back at the previous Conversation and underline some of the structures in the Grammar Focus box. (Answer: *be sure to*, *don't forget to*, *try not to*, *make sure to*)

A

- Have Ss label the three pictures: *alarm system*, *cell phone*, *laptop computer*. Then explain the task.
- Ss complete the task individually or in pairs. Go around the class and give help as needed. Remind Ss to write one more suggestion for each item. Then elicit answers.

Answers/Possible answers

1. LC	3. AS	5. AS	7. CP
2. AS	4. LC	6. CP / LC	

AS: *Don't forget to pay the bill.*
CP: *Be sure to turn it off in a movie theater.*
LC: *Remember to save your work often.*
(Note: Additional suggestions are italicized.)

B *Group work*

- Model the activity with several Ss. In small groups, Ss take turns giving suggestions for using the three items in part A. If you prefer, use more familiar objects (e.g., *bicycle*, *washing machine*, *car*, *photocopier*, *tape recorder*, *hair dryer*).
- ***Option:*** Play a game. Ss give advice and the rest of the class guesses what the advice refers to.

7 CONVERSATION Can I borrow your phone?

A Listen and practice.

Jenny: Can I borrow your phone to call my boss?
Richard: I can't believe you still don't have a cell phone. Here you go.
Jenny: Thanks. Now, what do I need to do?
Richard: First of all, be sure to turn it on. And don't forget to dial the area code.
Jenny: OK, I can see the number, but I can't hear anything.
Richard: That's because you haven't pressed the "call" button.
Jenny: Oh, good. It's ringing.
Richard: Try not to get too excited. You'll probably get his voice mail.
Jenny: You're right. It's a recording.
Richard: Make sure to hit the "end" button or else you'll leave our conversation on his voice mail!

B Listen to the rest of the conversation. Who does Jenny want to call next?

8 GRAMMAR FOCUS

Imperatives and infinitives for giving suggestions

Be sure to turn it on.
Don't forget to dial the area code.
Make sure to hit the "end" button.
Remember to pay the bill every month.
Try not to talk for too long.

A Look at these suggestions. Which ones refer to an alarm system (**AS**)? a cell phone (**CP**)? a laptop computer (**LC**)? (More than one answer is sometimes possible.) Then think of another suggestion for each thing.

1. Try to keep it closed to protect the screen. ....
2. Don't forget to write down your secret code. ....
3. Remember to turn it off as soon as you come in the door. ....
4. Try not to get it wet or the keys may get stuck. ....
5. Make sure to set it each time you leave home. ....
6. Remember to recharge the batteries before they die. ....
7. Be sure to turn it off before bed or a call may wake you up. ....

B *Group work* Take turns giving suggestions for using the items in part A. Use these phrases.

Make sure to . . .	Try to . . .	Remember to . . .
Be sure not to . . .	Try not to . . .	Don't forget to . . .

9 SPEAKING Free advice

A Listen to people give advice about three of the things below. Write the name of each item in the chart.

Item	Advice
1.	....
2.	....
3.	....

B Listen again. Complete the chart. Then compare with a partner.

C ***Pair work*** What do you know about the other things in part A? What advice can you give about them?

10 INTERCHANGE 7 Talk radio

Give callers to a radio program some advice. Go to Interchange 7.

11 WRITING A note giving instructions

A Imagine a friend is going to stay in your home while you're on vacation. Think of three unusual things you want him or her to do. Then write a note giving instructions.

Su Jin,
Thanks again for agreeing to house-sit for me. Please remember to do these three things: First, make sure to feed Owen, my pet snake, or else he'll escape and move around the house. Also, don't forget to . . .

B ***Group work*** Take turns reading your notes aloud. Who gave the most unusual instructions?

9 SPEAKING

***Learning objectives:** practice listening for specific information; give advice using imperatives and infinitives*

A [CD 2, Track 7]

- Focus Ss' attention on the pictures. Explain the task. In pairs or small groups, Ss brainstorm the kinds of vocabulary and advice they expect to hear about each item.
- Play the audio program. Ss listen and write the three items in the chart in the order they are talked about. Then Ss compare answers in pairs.

Audio script *(See page T-228.)*

B

- Play the audio program again, pausing after each speaker to give Ss time to write the advice. Then elicit answers.

Answers

Item	*Advice*
1. camcorder	It's best to use a stand. Be careful when you put in the battery.
2. in-line skates	Remember to wear protective gear. Make sure to skate on a flat surface.
3. ATM card	Be sure to put it in correctly. Then punch in your secret code. Remember to press "enter." Don't forget to count your money before you walk away from the machine.

For grammar recognition practice, play ***Stand Up, Sit Down*** on page T-151. Play the advice for the skates and the ATM card. Ss listen for expressions taught in the Grammar Focus (e.g., *be sure to, remember to*).

C *Pair work*

- Explain the task. In pairs, Ss talk about the other items in part A (*CD Walkman, motorbike,* and *personal watercraft*). Go around the class and give help as needed.
- Pairs share their best piece of advice for each item with the rest of the class.
- Find out which Ss have used the things in part A. Ask: "Do you own any of these things?"

10 INTERCHANGE 7

See page T-121 for teaching notes.

11 WRITING

***Learning objective:** write a note giving instructions using imperatives and infinitives*

A

- Explain the situation and the term *to house-sit* (*when you go away, you ask someone to stay in your house for you*). Ask: "Has anyone in the class ever house-sat?"
- Ss read the example paragraph silently. Point out the initial sentence of thanks and the use of sequence markers (*First, Also . . .*). Remind Ss of the meaning of *or else*.
- Give Ss time to think of three unusual things. Tell them to focus on giving someone directions or advice.
- Ss write a first draft. Tell them to use imperatives and infinitives where possible.
- ***Option:*** This part can also be assigned as homework.

B *Group work*

- In groups, Ss take turns reading their notes aloud to the rest of the group. Ss discuss the notes and make suggestions for revision. Go around the class and give help as needed.
- Ss revise their drafts based on the group feedback and their own ideas.
- ***Option:*** Have Ss put their final drafts on a bulletin board or wall, exchange them with other Ss, or give them to you to read.

TIP To increase Ss' self-confidence and create an English-speaking atmosphere in the classroom, display Ss' work on the classroom walls, if possible.

12 READING

***Learning objectives:** read an article about technology in the future; develop skills in identifying paragraph topics and reading for specific information*

- Books closed. Draw this on the board:

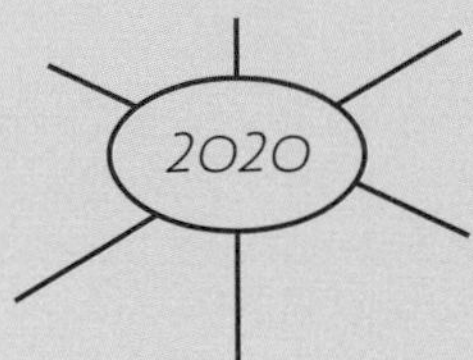

- Ask Ss how they think life will be different in the year 2020. Write the ideas they give on the lines coming out of the circle.
- Books open. Focus Ss' attention on the title of the article. Explain that they are going to find out if the text mentions their ideas.
- Explain the pre-reading task. Make sure Ss understand all the headings. Then give them time to scan the article to find the answers. Remind Ss to look for the information quickly, and not to worry about words they don't know. Then check answers. (Answers: Paragraph 1: Getting Around, Paragraph 2: Shopping, Paragraph 3: Eating, Paragraph 4: Working, Paragraph 5: Communicating, Paragraph 6: Relaxing)
- Ask Ss if the text includes any of their ideas from the pre-reading activity. Discuss briefly.

A

- Ss read the article silently.
- Elicit or explain any new vocabulary. Encourage other Ss to explain the words, using different words, pictures, or mime.

Vocabulary

daydream: think about nice things; not concentrating on the present moment
behind the wheel of your car: driving
automatic pilot: a setting that allows a machine to work or move by itself
head for: go toward
groceries: food that you buy in a store or supermarket
diagnostic machine: a machine that checks the status of something or someone
set: program a machine to do an operation
classic: a very well-known, old movie

- Have Ss look up any other new words in their dictionaries for homework.
- Explain the task. Tell Ss to read the text again and to check (✓) the appropriate column. If a sentence is false, Ss write the correct information. Model the first sentence with the class.

Possible answers

2. F Money is automatically deducted from your bank account.
3. T
4. F Your diagnostic machine finds out which food your body needs./Your food-preparation machine makes you a salad.
5. F You have a home office./You never have to commute to work anymore.
6. F Your computer translates messages.
7. T
8. F You have a list of new movies on your TV.

B *Pair work*

- In pairs, Ss take turns asking and answering the questions. Go around the class and give suggestions or ask additional questions, if necessary.
- ***Option:*** Set the scene. Student A lived 50 years ago and Student B lives in the year 2020. They meet in a time machine and ask each other questions about some of the topics in the article (e.g., *How do you shop? What do you eat?*). Give pairs time to prepare. Then have them role-play in groups or in front of the class.

End of Cycle 2

Do your students need more practice?

Assign . . .	*for more practice in . . .*
Workbook Exercises 7–11 on pages 40–42	Grammar, Vocabulary, Reading, and Writing
Lab Guide Exercises 5–6 on page 10	Listening, Pronunciation, Speaking, and Grammar
Video Activity Book Unit 7	Listening, Speaking, and Cultural Awareness
CD-ROM Unit 7	Grammar, Vocabulary, Reading, Listening, and Speaking

12 READING

A Day in Your Life – In the Year 2020

Scan the article. Then add the correct heading to each paragraph.

Communicating   Shopping   Relaxing   Eating   Getting Around   Working

People used to know more or less how their children would live. Now things are changing so quickly that we don't even know what our own lives will be like in a few years. What follows is how experts see the future.

....

You're daydreaming behind the wheel of your car, but that's OK. You have it on automatic pilot, and with its high-tech computers, your car knows how to get you home safely.

....

You head for the kitchen when you get home. You ordered groceries by computer an hour ago, and they've been delivered. You paid for them before they arrived. The money was automatically deducted from your bank account. Nobody uses cash anymore.

....

What's for lunch? In the old days, you used to stop off to get a hamburger or pizza. Now you use your diagnostic machine to find out which foods your body needs. Your food-preparation machine makes you a salad.

....

After lunch, you go down the hall to your home office. Here you have everything you need to do your work. You never have to commute to work anymore.

....

Your information screen says that you've received a message from a co-worker in Brazil. You set your computer to translate Portuguese into English. Your co-worker's face appears on the screen, and the translation appears at the bottom.

....

You finish working and go back to your living room. You turn on the television and look through the list of new movies. It's like having a video store in your home. How about a classic tonight? Maybe *Back to the Future*?

A Read the article. Check (✓) True or False for each statement about the future. Then write true information for each false statement.

True	False	
☐	☑	1. You need to pay attention while driving. *Your car has automatic pilot.*
☐	☐	2. You pay for your groceries when they arrive. ....
☐	☐	3. People don't use cash anymore. ....
☐	☐	4. You usually buy a hamburger or pizza for lunch. ....
☐	☐	5. You need to go to the office every day. ....
☐	☐	6. You and your co-workers have to speak the same language. ....
☐	☐	7. When you get a message, you can see the sender's face. ....
☐	☐	8. You have to go to a video store to rent movies. ....

B ***Pair work*** Which changes sound the most interesting? the most useful? Are there any changes that you don't like?

8 Let's celebrate!

1 SNAPSHOT

Holidays and Festivals
Chinese New Year
January or February
Chinese people celebrate with firecrackers and lion dances.
Valentine's Day
February 14
People in many countries give chocolates, flowers, or jewelry to the people they love.
Children's Day
May 5
Japanese families put up colored streamers shaped like fish, in honor of their children.
Day of the Dead
November 2
Mexican families offer food to the dead and then have a meal in a cemetery.

Source: *Reader's Digest Book of Facts*

Which of these holidays celebrate people? Which celebrate events?
Do you celebrate these or similar holidays in your country?
What other special days do you have? What's your favorite holiday or festival?

2 WORD POWER

Pair work Complete the word map. Add one more word to each category. Then describe a recent celebration using some of the words.

anniversary
cake
cards
dancing
fireworks
flowers
fruit punch
parade
party
presents
roast turkey
wedding

A: I went to a friend's birthday party recently. There was live music and dancing.
B: What kind of music did they play?

Let's celebrate!

In Unit 8, students discuss holidays and special occasions. In Cycle 1, they describe celebrations and annual events using relative clauses of time. In Cycle 2, they describe customs using adverbial clauses of time.

Cycle 1, Exercises 1–7

1 SNAPSHOT

***Learning objective:** learn vocabulary for talking about holidays and festivals*

- Books closed. Introduce the topic of special days by asking Ss to brainstorm public holidays in their country.
- If necessary, review dates with Ss. Point out that the preposition *in* is used with months (*in December*) and the preposition *on* is used with days and dates (*on December 25th*). Remind Ss how to say dates (e.g., *December twenty-fifth*).

For more practice with dates, play ***Line Up!*** on page T-144. Each S chooses a holiday and lines up in order of its date. Alternatively, Ss line up in order of their birthdays.

- Books open. Ask Ss to read the information in the Snapshot, using their dictionaries if necessary. Elicit or explain any vocabulary.

Vocabulary

lion dance: dance performed by several people wearing a lion costume – one wears the head of the lion and the others the body and tail
costume: a mask or clothing worn on special occasions
streamer: a long colored piece of cloth or paper
cemetery: an area of ground where people are buried

- Read the questions and have Ss discuss them in groups. Encourage Ss to ask follow-up questions. For example, after the last question, Ss could ask: "Why is it your favorite holiday? What makes it so special for you? What do you do on that day?"

2 WORD POWER

***Learning objective:** learn vocabulary for discussing celebrations*

Pair work

- Explain the task and model the first word (*anniversary*). Then have Ss complete the word map in pairs. Remind them to add one more word to each category. Then elicit Ss' answers.

TIP For an alternative way to go over answers, write the words on cards and ask Ss to organize them into the correct groups.

Answers

Special occasions	**Activities**
anniversary	dancing
party	fireworks
wedding	parade
birthday	*barbecue*
graduation	*singing*
Special food and drink	**Things we give/receive**
cake	cards
fruit punch	flowers
roast turkey	presents
champagne	*candy*
meat pies	*jewelry*

(Note: Additional examples are italicized.)

- Model the correct pronunciation of the words in the list. If necessary, explain any unfamiliar words.
- Point out the example conversation. Then Ss take turns asking and answering questions about celebrations they attended recently (e.g., *What kind of music did they play? Where was it? What was the food like?*).
- ***Option:*** To review the new vocabulary, play ***Scrambled Letters***. Write these words on the board and have Ss unscramble them:

1. kutyer	t-----	(turkey)
2. slofewr	f------	(flowers)
3. burFerya	F-------	(February)
4. gwidned	w------	(wedding)
5. yarJnau	J------	(January)
6. recarfikserc	f-----------	(firecrackers)
7. rerinyvarsan	a----------	(anniversary)
8. gandcin	d-------	(dancing)
9. rejlyew	j------	(jewelry)
10. chupn	p----	(punch)

When Ss finish, have them tell you the meaning.

3 PERSPECTIVES

Learning objectives: *discuss favorite holidays; see relative clauses of time in context*

A [CD 2, Track 8]

- Books closed. Explain that Ss will hear three people discuss their favorite day of the year.
- Play the audio program. Ss take notes on which holiday each speaker mentions and one thing he or she does on that day. Elicit Ss' answers.

Answers/Possible answers

1. Thanksgiving – cook a large turkey
2. Valentine's Day – give gifts
3. New Year's Eve – have a party at someone's house

- Write these sentences on the board:
  Thanksgiving: It's a day when ______________
  February 14: It's the day when ______________
  New Year's Eve: It's a night when ______________
- Play the audio program again. Ss listen and complete the sentences. Elicit answers.
- Books open. Have Ss check their answers by reading the information in the boxes. Elicit or explain any new vocabulary.

Vocabulary

harvest: the gathering or collecting of grains and vegetables from a farm
cranberry: a small, round red fruit with a sour taste
look forward to: anticipate with positive feelings
I can't wait . . . : I'm really excited about . . .

- Play the audio program again while Ss listen and read along silently. Ask them to pay special attention to the emotions expressed by the speakers.

To practice speaking and pronunciation, try ***Say It With Feeling!*** on page T-150.

B Pair work

- Ss discuss the questions in pairs. Encourage them to ask follow-up questions (e.g., *Why do you like the holiday?*).
- ***Option:*** Ask Ss what they know about the origins of these three holidays. Alternatively, have Ss find out about the holidays for homework and report to the class.

4 GRAMMAR FOCUS

Learning objective: *practice using relative clauses of time*

[CD 2, Track 9]

- Ask Ss to complete these sentences from memory: *Thanksgiving is a day when . . . / February 14 is the day when . . . / New Year's Eve is a night when . . . .* Then write them on the board.
- Point out that a relative clause of time is formed with *when*, which refers to the noun phrase (e.g., *the days*, *the month*, *the season*, *the time*) that comes before it. Underline the word *when* in the example sentences. Then elicit some more examples from Ss.
- Play the audio program to present the sentences in the box. Ss listen and repeat.

A

- This exercise requires Ss to use real-world knowledge. Most Ss will know enough to match some of the phrases, so they can probably complete the task by process of elimination.
- Read the question and the instructions. Then ask for Ss' suggestions for the first item. Ss complete the task individually. Check Ss' answers.

Answers

1. b 2. f 3. c 4. e 5. d 6. a

B

- Model how to complete the first sentence with the class (e.g., *Winter is the season when it snows / when it's cold / when people can ski.*). Then Ss write their own sentences with relative clauses. Go around the class and give help as needed.
- After Ss compare answers with a partner, go over answers with the class. Accept any sentences that are logical and grammatically correct.

Possible answers

1. Winter is the season **when it's cold and snowy**.
2. Birthdays are days **when someone gets a cake and presents**.
3. Spring is the time of year **when flowers blossom**.
4. Mother's Day is a day **when people honor their mothers**.
5. July and August are the months **when many people go to the beach**.
6. A wedding anniversary is a time **when couples celebrate their marriage**.

- ***Option:*** Ss form groups and play a game. Without mentioning the name of the holiday, they write sentences about a holiday in their country (e.g., *It's a day when people honor teachers.*). Then Ss exchange sentences and guess the name of the holiday (e.g., *Is it Teacher's Day?*).

3 PERSPECTIVES Special days

A Listen to people discuss some special days of the year.

"My favorite holiday is Thanksgiving. It's a day when North Americans celebrate the harvest. Everyone in the family gets together at our house. I cook a large turkey and serve it with cranberry sauce."

"February 14 is the day when people give cards and presents to the ones they love. I'm really looking forward to Valentine's Day this year! I already have the perfect gift for my boyfriend."

"I can't wait until the end of the year! New Year's Eve is a night when I have fun with my friends. We usually have a party at someone's house. We stay up all night and then go out for breakfast in the morning."

B ***Pair work*** Look at the statements again. Do you like any of the holidays? Which ones?

4 GRAMMAR FOCUS

Relative clauses of time

Thanksgiving is **a day**	**when** North Americans celebrate the harvest.
February 14 is **the day**	**when** people give cards to the ones they love.
New Year's Eve is **a night**	**when** I have fun with my friends.

A How much do you know about these days and months? Complete the sentences in column A with information from column B. Then compare with a partner.

A	*B*
1. New Year's Day is a day when	a. Brazilians celebrate Carnaval.
2. April Fools' Day is a day when	b. people have parties with family and friends.
3. May and June are the months when	c. many young adults choose to get married.
4. Valentine's Day is a day when	d. people in many countries honor workers.
5. Labor Day is a day when	e. people express their love to someone.
6. February is the month when	f. people sometimes play tricks on friends.

B Complete these sentences with your own information. Then compare with a partner.

Winter is the season . . .
Birthdays are days . . .
Spring is the time of year . . .

Mother's Day is a day . . .
July and August are the months . . .
A wedding anniversary is a time . . .

5 LISTENING *Carnaval time*

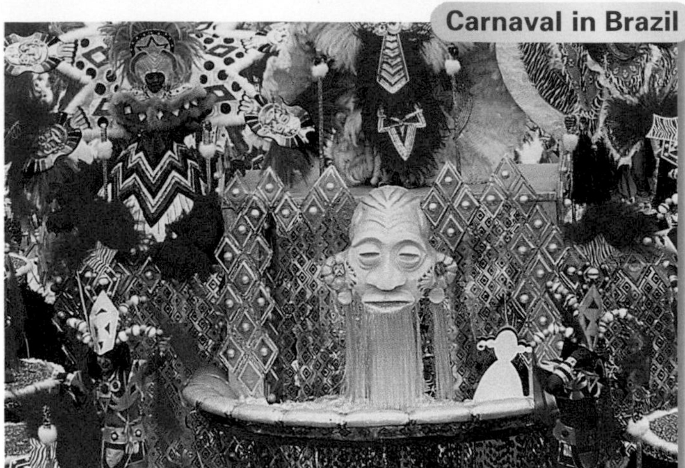
Carnaval in Brazil

A Mike has just returned from Brazil. Listen to him talk about Carnaval. What did he enjoy most about it?

B Listen again and answer these questions.

What is Carnaval?
How long does it last?
When is it?
What is the samba?

6 SPEAKING *Special days*

A *Pair work* Choose your three favorite holidays. Tell your partner why you like each one.

A: I really like New Year's Day.
B: What do you like about it?
A: Well, it's a day when I make my New Year's resolutions.

B *Class activity* Take a class vote. What are the most popular holidays in your class?

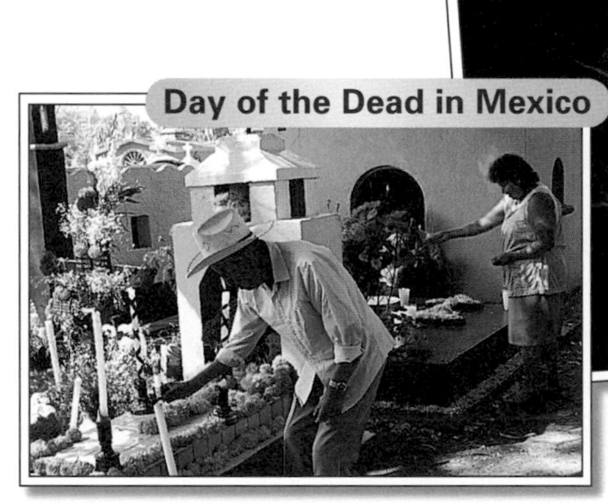
Day of the Dead in Mexico

Chinese New Year

7 WRITING *A travel guide*

A Write a paragraph for a travel magazine about a festival or celebration where you live. When is it? How do people celebrate it? What should a visitor be sure to see and do?

The annual fireworks festival in Yenshui, Taiwan, occurs on the last day of the New Year celebration. This is the first full moon of the new lunar year. It's a day when people explode fireworks in the streets, paint their faces, and dress up as . . .

B *Pair work* Read your partner's paragraph. What do you like about it? Can you suggest anything to improve it?

5 LISTENING

Learning objectives: *learn about Carnaval in Brazil; develop skills in listening for specific information*

A ▶ ***[CD 2, Track 10]***

- Books closed. Find out what the class knows about Carnaval. Write their ideas on the board.
- Set the scene. A man went to Brazil and is talking about his experiences there. Play the audio program. Ss listen to find out what he enjoyed most.

Audio script *(See page T-228.)*

Answer

The best part about Carnaval is the big parade.

B ▶

- Books open. Focus Ss' attention on the picture and questions. Ss listen for the answers and take notes. They should write only key words and phrases.
- Play the audio program again. Ss listen, take notes, and compare answers with a partner.

Answers

Carnaval is a party.
It lasts for four (whole) days.
It's in late February or early March.
The samba is a dance.

- ***Option:*** Ask Ss to share other information about Carnaval with the class.

6 SPEAKING

Learning objective: *talk about holidays using relative clauses of time*

- ***Option:*** To prepare for this activity, encourage Ss to bring photos to show during their discussions.
- Focus Ss' attention on the pictures. If anyone knows about one of the holidays, the rest of the class asks questions about it.

A *Pair work*

- Write these discussion topics on the board:
  date *origin* *activities* *place*
  special food and drink *things we give/receive*
  what you like about it *what else people do*
- Elicit questions (e.g., *What's the food like?*).
- As Ss work, go around the class and write down errors. Then go over them at the end of the activity.
- ***Option:*** Have each S prepare a short presentation. When each S finishes, encourage the rest of the class to ask follow-up questions. In large classes, Ss can give their presentations in groups.

To practice questions and answers about holidays, play ***Ask the Right Question*** on page T-146. Prepare different statements about holidays and celebrations (e.g., *Valentine's Day is on February 14. Halloween is a day when children dress up.*).

B *Class activity*

- Have Ss write the holiday they discussed on the board. If it is already there, don't write it again.
- Explain the task. In pairs or groups, Ss rate each holiday on the list, and award points out of three (1 = poor, 2 = OK, 3 = excellent).
- Read the holidays on the board and ask each pair or group to tell you how many points they gave the holiday. Have a S write the points on the board and then count the totals at the end of the activity. Which holiday was most popular? Elicit reasons.

7 WRITING

Learning objective: *write a paragraph for a travel guide using relative clauses of time*

A

- Explain the task. Then read the example paragraph. Point out that Ss should use the discussion topics from Exercise 6 to get ideas.
- Ss use their notes to write a first draft. Go around the class and give help as needed.

B *Pair work*

- Ss exchange paragraphs with a partner and ask follow-up questions. Then they work individually to revise their drafts.

End of Cycle 1

Do your students need more practice?

Assign . . .	*for more practice in . . .*
Workbook Exercises 1–4 on pages 43–45	Grammar, Vocabulary, Reading, and Writing
Lab Guide Exercises 1–3 on page 11	Listening, Pronunciation, Speaking, and Grammar

8 CONVERSATION

Learning objectives: *practice a conversation about wedding customs; see adverbial clauses of time in context*

- ***Option:*** To prepare for this activity, encourage Ss to bring wedding photos to class.

A *[CD 2, Track 11]*

- Books closed. Ask if any Ss in the class are married or if anyone has been to a wedding recently. If Ss brought photos to class, have them show the photos.
- Ask these questions about weddings: "In your country, where do weddings normally take place? Is there a ceremony and a reception? How are they different? Do the bride and groom wear special clothes? Who gives gifts? Do guests give speeches at the reception?"
- Books open. Focus Ss' attention on the photo. Ask: "What is the bride wearing? How are the guests dressed?"
- Books closed. Play the audio program. Ss listen to find out about traditional Japanese weddings. Elicit some information Ss heard.

> ***TIP*** Be sure to point out useful language features in the Conversations. If Ss are aware of these features, they will be more likely to use them during speaking activities.

- Explain that to keep a conversation going, it is important to (1) add follow-up information, (2) ask for more information, and (3) show interest.
- Now point out these conversational features. Play the first few lines of the audio program, pausing after *Those pictures were taken right after the ceremony.* Ask: "How did Emiko keep the conversation going?" (Answer: She gave extra information.)
- Play the next line (*Where was the ceremony?*). Ask: "How did Jill keep the conversation going?" (Answer: She asked a follow-up question.)
- Play the next line (*At a shrine.*). Point out that Emiko not only gave the answer, but she also added some more information. Ask: "What did she say?" Play the next line and elicit the answer. (Answer: *When people get married . . .*)
- Play the next line. Ask: "How did Jill show interest?" (Answer: She said, *"That's interesting."* and asked a follow-up question.)
- Books open. Ss read the conversation and underline the places where someone gives extra information. Then ask Ss to circle the places where someone asks a follow-up question or shows interest.
- Ss practice the conversation in pairs.

B

- Play the rest of the audio program. Ss listen and find out what the guests received. Then check answers.

Audio script *(See page T-228.)*

Answer

The bride and groom gave each guest a ceramic box filled with sweets.

9 PRONUNCIATION

Learning objective: *notice and practice stress and rhythm in sentences*

A *[CD 2, Track 12]*

- Explain that in English, stressed words or syllables occur with a more or less regular rhythm or beat, called *stress-timed rhythm*. The other words or syllables in the sentence are reduced to maintain the regular rhythm of the stressed words or syllables.
- Play the audio program and focus Ss' attention on the stressed words and syllables. Point out that the most important words, including main verbs, nouns, adjectives, and adverbs, are usually stressed. Auxiliary or modal verbs, articles, pronouns, and prepositions are usually not stressed.
- Ss listen to the sentence again and repeat. Have Ss tap a pen on the desk and beat out the rhythm.

B

- Explain the task. Ss listen to three sentences and mark where they hear the stress. Play the audio program. Then go over answers with the class.

Answers

(stressed syllables in bold)
After the **cer**emony, there's a re**cep**tion with **fam**ily and **friends**.
Before the **guests leave**, the **bride** and **groom give** them **pre**sents.
The **guests** usually give **money** to the **bride** and **groom**.

- Ss practice the sentences.

! For another way to practice stress and rhythm, try ***Walking Stress*** on page T-152.

8 CONVERSATION Wedding day

A Listen and practice.

Jill: Your wedding pictures are really beautiful, Emiko.
Emiko: Thank you. Those pictures were taken right after the ceremony.
Jill: Where was the ceremony?
Emiko: At a shrine. When people get married in Japan, they sometimes have the ceremony at a shrine.
Jill: That's interesting. Were there a lot of people there?
Emiko: Well, usually only family members and close friends go to the ceremony. But afterward we had a reception with family and friends.
Jill: So, what are receptions like in Japan?
Emiko: There's a big dinner, and after the food is served, the guests give speeches or sing songs.
Jill: It sounds like fun.
Emiko: It really is. And then, before the guests leave, the bride and groom give them presents.
Jill: The guests get presents?
Emiko: Yes, and the guests give money to the bride and groom.

B Listen to the rest of the conversation. What did the bride and groom give each guest?

9 PRONUNCIATION Stress and rhythm

A Listen and practice. Notice how stressed words and syllables occur with a regular rhythm.

When people get married in Japan, they sometimes have the ceremony at a shrine.

B Listen to the stress and rhythm in these sentences. Then practice them.

After the ceremony, there's a reception with family and friends.

Before the guests leave, the bride and groom give them presents.

The guests usually give money to the bride and groom.

10 GRAMMAR FOCUS

Adverbial clauses of time

When people get married in Japan,	they sometimes have the ceremony at a shrine.
After the food is served,	the guests give speeches or sing songs.
Before the guests leave,	the bride and groom give them presents.

A What do you know about wedding customs in North America? Match these phrases with the information below.

1. Before a man and woman get married, they usually ....
2. When a couple gets engaged, the man often ....
3. Right after a couple gets engaged, they usually ....
4. When a woman gets married, her family usually ....
5. When people are invited to a wedding, they almost always ....
6. Right after a couple gets married, they usually ....

a. pays for the wedding and reception.
b. go on a short trip called a "honeymoon."
c. give the bride and groom a gift or some money.
d. gives the woman a diamond ring.
e. begin to plan the wedding.
f. "date" each other for about a year.

B ***Pair work*** What happens when people get married in your country? Complete the statements in part A with your own information. Pay attention to stress and rhythm.

11 INTERCHANGE 8 *Once in a blue moon*

How do your classmates celebrate special events? Go to Interchange 8.

12 SPEAKING *That's an interesting custom.*

A ***Group work*** Do you know any interesting customs related to the topics below? Explain a custom and discuss it with your classmates.

births marriages courtship seasons good luck

A: I know a custom from the Philippines. When a boy courts a girl, he stands outside her house and sings to her.
B: What kinds of songs does he sing?
C: Romantic songs, of course!

B ***Class activity*** Tell the class the most interesting custom you talked about in your group.

10 GRAMMAR FOCUS

Learning objective: *learn and practice adverbial clauses of time*

▶ ***[CD 2, Track 13]***

***Adverbial clauses with* before, when, *and* after**

- Write the words *before*, *when*, and *after* on the board. Model how we use them as adverbs before a noun (e.g., *These photos were taken before the ceremony.*).
- Now write this adverbial clause on the board:
  Before two people get married, they plan the wedding.
  Point out that:
  1. The first half of the sentence is an adverbial clause (adverb + subject + verb).
  2. An adverbial clause is subordinate. It cannot occur on its own and is always attached to a main clause.
     Before two people get married, (= the subordinate clause) they plan the wedding. (= the main clause)
  3. Adverbial clauses of time can appear either before or after the main clause. We use a comma if the adverbial clause comes first.
     Before they marry, couples send invitations.
     Couples send invitations before they marry.
- Refer Ss to the Conversation on page 53. Tell them to look for examples of adverbial clauses with *before*, *when*, or *after*. (Answers: 1. When people get married in Japan 2. After the food is served 3. Before the guests leave)
- ***Option:*** Ask Ss to change the order of the three sentences, so that the adverbial clause follows the main clause.
- Play the audio program to present the sentences in the box. Ss listen and read silently.

A

- Read the instructions. Elicit or explain any new vocabulary.

Vocabulary

right (before/after): immediately (before/after)
wedding reception: the party after the wedding ceremony
honeymoon: the vacation a bride and groom take after their wedding
date: have a romantic relationship
get engaged: formally agree to get married

- Model the first item. Ss complete the task individually and then compare answers in pairs. Elicit answers.

Answers

1. f 2. d 3. e 4. a 5. c 6. b

- ***Option:*** To review rhythm and stress, have Ss mark the stress in the sentences and then practice saying them.

B *Pair work*

- Explain the task. Ss complete the phrases in part A with information about marriage customs in their country.
- Pairs write sentences with their own information. Remind Ss to use the stress and rhythm patterns they practiced in Exercise 9.

11 INTERCHANGE 8

See page T-122 for teaching notes.

12 SPEAKING

Learning objective: *talk about interesting customs using adverbial clauses of time*

A *Group work*

- ***Option:*** If necessary, briefly review these typical language mistakes:
  1. *wedding and marriage.* A *wedding* is one day only; *marriage* is the time after the wedding.
  2. *customs and costumes. Customs* are habits; *costumes* are clothes and masks worn for a special occasion.
  3. *get married to*, *be married to*, and *marry*. On the day of the wedding, a woman *marries*, or *gets married to*, a man. After that, she *is married* to him.
- Write these topics on the board:
  food   location   colors   music   traditions
- Explain the activity and model the conversation with Ss. Give Ss time to think of some customs they know. Then elicit suggestions about births, marriages, courtship (dating), seasons, and good luck.
- Ss discuss the customs they know in groups. Encourage them to ask follow-up questions, give extra information, and show interest.

B *Class activity*

- Ask groups to share some interesting information with the class.

To practice talking about customs, play ***True or False?*** on page T-148.

13 READING

***Learning objectives:** read an article about customs in different countries; develop skills in scanning for specific information and understanding reference words*

- Books closed. Ask Ss if they know about any festivals that honor the dead, are from India, or fight against evil spirits. Ss should already know about Day of the Dead from the Snapshot.
- Elicit or explain any new vocabulary.

Vocabulary

ribbon: a long, narrow strip of material used as decoration
ancestor: a member of your family from long ago
grave: a place where someone is buried, usually in a cemetery
silk: a soft, smooth material
bracelet: a piece of jewelry worn around the wrist
loyal: always supportive; faithful
fireworks: colorful explosions in the air as a show
dried: dehydrated; with the water removed
evil: with bad or cruel intention; the opposite of good

TIP To teach Ss words for materials, jewelry, and other small objects, bring realia (e.g., *a ribbon, silk, a bracelet*) to the classroom.

- Books open. Divide the class into three groups: A, B, and C. Ask each group to look at one of the pictures in the book and make a list of nouns, adjectives, and verbs to describe what is happening in each picture. Give Ss a time limit of three minutes and then ask Ss to guess what is happening.
- Have Ss read the text quickly and find out which paragraph refers to each picture. (Answers: picture 1 = paragraph 1; picture 2 = paragraph 2; picture 3 = paragraph 5)

A

- Explain the task and model the first question with the Ss. Then Ss work individually to complete the rest of the task. Go around the class and give help as needed.
- ***Option:*** Ss compare answers in groups.
- Elicit Ss' responses to check answers.

Answers

1. They dress them up in flowers and ribbons.
2. Koreans celebrate Chusok to give thanks for the harvest.
3. Indian women give bracelets to men in exchange for loyalty.
4. Families in Argentina get together and have a big meal and meet for parties.
5. Japanese families throw dried beans around their homes (shouting, "Good luck in! Evil spirits out!"). Then they eat the beans.

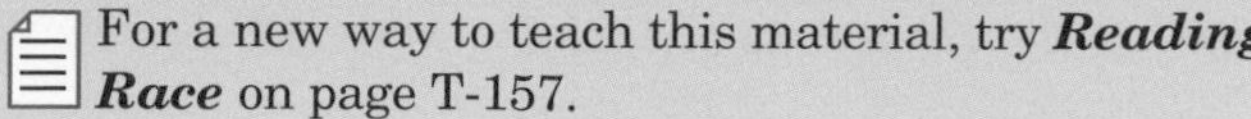

For a new way to teach this material, try ***Reading Race*** on page T-157.

B

- Explain the task and model the first example. Ss complete the task individually and then compare answers in pairs.

Answers

1. animals
2. Chusok (or August 15)
3. ancestors'
4. men
5. New Year's Eve (or December 31)
6. beans

C *Pair work*

- Read the question. In pairs, Ss talk about customs in their own countries or in other countries. Go around the class and give help as needed.
- ***Option:*** Books closed. Draw five mind maps on the board. In the middle of each one, write the name of a celebration mentioned in the text. Ask Ss to tell you some key words about each from memory. Then have Ss complete the mind maps on the board.

End of Cycle 2

Do your students need more practice?

Assign . . .	*for more practice in . . .*
Workbook Exercises 5–10 on pages 46–48	Grammar, Vocabulary, Reading, and Writing
Lab Guide Exercises 4–8 on pages 11–12	Listening, Pronunciation, Speaking, and Grammar
Video Activity Book Unit 8	Vocabulary, Listening, and Cultural Awareness
CD-ROM Unit 8	Grammar, Vocabulary, Reading, Listening, and Speaking

Evaluation

Assess Ss' understanding of Units 7 and 8 with the quiz on pages T-206 and T-207.

Assess Ss' understanding of Units 1–8 with one of the tests on pages 143–152 of the *Interchange Third Edition/Passages Placement and Evaluation Package.*

13 READING

Unique CUSTOMS

Look at the photos. What do you think is happening in each picture?

1 January 17 is **St. Anthony's Day** in Mexico. It's a day when people ask for protection for their animals by bringing them to church. But before the animals go into the church, the people usually dress them up in flowers and ribbons.

2 On August 15 of the lunar calendar, Koreans celebrate **Chusok**, also known as Korean Thanksgiving. It's a day when people give thanks for the harvest. Korean families honor their ancestors by going to their graves to take them rice and fruit and clean the gravesites.

3 Long ago in India, a princess who needed help sent her silk bracelet to an emperor. Although he did not arrive in time to help her, he kept the bracelet as a sign of the bond between them. Today in India, during the festival of **Rakhi**, men promise to be loyal to their women. In exchange, the women give them a bracelet of silk, cotton, or gold thread.

4 One of the biggest celebrations in Argentina is **New Year's Eve.** On the evening of December 31, families get together and have a big meal. At midnight, fireworks explode everywhere and continue throughout the night. This is a day when friends and families meet for parties, which last until the next morning.

5 On the evening of February 3, people in Japan celebrate the end of winter and the beginning of spring. This is known as **Setsubun**. Family members throw dried beans around their homes, shouting, "Good luck in! Evil spirits out!" After they throw the beans, they pick them up and eat one bean for each year of their age.

A Read the article. Then answer these questions.

1. How do people in Mexico dress their animals on St. Anthony's Day?
2. Why do Koreans celebrate Chusok?
3. Why do Indian women give men a bracelet for the festival of Rakhi?
4. What do families in Argentina do on New Year's Eve?
5. What do Japanese families do during Setsubun?

B What do these words refer to? Write the correct word(s).

1. them (par. 1, line 2)	....	4. them (par. 3, line 5)	....
2. It (par. 2, line 2)	....	5. This (par. 4, line 4)	....
3. their (par. 2, line 4)	....	6. them (par. 5, line 5)	....

C ***Pair work*** Do you know of a celebration or custom that is similar to those in the article? Describe it.

Units 7–8 Progress check

SELF-ASSESSMENT

How well can you do these things? Check (✓) the boxes.

I can	Very well	OK	A little
Describe uses and purposes using infinitives and gerunds (Ex. 1)	☐	☐	☐
Give instructions and advice using imperatives and infinitives (Ex. 2)	☐	☐	☐
Describe special days using relative clauses of time (Ex. 3)	☐	☐	☐
Listen to and understand information using adverbial clauses of time (Ex. 4)	☐	☐	☐
Ask and answer questions using adverbial clauses of time (Ex. 5)	☐	☐	☐

1 GAME *What is it?*

A ***Pair work*** Think of five familiar objects. Write a short description of each object's use and purpose. Don't write the name of the objects.

It's electronic. You connect it to your TV. It's used for playing movies. You can also use it to record TV shows.

B ***Group work*** Take turns reading your descriptions and guessing the objects. Keep score. The pair with the most correct answers wins.

2 ROLE PLAY *Stressful situations*

Student A: Choose one situation below. Decide on the details and answer Student B's questions. Then get some advice. Start like this: *I'm really nervous. I'm . . .*

going on a job interview
What's the job?
What are the responsibilities?
Who is interviewing you?

going on a first date
Who is it with?
Where are you going?
When are you going?

giving a speech
What is it about?
Where is it?
How many people will be there?

Student B: Student A is telling you about a situation. Ask the appropriate questions above. Then offer two pieces of advice.

Change roles and try the role play again.

useful expressions

Try to . . .	Try not to . . .
Remember to . . .	Be sure to . . .
Don't forget to . . .	Make sure to . . .

Units 7–8 Progress check

SELF-ASSESSMENT

Learning objectives: *reflect on one's learning; identify areas that need improvement*

- Ask: "What did you learn in Units 7 and 8?" Elicit Ss' answers.
- Ss complete the Self-assessment. Encourage them to be honest, and point out they will not get a bad grade if they check (✓) "a little."
- Ss move on to the Progress check exercises. You can have Ss complete them in class or for homework, using one of these techniques:
  1. Ask Ss to complete all the exercises.
  2. Ask Ss: "What do you need to practice?" Then assign exercises based on their answers.
  3. Ask Ss to choose and complete exercises based on their Self-assessment.

1 GAME

Learning objective: *assess one's ability to describe uses and purposes using infinitives and gerunds*

A Pair work

- Explain the task. Ss write descriptions of objects without saying what they are. Then Ss read their descriptions and classmates guess what the object is. Read the example and remind Ss to use expressions like *It's used to . . . / for . . .* in their descriptions.
- In pairs, Ss think of five well-known objects and write a short description of each one, without naming it. Give Ss a time limit.

B Group work

- Each pair joins another pair. Ss take turns reading their descriptions aloud and guessing the objects. Ss win a point for every object they guess correctly.
- ***Option:*** Ss win three points for every correct first guess. If they ask a question to get more information, they win only two points for the second guess. If they are correct on the third guess, they win only one point. The maximum that a team can win is 15 points.
- Pairs keep track of their scores throughout the game. The pair with the most points wins.

2 ROLE PLAY

Learning objective: *assess one's ability to give instructions and advice using imperatives and infinitives*

- Explain the roles. Student A faces some stressful situations soon and is very nervous. Student B is a friend who offers advice.
- Read the three stressful situations and the useful expressions. Then have Ss form pairs. Student As choose one of the situations and tell their partner which one they have chosen.
- Give Student As a few minutes to think about the details. Ask Student Bs to use the useful expressions to prepare some advice.
- Model the role play with a S, like this:
  T: What's your stressful situation?
  S: I'm really nervous. I'm going on a first date.
  T: Well, try not to be nervous. It'll be fine. Who are you going out with?
  S: A new friend of mine from class.
  T: That's great. Where are you going?
  S: We're going to the movies.
  T: Well, try to . . . and remember to . . .
- Student A begins by telling Student B about the situation. Student B asks questions and offers at least two pieces of advice.
- During the role play, go around the class and listen. Make a note of common errors.
- Suggest ways the role plays could be improved. Give examples of good communication that you heard.
- Ss change roles and try the role play again.

3 SPEAKING

Learning objective: *assess one's ability to describe special days using relative clauses of time*

A Pair work

- Explain the task. Ss choose one of the imaginary holidays listed (or create their own) and describe it. Read the example and the questions while Ss look at the pictures.
- In pairs, Ss use the questions provided to write a short description of the holiday. Set a time limit. Go around the class and give help as needed.
- Give Ss a few minutes to revise their draft for errors. Encourage them to add more details, if necessary.

B Group work

- Explain and model the task with several Ss. Read the example again and have Ss ask you for more information (e.g., *Do people eat anything special on World Smile Day?*).
- Ss complete the task in groups. Set a time limit. When time is up, ask each group to vote. What is their favorite new holiday? Why?
- ***Option:*** Ask groups to tell the class about the holiday they liked best.

LISTENING

Learning objective: *assess one's ability to listen to and understand information using adverbial clauses of time*

A [CD 2, Track 14]

- Read the instructions and the information in the chart. Then explain the task.
- Play the audio program, pausing after each custom. Ss listen and check (✓) True or False. Then go over answers with the class.

Audio script *(See pages T-228–229.)*

Answers

1. True 2. False 3. False 4. True

B

- Read numbers 2 and 3 in the chart in part A. Then play the audio program again. Ss listen and correct the information. Then elicit answers.

Answers

2. When people get married in Malaysia, they have to eat **uncooked** rice.
3. In Italy, **after** a couple gets married, a friend or relative releases two white doves.

DISCUSSION

Learning objective: *assess one's ability to ask and answer questions using adverbial clauses of time*

Group work

- Explain the task. Point out that Ss should try to continue the conversation for as long as possible by adding additional information and asking follow-up questions. Have Ss read the questions silently.
- In small groups, Ss discuss the questions and others of their own. Go around the class and listen. Take notes on errors you hear. Pay attention to Ss' ability to keep a conversation going.
- Go over the errors you heard. Give examples of good communication that you heard.

WHAT'S NEXT?

Learning objective: *become more involved in one's learning*

- Focus Ss' attention on the Self-assessment again. Ask: "How well can you do these things now?"
- Ask Ss to underline one thing they need to review. Ask: "What did you underline? How can you review it?"
- If needed, plan additional activities or reviews based on Ss' answers.

3 SPEAKING My own holiday

A ***Pair work*** Choose one of these imaginary holidays or create your own. Then write a description of the holiday. Answer the questions below.

World Smile Day

All-You-Can-Eat Cake Day

Be Late For Something Day

What is the name of the holiday? When is it? How do you celebrate it?

> World Smile Day is a day when you have to smile at everyone. It's on June 15, the last day of school. People have parties, and sometimes there's a parade!

B ***Group work*** Read your description to the group. Then vote on the best holiday.

4 LISTENING Marriage customs

A Listen to some information about unusual marriage customs. Check (✓) True or False for each statement.

	True	False
1. When two women of a tribe in Paraguay want to marry the same man, they have a boxing match.	☐	☐
2. When people get married in Malaysia, they have to eat cooked rice.	☐	☐
3. In Italy, before a couple gets married, a friend or relative releases two white doves.	☐	☐
4. In some parts of India, when people get married, water is poured over them.	☐	☐

B Listen again. Correct the statements that you marked false.

5 DISCUSSION In your country . . .

Group work Talk about marriage in your country. Ask these questions and others of your own.

How old are people when they get married?
What happens after a couple gets engaged?
What happens during the ceremony?
What do the bride and groom wear?
What kind of food is served at the reception?
What kinds of gifts do people usually give?

a Korean wedding

WHAT'S NEXT?

Look at your Self-assessment again. Do you need to review anything?

9 Back to the future

1 SNAPSHOT

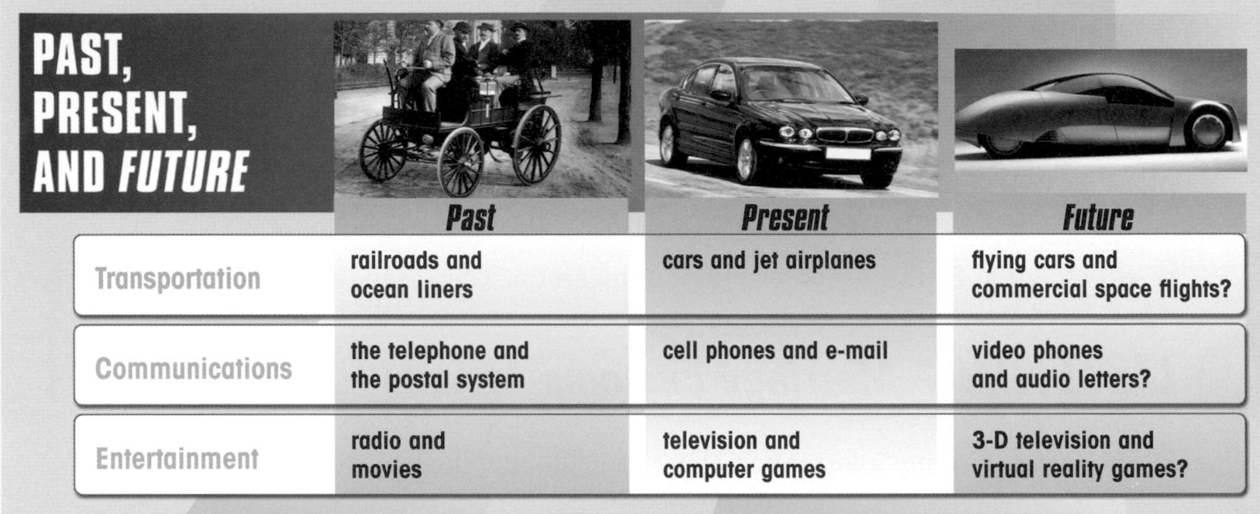

PAST, PRESENT, AND *FUTURE*

	Past	Present	Future
Transportation	railroads and ocean liners	cars and jet airplanes	flying cars and commercial space flights?
Communications	the telephone and the postal system	cell phones and e-mail	video phones and audio letters?
Entertainment	radio and movies	television and computer games	3-D television and virtual reality games?

Sources: *New York Public Library Book of Chronologies*; *New York Public Library Desk Reference*

Which of these past and present developments are the most important? Why?
Do you think any of the future developments could happen in your lifetime?
How will clothing and music be different in the future? Suggest two differences.

2 CONVERSATION This neighborhood has changed!

A Listen and practice.

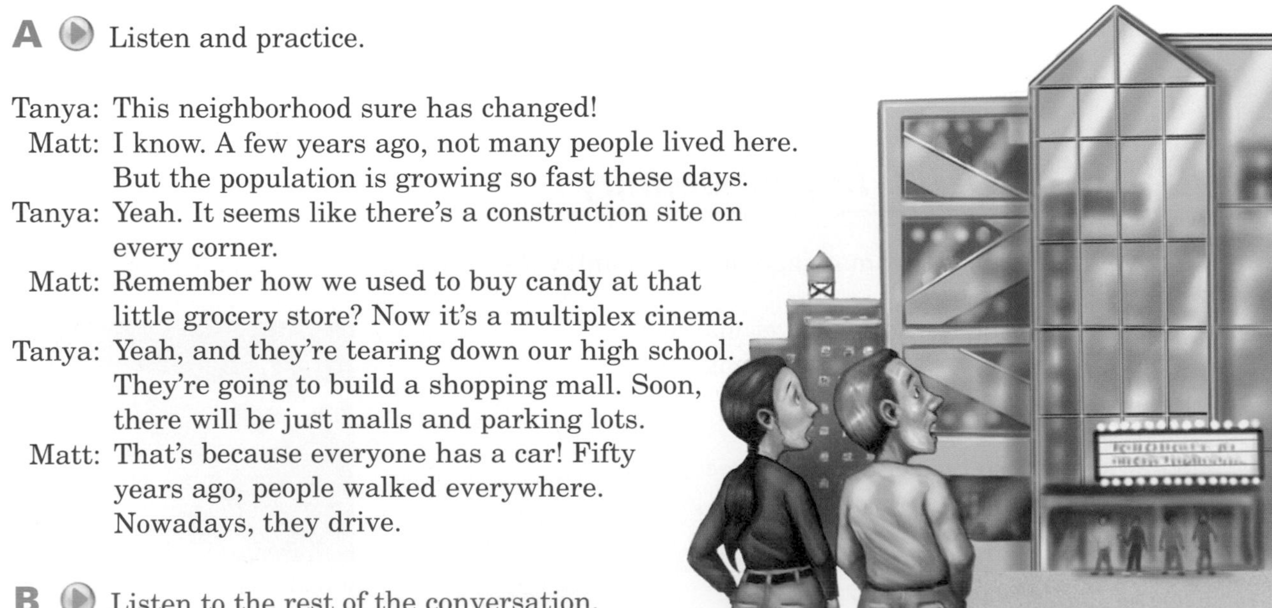

Tanya: This neighborhood sure has changed!

Matt: I know. A few years ago, not many people lived here. But the population is growing so fast these days.

Tanya: Yeah. It seems like there's a construction site on every corner.

Matt: Remember how we used to buy candy at that little grocery store? Now it's a multiplex cinema.

Tanya: Yeah, and they're tearing down our high school. They're going to build a shopping mall. Soon, there will be just malls and parking lots.

Matt: That's because everyone has a car! Fifty years ago, people walked everywhere. Nowadays, they drive.

B Listen to the rest of the conversation. What else has changed in their neighborhood?

Back to the future

In Unit 9, students discuss life in different times. In Cycle 1, they review the past, present, and future tenses. In Cycle 2, they talk about consequences using conditional sentences with if *clauses.*

Cycle 1, Exercises 1–7

SNAPSHOT

Learning objective: *talk about developments of the past, present, and future*

- Focus Ss' attention on the title and find out if the class knows where it comes from. (Answer: It's the same title as the 1985 American movie *Back to the Future*. Michael J. Fox stars as a young man who goes back in time and meets his own parents when they were in high school.)
- Books closed. Write these categories on the board:
  Transportation Communications Entertainment
  Ask: "Can you think of some ways life 100 years ago was different from life today? How do you think it will be different in the next 50 years?"
- Books open. Ss read the Snapshot, starting with the past.
- Check comprehension by using the pictures and asking one or two questions (e.g., *How did people use to travel?*).
- Elicit or explain any new vocabulary.

Vocabulary

ocean liners: large ships that cross the ocean
3-D (three-dimensional): having or showing length, depth, and height

- Ss discuss the questions in small groups.

CONVERSATION

Learning objectives: *practice a conversation about changes; see examples of past, present, and future tenses in context*

A [CD 2, Track 16]

- Ss cover the text and look at the picture. Ask: "What buildings can you see? How old are the people? Why do you think they look surprised?"
- Books closed. Set the scene. Tanya and Matt are discussing how things have changed in the neighborhood where they grew up.
- Write these questions on the board:
  1. Have things changed a little or a lot?
  2. Have things changed for better or for worse?
- Play the audio program. Encourage Ss to listen and take notes. Then elicit answers and examples. (Answers: 1. a lot 2. for worse)
- Write this on the board:

In the past	*Now*
1. There was a grocery store.	*It's a . . .*
2. There was a high school.	*They're . . .*
3. People walked everywhere.	*They . . .*

- Play the audio program again. Ss listen and complete the sentences.
- Check Ss' answers to the questions on the board. (Answers: 1. multiplex cinema 2. tearing it down; going to build a shopping mall 3. drive)
- Books open. Play the audio program again while Ss read along silently. Elicit or explain any new words or expressions.
- Ss practice the conversation in pairs.

TIP To prevent Ss from reading the Conversation to each other, have them stand up and face each other. They will find it more natural to look at each other and will enjoy the chance to stand.

! To practice this Conversation in different situations, try ***Substitution Dialog*** on page T-151. Ss create their own substitutions or replace the underlined words with these:
1. neighborhood: city/village/. . .
2. a few years ago: 10 years ago/5 years ago/. . .
3. construction site: mall/high-rise/. . .
4. multiplex cinema: DVD store/shopping center/. . .

B

- Read the question. Then play the rest of the audio program and check answers.

Audio script *(See page T-229.)*

Answer

The old bookstore is now a pizzeria.

- ***Option:*** Ask Ss what has changed in their neighborhoods. Write Ss' ideas on the board. Then take a class vote to find out the three most important changes.

GRAMMAR FOCUS

Learning objective: *practice describing events using time contrasts between the past, present, and future*

[CD 2, Track 17]

- Play the audio program to present the sentences in the box. Ss listen and repeat.
- Elicit the types of tenses used for referring to the three different time periods presented here (e.g., *past*, *present*, *future*). Point out the modal *might*, and explain that it indicates possibility.
- Elicit time expressions that we use with each tense and write them on the board:

Past	Present	Future
A few years ago	These days	Soon
In the past	Today	In twenty years
In the nineteenth century	Nowadays	In the future
In the 1960s	This year	In the next hundred years
		In a year

- Refer Ss to the previous Conversation. How many examples can they find of past, present, and future tenses? (Answer: past – four, present – six, future – two) Elicit more examples of each tense.

TIP To prevent some Ss from dominating the lesson, divide your class into rows or sections. Explain that you will accept an answer from each group in turn.

To practice recognizing different tenses in the Conversation, try ***Stand Up, Sit Down*** on page T-151. Play the audio program and have Ss listen for examples of past, present, or future tense verbs.

A

- Go over the phrases in column A and then the information in column B. Explain any new vocabulary.
- Ss complete the task individually and compare answers with a partner. Then elicit Ss' responses.

Answers

1. d	3. g	5. b	7. h
2. a	4. f	6. c	8. e

B

- Explain the task. Ss work individually to complete the phrases in part A with appropriate information. Go around the class and monitor Ss' use of tenses.
- If Ss have problems with particular tenses, they should review them on their own. For the past tenses, have Ss study Unit 1; for the future tenses, refer Ss to Unit 5.
- Ss form pairs and compare their sentences.

For more practice with time expressions and tenses, play ***Tic-Tac-Toe*** on page T-148. Write time expressions (e.g., *these days*, *in the past*, *soon*) in the boxes. Ss use the expressions in a sentence with the correct verb tense (e.g., *Soon, there will be another presidential election.*).

PRONUNCIATION

Learning objectives: *notice and practice intonation in statements beginning with a time phrase; personalize phrases using different tenses*

A [CD 2, Track 18]

- Play the audio program. Have Ss look at the arrows while listening to the intonation patterns.
- Play the audio program again, pausing for Ss to repeat each statement. Then check a few Ss' intonation.

TIP To help Ss feel the intonation, have them stand up when they repeat the sentences. Ask them to stand on their toes for rising intonation and to slouch for falling intonation.

B *Pair work*

- Explain the task. Ss complete each statement with appropriate information about themselves. Point out that Ss can either use a different topic (e.g., *As a child, I used to ride my bike everywhere. Five years ago, I lived and worked in Korea.*) or one topic to contrast three time periods (e.g., *As a child, I used to read a lot. Nowadays, I surf the Internet. Next year, I'm going to write a novel.*).
- Ss complete the statements individually. Set a time limit of about five minutes. Go around the class and give help as needed.
- In pairs, Ss take turns reading their sentences aloud. Go around the class and listen to their intonation.

3 GRAMMAR FOCUS

Time contrasts

Past	*Present*	*Future*
A few years ago, not many people **lived** here.	These days, the population **is growing** so fast.	Soon, there **will be** a lot of shopping malls.
People **used to shop** at grocery stores.	Today, people **shop** at supermarkets.	In twenty years, people **might buy** groceries by computer.
Fifty years ago, people **walked** everywhere.	Nowadays, people **drive** their cars instead.	In the future, people **are going to use** cars even more.

A Match the phrases in column A with the appropriate information from column B. Then compare with a partner.

A	*B*
1. Before the automobile, ...	a. people used to shop at small stores.
2. Before there were supermarkets, ...	b. pollution is becoming a serious problem.
3. About five hundred years ago, ...	c. most people are going to work at home.
4. In most offices today, ...	d. people didn't travel as much from city to city.
5. In many cities nowadays, ...	e. there will probably be cities in space.
6. Soon, ...	f. people work more than 40 hours a week.
7. In the next hundred years, ...	g. people played the first game of golf.
8. Sometime in the future, ...	h. doctors might find a cure for the common cold.

B Complete the phrases in part A with your own information. Then compare with a partner.

4 PRONUNCIATION Intonation in statements with time phrases

A Listen and practice. Notice the intonation in these statements beginning with a time phrase.

In the past, very few people used computers.

Today, people use computers all the time.

In the future, there will be a computer in every home.

B *Pair work* Complete these statements with your own information. Then read your statements to a partner. Pay attention to intonation.

As a child, I used to . . .
Five years ago, I . . .
Nowadays, I . . .

Next year, I'm going to . . .
In five years, I'll . . .
In ten years, I might . . .

5 LISTENING *For better or for worse*

A Listen to people discuss changes. Check (✓) the topic each person talks about.

Topic		Change	Better or	worse?
1. ☐ population	☐ environment	....	☐	☐
2. ☐ transportation	☐ cities	....	☐	☐
3. ☐ families	☐ shopping	....	☐	☐

B Listen again. Write down the change and if things are better or worse now.

6 SPEAKING *Changing times*

Group work How have things changed? How will things be different in the future? Choose two of these topics. Then discuss the questions below.

education	fashion	housing	shopping	technology
entertainment	food	medicine	sports	transportation

What was it like in the past?
What is it like today?
What will it be like in the future?

A: In the past, a lot of people made their own clothes.
B: Nowadays, they often order things online.
C: In the future, . . .

7 WRITING *A description of a person*

A ***Pair work*** Interview your partner about his or her past, present, and hopes for the future.

B Write a paragraph describing how your partner has changed. Make some predictions about the future. Don't write your partner's name.

She used to be the quietest girl in the class. Now, she's in the drama club and loves to watch soap operas. One day, she'll be a successful actress. She'll be famous, and will star in movies and on TV. I think she'll . . .

C ***Class activity*** Read your paragraph to the class. Can they guess who it is about?

5 LISTENING

Learning objective: *develop skills in listening for main ideas and making inferences*

A [CD 2, Track 19]

- Focus Ss' attention on the left side of the chart. Explain that Ss will listen for and check (✓) the topic of each conversation. Play the audio program. Ss listen and complete the task.
- Go over answers with the class. Ask Ss which words helped them choose the answer (e.g., *trees*).

Audio script *(See page T-229.)*

Answers

1. environment 2. transportation 3. families

B

- Explain the task. Ss listen and take note of the change each speaker mentions. Is it for better or for worse?
- Play the audio program again. Ss complete the chart.
- Ss compare answers in small groups. If Ss disagree or want to listen again, play the audio program again. This time, pause for a few seconds after each conversation to give Ss time to complete the chart. Then elicit answers from the class.

Answers

Change	*Better or worse?*
1. the city has planted trees	better
2. used to be a good bus system, but isn't anymore	worse
3. used to be many children; now it's too quiet	worse

6 SPEAKING

Learning objective: *talk about changes using time contrasts between the past, present, and future*

Group work

- Explain the task. Go over the list of topics and the questions. Groups choose two topics to discuss.
- Use the questions and the example conversation to model the activity with several Ss.
- Ss form groups and complete the task. Set a time limit of about ten minutes. If possible, mix older Ss with younger Ss. Go around the class and note common errors. Then point out the errors after the activity.

TIP To increase Ss' speaking time, ask them to try the activity again. Be sure to give Ss a new challenge (e.g., *focusing on intonation, working with a new group, or adding more details*).

7 WRITING

Learning objective: *write a paragraph describing someone using time contrasts*

A Pair work

- Explain the task. Ss interview each other about their past, present, and hopes for the future. Encourage Ss to be imaginative during their interviews.
- Conduct a quick brainstorming activity with the whole class to help pairs with their interviews. Elicit possible interview questions (e.g., *What did you use to be like? What are you doing nowadays? What are you going to do in the next five years?*).
- In pairs, Ss take turns interviewing each other using the questions and others of their own.

B

- Present the example paragraph. Then Ss write a paragraph about how their partner has changed. Remind Ss that they shouldn't write their partner's name anywhere in their description.
- Ss use their notes to write a description of their partner.
- ***Option:*** This part could be done for homework.

C Class activity

- Collect and shuffle the papers. Give one to each S to read. Ss try to guess who the description is about.

End of Cycle 1

Do your students need more practice?

Assign . . .	*for more practice in . . .*
Workbook Exercises 1–4 on pages 49–51	Grammar, Vocabulary, Reading, and Writing
Lab Guide Exercises 1–6 on pages 13–14	Listening, Pronunciation, Speaking, and Grammar

8 PERSPECTIVES

Learning objectives: *discuss the consequences of making money; see conditional sentences with* if *clauses in context*

- Books closed. Draw this mind map on the board:

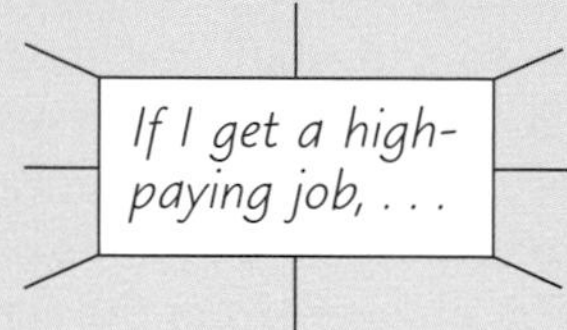
If I get a high-
paying job, . . .

- Lead a class discussion. Ask: "Who wants to make a lot of money? Why? If you get a high-paying job, how will your life change for better? for worse?"
- Elicit answers from the class. Ask a S to write the ideas on the board. Don't worry about Ss' grammar at this point, simply help generate ideas and get Ss interested in the topic.

A [CD 2, Track 20]

- Books open. Have Ss read the statements silently and compare them with the mind map. Which of the consequences did Ss mention in their discussion?
- Go over each statement and explain any new vocabulary. Then play the audio program while Ss listen and read silently. Point out the pronunciation of contractions with *will*.
- Ss practice reading the statements in pairs.

B *Pair work*

- Explain the task. In pairs, Ss go over each statement and discuss whether the consequences are advantages or disadvantages.

9 GRAMMAR FOCUS

Learning objective: *practice using conditional sentences with* if *clauses*

[CD 2, Track 21]

- Write this example from the Perspectives section on the board:
  Possible situation — Consequence
  If you get a high-paying job, you won't have to work as hard.
  Underline the verbs *get* and *won't have to work*.
- Explain that *If you get a high-paying job* is a possible situation, i.e., it may happen one day. The rest of the sentence is a consequence of getting a high-paying job.
- Point out that we can say these in a different order: *You won't have to work as hard if you get a high-paying job.*
- Elicit or explain the rules:
  1. If + simple present, subject + will/won't
     If you eat candy, you'll gain weight.
     This is the most typical structure used with possible future situations and consequences.
  2. If + simple present, subject + may/might
     If you eat candy, you might gain weight.
     We can also use *may* and *might* as consequences, to show that the consequence is less likely.
  3. will + be able to/will + have to
     If you save some money, you'll be able to travel. (possibility)
     If you travel abroad, you'll have to get a visa. (necessity)
     We cannot say *will can* or *will must*. Instead, we say "will be able to" and "will have to."
- Refer Ss to the Perspectives section and have them find two examples of each pattern.
- Play the audio program to present the sentences in the box. Then use another situation (e.g., *If you study English, . . .*) and encourage Ss to think of new consequences.

For more practice, play the ***Chain Game*** on page T-145. Ss begin with a phrase like *If I win the lottery, . . .* and add consequences.

A

- Ask Ss to read the *if* clauses in column A and the consequences in column B. Explain any new vocabulary.
- Point out that there may be more than one correct answer for some items. Ss complete the task and compare answers in pairs. Then go over answers with the class.

Answers

1. a, b 2. a, b, c 3. e 4. a 5. d

B

- Model the task by asking for suggestions to complete the first *if* clause in part A. Then Ss complete the task individually before practicing with a partner.
- ***Option:*** Have pairs share some of their best sentences with the class.

8 PERSPECTIVES *Who wants to make money?*

A Listen to some possible consequences of getting a high-paying job. Check (✓) the statements you agree with.

If you get a high-paying job, ...

.... you won't have to work as hard
.... you'll be able to travel first class
.... you might have to pay higher taxes
.... you'll be able to donate more to charities
.... more people may want to be your friend
.... you'll be able to buy things you want
.... you might be on TV or in the newspapers
.... people will ask you for a loan
.... you'll have a lot more free time
.... you'll be able to buy your parents a new car

B ***Pair work*** Look at the statements again. Which are advantages of getting a high-paying job? Which are disadvantages?

"I think the first one is an advantage. I don't like to work very hard."

9 GRAMMAR FOCUS

Conditional sentences with if *clauses*

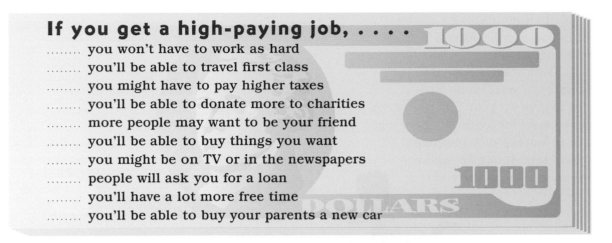

Possible situation + simple present	*Consequence + future with* **will**, **may**, *or* **might**
If you get a high-paying job,	you **won't have to work** as hard.
If you don't have to work as hard,	you**'ll have** a lot more free time.
If you have a lot more free time,	you **might get** bored.
If you get bored,	you **may have to look for** another job.

A Match the clauses in column A with the appropriate information from column B. Then compare with a partner.

A	*B*
1. If you eat less sugar, ...	a. you may feel more relaxed.
2. If you walk to work every day, ...	b. you might feel healthier.
3. If you don't get enough sleep, ...	c. you'll stay in shape without joining a gym.
4. If you own a pet, ...	d. you'll have more money to spend on yourself.
5. If you don't get married, ...	e. you won't be able to stay awake in class.

B Add your own information to the clauses in column A. Then practice with a partner.

"If you eat less sugar, you'll lose weight."

10 WORD POWER Consequences

A ***Pair work*** Can you find two consequences for each possible event? Complete the chart with information from the list.

be able to buy expensive clothes
feel better about yourself
feel hungry a lot
feel jealous sometimes
feel safer in your home
have to give up your favorite snack
get requests for loans from friends
have to learn a new language
have to take it out for walks
lose touch with old friends

Possible event	Consequences
buy a large dog	....
fall in love	....
go on a diet	....
inherit a lot of money	....
move to a foreign country	....

B ***Group work*** Share your answers with the group. Can you think of one more consequence for each event?

11 SPEAKING Unexpected consequences

A ***Group work*** Choose three possible events from Exercise 10. One student completes an event with a consequence. The next student adds a consequence. Suggest at least five consequences.

A: If you buy a large dog, you'll have to take it out for walks every day.
B: If you take it out for walks every day, you might have an accident.
C: If you have an accident, you may have to go to the hospital.
D: If you go to the hospital, you won't be able to take care of your dog.
A: If you aren't able to take care of your dog, you'll probably have to give it away.

B ***Class activity*** Who has the most interesting consequences for each event?

12 INTERCHANGE 9 Consider the consequences

Give your opinion about some issues. Go to Interchange 9 at the back of the book.

10 WORD POWER

Learning objective: *learn vocabulary for talking about possible events and consequences*

A Pair work

- Explain the task. Have Ss read the items in the list and the possible events in the chart. Then elicit or explain any new words or expressions.

Vocabulary

loan: money that is borrowed
lose touch: not speak to or see someone for a long time
fall in love: begin to love someone
inherit: receive something from someone who has died

- Model the task with the first event (*buy a large dog*). Elicit Ss' suggestions for the two most likely consequences (*feel safer in your home; have to take it out for walks*). Tell Ss that there may be more than two appropriate answers for some events.
- Ss form pairs and complete the chart. Go around the class and give help as needed. Then ask Ss who finish early to write some of their ideas on the board.

Possible answers

buy a large dog
feel safer in your home; have to take it out for walks
fall in love
feel better about yourself; feel jealous sometimes
go on a diet
feel hungry a lot; have to give up your favorite snack
inherit a lot of money
be able to buy expensive clothes; get requests for loans from friends
move to a foreign country
have to learn a new language; lose touch with old friends

B Group work

- Ss discuss the question in small groups. Set a time limit of about five minutes. Then invite groups to write interesting consequences on the board.

Possible answers

buy a large dog
have to find someone to take care of it when you go away
fall in love
be able to share things with someone all the time
go on a diet
start to feel thinner
inherit a lot of money
be able to take a cruise around the world
move to a foreign country
learn about a new culture

For more practice with this vocabulary, play ***Split Sentences*** on page T-146. Prepare cards using new words and phrases from the unit.

11 SPEAKING

Learning objective: *talk about consequences using conditional sentences with* if *clauses*

A Group work

- Read the instructions. Then model the activity by reading the example conversation with a few Ss.
- Ss form groups and choose three possible events from Exercise 10. Then they describe a chain of events with at least five consequences. Set a time limit of about ten minutes for this activity.
- ***Option:*** Ask groups to write down their sentences.

B Class activity

- Ask groups to share their most interesting chain of events with the class. Then vote on the most interesting consequence for each event.
- ***Option:*** Do the activity again as a whole class. If possible, the class sits in a circle. Explain that each S thinks of a possible event with one consequence and writes it at the top of a piece of paper. Ss pass their paper to the left, read the previous sentence, and write another one. For example:
  1. If you win the lottery, you'll be able to take a long vacation.
  2. If you take a long vacation, you might go to Europe.

  The activity continues until the paper returns to the original writer.
- ***Option:*** In pairs, Ss play ***Optimist, Pessimist***. Student A is the optimist and Student B is the pessimist. Student A begins with a plan and Student B finds a reason why it's not a good idea. For example:
  A: Tomorrow I'm going to play tennis.
  B: But what will you do if it rains?
  A: If it rains, then I'll go to the movies.
  B: But what will you do if the movie theater is closed?
  The S who keeps the conversation going wins.

12 INTERCHANGE 9

See page T-123 for teaching notes.

13 READING

Learning objectives: *read an article about falling in love; develop skills in reading for specific information and recognizing sources*

- ***Option:*** Books closed. Play a quick warm-up game to introduce the topic.
  1. At the top, center of the board write: LOVE IS . . . Explain that there used to be a famous cartoon series that always began with these words. (For example, *Love is . . . giving someone your last chocolate, forgiving*, etc.)
  2. Draw a vertical line down the middle of the board and ask the class to stand in two lines, A and B.
  3. In turn, Ss go to the board and complete the sentence. While Ss in line A write on the left, Ss in line B write on the right.
  4. Set a time limit. When Ss finish, compare the answers. The group with the most ideas wins.
- To complete parts A and B, Ss will need to know the following vocabulary. Have Ss look up these words before class or go over the meanings in class.

Vocabulary

have a crush on: feel a strong but temporary attraction to someone
be attracted to: like someone and want to have a relationship with him/her
interrupt: stop someone from speaking by suddenly saying something
avoid: stay away from
still (adv.): continuing until now
nevertheless: in spite of what was just said; however
admit: recognize or accept as true
trust: have confidence or believe in someone

! For another way to teach this vocabulary, try ***Vocabulary Mingle*** on page T-153.

- Read the pre-reading question and briefly discuss it as a class.

A

- Explain the task. Ss read the text silently and check (✓) the correct answer. Tell them they don't need to understand every word. Elicit answers from the class.

Answer

a magazine

- Ask Ss if there are any other words they don't understand. With the help of other Ss, explain new vocabulary.

B

- Read the instructions. Tell Ss to read the article again and make notes in the chart. Go around the class and give help as needed.
- Copy the empty chart onto the board. Then ask a few Ss to fill it in.

Answers

Falling in love	*Staying in love*
1. talk to or telephone the person for no reason	1. might not call the person as much
2. bring the person into every conversation	2. might not talk about the person as much
3. have an interest in things you used to avoid	3. can be yourself, be totally honest, and trust the person

C *Pair work*

- Ss discuss the questions in pairs. Then have a class discussion

End of Cycle 2

Do your students need more practice?

Assign . . .	*for more practice in . . .*
Workbook Exercises 5–10 on pages 52–54	Grammar, Vocabulary, Reading, and Writing
Lab Guide Exercises 7–8 on page 14	Listening, Pronunciation, Speaking, and Grammar
Video Activity Book Unit 9	Listening, Speaking, and Cultural Awareness
CD-ROM Unit 9	Grammar, Vocabulary, Reading, Listening, and Speaking

13 READING

Are you in love?

What is the difference between "having a crush" on someone and falling in love?

You think you're falling in love. You're really attracted to a certain person. But this has happened before, and it was just a "crush." How can you tell if it's real this time? Here's what our readers said:

If you're falling in love, . . .

- you'll find yourself talking to or telephoning the person for no reason. (You might pretend there's a reason, but often there's not.)
- you'll find yourself bringing this person into every conversation. ("When I was in Mexico – ," a friend begins. You interrupt with, "My boyfriend made a great Mexican dinner last week.")
- you might suddenly be interested in things you used to avoid. ("When a woman asks me to tell her all about football, I know she's fallen in love," said a TV sports announcer.)

OK, so you've fallen in love. But falling in love is one thing, and staying in love is another. How can you tell, as time passes, that you're still in love? If you stay in love, your relationship will change. You might not talk as much about the person you are in love with. You might not call him or her so often. But this person will nevertheless become more and more important in your life.

You'll find that you can be yourself with this person. When you first fell in love, you were probably afraid to admit certain things about yourself. But now you can be totally honest. You can trust him or her to accept you just as you are. Falling in love is great – staying in love is even better!

A Read the article. Where do you think it is from? Check (✓) the correct answer.

☐ a newspaper ☐ a magazine ☐ an advice column ☐ an advertisement

B What things happen when you're falling in love compared to staying in love? Complete the chart.

Falling in love	Staying in love
1.	1. ....
2.	2. ....
3.	3. ....

C ***Pair work*** Which is more difficult – falling in love or staying in love? Can you think of other signs of being in love?

10 I don't like working on weekends!

1 SNAPSHOT

EIGHT IMPORTANT JOB SKILLS	
Here are some skills that employers look for.	
☐ 1. Can you **solve problems?**	☐ 5. Are you good at **math and science?**
☐ 2. Do you **work well with people?**	☐ 6. Can you **manage money well?**
☐ 3. Can you **use a computer?**	☐ 7. Do you **speak other languages?**
☐ 4. Can you **teach others** how to do things?	☐ 8. Can you **manage other people?**

Source: U.S. Department of Labor

Which of these skills do you think are most important? Why?
Check (✓) the skills that you think you have.
Look at the skills you checked. What jobs do you think you might be good at?

2 CONVERSATION *I need a job!*

A Listen and practice.

Dan: I'm so broke. I really need to find a job!
Brad: So do I. Do you see anything good listed on the Internet?
Dan: How about this? A door-to-door salesperson to sell baby products.
Brad: Like diapers and things? No, thanks. And anyway, I'm not good at selling.
Dan: Well, I am! I might check that one out. Oh, here's one for you. An assistant entertainment director on a cruise ship.
Brad: That sounds like fun. I like traveling, and I've never been on a cruise ship.
Dan: It says here you have to work every day while the ship is at sea.
Brad: That's OK. I don't mind working long hours if the pay is good. What's the phone number?
Dan: It's 555-3455.

B Listen to Brad call about the job.
What else does the job require?

I don't like working on weekends!

In Unit 10, students discuss jobs, abilities, and personality traits. In Cycle 1, they talk about job skills using gerunds and short responses. In Cycle 2, they talk about the kinds of jobs they want and don't want using clauses with because.

Cycle 1, Exercises 1–7

SNAPSHOT

Learning objective: *talk about the job skills that are most important to employers*

- Books closed. In pairs, Ss brainstorm a list of all the jobs they know. Set a time limit. Then have Ss count the jobs and find out who listed the most.
- Ask: "Which job skills do you think are important today?" Elicit some ideas from Ss (e.g., *Employees should be good at . . . / They should know how to . . .*).
- Books open. Ss read the information in the Snapshot.
- Read the first discussion question aloud. Then Ss discuss it in pairs. When Ss finish, have them form groups to discuss which skills are most important and why.

For more practice ranking, try ***Vocabulary Steps*** on page T-154. Ss draw eight steps and put the most important skill at the top of the staircase.

- Ss work individually to check (✓) which skills they think they have. Then have them compare in small groups. Alternatively, Ss take turns interviewing each other in pairs.
- Groups answer and discuss the third question.

CONVERSATION

Learning objectives: *practice a conversation about jobs and job requirements; see gerunds and short responses in context*

A [CD 2, Track 22]

- Focus Ss' attention on the picture. Ask: "Where are they? What are they doing? Why?" Accept any reasonable responses.
- Play the first two lines of the audio program and elicit Ss' answers.
- Books closed. Write this question on the board: *Which two jobs do they find on the Internet?*
- Play the audio program. Ss listen. Then check Ss' answers to the question. (Answers: door-to-door salesperson to sell baby products; assistant entertainment director on a cruise ship)
- Write these questions on the board:
  1. What's the phone number for the cruise ship job?
  2. What are the working hours like?
- Play the audio program. Ss listen. Then elicit answers. (1. 555-3455 2. long)
- Books open. Elicit or explain any unfamiliar words or expressions.

Vocabulary

broke: without money; poor
door-to-door salesperson: someone who goes from house to house selling products
diaper: underwear for babies or young children
check something out: look into; get more information
entertainment director: a person in charge of the entertainment (e.g., movies, talent shows)
cruise ship: a large luxury boat that makes long journeys
at sea: traveling on the ocean
I don't mind . . . : . . . doesn't bother me.

- Play the audio program again. Ss listen and read silently.
- Ss practice the conversation in pairs.

To practice this Conversation with various partners, try the ***Onion Ring*** technique on page T-151.

B

- Explain the task. Then play the second part of the audio program.

Audio script *(See page T-229.)*

- Have Ss compare responses in pairs. Then elicit answers from the class.

Answer

The job requires someone who speaks more than one language.

3 GRAMMAR FOCUS

***Learning objective:** practice making statements with gerunds and giving short responses*

[CD 2, Track 23]

Gerunds (verb + -ing)

- Refer Ss to the previous Conversation. Ask them to complete Brad's sentences:
  1. I'm not good at ________________ .
  2. I like ________________ .
  3. I don't mind ________________ .
- Elicit answers. (Answers: 1. selling 2. traveling 3. working long hours) Explain that *selling*, *traveling*, and *working* are gerunds. They are made up of a base verb and *-ing*. They function as nouns.
- Focus Ss' attention on the left column of the Grammar Focus box. Point out some verbs or phrases (e.g., *I like*, *I hate*, *I'm good at*) that are followed by a gerund. Elicit other examples from the box (e.g., *I don't mind*, *I'm not good at*, *I can't stand*). Then point out the examples in the far right column.

Short responses to show agreement/disagreement

- Refer Ss to the Conversation again. Ask Ss: "Who says the phrase *So do I*? Is he agreeing or disagreeing?" (Answers: Brad; He's agreeing. He also needs a job.)
- Explain that short responses with *so* and *neither* are ways of agreeing. For example, we use:
  1. So to agree with a positive statement.
     A: I need to find a job. *B: So do I.*
  2. Neither to agree with a negative statement.
     A: I don't like working long hours. *B: Neither do I.*
- With both *so* and *neither*, we use the verb from the original statement. The subject (noun or pronoun) comes *after* the verb.
- Do a quick drill with the class, like this:
  1. Responses with *so*
     T: I'm good at singing.
     S1: So am I. (= I'm good at it, too.)
  If there is no auxiliary or modal, we use *do* or *did*.
     T: I hate working overtime.
     S2: So do I. (= I hate it, too.)
     T: We used to live in New York.
     S3: So did we. (= We lived there, too.)
- Repeat the drill with *neither*:
  2. Responses with *neither*
     T: I'm not good at skiing.
     S4: Neither am I. (= I'm not good at it either.)
- Point out the six ways to disagree. Then play the audio program to present the language in the box.

For more practice with gerunds, play ***True or False?*** on page T-148. Ss make up sentences about themselves.

A Pair work

- Explain the task. Ss match the phrases in columns A and B to make statements about themselves.
- Make sure Ss understand the vocabulary in column B. Then Ss work individually to complete the task.
- Model the example conversation. Then Ss read their statements to each other and give short responses.
- Go around the class and give help as needed. Take note of common problems and go over them with the whole class after the activity.
- ***Option:*** Ss repeat the activity with a new partner.

B Group work

- Explain the task. Model an example conversation with a S:
  T: I'm really interested in working abroad.
  S: Really? Where would you like to work?
  T: Maybe in Mexico or in Chile.
- Refer Ss to the Conversation on page 53. Remind them how Jill and Emiko showed interest by asking follow-up questions and giving additional information.
- Ss work individually to complete the phrases in part A with their own information. Then Ss take turns reading their statements in groups. Other Ss ask questions to get more information.
- ***Option:*** Ss earn one point for each follow-up question they ask. Ss keep track of their own scores.

PRONUNCIATION

***Learning objective:** notice and practice released and unreleased sounds*

A [CD 2, Track 24]

- Explain that, at the end of a word, the sounds /t/ and /d/ are not released, i.e., they are not fully articulated, when they are followed by a consonant sound. Play the audio program. Ss listen and notice how the sound is hardly heard.
- Repeat the above steps for released sounds. Point out that the /t/ and /d/ sounds are released when they are followed by a vowel sound.

B Pair work

- Explain the task. Ss write their sentences individually and then practice them in pairs. Go around the class and give help as needed.

3 GRAMMAR FOCUS

Gerunds; short responses

Affirmative statements with gerunds	*Agree*	*Disagree*
I like traveling.	So do I.	Oh, I don't.
I hate working on weekends.	So do I.	Really? I like it.
I'm good at using a computer.	So am I.	Gee, I'm not.
Negative statements with gerunds		
I don't mind working long hours.	Neither do I.	Well, I do.
I'm not good at selling.	Neither am I.	I am!
I can't stand making mistakes.	Neither can I.	Oh, I don't mind.

Other verbs or phrases followed by gerunds
love
enjoy
be interested in

A *Pair work* Match the phrases in columns A and B to make statements about yourself. Then take turns reading your sentences and giving short responses.

A	*B*
1. I don't like	a. talking on a cell phone.
2. I'm not very good at	b. working with a group or team.
3. I'm good at	c. solving other people's problems.
4. I hate	d. sitting in long meetings.
5. I can't stand	e. commuting by bicycle.
6. I'm interested in	f. eating lunch out every day.
7. I don't mind	g. managing my time.
8. I enjoy	h. learning foreign languages.

A: I don't like commuting by bicycle.
B: Neither do I.

B *Group work* Complete the phrases in column A with your own information. Then take turns reading your statements. Ask questions to get more information.

PRONUNCIATION Unreleased and released /t/ and /d/

A Listen and practice. Notice when the sound /t/ or /d/ at the end of a word is followed by a consonant, it is unreleased. When it is followed by a vowel sound, it is released.

Unreleased	*Released*
She's not good at math and science.	He's not a good artist.
I hate working on Sundays.	They really hate it!
You need to manage money well.	I need a cup of coffee.

B *Pair work* Write three sentences starting with *I'm not very good at* and *I don't mind*. Then practice the sentences. Pay attention to the unreleased and released sounds /t/ and /d/.

5 LISTENING Job hunting

A Listen to people talk about the kind of work they are looking for. Check (✓) the job that would be best for each person.

1. Bill	2. Shannon	3. Ben
☐ flight attendant	☐ lawyer	☐ marine biologist
☐ teacher	☐ bookkeeper	☐ model
☐ songwriter	☐ doctor	☐ architect

B Listen again. Answer these questions.

1. What is Bill's attitude toward making money?
2. What does most of Shannon's family do for a living?
3. What has Ben done to break into movies?

6 SPEAKING Chores

A ***Pair work*** Interview your partner about these chores. Check (✓) his or her answers.

How do you feel about . . . ?	I enjoy it.	I don't mind it.	I hate it.
doing your homework	☐	☐	☐
washing the dishes	☐	☐	☐
cleaning your room	☐	☐	☐
making phone calls	☐	☐	☐
washing your clothes	☐	☐	☐
organizing your desk	☐	☐	☐
typing your school reports	☐	☐	☐
buying groceries	☐	☐	☐
ironing your clothes	☐	☐	☐
commuting to and from school	☐	☐	☐

B ***Pair work*** Imagine the government is offering a robot to all students. Each robot can do four chores for two students. Decide which chores you want your robot to do.

A: I want the robot to do my homework for me.
I can't stand doing my homework.
B: Neither can I. But I hate cleaning my room even more!

C ***Group work*** There is a shortage of robots. Each robot can only do two chores for four students. Discuss the things you want your robot to do.

7 INTERCHANGE 10 Dream job

Decide which job to apply for. Go to Interchange 10 at the back of the book.

5 LISTENING

Learning objective: *develop skills in listening for main ideas and making inferences*

A [CD 2, Track 25]

- Ask Ss what *job hunting* means (= looking for a job). Ask if anyone has ever gone job hunting and put them in the "hot seat." Have the rest of the class ask them questions.
- Explain the situation. Three people are being asked about the kind of work they are looking for. Note that the speakers don't say exactly which job they are looking for. Ss need to listen and make inferences.
- Play the first item in the audio program. Have Ss tell you which job would be best for Bill. Ask how they chose the answer. (Answers: flight attendant; He wants to travel and see the world.)
- Play the rest of the audio program, pausing after each speaker. Then check answers. Again, ask Ss why they chose the answers.

Audio script *(See page T-229–230.)*

Answers

1. flight attendant 2. doctor 3. model

B

- Read the questions and play the audio program again, pausing after each speaker. Ss listen and answer the questions. Have Ss compare answers in pairs. Then go over answers with the class.

Possible answers

1. He's not interested in making a lot of money right now.
2. Everyone in her family is in law or business.
3. He has worked out/gone to the gym, taken acting lessons, and just had pictures taken.

6 SPEAKING

Learning objective: *talk about chores using gerunds and short responses*

A Pair work

- Have Ss read the list of chores silently. Elicit and explain any unfamiliar vocabulary. Then explain the task.
- Remind Ss about pronunciation. Point out that *How do you feel about . . . ?* ends in the sound /t/. If the next word begins with a consonant (e.g., *doing*), Ss should not release the /t/. If the next word begins with a vowel (e.g., *organizing*), Ss need to release the /t/.
- ***Option:*** Read the questions aloud. Ss repeat the correct pronunciation and intonation.
- Ss form pairs and take turns interviewing each other. They should check (✓) their partner's answers.

B Pair work

- Explain the task. In pairs, Ss agree on which four chores from the list they want the robot to do.
- Read the example conversation with a S. Remind Ss to use the structure *I want the robot to (+ base verb) for me*, and to add extra information when answering (e.g., *I can't stand . . .* or *neither can I*). Practice the conversation with several Ss.

> **TIP** To check that Ss understand the instructions, use concept questions. For example, ask Ss: "Are you going to work in pairs or groups? Are you going to make note of your choices? What will you do when you finish?"

- Ss form pairs and choose four chores they want the robot to do for them. Go around the class and give help as needed.

C Group work

- Explain the task. Each pair joins another pair. The robot can only do two chores for four Ss. In groups, Ss discuss until they come to an agreement.
- Have each group tell the class which two chores they want the robot to do. Then find out if the groups chose similar chores.

7 INTERCHANGE 10

See page T-124 for teaching notes.

End of Cycle 1

Do your students need more practice?

Assign . . .	for more practice in . . .
Workbook Exercises 1–6 on pages 55–57	Grammar, Vocabulary, Reading, and Writing
Lab Guide Exercises 1–6 on pages 15–16	Listening, Pronunciation, Speaking, and Grammar

8 WORD POWER

Learning objective: *learn adjectives for describing personality traits*

A

- Focus Ss' attention on the pictures. Explain the subtitle *Personality traits*.
- Read the instructions and explain the difference between *positive* (good) and *negative* (bad). Point out the first adjective (*bad-tempered*) in the chart is negative, so the letter *N* is written in the blank. Ask Ss to find a positive adjective and to write *P* next to it.
- Ss complete the task individually, without using a dictionary. Go around the class and give help as needed.

> **TIP** To monitor your Ss equally, vary your routine. For example, if you always start at the front of the class, start from the back sometimes.

- ***Option:*** When Ss finish, tell them to compare answers in pairs. Encourage them to use their dictionaries to check the meaning of any words they aren't sure about.
- Elicit answers from the class. Model the pronunciation of adjectives that Ss have problems with.

Answers

bad-tempered	N	hardworking	P
creative	P	impatient	N
critical	N	level-headed	P
disorganized	N	moody	N
efficient	P	punctual	P
forgetful	N	reliable	P
generous	P	strict	N

B *Pair work*

- Write these words on the board:
neighbor, parents, children, friend, classmate, teacher, brother, sister, co-worker, boss
- Read the instructions and the example sentence. Encourage Ss to make similar statements using adjectives from the list and people from the board.
- Ss form pairs and talk about people they know with these personality traits. Remind Ss to give additional information and ask follow-up questions.

To review the vocabulary in the next class, play ***Mime*** on page T-148.

C *[CD 2, Track 26]*

- Explain the task and play the audio program. Ss listen and complete the chart. Then go over answers with the class.

Audio script *(See page T-230.)*

Answers

1. serious	3. moody
2. generous	4. bad-tempered

9 PERSPECTIVES

Learning objectives: *discuss job profiles; see clauses with* because *in context*

A *[CD 2, Track 27]*

- Books closed. Write these questions on the board:
What kind of work would you like to do?
What kind of job would you be good at? Why?
- Ss work in pairs or groups to answer the questions. Alternatively, have a class discussion.
- Set the scene. Three people are answering the question *What kind of work would you like to do?* Play the audio program. Ss listen to find out what job each person talks about. (Answers: journalist, stockbroker, teacher)
- Elicit or explain any new vocabulary.

Vocabulary

journalist: someone who writes for newspapers or magazines

stockbroker: someone who buys and sells stock, or part of the ownership of a company

- Write these questions on the board:
Which speaker . . .
can't make decisions quickly?
is creative but impatient?
used to work as a reporter?
doesn't mind working hard?
- Play the audio program again. Ss listen and answer the questions. Elicit answers. (Answers: 2, 3, 1, 2)
- Books open. Play the audio program again. Ss listen and read silently.

B *Pair work*

- In pairs, Ss discuss which job they would choose. Elicit answers from the class.

8 WORD POWER Personality traits

A Which of these adjectives are positive (**P**)? Which are negative (**N**)?

bad-tempered	...N...	hardworking	....
creative	....	impatient	....
critical	....	level-headed	....
disorganized	....	moody	....
efficient	....	punctual	....
forgetful	....	reliable	....
generous	....	strict	....

bad-tempered

disorganized

B ***Pair work*** Tell your partner about people you know with these personality traits.

"My neighbor is bad-tempered. Sometimes she . . . "

C Listen to four conversations. Then check (✓) the adjective that best describes each person.

1. a boss
   - ☐ creative
   - ☐ forgetful
   - ☐ serious
2. a co-worker
   - ☐ unfriendly
   - ☐ generous
   - ☐ strange
3. a teacher
   - ☐ moody
   - ☐ patient
   - ☐ hardworking
4. a relative
   - ☐ bad-tempered
   - ☐ disorganized
   - ☐ reliable

9 PERSPECTIVES Job profiles

A Listen to these people answer the question, "What kind of work would you like to do?" What job does each person talk about?

"Well, I think I'd make a good journalist because I'm good at writing. When I was in college, I worked as a reporter for the school newspaper. I really enjoyed writing different kinds of articles."

"I know what I *don't* want to do! A lot of my friends work in the stock market, but I could never be a stockbroker because I can't make decisions quickly. I don't mind working hard, but I'm terrible under pressure!"

"I'm still in school. My parents want me to be a teacher, but I'm not sure yet. I guess I could be a teacher because I'm very creative. I'm also very impatient, so maybe I shouldn't work with kids."

B ***Pair work*** Look at the interviews again. Which job would you choose?

10 GRAMMAR FOCUS

Clauses with because

The word **because** *introduces a cause or reason.*

I'd make a good journalist **because I'm good at writing.**
I could be a teacher **because I'm very creative.**
I wouldn't want to be a teacher **because I'm very impatient.**
I could never be a stockbroker **because I can't make decisions quickly.**

A Complete the sentences in column A with appropriate information from column B. Then compare with a partner.

A	*B*
1. I wouldn't want to be a nurse	a. because I don't like hospitals.
2. I'd like to be a novelist	b. because I really enjoy traveling.
3. I could never be an accountant	c. because I have a terrible memory.
4. I would make a bad waiter	d. because I'm terrible with numbers.
5. I could be a flight attendant	e. because I love creative writing.

B ***Group work*** Think about your personal qualities and skills. Then complete these statements. Take turns discussing them with your group.

I could never be a . . . because . . .
I wouldn't mind working as a . . . because . . .
I'd make a good . . . because . . .

"I have a terrible memory."

C ***Class activity*** Choose some statements made by members of your group. Share them with the rest of the class.

11 WRITING *A cover letter for a job application*

A Imagine you can apply for one of the jobs in this unit. Write a short cover letter for a job application.

Attention: Mr. Yoshioka, Personnel Director, Executive Air Lines

Dear Mr. Yoshioka,
I am responding to your recent advertisement in *The Post* for a bilingual international flight attendant. I think I'd make a good flight attendant for Executive Air Lines because I'm a very friendly person and I really love traveling. I also enjoy meeting people. As you can see from my résumé, I've had a lot of experience working with tourists. I worked at . . .

B ***Pair work*** Exchange papers. If you received this letter, would you invite the applicant for a job interview? Why or why not?

10 GRAMMAR FOCUS

Learning objective: *practice using clauses with* because

[CD 2, Track 28]

- Write these statements on the board:

I could be a teacher because . . .	*I'm terrible under pressure.*
I couldn't be a stockbroker because . . .	*I'm good at writing.*
I'd make a good journalist because . . .	*I'm very creative.*

Because

- Ask Ss to look back at the Perspectives section and match the phrases on the board.
- Explain that the conjunction *because* can connect two independent clauses into one sentence. *Because* answers the question "Why?"
- Point out that the clauses starting with *because* can come either before or after the main clause (e.g., *Because I'm good at writing, I'd make a good journalist. / I'd make a good journalist because I'm good at writing.*). Point out the comma in the first example. No comma is used, however, when *because* is in the middle of the sentence.

Could/would

- Explain that *could* and *would* are used to talk about hypothetical situations. Point out that *would* is reduced to *'d* when speaking.
- Play the audio program to present the sentences in the box.
- ***Option:*** Play this game to practice the new structure and vocabulary.
  1. Write one sentence on the board, e.g., *I'd make a good journalist because I'm creative.*
  2. Invite a S to come to the board and change or add one word only, e.g., *I'd make a good journalist because I'm organized.*
  3. The next S changes another word in the sentence, e.g., *I'd make a good teacher because I'm organized./ I'd be a good journalist because I'm organized.*

  Ss can play this in teams on the board. The team that makes the most changes wins.

A

- Explain the task. Ss complete the task individually and then compare answers in pairs. Check Ss' answers.

Answers

1. a 2. e 3. d 4. c 5. b

B Group work

- Write these expressions on the board:
  Really? Why is that?
  Do you think so? I think . . .
  I don't agree. In my opinion, . . .
  But maybe you have other skills, like . . .
- Explain the task. Then model how to complete the statements using examples from several Ss. Give Ss a few minutes to do the first part of the task. They can write their statements in their books or on paper.
- Have Ss form groups and take turns reading their statements aloud. Remind Ss to ask questions to get more information, especially reasons and explanations.

TIP To make sure that all Ss ask follow-up questions, have them put three small coins (or paper clips) in front of them on the desk. Each time they ask a follow-up question, they can take a coin back from the pile.

C Class activity

- Groups take turns sharing some of the interesting statements from part B with the class.

11 WRITING

Learning objective: *write a cover letter for a job application using gerunds and clauses with* because

A

- ***Option:*** Ss quickly review the unit and list all the jobs they can find.
- Explain the task. Read the example paragraph, choose a S to read it, or give Ss time to read it silently.
- Encourage Ss to brainstorm the type of job they want to write about – one they would be interested in applying for. Tell Ss to write down their ideas in the form of words, mind maps, or notes, and to include examples, reasons, and explanations. Go around the class and give help as needed.
- Ss use their notes to write a cover letter.
- ***Option:*** This part of the task could be done for homework.

B Pair work

- Ss form pairs and read each other's letters. Then they decide if they would invite their partner for a job interview. They should explain why or why not, and give feedback to their partner.

For a more detailed way to teach this Writing, try ***Cover Letter Gap-Fill*** on page T-158.

12 READING

Learning objectives: *read an article about personality types; develop skills in distinguishing main ideas from supporting ideas and making inferences*

- Books closed. Brainstorm with the class. On the board, write: *How to find a good job.* Then elicit examples and write suggestions on the board. For example:
  How to find a good job:
  - look at ads in the newspaper
  - ask friends for advice
  - think about your abilities
  - go to an employment agency
  - post your résumé online
  - consider your interests

For an alternative way to present this topic, try ***Running Dictation*** on page T-153. Use the first two paragraphs of the article.

A

- Books open. Read the title and the pre-reading question. Elicit the answer. (Answer: Artistic)
- Have Ss read the article without using their dictionaries. Tell them to circle, underline, or highlight any words or expressions whose meanings they can't guess from context.
- ***Option:*** Ss work in pairs or small groups to help each other understand any words they weren't able to guess.
- Elicit or explain any new words.

Vocabulary

rush: do something very quickly
classified ads: section in a newspaper containing advertisements for different products or services, including job listings
psychologist: someone trained in psychology, or the study of the mind
certain: some; specific; not all
curious: interested in learning about new things
enterprising: good at thinking of and doing new things
outgoing: friendly and willing to meet new people
imaginative: with new and interesting ideas
persuade: make another person decide to do something by giving good reasons
keep track of: pay attention to something so you know what's happening
counselor: someone who gives advice to people with problems

- Explain the task. Elicit the difference between a main idea (the most important and general idea in a paragraph) and a supporting idea (an idea that gives an example, explains, or adds information about the main idea). Ask a S to find and read the first sentence. Then elicit the answer.
- Ss complete the task individually and then check their answers in pairs. Then go over answers with the class.

Answers

1. Supporting idea
2. Main idea
3. Supporting idea
4. Main idea
5. Supporting idea

B

- Explain the task. Pronounce each heading listed in the chart and have Ss repeat the correct pronunciation and word stress.
- Ss complete the task individually and then explain their answers to a partner. Alternatively, write the categories on the board and ask Ss to write possible jobs in each category. Discuss answers as a class.

Possible answers

Realistic: mechanic, engineer
Investigative: detective, systems analyst
Artistic: interior decorator, novelist
Social: teacher, counselor
Enterprising: business manager, salesperson
Conventional: accountant, administrator

C *Group work*

- Ss form small groups to take turns asking and answering the questions. Go around the class and give help as needed. Encourage Ss to give examples and reasons, and to ask follow-up questions.
- ***Option:*** Ss form small groups. Each group has a small object to throw. Ss use adjectives that begin with the first letter of their name. For example, the first student says, "I'm Pedro, I'm practical," and then throws the object to another S. This S says, "I'm Olga, I'm outgoing." The S who can keep going the longest wins.

End of Cycle 2

Do your students need more practice?

Assign . . .	***for more practice in . . .***
Workbook Exercises 7–10 on pages 58–60	Grammar, Vocabulary, Reading, and Writing
Lab Guide Exercises 7–8 on page 16	Listening, Pronunciation, Speaking, and Grammar
Video Activity Book Unit 10	Listening, Speaking, and Cultural Awareness
CD-ROM Unit 10	Grammar, Vocabulary, Reading, Listening, and Speaking

Evaluation

Assess Ss' understanding of Units 9 and 10 with the quiz on pages T-208 and T-209.

12 READING

Find the Job That's Right for You!

Look at the photo and skim the list below. What personality type do you think best describes the person in the picture?

1 Nearly 50% of all workers in the United States have jobs they aren't happy with. Don't let this happen to you! If you want to find the right job, don't rush to look through the classified ads in the newspaper. Instead, sit down and think about yourself. What kind of person are you? What makes you happy?

2 According to psychologist John Holland, there are six types of personalities. Nobody is just one personality type, but most people are mainly one type. For each type, there are certain jobs that might be right and others that are probably wrong.

3 Considering your personality type can help you make the right job decision. Liz is a good example. Liz knew she wanted to do something for children. She thought she could help children as a school counselor or a lawyer. She took counseling and law courses – and hated them. After talking to a career counselor, she realized the problem was that she's an Artistic type. Liz studied film, and she now produces children's TV shows – and loves it.

The **Realistic** type is practical and likes working with machines and tools.

The **Investigative** type is curious and likes to learn, analyze situations, and solve problems.

The **Artistic** type is imaginative and likes to express himself or herself by creating art.

The **Social** type is friendly and likes helping or training other people.

The **Enterprising** type is outgoing and likes to persuade or lead other people.

The **Conventional** type is careful and likes to follow routines and keep track of details.

A Read the article. Then find these sentences in the article. Decide whether each sentence is the main idea or a supporting idea in that paragraph. Check (✓) the correct boxes.

	Main idea	Supporting idea
1. Nearly 50% of all workers . . . they aren't happy with. (par. 1)	☐	☐
2. According to psychologist . . . types of personalities. (par. 2)	☐	☐
3. For each type, there are . . . that are probably wrong. (par. 2)	☐	☐
4. Considering your personality . . . the right job decision. (par. 3)	☐	☐
5. After talking to a career counselor, . . . an Artistic type. (par. 3)	☐	☐

B For each personality type, write two examples of appropriate jobs. Then explain your answers to a partner.

Realistic	Investigative	Artistic	Social	Enterprising	Conventional
....	....	....	....	....	....
....	....	....	....	....	....

C ***Group work*** What personality type do you think you are? Does your group agree?

Units 9–10 Progress check

SELF-ASSESSMENT

How well can you do these things? Check (✓) the boxes.

I can	Very well	OK	A little
Ask and answer questions about changes using time contrasts (Ex. 1)	☐	☐	☐
Describe possibilities using conditional sentences with *if* clauses (Ex. 2)	☐	☐	☐
Listen to and understand descriptions of abilities and personality traits (Ex. 3)	☐	☐	☐
Ask and answer questions about job preferences and skills using gerunds (Ex. 4)	☐	☐	☐
Give reasons using clauses with *because* (Ex. 4)	☐	☐	☐

1 SPEAKING *Past, present, and future*

A ***Pair work*** Think of one more question for each category. Then interview a partner.

Appearance	What did you use to look like? Can you describe yourself now? What do you think you'll look like in the future?
Free time	Did you have a hobby as a child? What do you like to do these days? How are you going to spend your free time next year?

B ***Group work*** Share one interesting thing about your partner.

2 GAME *Truth and consequences*

A Add one event and one consequence to the lists below.

Event	Consequence
☐ you move to a foreign country	☐ buy you a gift
☐ it's sunny tomorrow	☐ feel jealous sometimes
☐ it's cold tomorrow	☐ have to learn a new language
☐ you give me $10	☐ go to the beach
☐ you don't call me later	☐ get really angry
☐ you go on a diet	☐ feel hungry a lot
☐ you fall in love	☐ stay home
☐	☐ ....

B ***Class activity*** Go around the class and make sentences. Check (✓) each *if* clause after you use it. The student who uses the most clauses correctly wins.

Units 9–10 Progress check

SELF-ASSESSMENT

Learning objectives: *reflect on one's learning; identify areas that need improvement*

- Ask: "What did you learn in Units 9 and 10?" Elicit Ss' answers.
- Ss complete the Self-assessment. Encourage them to be honest, and point out they will not get a bad grade if they check (✓) "a little."
- Ss move on to the Progress check exercises. You can have Ss complete them in class or for homework, using one of these techniques:
  1. Ask Ss to complete all the exercises.
  2. Ask Ss: "What do you need to practice?" Then assign exercises based on their answers.
  3. Ask Ss to choose and complete exercises based on their Self-assessment.

1 SPEAKING

Learning objective: *assess one's ability to ask and answer questions about changes using time contrasts*

A *Pair work*

- Explain the task. Ss will talk about two categories (appearance and free time) using past, present, and future tenses. If helpful, make a list on the board of tenses that Ss might use during their conversation (past simple, *used to*, present simple, present continuous, future with *will*, *might*, and *be going to*).
- Have Ss read the questions silently. Then they add one more question to each category.
- Ss form pairs and use their questions to interview each other. Remind Ss to give additional information and ask follow-up questions.

B *Group work*

- Have each pair join another pair. Ask them to share at least one interesting thing about their partners. Again, encourage Ss to ask follow-up questions.
- ***Option:*** Ss earn one point for every follow-up question they ask.
- As Ss discuss in groups, go around the class and write down any errors you hear. Pay attention to Ss' ability to keep a conversation going and to use different tenses.
- Go over any errors you noticed with the whole class. Be sure to praise examples of good communication.

2 GAME

Learning objective: *assess one's ability to describe possibilities using conditional sentences with* if *clauses*

A

- Briefly review how to make conditional sentences, using *may*, *might*, or *will*. Write an event on the board and elicit some possible consequences from Ss, e.g.:

Event	*Consequence*
If you join a gym . . .	*you may lose weight.*
	you might make new friends.

- Ask Ss to read the list of events and consequences. Elicit or explain any unfamiliar vocabulary. Then Ss work individually to add one event and one consequence to the lists in the chart. Remind Ss that the event and consequence must match each other.

B *Class activity*

- Explain and model the task with a few Ss. Read one event (e.g., *If you move to a foreign country . . .*) and ask a S to complete the clause with a consequence (e.g., *you may have to learn a new language*). Check (✓) the *if* clause you used and allow the S to read another event. Then repeat the activity with another S, using a different clause.
- Ss get up and move around the class, making sentences together and checking (✓) the *if* clauses they use. The first person to use all the clauses correctly wins.

3 LISTENING

Learning objective: *assess one's ability to listen to and understand descriptions of abilities and personality traits*

A [CD 2, Track 29]

- Read the instructions aloud and focus Ss' attention on the left side of the chart. Explain the task. Ss listen to find out what jobs Louisa and Tim are talking about.
- Play the audio program, pausing after each discussion. Ss listen and complete the left side of the chart only. Then elicit Ss' responses.

Audio script *(See page T-230.)*

Answers

1. Louisa	politician	bad
	architect	good
2. Tim	restaurant manager	bad
	teacher	good

B

- Explain that now Ss will listen for the reasons that Louisa and Tim give.
- Play the audio program again. Ss listen and complete the rest of the chart. Then go over answers with the class.

Answers

1. Louisa	not good at working with people
	creative; likes drawing; could work alone
2. Tim	disorganized
	likes working with kids; patient; hardworking

4 DISCUSSION

Learning objectives: *assess one's ability to ask and answer questions about job preferences and skills using gerunds; assess one's ability to give reasons using clauses with* because

A

- Focus Ss' attention on the photos and read the questions below. Explain any new vocabulary.
- Explain the first task. Ss use the questions to help them write their own job profile. Tell them to write the profile on a separate piece of paper.
- Ask a S to help you prepare a sample job profile on the board, like this:
  Personal Job profile for . . . (name of S)
  Skills
  - can type 45 words a minute
  - speaks Spanish, Portuguese, and English
  - knows how to use accounting software programs
  - is good with numbers
  Job Preferences
  - likes working 9 to 5
  - prefers having an office job
  - enjoys wearing a suit to work
- Give Ss a few minutes to complete the task. Go around the class and give help as needed.
- Ask two Ss to read the example conversation.
- Ss work in pairs to compare their profiles. Go around the class and give help as needed.

B *Group work*

- Explain the task. S1 reads his or her job profile. The group discusses the profile and suggests suitable jobs. Remind Ss that they should give reasons for their suggestions. Allow the S to respond before the group continues with the next profile.
- Ask two Ss to read the example conversation.
- Ss form groups and take turns discussing job profiles and possible jobs. Go around the class and take note of any errors you hear.
- ***Option:*** Ask one or two Ss to tell the class which jobs the group suggested and why.

WHAT'S NEXT?

Learning objective: *become more involved in one's learning*

- Focus Ss' attention on the Self-assessment again. Ask: "How well can you do these things now?"
- Ask Ss to underline one thing they need to review. Ask: "What did you underline? How can you review it?"
- If needed, plan additional activities or reviews based on Ss' answers.

3 LISTENING Good or bad?

A Listen to Louisa and Tim discuss four jobs. Write down the jobs and check (✓) if they would be good or bad at them.

	Job	Good	Bad	Reason
1. Louisa	....	☐	☐	....
	....	☐	☐	....
2. Tim	....	☐	☐	....
	....	☐	☐	....

B Listen again. What reasons do they give?

DISCUSSION Job profile

A Prepare a personal job profile. Write your name, skills, and job preferences. Think about the questions below. Then compare with a partner.

Are you good at . . . ?
communicating with people
solving problems
making decisions quickly
speaking foreign languages

Do you . . . ?
have any special skills
have any experience
have a good memory
manage money well

Do you like . . . ?
traveling
working with a team
wearing a uniform
working long hours

A: Are you good at communicating with people?
B: Sure. I enjoy talking to people.
A: So do I. I like meeting new people and . . .

B ***Group work*** Make suggestions for possible jobs based on your classmates' job profiles. What do you think of their suggestions for you?

A: Hmm. Juan could be an executive because he likes solving problems and making decisions quickly.
B: No way! I could never be an executive. I'm too disorganized!

WHAT'S NEXT?

Look at your Self-assessment again. Do you need to review anything?

11 It's really worth seeing!

1 SNAPSHOT

FAMOUS LANDMARKS

The Great Wall of China was begun in 214 B.C. It is the largest structure ever built.

The Colosseum in Rome was opened in 80 A.D. It was sometimes filled with water for ship battles.

Machu Picchu in Peru was constructed around 1400 A.D. It was probably a home for the Inca royal family.

The Statue of Liberty in New York was opened in 1886. It was a gift to the United States from the people of France.

The Eiffel Tower in Paris was completed in 1889. It was built for the 100th anniversary of the French Revolution.

Source: *World Book Encyclopedia*

Which landmark did people live in? Which was a gift? Which was used for events?
What else do you know about these places?
What are the three most famous landmarks in your country?

2 PERSPECTIVES The Empire State Building

A How much do you know about the Empire State Building? Check (✓) the statements you think are true.

- ☐ 1. The Empire State Building was designed by an American architect.
- ☐ 2. It was officially opened by the president of the United States in 1931.
- ☐ 3. It is located in New York City.
- ☐ 4. The construction of the building took five years.
- ☐ 5. It cost $2 million to build.
- ☐ 6. There are 102 floors in the building.
- ☐ 7. It is the tallest building in the world.
- ☐ 8. It was featured in the movie *King Kong*.

B Now listen and check your answers. What information is the most surprising?

It's really worth seeing!

Cycle 1, Exercises 1–6

In Unit 11, students discuss remarkable places in the world. In Cycle 1, they talk about famous landmarks, monuments, and works of art using the passive with by *(simple past). In Cycle 2, they talk about key features of countries around the world using the passive without* by *(simple present).*

SNAPSHOT

Learning objectives: *read about famous landmarks; see the passive with* by *in context*

TIP To create interest in the topic, bring (or ask Ss to bring) realia to class. A large world map, photos, postcards, or information from the Internet about cities and countries around the world would be helpful.

- ***Option:*** Explain that this unit is about famous places in the world. As a warm-up, have Ss skim the unit to find all the countries listed.
- ***Option:*** Elicit the meaning of a *landmark* (= a familiar object or building). To prepare Ss for the topic, ask about places near your school: "What is one place that everyone who lives or works around here knows? Is it a landmark? Is there a monument, statue, or clock that is famous around here? If so, where is it?"
- Books closed. Write these landmarks and countries on the board. Ask Ss to match the landmark with the country:

Landmark	Country
The Great Wall	France
The Colosseum	China
Machu Picchu	Italy
The Statue of Liberty	U.S.A.
The Eiffel Tower	Peru

- Books open. Ss read the Snapshot to find the answers. Point out that B.C. means "before Christ" and A.D. is an abbreviation for *anno Domini*, Latin for "in the year of God." Elicit answers. (Answers: China, Italy, Peru, U.S.A., France)
- Ask: "Has anyone ever visited any of these places?"
- Elicit or explain any unfamiliar vocabulary.

Vocabulary

structure: any type of construction, e.g., a bridge, a wall, a building, a tower
ship battles: fights between ships
constructed: built
royal family: a family of kings and queens
completed: finished
the French Revolution: a period when the ordinary people of France threw the royal family out of power

- Ss discuss the questions in pairs or small groups. Then elicit Ss' answers. For the second question, don't say too much about the Great Wall or Machu Picchu. They will be presented in Exercise 6. The following information may be helpful:

  the Great Wall of China: You can visit it from Beijing; it has a roadway along the top.

  the Colosseum: It had a seating capacity of 87,000; it was used in ancient Rome as a place for gladiator fights; it was a battleground in World War II.

  Machu Picchu: It is situated on a mountain near the Cusco in Peru; no one knows why it was abandoned.

  the Statue of Liberty: It was designed by the French sculptor F.A. Bartholdi and built in France; it is the tallest statue (151 feet/45.3 meters) in the United States; it has 142 steps.

  the Eiffel Tower: It was designed by Gustav Eiffel, a French engineer; it has an elevator to the top, where you can get a good view of Paris; it was originally intended to be a temporary structure.

2 PERSPECTIVES

Learning objectives: *learn about the Empire State Building; see the passive with* by *(past simple) in context*

A *[CD 2, Track 31]*

- Books closed. Ask Ss what they know about the Empire State Building. Has anyone been there?
- Books open. Explain that Ss will hear statements about the building – some true and some false. Play the audio program. Ss listen and read silently.
- Ss read the information again and check (✓) the statements they think are true.

B

- Play the second part of the audio program. Ss listen and check their answers.

Audio script *(See page T-230.)*

Answers

True: 1, 2, 3, 6, 8

- As a class, discuss which facts are the most surprising.

3 GRAMMAR FOCUS

Learning objective: *practice using the passive with* by

[CD 2, Track 32]

Passive (simple past)

- Prepare six cards and write these words on them: *The president / the building / opened / was / by / in 1931.*
- Ask four Ss to hold up these cards:

S1	S2	S3	S4
The president	***opened***	*the building*	*in 1931.*

- Now explain that in English we can say the same thing in another way. Ask two more Ss to hold up these cards:

S3	S5	S2	S6	S1	S4
The building	***was***	***opened***	*by*	*the president*	*in 1931.*

- Elicit or explain the following rules:

Active

The president	*opened*	*the building.*
Subject +	verb +	object

Here, the emphasis is on the **president**. It wasn't John Smith who opened the building. It was the **president**.

Passive

The building was opened (by the president).
Object + *was/were* + past participle + (by + subject)

Here, the emphasis is on the **building**. The most important fact is that the **building was opened**.

- The passive is the best way to express an idea when:
  1. We don't know who did the action, e.g., ***My house was broken into*** *on Friday.*
  2. There is no "doer" of the action, e.g., ***He was killed*** *in an earthquake.*
  3. The fact is more important than the "doer" of the action, e.g., ***My dog was run over*** *by a car.*
- Remind Ss that the past passive verb is made up of: ***was/were + past participle***. We don't always use *by* to show "who" or "what" did the action.
- Have Ss look at the Snapshot and Perspectives sections on the previous page to find examples of the passive in the simple past tense. Ask two Ss to write them on the board as Ss say them. There are ten examples in total; two contain the word *by*.
- Play the audio program to present the sentences in the box. Tell Ss to pay attention to the pronunciation of *was*. Point out that it is usually unstressed in passive sentences.
- Ask Ss to suggest additional passive sentences about things that they know (e.g., *The movie* Psycho *was directed by Alfred Hitchcock. The* Mona Lisa *was painted by Leonardo da Vinci.*).

TIP To check that Ss understand how to form the structure, have them generate their own examples.

A

- Focus Ss' attention on the pictures and elicit information about each one (e.g., *What is it? What do Ss know about it?*).
- Go over the phrases in columns A and B. Elicit or explain any new vocabulary.
- Have Ss complete the task individually. If Ss are not familiar with the works, encourage them to use a process of elimination before comparing answers with a partner. Then go over answers with the class.

Answers

1. b 2. e 3. d 4. c 5. a

B *Pair work*

- Explain the following words and expressions:

Vocabulary

radium: a chemical element that is used to treat diseases, including cancer
high-definition television (HDTV): a special television system that shows sharp, clear images

- Explain the task. Point out that a date or year can appear in several places in a passive sentence – at the beginning, in the middle, or at the end:
In 1931, it was opened by the president.
It was opened in 1931 by the president.
It was opened by the president in 1931.
- As Ss complete the task individually, go around the class and give help as needed. Then Ss take turns reading their sentences in pairs. Elicit Ss' answers.

Possible answers

1. The Statue of Liberty was designed by Frédéric Bartholdi in 1884.
2. Radium was discovered by Marie Curie in 1898.
3. *One Hundred Years of Solitude* was written by Gabriel García Márquez in 1971.
4. The first digital HDTV (high-definition television) was produced by Woo Paik in 1991.
5. Frida Kahlo was played by Salma Hayek in the movie *Frida* in 2002.

For more practice using the passive with *by*, play ***Twenty Questions*** on page T-145.

4 INTERCHANGE 11

See page T-125 for teaching notes.

3 GRAMMAR FOCUS

Passive with by (simple past)

The passive changes the focus of a sentence.
For the simple past, use the past of* be *+ past participle.

Active	***Passive***
The president **opened** the building in 1931.	It **was opened by** the president in 1931.
An American architect **designed** the building.	It **was designed by** an American architect.

A Do you know who created these popular works? Match the phrases in column A with the appropriate information from column B. Then compare with a partner.

A	*B*
1. *The Kiss*	a. was composed by Georges Bizet.
2. The song "Yesterday"	b. was painted by Gustav Klimt.
3. The film *Schindler's List*	c. was written by Jane Austen.
4. The novel *Pride and Prejudice*	d. was directed by Steven Spielberg.
5. The opera *Carmen*	e. was recorded by the Beatles.

B ***Pair work*** Change these sentences into passive sentences with *by*. Then take turns reading them aloud.

1. Frédéric Bartholdi designed the Statue of Liberty in 1884.
2. Marie Curie discovered radium in 1898.
3. Gabriel García Márquez wrote *One Hundred Years of Solitude* in 1971.
4. Woo Paik produced the first digital HDTV (high-definition television) in 1991.
5. Salma Hayek played Frida Kahlo in the movie *Frida* in 2002.

4 INTERCHANGE 11 Who is this by?

Who created these well-known works? Go to Interchange 11.

5 PRONUNCIATION *The letter* o

A Listen and practice. Notice how the letter *o* is pronounced in the following words.

/o/	/ou/	/u:/	/ʌ/
not	no	do	one
top	don't	food	love
....	....	....	....
....	....	....	....

B How is the letter *o* pronounced in these words? Write them in the correct column in part A. Then listen and check your answers.

come done lock own shot soon who wrote

6 LISTENING *Ancient monuments*

Listen to three tour guides describe some very old monuments. Take notes to answer the questions below. Then compare with a partner.

1

the Pyramids

2

Machu Picchu

3

the Great Wall of China

Who built them?
Why were they built?

How big is the city?
When was it discovered?

Why was it built?
How long is it?

WORD POWER *Where is it from?*

A Complete the chart. Then add one more word to each category.

cars
cattle
chickens
✓ coffee
corn
✓ lobsters
microchips
oysters
rice
sheep
shrimp
televisions

Farmed	Grown	Manufactured	Raised
lobsters	*coffee*	....	....
....	....	....	....
....	....	....	....
....	....	....	....

B ***Group work*** Talk about things that are found in your country.

"We grow coffee. We also manufacture cars."

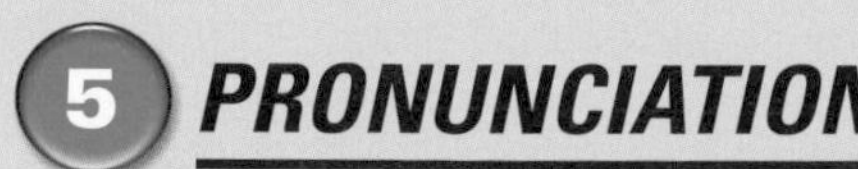

5 PRONUNCIATION

Learning objective: *notice the different ways the letter* o *is pronounced*

A [CD 2, Track 33]

- Books closed. Write these words on the board and read them aloud. Ask: "What is different about the letter *o* in each word?"
  not *no* *do* *one*
- Books open. Point out the letter *o* is pronounced in different ways in English. Play the audio program. Ss listen to how the letter *o* is pronounced.
- Play the audio program again. Ask individual Ss to repeat to check their pronunciation.

B

- Explain the task. Ss read the words and write them in a column in part A. Then play the rest of the audio program. Ss check their answers.

Answers

/ɒ/ = lock, shot
/u:/ = soon, who
/ou/ = own, wrote
/ʌ/ = come, done

- ***Option:*** Have Ss find examples of five words on page 73 containing the letter *o* (e.g., *focus*, *open*, *popular*, *appropriate*, *song*, *novel*, *opera*, *composed*, *movie*) and practice the pronunciation of these words.

For more practice, play ***Run for It!*** on page T-148. Assign each wall an *o* sound, then say words containing the letter *o*. For more of a challenge, write them on the board.

6 LISTENING

Learning objective: *develop skills in listening for main ideas and specific information*

[CD 2, Track 34]

- Give Ss time to look at the pictures and questions. Then ask Ss to predict the answers and tell a partner what else they would like to know about these places.
- Explain the task. Ss will hear three tour guides talk about these places. Ss listen for the answers.
- Play the audio program. Ss listen to check their predictions and take notes. Have Ss compare answers in pairs. Then go over answers with the class.

Audio script *(See page T-230–231.)*

Possible answers

1. The Pyramids were built by the Egyptians. They were built as burial places for kings.
2. Machu Picchu covers about 13 square kilometers, or 5 square miles. It was discovered in 1911.
3. The Great Wall was built to protect a Chinese kingdom. It is about 2,000 miles, or 3,400 kilometers, long.

End of Cycle 1

Do your students need more practice?

Assign . . .	*for more practice in . . .*
Workbook Exercises 1–4 on pages 61–63	Grammar, Vocabulary, Reading, and Writing
Lab Guide Exercises 1–2 on page 17	Listening, Pronunciation, Speaking, and Grammar

Cycle 2, Exercises 7–13

7 WORD POWER

Learning objective: *learn vocabulary for discussing products found in a country*

A

- Ss complete the chart and add one more word to each category. While Ss work, draw the chart on the board.
- Elicit answers while a S writes them on the board.

Answers

Farmed	*Grown*	*Manufactured*	*Raised*
lobsters	coffee	cars	cattle
oysters	corn	microchips	chickens
shrimp	rice	televisions	sheep
fish	*bananas*	*textiles*	*pigs*

(Note: Additional examples are italicized.)

B Group work

- Ss work in groups to make as many sentences as they can. Then groups share some sentences with the class.

8 CONVERSATION

Learning objectives: *practice a conversation between people asking for and giving information; see the passive with* by *in context*

A ▶ ***[CD 2, Track 35]***

- Books closed. Set the scene. A man is calling for information about the European Union (= a group of European countries that act together in political and economic matters). Write these questions on the board:
  1. Who does he think he's talking to?
  2. Who is he really talking to?
  3. What was the problem?
- Play the audio program. Ss listen. Then elicit answers to the questions. (Answers: 1. a travel agent 2. someone at a hair salon 3. He had the wrong number.)
- ***Option:*** Ask the class: "Has anything like this ever happened to you?" If so, have Ss explain.
- Write this comprehension question on the board:
  What three things does the man ask about the EU?
- Play the audio program again and check answers. (Answers: currency, language, and credit cards)
- Books open. Play the audio program again while Ss look at the picture and read silently.
- Explain that *I really have no idea* means *I don't know*. Also, point out that *How would I know?* is rude. It suggests that the woman thinks the man's question is stupid.
- Ss practice the conversation in pairs.

To improve pronunciation and have fun with this Conversation, try ***Say It With Feeling!*** on page T-150. Encourage Ss to use actions, too.

B ***Pair work***

- Explain the task. Then have Ss look at the Conversation and tell you which parts they could change (e.g., *the country, the information he wants, and the place he is calling*). On the board, write the main topics in the conversation:
  greeting currency language credit cards
  misunderstanding (you're a travel agent) real place
- Books closed. Pairs take turns role-playing the Conversation using their own words and information about another country. Ss can write the information or speak from memory.

9 GRAMMAR FOCUS

Learning objective: *practice using the passive without* by

▶ ***[CD 2, Track 36]***

- Explain that, as Ss saw with the simple past passive, we change the emphasis when we use the simple present passive. Instead of saying: "**They** use the euro in most of the European Union," we can say "**The euro** is used in most of the European Union." The focus changes from "they" (which is not clear) to "the euro" (which is what we're interested in). Play the audio program to present sentences in the box.
- Write these passive sentences on the board to demonstrate how the *by* phrase is omitted here:
  The euro is used in most of the EU (by the people).
  Cars are manufactured in Europe (by manufacturers).
- Explain that the "doer" of the action in each of these sentences is obvious or not important, so the *by* phrase can be easily omitted.
- Refer Ss to the previous Conversation and ask them to underline the examples of the present simple passive. There are three questions and one statement.

A

- Explain the task and read the verbs in parentheses. Have Ss check any new words in their dictionaries.
- Ss complete the passage individually. If necessary, refer Ss to the list of participles in the appendix at the back of the book. Then go over answers with the class.

Answers

Many crops **are grown** in Taiwan. Some crops **are consumed** locally, but others **are exported**. Tea **is grown** in cooler parts of the island and rice **is cultivated** in warmer parts. Fishing is also an important industry. A wide variety of seafood **is caught**. Many people **are employed** in the electronics and textile industries.

B

- Explain and model the task by eliciting the answer to the first item. Tell Ss that each verb can be used only once.
- Ss work individually. Then go over answers.

Answers

1. are spoken	3. is made up of	5. are manufactured
2. is grown	4. are raised	6. is used

C ***Pair work***

- Ss use the passive of the verbs in part B to talk about their country (or another country they know).
- ***Option:*** Ss share their ideas with the class.

8 CONVERSATION *I need some information.*

A Listen and practice.

Kelly: Hello?
John: Oh, hello. I need some information. What currency is used in the European Union?
Kelly: Where?
John: The European Union.
Kelly: I think the euro is used in most of the EU.
John: Oh, right. And is English spoken much there?
Kelly: I really have no idea.
John: Huh? Well, what about credit cards? Are they accepted everywhere?
Kelly: How would I know?
John: Well, you're a travel agent, aren't you?
Kelly: What? This is a hair salon. You have the wrong number!

B *Pair work* Use information about a country you know to act out the conversation.

9 GRAMMAR FOCUS

Passive without by (simple present)

For the simple present, use the present of **be** *+ past participle.*

Active	*Passive*
They **use** the euro in most of the European Union.	The euro **is used** in most of the EU.
They **speak** English in many European countries.	English **is spoken** in many European countries.
They **manufacture** a lot of cars in Europe.	A lot of cars **are manufactured** in Europe.

A Complete this passage using the simple present passive form.

Many crops .... (grow) in Taiwan. Some crops .... (consume) locally, but others .... (export). Tea .... (grow) in cooler parts of the island and rice .... (cultivate) in warmer parts. Fishing is also an important industry. A wide variety of seafood .... (catch). Many people .... (employ) in the electronics and textile industries.

B Complete the sentences. Use the passive of these verbs.

grow   make up   manufacture   raise   speak   use

1. French and English .... in Canada.
2. A lot of rice .... in Vietnam.
3. The U.S. .... of 50 states.
4. A lot of sheep .... in New Zealand.
5. Cars and computers .... in Korea.
6. The U.S. dollar .... in Ecuador.

C *Pair work* Use the passive of the verbs in part B to talk about your country and other countries you know.

10 LISTENING Colombia

A Listen to a short talk about Colombia. Complete the chart.

Facts about Colombia	
Location	....
Population	....
Language	....
Industries	....
Agricultural products	....

B Listen again. Check (✓) the things the speaker mentions about Colombia.

- [ ] beaches
- [ ] volcanoes
- [ ] snow-capped mountains
- [ ] rivers
- [ ] lakes
- [ ] hot lowland plains

11 SPEAKING True or false?

A ***Pair work*** Choose a country. Then answer these questions. Include one false statement.

Where is it located?
What cities are found there?
What languages are spoken?
What currency is used?
What famous tourist attraction is found there?
What products are exported?

B ***Class activity*** Give a short talk like the one in Exercise 10 about the country you chose. Can the class identify the false statement?

12 WRITING A guidebook introduction

A Make an information chart like the one in Exercise 10 about a country you know. Then write an introduction for a guidebook about the country.

Vietnam is located in Southeast Asia. It has a population of over 80 million people. Vietnamese is the official language. The country has many beautiful beaches, high mountains, and busy cities. Rice is grown in . . .

B ***Group work*** Exchange papers. Is any important information missing? Do you want to visit the country?

10 LISTENING

Learning objective: *develop skills in listening for specific information*

A [CD 2, Track 37]

- Present the map, pictures, and chart. In pairs, ask Ss to predict some words they think they will hear during the talk.

To help Ss make predictions before listening, play ***Prediction Bingo*** on page T-146.

- Tell Ss to listen and take notes to complete the chart. Then play the audio program.

Audio script *(See page T-231.)*

- Draw the chart on the board. Have a few Ss write the answers they are sure about.

Answers

Location northwest South America, with coasts on the Atlantic and Pacific oceans
Population around 36 million
Language Spanish
Industries textiles and clothing; mining and oil
Agricultural products coffee, flowers, sugar, bananas, rice, corn, and cotton

B

- Play the audio program again. This time, Ss listen and check (✓) the other things the speaker mentions. Have Ss compare answers in pairs. Then elicit answers from the class.

Answers

beaches (coastlines); snow-capped mountains; hot lowland plains

For more practice using the passive voice, play ***Ask the Right Question*** on page T-146. On the board, write a passive sentence (e.g., *The euro is used in Italy.*). Elicit a passive question that the statement answers (e.g., *What currency is used in Italy?*). On each index card, Ss write one passive statement.

11 SPEAKING

Learning objective: *talk about a country using the simple present passive and vocabulary for discussing products*

A Pair work

- Explain the task. In pairs, Ss choose a country and write answers to the questions. Set a time limit of about five minutes. If Ss want to research a country, this part could be assigned as homework.
- Help Ss brainstorm other information they could include (e.g., *geographical features*, *religion*, *capital city*). For more ideas, refer Ss to Exercises 7A and 10A.
- Remind Ss to include one statement that is false.

B Class activity

- Ss take turns giving a short talk about the country they chose. Encourage Ss to present the information without simply reading their notes from part A. The class listens and guesses which statement is false.
- Alternatively, divide the class into two teams and keep score. Each correct answer equals one point. The team with the most points wins.

For more speaking practice, try the ***Country Profiles Quiz*** on page T-158.

12 WRITING

Learning objective: *write an introduction to a guidebook using the simple present passive and vocabulary for discussing products*

If possible, bring a guidebook written in English to class, or pages of guidebooks from the Internet.

A

- Explain the task and read the example paragraph. Point out that both active and passive sentences are used in the example.
- Ask Ss to choose a country to write about. They can choose one that they already know about or research another country. If Ss research a country, this part could be assigned as homework.
- Ss gather information and make a chart like the one in Exercise 10. Then they use their notes to write a draft of their introduction.

To help Ss organize their writing, try ***Mind Mapping*** on page T-154.

B Group work

- In groups, Ss exchange papers and take turns reading them aloud. Encourage Ss to ask for more information and to say if they want to visit the country. Why?

13 READING

***Learning objectives:** read an article about some unusual museums; develop skills in guessing meaning from context and understanding text organization*

- Books closed. Write the word *Museums* in a box in the middle of the board and ask Ss what kinds of museums are in their city, town, or country. Elicit ideas and write them on the board as a mind map:

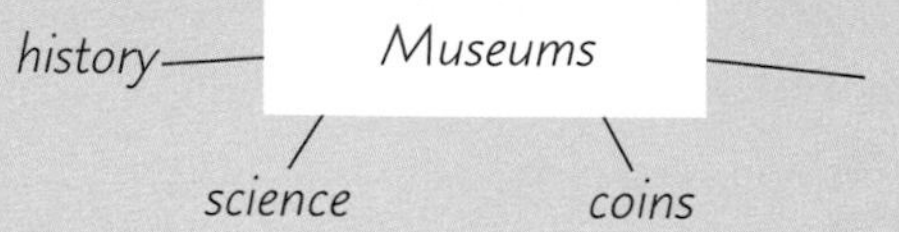

- Ask Ss if they have ever been to or heard about any unusual museums.
- Books open. Ask Ss what they see in the pictures. Explain the pre-reading task and tell Ss to scan the article as quickly as possible for the answers. Then elicit answers. (Answers: very old objects – the Museum of Gold; a working factory – the Chocolate Museum; historic cooking tools – the Kimchi Museum)

> **TIP** To help Ss scan quickly and focus on key words only, have Ss who finish raise their hands and leave them up. This will encourage those who haven't finished to work more quickly.

A

- Explain that they are going to guess the meanings of some new words and expressions from context. As an example, read the first paragraph aloud and ask Ss to guess the meaning of *off the beaten path*.
- Ss complete the exercise individually. Then go over answers with the class. Ask Ss how they guessed the correct answers.

Answers

1. do something unusual	4. very old
2. started	5. free of charge
3. attractive	6. thick and sticky

- Elicit other new words in the text. Tell Ss to use their dictionaries or work in pairs to guess the meaning from context.

Vocabulary

eye-opening: surprising; interesting
highlight: attract attention to; emphasize
utensils: devices or tools with a particular use
souvenir: something you buy or keep to remember a place you visited
exhibit: an object on show in a museum or art gallery
sparkle: shine brightly; for example, a diamond sparkles in the light
item: an object
copper: a soft, red-brown metal
sample: take or try a small amount of something

B

- Explain the task. Tell Ss that they need to guess the paragraph, but not the exact place in the paragraph where each sentence could go. Model the task with the first sentence. Then ask Ss how they guessed the correct answer.
- Ss complete the task individually. Then go over answers with the class. Ask Ss how they guessed the answers.

Answers

a. 2 b. 4 c. 3 d. 1

C *Pair work*

- Have Ss discuss the questions in pairs.
- ***Option:*** As a follow-up, Ss write a paragraph about a museum in their city, town, or country. These can be displayed in the classroom or given to you to check.

To review vocabulary from this reading, play ***Tic-Tac-Toe*** on page T-148.

End of Cycle 2

Do your students need more practice?

Assign . . .	*for more practice in . . .*
Workbook Exercises 5–10 on pages 64–66	Grammar, Vocabulary, Reading, and Writing
Lab Guide Exercises 3–7 on page 17	Listening, Pronunciation, Speaking, and Grammar
Video Activity Book Unit 11	Listening, Speaking, and Cultural Awareness
CD-ROM Unit 11	Grammar, Vocabulary, Reading, Listening, and Speaking

13 READING

A Guide To Unusual Museums

Look at the pictures and scan the article. Where do you think you can see very old objects? a working factory? historic cooking tools?

1 Do you like museums? Have you been to the Louvre in Paris, the Museum of Anthropology in Mexico City, or any of those other "must see" museums? Well, now it's time to go off the beaten path.

The Kimchi Museum
Seoul, Korea

2 If you don't know about kimchi, a trip to the Kimchi Museum is an eye-opening experience. The museum was founded in 1986 to highlight Korea's rich kimchi culture. The exhibit includes displays of cooking utensils and materials related to making, storing, and eating the famous pickled vegetables. The museum also provides details about the history and nutritional benefits of Korea's most beloved side dish. Finally, stop by the souvenir shop to try various types of kimchi.

The Museum of Gold
Bogotá, Colombia

3 If you want to see beautiful objects, the Museum of Gold is *the* place. It holds one of South America's most stunning collections. Because the exhibits sparkle so brightly, you can actually take photographs without using a flash on your camera! Not everything is made of gold, though. Among the exhibits are ancient pre-Columbian items. Many of them are made from a mixture of gold and copper, known as *tumbaga*.

The Chocolate Museum
Cologne, Germany

4 The Chocolate Museum will teach you everything about chocolate – from cocoa bean to candy bars. You'll learn about chocolate's 3,000-year history and discover how it was once used as money in South America. A real chocolate factory shows you how chocolate is made. After you've finished the tour, you can sample a complimentary drink of rich, gooey pure chocolate – perfect for those with a sweet tooth.

A Read the article. Find the words in *italics* in the article. Then circle the meaning of each word or phrase.

1. When you *go off the beaten path*, you **do something unusual / go somewhere far away**.
2. When something is *founded*, it is **started / discovered**.
3. When something is *stunning*, it is extremely **attractive / large**.
4. When something is *ancient*, it is **very old / common**.
5. When something is *complimentary*, it is **free of charge / very expensive**.
6. When something is *gooey*, it is **light and refreshing / thick and sticky**.

B Where do these sentences belong? Write the number of the paragraph where each sentence could go.

.... a. Don't forget to buy your favorite kind to bring home for dinner!
.... b. Did you know that it wasn't popular in Europe until the nineteenth century?
.... c. The museum also features coins, jewelry, and pieces of rare art.
.... d. There are some museums that try to be a little different.

C ***Pair work*** Which of these museums would you most like to visit? Why?

12 It could happen to you!

1 SNAPSHOT

Success Stories

Michael Jeffrey Jordan

Born: February 17, 1963, in Brooklyn, New York
Education: B.A. from the University of North Carolina

Accomplishments:
- Generally considered the greatest basketball player of all time
- Star of three films and author of two books

Madonna Louise Veronica Ciccone

Born: August 16, 1958, in Bay City, Michigan
Education: Two years at the University of Michigan

Accomplishments:
- One of the most successful artists in the history of pop music
- Won a Golden Globe award for her role in *Evita*

William Henry Gates III

Born: October 28, 1955, in Seattle, Washington
Education: Harvard University dropout

Accomplishments:
- At 19, founded Microsoft Corporation, the world's leading software company
- At 31, became the world's youngest billionaire

Sources: *www.biography.com; www.people.com*

What else do you know about these people?
Which is the most impressive accomplishment of each person?
Name three successful people from your country. What have they accomplished?

2 PERSPECTIVES *It happened to me!*

A Listen to what happened to these people. Check (✓) the things that have happened to you.

- ☐ "I was watching a really good movie, but I fell asleep before the end."
- ☐ "I was working at a boring job when someone offered me a much better one."
- ☐ "While I was shopping one day, a celebrity walked into the store."
- ☐ "I was traveling in another country when I met an old school friend."
- ☐ "While I was waiting in line, a TV reporter asked to interview me for the news!"
- ☐ "I was getting off a bus when I slipped and fell in some mud."
- ☐ "While I was walking down the street, I found a wallet full of money."

B Look at the statements again. Which events are lucky? Which are unlucky?

"I hate to fall asleep during a good movie. That's definitely unlucky!"

It could happen to you!

In Unit 12, students discuss personal experiences. In Cycle 1, they talk about events, accidents, and accomplishments in their lives using the past continuous and the simple past. In Cycle 2, they talk about events using the present perfect continuous.

Cycle 1, Exercises 1–6

SNAPSHOT

Learning objectives: *read three success stories; learn vocabulary for talking about accomplishments*

- Books closed. Write these questions on the board:
  True or False?
  1. Michael Jordan has written three books.
  2. Madonna was born in New York.
  3. Bill Gates dropped out of college.
- Books open. Ss skim the Snapshot to check their answers. Elicit answers from the class. (Answers: 1. F 2. F 3. T)
- Ask Ss to read the three profiles, underlining any words they don't know.
- Explain new words by giving definitions or examples (e.g., *dropout* = a student who leaves school before finishing, William Henry Gates *III* = his father and grandfather had the same name). Alternatively, tell Ss to ask their classmates for definitions or examples of any words they can't understand from context. Then Ss discuss the questions in small groups. Go around the class and give help as needed.

For another way to teach this Snapshot, try ***Jigsaw Learning*** on page T-152. In groups of three, each S reads about one person and then shares the information with the others.

- Elicit feedback from Ss about the third question. Ask Ss: "Who is it? Is this person still living? What has he or she done to become famous? What accomplishments do you admire? Do you respect the person's success?"

For more practice with this topic, play ***Twenty Questions*** on page T-145.

- ***Option:*** As a follow-up, find out if there are any common threads (e.g., *personality traits, certain types of accomplishments*) that connect people to success and fame.

PERSPECTIVES

Learning objectives: *discuss lucky and unlucky events; see the past continuous in context*

A [CD 2, Track 38]

- Books closed. Ask the class: "Have you ever met or seen a famous person?" Elicit some experiences.
- Explain the task. Ss listen to people talk about things that have happened to them. As Ss listen, they write down what each person says. Play the audio program, pausing after each speaker to give Ss time to write.
- Books open. Ss read the statements and correct their notes.
- Play the audio program again. This time, Ss read and check (✓) the things that have happened to them. Point out that it does not have to be exactly the same event, but something similar.
- In groups, ask Ss to discuss which things have happened to them. What happened? When? What did the S do? Encourage the rest of the group to ask for more information.

TIP To prevent Ss from using their first language when working in groups, explain that they must ask for "time out" when they want to use their L1. If necessary, place a limit on the number of "time outs."

B

- Explain the task and read the example sentence. Remind Ss to give additional information (e.g., *Why was it lucky or unlucky?*).
- In pairs, Ss read each sentence again and talk about whether the event was lucky or unlucky.

3 GRAMMAR FOCUS

Learning objective: *practice using the past continuous and the simple past*

[CD 2, Track 39]

- To explain the use of the past continuous, ask Ss to mime an action. Then suddenly turn off the light. Ask Ss: "What happened?" (Answer: You turned off the light.) Then ask Ss: "What were you doing when I turned off the light?" Help Ss to express their answers in the past continuous (e.g., *I was writing / typing / eating when the light was turned off.*).

TIP To explain the use of a tense, use a simple memorable action, or something visual like a time line (see below).

- Briefly explain the past continuous.

Past continuous

Point out that the past continuous is often used with the simple past. Both actions happened at the same time, but one action (the past continuous) started earlier and was in progress when the other action (the simple past) happened.

Earlier action   *Later action (interrupting the first)*

8:00   *8:15*

I was eating when the phone rang.

- Point out that *when* and *while* are often interchangeable when referring to a point or a period in time – for example:
  When / While I *was waiting* in line, it started to rain.
  It started to rain *while/when* I *was waiting* in line.
- Refer Ss to the Perspectives section. Ask them to underline the simple past phrases (e.g., *I fell asleep before the end, someone offered me a much better one*).
- Ask Ss to look at the other half of each sentence (e.g., *I was watching a movie, I was working at a boring job*). Elicit the form and explain that these are examples of the past continuous tense:
  Subject + was/were + verb + *-ing*
  I   *was*   *watching*
- Play the audio program to present the sentences in the box. Ss listen and repeat.

A

- Focus Ss' attention on the illustration and use the first item to model the task. Then Ss work individually to complete the task. Go around the class and give help as needed.
- Ss compare answers in pairs. Then elicit answers from the class.

Answers

1. My brother **was snowboarding** when he **broke** his leg in several places.
2. Several years ago, I **was having** problems with math, so I **found** a tutor to help me.
3. The couple **had** their first child when they **were living** in a tiny apartment.
4. While I **was driving** in Ireland a few years ago, I **realized** I was on the wrong side of the road!
5. Ulrike **was reading** a good book, but someone **told** her the ending.
6. While my mother **was cooking** dinner last night, the phone **rang** three times and then **stopped.**
7. Tracy and Eric **met** when they **were working** at the same restaurant in Vancouver.

For more practice with the past continuous, play ***Mime*** on page T-148. Write sentences on slips of paper and have Ss act them out for the rest of the class to guess.

B

- Point out that the past continuous is also used to say someone was in the middle of doing something at a certain time:
  My family was living in Chile this time last year.
  I was waiting for you at 8:00. Where were you?
- Explain the task and elicit sentences from the class. Write some of them on the board.
- Now Ss write sentences about themselves. Encourage them to include interesting information. Go around the class and check Ss' sentences before they begin part C.

C Pair work

- Explain the task and have two Ss model the example conversation. Then write these useful expressions on the board:
  Oh, really? That's interesting.
  Why were you/did you . . . ?
  Wow! That's incredible./Oh no! That's terrible.
- Ss take turns reading their sentences aloud in pairs. Remind them to respond and ask follow-up questions to get more information. Go around the class and write down any errors.
- Go over any errors you noticed with the whole class.

3 GRAMMAR FOCUS

Past continuous vs. simple past

Use the past continuous for an action in progress in the past.
Use the simple past for a completed action.

I **was watching** a good movie, but I **fell** asleep before the end.
I **was working** at a boring job when someone **offered** me a much better one.
While I **was shopping** one day, a celebrity **walked** into the store.

A Complete these sentences. Then compare with a partner.

1. My brother .... (snowboard) when he .... (break) his leg in several places.
2. Several years ago, I .... (have) problems with math, so I .... (find) a tutor to help me.
3. The couple .... (have) their first child when they .... (live) in a tiny apartment.
4. While I .... (drive) in Ireland a few years ago, I .... (realize) I was on the wrong side of the road!
5. Ulrike .... (read) a good book, but someone .... (tell) her the ending.
6. While my mother .... (cook) dinner last night, the phone .... (ring) three times and then .... (stop).
7. Tracy and Eric .... (meet) when they .... (work) at the same restaurant in Vancouver.

B Complete these statements with interesting information about yourself. Use the simple past or the past continuous.

1. During my childhood, . . .
2. When I was going to elementary school, . . .
3. I met my best friend while . . .
4. Two years ago, . . .
5. Last month, . . .

C ***Pair work*** Take turns reading your sentences from part B. Then ask and answer follow-up questions.

A: During my childhood, my family was living in Chile.
B: Oh, really? That's interesting. What were they doing there?
A: My father was working for a mining company.

4 LISTENING *Lucky breaks*

A Listen to these stories about lucky breaks. What were the people doing before they got their lucky breaks? What was their lucky break?

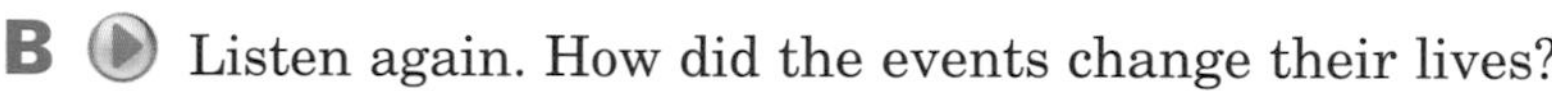

	What they were doing	Lucky break
1. Yang Zhifa	....	....
2. Gwyneth Paltrow	....	....

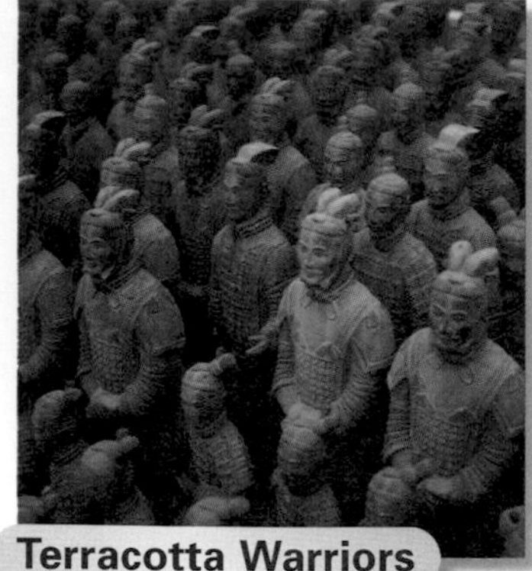

Terracotta Warriors

B Listen again. How did the events change their lives?

5 WORD POWER *Storytelling*

A Some adverbs are often used in storytelling to emphasize that something interesting is about to happen. Which of these adverbs are positive (**P**)? Which are negative (**N**)? Which are neutral (**E**)?

coincidentally	....	strangely	....
fortunately	....	suddenly	....
luckily	....	surprisingly	....
miraculously	....	unexpectedly	....
sadly	....	unfortunately	....

B ***Pair work*** Complete these statements with adverbs from part A to make up creative sentences.

I was walking down the street when, . . .
It started out as a normal day, but, . . .
We were on our way to the party when, . . .

A: I was walking down the street when, unexpectedly, it started to rain.
B: Or, I was walking down the street when, suddenly, I found twenty dollars!

6 WRITING *A short story*

A Write a short story about something that happened to you recently. Try to include some of the adverbs from Exercise 5.

I was visiting the coast last year when, unexpectedly, I got a chance to go kayaking. Fortunately, it was a perfect day and I was having a great time. The water was calm and I was beginning to feel a little tired when, suddenly, . . .

B ***Group work*** Take turns reading your stories. Answer any questions from the group.

4 LISTENING

Learning objective: *develop skills in listening for specific information and making inferences*

A **[CD 2, Track 40]**

- Explain the task and present the information in the chart. Ask Ss: "What do you know about the Terracotta Warriors in China? What do you know about Gwyneth Paltrow?"
- Play the audio program. Ss listen and complete the chart. Then elicit Ss' answers.

Audio script *(See page T-231.)*

Possible answers

1. He was looking for water/drilling a well when he hit something hard. He discovered an important archaeological site.
2. She was at a movie theater/waiting in line to buy popcorn when she noticed Steven Spielberg. He offered her a part in a movie.

B

- Play the audio program again. Ss listen and answer the question. Then Ss compare their answers.

Possible answers

Before the discovery, Yang Zhifa was an ordinary farmer. Today he sits in the museum, signs autographs, and poses for pictures.
Gwyneth Paltrow got her first movie role. This led to a career as an international actress.

For another way to teach this Listening, try ***Mixed-Up Stories*** on page T-158.

5 WORD POWER

Learning objective: *learn some useful adverbs for telling stories*

A

- Read the instructions and model the task. Ask Ss to find a word that has a positive meaning (e.g., *fortunately*) and to write *P* next to it.
- Tell Ss to look for positive adverbs first and then negative and neutral words. Ss complete the chart individually. Go around the class and give help as needed. Then go over answers.

Answers

P – fortunately, luckily, miraculously
N – sadly, unfortunately
E – coincidentally, strangely, suddenly, surprisingly, unexpectedly

B ***Pair work***

- Explain the task and model the example conversation with a S. Elicit other suggestions from the class.
- Ss form pairs and make up creative sentences. Then each pair joins another pair to share their ideas.
- ***Option:*** Have Ss use adverbs to describe a lucky break from Exercise 4.

For more practice with adverbs, play the ***Chain Game*** on page T-145. Have Ss add sentences to a story, rather than make one long sentence.

6 WRITING

Learning objective: *write a short story using adverbs and the past continuous*

A

- Remind Ss that they have read and talked about lucky breaks, accomplishments, accidents, coincidences, and funny events. Explain that now they are going to write a story about something that has happened to them.
- Ss read the example paragraph and write their own story.

B ***Group work***

- Ss exchange stories and read them aloud. Encourage Ss to ask follow-up questions and give additional information whenever possible.
- ***Option:*** Have Ss revise their stories and give them to you to check or grade.

End of Cycle 1

Do your students need more practice?

Assign . . .	***for more practice in . . .***
Workbook Exercises 1–5 on pages 67–69	Grammar, Vocabulary, Reading, and Writing
Lab Guide Exercises 1–4 on page 18	Listening, Pronunciation, Speaking, and Grammar

7 CONVERSATION

Learning objectives: *practice a conversation between people catching up on news; see the present perfect continuous in context*

A [CD 2, Track 41]

- Focus Ss' attention on the picture. Ask: "Where are they? What do they look like? Do you think this is their first meeting?" Accept any reasonable answers.
- Books closed. Ask: "Is this their first meeting? How do you know?" Play the first few lines of the audio program. Then elicit answers. (Answer: No. They know each other, but haven't seen each other in ages.)
- Write these questions on the board:
  What are Gina and Pete doing?
  How long have they been doing it?
- Play the audio program. Ss listen and answer the questions. Then elicit answers. (Answers: **Gina:** working two jobs and saving for a trip, for six months; **Pete:** spending money and modeling, since he graduated)
- Books open. Play the audio program again. Focus Ss' attention on the pronunciation of *been* (= /bɪn/). Elicit or explain any new words and expressions.

Vocabulary

in ages: for a long time
lately: recently
How come?: Why?
I'm almost out of money!: I have very little money left.

- Ask Ss to read the conversation and find examples of follow-up questions (e.g., *How come?*), additional information (e.g., *Since I graduated. But I haven't been . . .*), and reactions (e.g., *Well, that's exciting.*).
- Ss practice the Conversation in pairs.

! For another way to practice this Conversation, try ***Musical Dialog*** on page T-150.

B

- Explain the task. Play the rest of the audio program. Ss listen and answer the question. Then elicit answers from the class.

Audio script *(See page T-231.)*

Possible answer

The man has been looking for a house to buy and finally found one last month. The woman just got back from a vacation in Italy; she just got engaged to a man she met there.

8 GRAMMAR FOCUS

Learning objective: *practice using the present perfect continuous*

[CD 2, Track 42]

- Refer Ss to the previous Conversation. Ask them to find examples of statements with *have/haven't been.* Then write this chart on the board:

1	2	3	4	5
I	've	been	working	two jobs
I	've (only)	been	spending	money
I	haven't	been	getting	any work

- Elicit how the present perfect continuous is formed by asking Ss what they see in each column:
  Subject + *have/has* (not) + been + verb + *-ing* + (rest)
  Briefly explain the use of the present perfect continuous and write the following on the board. Point out the use of time expressions (e.g., *for*, *since*, *all year*, *this week*).
  1. *The present perfect continuous is used to describe an action that started in the past and continues into the present:*
     I've been working two jobs for the last six months.
  2. *The present perfect continuous can also be used without a time expression to describe an activity that started in the past but is still in progress:*
     I've been thinking about taking a trip.
- Elicit additional sentences. Then play the audio program to present the examples in the box.

A

- Explain the task and model the first item. After Ss complete the task, elicit answers.

Answers

1. A: What **have** you **been doing** lately?
   B: Well, **I've been spending** my free time at the beach.
2. A: **Have** you **been working** part time this year?
   B: Yes, I have. **I've been making** drinks at Coffee Time for the past few months.
3. A: How **have** you **been feeling** lately?
   B: Great! **I've been getting** a lot of sleep. And I **haven't been eating** as much since I started my diet.
4. A: **Have** you **been getting** enough exercise lately?
   B: No, I haven't. **I've been studying** a lot for a big exam.

B *Pair work*

- Ss work in pairs to ask the questions in part A and respond with their own information.

7 CONVERSATION What have you been doing?

A Listen and practice.

Pete: Hey, Gina! I haven't seen you in ages. What have you been doing lately?
Gina: Nothing exciting. I've been working two jobs for the last six months.
Pete: How come?
Gina: I'm saving up money for a trip to Morocco.
Pete: Well, that's exciting.
Gina: Yeah, it is. What about you?
Pete: Well, I've only been *spending* money. I'm pursuing a full-time modeling career.
Gina: Really? How long have you been modeling?
Pete: Since I graduated. But I haven't been getting any work. I need a job soon. I'm almost out of money!

B Listen to two other people at the party. What has happened since they last saw each other?

8 GRAMMAR FOCUS

Present perfect continuous

Use the present perfect continuous for actions that start in the past and continue into the present.

What **have** you **been doing** lately?	**I've been working** two jobs for the last six months.
How long **have** you **been modeling**?	**I've been modeling** since I graduated.
Have you **been saving** money?	No, I **haven't been saving** any money. I**'ve been spending** it!

A Complete the conversations with the present perfect continuous. Then practice with a partner.

1. A: What .... you .... (do) lately?
   B: Well, I .... (spend) my free time at the beach.
2. A: .... you .... (work) part time this year?
   B: Yes, I have. I .... (make) drinks at Coffee Time for the past few months.
3. A: How .... you .... (feel) recently?
   B: Great! I .... (get) a lot of sleep. And I .... (not eat) as much since I started my diet.
4. A: .... you .... (get) enough exercise lately?
   B: No, I haven't. I .... (study) a lot for a big exam.

B ***Pair work*** Take turns asking the questions in part A. Give your own information.

9 PRONUNCIATION Contrastive stress in responses

A Listen and practice. Notice how the stress changes to emphasize a contrast.

A: Has your brother been studying German?

B: No, I've been studying German.

A: Have you been teaching French?

B: No, I've been studying French.

B Mark the stress changes in these conversations. Listen and check. Then practice the conversations.

A: Have you been studying for ten years?

B: No, I've been studying for two years.

A: Have you been studying at school?

B: No, I've been studying at home.

10 SPEAKING Tell me about it.

Group work Add four questions to this list. Then take turns asking and answering the questions. Remember to ask for further information.

Have you been . . . lately?

taking driving lessons
working out
learning a new hobby
working long hours
reading any interesting books
doing anything unusual
traveling
dating anyone

useful expressions

Really? I didn't know that!
Oh, I see.
Gee, I had no idea.
Wow! Tell me more.

A: Have you been taking driving lessons lately?
B: Yes, I have. I've been going every week.
C: How have the lessons been going?
B: Great! I think I'm becoming an excellent driver.

11 INTERCHANGE 12 Life is like a game!

Play a board game. Go to Interchange 12.

9 PRONUNCIATION

Learning objective: *notice how stress is used in responses to emphasize a contrast*

A [CD 2, Track 43]

- Explain that you can change the meaning of a sentence by stressing different words. Play the audio program. Point out the extra stress on the contrasting words in the example conversations.
- Remind Ss that stress is shown in English by making a word or syllable higher, longer, and louder.
- Play the audio program again, pausing after each line for Ss to repeat. Check individual Ss' pronunciation and proper use of contrastive stress.

TIP During choral repetition, it is difficult to hear if Ss are using the correct pronunciation. It is important to interrupt the choral drill occasionally and ask individuals to try it.

B

- Ss read the example conversations in pairs. Then they mark the words that need to be stressed to show contrast.
- Play the audio program and have Ss check their answers. Ask Ss to correct any errors they made.

Answers

A: Have you been studying for ten years?
B: No, I've been studying for **two** years.
A: Have you been studying at school?
B: No, I've been studying at **home**.

- Ss practice the conversations in pairs.

For more practice with contrastive stress, play ***True or False?*** on page T-148. Ss look through the last two units and make sentences about the people and pictures. Partners use contrastive stress to correct the false statements.

10 SPEAKING

Learning objective: *talk about recent activities using the present perfect continuous tense*

Group work

- Explain the task. Point out the useful expressions box and ask Ss to add other expressions. Then write new expressions on the board for the class to use.
- Elicit suggestions for additional questions. Encourage them to use their imaginations. Write as many of the Ss' ideas as possible on the board (e.g., *How long have you been studying English? How long have you been living here? Have you been working as a . . . for a long time?*).
- Use the example conversation to model the task. Then ask Ss some of the questions in the list. Encourage Ss to ask follow-up questions and give additional information.
- Set a time limit of about ten minutes. Remind Ss to use contrastive stress when necessary.
- Ss form groups and take turns asking and answering questions. Go around the class and give help as needed.

TIP To increase Ss' talking time, re-group them and have them share their ideas with other classmates. Possible ways to re-group Ss: (a) have each group join another group, (b) have each group send one member to the next group, (c) assign a letter (a–e) to each S in a group and form new groups of all a's, all b's, etc.

- ***Option:*** For more practice, tell Ss to imagine they are going to a school reunion party. First, have Ss read the Conversation on page 81 again. Then have pairs role-play a similar conversation using their own words and information. Tell them to pretend that they haven't seen each other for over several years.

To make the role play more fun, try ***Musical Dialog*** on page T-150.

11 INTERCHANGE 12

See page T-126 for teaching notes.

12 READING

Learning objectives: *read an article about some gifted children; develop skills in skimming and reading for specific information*

- Books closed. Write the word *prodigy* on the board and ask the class if anyone can explain it. If not, tell the class: "It means a child who shows great ability at a young age." For example, Mozart was a child prodigy. Ask Ss if they know about any other child prodigies.
- Books open. Explain the pre-reading task. Then give Ss one minute to answer the questions. (Answers: an artist, Alexandra Nechita; a musician, Sarah Chang; a college graduate, Michael Kearney)

! For another way to teach this Reading, replace the pre-reading task and part A with ***Reading Race*** on page T-152. Books closed. Dictate the questions to Ss or write them on the board. Ss go around the class and answer them.

A

- Explain the task. Then Ss read the article about the three child prodigies.
- Tell Ss to use their dictionaries after they finish reading the text only if there are words they don't know or can't guess from context. Ask Ss to share any definitions they looked up with the rest of the class.

Vocabulary

praise: expression of strong admiration or approval
perform: do an artistic act for the public (music, theater, etc.)
soloist: a person who performs music alone
orchestra: a group of musicians playing different instruments together, usually classical music
record: copy sound or images onto magnetic tape
warn: tell someone about a possible danger
prove: show or demonstrate
teens: People aged between 13 and 19 years old
inks: colored liquids used for writing or drawing
watercolors: paints that can be mixed with water

- Have Ss who finish early write their answers on the board.

Answers

1. "the most wonderful, perfect violinist"
2. her father
3. Juilliard School of Music
4. that he might have learning difficulties
5. teaching and working on his Ph.D.
6. inks, watercolors, and oil paints
7. she had her first art exhibit
8. Picasso's

B *Pair work*

- Present the questions. Ss discuss them in pairs. Go around the class and give help as needed.
- ***Option:*** Student A is a journalist. Student B is one of the prodigies. Role-play an interview for a newspaper or TV program.

End of Cycle 2

Do your students need more practice?

Assign . . .	*for more practice in . . .*
Workbook Exercises 6–10 on pages 70–72	Grammar, Vocabulary, Reading, and Writing
Lab Guide Exercises 5–7 on page 18	Listening, Pronunciation, Speaking, and Grammar
Video Activity Book Unit 12	Listening, Speaking, and Cultural Awareness
CD-ROM Unit 12	Grammar, Vocabulary, Reading, Listening, and Speaking

Evaluation

Assess Ss' understanding of Units 11 and 12 with the quiz on pages T-210 and T-211.

12 READING

CHILD Prodigies

Look at the pictures and skim the article. Which child do you think is an artist? a musician? a college graduate?

Other musicians have described Sarah Chang as "the most wonderful, perfect violinist" they've ever heard. What makes this praise especially surprising is Sarah's age. She's only in her twenties, and people have been describing her this way since she was a child. On Sarah's fourth birthday, her father gave her a violin. By age 5, she was accepted at the famous Juilliard School of Music in New York City. By 8, she was performing as a violin soloist with major orchestras. Since then, Sarah has performed around the world and recorded many albums.

Before Michael Kearney was born, the doctors warned his parents that he might have learning difficulties. He's been proving them wrong ever since! By the time he was 4 months old, Michael could say full sentences like, "What's for dinner, Mom?" By 10 months, he could read words. Studying at home with his parents, Michael completed four grade levels each year. At 10, he graduated from college with honors. And at 14, he received a Master's degree. Now in his late teens, he is teaching and working on his Ph.D.

When Alexandra Nechita was 2, her parents gave her some crayons and coloring books. Alexandra was soon working in inks, watercolors, and by the time she was 7, oil paints. At 8, Alexandra had her first art exhibit. Now a young adult, Alexandra is one of the most recognized artists in the world. Her paintings are often compared to those of Picasso and other great artists. They have sold for as much as $80,000. She has been on TV many times, and several books of her paintings have been published.

A Read the article. Then answer these questions.

1. How do other musicians describe Sarah? ....
2. Who gave Sarah her first violin? ....
3. Where did Sarah go to school? ....
4. What did doctors tell Michael's parents? ....
5. What is Michael doing now? ....
6. What materials has Alexandra worked with? ....
7. What happened to Alexandra when she was 8? ....
8. Whose work has Alexandra's been compared to? ....

B ***Pair work*** Which of the three prodigies do you think is the most amazing? If you were a prodigy, what would you like to be really good at? Why?

Units 11–12 Progress check

SELF-ASSESSMENT

How well can you do these things? Check (✓) the boxes.

I can	Very well	OK	A little
Describe accomplishments using the passive with *by* (Ex. 1)	☐	☐	☐
Listen to and understand facts using the passive with and without *by* (Ex. 2)	☐	☐	☐
Describe situations using the passive without *by* (Ex. 3)	☐	☐	☐
Ask and answer questions using the past continuous and the simple past (Ex. 4, 5)	☐	☐	☐
Ask and answer questions using the past perfect continuous (Ex. 5)	☐	☐	☐

1 SPEAKING Right or wrong?

A List six novels, movies, songs, albums, or other popular works. Then write one *who* question for each thing.

The Matrix movies

Who played Neo in the Matrix movies?

B ***Pair work*** Take turns asking your questions. Use the passive with *by* to answer.

A: Who played Neo in the *Matrix* movies?
B: I think Neo was played by Keanu Reeves.

2 LISTENING Facts about Spain

A Listen to people on a game show answer questions about Spain. What are the answers? Complete the chart.

1. Currency	....	**4.** A popular sport	....
2. Bordering countries	....	**5.** Two main crops	....
3. Capital	....	**6.** Two industries	....

B Listen again. Keep score. How much money does each contestant have?

Units 11–12 Progress check

SELF-ASSESSMENT

Learning objectives: *reflect on one's learning; identify areas that need improvement*

- Ask: "What did you learn in Units 11 and 12?" Elicit Ss' answers.
- Ss complete the Self-assessment. Encourage them to be honest, and point out they will not get a bad grade if they check (✓) "a little."
- Ss move on to the Progress check exercises. You can have Ss complete them in class or for homework, using one of these techniques:
  1. Ask Ss to complete all the exercises.
  2. Ask Ss: "What do you need to practice?" Then assign exercises based on their answers.
  3. Ask Ss to choose and complete exercises based on their Self-assessment.

SPEAKING

Learning objective: *assess one's ability to describe accomplishments using the passive with* by

A

- Explain the task. Elicit some titles for the categories given and write them on the board. Then write a question using *who* (e.g., *Who played Neo in the Matrix movies? Who wrote . . . ? Who sang . . . ?*) next to each work listed on the board.
- Give Ss a few minutes to write six titles on a piece of paper. Then they should write one *who* question for each work. Remind Ss to underline titles of books, albums, and movies and to put titles of songs in quotation marks.

B *Pair work*

- Explain the task. Ask two Ss to read the example conversation. Point out that Ss must use the passive with *by* to answer the questions.
- Ss form pairs and take turns asking and answering their questions. Set a time limit of ten minutes. Go around the class and give help as needed.
- ***Option:*** Collect Ss' questions and use them as a class quiz, with Ss working in teams. Teams get one point for every correct answer. The team with the most points wins.

LISTENING

Learning objective: *assess one's ability to listen to and understand facts using the passive with and without* by

A *[CD 3, Track 1]*

- In pairs, ask Ss to discuss what they know about Spain. Don't go over answers at this point.
- Explain the task. Ss listen to a game show and complete the chart with information about Spain.
- Go over the chart. If Ss already know the information, tell them to write it on a separate piece of paper and check or correct it while they listen.
- Play the audio program. Ss complete the chart. After Ss compare notes in pairs, elicit answers from the class. Encourage Ss to use the passive to answer.

Audio script *(See page T-231–232.)*

Answers

1. the euro
2. France and Portugal
3. Madrid
4. bullfighting
5. olives and wheat
6. textiles and automobiles

B

- Explain the task. Ss listen again to find out how much money each contestant has. Remind Ss to keep score on a piece of paper.
- Play the audio program again. Then go over answers with the class.

Answers

Contestant A: $300
Contestant B: $200
Contestant C: $100

- ***Option:*** Elicit other information about Spain.

3 GAME

Learning objective: *assess one's ability to describe situations using the passive without* by

Group work

- Books closed. Model the task by demonstrating a sentence-making competition. Write this situation on the board:
  theft in a department store
- Elicit sentences from the class that explain what happened as a result of the situation. Ask a S to write them on the board (e.g., *some earrings were stolen, the police were called, a man was arrested*). If necessary, remind Ss that we use *steal* for objects and *rob* for places and people.
- Books open. Focus Ss' attention on the three situations and explain that Ss must use the passive without *by* to write as many sentences as possible for each situation.
- Ss work in small groups to write sentences for each situation. Set a time limit of ten minutes.
- Ask Ss to read the sentences they wrote for each situation. The group that wrote the most sentences wins.
- ***Option:*** Groups exchange papers and read each other's sentences to find out what they missed.

ROLE PLAY

Learning objective: *assess one's ability to ask and answer questions using the past continuous and the simple past*

- Explain the task. Student A is a suspect, or a person the police believe has stolen the painting. Student B is a police detective.
- Have Ss form pairs. Tell Student As to make up an alibi, or a story to show they were in another place at the time of the crime. They should take notes to explain what they were doing when the painting disappeared.
- While Student As write notes, go over the questions in the notebook with Student Bs. Tell them to add two questions to the notebook.
- Ss work in pairs. If possible, have them stand on either side of a desk, which will represent the police station desk. Set a time limit of about ten minutes.
- During the role play, go around the class and listen. Take note of any common errors. When time is up, suggest ways the role plays could be improved. Give examples of good communication that you heard.
- Ss change roles and try the role play again.
- ***Option:*** Find out who had the most creative alibi.

DISCUSSION

Learning objectives: *assess one's ability to ask and answer questions using the past continuous and the simple past; assess one's ability to ask and answer questions using the past perfect continuous*

A *Group work*

- Read the questions to model the correct pronunciation, intonation, and stress. Ss listen and repeat.
- Read the useful expressions in the box. Ask Ss to add other expressions.
- Model the activity by asking the class some of the questions in the list. Then ask follow-up questions and encourage Ss to give additional information.
- Ss form groups and take turns asking and answering questions. Set a time limit of about ten minutes.

B *Class activity*

- Ask Ss from each group to tell the class what they learned about their classmates.
- After each group presents their information, encourage the rest of the class to ask follow-up questions.

WHAT'S NEXT?

Learning objective: *become more involved in one's learning*

- Focus Ss' attention on the Self-assessment again. Ask: "How well can you do these things now?"
- Ask Ss to underline one thing they need to review. Ask: "What did you underline? How can you review it?"
- If needed, plan additional activities or reviews based on Ss' answers.

GAME Sentence-making competition

Group work Use the passive to write results for these situations. Then compare with the class. Which group wrote the most sentences?

Your roommate cleaned the apartment.	There was a big storm yesterday.	Someone broke into your house last night.
The dishes were done.	*The airport was closed.*	*The window was broken.*

ROLE PLAY Alibis

A famous painting has been stolen from a local museum. It disappeared sometime last Sunday afternoon between 12 P.M. and 4 P.M.

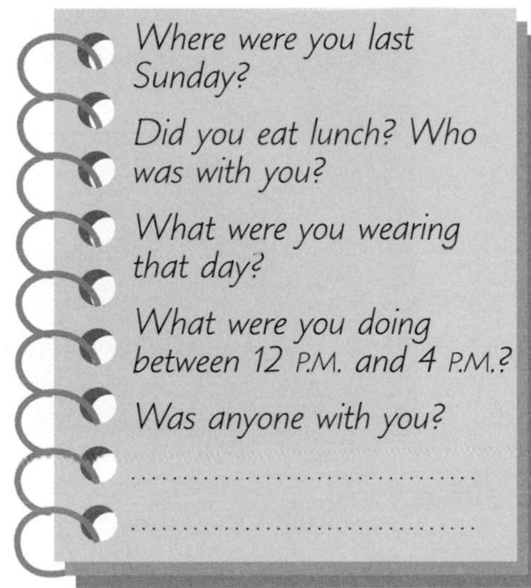

Where were you last Sunday?
Did you eat lunch? Who was with you?
What were you wearing that day?
What were you doing between 12 P.M. and 4 P.M.?
Was anyone with you?

Student A: Student B suspects you stole the painting. Make up an alibi. Take notes on what you were doing that day. Then answer Student B's questions.

Student B: You are a police detective. You think Student A stole the painting. Add two questions to the notebook. Then ask Student A the questions.

Change roles and try the role play again.

DISCUSSION Really? How interesting.

A ***Group work*** What interesting things can you find out about your classmates? Ask these questions and others of your own.

Have you been doing anything exciting recently?
Are you studying anything right now?
How long have you been studying it?
Have you met anyone interesting lately?
Who is your best friend? How did you meet?
Where were you living ten years ago? Did you like it there? What do you remember about it?

useful expressions

Really? I didn't know that!
Oh, I see.
Gee, I had no idea.
Wow! Tell me more.

B ***Class activity*** Tell the class the most interesting thing you learned.

WHAT'S NEXT?

Look at your Self-assessment again. Do you need to review anything?

13 Good book, terrible movie!

1 SNAPSHOT

Movie Mania
Successful movies in their categories:
Movie Type | Film Title
Drama | ☐ Titanic
Science Fiction | ☐ Star Wars
Horror | ☐ Jurassic Park
Fantasy | ☐ The Lord of the Rings: The Two Towers
War | ☐ Saving Private Ryan
Comedy | ☐ Home Alone
Animated | ☐ The Lion King
Action | ☐ Spider-Man

Source: *www.the-movie-times.com*

Check (✓) the movies you have seen. Did you enjoy them?
Which type of movie is your favorite? Why?
What are the three best movies you've seen in the past few years?

2 CONVERSATION *What's playing?*

A Listen and practice.

Roger: Do you want to see a movie tonight?
Carol: Hmm. Maybe. What's playing?
Roger: How about the new James Bond film? I hear it's really exciting.
Carol: Actually, the last one was boring.
Roger: What about the movie based on Stephen King's new novel?
Carol: I don't know. His books are usually fascinating, but I don't like horror movies.
Roger: Well, what do you want to see?
Carol: I'm interested in the new Halle Berry movie. It looks good.
Roger: That's fine with me. She's a wonderful actress.

Halle Berry

B Listen to the rest of the conversation. What happens next? What do they decide to do?

Good book, terrible movie!

In Unit 13, students discuss books, movies, and TV programs. In Cycle 1, they talk about books and movies using participles as adjectives. In Cycle 2, they talk more about movies and famous Hollywood names using relative clauses.

Cycle 1, Exercises 1–7

1 SNAPSHOT

Learning objective: *learn vocabulary for talking about types of movies*

- Books closed. Write the movie types from the Snapshot on the board. Ask Ss to guess the most successful English movie in each category. Elicit movie titles, but do not say whether answers are right or wrong.
- Books open. Ss read the Snapshot to check their predictions. Ask Ss if anything surprises them about this information.
- ***Option:*** Elicit other movie types (e.g., *documentaries, thrillers, musicals*).
- Ss discuss the questions in small groups. Point out that for the third question, Ss' don't have to choose an English-language movie.

For another way to practice this vocabulary, try ***Vocabulary Steps*** on page T-154. Ss rank the movie types in order from *least favorite* to *favorite*.

2 CONVERSATION

Learning objectives: *practice a conversation about movies; see participles as adjectives in context*

A [CD 3, Track 3]

- Books closed. Ask the class: "What movies are playing in theaters now? Which movies have you seen? Which are good? bad?" If possible, bring movie listings from a local newspaper or the Internet to class.

TIP To help Ss see the value of what they are doing in class, link each exercise to the next (e.g., *You talked about movies in the Snapshot. Now you're going to hear two people talking about going to see a movie.*).

- Set the scene. Two people are trying to decide what movie to see tonight. Write these questions on the board:
  1. Who is choosier? (= more difficult to please)
  2. What do they decide to see?
- Play the audio program. Then elicit Ss' answers to the questions on the board. (Answers: 1. the woman 2. the new Halle Berry movie)
- ***Option:*** Ask Ss which of the three movies they would prefer to see.
- Write this on the board:

1. exciting	*the last James Bond film*
2. boring	*the new James Bond film*
3. fascinating	*the new Halle Berry movie*
4. interesting	*Stephen King's books*

- Play the audio program again. This time, Ss listen and match the adjectives to the movies or novels.
  Then elicit answers from the class. (Answers: 1. the new James Bond film 2. the last James Bond film 3. Stephen King's books 4. the new Halle Berry movie)
- Books open. Play the audio program again. Ss listen and read silently. Ask Ss to focus on how the two people reach an agreement.
- Ss practice the conversation in pairs.
- ***Option:*** Ss role-play a similar conversation. Student A makes suggestions. Student B is a bit choosy, but finally agrees. If possible, Ss talk about current movies.

B

- Read the questions. Then play the rest of the audio program. Ss listen and take notes. After Ss compare their responses, elicit answers from the class.

Audio script *(See page T-232.)*

Possible answers

Carol calls the theater and finds out the Halle Berry movie finished playing last night. They decide to watch TV instead.

3 GRAMMAR FOCUS

Learning objective: *practice using present participles and past participles as adjectives*

[CD 3, Track 4]

Present and past participles as adjectives

- Draw a picture of a man on the board. Explain that the man is watching a boring movie on TV. Draw a TV next to the man and write *boring* inside the TV.
- Ask Ss how the man feels while watching TV. Elicit the word *bored* and write it inside the man's body.

- Draw a book on the other side of the man. Explain that now he is reading an interesting book. Write *interesting* on the book and elicit how the man feels. Write *interested* inside his body.
- Ask Ss to add five more examples of adjectives that end in *-ing* and *-ed* to the picture. In pairs, have Ss take turns making sentences.
- Refer Ss to the Grammar Focus box. Point out that the adjectives ending in *-ing* are called present participles. They are outside factors that *cause* a feeling. Past participles end in *-ed* and express the feeling or reaction.
- Play the audio program to present the sentences in the box. If necessary, play it again and have Ss listen for correct pronunciation and stress.

A

- Focus Ss' attention on the photo of Johnny Depp and elicit adjectives about him. Then read the instructions and model the first item with the class.
- Ss complete the task individually. After Ss compare their responses, elicit answers from the class.

Answers

1. Johnny Depp is a very **amazing** actor.
2. I find animated films **amusing**.
3. I'm not **interested** in science fiction movies.
4. I'm **bored** by watching television.
5. I thought *Jurassic Park* was an **exciting** book.
6. I'm **fascinated** by J.R.R. Tolkien's novels.
7. It's **surprising** that horror movies are so popular.

B *Pair work*

- Explain the task. Have Ss skim the paragraph to check for unfamiliar words. Then Ss work in pairs to complete the description. Give Ss a time limit before checking answers.

Answers

I had a terrible time at the movies. First, my ticket cost $10. I was really **shocked** by the price. By mistake, I gave the cashier a $5 bill instead of a ten. I was a little **embarrassed.** Then there was trash all over the theater. The mess was **disgusting.** The people behind me talked during the movie, which was **annoying**. The story was hard to follow. I always find thrillers too **confusing.** I liked the special effects, though. They were **amazing**!

4 WORD POWER

Learning objective: *learn and classify synonyms for common adjectives*

A

- Explain the task. Ss write similar adjectives, or synonyms, under the words in each heading. To model the task, ask Ss to find a word in the list that means the same as *awful*. When you hear a correct response, have Ss write it in the first blank under the heading *awful*.
- Ss complete the task individually, using a dictionary if necessary. Then elicit answers.

Answers

Awful	*Wonderful*	*Stupid*	*Strange*
disgusting	fabulous	absurd	bizarre
dreadful	fantastic	dumb	odd
horrible	marvelous	ridiculous	unusual
terrible	outstanding	silly	weird

- ***Option:*** Model the correct pronunciation of the words in the chart. Ss listen and repeat.

B

- Explain the task. Refer Ss to Exercise 3. Then ask Ss to suggest similar sentences using the adjectives in the Word Power.
- Ss write six sentences using adjectives from the list in part A. Go around the class and take note of any errors. When Ss finish, go over any errors you noticed by writing them on the board and having the class correct them.
- Ss compare sentences in pairs. Encourage them to agree or disagree with each other.

For more practice with this vocabulary, play ***Bingo*** on page T-147.

3 GRAMMAR FOCUS

Participles as adjectives

Present participles	Past participles
Stephen King's books are **fascinating.**	I'm **fascinated** by Stephen King's books.
The last James Bond film was **boring.**	I was **bored** by the last James Bond film.
The new Halle Berry movie sounds **interesting.**	I'm **interested** in the new Halle Berry movie.

A Complete these sentences. Then compare with a partner.

Johnny Depp

1. Johnny Depp is a very .... actor. (amaze)
2. I find animated films .... (amuse)
3. I'm not .... in science fiction movies. (interest)
4. I'm .... by watching television. (bore)
5. I thought *Jurassic Park* was an .... book. (excite)
6. I'm .... by J.R.R. Tolkien's novels. (fascinate)
7. It's .... that horror movies are so popular. (surprise)

B ***Pair work*** Complete the description below with the correct form of these words.

amaze annoy confuse disgust embarrass shock

I had a terrible time at the movies. First, my ticket cost $10. I was really .... by the price. By mistake, I gave the cashier a $5 bill instead of a ten. I was a little .... Then there was trash all over the theater. The mess was .... The people behind me talked during the movie, which was .... The story was hard to follow. I always find thrillers too .... I liked the special effects, though. They were .... !

4 WORD POWER *Opinions*

A Complete the chart with synonyms from the list.

absurd	dumb	marvelous	silly
bizarre	fabulous	odd	terrible
disgusting	fantastic	outstanding	unusual
dreadful	horrible	ridiculous	weird

Awful	Wonderful	Stupid	Strange
....	....	....	....
....	....	....	....
....	....	....	....
....	....	....	....

B Write six sentences like the ones in part A of Exercise 3 about movies, actors, or novels. Then compare with a partner.

5 LISTENING *How did you like it?*

A Listen to people talk about books and movies. Do you think each person would recommend the book or movie?

B Listen again. Check (✓) the adjective that best describes what they say about each one.

1.	2.	3.	4.
☐ fascinating	☐ wonderful	☐ boring	☐ ridiculous
☐ silly	☐ odd	☐ terrific	☐ interesting
☐ strange	☐ boring	☐ dreadful	☐ exciting

6 PRONUNCIATION *Emphatic stress*

A Listen and practice. Notice how stress and a higher pitch are used to express strong opinions.

That's fascinating! He was amazing! Oh, that's terrible!

B ***Pair work*** Write four statements using these words. Then take turns reading them. Pay attention to emphatic stress.

dreadful fantastic horrible ridiculous

7 DISCUSSION *Let's go to the movies!*

A ***Pair work*** Take turns asking and answering these questions and others of your own.

What kinds of movies are you interested in? Why?
What kinds of movies do you find boring?
Who are your favorite actors and actresses? Why?
Are there actors or actresses you don't like?
What's the worst movie you have ever seen?
What are your three favorite movies in English? Why?
Are there any outstanding movies playing now?

A: What kinds of movies are you interested in?
B: I love action movies.
A: Really? Why is that?
B: They're exciting! What about you?
A: I think action movies are kind of silly. I prefer . . .

Now Showing
on Video and DVD
COMEDIES
THRILLERS
DRAMA
MYSTERIES
SCIENCE FICTION
CLASSICS
DOCUMENTARIES
ANIMATION

B ***Group work*** Compare your information. Whose taste in movies is most like yours?

5 LISTENING

Learning objective: *develop skills in making inferences*

A ▶ ***[CD 3, Track 5]***

- Explain the situation. Ss will hear people give opinions about books and movies. Then Ss decide whether or not each person would recommend the book or movie.
- Play the audio program. Ss listen and take notes. Then elicit answers from the class.

Audio script *(See page T-232.)*

Answers

1. yes 2. no 3. yes 4. no

- ***Option:*** Play the audio program again. This time, pause after each conversation and ask Ss to tell you what the speaker is describing (e.g., *a novel*).

B ▶

- Explain the task. Ss look over the adjectives listed and check (✓) the best adjective for each situation.
- Play the audio program again. Then elicit answers.

Answers

1. fascinating 2. boring 3. terrific 4. ridiculous

6 PRONUNCIATION

Learning objective: *notice how emphatic stress is used to express an opinion*

A ▶ ***[CD 3, Track 6]***

- Explain that in English words with more than one syllable, one syllable has the primary, or main, stress. Stress can be used to express strong opinions. Remind Ss that stress is shown by making the syllable higher, longer, and louder.
- Play the audio program. Ss listen and pay attention to the stress and pitch.
- Play the audio program again and have Ss repeat. Encourage them to exaggerate to show emotion.

B *Pair work*

- Explain the task. Ask Ss to write four sentences about movies. To show more emphatic stress, have Ss write two sentences about movies they hate and two about movies they love.
- Ss form pairs and take turns reading their sentences. Remind them to use stress and pitch to express their opinions.

> ***TIP*** To give Ss more practice with a pronunciation feature, ask them to practice or listen to other exercises (e.g., *Conversation, Grammar Focus, Listening*) again.

DISCUSSION

Learning objective: *discuss movies using participles as adjectives*

A *Pair work*

- Books closed. Ask Ss to brainstorm questions about movies. Then write some of them on the board:
  What's your favorite . . . (musical/comedy/drama)?
  How many movies do you watch every month?
  Do you usually rent movies or go to the theater?
- Books open. Ask Ss to read the list of questions and the example conversation. Encourage them to extend it as much as possible.

! For another way to practice this exercise, try ***Look Up and Speak!*** on page T-150.

- Books closed. Ss form pairs and practice asking and answering their questions. Encourage them to ask follow-up questions and add emphatic stress. Set a time of about ten minutes. Go around the class and give help as needed.

! For more speaking practice, try the ***Onion Ring*** technique on page T-151. Ss ask and answer questions about movies until you say, "Change!"

B *Group work*

- Each pair joins another pair. Ss compare their responses and decide who has a similar taste in movies.
- ***Option:*** Ask Ss to share this information with the class.

End of Cycle 1

Do your students need more practice?

Assign . . .	***for more practice in . . .***
Workbook Exercises 1–4 on pages 73–74	Grammar, Vocabulary, Reading, and Writing
Lab Guide Exercises 1–4 on page 19	Listening, Pronunciation, Speaking, and Grammar

8 PERSPECTIVES

***Learning objectives:** listen to people describe their Hollywood favorites; see relative clauses in context*

A ▶ *[CD 3, Track 7]*

- Books closed. Set the scene. Ss will hear three people talk about their favorite movies or actors.
- Play the audio program. Ss listen and guess what movie or actor each person is describing.

B ▶

- Play the second part of the audio program. Ss listen and check their answers.

Audio script *(See page T-232.)*

Answers

1. *Titanic* 2. Tom Hanks 3. *Home Alone*

- ***Option:*** Ask Ss if they are familiar with the movies and actor. What do they think of them?
- Books open. Play the audio program again while Ss listen and read silently. Elicit or explain any new vocabulary.

Vocabulary

iceberg: a large piece of frozen water in the ocean
sink: fall to the bottom of the ocean
in a row: consecutively; one after the other
burglar: a person who steals things from your home

GRAMMAR FOCUS

***Learning objective:** practice using relative clauses*

▶ *[CD 3, Track 8]*

Relative clauses

- Books closed. Read these sentences: "It's about an ocean liner which sinks. It's a movie that stars Kate Winslet. He's the actor who won two Academy Awards. It's about a boy that gets left behind."
- Point out that these sentences contain two clauses each: a main clause and a relative clause. Write this example on the board:
  Main clause — *Relative clause*
  He's the actor — *who won two Academy Awards.*
- Ask Ss to identify the two clauses in the other sentences. Then elicit or explain that:
  1. A relative clause joins two sentences together.
  2. A relative clause gives information about something in the main clause.

Relative pronouns: who/which/that

- Point out that the pronouns *who*, *which*, and *that* can be used to join two clauses together.
- Start with the relative pronoun *who*. Ask Ss to identify a sentence from the Perspectives section containing *who*.
- Ask Ss if the noun before *who* is a person or a thing. (Answer: person)
- Repeat these steps for *which* and *that*.
- Write these rules on the board:
  1. who is used to join clauses about people
  2. which is used to join clauses about things
  3. that is used to join clauses about people or things
- Play the audio program to present the sentences in the box.

A

- Ask Ss to look over the example conversations. Elicit or explain any new vocabulary (e.g., *hard to put down* = difficult to stop reading). Ss complete the task. Then check answers.

Answers

1. He's a movie director **who/that** made the film *Hulk.*
2. Yes, it's an action movie **which/that** stars Johnny Depp.
3. It's a musical about a girl **who/that** becomes a celebrity.
4. Yes! It was a great book **which/that** was hard to put down.

- Ss practice the conversations in pairs.

B *Pair work*

- Explain the task. Use the first item to model a completed sentence. Ss complete the task in pairs and then share their sentences with the class.

C *Group work*

- Explain the task. In groups, Ss discuss people and things they don't like. Go around the class and give help as needed.
- ***Option:*** Ss write paragraphs like the ones in the Perspectives section. Then, Ss read the paragraphs aloud and guess what or who is being described.

10 INTERCHANGE 13

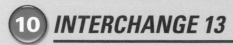

See page T-127 for teaching notes.

8 PERSPECTIVES *It's about . . .*

A Listen to these people talk about some of their Hollywood favorites. Can you guess what movie or actor each person is describing?

"I can't believe I saw it nine times! It's a movie that stars Kate Winslet. It's about an ocean liner which hits an iceberg and sinks."

"He's the actor who won an Academy Award two years in a row. He got the first Oscar for *Philadelphia*, and then he won again the very next year for *Forrest Gump*."

"I love this movie! It's a comedy about a boy that gets left behind when his family goes on vacation. And there are some burglars who try to break into the house. It's hilarious!"

B Now listen and check your answers.

9 GRAMMAR FOCUS

Relative clauses

Use **who** *or* **that** *for people.*

He's an actor. He won two Oscars.
He's an actor **who/that** won two Oscars.

Use **which** *or* **that** *for things.*

It's a movie. It stars Kate Winslet.
It's a movie **which/that** stars Kate Winslet.

A Rewrite B's answers using relative clauses. Then practice with a partner.

1. A: Who is Ang Lee?
   B: He's a movie director. He made the film *Hulk*.
2. A: Have you heard of *Pirates of the Caribbean*?
   B: Yes, it's an action movie. It stars Johnny Depp.
3. A: What's *Chicago*?
   B: It's a musical about a girl. She becomes a celebrity.
4. A: Did you enjoy John Grisham's latest novel?
   B: Yes! It was a great book. It was hard to put down.

B ***Pair work*** Complete these sentences with relative clauses. Then compare your information around the class.

1. Brad Pitt is an actor . . .
2. *Gladiator* is a movie . . .
3. Sting is a musician . . .
4. *The Simpsons* is a TV show . . .

C ***Group work*** Choose an actor, movie, musician, or TV show you *don't* like. Others agree or disagree.

10 INTERCHANGE 13 *Famous faces*

What do you know about movies and TV shows? Go to Interchange 13.

11 SPEAKING Scriptwriters

A ***Group work*** You are scriptwriters for a television studio. You have to write a new script for a TV detective show or mystery. Plan an interesting story. Make brief notes.

Where does the story take place?
Who are the main characters?
What are the main events?
How does the story end?

B ***Class activity*** Tell the class about your story.

"Our story is about two secret agents who are chasing after an alien from another planet. There are two main characters. . . . "

12 LISTENING A night at the movies

A Listen to two critics talk about a new movie. What do they like or not like about it? Rate each item in the chart from 1 to 3.

	Acting	Story	Photography	Special effects
Pauline	....	....	....	....
Colin	....	....	....	....

Ratings
1 = didn't like it
2 = OK
3 = liked it very much

B Look at the chart in part A. Guess how many stars each critic gave the movie. Then listen to the critics give their ratings.

★ poor ★★ fair ★★★ very good ★★★★ excellent

13 WRITING A movie review

A ***Pair work*** Choose a movie you both have seen recently and discuss it. Then write a review of it.

What was the movie about?
What did you like about it?
What did you *not* like about it?
How was the acting?
How would you rate it?

B ***Class activity*** Read your review to the class. Who else has seen the movie? Do they agree with your review?

We recently saw the movie *Chocolat*. It's a comedy about a mysterious woman who moves to a small French village. She opens up a shop that sells delicious chocolates. The acting is very good. The town mayor is an especially funny character who . . .

11 SPEAKING

Learning objective: *talk about ideas for a TV show using relative clauses*

A *Group work*

- Explain the task. Focus Ss' attention on the illustration and example in part B. Encourage Ss to be creative and use details to make their stories more exciting. Whenever possible, Ss should try to use relative clauses and adjectives.

For another way to teach this exercise, try ***Scriptwriters*** on page T-159.

- Read the questions that groups should use during the activity. Elicit suggestions for other questions and write them on the board.
- Ss form groups and write the main points of the story.

B *Class activity*

- Groups take turns telling their stories to the class. Encourage all members of the group to add details. Other classmates ask follow-up questions.

> **TIP** Instead of groups telling the class, ask each group to send a "messenger" to the next group and ask him or her to tell the story. Alternatively, ask Ss to form new groups.

- ***Option:*** Elicit ways to continue the example story.

12 LISTENING

Learning objective: *develop skills in listening for specific information and making inferences*

A *[CD 3, Track 9]*

- As a class, brainstorm aspects of a movie that critics sometimes discuss (e.g., *acting*, *story*, *costumes*, *music*).
- Write these expressions on the board and elicit the meanings:
  1. A standard story . . . the same old stuff.
  2. He was a totally believable character.
  3. The special effects were a weakness.
  4. Everything looked fake, not real.
- Ask Ss to decide if each expression means that the speaker liked the movie, didn't like it, or thought it was OK. (Answers: 1. OK 2. liked it 3. didn't like it 4. didn't like it)
- Explain the situation and the task. Make sure that Ss understand the rating system and words in the chart.
- Play the audio program. Ss listen and complete the chart. Ask Ss to compare answers in groups. If there are disagreements, go over those answers with the class.

Audio script *(See page T-232.)*

Answers

	Acting	*Story*	*Photography*	*Special effects*
Pauline	3	2	1	1
Colin	3	3	3	3

> **TIP** To avoid turning this into a "memory test," play the audio program a second time, segment by segment.

- ***Option:*** Play the audio program again. Ask Ss to take notes on what the critics did or didn't like about the movie and why. Then have Ss compare their notes in small groups.

B

- Explain the task. Ss guess based on the information in part A. Elicit Ss' answers, but don't tell the correct answers yet.
- Play the second part of the audio program. Ss listen and check their guesses. Elicit answers.

Audio script *(See page T-233.)*

Answers

Pauline: 2 stars Colin: 4 stars

13 WRITING

Learning objective: *write a movie review using relative clauses*

A *Pair work*

- Explain the task and go over the questions. Try to pair up Ss who have recently seen the same movie.
- Ss use the questions to discuss the movie in detail.

For another way to teach organization skills, try ***Mind Mapping*** on page T-154.

- Ss use their notes to write a movie review. Remind Ss to practice the language they learned in this unit.

B *Class activity*

- Ss take turns reading their reviews to the class. Others who have seen the movie should say whether or not they agree.

14 READING

Learning objectives: *read an about Harry Potter's creator; develop skills in understanding sequence and text organization*

For a new way to practice making predictions, try ***Cloud Prediction*** on page T-154. Draw this cloud on the board and write the following words and phrases inside:

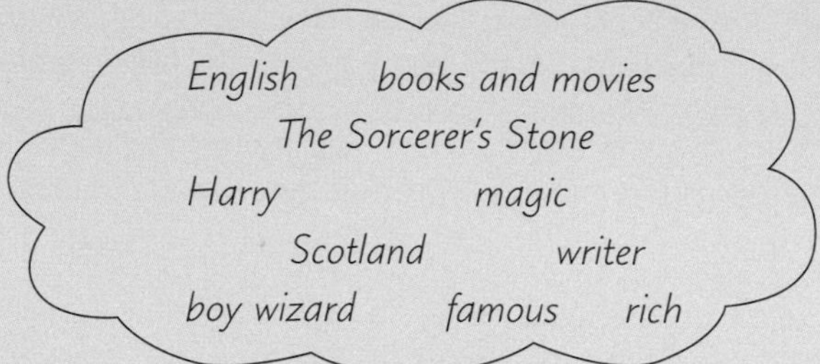

English
books and movies
The Sorcerer's Stone
Harry
magic
Scotland
writer
boy wizard
famous
rich

Ask Ss what they think the Reading is about. (Answer: J.K. Rowling, author of the Harry Potter novels)

- Go over the pre-reading question with Ss. Ask: "What kinds of words will you look for?" Elicit answers. (Answers: place names, words with capital letters) Then give them one minute to find the answer. Check the answer with the class. (Answer: on a train trip to London)
- Ss read the article individually, underlining any words they don't understand. Tell them to choose *three* of these words to check in a dictionary. If they want to know any other words, they should wait until after they finish part A. This will help them focus on main ideas and general understanding, rather than on individual words.

A

- Explain the task. Elicit the first event, then tell Ss to write the number *1* next to that sentence.
- Ss complete the task individually or in pairs. Then go over answers with the class.
- ***Option:*** Write each sentence from part A on a large card. Ask ten Ss to come to the front of the class, take a card, and line up in the correct order. Others check to see if they agree.

Answers

a. 8 c. 3 e. 6 g. 7 i. 9
b. 2 d. 10 f. 5 h. 1 j. 4

- Elicit or explain any new vocabulary.

Vocabulary

witchcraft, wizardry: using magic to make things happen (a **witch** is a female magical person; a **wizard** is a male magical person)
phenomenon: something special because it is very different or unusual
make up: invent; create
cast: the characters in a book or movie
battle: fight; combat
darkness: evil
unexpected: surprising

B

- Explain the task. The sentences were taken from the text. Ss need to identify the paragraphs they were taken from. Model sentence A with the class as an example. Ask Ss how they found the answer. (Answer: The sentence refers to school, so it must come from paragraph 2.)
- Ss complete the task individually. Go around and give help as needed.
- Ss discuss their answers in pairs. Then go over answers with the class.

Answers

a. paragraph 2 d. paragraph 6
b. paragraph 1 e. paragraph 3
c. paragraph 5 f. paragraph 4

C *Pair work*

- Ss discuss the questions in pairs. Then ask them to share some of the ideas they discussed with the rest of the class.
- ***Option:*** Divide the class into two groups, interviewers and authors. Interviewers write questions and authors answer based on J.K. Rowling's life and books. Ss role-play in pairs. Tell authors to make up answers they don't know.

End of Cycle 2

Do your students need more practice?

Assign . . .	*for more practice in . . .*
Workbook Exercises 5–10 on pages 75–78	Grammar, Vocabulary, Reading, and Writing
Lab Guide Exercises 5–7 on page 19	Listening, Pronunciation, Speaking, and Grammar
Video Activity Book Unit 13	Listening, Speaking, and Cultural Awareness
CD-ROM Unit 13	Grammar, Vocabulary, Reading, Listening, and Speaking

TIP To raise Ss' awareness of their progress, occasionally discuss with the class how they feel they are progressing. Ask them what kinds of problems they face and how they learn best. Then suggest ideas or solutions. Encourage Ss to share their ideas.

14 READING

The Magic of Potter

Scan the article. Where was author J.K. Rowling when she got the idea for Harry Potter?

1 There was a time when no one knew the name Harry Potter. Now the adventures of this extraordinary student at Hogwarts School of Witchcraft and Wizardry are read in over 45 languages, including Russian, Thai, and even ancient Greek. No one can explain the Harry Potter phenomenon – not even J.K. Rowling, his creator.

2 J.K. Rowling was born in England in 1965. From a young age, she knew she wanted to be a writer. When she was 6, she wrote her first story – about a rabbit that gets sick. At school, she used to make up stories to tell her friends.

3 After graduating from college, she worked as a secretary. But she didn't give up her dream. She spent her lunch hour writing stories, mainly for adults. Then in 1990, on a train trip to London, she got the idea for the boy wizard. She says he just appeared in her head. She soon created a whole cast of unique characters to help Harry battle the forces of darkness.

4 She kept working on the story while she was teaching English in Portugal, where she married, had her first child, and divorced a year later. When she returned to England, she brought back a suitcase of Harry Potter stories.

5 After returning home, she was broke and living in a small, cramped apartment. She continued writing, and in 1995, finished the first book in the series, *Harry Potter and the Sorcerer's Stone.* It was published in 1997 and became an unexpected bestseller.

6 Rowling's life has changed dramatically. She has become internationally famous and now earns around $40 million a year. She remarried, had a second child, and currently lives in Scotland.

A Read the article. Then number these sentences from 1 (first event) to 10 (last event).

.... a. She completed her first book.
.... b. She finished school.
.... c. She worked as a secretary.
.... d. Her second child was born.
.... e. She got married for the first time.
.... f. She moved to Portugal.
.... g. She had no money.
.... h. She made up her first story.
.... i. The first Harry Potter book was published.
.... j. She got the idea for Harry Potter.

B Where do these sentences belong? Write the number of the paragraph where each sentence could go.

.... a. She hated going to school, but always loved to read.
.... b. When asked about this popularity, she has said, "I really wrote it for myself."
.... c. There were times when she couldn't even afford to eat.
.... d. Despite her fame and fortune, she's been able to keep her private life.
.... e. She didn't have a pen or paper with her, so she had to memorize it.
.... f. It was filled with ten versions of the first chapter of the book!

C ***Pair work*** Have you ever read a Harry Potter book? What else do you know about this famous character?

14 So that's what it means!

1 SNAPSHOT

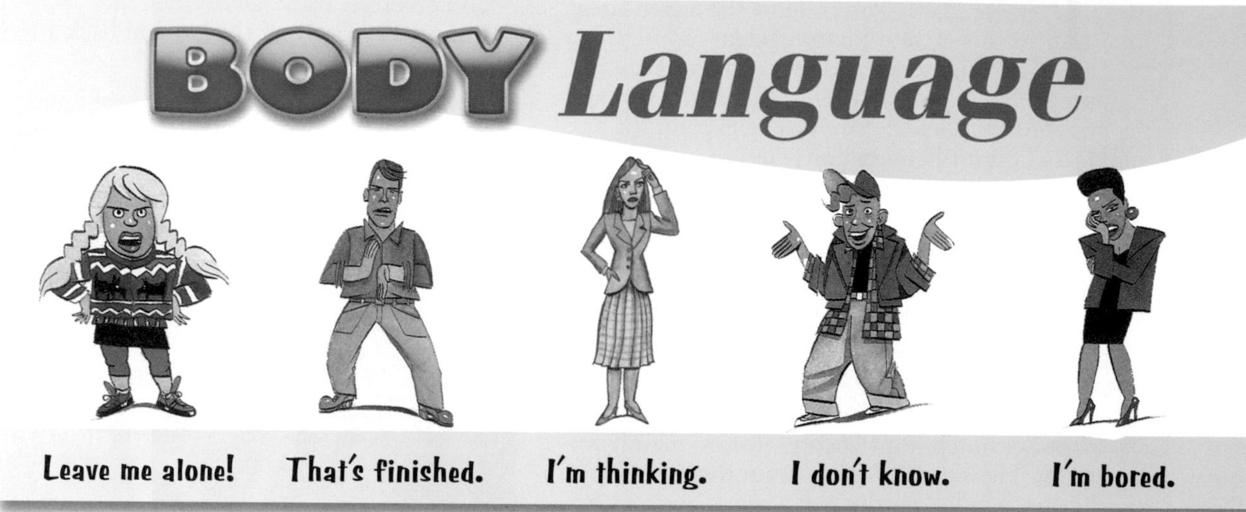

BODY Language
Leave me alone!
That's finished.
I'm thinking.
I don't know.
I'm bored.

Source: *Bodytalk*

Do people in your country use these gestures? Do you?
What other gestures can you use to communicate these meanings?
What are three other gestures you sometimes use? What do they mean?

2 WORD POWER Feelings and gestures

A What is this man doing in each picture? Match each expression with a picture. Then compare with a partner.

1. He's biting his nails. ....
2. He's rolling his eyes. ....
3. He's scratching his head. ....
4. He's tapping his foot. ....
5. He's twirling his hair. ....
6. He's wrinkling his nose. ....

a b c

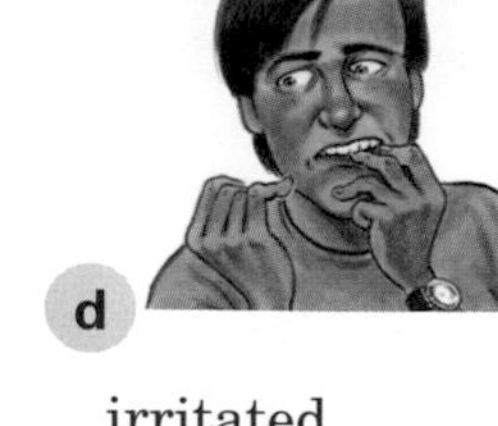

d e

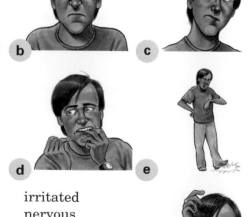

B *Group work* Use the pictures in part A and these adjectives to describe how the man is feeling.

annoyed	confused	embarrassed	frustrated	irritated
bored	disgusted	exhausted	impatient	nervous

"In the first picture, he's twirling his hair. He looks nervous."

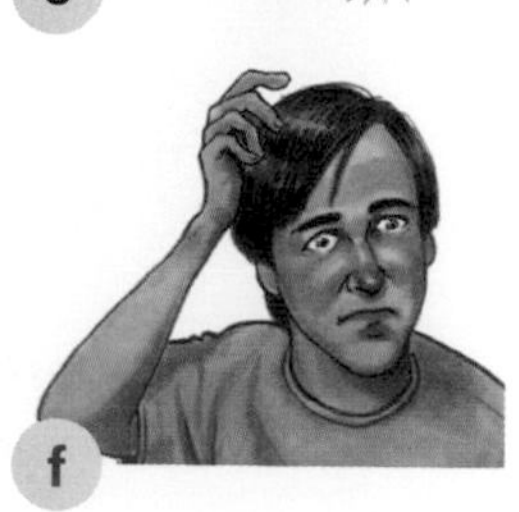

f

So that's what it means!

In Unit 14, students discuss communication, including such topics as body language, gestures, and international signs. In Cycle 1, they explain gestures using modals and adverbs. In Cycle 2, they talk about signs using terms of permission, obligation, and prohibition.

Cycle 1, Exercises 1–7

SNAPSHOT

Learning objective: *talk about gestures and body language*

- Books closed. Demonstrate one or two common gestures to see if the class can guess their meanings (e.g., *making a phone call*, *drinking*, *eating*). Avoid using the gestures presented on pages 92–94, as Ss will be asked to figure those out while doing various tasks.
- Books open. Ss look at the pictures and read the information in the Snapshot.
- ***Option:*** Just for fun, ask a few Ss to mime the gestures in the Snapshot.
- Read the questions. Ss work in pairs or groups to discuss them. Go around the class and give help as needed. Then ask Ss to share their ideas.

WORD POWER

Learning objective: *learn vocabulary for describing feelings and gestures*

A

- Explain the task. Then model one example by asking Ss what the man is doing in the first picture. (Answer: He's twirling his hair.) Tell Ss to write the letter *a* next to number 5.
- Ss complete the task individually, without using their dictionaries. Remind Ss to look for clues (e.g., *hair*, *foot*) to help them find the answers. Go around the class and give help as needed. Then elicit Ss' answers.

Answers

1. d 2. c 3. f 4. e 5. a 6. b

- Model the pronunciation of each expression. Ss listen and repeat.
- ***Option:*** Ask Ss if they ever bite their nails, roll their eyes, twirl their hair, etc. Find out which are the most common gestures in the class.

For more practice with this vocabulary, play ***Mime*** on page T-148.

B *Group work*

- Explain the task. Ss look at the pictures in part A and describe how the man is feeling.
- Have Ss look at the adjectives and help with any new vocabulary. Model the pronunciation of each word. Point out that if the sound /t/ or /d/ appears before *-ed*, Ss should add an extra syllable (e.g., *disgusted* and *exhausted* have three syllables, while *annoyed* and *confused* have two syllables).

TIP To show the number of syllables in a word, use your fingers (one for each syllable). If you hear a S make a mistake, like em-bar-ras-sed, indicate where the error lies by pointing to your fourth finger silently.

- To model the task, read the example sentence. Ask: "In the first picture, how do you think the man feels?" Elicit suggestions (e.g., *frustrated*, *annoyed*).
- Ss discuss each picture in small groups. Tell Ss that there may be more than one answer. Go around the class and give help as needed. Then elicit Ss' answers.
- ***Option:*** Encourage Ss to explain to the class any gestures that represent different feelings in other cultures.

Possible answers

a. bored, frustrated, irritated, nervous
b. disgusted
c. annoyed, frustrated, irritated
d. impatient, nervous
e. impatient, nervous
f. bored, confused

For more practice with this vocabulary, play ***Bingo*** on page T-147.

3 CONVERSATION

Learning objectives: *practice a conversation about body language; see modals and adverbs in context*

A [CD 3, Track 10]

- Focus Ss' attention on the illustration. Ask: "Where are they? What is the man from India doing? How is the other man reacting?" Elicit ideas.
- Books closed. Play the audio program and have Ss listen to check their answers. (Answers: They are at a school/university. The Indian man is moving his head from side to side. The other man is confused.)
- Write this on the board:
  Three people guess what Raj means. Which guess is correct?
  1. Maybe it means that Raj doesn't understand.
  2. It might mean that Raj doesn't agree.
  3. It could mean that Raj agrees.
- Play the audio program again. Ss listen to check their answer. Then ask Ss which guess is correct. (Answer: 3. It could mean that Raj agrees.)
- Books open. Play the audio program again, pausing after each line so the class can repeat. Elicit or answer any questions about vocabulary.

Vocabulary

noticed: saw
actually: in fact

- Ss practice the conversation in groups of three.
- ***Option:*** Challenge groups to substitute a different gesture and to use their own information when trying the conversation again.

B

- Read the question aloud. Then play the second part of the audio program. Ss listen and take notes.

Audio script *(See page T-233.)*

- Elicit answers from the class.

Possible answer

Raj finds the way people end a conversation unusual. For example, they'll say things like, "Hey, let's get together soon." He thought it was an invitation, but it's just a way of saying good-bye.

GRAMMAR FOCUS

Learning objective: *practice using modals and adverbs to talk about meaning*

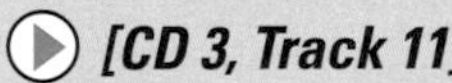

[CD 3, Track 11]

Modals and adverbs

- Draw this on the board:

Slight possibility

MODALS	↑	*ADVERBS*
It might/may mean		*Maybe/Perhaps it means*
It could mean		*It possibly/probably means*
It must mean	↓	*It definitely means*

Strong possibility

- Explain that when we are not sure about the meaning, we use modals of possibility (*might, may, could*) or adverbs (*maybe, perhaps, possibly, probably*). When we are sure about the meaning, we use the modal *must* or the adverb *definitely*.
- Ask: "Do modals use the base form of the verb or the infinitive?" Elicit the answer. (Answer: the base form)
- Explain that *maybe* and *perhaps* go at the beginning of the sentence. Elicit where *possibly, probably,* and *definitely* go in a sentence. (Answer: after the subject)
- Play the audio program to present the sentences in the box. Elicit additional examples from the class.

Pair work

- Explain the task. Ss look at the pictures and then match each gesture with a possible meaning in the box. Use the first gesture as a model.
- Ss work individually to write a sentence describing each gesture. Go around the class and give help as needed.
- When Ss finish, model the example conversation with a S. Then Ss work in pairs to compare their sentences.
- Find out which gestures Ss didn't agree on. Elicit other pairs' responses to check answers.

Answers

1. That sounds crazy!	4. Peace.
2. Come here.	5. Good luck!
3. Be quiet.	6. I can't hear you.

- ***Option:*** Ask Ss to rephrase their sentences. For example, if they used a modal, they should change it to an adverb.

3 CONVERSATION Have you met Raj?

A Listen and practice.

Ron: Have you met Raj, the student from India?
Emily: No, I haven't.
Ron: Well, he seems really nice, but there's one thing I noticed. He moves his head from side to side when you talk to him. You know, like this.
Emily: Maybe it means he doesn't understand you.
Ron: No, I don't think so.
Emily: Or it could mean he doesn't agree with you.
Peter: Actually, people from India sometimes move their heads from side to side when they agree with you.
Ron: Oh, so that's what it means!

B Now listen to Raj talk to his friend. What does he find unusual about the way people in North America communicate?

4 GRAMMAR FOCUS

Modals and adverbs

Modals	*Adverbs*
It **might/may** mean he doesn't understand you.	**Maybe/Perhaps** it means he doesn't understand you.
It **could** mean he doesn't agree with you.	It **possibly/probably** means he doesn't agree with you.
That **must** mean he agrees with you.	That **definitely** means he agrees with you.

Pair work What do these gestures mean? Take turns making statements about each gesture using the meanings in the box.

possible meanings
Good luck!
Be quiet.
Peace.
That sounds crazy!
I can't hear you.
Come here.

A: What do you think the first gesture means?
B: It probably means . . . , or it might mean . . .

5 SPEAKING What does it mean?

A Imagine you are in a foreign country and you don't speak the language. Think of gestures to communicate these meanings.

Go away.	I don't understand.
Help!	It's delicious.
Please repeat.	How much does this cost?
I'm lost.	Someone stole my wallet.
I'm hungry.	Where's the bathroom?

B ***Pair work*** Take turns acting out your gestures. Can your partner guess what you are trying to say?

C ***Group work*** What else could your gestures mean? For each gesture you acted out in part B, think of one more possible meaning.

A: This probably means "go away," but it might also mean you don't like something.
B: It could also mean . . .

6 PRONUNCIATION Pitch

A Listen and practice. Notice how pitch is used to express certainty or doubt.

	Resolved	*Unresolved*
A: Do you think her gesture means "go away"?	B: Definitely.	B: Probably.
A: Do you understand what her gesture means?	B: Absolutely.	B: Maybe.

B ***Pair work*** Take turns asking yes/no questions. Respond by using *absolutely*, *definitely*, *maybe*, *probably*, and your own information. Pay attention to pitch.

7 INTERCHANGE 14 What's going on?

Interpret people's body language. Go to Interchange 14.

5 SPEAKING

Learning objective: *talk about gestures using modals and adverbs*

A

- Focus Ss' attention on the picture and elicit ideas. Ask: "Where are they? What are they doing?" (Answers: in class, playing charades)
- Explain the situation. Use the first expression to model the task. Then ask a S to act it out in a different way. Remind Ss that they must communicate without words, i.e., by using only gestures or facial expressions.
- Ss work individually to think of a gesture for each expression.

B *Pair work*

- Ask a S to act out an expression. Then model how to make guesses about meaning. The S who is acting cannot speak, but can mime to indicate whether a guess is right, wrong, or close.
- Ss take turns acting out gestures in pairs. When guessing, remind Ss to use complete sentences with modals or adverbs.

> **TIP** By closely observing Ss during the Speaking activity, you can decide if further grammar practice or clarification is needed.

C *Group work*

- Ss form groups and take turns acting out the gestures they used in part B. For each gesture, Ss discuss what else the gesture could mean.
- ***Option:*** Follow up the activity with a class discussion. Ask: "How do gestures differ from culture to culture? Have you ever been in a foreign country and didn't speak the language? What was it like?"

6 PRONUNCIATION

Learning objective: *notice the use of pitch to express certainty or doubt*

A *[CD 3, Track 12]*

Resolved

Point out that we can show certainty in three ways – by saying something higher, longer, or louder:

1. We can raise our voice and say the main syllables at a higher pitch and end with a falling pitch.
2. We can make the stressed syllable last longer.
3. We can say the main syllables of each word more loudly.

- Have Ss practice saying *definitely* and *absolutely* using a high pitch. Listen carefully. Do the Ss sound certain when they say *definitely* and *absolutely*?

Unresolved

- Now explain that we express doubt or uncertainty in two ways:
  1. We do not release the start of the word quickly, i.e., lengthening the sound of the first syllable.
  2. We raise the pitch of the last syllable, as if asking a question.
- Have Ss practice saying *probably* and *maybe*.
- Play the audio program. Ss listen and practice.
- Play the audio program again. After Ss practice together, ask individual Ss to demonstrate for the class.

> **TIP** To make pronunciation practice more fun, involve Ss' senses. Have them exaggerate sounds (for word stress), stand up and sit down (for intonation), and blur syllables (for unreleased sounds). Above all, encourage Ss to have fun!

B *Pair work*

- Explain the task and elicit some examples of yes/no questions. Focus Ss' attention on illustrations in the unit and ask: "Is she angry? Do you think he's nervous?"
- Ss take turns asking and answering questions using the correct pitch and stress. Then ask a few Ss to demonstrate for the class.

7 INTERCHANGE 14

See page T-128 for teaching notes.

End of Cycle 1

Do your students need more practice?

Assign . . .	*For more practice in . . .*
Workbook Exercises 1–4 on pages 79–81	Grammar, Vocabulary, Reading, and Writing
Lab Guide Exercises 1–4 on page 20	Listening, Pronunciation, Speaking, and Grammar

Cycle 2, Exercises 8–13

8 PERSPECTIVES

***Learning objectives:** discuss international signs; see terms of permission, obligation, and prohibition in context*

A *[CD 3, Track 13]*

- Explain that Ss will talk about international signs. Draw a recognizable sign on the board and ask Ss what it means. Elicit other common signs from Ss.
- Ask Ss to cover the sentences and look only at the pictures. In pairs, Ss guess what each sign means. During the task, help Ss with any new vocabulary.
- Explain the task. As you play the audio program, Ss listen and point to the sign they hear. Play the first sentence to make sure Ss understand the instructions. Then play the rest of the audio program without stopping. Ss listen and point.
- Have Ss read the descriptions a–h. Then play the audio program again. This time, Ss write the correct letter under the picture. Go over answers with the class.

Answers

d, a, g, e, h, c, b, f

B *Pair work*

- Explain the task and elicit suggestions for the first sign. Ss complete the task in pairs. Remind them to give two suggestions for each sign.

Possible answers

a. on a beach, at a campsite
b. in a museum, in an art gallery
c. on an airplane, in a taxi
d. on an aluminum can, on a plastic bottle
e. at a construction site, in a factory
f. in a hotel room, at a campsite
g. in a park, on a sidewalk
h. in a place of worship, in someone's home

9 GRAMMAR FOCUS

***Learning objective:** practice using modals to express permission, obligation, and prohibition*

 *[CD 3, Track 14]*

Prohibition: can't, isn't allowed to

- Draw a picture of a man in jail on the board. Give him a name, and elicit ideas about things he **can't** or **isn't allowed to** do (e.g., *He can't visit his friends. He isn't allowed to go out.*). Then ask Ss what they can't or aren't allowed to do.

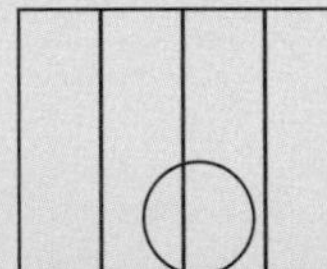

Permission: can, be allowed to

- Elicit what he **can** or **is allowed to** do (e.g., *He's allowed to write letters. He can exercise every day.*). Then ask Ss what they can or are allowed to do.

Obligation: have to, have got to

- Finally, ask what the prisoner **has (got) to** do, (e.g., *He has (got) to wear a prison uniform.*). Then elicit examples of obligations that Ss have.
- Play the audio program to present the sentences in the box. Refer Ss to the Perspectives section to find examples of the three functions.

A

- Ask Ss to cover the sentences and look only at the signs. Have Ss suggest what each sign means. Explain any new vocabulary (e.g., *lock*, *bike rack*, *hallway*, *campus*, *wastepaper basket*).
- Use the first school rule to explain and model the task. Then have Ss complete the task. Go around the class and give help as needed.
- Ss work in pairs to compare answers. If necessary, model the pronunciation as you go over answers with the class.

Answers

1. f	3. h	5. c	7. e
2. a	4. d	6. g	8. b

B *Pair work*

- Explain the task and have two Ss read the example conversation. In pairs, Ss discuss what each sign means. Remind them to use the language in the Grammar Focus box.

Possible answers

a. You ***aren't allowed to*** eat or drink in the classroom.
b. You ***have to*** turn out the lights when you leave.
c. You ***can't*** bring pets onto the campus.
d. You ***have (got) to*** keep the classroom door closed.
e. You ***can't*** open the windows.
f. You ***can*** lock your bikes in the bike rack.
g. You ***have to*** throw all trash in the wastepaper basket.
h. You ***aren't allowed to*** play ball in the hallway.

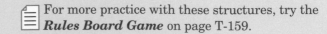

For more practice with these structures, try the ***Rules Board Game*** on page T-159.

8 PERSPECTIVES Signs

A What do you think these international signs mean? Listen and match each sign with the correct meaning.

 ....
 ....
 ....
 ....
 ....
 ....
 ....
 ....

a. You can camp here.
b. You aren't allowed to take photographs here.
c. You have to fasten your seat belts.
d. You can recycle this item.
e. You have to wear a hard hat to enter this area.
f. You can't drink the water here. It's not safe.
g. You have to have your dog on a leash here.
h. You've got to take off your shoes here.

B *Pair work* Where might you see the signs in part A? Give two suggestions for each one.

"You might see this one at a national park or . . ."

9 GRAMMAR FOCUS

Permission, obligation, and prohibition

Permission	*Obligation*	*Prohibition*
You **can** camp here.	You **have to** camp here.	You **can't** camp here.
You**'re allowed to** take off your shoes.	You**'ve got to** take off your shoes.	You **aren't allowed to** take off your shoes.

A Match these school rules with the correct sign. Then compare with a partner.

1. Lock your bikes in the bike rack. ....
2. No eating or drinking in the classroom. ....
3. No playing ball in the hallway. ....
4. Keep the classroom door closed. ....
5. No pets allowed on campus. ....
6. Throw all trash in the wastepaper basket. ....
7. Don't open the windows. ....
8. Turn out the lights when leaving. ....

a

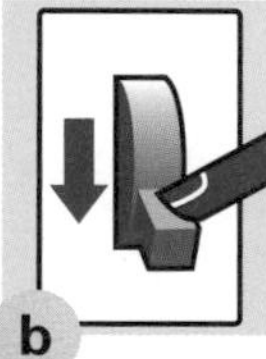
b

c

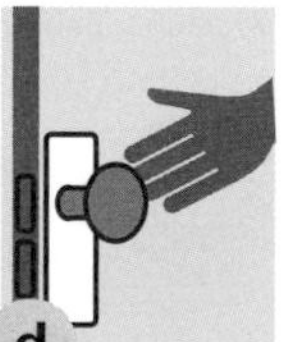
d

e

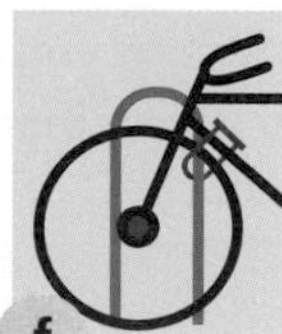
f

g

h

B *Pair work* Use the language in the grammar box to take turns talking about each sign.

A: This first sign means you aren't allowed to eat or drink in the classroom.
B: Yes, I think you're right. And the second one means you have to . . .

10 DISCUSSION Rules and regulations

A ***Pair work*** How many rules can you think of for each of these places?

on an airplane	in an art museum	at a zoo
in a library	in a movie theater	at work

"On an airplane, you have to wear your seat belt when the plane is taking off and landing."

useful expressions

You can/can't . . .
You are/aren't allowed to . . .
You have to . . .

B ***Group work*** Share your ideas. Why do you think these rules exist? Have you ever broken any of them? What happened?

11 LISTENING What's in a sign?

A Listen to three conversations about driving. Check (✓) True or False for each statement.

	True	False
1. The man hasn't had a parking ticket lately.	☐	☐
Parking isn't allowed there during working hours.	☐	☐
The fine for parking is $16.	☐	☐
2. The woman is driving faster than the speed limit.	☐	☐
There are other cars in her lane.	☐	☐
The lane is reserved for buses and taxis.	☐	☐
3. The other drivers are flashing their lights.	☐	☐
He's driving with his lights on.	☐	☐
The other drivers are giving him a warning.	☐	☐

B Listen again. Which drivers did something wrong?

12 WRITING A list of rules

A Write a list of rules and regulations for your school or classroom.

You aren't allowed to chew gum in class.

B ***Group work*** Share your lists. Then choose the ten best rules. Work together to write brief explanations of why each is necessary.

1. You aren't allowed to chew gum in class because it may bother other students.
2. You can keep a library book for only two weeks because someone else might want to check it out.
3. You have to leave the building to use your cell phone because . . .

10 DISCUSSION

Learning objective: *discuss rules using terms of permission, obligation, and prohibition*

A Pair work

- Explain the task. For each place, Ss think of as many rules as they can. Elicit ideas from Ss for the first place (e.g., *You have to wear a seat belt. You can't bring sharp objects on board.*).
- Ss work in pairs to think of rules for each place. Go around the class and give help as needed.

B Group work

- Read the instructions and questions. Each pair joins another pair to discuss the questions.
- ***Option:*** Ss share their group's ideas with the class.

Possible answers

on an airplane – You have to wear a seat belt. You can't bring sharp objects on board.
in a library – You can't talk loudly. You can borrow books for a certain amount of time. You aren't allowed to use a cell phone.
in an art museum – You can't touch the exhibits. You can't make a noise or use a cell phone.
in a movie theater – You have to throw away your trash after the movie. You have to turn off your cell phone. You can't talk loudly.
at a zoo – You can't feed the animals. You aren't allowed to touch the animals. You can take pictures.
at work – You have to wear a uniform. You have to arrive on time. You aren't allowed to sleep.

For more speaking practice, play ***Vocabulary Tennis*** on page T-147. Ss think of more places (e.g., *at school*, *at home*, *in a car*) and then brainstorm rules.

For a new way to practice the discussion questions, try the ***Onion Ring*** technique on page T-151.

11 LISTENING

Learning objective: *develop skills in listening for specific information and making inferences*

A [CD 3, Track 15]

- Set the scene. Ss will hear three conversations about driving. Ask the class: "Who knows how to drive?" Then brainstorm some rules of the road.
- Give Ss time to read the statements. Elicit or explain any new vocabulary (e.g., *parking ticket*, *fine*, *speed limit*, *flash your lights*).
- Play the audio program. Ss listen and complete the task. Then go over answers with the class.

Audio script *(See page T-233.)*

Answers

1. False, True, False
2. False, False, True
3. True, False, True

- ***Option:*** Play the audio program again. Ss listen and take notes to correct the false information. Then check answers with the class.

B

- Explain the task. Play the audio program again. This time, Ss listen to find out which drivers did something wrong. Have Ss compare answers with a partner. Then go over answers with the class.

Answers

All the drivers did something wrong:
Driver 1 parked in the wrong place.
Driver 2 was driving in the wrong lane.
Driver 3 was speeding, but slowed down.

12 WRITING

Learning objective: *write a list of rules using terms of permission, obligation, and prohibition*

A

- Explain the task and read the example sentence. Then have Ss brainstorm more classroom rules. If necessary, refer Ss to the ideas in part A of Exercise 9.

B Group work

- In groups, Ss share their lists and choose the ten best rules. Then they work together to explain the rules. Remind Ss to use the new language to give explanations with *because* for each rule.
- ***Option:*** Ss exchange lists and read them aloud. Alternatively, display them on the walls. Then take a class vote on which set of rules is the best.

13 READING

***Learning objectives:** read and discuss some common proverbs; develop skills in distinguishing main ideas from supporting ideas*

- ***Option:*** Books closed. Write an example of a common proverb on the board. Ask Ss: "What is this called?" Elicit the word *proverb* (= a popular phrase that gives advice or teaches some common wisdom).
- Books open. Read the title. Explain that *pearls of wisdom* are short sentences or phrases that are rich in wisdom or truth.
- Explain the pre-reading task. Ask Ss to try to match the proverbs without worrying about new words. Then go over answers with the class. (Answers: Give advice = A bird in the hand is worth two in the bush. Teach a lesson = Money doesn't grow on trees. Give a warning = Don't count your chickens before they hatch. Express a common truth = One person's meat is another one's poison.)

A

- Ss read the article. Tell them to circle or highlight words or expressions whose meanings they can't guess from context.
- When Ss finish, have them form small groups. Ask them to compare any words they couldn't guess and to help each other with definitions. Go around the class and give help as needed.

For a new way to teach this Reading, try ***Vocabulary Mingle*** on page T-153.

- Elicit any new words or expressions.

Vocabulary

pearl: a small, shiny, hard ball that forms inside some oyster shells and is valued as a jewel
wisdom: the ability to make good judgments based on experience
bush: a low tree with many leaves
hatch: the process of a baby bird or reptile coming out of an egg
poison: a toxic substance that can cause illness or death if swallowed, absorbed, or breathed into the body
sum up: make a summary; express the important facts briefly
source: origin
warning: a notice of a possible danger
outcome: a result

- Explain the task. Elicit the difference between a main idea and a supporting idea. Tell Ss that the main idea is one that answers the questions at the beginning of each paragraph. Then model the first sentence as an example.
- Ss complete the exercise individually. Go over answers with Ss, asking them to justify their answers.

Answers

1. Supporting idea
2. Main idea
3. Main idea
4. Supporting idea
5. Main idea

B *Class activity*

- Read the questions. If Ss are from different countries, have them explain the proverbs to each other. If Ss are from the same country, ask them to tell you five proverbs and explain them in English.
- ***Option:*** Ask Ss to work in pairs to choose one proverb from the text. They create a conversation using the proverb. For example:
  Son: Mom, can I have some more money to go out with my friends?
  Mom: No, I'm sorry. I already gave you $20 this week. Money doesn't grow on trees!
  Ask a few pairs to act out their conversation for the class.

End of Cycle 2

Do your students need more practice?

Assign . . .	*for more practice in . . .*
Workbook Exercises 5–9 on pages 82–84	Grammar, Vocabulary, Reading, and Writing
Lab Guide Exercises 5–6 on page 20	Listening, Pronunciation, Speaking, and Grammar
Video Activity Book Unit 14	Listening, Speaking, and Cultural Awareness
CD-ROM Unit 14	Grammar, Vocabulary, Reading, Listening, and Speaking

Evaluation

Assess Ss' understanding of Units 13 and 14 with the quiz on pages T-212 and T-213.

13 READING

Pearls of Wisdom

Look at these proverbs and the pictures below. Then match each proverb with a picture.

A bird in the hand is worth two in the bush.	*Don't count your chickens before they hatch.*
One person's meat is another one's poison.	*Money doesn't grow on trees.*

1 **Why do people use proverbs?** Many people love proverbs for their wisdom. Others enjoy the images in proverbs. But proverbs are most impressive because they express a lot of information in just a few words. A good proverb quickly sums up ideas that are sometimes hard to express. And the person listening immediately understands it.

2 **Where do proverbs come from?** Proverbs come from two main places – ordinary people and famous people. These two sources are not always distinct. Common and popular wisdom has often been used by famous people. And something said or written down by a well-known person has often been borrowed by the common man. For example, *"Bad news travels fast"* probably comes from the experience of housewives. However, *"All's well that ends well"* was written by William Shakespeare.

3 **What do proverbs tell us?** Proverbs are used everywhere in the world. If you can understand a culture's proverbs, you can better understand the culture itself. There are many different ways that we use proverbs in daily life. Here are some examples. Proverbs can:

Give advice
Meaning: Something you have is better than something you might get.

Give a warning
Meaning: Don't plan on a successful outcome until it actually happens.

Teach a lesson
Meaning: It's not easy to get money.

Express a common truth
Meaning: What one person loves, another person may hate.

A Read the article. Then find these sentences in the article. Decide whether each sentence is the main idea or a supporting idea in that paragraph. Check (✓) the correct boxes.

	Main idea	Supporting idea
1. Many people love proverbs for their wisdom. (par. 1)	☐	☐
2. But proverbs are most . . . just a few words. (par. 1)	☐	☐
3. Proverbs come from . . . and famous people. (par. 2)	☐	☐
4. If you can understand . . . the culture itself. (par. 3)	☐	☐
5. There are many . . . proverbs in daily life. (par. 3)	☐	☐

B ***Class activity*** Can you think of an interesting proverb from your country? What does it mean? Tell it to the class in English.

Units 13–14 Progress check

SELF-ASSESSMENT

How well can you do these things? Check (✓) the boxes.

I can	Very well	OK	A little
Ask for and give opinions using participles as adjectives (Ex. 1)	☐	☐	☐
Describe people and things using relative clauses (Ex. 2)	☐	☐	☐
Listen to and understand interpretations using modals and adverbs (Ex. 3)	☐	☐	☐
Explain gestures and meanings using modals and adverbs (Ex. 4)	☐	☐	☐
Talk about laws using terms of permission, obligation, and prohibition (Ex. 5)	☐	☐	☐

1 SURVEY *Entertainment opinions*

A Complete the first column of the survey with your opinions.

	Me	My classmate
A confusing movie	....	....
A boring TV show	....	....
A shocking news story	....	....
A fascinating book	....	....
An interesting celebrity	....	....
A singer you are amazed by	....	....
A song you are annoyed by	....	....

B ***Class activity*** Go around the class and find someone who has the same opinions. Write a classmate's name only once.

2 ROLE PLAY *Movie recommendations*

Student A: Invite Student B to a movie. Suggest two films. Then answer your partner's questions. Start like this: *Do you want to see a movie?*

Student B: Student A invites you to a movie. Find out more about the two movies. Then accept or refuse the invitation.

Change roles and try the role play again.

Units 13–14 Progress check

SELF-ASSESSMENT

***Learning objectives:** reflect on one's learning; identify areas that need improvement*

- Ask: "What did you learn in Units 13 and 14?" Elicit Ss' answers.
- Ss complete the Self-assessment. Encourage them to be honest, and point out they will not get a bad grade if they check (✓) "a little."
- Ss move on to the Progress check exercises. You can have Ss complete them in class or for homework, using one of these techniques:
  1. Ask Ss to complete all the exercises.
  2. Ask Ss: "What do you need to practice?" Then assign exercises based on their answers.
  3. Ask Ss to choose and complete exercises based on their Self-assessment.

1 SURVEY

***Learning objective:** assess one's ability to ask for and give opinions using participles as adjectives*

A

- Explain the task. Then go over the categories in the chart. Give Ss time to complete the *Me* column with their opinions.

B *Class activity*

- Model the task by asking a S a question from the survey, like this:
  T: What's the name of a movie you think was confusing?
  S: Well, I thought the movie *21 Grams* was confusing.
  T: (*writes* 21 Grams *in the* My Classmate *column*) Why were you confused?
  S: Well, there were three different stories and they were told out of order.
  T: Sounds interesting. When did you see it?
  S: Last winter.
- Explain the rules before Ss begin. Ss should write the classmate's name and answer in the *My Classmate* column. Ss can write each classmate's name only once. Ss should ask follow-up questions to try to find someone who has the same opinion.
- Ss stand up and move around the classroom, asking and answering questions about the categories in the chart. Go around the class and write down common errors.
- Elicit feedback from the class. Ask if anyone found another S with the same opinion. Go over any errors you noticed, and praise successful communication that you observed.

2 ROLE PLAY

***Learning objective:** assess one's ability to describe people and things using relative clauses*

- Explain the task. Student A invites Student B to a movie. Student B finds out about two movie choices and then either accepts or refuses the invitation.
- Brainstorm the kinds of questions someone who is invited to a movie might ask. Write suggestions on the board (e.g., *What kind of movie is it? What's it about? Who's in it? What time is it playing? Where is it playing?*).
- Have Ss form pairs. Tell Student As to think of two movies they would like to see. Explain that they should be prepared to answer the questions on the board.
- While Student As prepare their answers, remind Student Bs how to politely accept or refuse an invitation.
- Ss work in pairs to complete the task. Set a time limit of about five minutes.
- During the role play, go around the class and listen. Take note of any common errors. When time is up, suggest ways the role plays could be improved. Give examples of good communication that you heard.
- Ss change roles and try the role play again.

3 LISTENING

Learning objective: *assess one's ability to listen to and understand interpretations using modals and adverbs*

A [CD 3, Track 16]

- Explain the task. Ss write only a word or two for each person.
- Play the audio program, pausing after each person to give Ss time to write their answers. Ss listen and complete the task. Then elicit answers.

Audio script *(See page T-233.)*

Answers

1. a road sign
2. a movie
3. a lecture
4. a swimming pool

B

- Explain the task and give Ss time to read the choices.
- Play the audio program again, pausing after each person to give Ss time to check (✓) the best answer.
- After Ss compare answers in pairs, go over answers with the class.

Answers

1. He is confused.
2. She hated it.
3. He thought it was interesting.
4. She is frustrated.

GAME

Learning objective: *assess one's ability to explain gestures and meanings using modals and adverbs*

A

- Brainstorm some emotions and ideas that a person can communicate using only facial expressions and gestures. Write suggestions on the board (e.g., *I'm tired of waiting. I like that music a lot. Nice to meet you! I'm really shocked!*).
- Ss work individually to think of two emotions or ideas of their own. Tell them to write each one on a separate card or piece of paper.

B Group work

- Collect all the cards or pieces of paper. Then mix them up and place them facedown in one pile.
- Explain the rules. Ss take turns picking a card from the pile and acting out the meaning for the others in the group to guess. If Ss pick their own card, they should put it back and take another.
- Read the example conversation with Ss. Point out that Student B is the person acting out the meaning. He or she can speak only to say whether a guess is right, wrong, or close. Then ask a S to pick a card from the top of the pile to act out while the class guesses the meaning.
- Ss form small groups. Give each group some cards to place facedown in a pile. Remind Ss to use expressions with modals and adverbs (e.g., *could mean*, *might mean*, *may mean*, *probably means*).
- Ss take turns acting out meanings while the rest of the group guesses.

DISCUSSION

Learning objective: *assess one's ability to talk about laws using terms of permission, obligation, and prohibition*

Group work

- Explain the task. Give Ss time to read the laws silently. Answer any vocabulary questions.
- Ask three Ss to read the example conversation. Encourage Ss to say what they think about voting laws and how they differ from country to country. If possible, have Ss expand the conversations by discussing which law they think is better – their own law or the law in the U.S. – and why.
- Ss take turns discussing the other laws in small groups. Set a time limit of about ten minutes.

WHAT'S NEXT?

Learning objective: *become more involved in one's learning*

- Focus Ss' attention on the Self-assessment again. Ask: "How well can you do these things now?"
- Ask Ss to underline one thing they need to review. Ask: "What did you underline? How can you review it?"
- If needed, plan additional activities or reviews based on Ss' answers.

3 LISTENING *That's how I feel!*

A Listen to some people talking. Write what each person is talking about.

1. .... 2. .... 3. .... 4. ....

B Listen again. What does each person mean? Check (✓) the best answer.

1. ☐ He is confused.
   ☐ He is nervous.
2. ☐ She enjoyed it.
   ☐ She hated it.
3. ☐ He didn't understand it.
   ☐ He thought it was interesting.
4. ☐ She is frustrated.
   ☐ She is bored.

4 GAME *Charades*

A Think of two emotions or ideas you can communicate with gestures. Write them on separate cards.

I'm tired of waiting.

B ***Group work*** Shuffle your cards together. Then take turns picking cards and acting out the meanings with gestures. The student who guesses correctly goes next.

A: That probably means you're bored.
B: No.
C: It could mean you're impatient.
B: You're getting closer . . . .

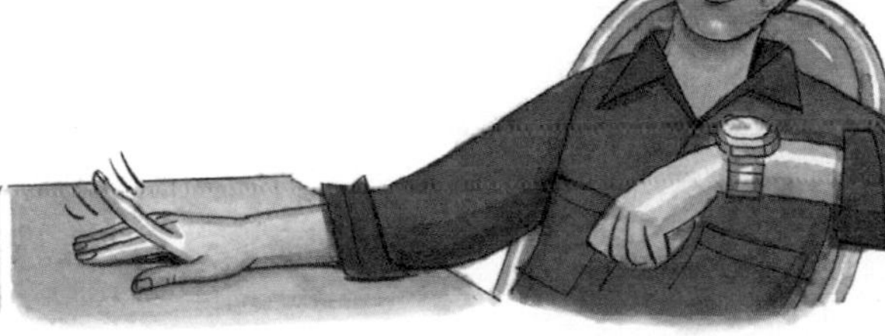
THUMP!
THUMP!
THUMP!

5 DISCUSSION *What's the law?*

Group work Read these laws from the United States. What do you think about them? Are they the same or different in your country?

- You're allowed to vote when you turn 18.
- In some states, you can get married when you're 16.
- You have to wear a seat belt in the front seat of a car.
- Young men don't have to serve in the military.
- You aren't allowed to keep certain wild animals as pets.
- In some states, you can't drive faster than 65 miles an hour.
- You have to have a passport to enter the country.

A: In the U.S., you're allowed to vote when you turn 18.
B: That's surprising! In my country, we *have* to vote when we're 18.
C: And in my country, we *can't* vote until we're 20.

WHAT'S NEXT?

Look at your Self-assessment again. Do you need to review anything?

15 What would you do?

1 SNAPSHOT

STORIES OF HONESTY

BUSINESSMAN RETURNS $750,000 TO OWNER

and is thanked with a brief phone call.

Fan Returns Soccer Star's Lucky T-shirt:

Player meets him to personally give $1,000 reward.

Student Uses Detective Work

to find owner of gold jewelry. "I thought it might have personal value," he told reporters.

Athlete Admits to Cheating

"I'm so sorry. I just wanted to win," he recently confessed. "I feel so ashamed."

Source: *The Los Angeles Times*

Do you know any other stories like these?
Have you ever found anything valuable? What did you do?
Do you think that people who return lost things should get a reward?

2 CONVERSATION *If I found $750,000 . . .*

A Listen and practice.

Phil: Look at this. Some guy found $750,000! He returned it and the owner simply thanked him with a phone call.
Pat: You're kidding! If I found $750,000, I wouldn't return it so fast.
Phil: Why? What would you do?
Pat: Well, I'd go straight to the mall and spend it. I could buy lots of nice clothes and jewelry.
Phil: Someone might also find out about it. And then you could go to jail.
Pat: Hmm. You've got a point there.

B Listen to the rest of the conversation. What would Phil do if he found $750,000?

What would you do?

Cycle 1, Exercises 1–5

In Unit 15, students discuss imaginary events and difficult situations. In Cycle 1, they talk about imaginary situations using unreal conditional sentences with if *clauses. In Cycle 2, they talk about predicaments using the past modals* would have *and* should have.

SNAPSHOT

Learning objective: *read and talk about examples of honesty*

- Books closed. Ask the class: "Have you ever lost something valuable and had it returned? What happened?" Ss discuss in pairs. Encourage them to ask their partners follow-up questions.
- Books open. Ss read the information in the Snapshot. Ask Ss which story they find the most interesting. Why? Elicit or explain any new vocabulary.

Vocabulary

honesty: being truthful; able to be trusted
reward: a present for finding something and returning it to the owner
detective: a police officer whose job is to discover information about crimes
admit: tell the truth about something you did
confess: admit
ashamed: embarrassed

- Read the questions. Then have Ss discuss them in groups. After ten minutes, ask Ss to change groups and share their ideas again.
- ***Option:*** Follow up with a longer discussion. Ask the class: "Do you agree that honesty pays? (= It's best to be honest.) What should happen to people who cheat and confess?"

CONVERSATION

Learning objectives: *practice a conversation about honesty; see unreal conditional sentences with* if *clauses in context*

A [CD 3, Track 18]

- ***Option:*** Focus Ss' attention on the illustration and ask them to brainstorm the things they see. After a set time limit, find out who has the most words (e.g., headline, newspaper, shopping bags, daydream).
- Books closed. Instead of Ss listening for specific information, tell Ss to simply listen carefully.
- Play the audio program. Then ask: "What kinds of things were the people talking about?" Have Ss write their answers on the board. (Answers: $750,000 returned; owner thanked with phone call; she'd go shopping; she could go to jail)

TIP To provide a break from sitting and involve Ss in their own learning, let Ss write their answers and brainstorm ideas on the board.

- Play the audio program again. Ss listen and take notes. Then Ss work in pairs to compare their notes with those on the board.
- Books open. Have Ss check their own notes against the picture and the conversation. How many Ss feel that they got most of the main ideas? some of the main ideas?
- Encourage Ss to check their dictionaries for the meanings of new words and expressions.
- Ss practice the conversation in pairs.

For a new way to practice this Conversation, try ***Disappearing Dialog*** on page T-151. Alternatively, use it with the Grammar Focus on page 101.

B

- Read the question. Then play the rest of the audio program. Ss listen and write their answers.

Audio script *(See page T-233.)*

- Elicit answers from the class.

Answer

Phil would take the money straight to the police.

- ***Option:*** Follow up with a discussion. Write these questions on the board: *What can you buy with $750,000? with $50,000? What are the risks of keeping money that you find? How honest are you?* Ss discuss in small groups or as a class.

3 GRAMMAR FOCUS

Learning objective: *practice using unreal conditional sentences with* if *clauses*

[CD 3, Track 19]

Unreal sentences with* if *clauses

- Books closed. Write these sentences on the board:
  Pat: If I __________ $750,000, I __________ return it so fast. I_____ go straight to the mall and spend it. I __________ buy lots of clothes.
- Have Ss fill in the blanks. To check answers, refer them to the previous Conversation. (Answers: found, wouldn't, 'd, could)
- Ask Ss if Pat is talking about a real or an unreal situation. (Answer: unreal)
- Books open. Elicit or explain this rule for forming unreal conditional sentences:
  1. Two types of verb forms are used in the clauses: (1) the simple past form in the *if* clause (*found*), (2) a modal verb in the main clause (*would*).
     If I found $750,000, I would buy clothes.
  2. The clauses can be used in either order. No comma is necessary when the *if* clause comes second.
     I would buy clothes if I found $750,000.
  3. We can use various modals in the main clause. The most common is *would*, or its contraction *'d*. We can also use *could* or *might*. *Might* expresses possibility while *could* expresses ability:
     If I found $750,000, I might go to the police. (= I'm not sure, but it's possible I would go to the police.)
     If I found $750,000, I could buy lots of jewelry. (= I would be able to buy lots of jewelry.)
- Play the audio program to present the sentences in the box. Ss listen and repeat. Then elicit examples of sentences with *if* clauses and modals.

For more practice with unreal conditionals, play the ***Chain Game*** on page T-145. Begin like this:
S1: If I won the lottery, I would buy a new car.
S2: If I won the lottery, I would buy a new car and I would . . .

A

- Explain the task and model the first conversation with a S. Then Ss work individually to complete the task. Go around the class and give help as needed. Finally, elicit Ss' responses to check answers.

Answers

1. A: If you **had** three months to travel, where **would** you **go**?
   B: Oh, that's easy! **I'd fly** to Antarctica. . . .
2. A: If your doctor **told** you to get more exercise, which sport **would** you **choose**?
   B: I'm not sure but I **might go** jogging. . . .
3. A: What **would** you **do** if your car **broke down**?
   B: If I couldn't afford to fix it, **I'd have to walk** . . .
4. A: **Would** you **break** into your house if you **locked** yourself out?
   B: If I **didn't have** another key, I**'d ask** a . . .

For another way to practice this structure, try ***Moving Dialog*** on page T-150. Have Student A ask the part A questions. Student B replies with his or her own information.

B Pair work

- Read the instructions and explain any new vocabulary. Then model the first question with a S.
- Ss take turns asking and answering the questions. Go around the class and give help as needed.

4 LISTENING

Learning objective: *develop skills in listening for main ideas and specific information*

A [CD 3, Track 20]

- Set the scene. Three friends are talking about predicaments, or unpleasant situations that are difficult to solve. Play the audio program. Ss listen and number the predicaments.

Audio script *(See page T-233–234.)*

- Go over answers with the class.

Answers

1. A friend lost all her money while traveling.
2. A friend has a serious shopping problem.
3. Two people were fighting in the street.

B

- Explain the task. Ss listen and write the suggestions given for each predicament.
- Play the audio program again, pausing for Ss to take notes. Then discuss the best suggestions.

Possible answers

(*These suggestions were given.*)

1. Jane and Burt would call their parents and ask them to send money. Burt might also try going to the American Express office to get a loan. Susan would probably sell her watch and camera or get a job as a waitress.
2. Jane would talk to her friend about it. Burt wouldn't say or do anything because it's none of his business. Susan would probably talk to her family.
3. Jane would call the police. Burt would try to break it up or get someone to help him. He'd also shout for someone to call the police.

3 GRAMMAR FOCUS

Unreal conditional sentences with if clauses

Unreal conditional sentences describe imaginary situations with simple past forms and consequences in the present.

What **would** you **do if** you **found** $750,000?

If I **found** $750,000,	I **would/I'd go** straight to the mall.
	I **could buy** lots of nice clothes and jewelry.
	I **might go** to the police.
	I **wouldn't return** it so fast.

A Complete these conversations. Then compare with a partner.

1. A: If you .... (have) three months to travel, where .... you .... (go)?
   B: Oh, that's easy! I .... (fly) to Antarctica. I've always wanted to go there.
2. A: If your doctor .... (tell) you to get more exercise, which sport .... you .... (choose)?
   B: I'm not sure, but I .... (go) jogging two or three times a week.
3. A: What .... you .... (do) if your car .... (break down)?
   B: If I couldn't afford to fix it, I .... (have to) walk everywhere.
4. A: .... you .... (break) into your house if you .... (lock) yourself out?
   B: If I .... (not have) another key, I .... (ask) a neighbor for help.

B ***Pair work*** Take turns asking and answering questions.

What would you do if . . . ?

you saw a burglar in your home
you found a diamond ring
you saw someone shoplifting
you won a million dollars in a lottery
your teacher gave you an A on a test by mistake
your friend wanted to marry someone you didn't trust

4 LISTENING Tough predicaments

A Listen to three people talk about predicaments. Number them in the order they are discussed.

Predicament	Suggestions
☐ Two people were fighting in the street.	....
☐ A friend lost all her money while traveling.	....
☐ A friend has a serious shopping problem.	....

B Listen again. What suggestions do the people give for each predicament? Take notes. Which is the best suggestion?

5 INTERCHANGE 15 Do the right thing!

What would you do in some difficult situations? Go to Interchange 15.

6 WORD POWER Antonyms

A Find nine pairs of opposites in this list. Complete the chart. Then compare with a partner.

✓ accept	borrow	dislike	find	lose	remember
admit	deny	divorce	forget	marry	save
agree	disagree	enjoy	lend	✓ refuse	spend

accept ≠ *refuse*	.... ≠	.... ≠ ....
.... ≠	.... ≠	.... ≠ ....
.... ≠	.... ≠	.... ≠ ....

B ***Pair work*** Choose four pairs of opposites. Write sentences using each pair.

I can never save money because I spend it all on clothes.

7 PERSPECTIVES I felt terrible.

A Listen to people talk about recent predicaments. Then check (✓) the best suggestion for each one.

"What a disaster! I spilled juice on my parents' new couch. They weren't home, so I just turned the cushions over. What should I have done?"

- ☐ You should have told them about it.
- ☐ You should have cleaned it immediately.
- ☐ You should have offered to buy them a new couch.

"I forgot my best friend's birthday. I felt terrible, so I sent him an e-mail to apologize. What would you have done?"

- ☐ I would have called him right away.
- ☐ I would have sent him a nice birthday present.
- ☐ I would have invited him out for a meal.

B ***Pair work*** Compare with a partner. Do you agree with each other?

5 INTERCHANGE 15

See page T-129 for teaching notes.

End of Cycle 1

Do your students need more practice?

Assign . . .	*for more practice in . . .*
Workbook Exercises 1–4 on pages 85–87	Grammar, Vocabulary, Reading, and Writing
Lab Guide Exercises 1 and 3 on page 21	Listening, Pronunciation, Speaking, and Grammar

Cycle 2, Exercises 6–13

6 WORD POWER

Learning objective: *learn verbs for describing events*

A

- Explain the task and read the example answer in the chart. Ss complete the task individually and then compare answers in pairs. Go over answers with the class and help Ss with correct pronunciation and stress.

Answers

admit–deny
enjoy–dislike
agree–disagree
borrow–lend
remember–forget
spend–save
divorce–marry
accept–refuse
find–lose

- ***Option:*** Ss work in pairs to brainstorm more verbs and their opposites (e.g., *come* and *go*, *give* and *take*).

TIP Draw a line down one side of the board and use this as your "Vocabulary Column." Add new words to it throughout the lesson. Keep track of what you have taught your Ss by reviewing the list at the end of each class.

B *Pair work*

- Explain the task and read the example sentence. Point out that Ss can use a simple statement, a question, or an unreal conditional sentence with an *if* clause.
- Ss work in pairs to choose four sets of verbs from the chart in part A. Then they write sentences using each pair. Go around the class and check Ss' sentences for correct grammar.

For more practice with this vocabulary, try ***Verb Word Search*** on page T-159.

7 PERSPECTIVES

Learning objectives: *discuss predicaments; see past modals* would have *and* should have *in context*

A [CD 3, Track 21]

- Focus Ss' attention on the picture and ask what happened. (Answer: He spilled juice on a couch and is deciding what to do about it.) Explain that Ss will hear two predicaments that really happened, not imaginary situations.
- Draw this chart on the board and ask Ss to copy it:

Predicament	What went wrong?	What did he do about it?
#1		
#2		

- Books closed. Play the audio program. Ss listen and complete the chart. Then have Ss open their books, read the predicaments, and check their answers.
- Play the audio program again. Point out the reduction of *have*, which sounds like *of*.
- Ss check (✓) the best suggestion for each predicament.

B *Pair work*

- Ss work in pairs to compare answers. Encourage them to explain their answers. Then take a class vote to find out which suggestions were most popular.
- ***Option:*** In pairs, Ss write new predicaments. Then each pair joins another pair, exchanges papers, and writes several suggestions for each predicament. The group then decides which suggestions are best.

8 GRAMMAR FOCUS

Learning objective: *practice using past modals to talk about actions in the past*

[CD 3, Track 22]

- Refer Ss to the Perspectives section. Ask the class: "Did he clean the couch? Did he call his friend?" (Answer: no) Point out that the *would have* and *should have* actions were imaginary or hypothetical (= they didn't really happen).
- Explain that we use *I would have* to give an opinion about an action in the past. We use *you should have* to make a suggestion about a past event. In both cases, our opinion or suggestion is too late.

Would have

- Ask Ss to find examples of *would have* from the Perspectives section. Ss write them on the board in columns, like this:

1	2	3	4	5
I	would	have	called	him . . .
I	would	have	sent	him . . .
I	would	have	invited	him . . .
What	would	you	have	done?

- Elicit the rules from Ss, by asking what they can see in each column.
  Statement:
  Subject + *would have* + past participle + (rest)
  Question:
  Wh- + *would* + pronoun + *have* + past participle?
- Have Ss think of more examples of *would have* + past participle (e.g., *I would have told him "I'm sorry."*). Have Ss use the negative too (e.g., *I wouldn't have called him.*).

Should have

- Repeat the above steps for *should have.*
- Play the audio program to present the sentences in the box. Ss listen and read silently.

A

- Explain the task and any new vocabulary (e.g., *change*, *ignore*, *campsite*). Tell Ss to look at the appendix at the back of their book for irregular past participle forms. Ss work individually to complete the sentences. Then go over answers with the class.

Answers

1. A: The cashier gave me too much change. What should I have **done**?
   B: You should have **said** something. You shouldn't have **taken** the money.
2. A: I ignored an e-mail from someone I don't like. What would you have **done**?
   B: I would have **replied** to the person. It just takes a minute!
3. A: I was watching a good movie when the phone rang. What should I have **done**?
   B: You should have **taken** the call and **told** the person you'd call later.
4. A: We left all our trash at the campsite. What would you have **done**?
   B: I would have **taken** it with me and **thrown** it away later.

- Ss practice the conversations in pairs.

B

- Explain the task. Read the sentences in each column and explain any new vocabulary (e.g., *cheat*, *messy*, *comb*, *warn*, *leave a note*, *exchange*). Then Ss work individually to match the situations with the most appropriate suggestions. After Ss compare answers in pairs, go over answers with the class.

Possible answers

1. a, b, d 2. b, d, e 3. a, d 4. c, d, f 5. d, g, h

C *Group work*

- Ss work in small groups to think of their own suggestions. Remind them to use past modals. Groups then choose their best suggestion for each situation.
- Ask groups to share their best ideas with the class.

9 PRONUNCIATION

Learning objective: *notice the reduction of the verb* have *in past modals*

A [CD 3, Track 23]

- Play the audio program. Point out how the reduced form for *have* /əv/ sounds like *of*. Play the audio program again, pausing for the class to practice.

B *Pair work*

- In pairs, Ss practice the conversations in part A of Exercise 8 again. Go around the class and give help as needed. Then go over any errors you noticed.

TIP To keep working on this feature, make it the "Sound of the Week" and focus on it for the next few classes.

8 GRAMMAR FOCUS

Past modals

Use* would have *or* should have *+ past participle to give opinions or suggestions about actions in the past.

What **should** I **have done**? — You **should have told** them about it. / You **shouldn't have hidden** it.

What **would** you **have done**? — I **would have called** him. / I **wouldn't have sent** him an e-mail.

A Complete these conversations. Then practice with a partner.

1. A: The cashier gave me too much change. What should I have .... (do)?
   B: You should have .... (say) something. You shouldn't have .... (take) the money.
2. A: I ignored an e-mail from someone I don't like. What would you have .... (do)?
   B: I would have .... (reply) to the person. It just takes a minute!
3. A: I was watching a good movie when the phone rang. What should I have .... (do)?
   B: You should have .... (take) the call and .... (tell) the person you'd call later.
4. A: We left all our trash at the campsite. What would you have .... (do)?
   B: I would have .... (take) it with me and .... (throw) it away later.

B Read the situations below. What would have been the best thing to do? Choose suggestions. Then compare with a partner.

Situations

1. The teacher borrowed my favorite book and spilled coffee all over it. ....
2. I saw a classmate cheating on an exam. So I wrote her a letter about it. ....
3. A friend of mine always has messy hair. So I gave him a comb for his birthday. ....
4. I hit someone's car when I was leaving a parking lot. Luckily, no one saw me. ....
5. My aunt gave me a wool sweater. I can't wear wool, so I gave it back. ....

Suggestions

a. You should have spoken to him about it.
b. I would have spoken to the teacher about it.
c. I would have waited for the owner to return.
d. I wouldn't have said anything.
e. You should have warned her not to do it again.
f. You should have left a note for the owner.
g. I would have told her that I'd prefer something else.
h. You should have exchanged it for something else.

C ***Group work*** Make another suggestion for each situation in part B.

9 PRONUNCIATION Reduction of have

A Listen and practice. Notice how **have** is reduced in these sentences.

What would you have (/əv/) done? I would have (/əv/) told the truth.

B ***Pair work*** Practice the conversations in part A of Exercise 8 again. Use the reduced form of **have**.

10 LISTENING *I'm calling about . . .*

A Listen to people calling Dr. Hilda, a counselor on a radio talk show. Complete the chart.

	Problem	What the caller did
Caller 1	....	....
Caller 2	....	....
Caller 3	....	....

B Listen again. According to Dr. Hilda, what should each caller have done?

C ***Group work*** Do you agree with Dr. Hilda? What would you have done?

11 SPEAKING *I shouldn't have . . .*

A Look at the five situations below. Think about the past month and write down an example for each situation.

1. something you shouldn't have bought
2. something you should have done
3. someone you should have called
4. something you shouldn't have said
5. someone you should have e-mailed or written

B ***Group work*** Talk about each situation in part A.

A: I bought a lamp at a garage sale. I shouldn't have bought it because I don't really like it.
B: I did something similar recently. I shouldn't have bought . . .

12 WRITING *A letter to an advice columnist*

Write a letter to an advice columnist about a real or imaginary problem. Put your letters on a bulletin board and choose one to write a reply to.

Dear Dr. Hilda,

I let a friend borrow my laptop and now it doesn't work. I took it to a repair shop, and they said it would be expensive to fix. When I asked my friend to help me pay the bill, she refused. Now she won't even speak to me! What did I do wrong? What should I have done?

Can't Do Anything Right

10 LISTENING

Learning objective: *develop skills in listening for specific information*

- Set the scene. Explain that many people call radio talk shows to ask for advice on personal problems. Ask Ss if they ever listen to such shows. If so, find out what kinds of problems people usually ask about. Encourage others to ask their own questions.

A [CD 3, Track 24]

- Explain the task. Ss will hear three people call a counselor on a radio talk show. Ss take notes about each caller and complete the chart.
- Play the audio program, pausing after each caller to give Ss time to take notes. Play the audio program again, if necessary. If Ss need more room to write notes, they can use a separate sheet of paper.

Audio script *(See page T-234.)*

- Have Ss compare answers in pairs or groups. Then elicit responses from individual Ss.

TIP To build Ss' confidence, have them compare answers before you ask them to speak in front of the whole class.

Possible answers

Caller 1
- daughter is dating older man; told her to stop seeing him

Caller 2
- borrowed father's new car and had an accident
- sent an e-mail; said someone had stolen car

Caller 3
- had a party where subject of politics came up
- got angry at a co-worker and asked him to leave

B

- Play the audio program again. This time Ss listen for Dr. Hilda's advice. Ask Ss to take notes.
- Go over answers with the class.

Possible answers

Caller 1
She should have spoken to the man; she should have asked him not to date her daughter; she should let her daughter date him and not worry about age.
Caller 2
He should have told the truth; his father would understand and be glad his son wasn't hurt.
Caller 3
He shouldn't have talked about politics; he shouldn't have gotten angry; he should apologize.

For a new way to teach this Listening, try ***Stand Up, Sit Down*** on page T-151. Ask Ss to stand up when they hear *would have* or *should have.*

C Group work

- Ss discuss Dr. Hilda's advice in small groups. Then ask Ss to share their ideas with the class.

11 SPEAKING

Learning objective: *talk about regrets using past modals*

A

- Read the instructions and situations. Ss should think about things they wish they hadn't done.
- Ss write five sentences. Go around the class and give help as needed.

B Group work

- Ss talk about their situations in small groups. Remind them to use the reduced form of *have*, and to ask follow-up questions to get more details.
- ***Option:*** One S plays Dr. Hilda. Others take turns calling her show and role-playing their situations.

12 WRITING

Learning objectives: *write a letter to an advice columnist; write a reply using past modals to give suggestions*

- ***Option:*** Focus Ss' attention on the letters on page 105.
- Write these questions on the board:
  Where were you? What happened?
  What was the problem? What did you do?
  How do you feel about the problem now?
- Explain the task. Ask a S to read the example letter. Then tell Ss to think of a fun or interesting situation and make notes.
- Ss use their notes to write a short letter to an advice columnist.
- Put Ss' letters on a bulletin board. Alternatively, collect the letters and give them to different Ss. Explain that Ss now play the role of Dr. Hilda, and reply to someone else's letter.
- When Ss finish, have them return the original letter and their reply to the writer.

13 READING

Learning objectives: *read and discuss letters to and from an advice columnist; develop skills in scanning and guessing meaning from context*

- Books closed. If possible, bring a real advice column from a local newspaper or magazine to show the class. If this is not possible, write *Advice Column* on the board. Find out how much the class knows about advice columns. If Ss are unfamiliar with advice columns, explain that in some countries, people write to an advice columnist about their personal problems. Both their letters and the columnist's replies are published at the same time. The writer's real name is rarely used.
- Ask Ss to predict the kinds of problems people write about.
- Books open. Give Ss two minutes to skim the letters – but not the replies. Ask: "Which of these problems did you predict?"
- Ss list the problems in note form. Go over answers with the class. (Possible answers: **Distraught Sister:** told her brother an untrue rumor she heard about his girlfriend. **Tired Mom:** is tired of supporting her adult son. **Confused Friend:** knows about something a friend's brother did, and wonders if she should tell the friend.)

A

- Explain the task. Ss match the problems with the replies. Point out that there is one extra reply. Tell them not to worry about new vocabulary.
- Check answers with the class.

TIP To provide variety, have Ss check answers in groups of three. If their answers differ, find out why and give help as needed.

Answers

Letter signed by:	*Amy's reply begins:*
Distraught Sister	Well, you learned a lesson.
Tired Mom	You're making it too easy . . .
Confused Friend	I would suggest you keep quiet.

B

- Explain the task. Model the first word as an example. Ask Ss to find the word *confront* in the article. Then ask: "Do you think *confront* is a verb, an adjective, or a noun?" (Answer: a verb) Then elicit the answer.
- Ss complete the task individually. Remind Ss to find the word in the article and look at the context before guessing its meaning.
- Go over answers with the class. For each word or expression, ask if Ss think it's a verb, an adjective, or a noun.

Answers

1. c 2. f 3. e 4. d 5. b 6. a

- Ask Ss if they have any questions about vocabulary. Encourage them to work together to explain any remaining words.

Vocabulary

rumor: information passed from one person to another that may not be true
break up: end a romantic relationship
meanwhile: at the same time something else is happening
skip: miss; be absent from without permission
willing: ready; prepared
damage: harm; break
gossip: information about other people's private lives
repair the damage: make everything all right

For another way to practice this vocabulary, try ***Vocabulary Mingle*** on page T-153.

C *Pair work*

- Ss work in pairs to discuss the questions. After about five minutes, ask Ss to share their ideas with the class.
- ***Option:*** In pairs, Ss choose one of the letters. Then they role-play a conversation.

End of Cycle 2

Do your students need more practice?

Assign . . .	*for more practice in . . .*
Workbook Exercises 5–9 on pages 88–90	Grammar, Vocabulary, Reading, and Writing
Lab Guide Exercises 2 and 4–7 on page 21	Listening, Pronunciation, Speaking, and Grammar
Video Activity Book Unit 15	Listening, Speaking, and Cultural Awareness
CD-ROM Unit 15	Grammar, Vocabulary, Reading, Listening, and Speaking

13 READING

Ask Amy

Scan the three letters to Amy. What problems do the writers ask for help with?

Dear Amy,
Someone told me that my brother's girlfriend was dating another guy. I felt I should let my brother know, and after I did, he decided to confront her with the story. They had a terrible argument and, although she denied the rumor, they broke up. Now it turns out that the rumor wasn't true, and my brother isn't speaking to me.

Distraught Sister

Dear . . . ,
You're making it too easy for him to stay where he is. Be firm and tell him he has two months to find a job and get his own place. He's old enough to take care of himself – but you have to be willing to let him go.

Amy

Dear Amy,
My son is 23 years old. He finished college last year, but he can't seem to find a job he likes. He still lives at home, and I'm worried that he's not trying hard enough to get a job and support himself. Meanwhile, I've been cooking his meals and doing his laundry.

Tired Mom

Dear . . . ,
I would suggest you keep quiet. Let them work things out for themselves. If you say something, you could damage your friendship with both of them.

Amy

Dear Amy,
I went to the movies with my best friend and her younger brother. She wasn't feeling well, so afterward, he drove me home. While we were driving, he told me he had skipped school that day, taken his mother's car, and gone to the beach! My dilemma is: Should I tell my friend about this?

Confused Friend

Dear . . . ,
You should have thought more carefully before you acted. It wasn't necessary to get angry. Next time, speak to the child immediately and warn him not to do it again.

Amy

Dear . . . ,
Well, you learned a lesson. You shouldn't have listened to gossip. And you shouldn't have passed it on. Now you have to repair the damage. Apologize sincerely and hope he will forgive and forget.

Amy

A Read the article. Then match the letters with the replies. (There is one extra reply.)

B Find the words in *italics* in the article. Then match each word or phrase with its meaning.

.... 1. *confront*
.... 2. *distraught*
.... 3. *dilemma*
.... 4. *firm*
.... 5. *work (things) out*
.... 6. *forgive and forget*

a. make a fresh start
b. find a solution
c. challenge in a direct way
d. strong and determined
e. a difficult problem
f. extremely worried or upset

C ***Pair work*** Do you agree with Amy's advice? What advice would you give? Think of a problem you are having. Ask your partner for advice.

16 What's your excuse?

1 SNAPSHOT

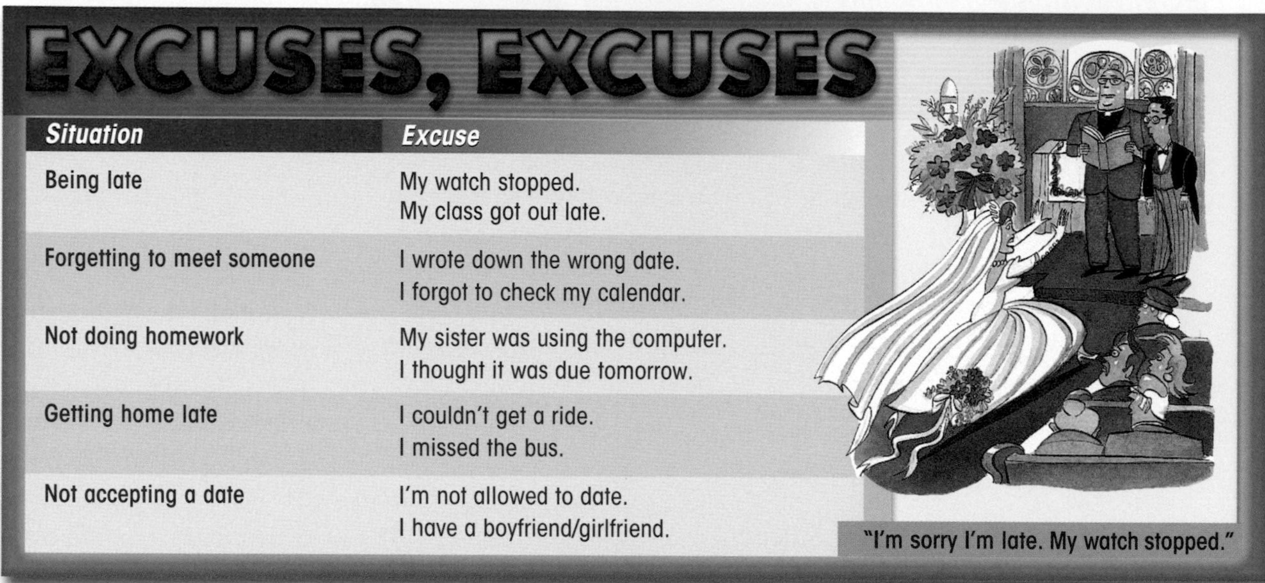

EXCUSES, EXCUSES

Situation	Excuse
Being late	My watch stopped. My class got out late.
Forgetting to meet someone	I wrote down the wrong date. I forgot to check my calendar.
Not doing homework	My sister was using the computer. I thought it was due tomorrow.
Getting home late	I couldn't get a ride. I missed the bus.
Not accepting a date	I'm not allowed to date. I have a boyfriend/girlfriend.

"I'm sorry I'm late. My watch stopped."

Have you ever heard any of these excuses? Have you ever used any of them?
Which are good excuses? Which are bad excuses?
What other excuses can you make for not accepting an invitation?

PERSPECTIVES Who said it?

A Who do you think made these requests? Listen and match each request with a person.

1. He asked me to play my music more quietly. ....
2. She told me not to come home after midnight. ....
3. She said to drink at least six glasses of water a day. ....
4. He said not to be late for practice again. ....
5. She asked me to pick up the kids after school. ....
6. He told me to bring a dictionary tomorrow. ....
7. He asked me not to tell anyone about his new girlfriend. ....

a. my doctor
b. my coach
c. my friend
d. my neighbor
e. my mother
f. my wife
g. my teacher

B ***Pair work*** Can you think of another request each person might make?

A: A doctor might also tell a patient to get more exercise.
B: . . . or to avoid eating greasy foods.

What's your excuse?

In Unit 16, students discuss honesty and practice giving reasons and explanations. In Cycle 1, they talk about excuses and requests using reported speech. In Cycle 2, they use reported speech to talk about statements that other people make.

Cycle 1, Exercises 1–4

1 SNAPSHOT

Learning objectives: *read examples of common excuses; talk about excuses*

- Books closed. Write these sentences on the board:
  I'm sorry I'm late. My watch stopped.
  I thought the homework was due tomorrow.
  Sorry. I missed the bus.
  I can't go out with you. I have a boyfriend/girlfriend.
- Ask Ss what the expressions have in common. (Answer: They are all excuses.)
- Elicit some more excuses by giving situations (e.g., *being late for class, forgetting to do homework*).
- Books open. Focus Ss' attention on the cartoon. Ask: "What happened? Is this a good excuse or a bad one? Do you think it's the truth?"
- Ss read the Snapshot silently. Answer any vocabulary questions (e.g., *calendar, due*) or elicit the meaning from other Ss.
- Give Ss a few minutes to look over the discussion questions and to think about their answers. Then Ss work in small groups to discuss them together. Go around the class and give help as needed.

2 PERSPECTIVES

Learning objectives: *discuss requests; see examples of reported speech for requests in context*

A  [CD 3, Track 25]

- Explain that Ss are going to hear some requests and decide who made each request.
- Play the first request in the audio program. Ask: "Who might make a request like this?" Elicit answers from the class.
- Play the audio program, pausing after each request to elicit ideas. Don't correct mistakes at this point.
- Ss read the sentences silently and match each request with a person.

TIP Ask a S who finishes early to write the answers on the board.

Answers

1. d 2. e 3. a 4. b 5. f 6. g 7. c

- If necessary, explain or elicit the difference between the verbs: *ask*, *tell*, and *say*.
  Ask is different because it leads to a question. Elicit the original questions from sentences 1 and 5, like this:
  My neighbor asked me, "Can you play your music more quietly?"
  My wife asked me, "Can you pick up the kids after school?"

  Point out that with *ask*, we have to say *who* we are asking (e.g., *she asked me/him/us/the boy/Ken*).
  Tell and *say* are very similar in meaning. The main difference is that *tell* is followed by a direct object, while *say* is not. For example:
  She told me, "Bring a dictionary tomorrow."
  She said, "Bring a dictionary tomorrow."
- Have Ss underline *asked me* and *told me* in the Perspectives section. Then play the audio program again. This time, focus Ss' attention on the use of *ask*, *tell*, and *say*.

B *Pair work*

- Explain the task. Ss look at the list of people. For each person, they think of another typical request.
- Model the example conversation with a S and elicit more examples for *doctor*. Remind Ss to use a direct object with *ask* and *tell*.
- Ss work in pairs to complete the task. Then each pair joins another pair to compare requests. Were there any similar requests? Which ones were different?
- Go around the class and write down any grammatical mistakes with *ask*, *say*, or *tell*. Then write the mistakes on the board and elicit corrections from the class.

3 GRAMMAR FOCUS

Learning objective: *practice using reported speech to make requests*

[CD 3, Track 26]

> ***TIP*** To explain reported requests, it's helpful to draw pictures. If you have an artistic S, ask him or her to draw them for you.

- Draw a simple figure on the board with a speech bubble coming from its mouth. In the bubble write: *Can you play your music more quietly?*
- Then refer Ss to the Perspectives section. Ask: "What did the neighbor ask?" Write the reported request on the board:
  He asked me to play my music more quietly.
- Explain that reported speech is used to talk about, or report, something that was asked or said in the past.
- Now draw a figure of a mother saying, "Don't come home after midnight." Elicit the reported request and write it on the board:
  She told me not to come home after midnight.
- Point out that the most common verbs for reporting requests are *ask*, *tell*, and *say*. They are used in the past tense to match the past action.
- Make sure Ss understand how to form a reported request by explaining that:
  1. All three of these verbs are followed by an infinitive (e.g., *She asked me/told me/said to phone her tonight.*).
  2. In a negative reported request, *not* is usually placed before the infinitive (e.g., *The teacher asked/told John not to be late.*).

- Play the audio program to present the sentences in the box. Ss listen and repeat.

A

- Ask Ss if they have ever thrown a surprise party. If so, have them tell what happened. Encourage other Ss to ask follow-up questions for more information.
- Explain the situation. Then use the first request and example sentence to model the task.
- Ss work individually to write the reported requests before comparing answers with a partner. Elicit answers from the class.

Possible answers

1. Amanda *told them* to meet at Albert's apartment at 7:30.
2. Amanda *asked them* to bring their favorite CDs.
3. She *said* not to bring any food.
4. She *asked them* to bring a small gift for Albert.
5. She *said* not to spend more than $10 on the gift.
6. Amanda *told them* to be careful not to say anything to him.

B *Group work*

- Tell Ss to imagine they are planning a party. Ss work individually to write four requests. Remind Ss to include requests with *Can you* and imperatives.
- Explain the task. Ss take turns reading their requests. Other Ss change the original requests into reported requests. Use the example conversation to model the task.
- Ss complete the task in small groups.

4 SPEAKING

Learning objective: *discuss recent requests using reported speech*

A

- Explain the task. Ss think of two things they were asked to do and two things they were asked *not* to do.
- Ss work individually to complete the chart. Go around the class and give help as needed.

B *Group work*

- Go over the task. Ss use the information in the chart and reported speech to talk about recent requests. Others ask follow-up questions to get more information. Elicit useful expressions (e.g., *What request has someone made recently? Who made it? When? Why? Did you perform the request?*).
- Ss complete the activity in small groups.

End of Cycle 1

Do your students need more practice?

Assign . . .	*for more practice in . . .*
Workbook Exercises 1–4 on pages 91–93	Grammar, Vocabulary, Reading, and Writing
Lab Guide Exercises 1–3 on page 22	Listening, Pronunciation, Speaking, and Grammar

3 GRAMMAR FOCUS

Reported speech: requests

Original request	Reported request
Can you play your music more quietly?	He **asked me to play** my music more quietly.
Don't come home after midnight.	She **told me not to come** home after midnight. She **said not to come** home after midnight.

A Amanda is having a surprise party for Albert. Look at what she told the guests. Write each request using *ask*, *tell*, or *say*. Then compare with a partner.

1. Meet at Albert's apartment at 7:30.
2. Can you bring your favorite CDs?
3. Don't bring any food.
4. Can you bring a small gift for Albert?
5. Don't spend more than $10 on the gift.
6. Be careful not to say anything to him.

Amanda told them to meet at Albert's apartment at 7:30.

B ***Group work*** Imagine you're planning a class party. Write four requests. Then take turns reading your requests and changing them into reported requests.

Juan: Bring something good to eat to the party!
Sonia: Juan told us to bring something good to eat.

Noriko: Can you help me clean up after the party?
Jin Sook: Noriko asked us to help her clean up.

4 SPEAKING What a request!

A Think of requests that people have made recently. Write two things people asked you to do and two things people asked you *not* to do.

Person	Request
my mom	*get a haircut*

B ***Group work*** Compare with others. Who has the most interesting or unusual requests? Who did what was asked?

A: My mom asked me to get a haircut.
B: What did you tell her?

5 WORD POWER Verb and noun pairs

A Find three words or phrases in the list that are usually paired with each verb. Then compare with a partner.

anger	a compliment	a criticism	a joke	your regrets
an apology	a concern	an excuse	a lie	sympathy
a complaint	your congratulations	an invitation	a reason	the truth

express	....	....	....
give	....	....	....
make	....	....	....
offer	....	....	....
tell	....	....	....

B ***Pair work*** In what situations do you do the things in part A? Write five sentences about things you *never*, *sometimes*, or *always* do. Then take turns reading your sentences and asking questions.

A: I never tell a lie.
B: Are you sure? What if someone asks how much you weigh?

6 CONVERSATION Are you doing anything on Saturday?

A Listen and practice.

Albert: Hi, Daniel. This is Albert.
Daniel: Oh, hi. How are things?
Albert: Just fine, thanks. Uh, are you doing anything on Saturday night?
Daniel: Hmm. Saturday night? Let me think. Oh, yes. My cousin just called to say he was flying in that night. I told him I would pick him up.
Albert: Oh, that's too bad! It's my birthday. I'm having dinner with Amanda, and I thought I'd invite more people and make it a party.
Daniel: Gee, I'm really sorry, but I won't be able to make it.
Albert: I'm sorry, too. But that's OK.

B ***Pair work*** Act out the conversation in part A. Make up your own excuse for not accepting Albert's invitation.

5 WORD POWER

Learning objective: *learn words and phrases that are paired with certain verbs*

A

- Explain the task. Elicit any new or unfamiliar vocabulary (e.g., *complaint*, *compliment*, *concern*, *criticism*, *regrets*, *sympathy*). If necessary, have Ss use their dictionaries.
- Help the class begin by asking about one or two of the verbs, like this:
  T: What word or phrase goes with the verb *express*?
  S1: I think you can "express anger" in English.
  T: You're right. That's one. What's another?
- Ss complete the chart individually or in pairs. Remind them to find three words or phrases for each verb. Go around the class and give help as needed.
- To check answers, write the verbs on the board and have Ss write their answers beside each verb.

Possible answers

express anger, a concern, your regrets
give a compliment, your congratulations, an excuse, a reason
make an apology, a complaint, a criticism, an excuse
offer your congratulations, sympathy
tell a joke, a lie, the truth

B *Pair work*

- Go over the instructions. Ask Ss to write five sentences about things they *never*, *sometimes*, or *always* do. Set a time limit. Then go around the class and give help as needed. To prepare for follow-up questions, tell Ss to include explanations in their sentences (e.g., I never tell jokes *because I'm not very good at telling them.*).
- When time is up, have two Ss read the example conversation to model the task. Remind Ss to ask follow-up questions. If helpful, elicit a few example questions and write them on the board:
  What happens when you express anger?
  Why don't you offer invitations/tell jokes more often?
  How would you express your sympathy to . . . ?
  In what situation would you tell a lie?
- Ss take turns asking and answering their questions in pairs. After about five minutes, ask pairs to share some of their responses with the class.

For more practice with this vocabulary, play ***Tic-Tac-Toe*** on page T-148.

6 CONVERSATION

Learning objectives: *practice a phone conversation between two friends; see examples of reported speech for statements in context*

A *[CD 3, Track 27]*

- Books closed. Explain the situation. Daniel is going to Albert's surprise birthday party. Amanda told him not to say anything to Albert. Now Albert is calling to invite Daniel to dinner that night! Ask Ss what they would do if that happened to them? Who would tell the truth? Who would tell a lie?
- Write these questions on the board:
  1. Does Daniel make an excuse? an apology?
  2. How does Albert respond? Does he express anger? regret?
- Play the audio program. Ss listen for the answers. (Answers: 1. He makes an excuse *and* an apology. 2. Albert expresses regret.)
- ***Option:*** Have a brief class discussion. Ask: "What should Daniel have done? What would you have done in Albert's situation?"
- Play the audio program again. Have Ss listen to find out what excuse Daniel makes. (Answer: Daniel tells Albert he's picking up his cousin at the airport.)
- Books open. Play the audio program again. Ss read silently as they listen. Ask Ss to listen for emotions expressed by the speakers (e.g., *That's too bad. Gee, I'm really sorry.*).
- Elicit or explain any new vocabulary.

Vocabulary

How are things?: How are you?
Oh, that's too bad!: I'm sorry to hear that something disappointing/bad has happened.
make it: be able to go to an event

- Ss practice the conversation in pairs. To imitate the feeling of talking on the phone, have them sit back-to-back.

For another way to practice this Conversation with more expression, try ***Say It With Feeling!*** on page T-150.

B *Pair work*

- Ss act out the conversation using their own words. Make sure the S playing Daniel makes up a new excuse for not being able to make it to dinner. Then have Ss change roles and repeat the task.

7 LISTENING

Learning objective: *develop skills in listening for detail*

A [CD 3, Track 28]

- Focus Ss' attention on the picture of Albert on the phone. Set the scene. Ss will hear four phone conversations in which Albert's friends make excuses for not coming to his birthday party.
- Tell Ss to look at the four names and the six excuses. Point out that there are two extra excuses. Then play the audio program. Ss listen and complete the task.

Audio script *(See pages T-234–235.)*

- Elicit Ss' responses to check answers.

Answers

1. d 2. e 3. b 4. a

- ***Option:*** Ask Ss how they would have reacted in Albert's situation.

B

- Play the rest of the audio program. Ss listen and take notes.

Audio script *(See page T-235.)*

- After pairs compare answers to the question, elicit responses from the class.

Possible answer

Albert came home singing "Happy Birthday" to himself. When he opened the door, all his friends shouted, "Surprise! Surprise! Happy birthday!" Albert was really surprised and said, "I can't believe it!" He immediately asked Amanda if she set it up (= planned the surprise birthday party for him).

- Ask Ss: "What do you think of surprise parties? Do they work for everyone?"

8 GRAMMAR FOCUS

Learning objective: *practice using reported speech to make statements*

[CD 3, Track 29]

- Write these excuses from Exercise 7 on the board:

Direct statement	*Reported statement*
"I'm not feeling well."	*She said she wasn't feeling well.*
"I have houseguests."	*She said she had houseguests.*

- Point out that the statements in the left column are what the friends actually said. The statements in the right column are "reports" of their excuses.
- Ask Ss to look at the underlined verbs. Elicit what happens when we report a statement. (Answer: We don't use the same tense to report someone's original sentence. Here, the original sentences use the present tense and the reported statements use the past tense.)
- Have Ss look at the sentences in the Grammar Focus box. Go over the direct statements with present and past form verbs and modals to show how the verbs move back one tense in the reported statements.
- Write the following on the board:

Direct statement	*Reported statement*	
be →	*was/were*	*present tense*
have/go →	*had/went*	
(made) →	*had (made)*	*past tense*
have (planned) →	*had (planned)*	*present perfect*
can	*could*	*modals*
will	*would*	
may	*might*	

- Play the audio program to present the direct and reported statements. Ss listen and repeat.

A

- Read the instructions and the first item, including the example answer. Ss work individually to write a reported statement for each excuse. Then Ss compare answers in pairs. Elicit Ss' responses.
- ***Option:*** If possible, ask eight Ss to write their answers on the board. Then correct the work as a class.

TIP Use gestures to help Ss self-correct their work. For example, form a T-shape with your hands to indicate the tense is wrong, or point behind your shoulder to say, "go back a tense."

Possible answers

1. Donna said/told her (that) she had to baby-sit her nephew that night.
2. William and Brigitte said/told her (that) they were going out of town for the weekend.
3. Mary said/told her (that) she had been invited to a wedding on Saturday.
4. James said/told her (that) he had promised to help Dennis move.
5. Anita said/told her (that) she couldn't come because she had the flu.
6. Mark said/told her (that) he would be studying for a test all weekend.
7. Eva and Randall said/told her (that) they had to pick someone up at the airport that evening.
8. David said/told her (that) he might have to work late on Saturday night.

B *Group work*

- Explain the task. Ss think of excuses to tell Sandra. In small groups, Ss take turns reading their excuses. Other Ss change the excuses into reported speech.
- Elicit some excuses from the class.

LISTENING He said, she said

A Listen to Albert inviting friends to his party on Saturday. What excuses do people give for not coming? Match the person to the excuse.

1. Scott ....
2. Fumiko ....
3. Manuel ....
4. Regina ....

a. She said that she wasn't feeling well.
b. He said he was taking his mother to a dance club.
c. She said she had houseguests for the weekend.
d. He said that he would be out of town.
e. She said she might go out with friends.
f. He said he was going away with his family.

B Listen. What happens on the night of Albert's birthday?

8 GRAMMAR FOCUS

Reported speech: statements

Direct statement	*Reported statement*	
I'**m not feeling** well.	She **said** (that)	she **wasn't feeling** well.
I **have** houseguests for the weekend.		she **had** houseguests for the weekend.
I **made** a tennis date with Kim.		she **had made** a tennis date with Kim.
I **have planned** an exciting trip.		she **had planned** an exciting trip.
We **can't come** tomorrow.	They **told me** (that)	they **couldn't come** tomorrow.
We **will be** out of town.		they **would be** out of town.
We **may go** out with friends.		they **might go** out with friends.

A Sandra is having a party at her house on Saturday. Look at these excuses. Change them into reported speech. Then compare with a partner.

1. Donna: "I have to baby-sit my nephew that night."
2. William and Brigitte: "We're going out of town for the weekend."
3. Mary: "I've been invited to a wedding on Saturday."
4. James: "I promised to help Dennis move."
5. Anita: "I can't come because I have the flu."
6. Mark: "I'll be studying for a test all weekend."
7. Eva and Randall: "We have to pick someone up at the airport that evening."
8. David: "I may have to work late on Saturday night."

Donna said she had to baby-sit her nephew that night.
Donna told her she had to baby-sit her nephew that night.

B ***Group work*** Imagine you don't want to go to Sandra's party. Take turns making excuses and changing them into reported speech.

A: I'm sorry I can't go. I have tickets to a concert that night.
B: Lucky guy! He said he had tickets to a concert that night.

9 PRONUNCIATION Reduction of had and would

A Listen and practice. Notice how **had** and **would** are reduced in the following sentences.

She said she'd made the bed. (She said she **had made** the bed.)
She said she'd make the bed. (She said she **would make** the bed.)

B Listen to four sentences. Check (✓) if you hear the reduced form of **had** or **would**.

1. ☐ had ☐ would
2. ☐ had ☐ would
3. ☐ had ☐ would
4. ☐ had ☐ would

10 SPEAKING Good intentions

A ***Group work*** What are some things you would like to do in the near future? Think of three intentions.

A: I'm going to learn how to sail.
B: That sounds fun. Are you going to take lessons?

B ***Class activity*** Report the best intentions you heard. Then predict which ones will happen.

"Tatyana said she was going to learn how to sail, but she doesn't want to take lessons."

11 WRITING A voice mail message

A Dan is out of town for the weekend. Listen to four voice mails he received. His roommate has written down the first message. Write down the three other messages.

Dan– Friday, 9 P.M.
Bill called. He said he would meet you in front of Pizza House at 6:30 P.M. on Monday.

B ***Pair work*** Compare your messages. Is any important information missing?

12 INTERCHANGE 16 Excuses, excuses

Make some plans. Student A find Interchange 16A; Student B find Interchange 16B.

9 PRONUNCIATION

Learning objective: *notice the reduction of* had *and* would *in reported speech statements*

A [CD 3, Track 30]

- Write these contractions of *I had* and *I would* on the board:
  I had = I'd   I would = I'd
- Explain that these two are easily confused. Play the audio program. Have Ss listen to the pronunciation of the reduced forms of *had* and *would* in the sentences. Then play the audio program again, pausing after each sentence for Ss to practice.
- ***Option:*** Ss read sentences 3, 4, and 6 from Exercise 8. Remind them to reduce *had* and *would*.

B

- Explain the task. Ss listen to four sentences and check (✓) if they hear reductions of *had* or *would*. Point out that they can only decide this by paying attention to the verb that comes *after* the contraction.
- Play the rest of the audio program. Ss listen and check the boxes. Then elicit answers.

Answers

1. would 2. had 3. had 4. would

10 SPEAKING

Learning objectives: *discuss future intentions; practice reported speech*

- Elicit or explain the meaning of the title *Good intentions*. Then focus Ss' attention on the picture. Ask: "What do you think the woman's intentions are?" Elicit answers from the class.

A Group work

- Explain the task. Ss think of three intentions. Then they discuss their intentions in small groups. Remind Ss to ask follow-up questions to get more information.
- ***Option:*** Award one point for every follow-up question a S asks. Ss keep track of their own scores.
- Go around the class and listen. Write down common errors. Then go over errors with the whole class.
- ***Option:*** Ss try the activity again in different groups.

TIP To increase Ss' speaking time, have them complete a task a second time with a new challenge (e.g., *focusing on pronunciation, grammar, fluency, or length of conversation*).

! For another way to teach this Speaking exercise, try ***Moving Dialog*** on page T-150. Ss begin like this:
S1: What would you like to do?
S2: I'm going to . . .

B Class activity

- Have Ss use reported speech to tell the class the best intentions they heard. Other Ss ask questions and make predictions about the intentions.

11 WRITING

Learning objectives: *write messages using reported speech; develop skills in listening for details and taking notes*

- Books closed. Ask Ss: "What do you think about answering machines and voice mail? Are they convenient? necessary? What's the best and worst thing about them?"

A [CD 3, Track 31]

- Books open. Explain the task. Play the first message on the audio program. Ss listen and read silently.
- Play the other messages, pausing after each one to give Ss time to write.

Audio script *(See page T-235.)*

B Pair work

- Ss compare messages in pairs. Then ask three pairs to write their messages on the board.

Answers

1. Friday, 9 P.M. Bill called. He said he would meet you in front of Pizza House at 6:30 P.M. on Monday.
2. Saturday, 11 A.M. Marie called. She said there was a French Club meeting on Tuesday at 2 P.M. She said she would see you then.
3. Your aunt Pauline called. She said she was arriving on Wednesday, May 5, late. She said to pick her up at the airport at 11:30. She said she was going to stay with you for three weeks.
4. Carla called. She said that she would meet you on Monday at 7 in front of the Seafood Grill on Water Street. She said she hoped your weekend was great.

12 INTERCHANGE 16

See pages T-130 and T-131 for teaching notes.

13 READING

Learning objectives: *read and discuss an article about lying; develop skills in summarizing and making inferences*

- Books closed. Ask Ss: "What's the opposite of *telling the truth*?" Elicit the answers *telling a lie* and *lying* from the class.
- Write the pre-reading questions on the board. If possible, start the discussion by giving an example of a real situation involving you or someone you know. Spend about five minutes getting Ss' opinions. Then have Ss discuss in small groups or as a class.
- ***Option:*** Books closed. Dictate the first paragraph to Ss. Read it twice at a normal speed. Ss take notes and then work in pairs to reconstruct the paragraph. When Ss finish, have them open their books to check their answers.
- Books open. Focus Ss' attention on the picture. Ask: "How do you think the woman *really* feels about what she's eating?"

A

- Ss read the article silently and then complete the summary. Tell them not to worry about new vocabulary. Go over answers with the class.

Answers

It isn't necessarily **wrong** to lie. It's probably OK to lie if you want to protect **a friendship** or **someone's feelings**. The main reasons for lying are to **hide something**, to **make an excuse**, to **make someone feel good**, or to **avoid sharing bad news**.

- Have Ss read the article again, underlining words or phrases they can't guess from context. When Ss finish, encourage them to check their dictionaries for the definitions.
- ***Option:*** Ss look up new words for homework.
- To make sure Ss understand important vocabulary, write the word or phrase on the board and tell the class to find it in the article. Have a S read the complete sentence in which it appears. Then ask Ss to give their own definition or an example for it.

Vocabulary

average: typical; normal
hide: not tell someone about something; keep something secret
instead: in place of something
the guys: male friends
stretch the truth: exaggerate or extend facts beyond the truth
avoid: *not* do something

B

- Explain the task. Read the first sentence and have Ss decide the reason for the lie. Ask Ss to complete the task and compare their answers in pairs. Then go over answers with the class.

Answers

1. #3 2. #4 3. #2 4. #1

C Group work

- Have Ss discuss the questions in small groups. Encourage them to think of recent situations when they said things that were not exactly true. Do they know the reason why they lied?
- Ask each group to report the most interesting ideas or stories they discussed.

For more practice with this topic, play ***True or False?*** on page T-148. Find out who is the best at telling white lies!

End of Cycle 2

Do your students need more practice?

Assign . . .	*For more practice in . . .*
Workbook Exercises 5–8 on pages 94–96	Grammar, Vocabulary, Reading, and Writing
Lab Guide Exercises 4–7 on page 22	Listening, Pronunciation, Speaking, and Grammar
Video Activity Book Unit 16	Listening, Speaking, and Cultural Awareness
CD-ROM Unit 16	Grammar, Vocabulary, Reading, Listening, and Speaking

Evaluation

Assess Ss' understanding of Units 15 and 16 with the quiz on pages T-214 and T-215.

Assess Ss' understanding of Units 9–16 with one of the tests on pages 153–162 of the *Interchange Third Edition/Passages Placement and Evaluation Package.*

For review or more practice with the topics in this book, try ***Talk About It!*** on page T-159.

13 READING

The Truth About Lying

Is it ever better to tell a lie rather than the truth? If so, when?

Most of us are taught to believe that lying is wrong. But it seems that everybody tells lies – not big lies, but what we call "white lies." If we believe that lying is wrong, why do we do it? Most of the time, people have very good reasons for lying. For example, they might want to protect a friendship or someone's feelings. So, when do we lie and who do we lie to? A recent study found that the average person lies about seven times a day. Here are some ways and reasons why.

#1 Lying to hide something: People often lie because they want to hide something from someone. For example, a son doesn't tell his parents that he's dating a girl because he doesn't think they will like her. Instead, he says he's going out with the guys.

#2 Lying to make an excuse: Sometimes people lie because they don't want to do something. For example, someone invites you to a party. You think it will be boring, so you say you're busy.

#3 Lying to make someone feel good: Often we stretch the truth to make someone feel good. For example, your friend cooks dinner for you, but it tastes terrible. Do you say so? No. You probably say, "Mmm, this is delicious!"

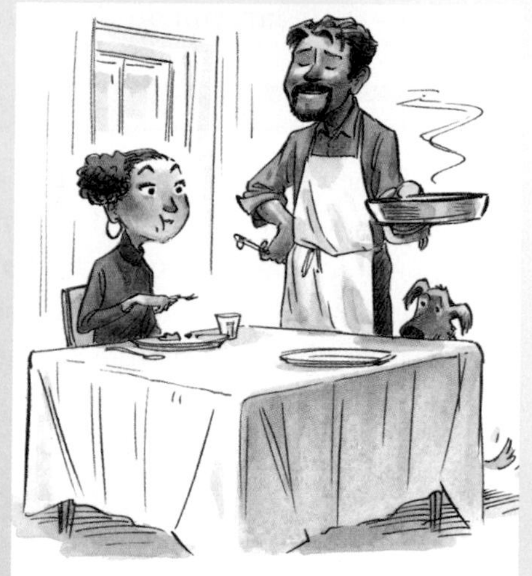

#4 Lying to avoid sharing bad news: Sometimes we don't want to tell someone bad news. For example, you have just had a very bad day at work, but you don't feel like talking about it. So if someone asks you about your day, you just say that everything was fine.

A Read the article. Then complete the summary with information from the article.

It isn't necessarily .... to lie. It's probably OK to lie if you want to protect .... or .... The main reasons for lying are to .... , to .... , to .... , or to ....

B Look at these situations. For each example, write the number of the appropriate reason.

.... 1. Your friend gives you an ugly shirt for your birthday. You say, "Oh, it's great!"
.... 2. You lost your job and are having trouble finding a new one. When an old friend calls to find out how you are, you say you're doing well.
.... 3. Someone you don't like invites you to a movie, so you say, "I've already seen it."
.... 4. You're planning a surprise party for a friend. To get him to come over at the right time, you ask him to stop by to see your new motorcycle.

C ***Group work*** Can you think of other reasons people tell white lies? What white lies have you told recently?

Units 15–16 Progress check

SELF-ASSESSMENT

How well can you do these things? Check (✓) the boxes.

I can	Very well	OK	A little
Speculate about imaginary events using unreal conditional sentences (Ex. 1)	☐	☐	☐
Talk about events in the past using past modals (Ex. 2)	☐	☐	☐
Ask for and give opinions or suggestions using past modals (Ex. 2)	☐	☐	☐
Listen to and understand requests (Ex. 3)	☐	☐	☐
Describe what people say and request using reported speech (Ex. 3, 4)	☐	☐	☐

1 DISCUSSION *Interesting situations*

A What would you do in these situations? Complete the statements.

If I found a valuable piece of jewelry in the park, ...

If a friend gave me a present I didn't like, ...

If I wasn't invited to a party I wanted to attend, ...

If a classmate wanted to copy my homework, ...

If someone took my clothes while I was swimming, ...

B ***Group work*** Compare your suggestions. For each situation, choose one to tell the class.

A: What would you do if you found some jewelry in the park?
B: I'd probably keep it. You'd never be able to find the owner.

2 SPEAKING *Dilemmas*

A Make up two situations like the one below. Think about experiences you have had or heard about at work, home, or school.

"A friend visited me recently. We had a great time at first, but she became annoying. She borrowed my clothes and refused to pay for things. After two weeks, I told her she had to leave because my parents were coming."

B ***Pair work*** Take turns sharing your situations. Ask for advice and suggestions.

A: What would you have done?
B: Well, I would have told her to leave after three days.

Units 15–16 Progress check

SELF-ASSESSMENT

Learning objectives: *reflect on one's learning; identify areas that need improvement*

- Ask: "What did you learn in Units 15 and 16?" Elicit Ss' answers.
- Ss complete the Self-assessment. Encourage them to be honest, and point out they will not get a bad grade if they check (✓) "a little."
- Ss move on to the Progress check exercises. You can have Ss complete them in class or for homework, using one of these techniques:
  1. Ask Ss to complete all the exercises.
  2. Ask Ss: "What do you need to practice?" Then assign exercises based on their answers.
  3. Ask Ss to choose and complete exercises based on their Self-assessment.

DISCUSSION

Learning objective: *assess one's ability to speculate about imaginary events using unreal conditional sentences*

A

- Explain the task and answer any vocabulary questions.
- Tell Ss to think of interesting suggestions for the first situation (e.g., *I'd put an ad in the paper. I'd leave a note in the park in case anyone came back to look for it.*).
- Ss work individually to write one suggestion for each situation. Set a time limit. Go around the class and give help as needed.

B *Group work*

- Explain the task. Ss work in groups to compare the statements they wrote in part A.
- Ask two Ss to read the example conversation. Encourage them to ask follow-up questions to continue the conversation.
- Explain that after discussing each situation, the group decides on the best suggestion. Then someone in the group writes it down.
- Ss form groups and choose a secretary. Set a time limit of about ten minutes for Ss to compare their suggestions and choose their favorites.
- Have groups read their best suggestions to the class. Encourage others to ask questions or to make comments.
- ***Option:*** Take a class vote on which suggestion they like best for each situation.

SPEAKING

Learning objectives: *assess one's ability to talk about events in the past using past modals; assess one's ability to ask for and give opinions or suggestions using past modals*

A

- Present the situation in the example by focusing Ss' attention on the picture. Then tell Ss to think of two similar situations based on experiences they have had at work, home, or school.
- Ss work individually to write two situations. Go around the class and give help as needed.

B *Pair work*

- Ask two Ss to read the example conversation. Encourage Ss to ask follow-up questions. Remind them to use the reduced form of *have*.
- Ss work in pairs to take turns reading their situations and asking for advice and suggestions.
- Go around the class and write down any common errors, especially past modals. When time is up, write the errors on the board and have Ss correct them. Praise correct uses of past modals that you heard.

3 LISTENING

Learning objectives: *assess one's ability to listen to and understand requests; assess one's ability to describe what people say and request using reported speech*

A ▶ [CD 3, Track 32]

- Explain the task. Ss listen to people making requests and match each request to the correct person.
- Play the audio program. Ss listen and complete the task. Then go over answers with the class.

Audio script *(See page T-235.)*

Answers

1. d. parent	4. e. classmate
2. c. neighbor	5. a. boss
3. b. doctor	6. f. teacher

B ▶

- Explain the task. Ss write each request. Then play the audio program again, pausing after each conversation to give Ss time to write.
- Ss complete the task. Then go over answers with the class.

Answers

1. Please pick up your things.
2. Can you move your car?
3. Don't take more than three a day.
4. Can I borrow your notes?
5. Please come into my office.
6. Please don't go until the bell rings.

C *Pair work*

- Explain the task. Then use reported speech and the first request to model the task for the class (e.g., *My mother asked me to pick up my things.*).
- Ss form pairs and take turns reporting the requests to each other. Go around the class and listen to make sure Ss are able to use reported requests.

GAME

Learning objective: *assess one's ability to describe what people say and request using reported speech*

A

- Explain the task and read the example. Give Ss time to think of and write three statements, one for each situation. Go around the class and give help as needed.

B *Class activity*

- Divide the class into groups of three. Tell each group to compare their statements and to choose one that they would like to talk about.
- ***Option:*** Ss continue to work in groups of three. The two Ss who did *not* experience the situation ask the third S detailed questions about it. They should find out as much as possible about the situation.
- Explain the task. In groups of three, Ss come to the front of the classroom and each read the same statement aloud. The rest of the class asks the three Ss questions. Make sure the class understands that only *one* of the Ss experienced the situation. The goal is to find out which of the three Ss *really* experienced the situation.
- Go over the three steps and the example questions with the class. Ask these questions to be sure that everyone in the class understands what to do: "How many contestants are telling the truth? How many are not? How can you find out who isn't telling the truth? What do you do when you discover someone isn't telling the truth?"
- Invite the first group to the front of the class to read their situation. Encourage the rest of the class to ask questions. Remind Ss to use reported speech when they discover who isn't telling the truth.

WHAT'S NEXT?

Learning objective: *become more involved in one's learning*

- Focus Ss' attention on the Self-assessment again. Ask: "How well can you do these things now?"
- Ask Ss to underline one thing they need to review. Ask: "What did you underline? How can you review it?"
- If needed, plan additional activities or reviews based on Ss' answers.

3 LISTENING Take a message.

A Listen to the conversations. Who would make these requests? Match conversations 1 to 6 to the correct person.

.... a. boss .... c. neighbor .... e. classmate
.... b. doctor .... d. parent .... f. teacher

B Listen again. Complete the requests.

1. Please ....
2. Can .... ?
3. Don't ....
4. Can .... ?
5. Please ....
6. Please don't ....

C ***Pair work*** Work with a partner. Imagine these requests were for you. Take turns reporting the requests to your partner.

4 GAME Tell the truth.

A Think of situations when you *expressed anger*, *gave an excuse*, or *made a complaint*. Write a brief statement about each situation.

I once complained about the food in a restaurant.

B ***Class activity*** Play a game. Choose three students to be contestants.

Step 1: The contestants compare their statements and choose one. This statement should be true about only one student. The other two students should pretend they had the experience.

Step 2: The contestants stand in front of the class. Each contestant reads the same statement. The rest of the class must ask questions to find out who isn't telling the truth.

Contestant A, what restaurant were you in?

Contestant B, what was wrong with the food?

Contestant C, what did the waiter do?

Step 3: Who isn't telling the truth? What did he or she say to make you think that?

"I don't think Contestant A is telling the truth. He said he couldn't remember the name of the restaurant!"

WHAT'S NEXT?

Look at your Self-assessment again. Do you need to review anything?

Interchange activities

interchange 1

***Learning objectives:** speak more fluently about the past with classmates; review questions with the past tense and* used to

A *Class activity*

- Focus Ss' attention on the title of this activity. Have Ss look at the information in the chart. Ask: "What do you think the word *profile* means?" (Answer: a description of the most important or interesting facts about someone)
- Explain that the things Ss learn about one another in this activity will help them form a profile of their classmates' personalities and past experiences.
- Read the instructions and go over the chart. Elicit questions 5–8.

Answers

5. Did you change schools when you were a child?
6. Did you use to fight a lot with your brothers and sisters?
7. Did you get in trouble a lot as a child?
8. Did you have a pet when you were little?

Interchange activities

interchange 1 ***CLASS PROFILE***

A ***Class activity*** Go around the class and find out the information below. Then ask follow-up questions and take notes. Write a classmate's name only once.

I used to look very different.

Find someone who	Name	Notes
1. used to look very different **"Did you use to look very different?"**	....	....
2. always listened to his or her teachers **"Did you always listen to your teachers?"**	....	....
3. wanted to be a movie star when he or she was younger **"Did you want to be a movie star when you were younger?"**	....	....
4. used to have a favorite toy **"Did you use to have a favorite toy?"**	....	....
5. changed schools when he or she was a child "..........?"	....	....
6. used to fight a lot with his or her brothers and sisters "..........?"	....	....
7. got in trouble a lot as a child "..........?"	....	....
8. had a pet when he or she was little "..........?"	....	....

B ***Group work*** Tell the group the most interesting thing you learned about your classmates.

Interchange 1

- Model the task with a S.
  T: Did you use to look very different?
  S: Yes. I used to have longer hair.
  T: Did you use to wear glasses?
  S: Yes. Now I wear contact lenses.
- Write the S's name in the Name column and the information in the Notes column. Explain that if a classmate says "no," they should ask another S the same question.
- Ask two Ss to model the task. Check that the class understands the instructions by asking questions like these: "When someone says 'yes,' what do you do? Do you write the person's name or the word 'yes' in the Name column?" (Answer: the person's name)
- Set a time limit of about ten minutes. Remind Ss to write down the name of any classmate who answers "yes" to a question in the chart and ask follow-up questions to get more information.
- Encourage Ss to get up and move around the classroom while asking and responding to one another's questions. Go around the class and take note of any problems that Ss may be having. Go over any errors at the end of the activity.

B *Group work*

- In small groups, Ss take turns sharing the most interesting information they learned about their classmates.

interchange 2 TOURISM CAMPAIGN

A *Pair work* Look at the photos and slogans below. What do you think the theme of each tourism campaign is?

B *Group work* Imagine you are planning a campaign to attract more tourists to one of the cities above or to a city of your choice. Use the ideas below or your own ideas to discuss the campaign.

best time to visit
famous historical attractions
special events or festivals
nicest area to stay
interesting places to see

A: Do you know when the best time to visit Rio is?
B: Probably in February or March because . . .

C *Group work* What will be the theme of your campaign? What slogan will you use?

Interchange 2

interchange 2

***Learning objectives:** discuss slogans and ways to attract tourists to a city; plan a tourism campaign for a city*

- ***Option:*** Bring some English-language travel brochures to class. Have Ss discuss the ads in pairs or small groups. Then ask Ss to share the most interesting ads/brochures with the rest of the class.
- Books closed. Ask Ss if they know the slogan for their city or another city (e.g., *Quito, Ecuador, is called The City of Eternal Spring*; *New York City is called The Big Apple.*).
- Explain that to attract more tourists to a city, a tourism board uses a theme to build a campaign, or a series of actions intended to achieve a specific goal. This theme usually involves something special about the city. In this activity, Ss plan a campaign to attract tourists to a city.

A *Pair work*

- Books open. Present the slogans for each city listed and explain any new vocabulary. Be careful not to give away the theme of each campaign.

Vocabulary

marvels: wonders
diner: a person who likes to eat well
paradise: an ideal location
banquet: feast (here, a large offering of high-quality music)

- Focus Ss' attention on the first photo and slogan. Ask: "What does this slogan mean? According to its slogan, what is special about Rio? art? culture? food? nature?"
- Ss discuss each slogan and theme in pairs. Then have each pair join another pair to compare answers.

Possible answers

Rio – culture (music and entertainment) and nature
Hong Kong – food
Cairo – culture and history
Salzburg – music

B *Group work*

- Read the instructions, list of ideas, and example conversation. Explain the task. Ss work in groups to choose a city and discuss how it is special. Encourage Ss to be as creative as possible.
- Ss choose a city and discuss each idea on the list. Go around the class and give help as needed.

TIP To make group work more effective, assign each student in the group a role (e.g., a secretary, a language monitor, a leader, and a person who will report back to the class).

C *Group work*

- Explain the task. Ss work in the same groups from part B to discuss possible themes and slogans.
- Groups take turns sharing their ideas with the rest of the class.
- ***Option:*** To turn this activity into a project, have Ss research a city and prepare a poster with photos and maps. Display Ss' work on a wall or bulletin board in the classroom, in a school magazine, or on the Web.

interchange 3 WISHFUL THINKING

A Complete this questionnaire with information about yourself.

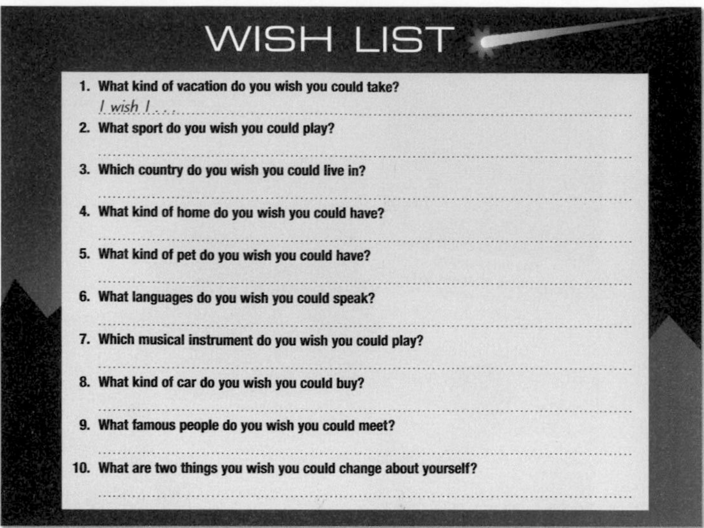

WISH LIST

1. What kind of vacation do you wish you could take?
   I wish I . . . .
2. What sport do you wish you could play?
3. Which country do you wish you could live in?
4. What kind of home do you wish you could have?
5. What kind of pet do you wish you could have?
6. What languages do you wish you could speak?
7. Which musical instrument do you wish you could play?
8. What kind of car do you wish you could buy?
9. What famous people do you wish you could meet?
10. What are two things you wish you could change about yourself?

B *Pair work* Compare your questionnaires. Take turns asking and answering questions about your wishes.

A: What kind of vacation do you wish you could take?
B: I wish I could go on a safari.
A: Really? Why?
B: Well, I could take some great pictures of wild animals!

C *Class activity* Imagine you are at a class reunion. It is ten years since you completed the questionnaire in part A. Tell the class about some wishes that have come true for your partner.

"Sue is a photographer now. She travels to Africa every year and takes pictures of wild animals. Her photos are in many magazines."

Interchange 3

interchange 3

Learning objective: *speak more fluently about how people would like to change their lives*

A

- Focus Ss' attention on the title of this activity. Explain that it refers to the false belief that something will happen just because you want it to. When people say, *"That's wishful thinking!"* they mean that it probably won't happen.
- Explain the task and read the ten questions in the chart. Ss repeat for correct pronunciation, stress, and intonation. Tell Ss to write a complete sentence beginning with *I wish (that) I could . . .* to answer each question. Go around the class and give help as needed. Tell Ss they can write either realistic or unrealistic wishes.
- ***Option:*** Ss can complete the chart in class or for homework.

B *Pair work*

- Explain the task and model the example conversation with Ss. Demonstrate how to keep the conversation going, like this:

  T: And how about you? What kind of vacation do you wish you could take?
  S: Me? I really wish I could go on a cruise.
  T: Really? Why?
  S: Well, I could visit many different tropical islands, and I'd have time to relax and read a lot of books.
- Tell Ss to take notes while interviewing their partners to use later in part C.
- Ss form pairs and take turns asking and answering the questions in part A. Encourage Ss to extend their conversations by asking for additional information. Go around the class and give help as needed.

C *Class activity*

- Read the instructions and explain that a class reunion is a meeting of former classmates. Read the description of Sue, who is now a professional photographer.
- Model the activity by asking Ss about their partners. Write the information on the board and demonstrate how to use it to make an interesting description:

  Wish List - #3: Terry wishes he could live in the U.S. He wishes he could live near the beach so he could swim and windsurf every day.

  Ten-Year Reunion Statement: Terry moved to California five years ago. His dream has finally come true. He goes swimming and windsurfing every day!
- Give Ss a few minutes to go over their notes from part B. Then encourage them to make up one or two interesting or amusing sentences to describe their partner ten years from now. Go around the class and give help as needed.
- Ss take turns reading their descriptions to the class.

interchange 4 RISKY BUSINESS

A How much do you really know about your classmates? Look at the survey and add two more situations to items 1 and 2.

	Name	Notes
1. Find someone who has		
a. cried during a movie		
b. had food poisoning		
c. been on TV		
d. studied all night for an exam		
e. lied about his or her age		
f.		
g.		
2. Find someone who has never		
a. driven a car		
b. used a recipe to cook		
c. had a cup of coffee		
d. played a video game		
e. eaten pizza		
f.		
g.		

B *Class activity* Go around the class and ask the questions in the survey. Write down the names of classmates who answer "yes" for item 1 and "no" for item 2. Then ask follow-up questions and take notes.

A: Have you ever cried during a movie?
B: Yes. I've cried during a lot of movies.
A: What kinds of movies?
B: Well, sad ones like *Casablanca* and . . .

A: Have you ever driven a car?
C: No, I haven't.
A: Why not?
C: Well, I'm too young. I don't have a driver's license.

C *Group work* Compare the information in your surveys.

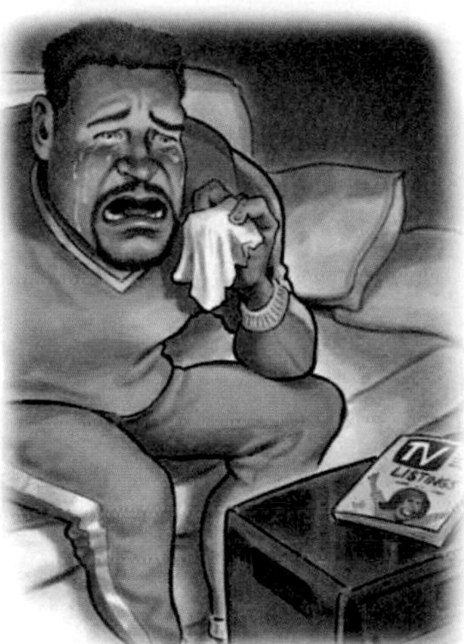

Interchange 4

interchange 4

Learning objective: *speak more fluently about experiences*

A

- Focus Ss' attention on the title. Explain that it is used to describe a situation or an action that could be dangerous in some way. In this activity, the phrase suggests that Ss might be taking a chance by telling about themselves and learning about their classmates.
- Read the question and instructions. Explain that a survey is a set of questions that you ask a large number of people to learn about their opinions or behavior. Ss will use this survey to discover what kinds of interesting experiences their classmates have had.
- Go over the situations listed in the chart. Elicit or explain any new vocabulary.
- Encourage Ss to be creative when they add two more situations to each item. Point out that this should be fun. The situations shouldn't embarrass or upset anyone.
- ***Option:*** Give some examples of things that people in the United States and Canada don't usually ask casual acquaintances about (e.g., *age, religion, politics, salary, cost of expensive or personal items*).
- Ss work individually to add four more situations. Go around the class and give help, especially on situations concerning cultural appropriateness.

B *Class activity*

- Explain the task and model the activity by reading the example conversations with Ss. Demonstrate when and how to write down classmates' names in the survey. If necessary, use the board to show how to take notes on additional information.
- ***Option:*** For lower-level classes, elicit the questions for each item from the class.
- Set a time limit of about ten minutes. Ss stand up and move around the class to ask and answer each other's questions. Go around the class and give help as needed. Encourage Ss to change partners frequently.
- When time is up, see if Ss have filled in most of the chart. If not, give them a few more minutes to complete the task.

C *Group work*

- Ss compare their information in groups. Help them get started by writing these questions on the board:
  I found out that . . . (name) has . . .
  Did you know that . . . (name) has never . . . ?
  Did anyone find someone who has/had never . . . ?
  When/Why/How did that happen?

interchange 5A FUN VACATIONS

Student A

A *Pair work* You and your partner are going to take a trip. You have a brochure for a ski trip, and your partner has a brochure for a surfing trip.

First, find out about the surfing trip. Ask your partner questions about these things.

the cost of the trip	what the price includes	the accommodations
surfing lessons	entertainment options	the nightlife

B *Pair work* Now use the information in this brochure to answer your partner's questions about the ski trip.

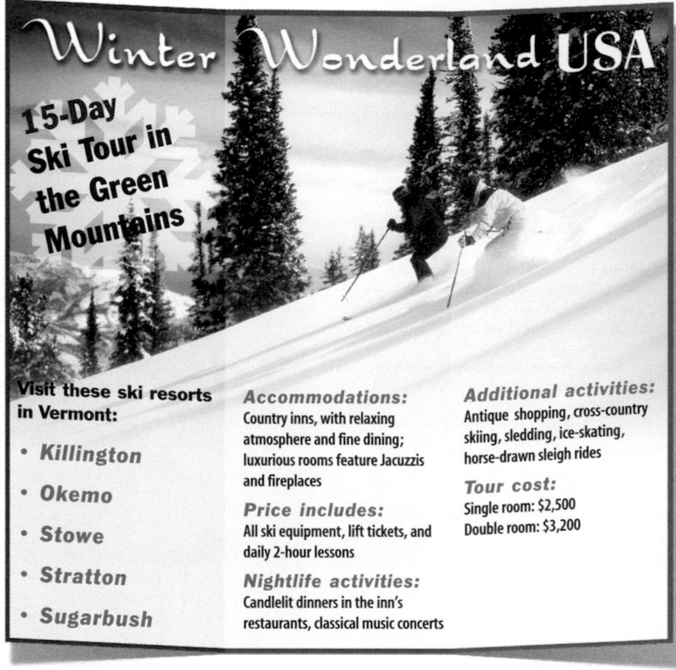

Winter Wonderland USA
15-Day Ski Tour in the Green Mountains
Visit these ski resorts in Vermont:
• Killington
• Okemo
• Stowe
• Stratton
• Sugarbush
Accommodations:
Country inns, with relaxing atmosphere and fine dining; luxurious rooms feature Jacuzzis and fireplaces
Price includes:
All ski equipment, lift tickets, and daily 2-hour lessons
Nightlife activities:
Candlelit dinners in the inn's restaurants, classical music concerts
Additional activities:
Antique shopping, cross-country skiing, sledding, ice-skating, horse-drawn sleigh rides
Tour cost:
Single room: $2,500
Double room: $3,200

C *Pair work* Decide which trip you are going to take. Then explain your choice to the class.

Interchange 5A

interchange 5A/B

Learning objective: *speak more fluently about vacation activities and plans*

- Books closed. Ask: "Has anyone ever taken a ski trip or a surfing trip?" If so, have the other Ss ask questions about the trip.
- Divide the class into pairs, preferably with Ss who didn't work together in Exercise 10. Then assign each S an A or B part.
- Books open. Tell Student A to look at page Interchange 5A and Student B to look at page Interchange 5B. Remind them not to look at each other's pages.
- Answer any questions about the instructions for the role play, the information in their brochures, or new vocabulary.

Vocabulary

Interchange 5A

Green Mountains: a range of the Appalachian Mountains in Vermont (a state in the northeastern region of the United States)
resorts: places where people can go for a vacation, with hotels, swimming pools, etc.
country inns: small hotels – often in large old houses – in areas outside cities
atmosphere: the feeling that an event, a situation, or a place gives you
luxurious: very comfortable, beautiful, and expensive
Jacuzzi: the trademark name for a hot tub, or a heated type of large bathtub that several people can sit in
lift tickets: tickets that show skiers have paid to ride up the mountain
candlelit dinners: dining in a room that has lighted candles on each table, considered romantic
antique: a piece of furniture, jewelry, etc., that is old and usually valuable
cross-country skiing: skiing through fields and woods on long, thin skis
sledding: using a vehicle that slides over snow, often used by children
sleigh rides: trips in a vehicle used for traveling on snow, pulled by horses
single: a hotel room for one person
double: a hotel room for two people

Interchange 5B

Southern California: the lower third of the western U.S. state of California
single/double rooms: (See definitions in Interchange 5A.)
Universal Studios: a movie theme park located in Hollywood
Disneyland: an amusement park in Southern California
Beverly Hills: a famous section of Los Angeles where many movie stars live

- If necessary, separate the two groups. Go over page Interchange 5A with Student As. When they understand what to do, they prepare their questions and roles. Then do the same with Student Bs and the information on page Interchange 5B.

A Pair work

- Model the role play with a Student B. Demonstrate how to start the activity by making up questions to ask about the surfing trip: "How much does the trip cost? What does the price include? What are the accommodations like? Are surfing lessons available? Will there be any entertainment/nightlife?"
- If Student B needs help answering the questions, elicit answers from other Student Bs.

interchange 5B ***FUN VACATIONS***

Student B

A *Pair work* You and your partner are going to take a trip. You have a brochure for a surfing trip, and your partner has a brochure for a ski trip.

First, use the information in this brochure to answer your partner's questions about the surfing trip.

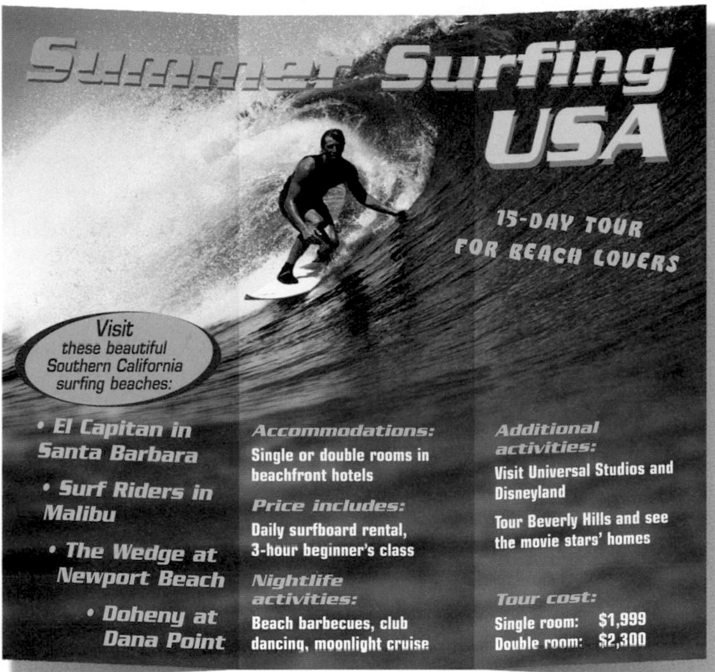

Summer Surfing USA
15-DAY TOUR FOR BEACH LOVERS
Visit these beautiful Southern California surfing beaches:
• El Capitan in Santa Barbara
• Surf Riders in Malibu
• The Wedge at Newport Beach
• Doheny at Dana Point
Accommodations:
Single or double rooms in beachfront hotels
Price includes:
Daily surfboard rental, 3-hour beginner's class
Nightlife activities:
Beach barbecues, club dancing, moonlight cruise
Additional activities:
Visit Universal Studios and Disneyland
Tour Beverly Hills and see the movie stars' homes
Tour cost:
Single room: $1,999
Double room: $2,300

B *Pair work* Now find out about the ski trip. Ask your partner questions about these things.

the cost of the trip	what the price includes	the accommodations
ski lessons	entertainment options	the nightlife

C *Pair work* Decide which trip you are going to take. Then explain your choice to the class.

Interchange 5B

- Set a time limit of five minutes for part A of the role play. Student As start by asking questions about the surfing trip. Student Bs answer by using the information on their page and making up information. Go around the class and take note of any common errors.
- When time is up, go over any errors you observed with the whole class.

B *Pair work*

- Student Bs ask questions about the ski trip. Set a time limit of five minutes. Go around the class and give help as needed. Remind Student As that they can make up additional information if they wish.

C *Pair work*

- Go over the instructions. Tell Ss to discuss what they would like to do and *not do* on their trips. Encourage Ss to ask follow-up questions and suggest additional information.
- Pairs take turns telling the class which trip they are going to take and why.

interchange 6

Learning objective: *speak more fluently when complaining and apologizing in this role play*

A *Pair work*

- Divide the class into pairs and assign each S an A or B part.
- Explain the task. Point out that this activity is a series of four different role plays. Ss should use their own language, expressions, and vocabulary. Tell pairs to look at each picture while they perform that particular role play.
- Give the class a few minutes to look at the four situations and cues. Point out that Student A and Student B will each get two chances to make a complaint and two chances to apologize.
- Answer any questions that Ss may have about the situations or vocabulary they might want to use.
- ***Option:*** For each picture, brainstorm words and write Ss' suggestions on the board. If necessary, add some of these words to the board:

  Picture 1
  hair salon, customer, hairstylist, shocked, upset, dye, pink, comb, spray bottle, fix

  Picture 2
  studying, backpack, strap, puppy, chew, bite, surprised

  Picture 3
  car accident, minor, head-on collision, one-way street, damaged, fender, fault, driving the wrong way, no-left-turn sign

  Picture 4
  supermarket, checkout line, cashier, grocery cart, bags, groceries, purse, no money/cash, embarrassed, upset, impatient, customers, waiting in line

- Model the first example conversation with a S to show how Student A could begin and how Student B might reply. Try to keep the conversation going for at least a minute. Encourage Ss to have fun by using appropriate gestures and facial expressions.

  S: My hair! You ruined my hair!
  T: Oh, I'm so sorry. I'll try to wash it out. But first, how about a nice cup of coffee or tea?
  S: Coffee! Tea! I want you to do something right now about this horrible hair color!
  T: All right. Uh, may I dye it again for you?
  S: Are you kidding?
  T: No, I admit that I made a terrible mistake and I'm very sorry. Please let me try to improve it.
  S: Well, can you make my hair blond . . . or red instead?
  T: I think so. Let's look at the colors on this chart and then I'll fix it for you. I promise.

- Have Ss practice each situation. Encourage Ss to stand up or move around.

B *Group work*

- Tell Ss to join another pair. Ss discuss experiences they have had that were similar to the situations in part A. Ss can also talk about other similar situations.
- ***Option:*** Call on one S from each group to share one of the stories from the group with the whole class. Ss can also write down their story for homework.

---

interchange 6 *THAT'S NO EXCUSE!*

A ***Pair work*** Look at these situations and act out conversations. Apologize and then give an excuse, admit a mistake, or make an offer or promise.

useful expressions
I'm sorry. / I didn't realize. / I forgot.
You're right. / I was wrong.
I'll . . . right away.
I'll make sure to . . . / I promise I'll . . .

1

Student A: You're the customer.
Student B: You're the hairstylist.

A: My hair! You ruined my hair!
B: Oh, I'm so sorry. I . . .

2

Student A: You own the puppy.
Student B: You own the backpack.

3

Student A: You're driving the red car.
Student B: You're driving the blue car.

4

Student A: You're the customer.
Student B: You're the cashier.

B ***Group work*** Have you ever experienced situations like these? What happened? What did you do? Share your stories.

Interchange 6

interchange 7 TALK RADIO

A *Group work* Look at the four problems that people called a radio program about. What advice would you give each caller? Discuss possible suggestions, and then choose the best one.

Caller 1: My family and I are going away on vacation and our house will be empty. How can we make our home safe from burglars?
Caller 2: One of my classmates wants to borrow my new CD player to take with him on vacation. I don't want to lend it to him. What can I say?
RADIO KZFM 98.1
KZFM 98
Caller 3: I'm going to meet my girlfriend's parents tomorrow for the first time. How can I make a good impression?
Caller 4: Our neighbor's dog barks all night and keeps everybody in the neighborhood awake. What can we do?

B *Pair work* Take turns "calling" a radio station and explaining your problems. Use the situations above or create new ones. Your partner should give you advice.

A: My family and I are going away on vacation and our house will be empty. How can we make our home safe from burglars?
B: Well, don't forget to lock all the windows. Oh, and make sure to . . .

Interchange 7

interchange 7

Learning objective: *speak more fluently when giving advice in this role play*

A *Group work*

- Books closed. To introduce the activity, ask Ss if they ever listen to radio programs where people call in with their problems. What do Ss think about them? Is the advice usually good? Why are they so popular?
- Books open. Explain the situation. Four people called a radio program with these problems. Have Ss look at the problems.
- Elicit or explain any new words and expressions (e.g., *burglars, lend, make a good impression, bark*) or have Ss check their dictionaries.
- Explain the task. Ss think of possible advice for each caller. Elicit Ss' suggestions for the first caller. Write some of their ideas on the board.
  - *Make sure to tell your neighbors.*
  - *Don't forget to lock the windows.*
  - *Get an automatic light switch so your house lights will go on and off each day.*
  - *Ask the post office to keep your mail until you return.*
  - *Stop daily newspaper delivery while you're gone.*
  - *Ask a friend or neighbor to check the house regularly*
- Ss form small groups and brainstorm advice for each caller. Remind them that *advice* is a noncount noun. To make it plural, we say "pieces of advice." Then give Ss a time limit.

TIP To keep Ss on task, remind them of the time throughout the activity (e.g., "You have two minutes left.").

- When time is up, have each group choose their best piece of advice for each situation.

B *Pair work*

- Explain that this activity gives each S four chances to ask for suggestions or give advice. Model the first caller's problem with a S. Sit back-to-back and pretend to hold a telephone in your hand. Read the example conversation with the S. Then elicit additional suggestions.
- Divide the class into pairs and give them time to brainstorm other problems to ask on a radio program. If Ss need help, brainstorm with the whole class and write ideas on the board. It may be helpful for Ss to think of broad categories (e.g., *health, dating and relationships, car problems, money and finance*).
- Set a time limit of eight minutes, or about two minutes for each situation. Remind "the host" to give at least four suggestions for each situation. Encourage Ss to be creative, improvise, and have fun.
- In pairs, Ss take turns calling about their problems. The "caller" starts first. Go around the class and listen. If Ss are having problems, stop the activity, go over the difficulties, and suggest solutions. If necessary, model one of the situations again.
- Continue the activity until Ss discuss all four situations and situations of their own.
- ***Option:*** Have Ss perform one or two situations for the class.

interchange 8 ONCE IN A BLUE MOON

A ***Class activity*** How do your classmates celebrate special days and times? Go around the class and ask the questions below. If someone answers "yes," write down his or her name. Ask for more information and take notes.

	Name	Notes
1. Does your family have big get-togethers?		
2. Do you ever buy flowers for someone special?		
3. Do you like to watch street parades?		
4. Do you wear your national dress at least once a year?		
5. Has someone given you money recently as a gift?		
6. Have you ever given someone a surprise birthday party?		
7. Do you like to celebrate your birthday with a party?		
8. Do you ever send birthday cards?		
9. Do you ever give friends birthday presents?		
10. Is New Year's your favorite time of the year?		
11. Do you ever celebrate a holiday with fireworks?		

A: Does your family have big get-togethers?
B: Yes, we do.
A: What do you do when you get together?
B: Well, we have a big meal. After we eat, we watch old home movies.

B ***Pair work*** Compare your information with a partner.

Interchange 8

interchange 8

Learning objectives: *speak more fluently about celebrations; practice asking follow-up questions, giving extra information, and showing interest*

A *Class activity*

- Read the instructions. Then ask Ss to read the questions in the chart for unknown words. Explain any new vocabulary.

Vocabulary

get-together: a friendly, informal party
national dress: a costume or outfit that is typical (or historical) in a particular country

- Call on Ss to read the questions aloud, and check for correct pronunciation, stress, and rhythm. If necessary, model the correct pronunciation.
- Explain the task. Ss stand up and go around the room, asking classmates questions. If the classmate answers "yes," they write the classmate's name in the column and ask some follow-up questions. Then they write some notes before talking to another classmate. Remind them to talk to as many Ss as possible.
- Point out the need to ask follow-up questions and to give extra information when answering. Elicit some expressions to show interest (e.g., *That sounds like fun! That's interesting. Really? Tell me more! Wow!*).
- To practice asking follow-up questions, model the first two or three questions and elicit Ss' suggestions.
  1. How many people usually come to your big get-togethers? Where does everyone meet? What do you usually do there? What kinds of food do you eat?
  2. Who do you buy flowers for? What kind? Why do you buy them?
  3. How often do you watch parades? What's the best parade you've ever seen? Why was it good?
- Ss complete the activity. Set a time limit of about ten minutes. Go around the class and give help, particularly if there are communication problems.

B *Pair work*

- Ss form pairs and compare their information. With a S, model how they should begin their discussion.

T: Let's start with the first question. Who has big family get-togethers?
S: Madhu's family has big get-togethers about once a month. They usually go over to his grandmother's on a Sunday afternoon. All of his sisters and aunts make special dishes, and the men are in charge of barbecuing the meat.
T: That's interesting. I found out that Sara also has big family get-togethers every summer. They usually meet at . . .

- ***Option:*** Ask pairs to tell the class some interesting things they learned about their classmates.

interchange 9 CONSIDER THE CONSEQUENCES

A Read over this questionnaire. Check (✓) the column that states your opinion.

	I agree.	I don't agree.	It depends.
1. If people watch less TV, they'll talk more with their families.	☐	☐	☐
2. If children watch a lot of violent programs on TV, they'll become violent themselves.	☐	☐	☐
3. If people work only four days a week, their lives will improve.	☐	☐	☐
4. If people have smaller families, they'll have better lives.	☐	☐	☐
5. If a woman works outside the home, her children won't be happy.	☐	☐	☐
6. If a woman becomes the leader of a country, a lot of things will change for the better.	☐	☐	☐
7. If cities provide free public transportation, there will be fewer cars on the road and less pollution.	☐	☐	☐
8. If there is a heavy fine for littering, our streets will be much cleaner.	☐	☐	☐
9. If teachers put all their lessons on the Internet, students will learn more.	☐	☐	☐
10. If teachers don't give tests, students won't study.	☐	☐	☐

B ***Group work*** Compare your opinions. Be prepared to give reasons for your opinions.

A: I think if people watch less TV, they'll talk more with their families.
B: I don't really agree.
C: Why not?
B: Well, if they don't watch TV, they'll do something else. They may read or spend all day on the computer.
C: I agree. Or they might go out and spend *less* time at home with their families.

I think that if they . . .
I agree with you.
I don't agree, because . . .

Interchange 9

interchange 9

Learning objective: *speak more fluently about consequences in an informal debate*

A

- Explain that the term *opinionated* means to have strong opinions. Ask: "Do you have strong opinions about issues like: violence on TV, the leader of the country, littering, or what teachers should do?" Explain that they are going to have a chance to give their views about these and other things.
- Tell Ss to read the instructions and go over the ten statements in the questionnaire. If Ss have questions about any words or phrases in the questionnaire, tell them to check their dictionaries. If necessary, explain any new words or phrases.

Vocabulary

It depends.: I can't decide. I would have different answers in different circumstances.
will become violent themselves: will be influenced by the violence they see and start doing things that hurt other people
heavy fine: a large amount of money that people pay the police or government for doing something wrong
littering: throwing trash on the ground

- Model the task. Read the first statement and ask Ss to raise their hands if they agree. Then tell those Ss to check (✓) the first column. Ask the rest of the class: "How many of you don't agree? How many think it depends?"
- Ss work independently to complete the questionnaire. Go around the class and give help as needed.

B *Group work*

- Explain the task. Focus Ss' attention on the picture. Then model the example conversation with several Ss.
- Give Ss a few minutes to look back at the choices they made in part A. Tell Ss to make a few notes (e.g., *examples*, *details*, *extra information*) to explain the reasons for their opinions.
- Ss compare opinions in small groups. Go around the class and listen. Don't interrupt the discussions if Ss are communicating freely and easily with one another.

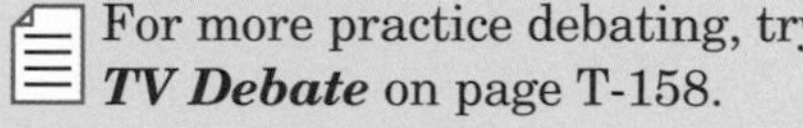

For more practice debating, try ***TV Debate*** on page T-158.

interchange 10

Learning objective: *speak more fluently about job skills in an interview situation*

A

- Explain the activity. Ss choose from three jobs and role-play an interview. They take turns asking questions and describing why they would be good for the job. Finally, they decide whether or not to hire their partner for the job.
- Give Ss a few minutes to read the job descriptions.
- Explain any new vocabulary.

Vocabulary

marketing manager: an employee who decides how to advertise a product, what price to charge for it, which brands are popular, etc.
responsibility: a task you must do
business degree: the qualification given to someone who has successfully completed a university/ college course of study in business
experience: knowledge or skill that you gain from doing a job or an activity
available: free; not busy
flexible hours: all different hours
take orders: do what you are told without complaining
maintain the calendar: look after the timetable
celebrity/a star: a famous person
cruise ship: a large luxury ocean liner that functions as a resort; a boat that people ride for travel and entertainment
"people person": someone who is sociable and outgoing
excursion: a trip

- Tell Ss to choose a job they would like to apply for. They should also think about why they want that job and why they think they would be good at it.

B *Pair work*

- Present the useful questions box. Then model how to start the role play with a S.

  T: Well, let's start with work experience. What kind of work experience do you have?
  S: Uh, I worked for three years as a marketing assistant.
  T: Oh? That sounds good. Where did you work?
  S: At MBA Sports.
  T: That's a good company. What kind of degree do you have?
  S: Actually, I don't have a college degree, but I learn fast. . . .

- Ss form pairs and decide who will interview first and for which job. Set a time limit of about five minutes. Encourage Ss to have fun and to be creative during their discussion. Go around the class and take note of things that pairs are doing well or that could be improved.
- When time is up, go over your observations with the class.
- Ss exchange roles and try the interview again. Encourage Ss to use their imaginations and to have fun. Go around the class and give help as needed.

C *Pair work*

- Tell Ss that their final task is to decide whether or not to hire their partner for the job. Remind them to explain their reasons.
- ***Option:*** Ss interview another S who wants the same job.
- ***Option:*** You may want to share some cultural information about hiring practices in North America. For example, by law, an employer is not allowed to discriminate against a person because of race, religion, age, gender, or marital status. To avoid this, employers cannot ask personal questions.

---

interchange 10 *DREAM JOB*

A Look at the following job descriptions. Choose one that you'd like to apply for.

Marketing Manager

Requirements:
- Must have a business degree or marketing experience
- Must be available to travel and work long hours
- Must enjoy sports and fitness activities

Responsibilities:
- Interviewing people about their sports preferences, writing reports, and working with famous athletes

Personal Assistant

Requirements:
- Must have excellent telephone skills
- Must be willing to work flexible hours
- Must be able to take orders and make important decisions

Responsibilities:
- Maintaining the calendar of a busy celebrity, scheduling meetings, and preparing the star for public appearances

Activities Director

Requirements:
- Must have experience working with tourists
- Must be a "people person"
- Must be outgoing and creative

Responsibilities:
- Organizing all leisure activities on a popular cruise ship, including planning daily excursions, special menus, and nightly entertainment

B *Pair work* Take turns interviewing each other for the job you each want. Give as much information as you can to show that you are the right person for the job.

useful questions

What kind of degree do you have?
What work experience do you have?
What hours can you work?
Do you mind working . . . ?
Are you interested in working with . . . ?
Why should I hire you for the job?

C *Pair work* Would you hire your partner for the job? Why or why not?

Interchange 10

interchange 11 WHO IS THIS BY?

A List one movie, one song, and one CD.

B ***Group work*** Take turns making a statement about each item. Does everyone agree with each statement?

A: The *Lord of the Rings* movies were filmed in New Zealand.
B: Are you sure? Weren't they filmed in Australia?
C: I'm pretty sure it was New Zealand.

C Now think of other famous creations and creators. Complete the chart. Make some of them true and some of them false.

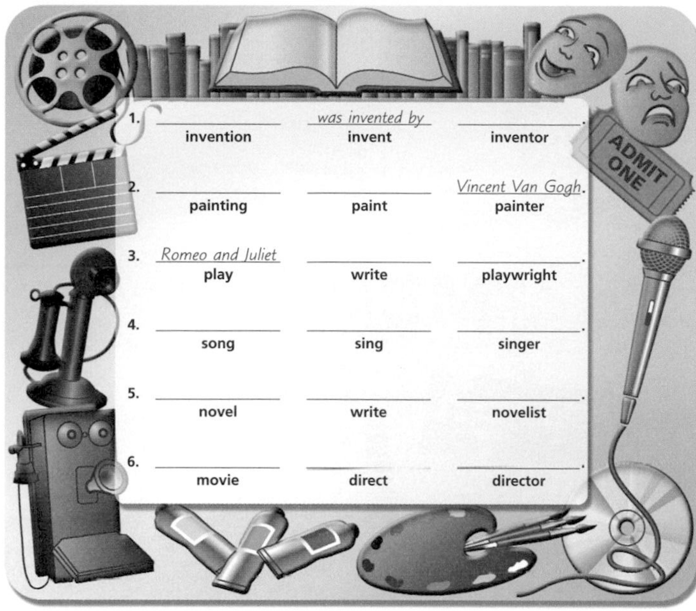

1. invention / was invented by / invent / inventor
2. painting / paint / Vincent Van Gogh. / painter
3. Romeo and Juliet / play / write / playwright
4. song / sing / singer
5. novel / write / novelist
6. movie / direct / director
ADMIT ONE

D ***Group work*** Make a statement about each item to your group members. Ask them to decide which statements are true and which are false.

A: The telephone was invented by Alexander Graham Bell.
B: I think that's false.
C: Really? I'm pretty sure it's true.

Interchange 11

interchange 11

Learning objective: *speak more fluently about works of art using the passive with and without* by

A

- Explain that Ss are going to make up statements about movies, books, songs, inventions, and works of art. First, Ss write down the name of a movie, a song, and a CD. Set a time limit.

B *Group work*

- Explain that Ss have to make one statement about each item they listed. Point out the first line of the example conversation (*The* Lord of the Rings *movies were filmed in New Zealand.*) as an example.
- To help Ss, draw the following, chart on the board:

The movie The song The CD	*was*	*written directed produced sung filmed recorded*	*in by*	*(date) (name)*
(name)	*won*	*an Oscar a Grammy an award*	*in for*	*(movie)*
(name)	*played*	*the role of the guitar/ drums*	*(name) on*	*(CD)*

- When Ss have written one sentence about each item, explain the task. In groups, Ss take turns making their statements. The others in the group listen and agree or disagree.
- Model the example conversation with Ss. Point out some ways to disagree politely with someone (e.g., *Are you sure?/I'm not sure. I think . . ./Wasn't it . . . ?/I don't agree.*). Then Ss begin the discussion.
- ***Option:*** If a group disagrees about a statement but doesn't know the answer, tell them to check the answer before the next class.
- ***Option:*** Have Ss share some new and interesting facts they learned with the class.

C

- Ask Ss to read the instructions silently and to look at the chart. Elicit or explain any new vocabulary.
- Point out the first example (*. . . was invented by . . .*). Elicit inventions and inventors from the class. Then give Ss time to complete the statements. Remind them to include some false statements.
- ***Option:*** Ss may do this part for homework.

D *Group work*

- Explain the task. Ask three Ss to read the example conversation.
- Ss form groups. Tell them to take turns reading the statements aloud and deciding which are true. If a statement is false or if Ss don't agree, they should discuss possible answers. Set a time limit of about five minutes. Go around the class and give help as needed.
- When time is up, Ss share their statements with the class.
- ***Option:*** Groups can compete against each other by reading their statements aloud. Other groups say which are true and get one point for each correct answer. After all groups have read their statements, total the points. The group with the most points wins.

interchange 12

Learning objective: *speak more fluently about your life experiences in this board game*

A *Group work*

- Divide the class into groups of four or five Ss each. Then go over the instructions to make sure the class understands how to play.
- Give Ss a few minutes to make small markers with their own initials on them. Tell Ss that the markers must be small enough to fit on the squares of the board game. Then make sure that each group has a coin to toss. Go around the class and help the Ss decide which side of the coin is *face up* and which side is *face down*.
- Model the example conversation with Ss. Then start again with a new sentence (e.g., *It's been a year since I've been teaching this class.*) and have Ss ask you follow-up questions.
- Set a time limit of about 20 minutes for the game. Ss take turns tossing the coins and moving their markers forward around the board. Go around the class and give help as needed. Remind groups to ask at least two follow-up questions after each S makes a statement.
- If more than one group finishes early, have them change players to form new groups and play again giving different answers.
- ***Option:*** Ss earn one point for each follow-up question they ask. Ss keep track of their own score.

interchange 12 *LIFE IS LIKE A GAME!*

A *Group work* Play the board game. Follow these instructions.

1. Use small pieces of paper with your initials on them as markers.
2. Take turns by tossing a coin:
   If the coin lands face up, move two spaces.
   If the coin lands face down, move one space.
3. Complete the sentence in the space you land on. Others ask two follow-up questions to get more information.

A: It's been a year since I started working.
B: Oh, really? Do you like your job?
A: Well, the job's just OK, but the money is great!
C: What do you do?
A: I'm a . . .

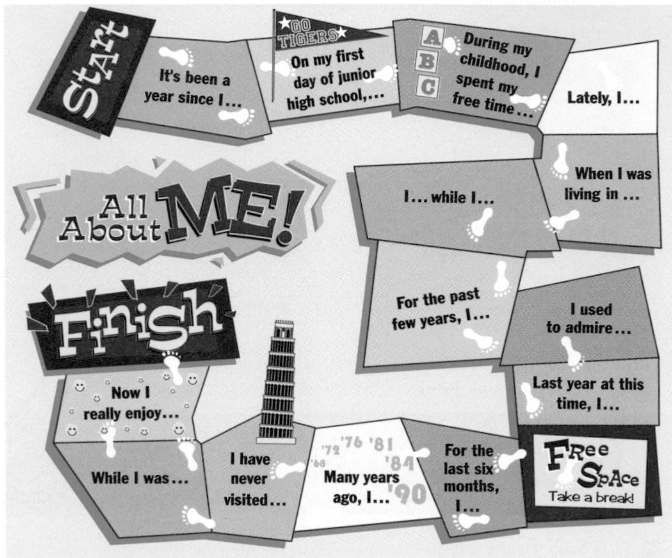

B *Class activity* Tell the class an interesting fact that you learned about someone in your group.

"Last year at this time, Daniel was hiking in the Swiss Alps!"

Interchange 12

- Stop the activity when time is up or, if the Ss are enjoying the game, let them continue playing until one S in each group finishes.

B *Class activity*

- Read the example sentence to model the activity. Then ask groups or individual Ss to share something interesting they learned about their classmates.

interchange 13 *FAMOUS FACES*

A Complete this questionnaire.

What is the name of a TV or movie star . . . ?	
1. that reminds you of someone in your family	....
2. that has beautiful eyes	....
3. who does things to help society	....
4. who has a beautiful speaking voice	....
5. who isn't good-looking but who is very talented	....
What is the name of a TV show or movie . . . ?	
6. that made you feel sad	....
7. that made you laugh a lot	....
8. which scared you	....
9. which had great music	....
10. that was about a ridiculous story	....

B ***Pair work*** Compare your questionnaires. Ask follow-up questions of your own.

A: What is the name of a TV or movie star that reminds you of someone in your family?
B: Tom Cruise.
A: Who does he remind you of?
B: My brother, Todd.
A: Really? Why?
B: Because he looks like my brother. They have the same smile.

Interchange 13

interchange 13

Learning objective: *speak more fluently about TV and movie stars, TV programs, and movies*

A

- Write these topics on the board: *TV stars, movie stars, TV programs,* and *movies.*
- Ss form pairs and brainstorm names associated with one of the topics. Give Ss a time limit of one or two minutes.
- Read the question and phrases in the questionnaire aloud. Explain any new vocabulary or have Ss check their dictionaries.
- ***Option:*** Model each of the ten questions in the chart (e.g., *What is the name of a TV or movie star that reminds you of someone in your family?*). Have Ss repeat to practice good pronunciation, intonation, and word stress.
- Ss complete the task individually. Go around the class and give help as needed.

B *Pair work*

- Explain the task. Have two Ss read the example conversation. Elicit more follow-up questions and write the suggestions on the board.
- Ss compare the information in their questionnaires in pairs. Encourage them to ask follow-up questions to get more details and information from their partners. Go around the class and take note of problems and successes.
- Share your observations and possible solutions with the class. Be sure to praise examples of good communication and fluent speech.

interchange 14

Learning objective: *speak more fluently about the events in a picture*

A *Pair work*

- Pre-teach some useful language by writing these expressions on the board:
  1. *She has her arms folded. His hands are open.*
  2. *He is winking and pointing at his chest.*
  3. *She is resting her chin on one hand.*
  4. *He has his hands on his hips.*
  5. *She is shaking her finger.*
- Ask Ss to match the body language with situations in the scene. Then go over answers. (Answers: 1. 1 2. 4 3. 3 4. 2 5. 5)
- Explain the task and give Ss a few minutes to look at the situations again.
- Model the example conversation with a S.
- Ss discuss the situations in pairs. Go around the class and give help as needed.

B *Group work*

- Each pair joins another pair. Tell groups to compare their ideas about what is happening in each situation. Explain that they should give reasons why they agree or disagree with one another.
- Set a time limit of about five minutes for groups to compare opinions. Go around the class and take note of how Ss are doing. If Ss have problems expressing their ideas, let them check their dictionaries.
- When time is up, elicit Ss' interpretations for each situation. Remind them that there are no right or wrong answers.

interchange 14 *WHAT'S GOING ON?*

A ***Pair work*** Look at this scene of a crowded restaurant. What do you think is happening in each of the five situations? Look at people's body language for clues.

A: Why do you think the woman in situation 1 looks upset?
B: Well, she might be having a fight with . . .

A: What do you think the man's gesture in situation 2 means?
B: Maybe it means he . . .

B ***Group work*** Compare your interpretations. Do you agree or disagree?

Interchange 14

Possible answers

1. The woman is upset. Her arms are folded and she's turned away from the man. She's slumped in the chair with her arms and legs crossed. Her body language shows that she is angry. The man looks like he's trying to explain something. His hands and arms are raised in a shrug, which makes him look like he might be apologizing for something.
2. The chef and the waiter are arguing. The chef looks angry. He's pointing a spoon at the waiter, which may mean the waiter has done something wrong. However, the waiter's body language – with his hands on his hips – shows that he probably doesn't agree with the chef.
3. One woman is pointing at the menu and asking the waitress about it. She looks irritated or annoyed by something. The waitress looks confused. The other woman at the table has her chin resting on her hand. This may mean that she's bored, impatient, or disgusted.
4. The man is trying to influence the host who seats people. He's handing him money while probably trying to explain that he is very important and should get a table right away. The man is also winking at the host, which means he's trying to be friendly. The host is rolling his eyes, which might mean that he's not impressed.
5. The two teenagers are arguing and teasing each other. The father doesn't seem to notice or care what they are doing. He might be hungry or bored, because he's eating a large piece of bread and not paying attention to the others. The mother looks annoyed with the children. She's shaking her finger at them.

interchange 15 DO THE RIGHT THING!

A What would you do in each of these situations? Circle **a**, **b**, or **c**. If you think you would do something else, write your suggestion next to **d**.

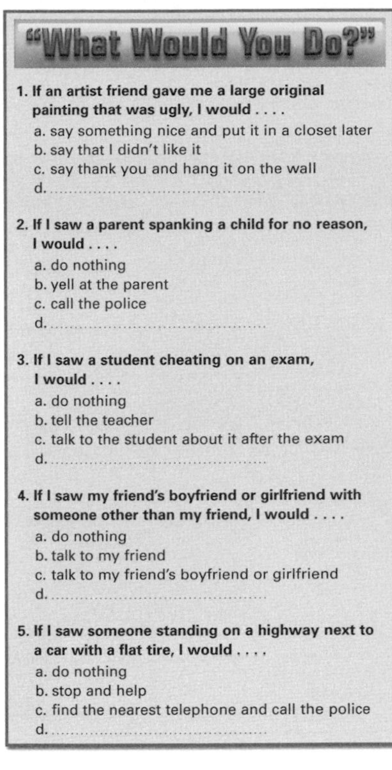

"What Would You Do?"

1. If an artist friend gave me a large original painting that was ugly, I would . . . .
a. say something nice and put it in a closet later
b. say that I didn't like it
c. say thank you and hang it on the wall
d. ....

2. If I saw a parent spanking a child for no reason, I would . . . .
a. do nothing
b. yell at the parent
c. call the police
d. ....

3. If I saw a student cheating on an exam, I would . . . .
a. do nothing
b. tell the teacher
c. talk to the student about it after the exam
d. ....

4. If I saw my friend's boyfriend or girlfriend with someone other than my friend, I would . . . .
a. do nothing
b. talk to my friend
c. talk to my friend's boyfriend or girlfriend
d. ....

5. If I saw someone standing on a highway next to a car with a flat tire, I would . . . .
a. do nothing
b. stop and help
c. find the nearest telephone and call the police
d. ....

B ***Group work*** Compare your choices for each situation in part A.

A: What would you do if an artist friend gave you an ugly painting?
B: Well, I would probably say that I didn't like it.
C: Really? I would . . .

C ***Class activity*** Take a class survey. Find out which choice was most popular for each situation. Talk about any other suggestions people added for **d**.

Interchange 15

interchange 15

Learning objective: *speak more fluently about difficult situations*

A

- Explain the task. Briefly go over the five situations and choices to make sure that Ss understand any new words or phrases.

Vocabulary

spank: hit (often on the bottom) with your open hand
yell: shout or say something very loudly because you are angry, excited, or frightened

- Give Ss a few minutes to complete the task individually. Remind them to write their own idea next to **d** if they don't choose **a**, **b**, or **c**. Go around the class and give help as needed, particularly with the Ss' own suggestions for **d**.

B *Group work*

- Divide the class into groups. Use the example conversation to model how Ss should compare choices and extend the discussion.
- Set a time limit of about ten minutes. Encourage groups to ask one another follow-up questions during their discussions. Go around the class and give help as needed.

C *Class activity*

- Read the first situation and choices. Ask Ss to raise their hands to show which answer they chose. Continue with the other situations, writing the numbers on the board to keep track of the Ss' choices. Are Ss surprised at the choices that were most popular? If so, ask some follow-up questions to discover why.
- For each situation, elicit suggestions for **d**. Encourage the rest of the class to give their comments and opinions.

interchange 16A EXCUSES, EXCUSES

Student A

A ***Pair work*** You and your partner want to get together. You also want to keep time open for other friends, so make up excuses for many of the days. Ask and answer questions to find a day when you are both free. Write your partner's excuses on the calendar.

A: Do you want to go out on the second?
B: I'm sorry. I'm going to my friend's wedding. Are you free on the first?
A: Well, I . . .

B ***Pair work*** Now work with another Student A. Discuss the excuses Student B gave you. Decide which excuses were probably true and which ones were probably not true.

A: Anna said that on the ninth she had to stay home and reorganize her clothes closet. That was probably not true.
B: I agree. I think . . .

Interchange 16A

interchange 16A/B

Learning objective: *speak more fluently about schedules and free time*

- To introduce the topic of giving excuses and telling white lies, have Ss look at the reading on page 111. Ask: "What do you think a *white lie* is?" (Answer: an untruth that is not very important, especially one that is told to avoid hurting someone's feelings)
- Divide the class into pairs. Then assign each S an A or B part. Tell Student As to look at page Interchange 16A and Student Bs to look at page Interchange 16B.

A *Pair work*

- Read the situation to the class. Then give pairs a few minutes to look over their calendars and to think of interesting excuses for the days they don't want to meet. Remind Ss not to look at their partner's page. Answer any questions about the instructions or the information in the calendars.
- Model the example conversation with a S to demonstrate how to ask questions and make excuses.
- Tell Ss to write the excuses that their partners give on their calendars. Ss will need these notes for the pair work in part B.
- Encourage Ss to have fun and not to give up until they agree on a date. Go around the class and give help as needed.
- Stop the activity when time is up or when all the pairs have agreed on a date.

B *Pair work*

- Divide the class into new pairs. Ask Student As to work together and Student Bs to work together.
- Explain the task. Ss use reported speech to tell their new partner about what their partner from part A said.
- Tell Ss to look at the excuses they wrote on their calendars in part A. Explain that they should use these notes to make statements with reported speech. Model the example conversation with a S. Then elicit a few additional examples from Ss and write them on the board.
- Pairs report the excuses they heard in part A and discuss whether the excuses were real or just "white lies." Go around the class and give help as needed.
- As a wrap-up, find out which day most pairs chose in part A. Why was that date the most popular? If pairs followed the information on their calendars closely, July 31 should have been the only date possible for them to get together.

interchange 16B EXCUSES, EXCUSES

Student B

A ***Pair work*** You and your partner want to get together. You also want to keep time open for other friends, so make up excuses for many of the days. Ask and answer questions to find a day when you are both free. Write your partner's excuses on the calendar.

A: Do you want to go out on the second?
B: I'm sorry. I'm going to my friend's wedding. Are you free on the first?
A: Well, I . . .

July

Sunday	Monday	Tuesday	Wednesday	Thursday	Friday	Saturday
					1	2 *Sue's wedding*
3 ← You want to keep these dates free. Make up excuses!	4 →	5 *movie with Bob*	6	7 ← You don't want to make plans in case you want to get away for a few days. Make up excuses!	8	9 →
10 *visit Mom and Dad*	11 *office party*	12	13 *photography workshop at school*	14	15 ← Maybe an old friend will call. Make up excuses!	16 →
17 *visit Grandma*	18	19 *museum with Craig*	20	21	22 *party at Amy's*	23 *baseball game with Jim*
24 *family get-together* / 31	25 You need a break. Make up an excuse!	26 *book group meeting*	27	28 *need to work late tonight*	29	30

B ***Pair work*** Now work with another Student B. Discuss the excuses Student A gave you. Decide which excuses were probably true and which ones were probably not true.

A. Joe said that on the sixth he had to stay home and reorganize his clothes closet. That was probably not true.
B: I agree. I think . . .

Interchange 16B

Units 1–16 Self-study

1 CHILDHOOD SUMMERS

A Listen to Kim and Jeff talk about their childhood summers. What three things do they have in common?

....

B Listen again. What were their summers like? Complete the chart.

	Their pets	Their favorite places	Their hobbies
1. Kim	....	....	....
2. Jeff	....	....	....

2 TOURIST INFORMATION

A Listen to some tourists ask for information at their hotel. Write what each person needs to do.

Needs	Responses
1. *exchange some money*	☐ a. There's one right across the street from here. ☐ b. It's past 10:00. They should be open now.
2.	☐ a. It stays open until 6 P.M. ☐ b. It opens at 9 A.M.
3.	☐ a. Only once a day. We really need more trains! ☐ b. You can follow this street all the way there.
4.	☐ a. It's eight blocks away. There aren't enough taxi stands in this area. ☐ b. Walk down to Grand Street. You can catch the subway there.
5.	☐ a. It costs twenty dollars a day. ☐ b. You can buy a special pass to go anywhere in the city.
6.	☐ a. Try the café on the corner. I think it's open until midnight. ☐ b. We need more vegetarian restaurants. The only one is on Ninth Avenue.

B Listen again. Check (✓) the correct response.

3 APARTMENT FOR RENT

A Listen to two people call about apartment advertisements.
Do you think the woman is going to rent the apartment? ☐ Yes ☐ No
Do you think the man is going to rent the apartment? ☐ Yes ☐ No

B Listen again. Which adjectives best describe each apartment?
Write **1** for the first apartment or **2** for the second apartment.

.... bright	.... dark	.... noisy	.... quiet	.... safe
.... dangerous	.... expensive	.... old	.... reasonable	.... spacious

4 HAVE YOU TRIED IT?

A Listen to two people shop for food. What foods have they tried?
Write **H** for Heidi or **P** for Peter.

.... ceviche .... red chili peppers .... Thai fried noodles .... coconut curry

B Listen again. How do you make ceviche? Number the pictures from 1 to 5.

☐ ☐ ☐ ☐ ☐

5 VACATION PLANS

A Listen to Cynthia discuss her vacation plans with Paul.
Check (✓) the things she talks about doing.

☐ fishing	☐ going abroad	☐ seeing another city
☐ camping	☐ staying home	☐ taking cooking lessons
☐ shopping	☐ going to the beach	☐ going to the mountains

B Listen again. For each activity you checked, write Paul's advice.

1. ....
2. ....
3. ....
4. ....
5. ....

6 SIMPLE REQUESTS

A Listen to people make requests. Check (✓) the thing each person talks about.

1.	☐ the radio	☐ the window	☐ the dog
2.	☐ the coat	☐ the shoes	☐ the magazine
3.	☐ the baby	☐ the grandfather	☐ the dog
4.	☐ the yard	☐ the TV	☐ the window
5.	☐ the TV	☐ the coat	☐ the lamp
6.	☐ the toys	☐ the books	☐ the dishes

B Listen again. Write the words that helped you choose each answer.

1. .... 3. .... 5. ....
2. .... 4. .... 6. ....

7 COMPUTER SUPPORT

A Listen to Janet call a computer support center for help. What is Janet's problem?

☐ She used the wrong keyboard.
☐ She didn't know the screen saver was on.
☐ She downloaded a virus.

B Listen again. Check (✓) the correct answer(s).

1. What does Janet use her laptop for?

☐ writing short stories ☐ writing e-mails ☐ playing DVDs
☐ surfing the Internet ☐ playing games ☐ downloading music

2. How can Janet protect her monitor?

☐ close her laptop ☐ turn on the screen saver ☐ leave her computer on all day

8 TRICK OR TREAT!

A Listen to someone talk about Halloween. Check (✓) True or False for each statement.

	True	False
1. October 31 is the day when people wear costumes.	☐	☐
2. During the 400s, people dressed up on October 31 to scare away the dead.	☐	☐
3. People believed that Halloween marked the end of spring.	☐	☐
4. In the U.S., Halloween is the time when adults "trick or treat."	☐	☐
5. On Halloween, children go to their neighbors' houses to ask for money.	☐	☐
6. These days, Halloween is a night when adults go to parties or parades.	☐	☐

B Listen again. For the statements you marked false, write the correct information.

9 TOO MUCH TECHNOLOGY?

A Listen to Jimmy and his grandfather talk about technology. Check (✓) the things his grandfather has used.

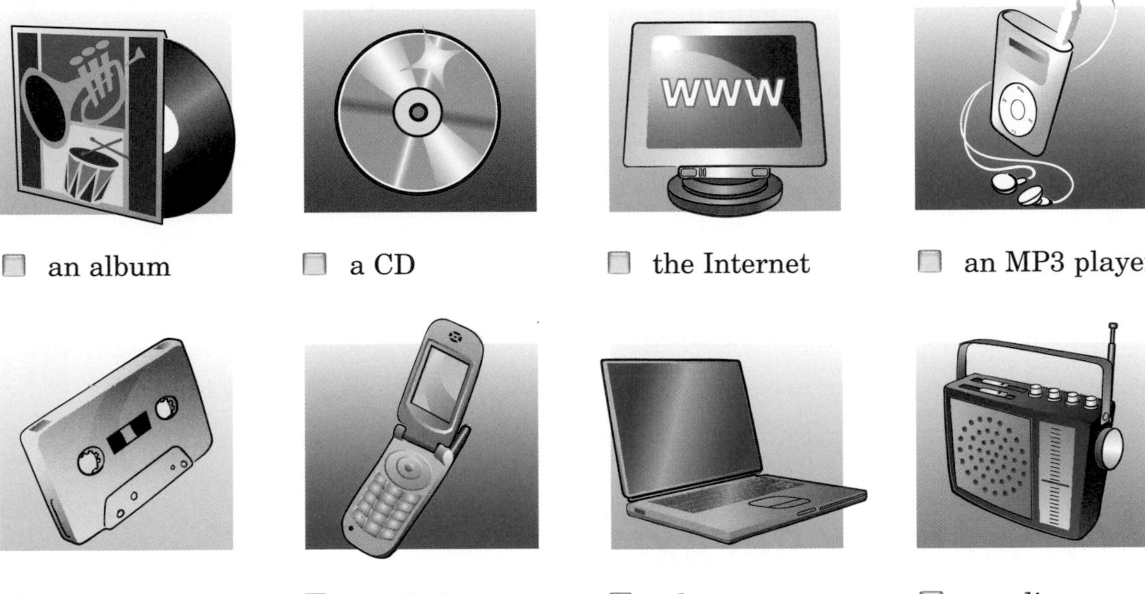

☐ an album ☐ a CD ☐ the Internet ☐ an MP3 player

☐ a cassette ☐ a cell phone ☐ a laptop ☐ a radio

B Listen again and answer these questions.

1. What does Jimmy think might happen to technology in the future?
2. What is one advantage of future technology?
3. What is one disadvantage of future technology?

10 ELECTION DEBATE

A Listen to an election debate. Write **A** for André or **J** for Jeri beside the adjective that best describes each person.

.... creative	.... hardworking	.... moody
.... critical	.... impatient	.... organized
.... efficient	.... level-headed	.... reliable

B Listen again and complete the chart.

	André			Jeri		
How good is each candidate at . . . ?	**good**	**OK**	**so-so**	**good**	**OK**	**so-so**
1. working with people	☐	☐	☐	☐	☐	☐
2. solving problems	☐	☐	☐	☐	☐	☐
How does each candidate like . . . ?	**likes**	**doesn't mind**	**hates**	**likes**	**doesn't mind**	**hates**
3. helping people	☐	☐	☐	☐	☐	☐
4. making mistakes	☐	☐	☐	☐	☐	☐

11 THE STATUE OF LIBERTY

A Listen to two tourists on a boat tour of New York Harbor. Why doesn't the man want to go inside the Statue of Liberty?

☐ It's closed to visitors. ☐ There's no elevator. ☐ There isn't enough time.

B Listen again. Correct the seven mistakes in the text.

The Statue of Liberty is located in New York Harbor. The people of ~~Canada~~ *France* gave the statue to the United States. The statue was designed by a French sculptor. Hundreds of people from all over the world visit the Statue of Liberty every year. There are 54 steps to the top of the crown. The statue was manufactured in the United States and shipped to New York. In 1986, it was assembled on Liberty Island, which took nine months. Visitors may climb the stairs to the top of the statue.

12 WHAT A LUCKY BREAK!

A Listen to Stacy and Richard talk about their careers. Who had a lucky break? ☐ Stacy ☐ Richard

B Listen again. Number the events for each person from 1 to 5.

Stacy	Richard
.... She moved to Los Angeles.	.... He sent his novel to publishers.
.... She was offered a position on a new show.	.... He tried to make a living as a writer.
.... She got a job as an assistant at a TV station.	.... He got a job at a hardware store.
.... She graduated from drama school.	.... He majored in English literature in college.
.... The regular announcer got sick.	.... His work was rejected eight times.

13 THIS BOOK LOOKS INTERESTING.

A Listen to people talk about a book. Match each character with two descriptions.

.... 1. the owner .... 3. the jockey
.... 2. the trainer .... 4. the horse

a. half blind c. millionaire e. small g. outspoken
b. cowboy d. odd-looking f. quiet h. well-educated

B Listen again. Complete these sentences with relative clauses from the conversation.

1. The owner was a man . . .
2. The trainer was a man . . .
3. The jockey was a man . . .
4. Seabiscuit was a horse . . .

14 POLICE PATROL

A Listen to four conversations. Number the pictures from 1 to 4.

☐ 

☐ 

☐ 

☐ 

B Listen again. Write each rule under the correct picture.

1. You can't park here.
2. You've got to put your dog on a leash.
3. Cars aren't allowed on this street.
4. You have to fasten your seat belt.

15 UNFORTUNATE SITUATIONS

A Listen to people describe situations. Check (✓) the correct response.

1. ☐ He should have locked the car.
   ☐ He shouldn't have left money in the car.
2. ☐ She should have spent the money.
   ☐ She shouldn't have gone shopping.
3. ☐ He should have written it down.
   ☐ He shouldn't have remembered the dinner.
4. ☐ She should have borrowed a friend's car.
   ☐ She shouldn't have lent her car to a friend.

B Listen again. Write your own response for each situation.

16 DON'T TELL ANYONE . . .

A Listen to a telephone conversation. What excuse did Susan give Bill?

☐ She had dinner plans. ☐ She was going to the movies. ☐ She wasn't feeling well.

B Listen again. Read the voice mail Grace left another friend. Then correct the six errors in her message.

Hi, it's Grace. I just talked to Bill, and you won't believe what happened! Bill said that Jack saw Susan and her father having lunch together last week. Bill and Susan were supposed to go shopping together, but Susan called the day before to say she couldn't make it. Well, Bill said he understood, and told her to stay home and get something to eat. But instead of staying home, she went out! Oh, by the way, don't say anything, OK? I promised Bill I wouldn't tell anyone.

Self-study audio scripts

1 Childhood summers

A Listen to Kim and Jeff talk about their childhood summers. What three things do they have in common?

JEFF: Hey, Kim, are these pictures of you when you were a kid?
KIM: Yeah. That's me with my dog. We used to spend a week at my uncle's beach house every summer.
JEFF: Hmm. When I was a kid, we used to take our dog and cat with us to the beach every year. Summers were always so much fun!
KIM: Yeah. I used to spend all day playing up in our tree house. I even brought my pet rabbit up there!
JEFF: Really? Our neighbors down the street had a great tree house. My brother and I used to sneak up there to play chess and read comic books.
KIM: Really? I remember that some kids used to leave their comic books in our tree house, but we never saw the kids.
JEFF: That's funny. What else did you use to do up there?
KIM: We used to climb up and make scrapbooks out of pictures we cut out of magazines. We also painted animals on the walls.
JEFF: Huh? What kinds of animals?
KIM: Dogs, horses, my rabbit . . .
JEFF: Wait a minute. Was your uncle's house on Glenn Avenue?
KIM: That was *you*?!

B Listen again. What were their summers like? Complete the chart.

2 Tourist information

A Listen to some tourists ask for information at their hotel. Write what each person needs to do.

1. MAN: Do you know when the banks open? I have to exchange some money.
2. WOMAN: Could you tell me what time the post office closes? I need to mail some postcards.
3. MAN: I'd like to buy some souvenirs. Can you tell me how to get to the outdoor market?
4. WOMAN: I need to go to the airport. Can you tell me where the nearest taxi stand is?
5. MAN: Do you know how much it costs to use the parking garage? I need to park my car.
6. WOMAN: I'd like to get something to eat. Could you tell me which restaurants serve dinner this late?

B Listen again. Check the correct response.

3 Apartment for rent

A Listen to two people call about apartment advertisements. Do you think the woman is going to rent the apartment? Do you think the man is going to rent the apartment?

MAN 1: [*phone rings*] Creative Rentals. Good morning.
WOMAN 1: Hello. I'm calling about the apartment you have for rent.
MAN 1: Yes. What can I tell you about it?
WOMAN 1: Where is it, exactly?
MAN 1: It's on King Street, just off the freeway.
WOMAN 1: Oh, near the freeway. Can you hear the traffic?
MAN 1: Yes, I'm afraid you do hear some. But the apartment has lots of space. It has three bedrooms and a very large living room.
WOMAN 1: I see. And is it in a new building?
MAN 1: Well, the building is over 50 years old.
WOMAN 1: Uh-huh. Well, I'll think about it. I wish it weren't so close to the freeway.
MAN 1: Well, if you want to see it, just give me a call.
WOMAN 1: OK, thank you.
MAN 1: Thanks for calling. Bye.

WOMAN 2: [*phone rings*] Town and City Rentals. How can I help you?
MAN 2: Hi. Umm . . . is that apartment you advertised still available?
WOMAN 2: Yes, it is.
MAN 2: Oh, good. Umm . . . listen. I, I can't pay too much, so the low price is really good for me.
WOMAN 2: Great.
MAN 2: Is it a big place?
WOMAN 2: No. It's two rooms, plus the kitchen and bathroom.
MAN 2: And is it a safe area to live?
WOMAN 2: Well, I can tell you I've lived in this neighborhood for five years and I've never heard about anybody having a problem.
MAN 2: Oh, that's good. Uh . . . let's see. Oh, yeah. Does the apartment have a lot of windows?
WOMAN 2: Windows? Yes, there are plenty of windows. But unfortunately, there's another building right next door. I wish the apartment were brighter, but there isn't much light, really.
MAN 2: Oh. Well, I'm never around during the day, anyway. Is it all right if I come look at it?
WOMAN 2: Sure. Just tell me when you want to see it.

B Listen again. Which adjectives best describe each apartment? Write **1** for the first apartment or **2** for the second apartment.

4 Have you tried it?

A Listen to two people shop for food. What foods have they tried? Write **H** for Heidi or **P** for Peter.

HEIDI: Over here, Peter! The fish looks so fresh. We could make ceviche this weekend. I love ceviche! Have you tried it?
PETER: No, I haven't. How do you make it?
HEIDI: Well, first you cut up the seafood in bite-size pieces.
PETER: So we'll need different kinds of fish?
HEIDI: Yeah. Let's get three kinds.
PETER: OK. Then what?
HEIDI: Then you mix the seafood with chili peppers.
PETER: Here are some red chili peppers, but I don't know what they're like. Have you tried this kind?
HEIDI: Yes, I tried them once. They were very spicy!
PETER: Good. I love spicy food. What next?
HEIDI: Next, you add lime juice and mix it in. After that, you put the seafood in the refrigerator to marinate.

PETER: You don't cook it?

HEIDI: No, you just marinate it overnight. Finally, you put the mixture on some lettuce and serve it!

PETER: OK, so what are we having tonight?

HEIDI: Oh! I know how to make a great dish – it's Thai fried noodles with chicken.

PETER: That sounds interesting. I'd like to try it, but I ate chicken for lunch. I really love coconut curry. Have you ever had it?

HEIDI: No, but it sounds good. Let's make that!

PETER: OK. Um, there are some spices right over there. Let's get some and then go. I'm getting hungry!

B Listen again. How do you make ceviche? Number the pictures from 1 to 5.

5 Vacation plans

A Listen to Cynthia discuss her vacation plans with Paul. Check the things she talks about doing.

PAUL: So, Cynthia, what are you doing with your time off?

CYNTHIA: I don't know. I haven't decided yet. I might go camping somewhere and just enjoy nature for a couple of weeks.

PAUL: Well, you'd better pack a first-aid kit and be careful. It could be dangerous!

CYNTHIA: Uh, yeah. Or maybe I'll go abroad and study a foreign language.

PAUL: Hmm. But there probably isn't enough time. You'll have to get a passport and maybe even a visa.

CYNTHIA: OK, so maybe I'll go to the beach and catch up on some reading.

PAUL: You shouldn't go to the beach at this time of year. It'll be too crowded!

CYNTHIA: Well, then I might go to another city and visit some museums and art galleries.

PAUL: You need to make a reservation right away! The plane ticket is going to be so expensive now!

CYNTHIA: Well, then I probably won't go anywhere. I'll just stay home and watch TV!

PAUL: That sounds boring. Why don't you do something more fun?

B Listen again. For each activity you checked, write Paul's advice.

6 Simple requests

A Listen to people make requests. Check the thing each person talks about.

1. MAN: Would you mind turning it down, please? I'm trying to read and I can't concentrate with it on so loud.
2. WOMAN: Can you pick them up? You need to put them away as soon as you take them off instead of just leaving them on the floor for someone to trip over.
3. MAN: Could you take him out for a walk? He hasn't been out for a couple of hours. Don't forget to keep him on the leash.
4. WOMAN: Would you please close it? When you leave it open, the wind blows and makes the room really cold.
5. MAN: Can you turn that on for me? It's getting dark in here, and I can't see what I'm reading.
6. WOMAN: Would you mind not leaving them on the counter when they're dirty? At least put them in the sink.

B Listen again. Write the words that helped you choose each answer.

7 Computer support

A Listen to Janet call a computer support center for help. What is Janet's problem?

MATT: [*phone rings*] Support center, this is Matt.

JANET: Uh, hi, Matt. I'm having problems with my laptop.

MATT: What's the problem?

JANET: I'm not really sure.

MATT: Well, what do you see when you turn your laptop on?

JANET: It comes on at first, but then it goes black after a while. I think the monitor may be broken. Or maybe I have a virus.

MATT: Hmm. What do you normally use your laptop for?

JANET: I use it for writing e-mails and surfing the Internet. I also use it to play computer games.

MATT: And how long do you usually leave it on?

JANET: Well, I also download music sometimes, so I leave it on all day while I'm doing other things.

MATT: Uh-huh. Always remember to turn on the screen saver when you're away from your laptop. Your monitor will last longer that way.

JANET: What's a screen saver?

MATT: It's something that comes on while you're not using your monitor, to protect it. Be sure to turn it on.

JANET: OK. And what does it look like when it comes on?

MATT: Well, it's black unless you download something else to use.

JANET: It's black? Oh, and what happens when you use the keyboard?

MATT: Your monitor comes back on when you use the keyboard. You can also move the mouse to "wake up" the monitor.

JANET: Uh, OK, well . . . I don't think I have a problem with my monitor anymore . . . it was just the, uh, screen saver.

MATT: Well, don't forget to download a new screen saver. Then next time your monitor goes black, you'll know it's really broken!

B Listen again. Check the correct answer(s).

8 Trick or treat!

A Listen to someone talk about Halloween. Check True or False for each statement.

MAN: One fall day, as you walk down the street, you might see ghosts, strange animals, and other weird things. What's going on? It's probably October 31st, or Halloween. Halloween is a day when people go out wearing costumes and colorful makeup.

Some people think that Halloween started in Ireland during the 400s. October 31st was the end of summer, and people believed that everyone who died during the year came back on that day. To scare away the dead, people put on costumes and went out into the streets to make noise.

Different cultures have different ways of celebrating Halloween. In the United States, it's the night when children dress up in costumes and go to neighbors' houses to "trick or treat," or ask for candy. Some adults wear funny or scary costumes and go to parties or parades. Halloween has become a fun holiday for both adults and children.

B Listen again. For the statements you marked false, write the correct information.

9 Too much technology?

A Listen to Jimmy and his grandfather talk about technology. Check the things his grandfather has used.

GRANDFATHER: What are you listening to, Jimmy? Is that a radio?
JIMMY: No, it's an MP3 player.
GRANDFATHER: An MP3 player? What's that?
JIMMY: It's a machine that plays music that I download from my computer.
GRANDFATHER: Hmm. When I was a child, we listened to the radio. Then, people listened to albums, and later, to cassettes. Everything changes so fast these days!
JIMMY: Yeah. Now, most people get music from CDs or the Internet. In five years, I bet there will be other ways.
GRANDFATHER: CDs, huh? Well, I guess if I don't pay attention, I'll miss out on a lot of new technology.
JIMMY: Right. Like just a few years ago, they made a cell phone that also surfs the Internet. Soon, we might not even need laptops or MP3 players – everything will be in one piece of technology.
GRANDFATHER: Do you really think so?
JIMMY: Yeah, and if all the technology is in one piece of equipment, you'll have fewer things to carry.
GRANDFATHER: Exactly! And if you don't need a laptop, an MP3 player, and a cell phone, you won't need such a big allowance, right?
JIMMY: Uh, well . . .

B Listen again and answer these questions.

10 Election debate

A Listen to an election debate. Write **A** for André or **J** for Jeri beside the adjective that best describes each person.

TEACHER: Welcome to our debate! The candidates for class president this year are André and Jeri. Please introduce yourselves and tell us why you'd be a good president.
ANDRÉ: Hi, I'm André. I think I'd be a great class president because I'm reliable, and I'm very creative.
JERI: Hi, everyone. I'm Jeri and I'm really good at organizing. I'm also efficient, and I'm hardworking.
TEACHER: How good are you at working with people? André?
ANDRÉ: I'm really good at working with people. And I'd make a good president because I am always level-headed. Most people think I'm easy to talk to.
TEACHER: And Jeri?
JERI: I'm OK at working with people. Sometimes I'm a little impatient, but I'm never critical.
TEACHER: OK! Next question. André, can you solve problems easily?
ANDRÉ: Well, it takes a lot of work to solve problems for a whole class, but I think I'm good at it. I really like helping people, and like I said, I'm very creative. Sometimes a problem just needs a creative solution!
TEACHER: OK, Jeri, what about you?
JERI: I like helping people, too. I'm so-so at solving problems, but if the solution doesn't work, I always ask someone for help. I can't stand making mistakes.
ANDRÉ: Oh, I don't mind. If you don't make mistakes, you won't learn anything!
TEACHER: That's a good point, André. Well, we're out of time. Thanks to our candidates for participating, and don't forget to vote on Thursday! [*applause*]

B Listen again and complete the chart.

11 The Statue of Liberty

A Listen to two tourists on a boat tour of New York Harbor. Why doesn't the man want to go inside the Statue of Liberty?

GUIDE: We are now approaching the famous Statue of Liberty, which has welcomed visitors to New York Harbor since 1886.
MAN: Wow! Look at it.
WOMAN: Incredible, isn't it?
GUIDE: The statue was given to the United States by the people of France. It was designed by the French sculptor Bartholdi.
MAN: It's really huge. Do we get to go inside?
WOMAN: I think we can climb the stairs all the way up to the crown.
MAN: Stairs? There's no elevator?
WOMAN: Well . . .
GUIDE: The Statue of Liberty is a major tourist attraction, and every year it is visited by millions of people from all over the world. There are 354 steps to the top of the crown.
MAN: Did you hear that? 354 steps!
WOMAN: Oh, come on, you can do it! People do it every day!
MAN: But . . .
GUIDE: The statue was manufactured in France, and shipped to New York in 1884. It arrived a year later. Then it was assembled on Liberty Island, where it stands today. Putting it together took four months.
MAN: I'm not feeling so good. . . .
WOMAN: Oh, stop! It'll be fun!
GUIDE: Please be back at the boat in 30 minutes. Unfortunately, the statue is currently closed to visitors. You may walk around the island, but you may not climb the stairs to the top.
MAN: Hey, let's go! What are you waiting for?

B Listen again. Correct the seven mistakes in the text.

12 What a lucky break!

A Listen to Stacy and Richard talk about their careers. Who had a lucky break?

RICHARD: How did you get into TV announcing, Stacy?
STACY: Well, when I graduated from drama school, I moved to Los Angeles to look for work as an actress. I was going to auditions every day, but I never got any parts. And I was running out of money.
RICHARD: So, what did you do?
STACY: I got a job as an assistant at a TV station. While I was working there, the regular announcer got sick and they asked me to fill in. I guess I did a good job, because within a few weeks, they offered me a position on a new show!
RICHARD: Wow, what a lucky break!
STACY: So, Richard, what did you do after you graduated?
RICHARD: Well, I majored in English literature in college.

STACY: Uh-huh.
RICHARD: So when I graduated, I tried to make my living as a writer.
STACY: Oh, really?
RICHARD: Yeah. See, I've written a novel and I've sent it to eight publishers, but they all, uh, rejected it. Say, would you like to read it? I have it right here with me.
STACY: Well, I'd love to read it, Richard, . . . but not right now. Uh, so do you have a job or anything?
RICHARD: Oh, yes. I'm in sales.
STACY: Oh? Where?
RICHARD: Actually, I've been working for the last month as a salesclerk in a hardware store. But when my novel sells, I know I'll be a best-selling author and I'll make lots of money.

B Listen again. Number the events for each person from 1 to 5.

13 This book looks interesting.

A Listen to people talk about a book. Match each character with two descriptions.

WOMAN: This book looks interesting.
MAN: Oh, I read that! It's fascinating. It's about a horse named Seabiscuit that won a big race.
WOMAN: What's so great about a horse winning a race?
MAN: Well, it happened at a time when the country was struggling with the Great Depression, and people became very excited by the story of this horse.
WOMAN: Why is that?
MAN: Well, it involved an unusual cast of characters. The horse's owner was a millionaire who was very loud and outspoken. And the trainer was a quiet man who used to be a cowboy in the American West.
WOMAN: Those two sound pretty different.
MAN: It gets better. The jockey was a well-educated fighter who was also half blind. And then Seabiscuit was a little odd-looking – he was considered too small to be a racehorse.
WOMAN: Hmm. They do sound unusual.
MAN: That's the point. All these strange characters came together to make Seabiscuit into a champion. The whole country was amazed.
WOMAN: Hmm. Maybe I'll read it.
MAN: Well, the movie is really good, too.
WOMAN: Oh, there's a movie?
MAN: Yeah, it's the one that stars Tobey Maguire.
WOMAN: Oh, I've heard about it! It's supposed to be fantastic!
MAN: Well, then, why don't we rent the DVD?
WOMAN: You don't mind seeing it again?
MAN: Not at all. You rent the DVD, and I'll make some popcorn.

B Listen again. Complete these sentences with relative clauses from the conversation.

14 Police patrol

A Listen to four conversations. Number the pictures from 1 to 4.

1. WOMAN 1: What's the problem, officer?
   OFFICER: Well, you can't park here.
   WOMAN 1: Oh. I didn't see a sign.
   OFFICER: There's a sign right there, behind the tree.
2. MAN 1: What is that police officer trying to tell us?
   WOMAN 2: Uh, it probably means he wants us to go over there.
   MAN 1: But we didn't do anything wrong.
   WOMAN 2: Oh, look, there's a sign. We've got to put Fluffy on a leash.
3. MAN 2: Excuse me, officer, can we drive through here?
   OFFICER: No, cars aren't allowed on this street. It's for pedestrians only.
   MAN 2: How can I get to the library from here?
   OFFICER: Go two more blocks to First Avenue. You can drive on that street.
4. WOMAN 2: Why is that traffic officer waving at us?
   MAN 1: I don't know. It must mean he wants us to stop.
   WOMAN 2: No, he's making a diagonal motion with his hand. He looks annoyed.
   MAN 1: Ohhh, it probably means we have to fasten our seat belts! I'm wearing mine . . . are you?
   WOMAN 2: Well, uh . . . no.

B Listen again. Write each rule under the correct picture.

15 Unfortunate situations

A Listen to people describe situations. Check the correct response.

1. MAN 1: I parked my car downtown and left my briefcase on the back seat. It had some money in it. I locked the car, of course, but when I came back, someone had broken the window and taken my briefcase.
2. WOMAN 1: I found a hundred-dollar bill in my neighbor's driveway. My neighbor was away, so the money probably wasn't his. Anyway, I took the money and went shopping. I bought a cool new jacket and a fabulous skirt. Now I feel bad.
3. MAN 2: My aunt invited me over for dinner. Unfortunately, I forgot to write it down. The day I was supposed to go to her house, a friend invited me to see a movie with him, and I completely forgot about dinner.
4. WOMAN 2: I lent my car to a friend who doesn't have a driver's license. While he was driving, he had an accident and caused more than five hundred dollars' worth of damage to my car.

B Listen again. Write your own response for each situation.

16 Don't tell anyone . . .

A Listen to a telephone conversation. What excuse did Susan give Bill?

GRACE: [*phone rings*] Hello?
BILL: Grace, it's Bill.
GRACE: What's up?
BILL: I'm so annoyed! Jack told me he saw Susan and her ex-boyfriend having dinner together!
GRACE: Really? When?
BILL: Last night. Susan and I were supposed to go to the movies. Then she called at the last minute and said she wasn't feeling well.
GRACE: Oh, so she told you she couldn't go.
BILL: Yeah. I said I understood. I told her that she should stay home and get some rest.
GRACE: Good, so you expressed your concern.
BILL: Yeah, but instead of staying home, she went out!
GRACE: That's terrible! She shouldn't have done that.
BILL: I know. She shouldn't have made an excuse. She should've just told me the truth! Listen, don't tell anyone, OK?
GRACE: Right. Uh, I have to go. I'll talk to you later.

B Listen again. Read the voice mail Grace left another friend. Then correct the six errors in her message.

Self-study answer key

1

A both had a dog; both used to go to the beach every summer; both used to play in a tree house

B

	pets	***places***	***hobbies***
1. Kim	dog	beach	make scrapbooks
	rabbit	tree house	paint
2. Jeff	dog	beach	play chess
	cat	tree house	read comic books

2

A 1. exchange some money
2. mail some postcards
3. buy some souvenirs
4. go to the airport
5. park his car
6. get something to eat

B 1. b; 2. a; 3. b; 4. a; 5. a; 6. a

3

A No; Yes

B 1: noisy; old; spacious
2: dark; reasonable; safe

4

A H: ceviche; red chili peppers; Thai fried noodles
P: coconut curry

B 2, 4, 5, 1, 3

5

A camping, going abroad, going to the beach, seeing another city, staying home

B 1. You'd better pack a first-aid kit and be careful.
2. You have to get a passport and a visa.
3. You shouldn't go to the beach.
4. You need to make a reservation.
5. Why don't you do something fun?

6

A/B 1. the radio (loud)
2. the shoes (them)
3. the dog (him, walk, leash)
4. the window (close, open, wind, cold)
5. the lamp (dark, reading)
6. the dishes (them, counter, dirty, sink)

7

A She didn't know the screen saver was on.

B 1. surfing the Internet; writing e-mails; playing games; downloading music
2. turn on the screen saver

8

A/B 1. True
2. True
3. False (end of *summer*)
4. False (*children* "trick or treat")
5. False (ask for *candy*)
6. True

9

A a radio; an album; a cassette

B 1. Everything will be in one piece of technology.
2. You'll have fewer things to carry.
3. You won't need a big allowance.

10

A A: creative; level-headed; reliable
J: efficient; hardworking; impatient; organized

B

	Andre	***Jeri***
1. working with people	good	OK
2. solving problems	good	so-so
3. helping people	likes	likes
4. making mistakes	doesn't mind	hates

11

A There's no elevator.

B

1. ~~Canada~~	France	5. ~~1986~~	1886
2. ~~Hundreds~~	Millions	6. ~~nine~~	four
3. ~~54~~	354	7. ~~may~~	may not
4. ~~the United States~~	France		

12

A Stacy

B Stacy: 2, 5, 3, 1, 4
Richard: 3, 2, 5, 1, 4

13

A 1. c, g; 2. b, f; 3. a, h; 4. d, e

B (Possible answers)
1. who was outspoken.
2. that used to be a cowboy.
3. who was half blind.
4. that won a big race.

14

A/B 4. You have to fasten your seat belt.
3. Cars aren't allowed on this street.
2. You've got to put your dog on a leash.
1. You can't park here.

15

A 1. He shouldn't have left money in the car.
2. She shouldn't have gone shopping.
3. He should have written it down.
4. She shouldn't have lent her car to a friend.

B Answers will vary.

16

A She wasn't feeling well.

B

1. ~~father~~	ex-boyfriend
2. ~~lunch~~	dinner
3. ~~week~~	night
4. ~~shopping~~	to the movies
5. ~~the day before~~	at the last minute
6. ~~something to eat~~	some rest

Games

How can you create a fun and lively atmosphere in the classroom?

Games provide stimulating ways to practice a variety of skills, including vocabulary, grammar, speaking, and listening. Classic and innovative games, such as Twenty Questions, Hot Potato, and Change Chairs, add enjoyment to learning. Depending on the teacher's goals, games can be used as a warm-up, as additional practice, or as a review.

These 20 Games can be adapted for use with different skills and with different levels. Unlike the Photocopiables, handouts are not usually required.

Games	Use to practice	Use with
1. Kim's Game	Vocabulary	Intro Level
2. Line Up!	Vocabulary, Grammar, Speaking	Levels Intro - 1
3. Sculptures	Vocabulary, Grammar	Levels Intro - 1
4. Concentration	Vocabulary, Grammar	Levels Intro - 1
5. Simon Says	Vocabulary, Listening	Levels Intro - 1
6. Change Chairs	Vocabulary, Listening	Levels Intro - 1
7. Chain Game	Vocabulary, Grammar, Listening	Levels Intro - 2
8. Twenty Questions	Grammar, Speaking, Listening	Levels 1 - 2
9. Ask the Right Question	Grammar	Levels 2 - 3
10. Split Sentences	Grammar	Levels 2 - 3
11. Just One Minute	Speaking, Listening	Levels 2 - 3
12. Prediction Bingo	Listening, Reading	Level 3
13. Bingo	Listening, Vocabulary	All levels
14. Hot Potato	Grammar, Speaking	All levels
15. Picture It!	Vocabulary	All levels
16. Vocabulary Tennis	Vocabulary	All levels
17. Run For It!	Grammar	All levels
18. Mime	Vocabulary, Grammar	All levels
19. Tic-Tac-Toe	Vocabulary, Grammar, Pronunciation	All levels
20. True or False?	Grammar, Speaking, Listening	All levels

1 KIM'S GAME

Aim: *Improve Ss' ability to remember vocabulary.*
Level: *Intro*
Preparation: *Bring objects (or pictures of objects) to class.*
Comment: *Use to review vocabulary.*

- Put the objects on your desk and cover them.
- Explain the task. Uncover the objects and ask Ss to look at them for three minutes. Then cover them. In pairs, Ss list the objects they remember. Set a three-minute time limit.
- Ss complete the task.
- Uncover the objects. The pair with the most correct words wins.

Variation 1: Write words on the board. Then erase them.

Variation 2: Put a picture with a lot of details on your desk. Ss use a specific structure (e.g., *there is/ there are*, prepositions of place) to write sentences about the objects.

2 LINE UP!

Aim: *Give Ss practice using a variety of skills in an active way.*
Levels: *Intro and 1*
Preparation: *None*
Comment: *Use to review vocabulary and practice grammar and speaking.*

- Review or teach these expressions:
  You're in front of / behind me.
- Write a question on the board. For example:
  What time do you get up?
- Explain the task. Ss go around the class and ask each other the question on the board. Then they stand in line according to the answers (e.g., in time order). Point out that the board is the beginning and the other end of the classroom is the end (e.g., of the day).
- Model the task with a few Ss.
- Explain that when two answers are the same, Ss stand in alphabetical order of their first names.
- Ss complete the task.
- Ask Ss to explain their position in line. For example: "I'm number 1. I get up at 5:00."

Variations: Use this game to practice the alphabet (e.g., *What's your last name?*), dates (e.g., *When's your birthday?*), lengths of time (e.g., *How long do you sleep each night?*), and structures (e.g., *How many phone calls have you made today?*).

Acknowledgment: *Idea adapted from* The Grammar Activity Book *by Bob Obee, Cambridge University Press.*

3 SCULPTURES

Aim: *Give Ss practice reviewing vocabulary in an active way.*
Levels: *Intro and 1*
Preparation: *List vocabulary you want to review.*
Comment: *Use to review vocabulary and grammar.*

- Divide the class into teams of three.
- Explain the task. Whisper an activity to one S (e.g., *play soccer*). This S whispers the activity to the other Ss on his or her team. The team has one minute to form a sculpture that illustrates the activity (e.g., S1 pretends to kick a ball, S2 pretends to be a goalkeeper). The other teams guess the activity. The first team to guess correctly gets a point.
- Model the task with one team.
- Play the game until you use all the vocabulary. The team with the most points wins.

Variation 1: Use this game to review vocabulary such as household chores, celebrations, or entertainment.

Variation 2: Ask Ss to use specific grammar structures when guessing the activity (e.g., present continuous, simple past).

4 CONCENTRATION

Aim: *Give Ss practice reviewing vocabulary and grammar in a fun way.*
Levels: *Intro and 1*
Preparation: *Make one set of cards for each group of Ss. Two cards in each set match (e.g., word + picture, word + definition, word + opposite).*
Comment: *Use to review vocabulary and grammar.*

- Ss work in groups of four. Give each group a set of cards. Ask the Ss to put all their cards face down on a desk.
- Explain the task. Ss take turns choosing two cards, turning them over, and saying the words. If the two cards match, they keep the pair of cards and take another turn. If the cards don't match, they put them face down again, and the next S takes a turn.
- Model the task with one group.
- Ss play the game. The S in each group with the most cards wins.

Variation: After Ss match cards, they use the word in a sentence with a specific verb tense (e.g., simple present).

5 SIMON SAYS

Aim: *Give Ss active practice developing listening skills.*
Levels: *Intro and 1*
Preparation: *None*
Comment: *Use to review vocabulary and practice listening.*

- Ss stand up.
- Explain the task. Give an instruction. If you start the instruction with "Simon says" (e.g., "Simon says touch your toes."), Ss follow the instruction. If you give the instruction without "Simon says" (e.g., "Touch your toes."), Ss do nothing.
- Explain that Ss sit down if they follow the instruction when you don't say "Simon says." They also sit down if they do the wrong action (e.g., they touch their knees instead of their toes).
- Model the game with a few instructions.
- Play the game. The last student standing wins.

Variation 1: Use this game to review action verbs (e.g., *sing*, *swim*) or sports (e.g., *play tennis*).

Variation 2: The winning S stands at the front of the class and gives the instructions for the next game.

6 CHANGE CHAIRS

Aim: *Review vocabulary and improve listening in an active way.*
Levels: *Intro and 1*
Preparation: *None*
Comment: *Use with classes of six or more Ss to review vocabulary and improve listening.*

- Ask Ss to move their chairs in a circle, facing the center. Stand in the middle.
- Explain the task. Give an instruction that starts with "Change chairs" (e.g., "Change chairs if you are wearing jeans."). All Ss wearing jeans stand up and change chairs.
- Model the task a few times.
- Ask one S to stand up. Take away his or her chair.
- Explain the task. The S without a chair stands in the center and gives the next instruction (e.g., "Change chairs if you have one brother."). This time, the S in the center also tries to sit down. The S left without a chair stands in the center and gives the next instruction.
- Model the task.
- Ss play the game.

Variation: Use this game to review specific categories of vocabulary (e.g., clothes, hobbies).

7 CHAIN GAME

Aim: *Give Ss listening practice while reviewing vocabulary.*
Levels: *Intro, 1, and 2*
Preparation: *None*
Comment: *Use to review vocabulary and practice grammar and listening.*

- Ss sit in circles in small groups.
- Explain the task. S1 makes a sentence. S2 repeats the sentence and adds to it. S3 repeats S2's sentence and adds to it. For example:
  S1: Last weekend I went dancing.
  S2: Last weekend I went dancing and read a book.
  S3: Last weekend I went dancing, read a book, and . . .
  Ss continue until a S can't remember what to say. Then the next S continues the sentence.
- Point out that the information in the sentence can be false.
- Model the game with one group.
- Ss play the game.

Variations: Use this activity to review specific groups of vocabulary, such as food (e.g., *I like . . .*), clothes (e.g., *I went to the store and I bought . . .*), or family members (e.g., *Tonight I'm going to call . . .*).

8 TWENTY QUESTIONS

Aim: *Give Ss practice asking yes/no questions.*
Levels: *1 and 2*
Preparation: *None*
Comment: *Use to practice grammar, speaking, and listening.*

- Ss work in small groups.
- Explain the task. One S in each group thinks of a famous person. The other Ss ask yes/no questions to guess the person. For example: "Is it a man? Is he a singer? Is he from Canada?" The S only answers "yes" or "no." The S who correctly guesses the person gets a point and thinks of the next famous person.
- Model the task. Think of a famous person and the class asks yes/no questions.
- Ss play the game. The S in each group with the most points wins.

Variation 1: Write famous people's names on pieces of paper (one name per paper, one paper per S). Attach the papers to the Ss' backs. Ss go around the room and ask yes/no questions to guess the name (e.g., "Am I a man?").

Variation 2: Use this game to practice present tense (e.g., *Is she an actress?*), past tense (e.g., *Was she an actress?*), or infinitives and gerunds (e.g., *Is it used to send information? Is it used for sending information?*).

9 ASK THE RIGHT QUESTION

Aim: *Give Ss practice making Wh-questions.*
Levels: *2 and 3*
Preparation: *Bring three index cards for each S.*
Comment: *Use to practice grammar.*

- Write this statement on the board:
  Evan's a chef at Ricky's Restaurant.
- Elicit Wh-questions that the statement could answer (e.g., "Where does Evan work? What does Evan do? Who's the chef at Ricky's Restaurant?").
- Give each S three index cards. Ss write one statement on each card that could answer several Wh-questions. Go around the class and give help as needed.
- Collect all the cards and mix them up. Then divide the class into two teams (A and B).
- Explain the game. S1 from Team A chooses a card and reads the statement aloud. S1 from Team B makes a Wh-question for it. If the question is correct, Team B gets a point. If it is not correct, S1 from Team A makes a Wh-question. If the question is correct, Team A gets a point. Then S2 from Team B chooses a card.
- Model the game a few times.
- Play the game until you use all the cards. The team with the most points wins.

10 SPLIT SENTENCES

Aim: *Help Ss understand complex sentences.*
Levels: *2 and 3*
Preparation: *Write ten complex sentences and split them in half. Make sets of the split sentences (one per three Ss). Put each set in an envelope.*
Comment: *Use to practice grammar.*

- Model the task with split sentences.
  For example:

If I found a wallet,	*I would call the police.*
If I saw a ghost,	*I would scream.*
If I were rich,	*I would share my wealth.*

- Ss work in teams of three. Give each group a set of split sentences.
- Ask each group to match the split sentences.
- Ss complete the task.
- The first team to match the split sentences correctly wins.

Variations: Use this game to practice specific complex structures, such as conditionals, passives, two-part verbs, and tag questions.

11 JUST ONE MINUTE

Aim: *Help Ss develop oral fluency and listening skills.*
Levels: *2 and 3*
Preparation: *Bring a clock or watch with a second hand to class.*
Comment: *Use to practice speaking and listening.*

- Write a topic on the board (e.g., customs, food, transportation).
- Explain the game. Ss work in pairs. S1 talks about the topic for one minute. Point out that S1 cannot repeat ideas, change the topic, or hesitate for more than five seconds. S2 listens for repetition, topic changes, or hesitations. After one minute, say, "Stop!" If S1 talked without any repetition, topic changes, or hesitations, he or she gets a point.
- Play the game. S2 tells S1 about any repetition, topic changes, or hesitations. If there are none, S1 gets a point.
- The Ss in each pair change roles. Write another topic on the board and S2 talks for one minute.
- Play the game with a few more topics. The S in each pair with the most points wins.

Variation 1: Write several topics on the board. S1 chooses a topic from the board.

Variation 2: At the end of each game, a S chooses the next topic.

12 PREDICTION BINGO

Aim: *Give Ss practice predicting the content of an audio program or text.*
Level: *3*
Preparation: *None*
Comment: *Use to practice listening or reading.*

- Tell Ss the topic of the audio program they will listen to or the text they will read (e.g., our lives in the future).
- Explain the task. Each S draws a bingo card with nine squares. Ss predict content words (i.e., nouns, verbs, adjectives) related to the topic individually. Then they write one word in each square.
  For example:

robots	*cell phones*	*computers*
school	*work*	*cars*
money	*travel*	*time*

- Ss listen to the audio program or read the text. When Ss hear or see a word that's on their bingo card, they circle it.
- The S with the most circled words wins.

Variation: Ss make bingo cards in pairs. Then they exchange cards with another pair.

13 BINGO

Aim: *Help Ss improve listening and vocabulary in a fun way.*
Levels: *All*
Preparation: *Prepare a list of at least 15 words you want to review.*
Comment: *Use to practice listening and vocabulary.*

- Tell Ss to draw a bingo card on a piece of paper:

- Read and spell each word on your list. Then make a sentence with it. For example, say: "Family. F-A-M-I-L-Y. There are three people in my family."
- Ss listen and write each word in a different square on their bingo cards. Point out that they can write the words in any order.
- Play the game. Read out the words from your list in a different order. As you read each word aloud, spell it and use it in a sentence. Ss circle the words on their cards. (Note: Cross the words off your list, so you can check Ss' cards later.) The first S to circle all the words in one row shouts "Bingo!" If the words are correct, the student wins.

Variation 1: Use this game to review vocabulary, the alphabet, sounds, numbers, or grammar (e.g., verb forms).

Variation 2: Instead of reading out the word, read out a definition. For example, when you say "This is the opposite of *hot*," Ss circle *cold*.

14 HOT POTATO

Aim: *Give Ss practice asking and answering questions.*
Levels: *All*
Preparation: *Write questions on ten pieces of paper (one per paper). Then wrap the papers around each other to make a paper ball. Bring music and a cassette or CD player to class.*
Comment: *Use to practice grammar and speaking.*

- Ss sit in a circle.
- Explain the game. While you play music, Ss throw the paper ball to each other. When you stop the music, the S holding the ball takes off the outside piece of paper, reads the question, and answers it. Then start the music and the Ss throw the paper ball again.
- Model the game, then play the game until Ss answer all ten questions.

Variation: Use this game to practice specific structures (e.g., present perfect, passives, and conditionals).

15 PICTURE IT!

Aim: *Help Ss understand vocabulary in a visual way.*
Levels: *All*
Preparation: *Make sets of vocabulary cards (one per four Ss). Put each set in an envelope.*
Comment: *Use to review vocabulary.*

- Ss work in groups of four. Give each group a set of cards.
- Explain the rules. One S in each group chooses a card and draws a picture of the word on a piece of paper. The other Ss try to guess the word. The first S to guess the word correctly gets a point and chooses the next card.
- Point out that the S drawing the picture cannot write numbers or letters, talk, or make gestures.
- Model the task by drawing a picture of a word on the board. The class guesses the word.
- Play the game until Ss use all the cards. The S in each group with the most points wins.

Variation: Use one set of cards. Divide the class into two teams (A and B). One S from Team A chooses a card and draws the picture on the board. The Ss in Team A have two minutes to guess the word. If they guess correctly, Team A gets a point. Repeat with Team B and continue until Ss use all cards. The team with the most points wins.

16 VOCABULARY TENNIS

Aim: *Help Ss review categories of words in a fun way.*
Levels: *All*
Preparation: *None*
Comment: *Use to review vocabulary.*

- Divide the class into two teams (A and B).
- Explain the game. Call out a category (e.g., jobs). Team A "serves" by saying a word in that category (e.g., teacher). Team B "returns the serve" by saying a different word from that category (e.g., nurse). The teams take turns saying words from the category.
- The game continues until one team can't think of any more words. The other team gets a point.
- Call out a different category (e.g., colors, furniture, leisure activities, adjectives) and play the game again.
- The team with the most points wins.

Variation: Bring a balloon to class. Teams A and B stand on opposite sides of the room. When Team A says a word, it "serves" the balloon to Team B. Team B must say a different word before the balloon reaches its side of the room. If Team B doesn't say a word or drops the balloon, Team A gets a point.

17 RUN FOR IT!

Aim: *Help Ss practice prepositions of time.*
Levels: *All*
Preparation: *Prepare a list of sentences with missing prepositions. Write each missing preposition on a separate card and post the cards around the classroom walls.*
Comment: *Use to practice grammar.*

- Divide Ss into two teams (A and B). Assign each member of the teams a number (e.g., S1, S2).
- Read out the first sentence without saying the preposition (e.g., "I always get up BLANK 6 A.M. on weekdays."). S1 from each team runs to find the card containing the missing preposition. The first S to reach the correct card gets a point for his or her team.
- Play the game until you use all the sentences. The team with the most points wins.

Variation 1: Use this game to review prepositions of place or time, modals, and auxiliaries (e.g., *do*, *did*, *have*).

Variation 2: If Ss cannot move freely around the room, they can point to the correct wall.

18 MIME

Aim: *Help Ss personalize and review vocabulary and grammar in an active way.*
Levels: *All*
Preparation: *Make sets of vocabulary cards (one per four Ss). Put each set in an envelope.*
Comment: *Use to review vocabulary and grammar.*

- Ss work in groups of four. Give each group a set of cards.
- Explain the rules. One S in each group chooses a card and mimes the activity (e.g., wash your hair, watch a comedy on TV). The first S to guess the activity correctly keeps the card and chooses the next one.
- Point out that Ss cannot speak while they are miming words.
- Ss continue until they use all the cards. The S with the most cards wins.

Variation 1: Use this game to review specific structures, such as present continuous (e.g., *She is washing her hair.*) or simple past vs. past continuous (e.g., *He was cooking when the phone rang.*).

Variation 2: Ss make sets of vocabulary cards in small groups. Then they exchange cards with another group, and mime the activities on the new cards.

19 TIC-TAC-TOE

Aim: *Help Ss review words in a fun way.*
Levels: *All*
Preparation: *Make a list of words you want to review.*
Comment: *Use to review vocabulary and practice grammar and pronunciation.*

- Draw a chart with nine squares on the board. Write one word in each square. For example:

know	give	think
fall	feel	buy
catch	sing	swim

- Divide the class into two teams (X and O).
- Explain the game. Team X chooses a word on the board (e.g., *buy*) and uses it in a specific way (e.g., changes the verb tense or uses it in a sentence). If the answer is correct, replace the word *buy* with an X. If the answer is incorrect, Team O tries to give the correct answer. If Team O's answer is correct, replace the word *buy* with an O. If neither team gives the correct answer, tell Ss the answer. Then replace the word *buy* with a different word.
- Play the game. The first team to get a straight line of three Xs or Os (across, down, or diagonally) wins.

Variation: Use this game to review question words (e.g., *what*, *where*), modals (e.g., *would*, *could*), adverbs of frequency, pronunciation (e.g., pronunciation of words, rhyming words), and vocabulary.

20 TRUE OR FALSE?

Aim: *Give Ss practice using grammar in a personalized way.*
Levels: *All*
Preparation: *None*
Comment: *Use to practice grammar, speaking, and listening.*

- Each S writes six statements about themselves. Three statements are true and three are false. For example:
  I can sing really well.
  I have three sisters.
- Explain the game. Ss take turns reading their statements aloud in small groups. The other Ss guess which statements are true and which are false. Ss get one point for each correct guess.
- Ss play the game. The S in each group with the most points wins.

! Fresh ideas

How can you tailor your classes to your students' needs, learning styles, and ages?

Fresh ideas provide innovative ways to teach a variety of exercises in the Student's Book. Techniques such as Disappearing Dialog, Onion Ring, and Jigsaw Learning make classes livelier, more interactive, and more varied. Depending on the exercise, these techniques can either supplement or replace the suggestions in the page-by-page teaching notes.

These 20 Fresh ideas can be adapted for use with different exercises and with different levels. Unlike the Photocopiables, handouts are not usually required.

Fresh ideas	Use with	Use with
1. Look Up and Speak!	Conversations	All levels
2. Say It With Feeling!	Conversations	All levels
3. Moving Dialog	Conversations	All levels
4. Musical Dialog	Conversations	All levels
5. Substitution Dialog	Conversations, Grammar Focuses	All levels
6. Disappearing Dialog	Conversations, Grammar Focuses	All levels
7. Onion Ring	Conversations, Discussions	All levels
8. Stand Up, Sit Down	Listenings	All levels
9. Walking Stress	Pronunciations	All levels
10. Question Exchange	Grammar Focuses	All levels
11. Reading Race	Readings, Perspectives	All levels
12. Jigsaw Learning	Readings, Listenings	Levels 1 - 3
13. Running Dictation	Readings, Perspectives	Levels 1 - 3
14. Vocabulary Mingle	Readings, Perspectives	Levels 1 - 3
15. Time Out!	Role Plays	Levels 1 - 3
16. Pass the Paper	Writings	Levels 1 - 3
17. Mind Mapping	Writings, Word Powers	Levels 1 - 3
18. Picture Dictation	Snapshots, Word Powers	Levels 1 - 3
19. Vocabulary Steps	Snapshots, Word Powers	All levels
20. Cloud Prediction	Conversations, Listenings, or Readings	All levels

1 LOOK UP AND SPEAK!

Aim: *Encourage Ss to look at their partners while practicing Conversations.*
Levels: *All*
Preparation: *None*
Comment: *Use with Conversations.*

- Point out that it's important to look at your partner when speaking.
- Explain the task. Ss work in pairs. S1 looks briefly at the first line of the conversation and tries to remember it. Then S1 looks up at S2 and says the line. S2 looks briefly at the next line of conversation, tries to remember it, and then looks up and says it.
- Model the task with one or two Ss.
- Ss complete the task in pairs.

Note: This technique works best when Ss stand up and face each other. It's a useful way to help Ss develop eye contact while speaking.

2 SAY IT WITH FEELING!

Aim: *Improve Ss' pronunciation, intonation, and understanding of a Conversation in an enjoyable way.*
Levels: *All*
Preparation: *None*
Comment: *Use with Conversations.*

- Explain the task. Ss listen to the audio program, focusing on the speakers' intonation and emotions (e.g., anger, surprise).
- Play the audio program. Ask Ss to repeat selected phrases with the correct intonation. Encourage them to exaggerate the intonation. They can also add gestures, if appropriate.
- Ss practice the conversation in pairs, using lots of intonation. Then they change roles and practice again.

Option: Ask pairs of Ss to perform the conversation in front of the class. The class votes for the best performance.

3 MOVING DIALOG

Aim: *Give Ss more speaking practice with different Ss.*
Levels: *All*
Preparation: *None*
Comment: *Use with Conversations.*

- Explain the task. Ss stand in two lines (A and B), facing each other. Then they practice the conversation.
- When you clap, the Ss in line A all move one step to their right. One S at the end of line A will not have a partner. He or she runs quickly to the beginning of line A.
- Ss practice the conversation with new partners.
- Continue as many times as needed.

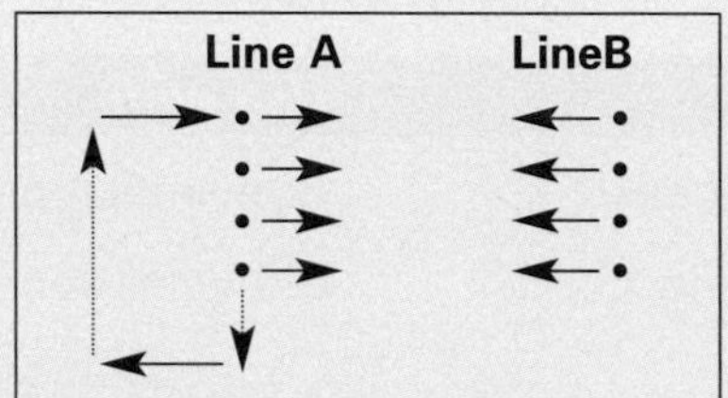

4 MUSICAL DIALOG

Aim: *Give Ss conversation practice in a natural and fun setting.*
Levels: *All*
Preparation: *Bring party music and a cassette or CD player to class.*
Comment: *Use with Conversations that could take place at a party (e.g., introductions, invitations, or discussions about childhood, daily routines, or families).*

- Explain the task. Ss move around the room while you play music. When you stop the music, they begin conversations with the S closest to them. They use the conversation in the Student Book as a model, substituting information about themselves.
- Model the task with one or two Ss.
- Play the party music. Stop the music every 20 or 30 seconds for Ss to complete the task.
- Continue as many times as needed.

Variation: Play the music without stopping. When you turn up the volume, Ss shout to begin conversations with the Ss closest to them.

5 SUBSTITUTION DIALOG

Aim: *Give Ss controlled practice with new structures.*
Levels: *All*
Preparation: *Choose four to six words or phrases to substitute.*
Comment: *Use with Conversations or Grammar Focus exercises that involve conversations.*

- After completing the Conversation or Grammar Focus conversation, tell Ss to underline and number the words or phrases you chose. For example:
  Customer: I'd like a hamburger (1), please.
  Waiter: All right. And would you like a salad (2)?
- Write substitutions for the underlined words on the board. For example:
  (1) a chicken sandwich/some french fries/ . . .
  (2) some soup/an appetizer/ . . .
- Explain the task. Ss practice the conversation twice using the substitutions on the board. Then they practice it using their own ideas.
- Model the task. Then Ss complete the task in pairs.

6 DISAPPEARING DIALOG

Aim: *Give Ss confidence using new vocabulary and grammar.*
Levels: *All*
Preparation: *None*
Comment: *Use with Conversations or Grammar Focus exercises that involve conversations.*

- After completing the Conversation or Grammar Focus conversation, write all or part of it on the board.
- Explain the task. Ss work in pairs. They take turns practicing the conversation on the board repeatedly. As they practice, gradually erase words from the board.
- Ss practice the conversation. Erase one word per line each time they practice. For example:
  A: Good morning. How are you?
  B: I'm just fine. Thank you. . . .
  becomes
  A: Good morning. ______ are you?
  B: I'm just fine. ______ you. . . .
- Erase more words. Gradually Ss will be able to practice the conversation without support.

Variation: Divide the class into two teams. One S from each team reads the conversation while you erase the words. When a S can't remember a word, the other team gets a point. The team with the most points wins.

7 ONION RING

Aim: *Give Ss more practice speaking with different Ss.*
Levels: *All*
Preparation: *None*
Comment: *Use with Conversations or Discussions.*

- Divide the class into two groups, A and B.
- The groups stand in two circles, one inside the other. Ss in Group A bring their books and make a circle around the classroom, facing inward. Ss in Group B bring their books and make an inside circle. Each S in Group B faces a S from Group A.

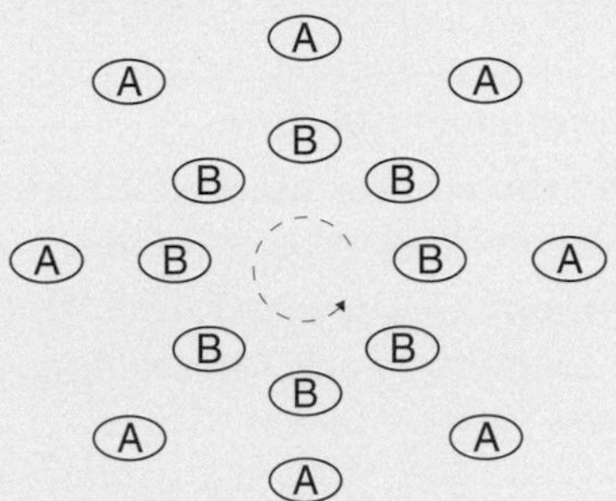

- Explain the task. Ss practice the conversation in pairs. When you say "Change!," Ss in Group B move to the left and practice the conversation with new partners from Group A.
- Ss practice the conversation. Call out "Change!" when most Ss complete the conversation.

Variation: Only Ss in Group A bring their books. Ss in Group B improvise the conversation.

8 STAND UP, SIT DOWN

Aim: *Focus Ss' attention on listening for specific sounds.*
Levels: *All*
Preparation: *None*
Comment: *Use with Listenings.*

- Ss complete the Listening exercises.
- Explain the task. Ss listen to the audio program again, focusing on a specific sound (e.g., [θ]). They stand up and sit down whenever they hear the sound.
- Model the task. Play a little of the audio program and demonstrate when to stand up and sit down.
- Play the audio program. Ss carry out the task.

Variation 1: Ss can also listen for other things, such as verb tenses (e.g., simple past), times, prices, pronouns, numbers, days, or types of words.

Variation 2: Divide the class into two groups (A and B). Each group listens for a different thing (e.g., Group A listens for [θ] and Group B listens for [ð]; Group A listens for simple past and Group B listens for past continuous).

9 WALKING STRESS

Aim: *Raise Ss' awareness of sentence stress in an active and fun way.*
Levels: *All*
Preparation: *None*
Comment: *Use with Pronunciations that focus on sentence stress.*

- Play the audio program. Focus Ss' attention on the sentence stress.
- Explain the task. Ss stand up and move to a place where they can move freely. Then model the task. Say: "I always go jogging on Sundays." Step forward on the first syllable in the words *always*, *jogging*, and *Sundays*.
- Read or play the other sentences. Check that Ss walk forward on the correct syllables.

Acknowledgment: *Idea adapted from* The Standby Book *by Seth Lindstromberg, Cambridge University Press.*

10 QUESTION EXCHANGE

Aim: *Give Ss practice making and answering questions.*
Levels: *All*
Preparation: *Write one verb or phrase for each S on pieces of paper.*
Comment: *Use with Grammar Focuses that involve questions.*

- After presenting the Grammar Focus, write the grammar structure on the board. For example: *How often do you ________ ?*
- Give each S a piece of paper with a different verb or phrase (e.g., *play sports*).
- Explain the task. Ss go around the room and find a partner. They take turns asking and answering questions using the structure on the board and the word or phrase on their piece of papers. For example: *How often do you play sports?*
  Then Ss exchange papers and find a new partner.
- Model the task with one or two Ss.
- Ss complete the task. Continue until Ss exchange papers with most of their classmates.
- Elicit interesting answers from the class.

Option: Encourage Ss to ask follow-up questions.

Acknowledgment: *Idea adapted from* Teaching Multilevel Classes *by Natalie Hess, Cambridge University Press.*

11 READING RACE

Aim: *Give Ss practice reading for specific information.*
Levels: *All*
Preparation: *Photocopy and enlarge the text. Cut the copy into paragraphs and post the paragraphs around the classroom walls. Prepare and copy a handout with 6 to 12 comprehension questions about the text (one handout per S).*
Comment: *Use with Readings or Perspectives that have several short texts.*

- Books closed. Distribute the handout and explain the task. Ss go around the class with their handouts, scan the texts, and answer the questions. The first S to correctly answer all the questions wins.
- Model the task with the first question. Then Ss complete the task.
- Ss check their answers by reading the texts in their Student's Books.

12 JIGSAW LEARNING

Aim: *Give Ss practice using all four skills in a collaborative way.*
Levels: *1, 2, and 3*
Preparation: *None*
Comment: *Use with Readings or Listenings that can be divided into three or four short texts.*

- Draw a chart on the board. List the texts at the top and things you want Ss to find on the left. For example:

	Text A	*Text B*	*Text C*
Topic			
Problem			

  Ss copy the chart on a piece of paper.
- Divide the class into three groups (A, B, and C).
- Explain the task. Ss complete the chart for their group only. For example, Group A only reads Text A and completes column A.
- Ss complete the task.
- Divide the class into new groups of three. Each group has one S each from groups A, B, and C. Ss share information to complete their charts.

Variation for Listenings: Bring three audio programs and cassette or CD players to class. Ss listen to the audio program in three groups and complete the column for their group. Then they form new groups and share their information.

13 RUNNING DICTATION

Aim: *Give Ss practice using all four skills in a collaborative way.*
Levels: *1, 2, and 3*
Preparation: *Photocopy and enlarge several copies of the text. Post the copies around the classroom walls.*
Comment: *Use with Readings or Perspectives.*

- Books closed. Ss work in pairs.
- Explain the task. S1 from each pair goes to the wall and memorizes part of the text. Then S1 comes back and dictates the information to S2, and S2 writes it down.
- Point out that Ss cannot shout across the room or remove the copies from the walls. When you call out "Change!," Ss change roles.
- Ss complete the task. The first pair to finish wins.
- Books open. Ss check their spelling.

14 VOCABULARY MINGLE

Aim: *Encourage Ss to find the meaning of unknown words.*
Levels: *1, 2, and 3*
Preparation: *None*
Comment: *Use with Readings or Perspectives.*

- Explain the first task. Ss read the text. When they find a word they don't know, they underline it with a straight line. If they think they know the meaning but are not sure, they underline it with a squiggly line.
- Ss complete the task individually.
- Explain the second task. Ss take their books and go around the room. They ask each other the meanings of the words they don't know or aren't sure of.
- Model the task with one or two Ss:
  T: What does *large* mean?
  S1: It means "big."
  T: Thanks.
- Ss complete the task.
- Help Ss with any remaining words they don't know.

Variation: Ss sit in small groups and ask each other the meanings of new words.

15 TIME OUT!

Aim: *Help students develop fluency and confidence.*
Levels: *1, 2, and 3*
Preparation: *None*
Comment: *Use with Role Plays.*

- Divide Ss into groups of six. Two Ss (S1 and S2) are the actors. The other four Ss help the actors.
- Explain the task. S1 and S2 perform the role play using the instructions in their Student's Books. If they don't know what to say or can't remember a word, they call "Time Out!" The role play stops and they ask the Ss in their group for help. They can also ask the other Ss in the group to replace them.
- Ss continue the role play until all Ss are actors.

Variation 1: S1 and S2 can bring in other Ss as new characters.

Variation 2: Ss can create new situations based on the role play.

Acknowledgment: *Idea adapted from* Strategic Interaction *by Robert J. Di Pietro, Cambridge University Press.*

16 PASS THE PAPER

Aim: *Help Ss generate ideas and plan compositions.*
Levels: *1, 2, and 3*
Preparation: *None*
Comment: *Use with Writings.*

- Before beginning their compositions, Ss work in groups of five or six. Ask Ss to write their name in the top right-hand corner of a blank piece of paper.
- Explain the task. Ss write a question related to the composition topic on their piece of paper (e.g., *Where did you go?*). Then they pass their paper to the right, and take the paper from their left. Each time Ss receive a paper, they write one question and pass the paper to the right.
- Ss complete the task. They continue until there are ten questions on each paper.
- Ss find their original papers, read the questions, and circle four or five they want to answer.
- Ss number the questions in the order they plan to answer them. Then they write their compositions.

17 MIND MAPPING

Aim: *Help Ss generate ideas and plan their compositions.*
Levels: *1, 2, and 3*
Preparation: *None*
Comment: *Use with Writings or Word Powers.*

- Write the composition theme (e.g., holidays) in a large circle on the board. Then elicit topics related to the theme and write them in smaller circles around the theme. For example:

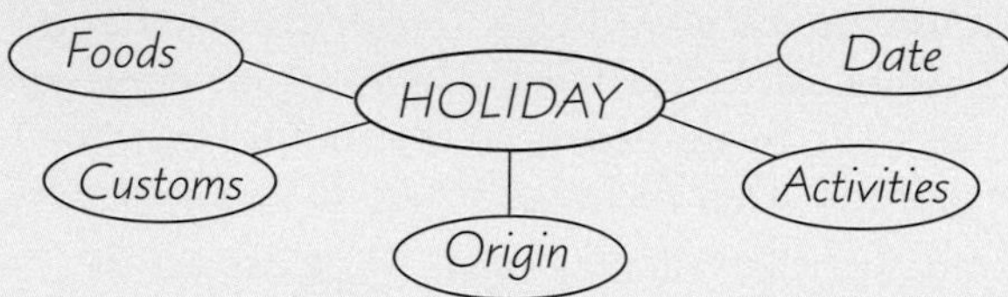

- Elicit words or phrases related to each topic. Write them in circles around the topics.
- Explain the task. Ss choose three topics to write about. They number them in the order they want to write about them.
- Brainstorm possible opening and closing sentences for the compositions.
- Ss write their compositions, using an opening sentence, three topics, and a conclusion.

Variation for Word Powers: Use the first two steps of this technique to review, categorize, and expand on vocabulary from Word Powers.

18 PICTURE DICTATION

Aim: *Develop Ss' vocabulary and listening skills.*
Levels: *1, 2, and 3*
Preparation: *None*
Comment: *Use with Snapshots and Word Powers that have pictures with a lot of details (e.g., clothes, maps, furniture).*

- Teach or review prepositional phrases of place (e.g., *in the middle, on the right / left, at the top / bottom, in the top / bottom right-hand / left-hand corner*).
- Explain the task. Ss work in pairs. S1 looks at the picture and S2 has a blank piece of paper. S1 describes the picture. S2 listens and draws it.
- Ss complete the task. Then they compare their drawings with the picture in the Student's Book.

Option: Describe a picture, and the class draws it.

Variation: Photocopy the picture and post it on the wall. S1 from each pair goes to the wall and returns to S2. S1 describes the picture to S2, and S2 draws it.

19 VOCABULARY STEPS

Aim: *Help Ss review and personalize vocabulary in a category.*
Levels: *All*
Preparation: *Choose four to six words in a category.*
Comment: *Use with Snapshots or Word Powers.*

- After presenting the Snapshot or Word Power, write the words you chose on the board. For example, if the category is *seasons*, write the words *spring*, *summer*, *fall*, and *winter*. Then draw steps on the board:

- Explain the task. Ss rank the words individually according to a criterion (e.g., favorite). They write their favorite at the top of the steps and their least favorite at the bottom of the steps.
- Ss complete the task. Then they compare their answers in pairs.

Variation 1: Ask Ss to rank vocabulary using different criteria. For example: sports (most fun, most popular), things (most useful, most expensive), foods (tastiest, healthiest), or jobs (most difficult, most dangerous).

Variation 2: Ask higher-level Ss to rank the words collaboratively in small groups.

Acknowledgment: *Idea adapted from* Five-Minute Activities *by Penny Ur and Andrew Wright, Cambridge University Press.*

20 CLOUD PREDICTION

Aim: *Develop Ss' ability to predict content from key words.*
Levels: *All*
Preparation: *List six to ten key words from the text.*
Comment: *Use with Conversations, Listenings, or Readings.*

- Write the key words on the board, inside a large cloud.
- Explain the task. Ss work in pairs. They use the key words on the board to predict the main ideas of the Conversation or Listening.
- Point out that all predictions are acceptable.
- Ss complete the task. Elicit Ss' predictions.
- Ss listen to the audio program and check their predictions.

Variation for Readings: After eliciting predictions, Ss read the text and check their predictions.

Photocopiables

Where can you find interesting, easy-to-use handouts for your classes?
Photocopiables provide innovative ways to teach specific exercises in the Student's Book, and include such activities as word searches, information gaps, and board games. Depending on the exercise, these materials can either supplement or replace the suggestions in the page-by-page teaching notes.

There are 16 Photocopiables, one for each unit. Each activity includes a photocopiable handout, which is provided at the end of this section.

Units	*Exercises*	*Photocopiables*
1. A time to remember	Speaking on page 4	Ask the Right Questions
2. Caught in the rush	Word Power on page 8	Dictionary Skills
3. Time for a change!	Perspectives on page 16	Hear the Differences
4. I've never heard of that!	Grammar Focus on page 23	Participle Concentration
5. Going places	Discussion on page 34	Role Cards
6. OK. No problem!	Word Power on page 38	Requests Picture Game
7. What's this for?	Grammar Focus on page 45	Information Gap Crossword
8. Let's celebrate!	Reading on page 55	Reading Race
9. Back to the future	Activity on Interchange 9	TV Debate
10. I don't like working on weekends!	Writing on page 68	Cover Letter Gap-Fill
11. It's really worth seeing!	Speaking on page 76	Country Profiles Quiz
12. It could happen to you!	Listening on page 80	Mixed-Up Stories
13. Good book, terrible movie!	Speaking on page 90	Scriptwriters
14. So that's what it means!	Grammar Focus on page 95	Rules Board Game
15. What would you do?	Word Power on page 102	Verb Word Search
16. What's your excuse?	Review of Book 2	Talk About It!

1 ASK THE RIGHT QUESTIONS

Aim: *Give Ss practice asking and answering questions.*
Preparation: *Make one copy of Photocopiable 1 for every two Ss. Cut the copies in half.*
Comment: *Use instead of the Speaking on page 4.*

- Choose six questions from the handout and answer them. Draw a word map on the board and include your answers. For example:

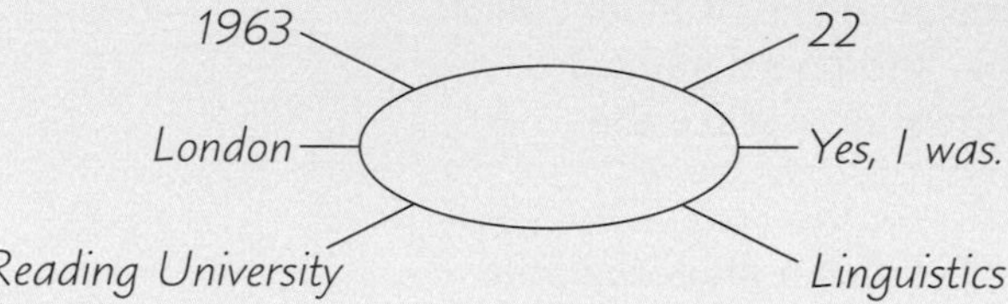

- Explain the task. Ss read the answers and guess the questions. Beginning with the year, elicit possible questions. Then continue with the other answers.
- Divide the class into two groups (A and B). Give Student A handouts to Group A and Student B handouts to Group B.
- Explain the task. Ss choose six questions to answer on their word maps. Then they fold their papers in half, so that only the word map is visible.
- Divide Ss into pairs with one S from Group A and one S from Group B. Pairs exchange word maps, read the answers, and guess the questions.
- Make sure that Ss do not write anything during the task.

Option: Ss change partners and repeat the task.

Acknowledgment: *Original idea from Ida Dolci, British Council.*

2 DICTIONARY SKILLS

Aim: *Give Ss practice using basic dictionary skills.*
Preparation: *Make one copy of Photocopiable 2 for every S.*
Comment: *Use after the Word Power on page 8.*

- Divide the class into small groups. Give one handout to each S.
- Explain the task. Ss match the sentences at the top of the handout with answers in the dictionary entries below.
- Ss complete the task. Elicit answers.

Option: Using the *Cambridge Dictionary of American English*, Ss check their answers to the Word Power on page 8.

Answers

1. a 2. d 3. e 4. f 5. b 6. g 7. c

3 HEAR THE DIFFERENCES

Aim: *Give Ss practice listening for differences.*
Preparation: *Make one copy of Photocopiable 3 for every two Ss. Cut the copies in half.*
Comment: *Use before the Perspectives on page 16.*

- Give each S a handout. Explain the task. Ss find the differences between the sentences they read and the sentences they hear. There is one difference in each sentence.
- Play the first sentence as an example. Ask: "What's the difference between the audio program and the written sentence?" Elicit answers.
- Play the audio program. Ss complete the task.
- Go over answers with the class.

Option: Before the activity, try ***Running Dictation*** on page T-153.

Answers

1. pets (not *dogs*)
2. big (not *bright*)
3. rooms (not *floors*)
4. expenses (not *problems*)
5. parking (not *closet*)
6. houses (not *apartments*)
7. as (not *so*)
8. aren't (not *are*)
9. closet (not *closed*)
10. privacy (not *private sea*)

4 PARTICIPLE CONCENTRATION

Aim: *Give Ss practice matching verbs and past participles.*
Preparation: *Make one copy of Photocopiable 4 for every four Ss. Cut the copies and put each set of cards in an envelope.*
Comment: *Use after the Grammar Focus on page 23.*

- Ss work in groups of four. Give each group an envelope. Tell Ss to shuffle the cards and arrange them face down on a desk.
- Explain the task. Ss take turns turning over two cards. If the words on the cards match (e.g., *eat* and *eaten*), the S keeps the cards and plays again. If not, the S replaces them and the next player takes a turn. The player with the most pairs at the end of the game wins.
- Encourage Ss to pronounce the words as they turn them over.
- As Ss play the game, go around the class and give help as needed.

Option: Ss take turns using the past participle cards to ask each other questions beginning with *Have you ever . . . ?*

5 ROLE CARDS

Aim: *Give Ss practice reaching a consensus.*
Preparation: *Make one copy of Photocopiable 5 for every four Ss. Cut the copies and divide the cards into five piles: A, B, C, D, and the maps.*
Comment: *Use with the Discussion on page 34.*

- Divide the class into four groups (A, B, C, and D). Give A cards to Group A, B cards to Group B, and so on.
- Explain the task. Each group plans a vacation. They discuss the questions in part A of Dream Vacation on page 34 and take notes.
- Ss complete the task and then form new groups, each with one student from group A, B, C, and D. Give each group a map. Tell Ss to discuss ideas until they all agree on a plan.
- Ss return to their original groups and compare plans.

Option: Ss write a letter to a friend about their vacation plans.

6 REQUESTS PICTURE GAME

Aim: *Give Ss practice making requests and giving excuses using pictures of two-part verbs.*
Preparation: *Make one copy of Photocopiable 6 for every four students. Cut the copies and put each set of cards in an envelope.*
Comment: *Use with the Word Power on page 38.*

Option: Brainstorm ways of making polite requests.

- Divide the class into groups of four Ss. Give each group an envelope. Tell Ss to shuffle the cards and put them in a pile face down on a desk.
- Explain the task. Ss take turns choosing a card and making an appropriate request. All Ss refuse the request by giving an excuse. Excuses may not be repeated. Then the group decides who gave the most creative excuse and gives that S the card. The player with the most cards wins.
- Model the task with one group.

  T: Could you hang up your towel, please?

  S1: I'm sorry. I'm not tall enough.

  S2: I'm sorry. I have to watch TV.

  S3: I'm sorry. I'm allergic to towels.

  T: OK, which excuse is the most creative?
- Ss complete the task. Go around the class and give help as needed.

7 INFORMATION GAP CROSSWORD

Aim: *Give Ss practice using* used to *and* used for.
Preparation: *Make one copy of Photocopiable 7 for every two Ss. Cut the copies in half.*
Comment: *Use after the Grammar Focus on page 45.*

- Divide the class into two groups (A and B). Give Part A of the handout to Group A and Part B of the handout to Group B.
- Explain that Group A has all the *across* words and Group B has all the *down* words.
- Explain the task. Ss write clues about the uses of the words on the left. For example, *A CD-ROM is used to store information/for storing information.*
- Ss complete the task. Go around the class and give help as needed.
- Divide Ss into pairs with one S from Group A and one S from Group B. Point out that they cannot look at each other's crossword puzzle.
- Ss take turns reading their clues aloud and guessing the words. Then they write the words to complete the puzzle. Model the task with a S:
  T: What's the clue for one across?
  S: It's used to store information.
- Ss complete the task and then look at their partner's puzzle to check their answers.

8 READING RACE

Aim: *Give Ss practice scanning a text for specific information.*
Preparation: *Make one copy of Photocopiable 8 for every two Ss. Cut the copies in half. Hang copies of the Reading on page 55 on a classroom wall.*
Comment: *Use with the Reading on page 55.*

- Give each S a handout. Ss read the questions.
- Explain the task. On the word "Go," Ss go around the classroom and scan the text to find the answers. Then Ss return to their places and write the answers on the handout. The S with the most correct answers wins.
- Model the task. Then Ss complete the task. Set a time limit of ten minutes.
- Ss read the text to check their answers.

Answers

1. the end of winter and the beginning of spring
2. a silk bracelet 3. with flowers and ribbons
4. the next morning 5. to their ancestors' graves
6. to be loyal to their wives 7. January 17 8. 30
9. fireworks explode 10. Korean Thanksgiving

9 TV DEBATE

Aim: *Give Ss practice defending a position in a debate.*
Preparation: *Make one copy of Photocopiable 9 for every eight Ss. Cut up each page into two sets of four cards. Put each set in an envelope.*
Comment: *Use after Part B of Interchange 9.*

- Write on the board: *If children watch a lot of violent programs on TV, they'll become violent.*
- Divide the class into groups of four. Give each group an envelope.
- Explain the task. Each S takes one card. Ss with FOR cards defend the statement. Ss with AGAINST cards argue against it. Encourage Ss on the same side to help each other. Remind Ss to use their own words.
- In small groups, Ss debate for as long as possible.

Option: When the groups finish, have a class debate. Ss give their personal opinions.

10 COVER LETTER GAP-FILL

Aim: *Give Ss practice writing a cover letter by filling in the gaps in an existing letter.*
Preparation: *Make one copy of Photocopiable 10 for every S.*
Comment: *Use after the Writing on page 68.*

- Ss work in pairs. Give one handout to each S. Tell Ss to cover the box at the bottom.
- Explain the task. Without writing anything, Ss discuss which words could go in the gaps.
- Now have Ss look at the box and use the words to fill in the gaps in the letter.
- Elicit the answers.

Answers

1. Attention	6. experience	11. appreciate
2. Personnel	7. In addition	12. interview
3. Dear	8. taken	13. application
4. advertisement	9. aspects	14. Yours
5. résumé	10. personality	15. Enclosed

Option: Ask Ss to write a cover letter for a job they would enjoy.

11 COUNTRY PROFILES QUIZ

Aim: *Give Ss practice asking and answering questions about countries.*
Preparation: *Make one copy of Photocopiable 11 for every four Ss. Cut the copies and put each set of cards in an envelope.*
Comment: *Use instead of the Speaking on page 76.*

- Divide the class into groups of four. Give each group an envelope.
- Explain the task. Each S takes one card. Ss take turns asking and answering questions about the countries on the cards.
- Tell Ss to listen carefully and try to remember the information without taking notes.
- Ss complete the task. Go around the class and give help as needed.
- Ss put the cards away. Ask these questions: "1. Which countries are located in Asia? 2. Which has the smallest population? 3. the largest? 4. Which are mainly Catholic? 5. Which uses the *real*? 6. Which export shoes? 7. Where is Spanish spoken? 8. Where is rice grown?" The first group to answer correctly gets a point.

Answers

1. Indonesia and Korea	5. Brazil
2. Dominican Republic	6. Brazil and Korea
3. Indonesia	7. Dominican Republic
4. Dominican Republic and Brazil	8. Indonesia and Korea

12 MIXED-UP STORIES

Aim: *Give Ss practice making predictions, listening, and sequencing events in a story.*
Preparation: *Make one copy of Photocopiable 12 for every four Ss. Cut the copies and put each set of slips in an envelope.*
Comment: *Use instead of the Listening on page 80.*

- Write the names *Yang Zhifa* and *Gwyneth Paltrow* on the board. Ask what Ss know about them. Tell Ss they are going to listen to how they got their lucky breaks.
- Divide the class into groups of four. Give each group an envelope.
- Explain the task. Ss read the slips and write the initials of the person each sentence describes.
- Ss complete the task. Then play the audio program. Ss listen and check their answers.

Answers

YZ: a, b, d, f, g, m, n   GP: c, e, h, i, j, k, l

- Have Ss put the events in chronological order.
- Play the audio program again. Ss listen and check their answers.

Answers

YZ: f, a, n, m, d, g, b   GP: e, h, i, j, k, l, c

13 SCRIPTWRITERS

Aim: *Give Ss practice building information about characters in a murder story.*
Preparation: *Make one copy of Photocopiable 13 for every S.*
Comment: *Use instead of the Speaking on page 90.*

- Divide the class into groups of four. Give one handout to each S.
- Explain the task. Ss create characters in a murder story. Ss write an answer to a question on the back of the handout, pass the handout to the S on their left, and take the handout from the S on their right. Then they read what is written and answer the next question until all the questions are answered.
- Ss begin by circling whether the character is male or female.
- Ss complete the task. Encourage them to be creative.
- When Ss finish, they choose a name for their character and write it in the circle. Then they invent a story involving all four characters. Write these questions on the board: *How do the characters know each other? Who is murdered? Why? When? Where? How? Who is the murderer? What happens in the end?*
- Ss complete the task and share their stories with the class.

Option: Ss write the story for homework.

14 RULES BOARD GAME

Aim: *Give Ss a review of new structures and vocabulary.*
Preparation: *Make one copy of Photocopiable 14 for every four Ss. Bring one die and four markers for every group.*
Comment: *Use after the Grammar Focus on page 95.*

- Ss work in groups of four. Give each group a handout, a die, and four markers.
- Model the game with one group. Ss put their markers on Start. S1 rolls the die and moves his or her marker the number of squares indicated on the die. Then S1 makes a sentence about the picture and says where you might see the sign.
- Point out that Ss can move the marker in any direction. Also, they must say the sentences, not write them. If the sentence is correct, the S writes his or her initials in that square. Then S2 takes a turn.
- Go around the class and give help as needed. The game ends when all the squares have initials. The S with the most initialed squares wins.

Acknowledgment: *Idea adapted from* The Grammar Activity Book *by Bob Obee, Cambridge University Press.*

15 VERB WORD SEARCH

Aim: *Give Ss a review of new verbs.*
Preparation: *Make one copy of Photocopiable 15 for every S.*
Comment: *Use after the Word Power on page 102.*

- Give each S a handout. Tell Ss that there are 18 verbs (9 pairs of opposites) in the word search. The verbs can go across, down, or diagonally. Point out the verb *accept* as an example. Then tell them that the opposite (*refuse*) is also in the word search.
- Explain the task. Ss find the verbs and circle them. Then they write them in the box below.
- Ss complete the task. The S that finds all the verbs first wins.
- Elicit the answers.

Answers

accept, admit, agree, borrow, deny, disagree, dislike, divorce, enjoy, find, forget, lend, lose, marry, refuse, remember, save, spend

16 TALK ABOUT IT!

Aim: *Give Ss practice discussing a variety of topics.*
Preparation: *Make one copy of Photocopiable 16 for every four Ss. Bring one die and four markers for every group.*
Comment: *Use after Unit 16.*

- Ss work in groups of four. Give each group a handout, a die, and four markers.
- Model the game with one group. Ss put their markers on Start. S1 rolls the die and moves his or her marker the number of squares indicated on the die. Then S1 talks about the subject of that square for about a minute. Other Ss ask questions. Then S2 takes a turn.
- Go around the class and give help as needed. Allow enough time for most Ss to complete the board.

Acknowledgment: *Idea adapted from* Keep Talking *by Friederike Klippel, Cambridge University Press.*

PHOTOCOPIABLE 1 *Ask the Right Questions*

Student A

Answer six questions.

Write your answers in the word map.

- ☐ When were you born?
- ☐ Where did you grow up?
- ☐ Were you a happy child?
- ☐ How old were you when you started elementary school?
- ☐ Did you study English as a child?
- ☐ Where did your parents grow up?
- ☐ Where did you go to high school?
- ☐ When did you graduate from high school?
- ☐ When was your mother born?

fold here

Student B

Answer six questions.

Write your answers in the word map.

- ☐ Where were you born?
- ☐ Were you an unhappy child?
- ☐ What was your major?
- ☐ When was your father born?
- ☐ When did you first study English?
- ☐ Did you have a pet?
- ☐ Where did you grow up?
- ☐ Where was your wife/husband born?
- ☐ How old were you when you finished high school?

fold here

PHOTOCOPIABLE 2 Dictionary Skills

Look at the top half of a dictionary page. Then write the correct letter next to each sentence.

1. This is the headword. It shows the spelling of the word. __a__
2. This shows the pronunciation of the word. ____
3. This gives information about the grammar of the word. ____
4. This word is related to the headword. ____
5. This shows a synonym of the headword. ____
6. This sentence gives a detailed definition of a word. ____
7. This sentence gives an example of how to use a word. ____

new NOT USED /nuː/ *adj* [*-er/-est* only] not previously used or owned • *They sell new and used cars/books/clothing.*

new RECENTLY DISCOVERED /nuː/ *adj* [*-er/-est* only] recently discovered or made known • *This new treatment offers hope to many sufferers.* ○ *Astronomers reported finding millions of new stars.* • If someone or something is **newfound**, they have recently happened or been discovered by you; *newfound friends* ○ *newfound respect*

newfangled /ˈnuːˈfæŋ ·gəld/ *adj* [not gradable] *esp. disapproving* recently created or invented • *I hate those newfangled alarm clocks that buzz.*

a ← **news** INFORMATION /nuːz/ *n* [U] recent information

b ← about people you know • *Why don't you call them and see if there's any news?*

c ← ○ *I've got some bad news for you.* ○ *We just heard the good news – congratulations on your engagement!* • *She's expecting a baby? That's* **news to** *me* (= I am very surprised). **newsy** /ˈnuː·zi/ *adj* full of news • *a long,*

d ← *newsy letter*

news REPORTS /nuːz/ *n* [U] a printed or

e ← broadcast report of information about important events in the world, the country, or the local area • *the nightly news* ○ *I'm pretty disgusted with TV news coverage.* ○ *Where were you when the news of the assassination broke?* • A **newscast** is a radio

f ← or television program consisting of news reports. A **newscaster** is someone who reads the reports on a television or radio news program. • A **news conference** is a meeting in which someone makes a statement to reporters or answers questions from them. • A **newsletter** is a printed document with information about the activities of a group, sent regularly to members or friends. • A **newspaper** is a regularly printed document consisting of news reports, articles, photographs, and advertisements that are printed on large sheets of paper folded together but not permanently joined. • A **newsstand** is a small structure where → g

newspapers and magazines are sold. If something is **newsworthy**, it is considered important enough to be in news reports.

newt /nuːt/ *n* [C] a small animal with a long body and tail, short, weak legs, and cold, wet skin; a type of SALAMANDER

next /nekst/ *pronoun, adj* [not gradable] being the first one after the present one or after the one just mentioned, or being the first after the present moment • *Go straight at the traffic light and then take the next right.* ○ *The next time you want to borrow my dress, ask me first.* ○ *She was next in line after me.* ○ *They're getting married next week/month/year.* ○ *The next day/morning we left for Calgary. If I can't have cake, ice cream is* **the next best thing** (= almost as good). • If you live **next door** to someone, no one else's home is between your home and their home: *next-door neighbors* • Something that is **next door** to something else is in the space directly to one side of it: *I can hear everything the guy in the cubicle next door says.* • Someone's **next of kin** are their closest relatives, who will be informed if they die.

Source: *Cambridge Dictionary of American English*

PHOTOCOPIABLE 3 Hear the Differences

1. Apartments are too small for dogs.
2. Apartments aren't bright enough for families.
3. Apartments don't have as many floors as houses.
4. Apartments have just as many problems as houses.
5. Apartments don't have enough closet spaces.
6. Apartments cost too much money.
7. Houses aren't so safe as apartments.
8. Houses are as convenient as apartments.
9. Houses don't have enough closed space.
10. Houses don't have as much private sea as apartments.

1. Apartments are too small for dogs.
2. Apartments aren't bright enough for families.
3. Apartments don't have as many floors as houses.
4. Apartments have just as many problems as houses.
5. Apartments don't have enough closet spaces.
6. Apartments cost too much money.
7. Houses aren't so safe as apartments.
8. Houses are as convenient as apartments.
9. Houses don't have enough closed space.
10. Houses don't have as much private sea as apartments.

PHOTOCOPIABLE 4 Participle Concentration

eat	be	speak	heard	lost
have	drink	find	made	seen
hear	lose	eaten	been	spoken
make	see	had	drunk	found

A

You have two weeks' vacation in December. You love the sea and would like to visit a Caribbean island. You know about some very cheap trips to Margarita and the Dominican Republic where hotel accommodations are included. You want to spend every day by the sea, relax, enjoy the sun, and swim. You don't want to spend much money. You prefer to take a tour and stay in cheap hotels. You hate camping and hiking.

B

You have three weeks' vacation in December. You love adventure vacations. Your dream is to visit Costa Rica, because there are many things to do there. For example, you can go to the beach, go scuba diving, go rafting, go mountain climbing, go to the rainforest, or go hiking and backpacking in the national parks. You are not worried about money. You just want to have a good time and a great adventure!

C

You have ten days' vacation left this year. You can take your vacation whenever you want. Every year you go to Mexico for your vacation. You love it because there are many things to see and do. You know the country very well and you want to go again. You usually rent a car. You spend a few days at the beach, a few days in the mountains, and a few days visiting historical places, such as the Mayan ruins. You like a vacation that has variety and freedom.

D

You want to spend the month of December traveling through Central America and the Caribbean. However, you don't want to spend much money. You would like to travel as cheaply as possible (for example, by camping rather than staying in hotels, and by hiking rather than using expensive transportation). You love sunshine, so you want to spend at least one week by the sea, maybe camping on the beach. You also love ancient cultures and want to see the ruins in Guatemala.

MAP OF AREA

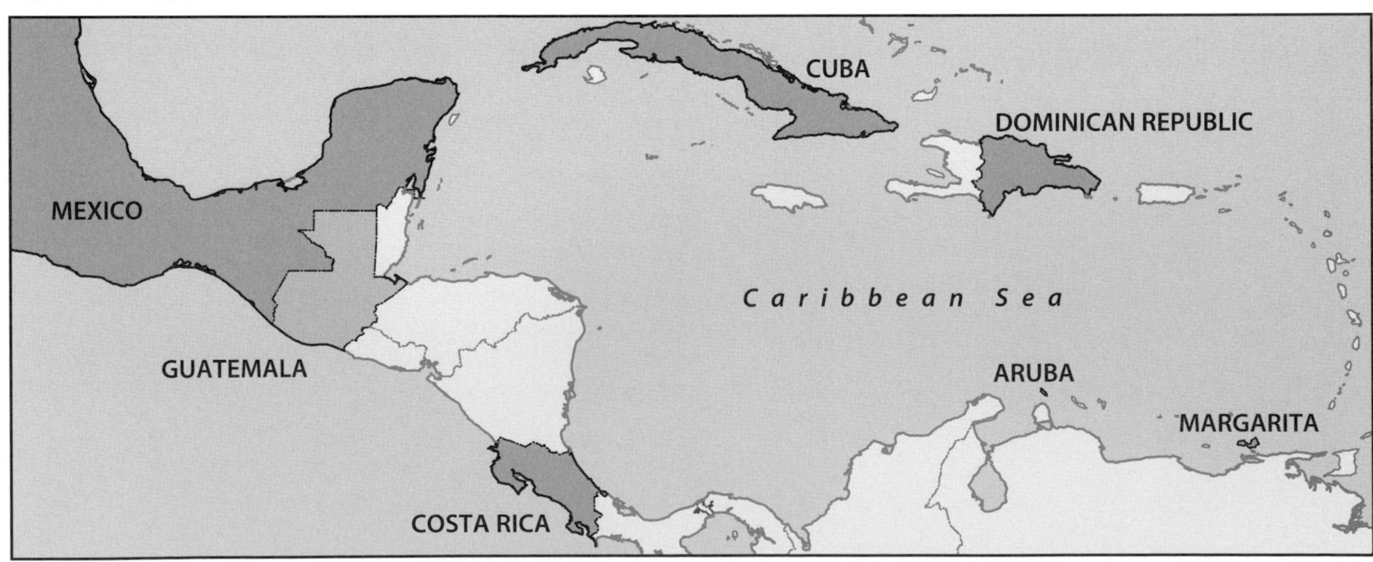

PHOTOCOPIABLE 6 Requests Picture Game

Part A
Across
1. A CD-ROM
4. A cell phone
7. Dictionaries
9. Robots
11. Cameras
13. A scanner
14. A computer

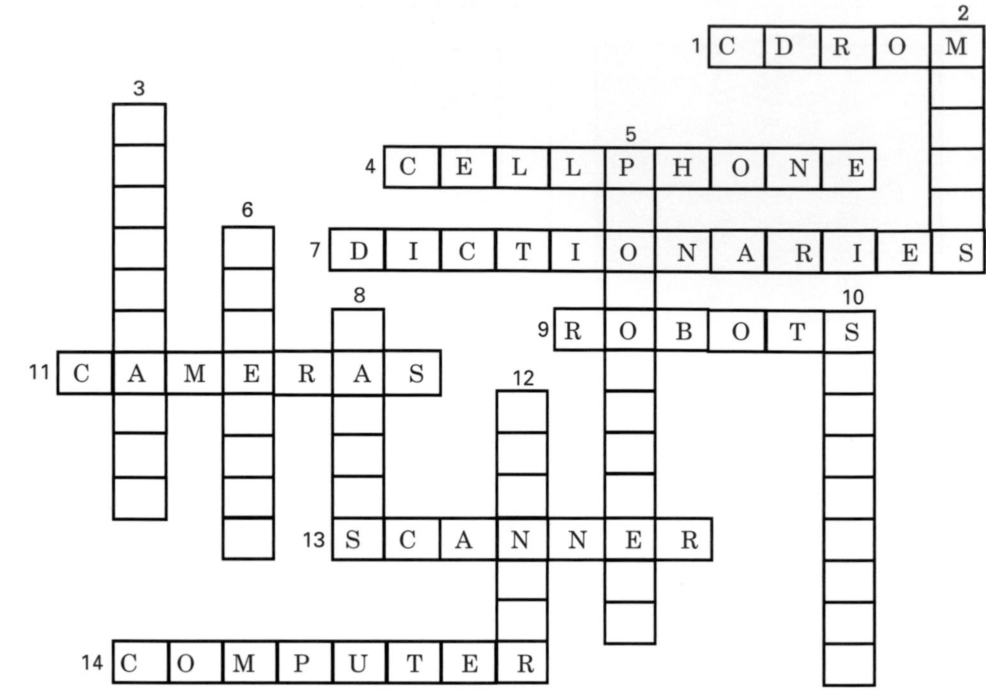

Part B
Down
2. Modems
3. A calculator
5. Photocopiers
6. The Internet
8. Pagers
10. A satellite
12. A printer

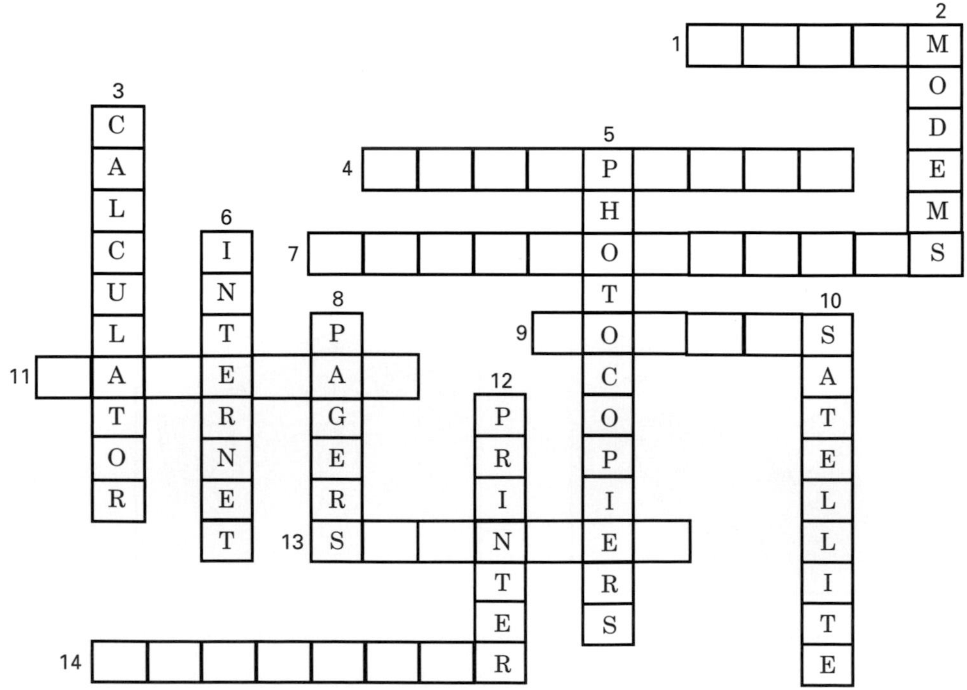

PHOTOCOPIABLE 8 Reading Race

1. What do people celebrate on Setsubun?
2. What did the Indian princess send to the emperor?
3. How do people decorate their animals before taking them to church?
4. When do New Year's Eve parties finish in Argentina?
5. Where do Koreans go on Chusok?
6. What do Indian men promise during the festival of Rakhi?
7. When is St. Anthony's Day?
8. If you are 30 years old, how many beans should you eat on Setsubun?
9. What happens at midnight on New Year's Eve in Argentina?
10. What is another name for Chusok?

---

1. What do people celebrate on Setsubun?
2. What did the Indian princess send to the emperor?
3. How do people decorate their animals before taking them to church?
4. When do New Year's Eve parties finish in Argentina?
5. Where do Koreans go on Chusok?
6. What do Indian men promise during the festival of Rakhi?
7. When is St. Anthony's Day?
8. If you are 30 years old, how many beans should you eat on Setsubun?
9. What happens at midnight on New Year's Eve in Argentina?
10. What is another name for Chusok?

PHOTOCOPIABLE 9 TV Debate

FOR

How can we blame television? Many years ago, we didn't have television, but there were many violent people. Computer games and movies will make children more violent than TV.

FOR

It depends on the parents. If parents talk to their children after they watch a violent program, there won't be a problem. Of course, parents can also make their children stop watching violent programs.

AGAINST

We have proof. In the U.S., there is a lot of violent television. As a result, many children take guns to school and attack students and teachers.

AGAINST

Television puts bad ideas into children's heads. Children and adults get ideas for terrible crimes because they watch violent programs.

FOR

How can we blame television? Many years ago, we didn't have television, but there were many violent people. Computer games and movies will make children more violent than TV.

FOR

It depends on the parents. If parents talk to their children after they watch a violent program, there won't be a problem. Of course, parents can also make their children stop watching violent programs.

AGAINST

We have proof. In the U.S., there is a lot of violent television. As a result, many children take guns to school and attack students and teachers.

AGAINST

Television puts bad ideas into children's heads. Children and adults get ideas for terrible crimes because they watch violent programs.

PHOTOCOPIABLE 10 Cover Letter Gap-Fill

(1) ____________: Mr. Yoshioka, (2) ____________ Director, Executive Air Lines

(3) ____________ Mr. Yoshioka,

I am responding to your recent (4) ____________ in *The Post* for a bilingual international flight attendant.

I think I'd make a good flight attendant for Executive Air Lines because I'm a very friendly person and I really love traveling. I also enjoy meeting people. As you can see from my (5) ____________ , I've had a lot of (6) ____________ working with tourists. I worked at the National Gallery last summer as a museum guide and interpreter for Japanese visitors. (7) ____________ , I'm very good with languages. I'm fluent in English and Japanese and have also (8) ____________ some French and German courses.

Because I have several friends who are flight attendants, I understand the positive and negative (9) ____________ of the job. I have seen how rewarding and challenging the work is. Moreover, I think my (10) ____________ is well-suited for a career in service: I am an efficient, hardworking, patient, and reliable person.

I'd (11) ____________ the opportunity to schedule an (12) ____________ with you. I will be in Tokyo in August, and I truly hope that a meeting will be possible at that time.

Thank you for considering my (13) ____________ .

(14) ____________ truly,

Stan Nakamura

(15) ____________ : CV

Yours	application	advertisement	appreciate	résumé
aspects	interview	Personnel	personality	experience
Enclosed	In addition	taken	Dear	Attention

A
DOMINICAN REPUBLIC
Location: the Caribbean
Population: 9 million
Language: Spanish
Currency: peso
Religion(s): Roman Catholic
Exports: sugar, coffee, gold, silver
Products/Industries: gold, silver, sugar, coffee
Interesting fact: The capital city, Santo Domingo, is the oldest city in the Americas.

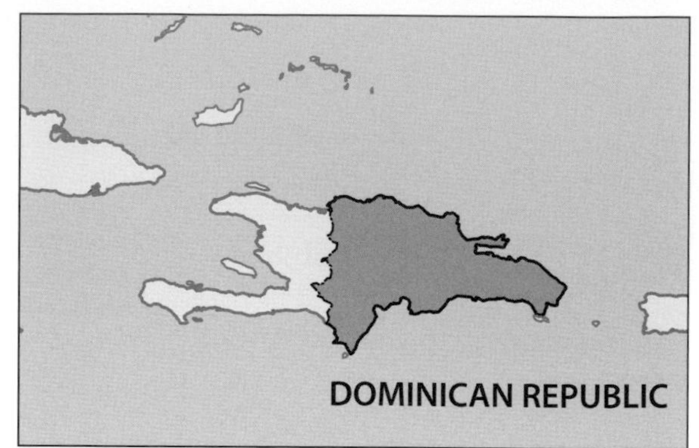

B
INDONESIA
Location: Southeastern Asia
Population: 238 million
Language: Bahasa Indonesia
Currency: rupiah
Religion(s): Muslim (88%), Christian (8%)
Exports: petroleum, gas, coffee
Products/Industries: rice, fish, coffee
Interesting fact: The country is composed of over 17,000 islands.

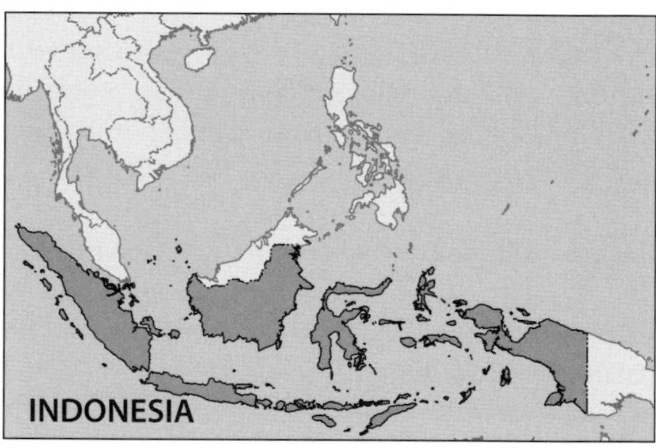

C
BRAZIL
Location: South America
Population: 184 million
Language: Portuguese
Currency: real
Religion(s): Roman Catholic
Exports: transport equipment, coffee, footwear
Products/Industries: petroleum, iron ore, timber
Interesting fact: Eighty-seven indigenous groups have become extinct since 1900.

D
KOREA
Location: Eastern Asia
Population: 48 million
Language: Korean
Currency: won
Religion(s): Buddhist (26%), Christian (26%)
Exports: electrical machinery, textiles, footwear
Products/Industries: rice, fish, chemicals
Interesting fact: Over 60% of Koreans are named Kim, Lee, or Park.

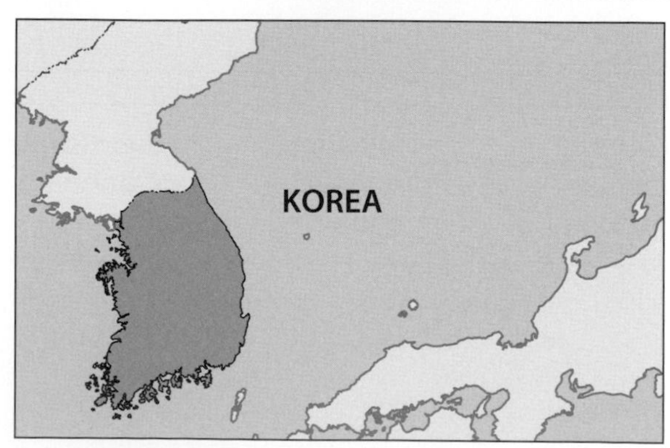

PHOTOCOPIABLE 12 Mixed-Up Stories

_____ (a) was very poor.

_____ (b) poses for pictures and signs autographs.

_____ (c) accepted the offer right away.

_____ (d) found pieces of pottery and ancient weapons.

_____ (e) had to go to drama school and learn how to act.

_____ (f) was an ordinary farmer.

_____ (g) now spends a lot of time in the museum.

_____ (h) had a lucky break at the age of 18.

_____ (i) was at a movie theater when the lucky break happened.

_____ (j) was waiting in line to buy popcorn.

_____ (k) noticed that Steven Spielberg was also in line.

_____ (l) was offered a role in the movie *Hook*.

_____ (m) hit something hard when drilling a well.

_____ (n) was looking for water one morning.

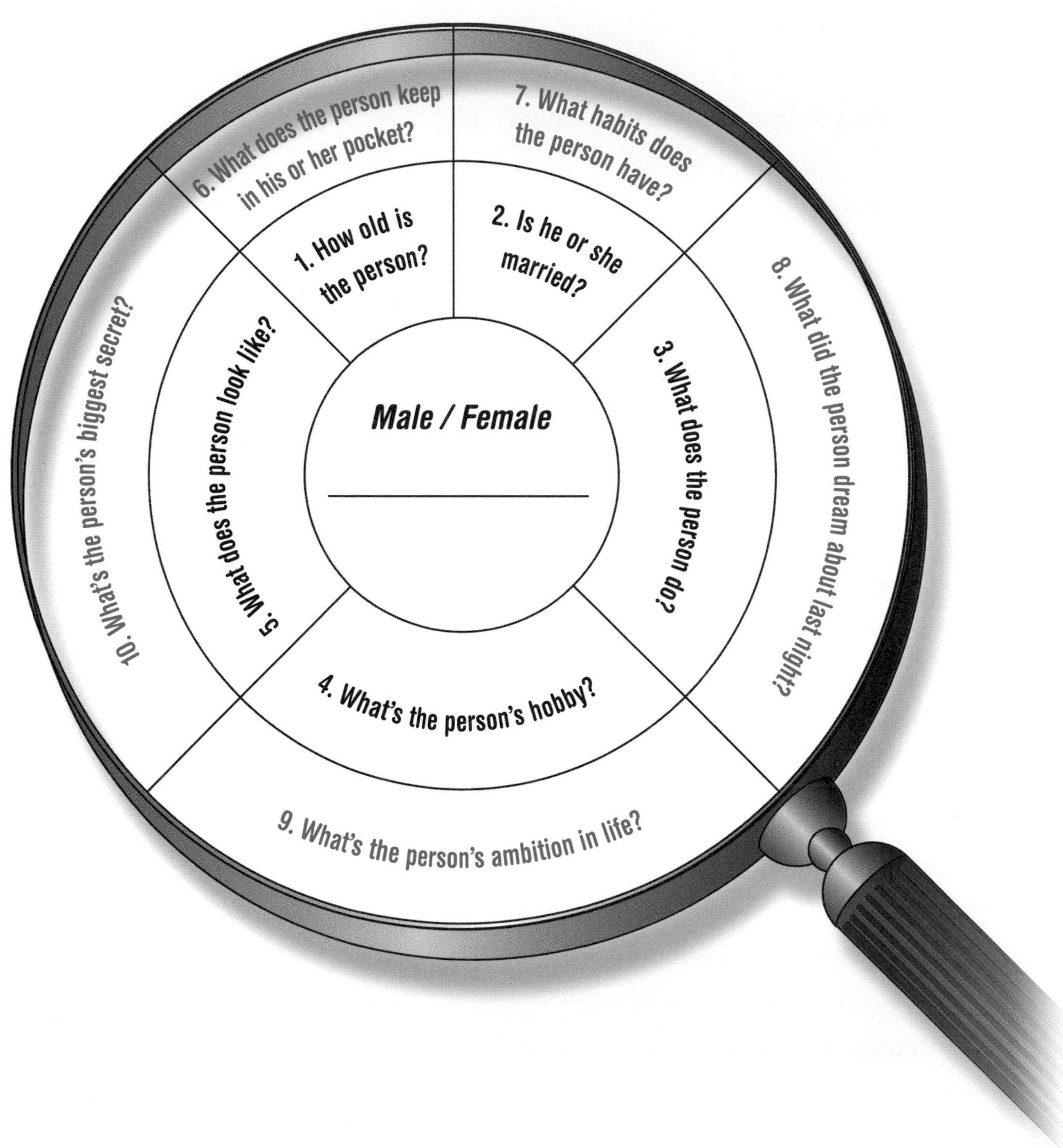
Male / Female
1. How old is the person?
2. Is he or she married?
3. What does the person do?
4. What's the person's hobby?
5. What does the person look like?
6. What does the person keep in his or her pocket?
7. What habits does the person have?
8. What did the person dream about last night?
9. What's the person's ambition in life?
10. What's the person's biggest secret?

Go again!
Lose a turn.
START!
Go back to your last square.
Move two squares in any direction.

PHOTOCOPIABLE 15 Verb Word Search

C	O	R	A	C	C	E	P	T	L	T	I	W	D	M
L	E	N	D	H	Z	U	X	O	P	Y	B	Y	I	C
O	P	J	M	X	A	O	R	U	H	G	N	N	S	J
S	W	K	I	U	A	B	F	F	V	N	A	T	L	X
E	F	L	T	E	G	D	I	N	O	X	O	F	I	S
K	T	I	U	Q	R	V	N	D	E	R	L	Y	K	P
J	O	P	M	E	E	H	D	I	S	A	G	R	E	E
R	E	F	U	S	E	B	X	V	W	G	L	E	U	N
E	C	Z	E	R	F	O	Q	O	X	G	R	S	T	D
M	O	I	M	R	B	O	R	R	O	W	D	S	T	W
E	A	B	M	U	X	E	P	C	L	E	N	Y	O	K
M	A	R	T	O	S	A	V	E	V	I	N	W	U	J
B	E	G	R	I	C	N	U	E	S	H	A	J	N	O
E	X	A	R	Y	O	E	E	M	N	A	L	P	O	B
R	E	N	R	U	M	E	M	T	O	I	D	E	N	Y

accept ≠ ______ ______ ≠ ______ ______ ≠ ______

______ ≠ ______ ______ ≠ ______ ______ ≠ ______

______ ≠ ______ ______ ≠ ______ ______ ≠ ______

PHOTOCOPIABLE 16 Talk About It!

- START
- some games you used to play
- 2 wedding customs in your country
- 4 advantages of living in an apartment
- Lose A Turn
- something you won or found
- 5 qualities of a good teacher
- your plans for next weekend
- 5 chores you hate doing
- your hobbies and interests
- how to prepare your favorite snack
- 3 interesting facts about your country
- 3 traffic problems in your city or town
- Move Forward 2 spaces
- 5 problems neighbors have
- 3 famous landmarks
- a birthday party you went to
- 5 common excuses people make
- how you celebrate the New Year
- 3 things you wish you could change
- Move Back 3 spaces
- your idea of a dream job
- 5 different uses for a computer
- 2 movies you like
- a vacation you remember
- Go Again!
- an actor or actress you like
- 5 gestures used in your country
- fashion today
- something lucky that happened to you
- 4 rules in your school or office
- your house or apartment
- 4 things you would pack for a vacation abroad
- 2 successful people
- Move Back 3 spaces
- an unusual museum
- Go Again!
- the city or town where you live
- your 2 favorite dishes
- 3 ways your city has changed
- Lose A Turn
- 3 things grown or produced in your country
- 4 common wishes people have
- your first school
- your idea of a dream vacation
- Move Forward 2 spaces
- your favorite celebration
- something you'd do if you won the lottery
- a favorite childhood memory
- START AGAIN

Unit 1 Language summary

Vocabulary

Nouns
background
bicycle
(summer) camp
childhood
comic book
competition
degree
diploma
hero
immigrant
interest
memory
movie star
occupation
personal ad
politics
possession
rabbit
scrapbook
snake
taste
toy
tree house
trumpet

Adjectives
good (at)
messy
neat
online
outdoor
professional
two-story

Verbs
be into (something)
collect
follow
get (in trouble)
get (to know)
keep fit
refer
remember
skate

Adverb
regularly

Expressions

Greeting someone
Hi./Hello.

Introducing yourself
My name is . . . ./I'm . . . .
Nice to meet you.
Good to meet you, too.

Exchanging personal information
Could you tell me (a little) about yourself?
Sure. What do you want to know?
Are you from . . . ?
Yes, I am./No, I'm not.
Where were you born?
I was born in . . . .
Did you grow up there?
Did you go to school in . . . ?
Yes, I did./No, I didn't.

Talking about past activities
Where did you learn to . . . ?
How old were you when you began to . . . ?
I was . . . years old.
What/Where did you use to . . . ?
When I was a kid, I used to . . . .

Talking about past abilities
How well did you . . . ?
I was pretty good.

Apologizing
I'm (really) sorry.

Asking for and agreeing to a favor
Can you . . . ?
Sure.

Unit 2 Language summary

Vocabulary

Nouns
area
banquet
certificate
counter
culture
district
editor
highway
(tourist) information center
marvel
motorist
nature
paradise
pedestrian
rating
road
shopping mall
sign
slogan
theme

Compound nouns
bicycle lane
bicycle stand
bus lane
bus station
bus stop
bus system
cash machine
newsstand
nightclub
parking garage
parking space
rush hour
streetlight
subway line
subway station
subway stop
subway system
taxi lane
taxi service
taxi stand
tourism campaign
traffic jam
train station
train stop
train system

Pronoun
whom

Adjective
duty-free

Verbs
allow
cause
concern
cost
provide
sightsee
solve
stay (open)

Adverbs
upstairs

Adverbs of quantity
fewer
less
more
not enough
too many
too much

Expressions

Expressing concern
There are too many . . . ./There is too much . . . .
There should be fewer . . . ./There should be less . . . .
We need more . . . .
There aren't enough . . . ./There isn't enough . . . .

Getting someone's attention
Excuse me.

Asking for information
Could you tell me where . . . ?
Can you tell me how often . . . ?
Do you know what time/when . . . ?
Just one more thing.

Thanking someone
Thanks (a lot).

Expressing probability
It should . . . .

Unit 3 Language summary

Vocabulary

Nouns
(room and) board
expense
housework
list
PIN number
safari
vegetable
wish

Adjectives
afraid
bright
comfortable
cramped
dingy
huge
inconvenient
modern
private
separate
shabby
two-car
wild

Verbs
add
expect
locate
make (changes)

Preposition
per

Expressions

Giving an opinion
The . . . isn't . . . enough.
The . . . is too . . . .
There aren't enough . . . ./There isn't enough . . . .
It's not as . . . as . . . .
It doesn't have as many . . . as . . . ./It has just as many . . . as . . . .

Exchanging personal information
Where are you living now?
I'm still . . . .

Expressing regret about a present situation
I'm afraid so.
I wish (that) I could . . . .
I wish I didn't . . . .
I wish life were easier.

Agreeing
Me, too.

Unit 4 Language summary

Vocabulary

Nouns

Food and beverages

bagel
eggplant
guacamole (dip)
lime
peanut butter
(chili) pepper
popcorn
pork
salt
sauce
snail
spice
sugar
vinegar

Other

appetizer
barbecue
bowl
charcoal
cookbook
diet
exam
ingredient
mixture
pan
plate
(food) poisoning
recipe
side
skewer
slice
tablespoon
video game

Adjectives

barbecued
crispy
diced
ethnic
marinated
melted
raw
shredded
strange
tempting
toasted
uncooked

Verbs

Cooking methods

bake
barbecue
boil
fry
roast
steam
toast

Other

close
cover
cry
cut up
marinate
mash
melt
mix
refrigerate
spread
turn over

Adverbs

from time to time
lightly
overnight

Expressions

Talking about food and beverages

Have you ever eaten . . . ?
  Yes, I have./No, I haven't.
It's/They're . . . !
This/It sounds . . . ./They sound . . . .

Ordering in a restaurant

Have you decided yet?
  Yes. I'll have . . . .
And you?
  I think I'll have . . . .

Making and declining an offer

Why don't you try some?
  No, thanks./No, I don't think so.

Describing a procedure

First, ...
Then, ...
Next, ...
After that, ...
Finally, ...

Stating a preference

I usually like to . . . .
I prefer to . . . .

Unit 5 Language summary

Vocabulary

Nouns
Activities
antique shopping
camping
eating out
fishing
reading
sledding

Other
accommodation
ATM card
camper
condition
copy
credit card
document
equipment
fare
fireplace
first-aid kit
(art) gallery
guidebook
hiking boots
identification
inn
Jacuzzi
lift
medication
national park
nightlife
option
overnight bag
plane ticket
resort
route
safety
sleigh
specialty
stall
suitcase
surfboard
tap
tour
vaccination
visa
windbreaker
wonderland

Adjectives
candlelit
(a) couple (of)
cross-country
exact
excited
horse-drawn
luxurious
necessary
required
round-trip

Verbs
Modals
had better
must
ought to
should

Other
avoid
bring back
carry
check out
discover
feature
fix up
include
mention

Adverbs
by myself
in advance

Conjunction
whether

Expressions

Talking about definite plans
Have you made any plans?
  I'm going to . . . .

Talking about possible plans
I guess I'll . . . .
Maybe I'll . . . .
I think I'll . . . .
I'll probably . . . .

Asking about length of time
For how long?
How long are you going to . . . ?
How many days will you . . . ?

Describing necessity
You must/You need to/You (don't) have to . . . .

Giving suggestions
You'd better/You ought to/You should/You shouldn't . . . .

Making and accepting an offer
Why don't you . . . ?
  Do you mean it? I'd love to!

Unit 6 Language summary

Vocabulary

Nouns
association
effort
enjoyment
flower
groceries
guest
guideline
hallway
household chore
laptop
mess
program
seat
security
sound
stereo
stranger
survey
tenant
toothbrush
towel
trash

Adjectives
following
pleasant

Verbs
Two-part verbs
clean up
go through
hang up
keep clean
let out
pick up
put away
take off
take out
throw out
turn down
turn off
turn on

Other
admit
apologize
bother
clear
contact
criticize
feel (free)
lend
lock
make sure
mind
nag
promise
realize

Adverbs
as soon as
badly
loudly
quietly

Expressions

Making and agreeing/objecting to a request
Please . . . .
  OK. No problem!
  Oh, but . . . .
Can/Could you . . . ?
  Sure, no problem.
  I'd be glad to.
Would you please . . . ?
  OK. I'll . . . .
Would you mind . . . ?
  Sorry. I'll . . . right away.

Giving an excuse
I'm sorry. I didn't realize . . . .

Admitting a mistake
I'm sorry. I forgot.
You're right. I was wrong.

Making an offer
I'll . . . right away.

Making a promise
I promise I'll . . . ./I'll make sure to . . . .

Expressing annoyance
Goodness!

Expressing surprise
Are you kidding?

Unit 7 Language summary

Vocabulary

Nouns

Machines/Appliances

answering machine
battery
calculator
camcorder
CD-ROM
robot
satellite
Walkman

Other

area code
assignment
bill
boss
burglar
button
caller
criminal
disk drive
dropout
engineer
evader
(DNA) fingerprinting
geek
hacker
hardware
impression
instruction
invention
keyboard
letter
monitor
mouse
percentage
recording
robotics
screen
task
technology
technophile
term
transmission
voice mail
watercraft
Web site
whiz
World Wide Web

Adjective

empty

Verbs

affect
browse
check
cut and paste
dial
double-click (on)
download
drag and drop
entertain
escape
feed
highlight
house-sit
influence
perform
press
protect
receive
recharge
ring
scan
set
store
transmit
understand

Expressions

Describing a use or purpose

What's this for?
  It's used for . . . ./It's used to . . . .
  I can use it for . . . ./I can use it to . . . .
What are these for?
  They're used for . . . ./They're used to . . . .
  You can use them for . . . ./You can use them to . . . .

Giving advice

First of all, be sure to . . . .
And don't forget to . . . .
Make sure to . . . .
Remember to . . . .
Try not to . . . .

Unit 8 Language summary

Vocabulary

Nouns

Holidays, festivals, and celebrations

April Fools' Day
Carnaval
Children's Day
Chinese New Year
Day of the Dead
Labor Day
Mother's Day
New Year's Day
New Year's Eve
Thanksgiving
Valentine's Day

Other

boyfriend
bride
cemetery
ceremony
courtship
cranberry sauce
custom
dancing
diamond ring
firecracker
fireworks
fruit punch
get-together
groom
harvest
home movie
honeymoon
luck
marriage
reception
resolution
samba
shrine
speech
streamers
trick
turkey

Adjectives

national
romantic
surprise

Verbs

be like
court
date
get (engaged/married/ together)
honor
last
look forward
occur
picnic

Adverbs

at least
in honor (of)

Expressions

Describing holidays, festivals, and celebrations

. . . is a day/a night when . . . .
. . . is the day when . . . .
. . . is the month when . . . .
. . . is the season when . . . .
A . . . is a time when . . . .
Before . . . , ...
After . . . , ...
When . . . , ...

Asking about customs

How old are people when they . . . ?
Is there . . . ?
Where is the . . . usually held?
What happens during the . . . ?
What do . . . wear?
What kind of food is served?

Unit 9 Language summary

Vocabulary

Nouns
accident
advantage
automobile
catalog
charity
cinema
(common) cold
communication
consequence
construction site
cure
disadvantage
environment
fine
first class
housing
jet airplane
leader
ocean liner
postal system
railroad
reality game
space flights
tax

Adjectives
audio
bored
commercial
flying
high-paying
multiplex
3-D
unexpected
violent
virtual

Verbs
Modals
may
might
Other
consider
donate
inherit
litter
star
tear down

Adverbs
instead
nowadays
soon

Expressions

Talking about the past
In the past, ...
People used to . . . .
. . . years ago, people . . . .

Talking about the present
These days, ...
Today, people . . . .
Nowadays, people . . . .

Talking about the future
Soon, there will be . . . .
In . . . years, people might/may . . . .
In the future, people are going to . . . .

Describing situations and possible consequences
If I . . . , I won't have to . . . .
If you don't . . . , you'll have to . . . .
If they . . . , they might . . . .
If you . . . , you may have to . . . .

Unit 10 Language summary

Vocabulary

Nouns

Jobs/Occupations

accountant
architect
artist
bookkeeper
(entertainment) director
journalist
marine biologist
model
novelist
reporter
songwriter
stockbroker

Other

activity
article
attitude
calendar
co-worker
cruise ship
decision
diaper
employer
excursion
experience
marketing
personnel
pressure
product
requirement
résumé
stock market

Adjectives

assistant
bad-tempered
bilingual
creative
critical
disorganized
door-to-door
forgetful
generous
hardworking
impatient
level-headed
moody
patient
punctual
recent
reliable
strict
unfriendly

Verbs

break (into)
commute
do for a living
hire
interview
iron
maintain
make (a decision/ a mistake)
manage
organize
schedule

Prepositions

to and from
toward

Expressions

Talking about possible occupations

I'd make a good/bad . . . because I'm . . . and I like/don't like . . . .
I wouldn't want to be a/an . . . because I'm too . . . .
I could (never) be a/an . . . because I'm good/not good at . . . .
I wouldn't mind working as a/an . . . because I really like . . . .

Expressing feelings and opinions

I like/hate/enjoy . . . .
I'm interested in . . . .
I'm not good at . . . .
I don't mind . . . .
I can't stand . . . .

Agreeing with feeling and opinions

So do I.
So am I.
Neither am I.
Neither do I.
Neither can I.

Disagreeing with feeling and opinions

Oh, I don't./Really? I . . . .
Gee, I'm not.
I am!
Well, I do.
Oh, I don't mind.

Unit 11 Language summary

Vocabulary

Nouns
battle
cattle
corn
crop
currency
electronics industry
hair salon
landmark
lobster
microchip
novel
opera
oyster
plain
playwright
president
radium
revolution
sheep
structure
textile industry
travel agent
variety

Adjectives
agricultural
digital
high-definition
lowland
official
royal
snow-capped
wide

Verbs
catch
compose
construct
consume
cultivate
direct
employ
export
farm
fill
film
make up
manufacture
produce
raise
record

Adverb
officially

Expressions

Describing works of art, inventions, and discoveries
. . . was built/composed/created/designed/directed/ painted/recorded/written by . . . .
. . . was developed/discovered/invented/produced by . . . .

Asking about a country
Where is . . . located?
What languages are spoken in . . . ?
What currency is used in . . . ?
Is English spoken (much) there?
Are credit cards accepted (everywhere)?

Responding to difficult questions
I'm not sure. Isn't it . . . ?
I think . . . , but I'm not sure.
I really have no idea.
How would I know?

Expressing confusion
Huh?
What?
Where?

Unit 12 Language summary

Vocabulary

Nouns
accomplishment
author
billionaire
ending
mining company
mud
role
software
tutor

Adjectives
asleep
calm
face down
face up
leading
modeling (career)
normal
tiny
unlucky

Verbs
be on one's way
be out (of)
break
get/have a chance
kayak
model
pursue
slip
snowboard
toss

Adverbs
coincidentally
fortunately
generally
luckily
miraculously
sadly
strangely
suddenly
surprisingly
unexpectedly
unfortunately

Expressions

Talking about past events
I was . . . , but I never . . . .
I was . . . when I . . . .
While I was . . . , ...

Exchanging personal information
Have you been doing anything exciting recently?
  Yes, I have./No, I haven't.
What have you been doing lately/these days?
  I've been . . . .
How long have you been doing that?
  For . . . .
How have you been?
  Great! What about you?

Greeting someone after a long time
I haven't seen you in ages.
Has it been . . . since I last saw you?

Expressing interest and surprise
That's definitely lucky!
Wow! Tell me more.
Oh, really? That's interesting.
Really? I didn't know that!
Oh, I see.
Gee, I had no idea.

Asking for a reason
How come?

Unit 13 Language summary

Vocabulary

Nouns

Movie types

action
adventure
animated
classic
comedy
documentary
drama
fantasy
horror
musical
mystery
romance
science fiction
thriller
war

Other

acting
alien
bill
category
character
critic
director
iceberg
mania
mayor
photography
script
smile
society
special effect
story
studio
title
village

Adjectives

absurd
bizarre
disgusting
dreadful
dumb
fair
fascinating
hilarious
horrible
main
marvelous
odd
outstanding
poor
ridiculous
silly
stupid
talented
weird
wonderful

Verbs

amaze
amuse
annoy
be based (on)
bore
chase
confuse
disgust
embarrass
excite
fascinate
get left (behind)
interest
laugh
put down
rate
remind
scare
shock
sink
surprise
take place

Adverbs

by mistake
in a row

Expressions

Giving opinions about movies, books, and people

I'm interested in . . . .
I thought . . . was an exciting book.
I'm fascinated by . . . .
I think . . . is a wonderful actress.
I find . . . fascinating.

Describing movies, books, and people

It's the movie which/that . . . .
It was a great book which/that . . . .
It's about a man/woman who/that . . . .
He's/She's . . . who/that . . . .

Unit 14 Language summary

Vocabulary

Nouns
bike rack
fight
gesture
gum
hard hat
lane
leash
nail
obligation
parking ticket
peace
permission
prohibition
regulation
rule
seat belt
situation
speed limit
warning
wastepaper basket

Adjectives
annoyed
confused
disgusted
embarrassed
frustrated
irritated
nervous
reserved

Verbs
Modals
can
could
have (got) to

Other
bite
camp
chew
exist
fasten
flash
go away
land
notice
recycle
repeat
roll
scratch
steal
tap
throw
turn out
twirl
wrinkle

Adverbs
absolutely
perhaps
possibly

Preposition
from (side to side)

Expressions

Hypothesizing
It might/may mean . . . .
It could mean . . . .
Maybe/Perhaps it means . . . .

Making a logical assumption
That must mean . . . .
That probably means . . . .

Disagreeing
I don't think so.

Expressing permission
You can . . . .
You're allowed to . . . .

Expressing prohibition
You can't . . . .
You aren't allowed to . . . .

Expressing obligation
You have to . . . .
You've got to . . . .

Unit 15 Language summary

Vocabulary

Nouns
advice column
businessman
campsite
comb
counselor
cushion
flat tire
garage sale
honesty
jail
owner
predicament
radio talk show
repair shop
reward
shopping problem
truth
value

Adjectives
ashamed
brief
original
tough

Verbs
afford
break down
cheat
confess
deny
dislike
divorce
exchange
hide
ignore
reply
shoplift
spank
spill
throw away
trust
warn
yell

Adverbs
immediately
personally
simply
straight

Expressions

Describing imaginary situations and consequences in the present
What would you do if . . . ?
If I . . . , I'd/I could/I might/I wouldn't . . . .

Saying someone is right
Hmm. You've got a point there.

Expressing disbelief
You're kidding!

Giving opinions or suggestions about actions in the past
What should I have done?
You should have . . . .
You shouldn't have . . . .
What would you have done?
I would have . . . .
I wouldn't have . . . .

Unit 16 Language summary

Vocabulary

Nouns
anger
apology
coach
compliment
criticism
houseguest
intention
lie
regret
ride
sympathy

Adjective
due

Verbs
express
fly (in)
get (out)
have (the flu)
make (a date/plans)
reorganize
sail
weigh

Adverb
out of (town)

Expressions

Reporting requests
. . . asked/told me to . . . .
. . . said to . . . .
. . . asked/told me not to . . . .
. . . said not to . . . .

Reporting statements
. . . said (that) . . . .
. . . told me (that) . . . .

Exchanging personal information
How are things?
  Just fine, thanks.

Talking on the phone
Hi, ... This is . . . .
  Oh, hi.

Expressing regret
That's too bad.
I'm really sorry.
  I'm sorry, too.

Oral quizzes

The questions found in the Question bank (pages T-194 to T-197) may be used to assess students' mastery of the material presented in *Interchange Third Edition*, Level 2. Each set of questions covers material from one unit.

When to give a quiz

- Oral quizzes may be given before or after Ss take the written quiz.
- Ask Ss the appropriate questions after the class has completed two units of material.
- Alternatively, questions may be asked after Ss have completed three or more units.

Before giving a quiz

- Photocopy the oral quiz scoring sheet – one for each S in the class.
- Depending on the number of Ss to be quizzed and the amount of time needed to assess each one, schedule about 20–30 minutes of a class period for the quiz.
- Become familiar with the aspects of speaking that the quiz measures (i.e., comprehension, fluency, grammar, vocabulary, and pronunciation).
- Tell the Ss that they are going to have an oral quiz. Explain that the goal is to answer questions and talk about the topics in the unit.
- Review vocabulary from the unit and prepare a list of words to include in the oral quiz. For specified questions, hold up or point at objects to indicate what Ss will describe or discuss.

How to give a quiz

- Point out that the purpose of the quiz is not for Ss to compete for the highest score; rather, the quiz will inform Ss (and the teacher) about how well they learned the material and what material, if any, may need extra review and practice.
- Tell Ss that they are not allowed to use their Student's Books or dictionaries during the quiz.
- When asking yes/no questions, it is often best to choose information that will elicit a negative answer. This will allow a follow-up question, or lead the S to provide the correct information.
- When selecting from among the questions provided, don't feel it's necessary to ask them all. You may also include questions and follow-up prompts of your own.
- It's often useful to vary the sequence of the questions you ask so that other Ss don't know exactly what to expect.
- The most effective (but time-consuming) way to use this quiz is to ask questions to one S at a time. When necessary, ask follow-up questions to encourage fuller answers. Try to help Ss feel like equal partners in the interaction, rather than feeling as if they are being interviewed or quizzed.
- Encourage Ss to ask questions to you or to other classmates. For specified questions, name or gesture toward a S or group of Ss. For example, tell the S: "Now ask me . . . " or "Now ask David . . . ."

Alternative presentation

- Choose questions to ask a group of two or three Ss. Be prepared to score Ss simultaneously, using a separate oral quiz scoring sheet for each S.

How to score a quiz

- Assign each S a number from 0 to 5 for each of the five areas. Reserve 0 for Ss who fail to take the quiz. Using this system, a maximum score of 25 points is possible by adding scores in each area.
- As Ss are assessed based on what is taught in a particular unit, they could get the maximum score on the oral quiz. This suggests that a S has mastered the content, structures, and vocabulary specific to that unit. Although some aspects of language (e.g., pronunciation) are not unit-specific, the scores should be based on the kind of speech and communication modeled in the unit.
- If a letter grade system is useful to the teacher and the Ss, this scoring system can be used:

  23–25 = A or Excellent
  20–22 = B or Very Good
  17–19 = C or Good
  16 or below = Needs improvement
- To keep quiz results in one place, use the form on page T-199 to record Ss' scores.
- If the results of the oral quiz are used with the results of the written quiz, add the scores together and divide by two.
- In addition to a numeric score, it's very important to provide Ss with written comments, including positive feedback. Praise Ss on their strengths and suggest areas for improvement.

Oral quiz scoring sheet

Name: ______________________

Date: ______________________

Score: ______________________

		Poor	Fair	Good	Very good	Excellent
Comprehension	0	1	2	3	4	5
Fluency	0	1	2	3	4	5
Grammar	0	1	2	3	4	5
Vocabulary	0	1	2	3	4	5
Pronunciation	0	1	2	3	4	5
General comments						
Suggestions for improvement						

Comprehension = ability to understand questions and respond appropriately
Fluency = ability to speak quickly, naturally, and without many pauses
Grammar = ability to use correct grammar and sentence structures
Vocabulary = ability to understand and use vocabulary words and phrases
Pronunciation = ability to use correct stress, rhythm, and intonation patterns

Question bank

Unit 1 A time to remember

Where were you born? Were you born in [city/country]?

Where did you grow up? When did you move to [city/country]?

Did you take English classes in [city/country]? When did you first study English? What other languages can you speak?

Where did you go to elementary/high school? Were you a good student? What were your best/worst subjects?

Did you enjoy your childhood? Did you use to collect things? What sports or games did you use to play? Did you use to have a nickname? Where did you use to spend your vacations?

What's your favorite childhood memory?

Ask me to tell you about myself. *or* Ask [classmate] to tell you about him/herself.

Unit 2 Caught in the rush

What's your city or town like? What transportation services are available?

What kinds of transportation problems are there? (*Elicit count/noncount nouns and adverbs of quantity.*)

Could you tell me where the nearest hotel/restaurant/drugstore/hospital is?

Do you know where the restrooms/elevators/stairs are?

Can you tell me where the nearest cash machine is?

Do you know what time the banks/stores usually open/close?

Do you know where I can get a good meal/haircut/city map around here?

What would you tell a visitor about your city or town?

Ask me about my hometown. *or* Ask [classmate] about his/her hometown or the city or town where you live.

Unit 3 Time for a change!

Do you live in a house or an apartment? What's it like?

Is your house or apartment [adjective] enough for you? Is it too [adjective]? Does it have enough [noun]? Does it have as many/much [noun] as your old house or apartment?

What's your neighborhood like? Is it [adjective]? Is it as [adjective] as this neighborhood?

What do you wish you could change about your home/school or job/appearance/skills? Why?

Ask me what I would like to change about my life. *or* Ask [classmate] what he/she would like to change about his/her life.

Unit 4 I've never heard of that!

Have you ever been to a [type of restaurant]? (*Elicit* Yes.) What was it like?

Have you ever eaten [dish]? (*Elicit* Yes.) Did you enjoy it/them?

Have you ever tried ethnic food? What did you think of it?

Have you ever eaten something you didn't like? What was it?

Have you ever been on a diet? What did you eat? What did you stop eating? Did you lose any weight?

What's your favorite way to cook or eat [food]?

How do you cook [dish]?

How do you make [snack]?

Unit 5 Going places

What do you like to do on vacation? Where do you like to go?

What did you do on your last vacation?

Have you made any vacation plans for this year? (*Elicit* Yes.) What are you going to do?

Where are you going to go? When are you leaving? How long will you be away? Are you going to go with anyone?

What do you need to do before traveling abroad? (*Elicit modals for describing necessity.*)

What are some things you should have before taking a trip? (*Elicit modals for giving suggestions.*)

Ask [classmate] about his/her last/next vacation.

Give me advice about my next vacation. *or* Give [classmate] advice about his/her next vacation.

Unit 6 OK. No problem!

(***Note:*** *Bring a portable radio / stereo and other objects to class.*)

Turn down the radio/stereo. (*Indicate object and elicit* OK. I'll turn it down.)

Pick up the books/papers. (*Indicate object and elicit* All right. I'll pick them up.)

Turn the lights on/off. (*Indicate object and elicit* OK. I'll turn them on/off.)

Please put your jacket/dictionary/cell phone away. (*Indicate object and elicit* All right. I'll put it away.)

What requests can you make in the kitchen/bathroom/living room/bedroom?

What requests can you make of your neighbor?

How can you respond to a request/complaint from a neighbor?

Ask me to do something for you. *or* Ask [classmate] to do something for you.

Unit 7 What's this for?

What technology/inventions do you use every day?

What do/would you use a computer to do? Do/Would you use it for [activity]?

What is/are [technology] used for doing? How is/are [technology] used?

How do computers make your life easier/more difficult?

How do computers affect the way people work and spend free time?

What kinds of problems does technology cause?

Give me specific instructions on how to use [technology]. Is there anything I need to remember to do or *not* to do?

Unit 8 Let's celebrate!

What is your favorite holiday/festival? What do you like about it? How do people celebrate it? Is there any special food or drink?

What is your favorite season? What do you like about it? What do people do at that time of year?

What do you usually do on your birthday? How did you spend your last birthday?

Tell me about weddings in your country. What do couples do before their wedding? What do guests do during/after the ceremony? When do people give gifts? What kinds of gifts do they give?

Tell me about an unusual custom in your country. What do people do before/after the event?

Ask me to describe an interesting custom from another country. *or* Ask [classmate] to describe an interesting custom from another country.

Unit 9 Back to the future

How was life different 50/100 years ago? How did people use to shop/travel?

What did people do before supermarkets/the automobile/the Internet?

What did you do before personal computers/CD players/cell phones?

Nowadays, how do most people get around? Where do people usually shop?

These days, what do people do in the evening/on weekends?

Do you think there will be more cars/shopping malls/pollution in the future?

In ten years, what things might people be able to do with a personal computer?

In the future, what are people/cities going to need more of?

What will happen if you have more free time/inherit a lot of money? (*Elicit possible situation and consequence.*)

Tell me what will happen if I get a pet. *or* Tell [classmate] what will happen if he/she moves to a foreign country. (*Elicit possible situation and consequence.*)

Unit 10 I don't like working on weekends!

I like/love/enjoy traveling/studying. What about you? (*Elicit affirmative or negative response.*)

I hate cooking/cleaning. What about you?

I'm good at using a computer/learning languages. What about you?

I don't mind working on weekends/doing the laundry. What about you?

I'm not good at solving problems/saving money. What about you?

I can't stand making mistakes/being late. What about you?

What are your positive personality traits? What are your negative personality traits?

Would you make a good teacher/accountant/waiter/stockbroker/doctor? Why or why not?

Would you like to be a novelist/flight attendant/salesperson/lawyer/nurse? Why or why not?

Ask me what kind of work I would like to do. *or* Ask [classmate] what kind of work he/she would like to do.

Unit 11 It's really worth seeing!

Tell me about [building/landmark]. Who designed it? When was it built? How was/is it used?

Tell me about another famous building or landmark. Who designed it? When was it built? How was/is it used?

What's your favorite book/movie/painting/song? Who is it by?

What products are manufactured in [country]? Is/Are [product] made there/here?

What crops are grown in [country]? Is/Are [crop] grown there/here?

Name three countries where [language] is spoken.

Tell me about a country you know well.

Ask me to describe a country. *or* Ask [classmate] to descibe a country.

Unit 12 It could happen to you!

What were you doing the last time your phone rang?

Did you ever fall asleep when you were doing something? What were you doing?

Have you ever been caught in a rainstorm? What were you doing? What happened?

What have you been doing lately/in the evening/on weekends? How long have you been [activity]?

Have you been working/studying/exercising? How long have you been [activity]?

Unit 13 Good book, terrible movie!

What is the last movie you've seen? What did you like/dislike about it?

What new movie would you most like to see? Why?

Did you ever see [movie]? How did you like it? Why?

What kinds of movies are you interested in?

What is your favorite [language] movie? Why do you like it?

What's your favorite movie/musical/book? Tell me about it. (*Elicit relative clauses.*)

Who is your favorite actor/actress/director/author? Tell me about him/her. (*Elicit relative clauses.*)

Ask me about my taste in books and movies. *or* Ask [classmate] about his/her taste in books and movies.

Unit 14 So that's what it means!

(***Note:*** *Bring pictures of people using gestures or expressions and pictures of signs.*)

What does this gesture mean? *or* What do you think this gesture means? (*Make gesture or indicate picture.*)

Show me a gesture that means I don't understand/I'm hungry/Come here.

Show me a gesture that means you're bored/exhausted/nervous.

What does this sign mean? *or* What do you think this sign means? (*Indicate picture.*)

What does [rule] mean? Where might you find this rule?

What rules might you find on an airplane/at school/in a museum/at work?

Show me a gesture and ask what it means. *or* Show [classmate] a gesture and ask what it means.

Unit 15 What would you do?

What would you do if you found a wallet full of money in a taxi?

What would you do if you forgot your mother's or father's birthday?

What would you do if a friend borrowed money and never paid you back?

Which sport would you choose if your doctor told you to get more exercise?

Where would you go on vacation if you had enough time and money?

I'm going to tell you about some situations and then ask you questions.

- I borrowed a friend's computer, and it crashed while I was using it. I returned it without saying anything. What should I have done? What would you have done?
- I noticed I was missing some money. I think I know who stole it, but I didn't say anything. What should I have done? What would you have done?

Tell me about a recent predicament you were in. What did you do? What should/shouldn't you have done?

Ask me about a recent predicament. *or* Ask [classmate] about a recent predicament.

Unit 16 What's your excuse?

What are some common excuses for being late/not accepting an invitation?

What request might a doctor/neighbor/parent/teacher make?

What has someone asked you to do/*not* to do recently? How did you respond?

Invite [classmate] to do something with you. (*Elicit invitation.*) What did [classmate] say?

Ask [classmate] to do something for you. (*Elicit request.*) What did [classmate] say?

Ask [classmate] about his/her future intentions. (*Elicit question.*) What did [classmate] say he/she was going to do?

Written quizzes

The following eight quizzes may be used to assess students' mastery of the material presented in *Interchange Third Edition*, Level 2. Each quiz covers two units. These quizzes will inform the teacher about what material needs to be reviewed and give Ss a sense of accomplishment.

When to give a quiz

- Give the appropriate quiz after the class has completed two units and the accompanying Progress check.
- Alternatively, quizzes may be given before Ss complete the Progress check. This may help Ss know what material to review.

Before giving a quiz

- Photocopy the quiz – one for each S in the class.
- Schedule about 20–30 minutes of a class period for the quiz.
- Locate and set the recorded part A for the quiz listening section on the Class Audio Cassette or Audio CD.
- Tell Ss that they are going to have a "pencil and paper" quiz. Suggest that they prepare by reviewing the appropriate units and unit summaries. Ss should pay particular attention to the Conversations, Grammar Focus points, and Word Power exercises. Tell Ss that the quiz will also contain a short listening section and a short reading passage.

How to give a quiz

- Point out that the purpose of the quiz is not for Ss to compete for the highest score; rather, the quiz will inform Ss (and the teacher) about how well they learned the material and what material, if any, may need extra review and practice.
- On the day of the quiz, hand out one photocopy of the quiz to each S.
- Encourage Ss to take about five minutes to look through the quiz, without answering any of the items. Make sure Ss understand the instructions.
- Tell Ss that they are not allowed to use their Student's Books or dictionaries during the quiz.
- Tell Ss that about five minutes of the quiz time will be used for the listening section (part A). This is the first section of the quiz; however, it is up to the teacher to decide whether to give the listening section at the beginning or end of the time.
- To help Ss use their time efficiently and to finish on time, write the total time for the quiz on the board before beginning the quiz:
  Total time: 30 minutes
- After the quiz begins, revise the time shown on the board every five minutes or so to tell the class how much time is left.
- When giving the listening section of the quiz, direct the class to part A and go over the instructions. Advise Ss just to listen the first time they hear the audio recording, and then to listen and mark their answers during the second playing. Then play the audio recording straight through twice, without stopping or pausing.

Alternative presentation

- If the teacher does not wish to use the class time for the quiz, tell Ss to complete the whole quiz at home except for part A, the listening section. Advise the Ss to complete the quiz at home in 30 minutes and not to use their Student's Books or dictionaries. During the preceding or following class, take five minutes to play the audio recording and complete part A.

How to score a quiz

- Either collect the quiz and use the Quiz answer key to score it, or go over the answers with the class while allowing each S to correct his or her own quiz. Alternatively, tell the Ss to exchange quizzes with a partner and correct each other's answers as the teacher elicits or reads the answers aloud.
- Each quiz has a total score of 25 points (25 correct answers are possible at 1 point each). If a letter grade system is useful to the teacher and the Ss, this scoring system can be used:
  23–25 = A or Excellent
  20–22 = B or Very Good
  17–19 = C or Good
  16 or below = Needs improvement
- To keep quiz results in one place, use the form on page T-199 to record Ss' scores.
- If the results of the written quiz are being used with the results of the oral quiz, add the scores together and divide by two.

Class quiz scoring sheet

Students' Names	*Units 1-2*	*Units 3-4*	*Units 5-6*	*Units 7-8*	*Units 9-10*	*Units 11-12*	*Units 13-14*	*Units 15-16*	*Total*
1.									
2.									
3.									
4.									
5.									
6.									
7.									
8.									
9.									
10.									
11.									
12.									
13.									
14.									
15.									
16.									
17.									
18.									
19.									
20.									
21.									
22.									
23.									
24.									
25.									
26.									
27.									
28.									
29.									
30.									

Units 1–2 quiz

Name: ______________________

Date: ______________________

Score: ______________________

A Listen to the conversations. Check (✓) the correct answers.

1. Tom grew up in

☐ Japan. ☐ San Diego. ☐ San Francisco.

2. Carol used to

☐ collect old photos. ☐ read comic books. ☐ watch mysteries.

3. According to Helen, there

☐ isn't enough parking downtown.

☐ is too much traffic.

☐ aren't enough buses.

4. Anna can join a car pool by

☐ asking a neighbor for a ride.

☐ calling a phone number.

☐ riding to work with Steve.

B Complete the conversations. Use the past tense.

1. A: Where ______________________ ?

   B: I was born in Mexico City.

2. A: Did ______________________ in high school?

   B: No, he didn't study French in high school. He studied Spanish.

3. A: When ______________________ from college?

   B: They graduated from college in 2002.

C Circle the correct word or phrase.

1. Every summer, Sam used to go to the (**beach** / **paint** / **soccer ball**) with his friends.
2. I really enjoyed playing (**scrapbook** / **chess** / **bicycle**) when I was a teenager.
3. Ed had some unusual pets, including a rabbit and a (**comic book** / **snake** / **tree house**).

D Complete the conversation. Use the correct form of *used to* and the verbs given.

A: ______________________ (play) soccer when you were a child?

B: Yes, I ______________________ soccer every day after school.

A: And what things ______________________ (collect)?

B: Oh, I never ______________________ anything, but now I collect postcards.

E Put the words in the correct order to make sentences.

1. (lanes should more we bicycle have)

____ .

2. (pollution is and much there traffic too air)

____ .

3. (fewer should noise there less be cars and)

____ .

F Write indirect questions. Use these Wh-questions and the words given.

Example: When do the department stores open? (Do)

Do you know when the department stores open?

1. Where is the nearest restaurant? (Do)

____ ?

2. How much do newspapers cost? (Could)

____ ?

3. Where is the best bookstore in town? (Do)

____ ?

4. What time do the banks close? (Can)

____ ?

G Read the article. Then check (✓) the correct answers.

Dean Kamen is an inventor. He and his team developed the Segway™ Human Transporter (HT) – a battery-powered, two-wheeled electric transportation device. With a price of $3,995, it costs less than a car, is easier to ride than a motorcycle, and uses less space than a bicycle. And it's easy to operate: stand on the platform, lean forward to move ahead, lean back to stop or move backward, and twist the left handle to turn. To go faster, lean forward a little more. Some people compare it to ice skating because it moves so quietly and turns so smoothly.

The Segway HT weighs 32 kilograms (70 pounds) and can fit in the trunk of most cars. Fully charging the battery packs for four to six hours allows you to ride as many as 16 kilometers (10 miles).

Although it can only hold one passenger (or 100–200 pounds), the Segway HT is a great way to get around or do errands. In most cities, it can go wherever people walk, jog, or ride bikes.

The Segway is an environmentally friendly and energy-efficient machine of the twenty-first century. Wouldn't it be fun to have one?

1. Dean Kamen
   - ☐ invented the Segway HT.
   - ☐ wants to own a Segway HT.
   - ☐ doesn't think the Segway HT is energy efficient.
2. The Segway HT
   - ☐ is harder than riding a motorcycle.
   - ☐ is cheaper than buying a car.
   - ☐ has four wheels and runs on electricity.
3. This new transportation device
   - ☐ recharges in four to six hours.
   - ☐ weighs 100–200 pounds.
   - ☐ goes 16 miles per hour.
4. The Segway HT
   - ☐ can go wherever people drive cars.
   - ☐ can be used only on ice.
   - ☐ could replace a bicycle.

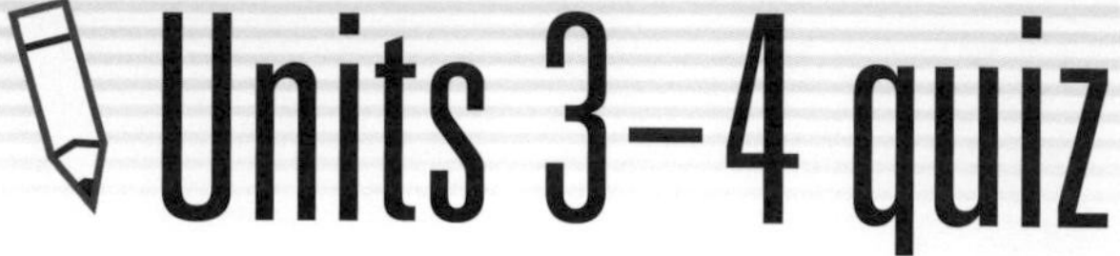

Units 3–4 quiz

Name: ______________________

Date: ______________________

Score: ______________________

A Listen to the conversations. Check (✓) the correct answers.

1. Jen likes her new apartment because
   - ☐ it has two bedrooms.
   - ☐ there's too much noise.
   - ☐ it's cheaper than her old apartment.
2. Seth wants to live downtown because
   - ☐ it's less expensive.
   - ☐ he works there.
   - ☐ there are more parking spaces.
3. Karen's apartment is
   - ☐ too small.
   - ☐ too spacious.
   - ☐ too private.
4. Doug wishes his new apartment were
   - ☐ nice and bright.
   - ☐ on the first floor.
   - ☐ not as cramped as his old apartment.

B Circle the correct word.

1. I love my neighborhood. It's very (**dangerous** / **inconvenient** / **safe**).
2. I live on a very busy street. It can get a little bit (**modern** / **noisy** / **spacious**).
3. It's (**comfortable** / **convenient** / **dingy**) to have parking spaces near my apartment.
4. Our house is modern and very bright. It has (**cramped** / **huge** / **private**) windows.

C Complete the sentences. Use *not enough* . . . or *not* . . . *enough* and the words given.

1. Our apartment is too small. There are ______________________ . (rooms)
2. People can see into our house. There is ______________________ . (privacy)
3. My apartment is very noisy. It's ______________________ for me. (quiet)

D Complete the sentences. Use *as* . . . *as*, *as many* . . . *as*, or *as much* . . . *as* and the words given.

1. My new apartment doesn't have ______________________ my old one. (windows)
2. Our house is just ______________________ your apartment. (convenient)
3. Modern apartments often don't have ______________________ older ones. (space)

E Complete the sentences. Use *wish* and the correct form of the underlined verbs.

Example: My parents <u>won't buy</u> me a car. I wish *they would buy me a car.*

1. I <u>don't like</u> my job. I wish ______________________ .
2. I <u>can't find</u> my cell phone. I wish ______________________ .
3. My boyfriend <u>isn't</u> in good shape. I wish ______________________ .

F Complete the conversation. Use the correct form of the verbs.

A: ________ you ever ________ (try) Spanish food?

B: Yes, I ________. I ________ (go) to a Spanish restaurant last week.

A: ________ you ________ (like) it?

B: Yeah, it ________ (be) delicious.

G Read Rosa's e-mail. Then check (✓) four true statements.

Hi Paula,

Greetings from Bangkok! Fernando and I are having a really good time! It's a great city for shopping. Yesterday, we went to a huge weekend market. It was full of really interesting things to buy, especially clothes. And the prices are great! Things here are not nearly as expensive as they are at home. Of course, Fernando tells me I'm spending too much money, but you know him. He never buys anything!

Have you ever eaten Thai food? It's delicious! We just had a wonderful dinner in one of the restaurants on the river. Fernando ordered green curry and rice, and I had my favorite dish, Mee Krob – crispy noodles with shrimp and chicken. For dessert, we had fried bananas. Everything was so good! It was also fun to watch the boats pass by!

One thing I've noticed is that some restaurants make their curries less spicy for foreigners. Yesterday, I told our waiter, "This curry isn't hot enough for us!" He smiled and said, "Some foreigners don't like spicy food." Then he brought us another curry that was much hotter.

Time to stop. We're flying home tomorrow, so I'll see you soon!

Rosa

☐ 1. Bangkok is a good place for shopping.

☐ 2. The market is open every day of the week.

☐ 3. You can buy most things except clothes in the market.

☐ 4. The prices in the market are very reasonable.

☐ 5. Some restaurants in Bangkok are right on the river.

☐ 6. Mee Krob is the Thai name for green curry.

☐ 7. All foreign visitors love Thailand's hot and spicy food.

☐ 8. Foreigners sometimes have to ask to have spicy food.

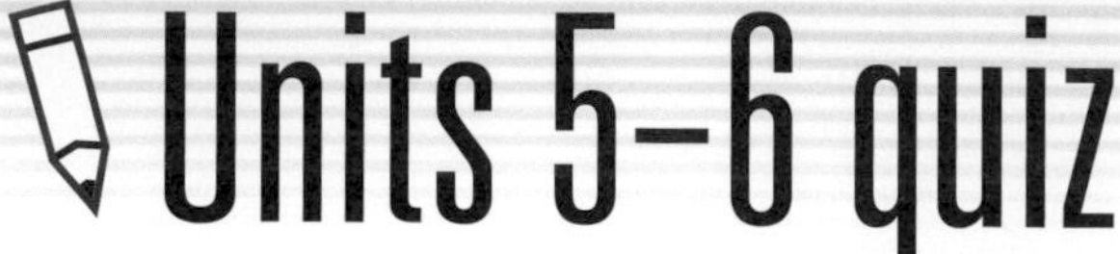

Units 5–6 quiz

Name: ____________________

Date: ____________________

Score: ____________________

A Listen to the conversations. Check (✓) the correct information.

1. ☐ Holly is going to visit Mike's grandparents.
   ☐ Mike is not going to go mountain climbing this year.
   ☐ Holly might go camping in August.
2. ☐ Holly is going mountain climbing this summer.
   ☐ Mike thinks Holly should go to Yosemite.
   ☐ Mike says Holly doesn't have to make reservations.
3. ☐ Kathy and Annette were roommates last year.
   ☐ Annette doesn't like being messy.
   ☐ Annette and Kathy are both very neat.
4. ☐ Annette can study while watching TV.
   ☐ Kathy likes to listen to music while studying.
   ☐ Annette's mother was always yelling at her.

B Complete the conversations. Use *be going to* or *will* and the verbs given.

1. A: What ________ you ______________ after class today? (do)
   B: I'm definitely ______________ a movie with a friend. (see)
2. A: When ________ they ______________ their vacation this year? (take)
   B: I think they ______________ on a cruise in June or July. (go)

C Circle the correct word or phrase.

1. You must take your (**first-aid kit** / **backpack** / **passport**) when you go to another country.
2. He needs to get new (**hiking boots** / **credit cards** / **suitcases**) before he goes backpacking next week.
3. We shouldn't forget to bring (**medication** / **luggage** / **cash**) for buying souvenirs.

D Complete the conversation. Use the correct modals for necessity and suggestion.

A: We ______________ make our plane reservations right away! It will be hard to find cheap flights later this month. (should / don't have to)

B: Good idea! And perhaps we ______________ buy round-trip tickets because they're usually cheaper. (have to / ought to)

A: And remember, you're going to drive the rental car, so you ______________ bring your driver's license. (need to / 'd better)

B: Of course. And you ______________ forget to pack your new digital camera. It will be fun learning how to use it. (must not / shouldn't)

E Circle the correct word.

1. Please clean (**off** / **up** / **on**) your bedroom. It's really a mess!
2. Could you please put (**over** / **off** / **away**) the groceries in the kitchen?
3. Can you turn (**down** / **out** / **on**) the TV while I'm on the phone?

F Rewrite the sentences. Use the correct form of the words given.

Example: Please take the cat out. (Can you)

Can you please take the cat out?

1. Close the door, please. (Could you)

____ ?

2. Please take out the garbage. (Would you)

____ ?

3. Don't sit there. (Would you mind)

____ ?

G Read the letter to Sally and her response. Then check (✓) the correct answers.

Dear Sally,

We live in a neighborhood where everyone knows each other and we all get along pretty well. However, a new family recently moved in, and now we have some problems.

The family's two teenagers play their music really loudly. When we politely asked, "Would you mind turning the music down?" they just looked at us.

Next, the family destroyed a beautiful tree. I hated to see them cutting it down. I ran out and shouted, "Could you please leave the tree alone?" but they chopped it down anyway.

They also have dogs that bark loudly all day. We've said many times: "Please keep your dogs inside at night so we can get some sleep." But they won't do it.

We don't know what to do anymore. How can we all get along?

Slowly losing our minds

Dear Slowly,

You have made polite requests with no results. The next time you hear loud music or barking dogs, call your local police. That should solve those problems. Unfortunately, there's nothing you can do about the tree. Try to stay polite and let the police take care of your neighbors.

Sally

1. How did the teens respond to the neighbor's request?
   - ☐ They said, "We're sorry. We'll try to be more quiet."
   - ☐ They said, "Are you kidding? We like loud music."
   - ☐ They didn't say anything.
2. What happened as the tree was being chopped down?
   - ☐ The new family asked to leave it alone.
   - ☐ The new family continued to cut it down.
   - ☐ The wood was used to build a doghouse.
3. What is the problem with the dogs?
   - ☐ They are kept inside all day.
   - ☐ They are outside barking all the time.
   - ☐ They aren't allowed to go outside.
4. What was Sally's advice?
   - ☐ Call the neighbors when the dogs bark.
   - ☐ Stop being polite to the neighbors.
   - ☐ Let the police solve the problems.

Units 7–8 quiz

Name: ______________________

Date: ______________________

Score: ______________________

A Listen to the conversations. Check (✓) the correct answers.

1. Stephanie says Richard is
   - ☐ a geek.
   - ☐ a hacker.
   - ☐ a mouse.
2. Barry asks Martha how to
   - ☐ play computer games.
   - ☐ scan photographs.
   - ☐ surf the Internet.
3. According to Eva,
   - ☐ she uses her computer to play games.
   - ☐ her roommates use her computer a lot.
   - ☐ her computer isn't working properly.
4. Heather shows Carlos how to use his new computer to
   - ☐ cut and paste.
   - ☐ drag and drop.
   - ☐ highlight text.

B Circle the correct word or phrase.

1. Microwave ovens are used (**to cooking** / **for cooking** / **for cook**) food very fast.
2. When you go to the beach, try (**not to get** / **to don't get** / **not getting**) the camcorder wet.
3. You can use my cell phone (**leaving** / **for leave** / **to leave**) a voice mail.
4. Don't forget (**for taking** / **taking** / **to take**) your ATM card with you.

C Correct the mistake in each sentence or pair of sentences.

1. I want to move some text. How do I cut and click?
2. When I need to find some information, I drag the net.
3. My father knows a lot about computers. He's a hacker.
4. Be sure to double-click with your disk drive.
5. The screen is too hard to read. I think I need a new keyboard.

D Complete the sentences in column A with information from column B. Then rewrite each pair of sentences using *when*.

A	*B*
_____ 1. Fall is the season . . .	a. some people stay up all night.
_____ 2. July and August are the months . . .	b. people celebrate Valentine's Day.
_____ 3. New Year's Eve is a night . . .	c. children often go back to school.
_____ 4. February 14 is the day . . .	d. many families take summer vacations.

1. *Fall is the season when* ______________________
2. ______________________
3. ______________________
4. ______________________

E Match the phrases with the most appropriate information.

_____ 1. Before a young man and woman speak,	a. they sometimes arrange another date.
_____ 2. Before they meet for the first time,	b. they usually talk on the telephone.
_____ 3. When they have their first date,	c. they might chat with each other on the Internet.
_____ 4. After they meet for the first time,	d. they often meet in a public place, such as a coffee shop.

F Read the article. Then check (✓) four true statements.

The Mid-Autumn Festival

While Chinese people celebrate a few holidays according to the western calendar, the lunar calendar is used for most others. Important holidays in the lunar calendar, which follows the cycles of the moon, include Chinese New Year and the Dragon Boat Festival. The moon is perhaps most important, however, for the Mid-Autumn Festival.

Fall is the season when the moon appears larger and brighter than during the rest of the year. This is because it's a time when the weather is dry and cool. The Mid-Autumn Festival occurs on the fifteenth day of the eighth lunar month. This is a day when the moon is full.

According to Chinese tradition, "When the moon is full, mankind is one." For this reason, it's considered a good time for family and friends to get together and celebrate the harvest.

When Chinese people celebrate the Mid-Autumn Festival, they often meet in beautiful places. They look at the moon and eat mooncakes, special cakes containing things like bean paste, egg yolk, sesame and lotus seeds, dates, pineapple, walnuts, and almonds. Mooncakes are very rich, so people usually eat them with oolong or jasmine tea.

☐ 1. The western calendar is used for most Chinese holidays.
☐ 2. The western calendar is used for the Mid-Autumn Festival.
☐ 3. The cool, dry weather in fall makes the moon seem unusually large and bright.
☐ 4. People celebrate the festival in bright sunshine because the weather is so cool.
☐ 5. August 15 is the day when people celebrate the festival.
☐ 6. The festival is a celebration of togetherness and the harvest.
☐ 7. Mooncakes contain beans, eggs, seeds, fruit, and nuts.
☐ 8. A lot of people like to drink tea with mooncakes.

Units 9–10 quiz

Name: ______________________

Date: ______________________

Score: ______________________

A Listen to the conversations. Check (✓) the correct information.

1. Sylvia
   - ☐ has some old letters from her grandmother.
   - ☐ is going to sell her old typewriter to John.
   - ☐ is happy with her laptop and new technology.
2. According to Harry, if Marsha stays in her apartment,
   - ☐ she may have to make a lot of repairs to it.
   - ☐ she'll have more time to save for a house.
   - ☐ she won't be able to afford a big old house.
3. Jim's dad
   - ☐ speaks both French and Spanish.
   - ☐ likes the idea of Jim becoming a flight attendant.
   - ☐ thinks Jim needs to take a vacation.
4. Mac
   - ☐ is going to be a counselor at a summer camp.
   - ☐ has a lot of patience to work with kids.
   - ☐ wants to get a job at a national park.

B Match the phrases with the appropriate information.

____ 1. About 200 years ago,	a. people usually wrote more personal letters.
____ 2. Before personal computers,	b. there might be cheap solar-powered cars.
____ 3. In many cities nowadays,	c. people often used horses for transportation.
____ 4. Sometime in the future,	d. there is too much traffic and noise pollution.

C Circle the correct word or phrase.

1. If you walk to work, you (**'ll have to** / **won't have to** / **may have to**) pay for the bus.
2. If you (**take** / **travel** / **don't go**) a vacation, you may feel better and more relaxed.
3. If you get married, you (**won't be** / **might take** / **will have**) less free time.

D Complete the conversations. Check (✓) the correct response.

1. A: I'm not very good at typing.

   B: ☐ Oh, I am! ☐ Well, I do. ☐ Really? I don't mind.
2. A: I like working with computers.

   B: ☐ So am I. ☐ Neither can I. ☐ So do I.

3. A: I don't mind driving to work every day.

   B: ☐ Oh, I don't. ☐ Neither do I. ☐ Really? I like it.

E Circle the correct word.

1. Fiona carefully plans her day so she's never late for appointments. She likes to be (**creative** / **punctual** / **forgetful**).
2. Jerry tries to help people and never says "no" when someone asks him for a favor. He seems like a really (**generous** / **impatient** / **disorganized**) person.
3. Amy and Sam get angry easily and almost never smile. Everyone thinks they're moody and (**level-headed** / **hardworking** / **bad-tempered**).

F Match the sentences with the appropriate information.

____	1. I'd like to work as an English teacher	a. because I'm too disorganized and can't stand hospitals.
____	2. I wouldn't want to be a flight attendant	b. because I'm very patient and enjoy helping people learn.
____	3. I would make a good waiter	c. because I have an excellent memory and like meeting people.
____	4. I could never become a doctor	d. because I don't like to travel or work with people.

G Read the job ads. Then write the letter of the best job for each person.

CLASSIFIEDS

A. *Assistant accountant*

Are you the type who likes to solve problems and analyze financial data? If so, this job is for you because it requires a creative person who is level-headed. You must be good at math and numbers. You need to be able to work alone as well as on team projects. Send résumé to National Accounting Firm.

B. *Office manager*

Immediate opening for an office manager with good computer skills. Excellent spoken and written English also needed. One other foreign language would be useful. We are looking for a creative person who works well with other people. Some evenings and Saturdays may be necessary. This is an interesting job for someone who is hardworking, organized, and good at solving problems. Contact Mr. Sawyer at Horizon Travel Agency for an interview.

C. *Sales clerk*

We have a vacancy for a sales clerk in our downtown department store. Five years' sales experience and high school diploma desired. Weekend work required. This is a good job for a reliable and patient person who likes meeting people and helping customers. Good salary, health benefits, and vacation time. Interviews next week from 9 A.M. to noon. Ask for Ms. Thompson.

____ 1. Carmen is a recent college graduate who has worked for eight years at several clothing stores in the local shopping mall.

____ 2. Joan doesn't mind working independently or with others. She's been a bookkeeper in a small family business for several years.

____ 3. Tony just finished a computer course. He has also studied Spanish for three years and doesn't mind working some evenings or on Saturdays.

____ 4. Sarah got excellent grades in math in high school and is a good problem-solver. She's taking an art class on Saturdays, so she can only work during the week.

Units 11–12 quiz

Name: ______________________

Date: ______________________

Score: ______________________

A Listen to the conversations. Check (✓) the correct answers.

1. The Egyptian pyramids
   - ☐ are buried in sand.
   - ☐ were built by Napoleon.
   - ☐ are not open to tourists.
2. Great Zimbabwe is
   - ☐ on the border of Zimbabwe and Zambia.
   - ☐ the largest monument in southern Africa.
   - ☐ a modern city with 20,000 people.
3. Easter Island
   - ☐ is close to Chile and Tahiti.
   - ☐ has some large statues.
   - ☐ has an unusual sculpture museum.
4. The city where the woman lived
   - ☐ is located where two rivers meet.
   - ☐ is known in English as the Golden City.
   - ☐ is over 500 years old.

B Rewrite the sentences as passive sentences with *by*.

Example: Prince recorded the song "Purple Rain."
The song "Purple Rain" was recorded by Prince.

1. George Lucas directed the *Star Wars* movies. ______________________
2. Tim Berners-Lee developed the World Wide Web. ______________________
3. Ian Fleming wrote the James Bond novels. ______________________
4. Gustave Eiffel designed the Eiffel Tower in Paris. ______________________

C Complete the sentences. Use the passive form of the verbs.

1. English ______________ (speak) in Australia and New Zealand.
2. Spanish and Portuguese ______________ (teach) at this school.
3. Rice ______________ (grow) in many Asian countries.

D Circle the correct word.

1. One of the crops grown in Guatemala is (**cattle** / **coffee** / **shrimp**).
2. (**Chickens** / **Microchips** / **Oysters**) are manufactured in California.

3. I planned to graduate this semester, but, (**luckily** / **suddenly** / **unfortunately**), I failed some of my exams.
4. I was looking for a job when, (**miraculously** / **sadly** / **strangely**), I won the lottery and went on vacation instead.

E Complete the sentences. Use the simple past or past continuous of the verbs.

1. I ________ (meet) my best friend while I ________________ (take) a business course.
2. We ________________ (sleep), but the storm ________ (wake) us up.
3. Ted ________________ (talk) when his cell phone suddenly ________ (go) dead.

F Complete the conversation. Use the present perfect continuous of the verbs.

A: Hi, Elena! I haven't seen you since New Year's Eve. ________ you ______ ________ (work) long hours?

B: Not exactly. I ________________ (go) to my job all day.

A: And at night?

B: Oh, our new baby ________________ (keep) us awake all night!

G Read the article. Then check (✓) the correct answers.

Ieoh Ming Pei was born in Guangdong, China, in 1917. I.M. Pei, as he is usually known, was a child prodigy. When he was only 17, he went to the United States to study architecture. He graduated from both MIT and Harvard Graduate School of Design. He also taught architecture at Harvard. In 1951, he was awarded a special prize called a Traveling Fellowship. He used it to visit Britain, France, Italy, and Greece. When he returned to the United States in 1954, he became a U.S. citizen. He got his lucky break in 1964 when he was asked by Jacqueline Kennedy to design the John F. Kennedy Library in Boston.

Since then, I.M. Pei has designed many of the world's most recognized buildings and landmarks. In 1983, he was chosen by French President Mitterand to expand and modernize the Louvre Museum in Paris. Pei's design made it the world's largest museum. His addition of three glass pyramids to its entrance became world famous immediately. During the 1980s and 1990s, he was commissioned to work on several more museums – in Cleveland, Ohio; in Kyoto, Japan; in Berlin, Germany; and in Luxembourg. But perhaps his most famous creation is in his native land – the 70-story Bank of China building in Hong Kong.

1. I.M. Pei is a citizen of
   - ☐ China.
   - ☐ France.
   - ☐ the United States.
2. In 1951, his prize allowed him to
   - ☐ study and teach at Harvard.
   - ☐ travel around Europe.
   - ☐ return to the United States.
3. The entrance to the Louvre is well known because
   - ☐ it's very large.
   - ☐ it looks very expensive.
   - ☐ it has three glass pyramids.
4. I.M. Pei has also designed a museum in
   - ☐ Kyoto.
   - ☐ Boston.
   - ☐ Hong Kong.

Units 13–14 quiz

Name: ______________________

Date: ______________________

Score: ______________________

A Listen to the conversations. Check (✓) the correct information.

1. Both Joe and Marian
   - ☐ were bored by the last *Lord of the Rings* movie.
   - ☐ thought *Spider-Man* was a better movie.
   - ☐ are interested in movies because of what they used to read.
2. Barbara
   - ☐ thought Ben Affleck was the actor who starred in *Cold Mountain*.
   - ☐ reads a lot of movie reviews in entertainment magazines.
   - ☐ doesn't think that Sharon Stone is still making films.
3. What does "mandatory" class attendance mean?
   - ☐ It means the teacher will lower your grade if you miss a class.
   - ☐ It means you must attend every class during the semester.
   - ☐ It could mean that you don't have to go to class every day.
4. What is true about the performance?
   - ☐ Brett has seen a Broadway musical before.
   - ☐ You're not allowed to receive phone calls.
   - ☐ You can take photos if you don't use a flash.

B Complete each sentence with the correct form of the word.

1. I think animated films are __________ (fascinate).
2. We're both __________ (interest) in reading Amy Tan's latest book.
3. I was __________ (surprise) to see Marisa and Michael at the party.
4. Renting a movie is a __________ (bore) way to spend Saturday night.

C Circle the correct word.

1. The musical was (**marvelous** / **terrible** / **outstanding**). I didn't enjoy it at all!
2. This book is (**disgusting** / **silly** / **fantastic**). I just started it, and I can't put it down.
3. People hated everything about the movie. What a (**bizarre** / **fabulous** / **dreadful**) film!

D Rewrite the sentences using *who*, *that*, or *which*.

1. Comedies are a type of movie. They usually make people laugh.

   ____

2. *Two and a Half Men* is a popular TV show. It stars Charlie Sheen.

   ____

3. Charlize Theron is an actress. She won an Oscar for her performance in *Monster*.

____

E Complete the conversations. Circle the correct word.

1. A: Look at Daniel sitting over there scratching his head and writing.
   B: Oh, (**maybe** / **may** / **might**) it means he's taking a test.
2. A: What does Hiroko's gesture mean?
   B: It (**probably** / **might** / **could**) means she wants you to go over there.
3. A: What does it mean when somebody does this?
   B: That's easy! That gesture (**perhaps** / **definitely** / **possibly**) means everything's OK.
4. A: Look! The woman is wrinkling her nose at what the waiter brought.
   B: (**Must** / **Perhaps** / **Could**) it means she doesn't like how the food looks.

F Rewrite the sentences. Use the correct form of the verbs.

Example: Park your bicycles here. (allow) *You're allowed to park your bicycles here.*

1. Turn out the lights before you leave. (have to) You ______________________________ .
2. No eating or drinking in the classroom. (can't) You ______________________________ .
3. Take off your shoes here. (allow) You ______________________________ .

G Read the article. Then check (✓) the correct answers.

Body Language: *What does it say?*

Much of what we say to others is communicated not only through words, but also through body language. This includes our posture, facial expressions, and gestures. Because body language plays such a significant role in communication, it's important to know what your body is telling other people. You should also know how to interpret other people's body language. Here are some examples of typical body language:

A smile is usually a sign of friendliness and interest. However, some people smile just to be polite. To get another clue from people's faces, notice how they use their eyes. Friendliness and interest are expressed when a person's eyes meet yours directly. If someone looks away for a moment and then back again, the person is probably paying attention to what you're saying. If this person continues to look away while you're talking, he or she might not be interested, or could be shy. People also use hand gestures during a conversation to describe the size of something or the way someone acted. Finally, be aware that when someone keeps pointing at you while talking, it could mean the person is angry or feels superior in some way.

1. People communicate with one another using
   ☐ only words. ☐ words and body language. ☐ only facial expressions.
2. Body language includes
   ☐ interpretations. ☐ words and gestures. ☐ posture, facial expressions, and gestures.
3. A smile can show friendliness, interest, and
   ☐ sometimes politeness. ☐ often attention. ☐ perhaps shyness.
4. Someone who points a finger directly at you may be
   ☐ friendly. ☐ interested. ☐ angry.

Units 15–16 quiz

Name: ____________________

Date: ____________________

Score: ____________________

A Listen to the conversations. Check (✓) the correct answers.

1. If Wanda won the lottery, she would

   ☐ keep working. ☐ get a job. ☐ quit her job.

2. If Phil had the same choice as last night's winner, he'd

   ☐ pay his car repair bills. ☐ choose the new car. ☐ take the boat trip.

3. Carl says he would have

   ☐ returned the big tip. ☐ kept the big tip. ☐ left a big tip.

4. According to Bruce, Tina should have

   ☐ told her students not to use their cell phones in class.

   ☐ switched off her cell phone.

   ☐ told the teacher about her grandmother.

B Complete the conversation. Use the correct form of the verbs.

A: My sister just graduated, but her new job doesn't start for two months.

B: Really? If I ________ (have) the time, I ________________ (borrow) some money and travel.

A: If I ________________ (not have) enough money, I ________________ (not ask) a friend for a loan.

B: What would you do?

A: I ________________ (stay) home and ________ (read).

C Complete the conversations. Use past modals of the verbs.

1. A: Last year, I gained a lot of weight, so I stopped eating for a week.

   B: Oh, I wouldn't ________________ (do) that. I would ________________ (go) on a special diet.

2. A: While I was parking, I hit someone else's car. I didn't leave a note.

   B: Oh, you should ________________ (admit) your mistake. You shouldn't ________________ (deny) responsibility.

D Complete the sentences with the correct form of the verbs *express*, *give*, *make*, *offer*, or *tell*.

1. Pam ________ a lot of jokes at Jennifer's birthday party last night.
2. When Tony found out I had failed my test, he ________ his sympathy.
3. We ________ our congratulations when we heard Beth was getting married.
4. When Justin doesn't want to do something, he never ________ a reason.

E Rewrite the conversation in reported speech using the verbs given.

John: Can you give me a ride to the airport?

Mary: I can drive you there in the evening.

John: Meet me outside my apartment at 8:00 P.M.

Mary: I will be there around eight.

John: Don't be late!

Mary: I don't have any other plans.

John: I'm very grateful.

John asked Mary to give him (ask) a ride to the airport. Mary ____________________ (tell) there in the evening. John ____________________ (ask) outside his apartment at 8:00 P.M. Mary ____________________ (say) there around eight. John ____________________ (tell) late. Mary ____________________ (tell) any other plans. John ____________________ (say) very grateful.

F Read the article. Then check (✓) the correct answers.

The Advice Sisters

Who would many young people go to these days for advice on a personal problem? The answer is "the advice sisters." Alison Blackman Dunham and Jessica Freedman are twin sisters who work together to provide a unique service. In their advice columns, both online and in print, Alison and Jessica offer a double take. In other words, each sister gives her own answer to each question. This means that the person who asks a question always receives two replies.

The advice sisters have co-authored a book and co-written several e-books. They have also worked together on an audiotape series about communicating more effectively at work, in life, and in love. Although they work together a lot, these two remarkable women also have separate careers. Alison is the owner of a public relations company in New York City. She is often quoted in career magazines and has written several books on managing life and career. Jessica, on the other hand, teaches writing and literature at several colleges. She owns an editing business, has written several books and film scripts, and is also a lawyer! When do the advice sisters ever find time to relax with their family and friends?

1. The advice sisters are
   - ☐ young sisters who need advice. ☐ business partners only. ☐ business partners and twins.
2. Their service is unusual because
   - ☐ it's only available online.
   - ☐ it provides two answers to each problem.
   - ☐ people with problems can choose which sister to consult.
3. The advice sisters
   - ☐ work together full-time. ☐ work together part-time. ☐ always work separately.
4. Jessica is also interested in
   - ☐ managing money. ☐ public relations. ☐ writing.

Quiz audio scripts

Units 1–2 *[CD 1, Track 14]*

A Listen to the conversations. Check the correct answers.

1.

TOM: Hi. I'm your new neighbor, Tom Jordan. I just moved into the building.
SARAH: Nice to meet you, Tom. I'm Sarah Hagen. Are you from around here?
TOM: No. I'm not from San Diego. I'm actually from San Francisco.
SARAH: Oh, were you born there?
TOM: No, I was born in Japan, but I grew up in San Francisco.
SARAH: Really? Do you speak Japanese?
TOM: Unfortunately not. I was only a baby when my family left Japan and moved to the States.

2.

GARY: How's your meal, Carol?
CAROL: It's really good. Do you want to try some?
GARY: No, thanks. So, tell me. What were you like as a child?
CAROL: Oh, when I was a kid, I was really into books. I used to read all the time.
GARY: What kinds of books?
CAROL: Well, I remember I used to read comic books a lot. And I loved reading mysteries.
GARY: Did you collect anything?
CAROL: No, I didn't use to collect anything, but now I collect old black-and-white photographs.

3.

HELEN: I had an interesting evening last night.
PAUL: Why? What did you do, Helen?
HELEN: Well, I went to a city council meeting on transportation.
PAUL: Oh. I wanted to go to that! What happened?
HELEN: First, several people talked about traffic problems. Some said there's too much traffic and then others talked about not having enough buses.
PAUL: That's true.
HELEN: And then I stood up and said there isn't enough parking downtown. We need more public parking garages.

4.

ANNA: Hey, Steve. Guess what? I had to wait 30 minutes for a bus this morning. My commute is getting worse and worse.
STEVE: It's because there are too many cars on the road. You know, Anna, I think you need to join a car pool.
ANNA: Car pool? What's that?
STEVE: It's a group of people who ride to work together in one car.
ANNA: Oh, right. That's a good idea. How do you join a car pool?
STEVE: There's a phone number you can call. You just leave your address and phone number and someone calls you back with the names and numbers of people in your neighborhood who want to carpool.
ANNA: I see. How do you know so much about this?
STEVE: I called that number five years ago!

Units 3–4 *[CD 1, Track 29]*

A Listen to the conversations. Check the correct answers.

1.

JEN: I just love my new apartment!
STUART: That's great, Jen. What do you like about it?
JEN: Everything. First of all, it's not as noisy as my old apartment.
STUART: Yeah, it was pretty noisy!
JEN: And another thing, it has two bathrooms! My family visits me often, so it'll be more convenient.
STUART: That's good. And what's the rent like?
JEN: That's what I like the most. It's not as expensive as my old apartment. I can finally start saving some money!

2.

SETH: I was late to work again today. There's just too much traffic.
GAIL: I know! And then there are never enough parking spaces.
SETH: Exactly! I can never find a place to park my car!
GAIL: So, Seth, why don't you move downtown? You could live near your office.
SETH: I'd like to. The problem is I really can't afford to live downtown. It's too expensive.
GAIL: But at least you could save some money by walking to work!

3.

KAREN: I wish I could find a new apartment. I'm ready for a change.
DENNIS: Why, Karen? What's wrong with the place you're living in now?
KAREN: Well, it's dingy and cramped. I don't know why I rented it in the first place. I mean, it's very safe and private, I just wish it weren't so small.
DENNIS: What kind of place are you looking for exactly?
KAREN: Someplace that's more spacious, but not too expensive.
DENNIS: Good luck!

4.

CHRISTIE: So, Doug, how do you like your new apartment?
DOUG: I love it! It's great.
CHRISTIE: What do you like about it?
DOUG: Do you remember how dark my old apartment was?
CHRISTIE: Yeah, it was kind of depressing.
DOUG: Well, my new apartment is on the top floor, so it's nice and bright.
CHRISTIE: Is there anything you don't like?
DOUG: Some of the apartments on the first floor have a small garden, and I'd like to grow flowers or maybe a few vegetables. So I kind of wish I lived on the first floor.
CHRISTIE: I guess you can't have everything.

Units 5–6 *[CD 1, Track 43]*

A Listen to the conversations. Check the correct information.

1.

MIKE: You know, Holly, summer's almost here. What are you doing for vacation?
HOLLY: Well, I'm going to visit my grandparents for a few weeks. They're getting older, and I want to spend more time with them.
MIKE: That's nice. My grandparents live too far away to visit. So, are you going anywhere else this summer?
HOLLY: Oh, I'm not sure. I think I'll spend a few days at the beach. How about you, Mike? Any plans?
MIKE: Me? I'm going to go mountain climbing with friends. I'm really looking forward to it!
HOLLY: Wow, that sounds exciting! Maybe I'll go camping in August. I'd love to visit a national park.

2.

HOLLY: Which national park do you recommend?
MIKE: For camping? Well, I think Yosemite National Park is the most beautiful. By the way, who are you going with?
HOLLY: My sister has been wanting me to go with her for a while. Do you think we'll need to make a reservation?
MIKE: Absolutely! August is the busiest month for park visitors. You ought to find out if campsites are still available.
HOLLY: Good idea. What else should we do before going camping?
MIKE: Well, you'd better check all your equipment before you leave home. And be sure to bring along a first-aid kit.

3.

KATHY: I'm so glad we're going to be roommates this year, Annette.
ANNETTE: Me, too! I've been looking forward to sharing an apartment.
KATHY: Yeah. And I really needed to find a new roommate. I had a lot of trouble with my last one.
ANNETTE: Oh, Kathy, what happened?
KATHY: Well, it was a bit like living with my mother. She was always telling me things like "Pick up your clothes!" and "Take out the trash."
ANNETTE: Um, I don't think there's anything wrong with being clean. I like to keep my room neat.
KATHY: Oh, no, Annette! *You* like to clean up all the time, too? Well, maybe you can keep everything picked up and put away for both of us!
ANNETTE: Mmm, no, I think we should pick up our own things and wash our own dishes. Maybe we just need to have a few rules. . . .

4.

KATHY: Rules?! You think we need to have rules?
ANNETTE: Sure, why not? Then we'll both know whose job it is to do things.
KATHY: OK, all right. As long as you don't ask me to change too much.
ANNETTE: What do you mean?
KATHY: Well, my mom was always yelling at me, "Kathy, can you turn the radio down?" and "Kathy, would you mind not leaving the TV on all the time?"
ANNETTE: Uh-oh. I need it to be really quiet when I'm studying. No music, no TV.
KATHY: And I can't study without listening to my CDs – turned up all the way!
ANNETTE: OK, Kathy, we have a little problem here. Maybe you could wear headphones when you listen to music.
KATHY: I guess I could do that.

Units 7–8 *[CD 2, Track 15]*

A Listen to the conversations. Check the correct answers.

1.

PETER: Hey, Stephanie, have you seen Richard recently? I've left him a few voice mails, but he never calls me back. Is he OK?
STEPHANIE: He never calls me back either. But don't worry about him. He bought a new computer last week.
PETER: So?
STEPHANIE: So he spends all day and night on his computer. He's become a total geek!
PETER: Really? He never used to like computers.
STEPHANIE: Well, he does now. He never goes out and has fun anymore!

2.

BARRY: Hey, Martha, can you come help me? I'm having computer problems.
MARTHA: You? But you're such a technophile. You're always surfing the net.
BARRY: Yeah, but I don't know how to do everything!
MARTHA: So, what's the problem, Barry? Whoa, what are all these photos doing on the table?
BARRY: I'm trying to scan them so I can e-mail them to friends.
MARTHA: Oh, scanning is easy! Place the photo here. Be sure to put it face down. And then double-click on this.
BARRY: That's it? That was easy!

3.

SYLVIO: Guess what, Eva? I just bought a really cheap plane ticket online!
EVA: Really? I always go to a travel agent to plan my vacations.
SYLVIO: Well, you can sometimes get cheaper tickets on the Internet. You should browse some Web sites. You have a computer at home, don't you?
EVA: Yeah, but I never use it.
SYLVIO: Why not? What's wrong with it?
EVA: Nothing! But my roommates are always playing games on it! When I tell them I need to use it, they say they're just going to finish the game. . . .

4.

HEATHER: How do you like your new computer, Carlos?
CARLOS: Actually, Heather, I prefer my old one.
HEATHER: Really? Why?
CARLOS: There are so many things I can't do! I don't know how to highlight text, drag and drop, or cut and paste. I could do all that on my old computer. And please don't tell me to read the manual.
HEATHER: Let's take one problem at a time.
CARLOS: OK. I want to highlight those two words.
HEATHER: Just use your mouse . . . like this . . . and then press this key here.
CARLOS: That was easy. Thanks.

Units 9–10 *[CD 2, Track 30]*

A Listen to the conversations. Check the correct information.

1.

JOHN: Sylvia, can you believe that 15 years ago, not many people had personal computers?

SYLVIA: I know. I remember being so happy when my parents gave me a manual typewriter for my eighteenth birthday.

JOHN: Yeah, I had one, too. It used to take forever to type something.

SYLVIA: Well, before typewriters, people used to write each other. My mother has some beautiful old handwritten letters.

JOHN: Those were the good old days, huh?

SYLVIA: Yes and no. Nowadays, e-mail makes it so easy to keep in touch with family and friends.

JOHN: So you wouldn't want to go back to those days?

SYLVIA: No, I'm very happy with my new laptop. Hey, do you want to buy my old typewriter? I think it's still up in the attic somewhere.

JOHN: No, thanks!

2.

MARSHA: I love old houses. I like that they have a past, you know, a history of every family that lived there.

HARRY: But, Marsha, if you buy an old house, you may have to make a lot of repairs to it.

MARSHA: Repairs? What kind of repairs?

HARRY: You might have to change the pipes and electrical wiring, or even put in a new heating system.

MARSHA: Well, that might be true, but just think of how wonderful it would be to live in such a beautiful old place.

HARRY: But if you stay in your apartment for a few more years, you won't have to worry about moving. You'll have a lot more time to save money for your dream home.

3.

DAD: So, Jim, have you thought any more about the kind of work you're interested in doing?

JIM: Well, I've been thinking how I love traveling and . . .

DAD: So do I, but that's what you do on vacation.

JIM: No, Dad, I mean, I want a job that involves traveling.

DAD: Oh? Like an airline pilot?

JIM: Well, not exactly . . . but, hey, you just gave me a good idea. I work well with other people, and I don't mind working long hours. . . . And I'm good at French and Spanish. So maybe I could become a flight attendant.

DAD: Mm. A flight attendant. Do you think your mom and I would get to fly at a special family rate?

JIM: I think so.

DAD: Great!

4.

MAC: Do you know yet what you're going to do this summer?

DIANA: Well, I think I'd make a good counselor because I really like working with children. I'm going to try to work at a summer camp.

MAC: Yeah, you'd be great working with kids at a camp. That kind of job isn't for me, though.

DIANA: But Mac, you like hiking and camping. And you're hardworking.

MAC: But I'd hate to have the responsibility of taking care of a group of children, and I'm way too impatient to work with kids.

DIANA: Well, what else would you enjoy doing?

MAC: I really enjoy working outdoors. I think I'm going to try to find a job working at a national park. I'd love to help park rangers take people on nature hikes and things like that.

Units 11–12 *[CD 3, Track 2]*

A Listen to the conversations. Check the correct answers.

1.

WOMAN: How was your trip to Egypt?

MAN: Oh, it was incredible. I finally got to visit the pyramids.

WOMAN: And what did you think?

MAN: I learned *so* much. Like, did you know that they were uncovered by Napoleon? Before he visited the country, they were buried in sand.

WOMAN: Really? Do they know who built them?

MAN: Yes, of course. They were built by the Egyptians.

WOMAN: And did you go inside a pyramid?

MAN: No. Most of the pyramids are closed to tourists. You can't go in, but I took a lot of photos from the outside. Do you want to see?

2.

MAN: Weren't you just on vacation in Africa?

WOMAN: Well, actually, I was there for work, but I was able to take a couple of great trips that I'll never forget.

MAN: Where did you go?

WOMAN: I went to Victoria Falls, on the border of Zimbabwe and Zambia. The falls are amazing! I really enjoyed the trip.

MAN: I'd love to go there! What about your other trip?

WOMAN: I visited a huge stone wall called Great Zimbabwe. The area inside the wall is supposed to be big enough to hold a city with 20,000 people. It's the largest monument in southern Africa.

MAN: So, what happened to the city?

WOMAN: No one really knows. I guess it's still a mystery.

3.

WOMAN: Welcome back. So, how was Easter Island?

MAN: I've never been anywhere like it. It's unique!

WOMAN: What's so special about it?

MAN: Well, first of all, it's very remote. Chile and Tahiti are over three thousand kilometers away! But it's known mainly for the giant statues.

WOMAN: Oh, yeah, I've seen photos of them.

MAN: They were built by Polynesians, who arrived there nearly two thousand five hundred years ago.

WOMAN: It sounds like you really enjoyed it.

MAN: I did. It was like an open-air museum, with the statues along the coast, archaeological sites, volcanic craters, and some fantastic beaches.

4.

MAN: What have you been doing? I haven't seen you in a long time.

WOMAN: I've been living abroad. I was working in Laos for a while.

MAN: Laos! I just read an article about Laos. I've always wanted to go there!

WOMAN: It's a beautiful country – especially the city where I lived. It was built at the point where the Mekong River meets the Khan River.

MAN: Yeah, I think I read about it. Isn't that the place with lots of temples?

WOMAN: Yeah! And fortunately, I had time to visit many of them. My favorite temple is called Golden City Monastery. It was built on the riverbank nearly five hundred years ago.

Units 13–14 *[CD 3, Track 17]*

A Listen to the conversations. Check the correct information.

1.

MARIAN: I wasn't surprised that the last *Lord of the Rings* movie won so many awards. It was fantastic! Did you like it, Joe?

JOE: Sure. The acting was good and the special effects were great.

MARIAN: It was an exciting movie, wasn't it?

JOE: Yeah, but you know, Marian, I think *Spider-Man* was even better.

MARIAN: What? You do? Why?

JOE: Well, I've always been interested in superheroes like Superman, Batman, and Spider-Man.

MARIAN: Did you use to read a lot of comic books when you were a kid?

JOE: Of course! I loved reading comics about superheroes who do good things with their special powers. How about you?

MARIAN: Well, I was fascinated by all Tolkien's novels, you know, *The Hobbit* and *The Lord of the Rings*.

JOE: Maybe that's why we like to see those types of movies today.

2.

GEORGE: OK, here's some good movie trivia for you, Barbara.

BARBARA: All right. What's the question?

GEORGE: Who is the actor that starred in *Cold Mountain*?

BARBARA: Oh, that's easy! It was Ben Affleck.

GEORGE: No, you're wrong! Jude Law was the actor who starred in that movie. And do you remember who his co-star was?

BARBARA: Wasn't it Sharon Stone?

GEORGE: Wrong again! You're terrible! Is she even making movies any more?

BARBARA: Well, I guess I haven't been to the movies in a while. How do you know so much about Hollywood news?

GEORGE: I guess I read a lot of entertainment magazines.

3.

YUKIKO: Do you understand what our teacher means when she says that attendance is "mandatory"?

GABRIEL: Well, I guess it probably means you have to go to class every day. You know, you won't be allowed to miss any classes this semester.

YUKIKO: Or maybe it means that the teacher will lower your grade if you miss a class. But what happens if I'm sick and I can't come to class?

GABRIEL: I don't know. Maybe we should ask her. Excuse me, Yukiko and I want to know what you meant when you said class attendance is mandatory.

TEACHER: Oh. That means you must attend every class during the semester.

4.

BRETT: I can't believe it, Lynn! This is the first time I've seen a Broadway musical!

LYNN: Pretty exciting, isn't it, Brett?

BRETT: It sure is. By the way, it says here in the program that you have to turn off your cell phone before the performance starts.

LYNN: Oh, that's right. Thanks for reminding me.

BRETT: And it says you aren't allowed to take any photos or videos during the performance.

LYNN: Uh-huh, I knew that. No cameras or video cameras are allowed.

BRETT: And did you know that you can't eat or drink anything in the theater?

LYNN: Yeah. If you want, we can go outside during the intermission to get a snack.

BRETT: That's a good idea.

Units 15–16 *[CD 3, Track 33]*

A Listen to the conversations. Check the correct answers.

1.

MEL: Hey, Wanda, did you hear about that teacher who won the lottery?

WANDA: Yes, I still can't believe he's going to keep teaching.

MEL: Why not? He loves his job! What's wrong with that?

WANDA: Well, if I won that much money, I'd quit my job immediately.

MEL: That's because you don't like your job. If you had a job that you really liked, you might not want to give it up.

WANDA: Maybe. But even if you like your job, there are so many other things to do in life.

2.

DONNA: Do you watch that TV game show, Phil? The one where the winner has to choose between two prizes?

PHIL: I watch it sometimes. Why?

DONNA: Well, I couldn't believe what last night's winner did. She must have been crazy!

PHIL: Why? What were her choices?

DONNA: A three-month boat trip on the Amazon River or a new car. I know which I'd choose!

PHIL: I'd take the car. You wouldn't believe the repair bills I have on my old car! Besides, I wouldn't be able to take three months off work. So, which did the winner choose, the car or the trip?

DONNA: Like you, she chose the car.

3.

CARL: How are you enjoying working at that new restaurant?

PATTY: I love it, Carl! The food's great, so it's crowded every night.

CARL: But what's the money like?

PATTY: Oh, it's much better than my last job. The customers are so happy with the food that the tips are pretty good! But I feel bad about something that happened last night.

CARL: Why? What happened?

PATTY: I served a group of foreigners. It must have been their first meal in this country. Anyway, they gave me a huge tip. I think they got confused with the currency.

CARL: So, what did you do?

PATTY: Nothing! What would you have done?

CARL: I would have told them the tip was too big.

4.

BRUCE: What's wrong, Tina? You look upset.

TINA: Actually, I am. I did something wrong, but I still don't know what I should have done.

BRUCE: What happened?

TINA: Well, my English teacher has a rule about cell phones. At the beginning of class, she always reminds us to switch them off.

BRUCE: I don't blame her. Cell phones shouldn't be allowed in classrooms.

TINA: Well, I agree, Bruce, but I was waiting for an important call from my parents. My grandmother is in the hospital. So I didn't switch off my cell.

BRUCE: Don't tell me! It rang in class!

TINA: Yeah, right during our final quiz.

BRUCE: What did she do?

TINA: She asked me to leave the room. I feel terrible. What should I have done?

BRUCE: I think you probably should have explained your predicament before the quiz.

Quiz answer key

Units 1–2

A (4 points)
1. San Francisco
2. read comic books
3. isn't enough parking downtown
4. calling a phone number

B (3 points)
1. were you born
2. he study French
3. did they graduate

C (3 points)
1. beach
2. chess
3. snake

D (4 points)
A: Did you use to play soccer when you were a child?
B: Yes, I used to play soccer every day after school.
A: And what things did you use to collect?
B: Oh, I never used to collect anything, but now I collect postcards.

E (3 points)
1. We should have more bicycle lanes.
2. There is too much traffic and air pollution. *or* There is too much air pollution and traffic.
3. There should be less noise and fewer cars. *or* There should be fewer cars and less noise.

F (4 points)
1. Do you know where the nearest restaurant is?
2. Could you tell me how much newspapers cost?
3. Do you know where the best bookstore in town is?
4. Can you tell me what time the banks close?

G (4 points)
1. invented the Segway HT
2. is cheaper than buying a car
3. recharges in four to six hours
4. could replace a bicycle

Units 3–4

A (4 points)
1. it's cheaper than her old apartment
2. he works there
3. too small
4. on the first floor

B (4 points)
1. safe
2. noisy
3. convenient
4. huge

C (3 points)
1. not enough rooms
2. not enough privacy
3. not quiet enough

D (3 points)
1. as many windows as
2. as convenient as
3. as much space as

E (3 points)
1. I wish I liked my job. *or* I wish I liked it.
2. I wish I could find my cell phone. *or* I wish I could find it.
3. I wish my boyfriend were in good shape. *or* I wish he were in good shape.

F (4 points)
A: Have you ever tried Spanish food?
B: Yes, I have. I went to a Spanish restaurant last week.
A: Did you like it?
B: Yeah, it was delicious.

G (4 points)
1. Bangkok is a good place for shopping.
4. The prices in the market are very reasonable.
5. Some restaurants in Bangkok are right on the river.
8. Foreigners sometimes have to ask to have spicy food.

Units 5–6

A (4 points)
1. Holly might go camping in August.
2. Mike thinks Holly should go to Yosemite.
3. Annette doesn't like being messy.
4. Kathy likes to listen to music while studying.

B (4 points)
1. A: What are you going to do after class today?
   B: I'm definitely going to see a movie with a friend.
2. A: When are they going to take their vacation this year?
   B: I think they'll go on a cruise in June or July.

C (3 points)
1. passport
2. hiking boots
3. cash

D (4 points)

A: We should make our plane reservations right away! It will be hard to find cheap flights later this month.
B: Good idea! And perhaps we ought to buy round-trip tickets because they're usually cheaper.
A: And remember, you're going to drive the rental car, so you need to bring your driver's license.
B: Of course. And you shouldn't forget to pack your new digital camera. It will be fun learning how to use it.

E (3 points)
1. up
2. away
3. down

F (3 points)
1. Could you close the door, please?
2. Would you please take out the garbage? *or* Would you please take the garbage out?
3. Would you mind not sitting there?

G (4 points)
1. They didn't say anything.
2. The new family continued to cut it down.
3. They are outside barking all the time.
4. Let the police solve the problems.

Units 7–8

A (4 points)
1. a geek
2. scan photographs
3. her roommates use her computer a lot
4. highlight text

B (4 points)
1. for cooking
2. not to get
3. to leave
4. to take

C (5 points)
1. I want to move some text. How do I cut and ~~click~~ *paste*?
2. When I need to find some information, I ~~drag~~ *surf* the net.
3. My father knows a lot about computers. He's a ~~hacker~~ *technophile*.
4. Be sure to double-click with your ~~disk drive~~ *mouse*.
5. The screen is too hard to read. I think I need a new ~~keyboard~~ *monitor*.

D (4 points)
1. c. Fall is the season when children often go back to school.
2. d. July and August are the months when many families take summer vacations.
3. a. New Year's Eve is a night when some people stay up all night.
4. b. February 14 is the day when people celebrate Valentine's Day.

E (4 points)
1. c
2. b
3. d
4. a

F (4 points)

3. The cool, dry weather in fall makes the moon seem unusually large and bright.
6. The festival is a celebration of togetherness and the harvest.
7. Mooncakes contain beans, eggs, seeds, fruit, and nuts.
8. A lot of people like to drink tea with mooncakes.

Units 9–10

A (4 points)
1. is happy with her laptop and new technology
2. she'll have more time to save for a house
3. likes the idea of Jim becoming a flight attendant
4. wants to get a job at a national park

B (4 points)
1. c
2. a
3. d
4. b

C (3 points)
1. won't have to
2. take
3. will have

D (3 points)
1. Oh, I am!
2. So do I.
3. Neither do I.

E (3 points)
1. punctual
2. generous
3. bad-tempered

F (4 points)
1. b
2. d
3. c
4. a

G (4 points)
1. C. Sales clerk
2. A. Assistant accountant
3. B. Office manager
4. A. Assistant accountant

Units 11–12

A (4 points)
1. are not open to tourists
2. the largest monument in southern Africa
3. has some large statues
4. is located where two rivers meet

B (4 points)
1. The *Star Wars* movies were directed by George Lucas.
2. The World Wide Web was developed by Tim Berners-Lee.
3. The James Bond novels were written by Ian Fleming.
4. The Eiffel Tower in Paris was designed by Gustave Eiffel.

C (3 points)
1. is spoken
2. are taught
3. is grown

D (4 points)
1. coffee
2. Microchips
3. unfortunately
4. miraculously

E (3 points)
1. I met my best friend while I was taking a business course.
2. We were sleeping, but the storm woke us up.
3. Ted was talking when his cell phone suddenly went dead.

F (3 points)

A: Hi, Elena! I haven't seen you since New Year's Eve. Have you been working long hours?
B: Not exactly. I've been going to my job all day.
A: And at night?
B: Oh, our new baby has been keeping us awake all night!

G (4 points)
1. the United States
2. travel around Europe
3. it has three glass pyramids
4. Kyoto

Units 13–14

A (4 points)
1. are interested in movies because of what they used to read
2. thought Ben Affleck was the actor who starred in *Cold Mountain*
3. It means you must attend every class during the semester.
4. You're not allowed to receive phone calls.

B (4 points)
1. fascinating
2. interested
3. surprised
4. boring

C (3 points)
1. terrible
2. fantastic
3. dreadful

D (3 points)
1. Comedies are a type of movie which (*or* that) usually make people laugh.
2. *Two and a Half Men* is a popular TV show which (*or* that) stars Charlie Sheen.
3. Charlize Theron is an actress who (*or* that) won an Oscar for her performance in *Monster*.

E (4 points)
1. maybe
2. probably
3. definitely
4. Perhaps

F (3 points)
1. You have to turn out the lights before you leave. *or* You've got to turn out the lights before you leave.
2. You can't eat or drink in the classroom.
3. You're allowed to take off your shoes here.

G (4 points)
1. words and body language
2. posture, facial expressions, and gestures
3. sometimes politeness
4. angry

Units 15–16

A (4 points)
1. quit her job
2. choose the new car
3. returned the big tip
4. told the teacher about her grandmother

B (3 points)

B: Really? If I had the time, I would borrow (*or* I'd borrow) some money and travel.
A: If I didn't have enough money, I wouldn't ask a friend for a loan.
B: What would you do?
A: I would stay (*or* I'd stay) home and read.

C (4 points)
1. B: Oh, I wouldn't have done that. I would have gone on a special diet.
2. B: Oh, you should have admitted your mistake. You shouldn't have denied responsibility.

D (4 points)
1. told (*or* made)
2. expressed (*or* offered)
3. offered
4. gives

E (6 points)

John asked Mary to give him a ride to the airport. Mary told John/him (that) she could drive him there in the evening. John asked Mary/her to meet him outside his apartment at 8:00 P.M. Mary said (that) she'd (*or* she would) be there around eight. John told Mary/her not to be late. Mary told John/him (that) she didn't have any other plans. John said (that) he was very grateful.

F (4 points)
1. business partners and twins
2. it provides two answers to each problem
3. work together part-time
4. writing

Audio scripts

1 A time to remember

2 CONVERSATION [p. 2]

B Listen to the rest of the conversation. What are two more things you learn about Ted?

TED: Hey, that was fun. Thanks for the lesson!
ANA: No problem. So, tell me a little about yourself. What do you do?
TED: I work in a travel agency.
ANA: Really! What do you do there?
TED: I'm in charge of their computers.
ANA: Oh, so you're a computer specialist.
TED: Well, sort of. Yeah, I guess so.
ANA: That's great. Then maybe you can give me some help with a computer course I'm taking.
TED: Oh, sure . . . but only if you promise to give me some more skating lessons.
ANA: It's a deal!

4 LISTENING [p. 3]

A Listen to interviews with two immigrants to the United States. Where are they from?

Yu Hong

INTERVIEWER: Where are you from originally, Yu Hong?
YU HONG: I'm from China . . . from near Shanghai.
INTERVIEWER: And when did you move here?
YU HONG: I came here after I graduated from college. That was in 1992.
INTERVIEWER: And what do you do now?
YU HONG: I'm a transportation engineer.
INTERVIEWER: I see. So you're an immigrant to the United States.
YU HONG: Yes, that's right.
INTERVIEWER: What are some of the difficulties of being an immigrant in the U.S.?
YU HONG: Oh, that's not an easy question to answer. There are so many things, really. I guess one of the biggest difficulties is that I don't have any relatives here. I mean, I have a lot of friends, but that's not the same thing. In China, on holidays or the weekend, we visit relatives. It isn't the same here.
INTERVIEWER: And what do you miss the most from home?
YU HONG: Oh, that's easy: my mom's soup! She makes great soup. I really miss my mother's cooking.

Ajay

INTERVIEWER: Where are you from, Ajay?
AJAY: I'm from India.
INTERVIEWER: And when did you move to the U.S.?
AJAY: It was in 1991.
INTERVIEWER: Are you studying here at the moment?
AJAY: Not now. I came here as a student and graduated two years ago. I'm working as a computer technician.
INTERVIEWER: Uh-huh. And what was it like when you first came here? Was it difficult?
AJAY: Yeah, it was at times. The main difficulty I had was with the educational system. Things are very different here. Teaching methods, everything is very different from what I was used to in India.
INTERVIEWER: And what do you miss the most from India?
AJAY: To tell you the truth, after you're here for a while, you don't miss anything very much. But I guess the weather and my family are the things I miss. And the quality of life. The quality of life is much nicer back home, frankly speaking.

B Listen again and complete the chart.

2 Caught in the rush

4 LISTENING [p. 9]

A Listen to someone talk about how Singapore has tried to solve its traffic problems. Check True or False for each statement.

MAN: Quite a number of things have been done to help solve traffic problems in Singapore. For example, motorists must buy a special pass if they want to drive into the downtown business district. They can go into the business district only if they have the pass displayed on their windshield.

Another thing Singapore has done is to make it more difficult to buy cars. People have to apply for a certificate if they want to buy a car. And the number of certificates is limited. Not everyone can get one. There is also a high tax on cars, so it costs three or four times as much to buy a car in Singapore as it does in, say, the United States or Canada. The other thing Singapore has done is to build an excellent public transportation system. Their subway system is one of the best in the world. And there is also a very good taxi and bus system.

B Listen again. For the false statements, write the correct information.

8 CONVERSATION [p. 11]

B Listen to the rest of the conversation. Check the information that Erica asks for.

ERICA: Excuse me. It's me again. I'm sorry. I need some more information – if you don't mind.
CLERK: Not at all.
ERICA: Thanks. Do you know how much a taxi to the city costs?
CLERK: Well, it depends on the traffic, of course. But it usually costs about $40.
ERICA: Forty dollars? I guess I'll take the bus. That means I have almost an hour till the next one. Where can I find an inexpensive restaurant in the airport? Maybe a fast-food place?
CLERK: Go upstairs and turn right. You'll see a snack bar on your left.
ERICA: Thanks very much. Have a nice day.
CLERK: You, too.

Units 1–2 Progress check

1 LISTENING [p. 14]

A Listen to an interview with Jeri, a fashion model. Answer the questions.

INTERVIEWER: Thanks for taking the time to speak with me, Jeri.
JERI: Oh, it's my pleasure.
INTERVIEWER: You have a beautiful accent. Where did you grow up?
JERI: I grew up in England, in a city called Brighton.
INTERVIEWER: How do you spell that?
JERI: B-R-I-G-H-T-O-N.
INTERVIEWER: Just like it sounds.
JERI: Yes.
INTERVIEWER: What was that like?
JERI: Brilliant. It's a lovely city, right by the sea. My family still lives there. My father owns a restaurant, and my mother teaches school.
INTERVIEWER: What did you want to be when you grew up?
JERI: Well, I never thought I'd be a model! I wanted to be a doctor or maybe a writer.
INTERVIEWER: Why not a model?
JERI: Well, I always thought I looked funny.
INTERVIEWER: I can't imagine it. Were you popular when you were growing up?
JERI: Not really. I wasn't unpopular, but I wasn't in the popular crowd at school. I had a nice group of friends, though.
INTERVIEWER: How did you like school?
JERI: Oh, I loved school. I was a great student. My mother actually taught at my primary school. I always thought that was terrific.
INTERVIEWER: What about your free time as a child. Did you have a hobby?
JERI: I used to paint. Actually, I still do. I have some paintings in a gallery right now.
INTERVIEWER: That's impressive.
JERI: Well, it's a very small exhibit. But it's something I really enjoy.
INTERVIEWER: Did you have a favorite game when you were growing up?
JERI: That's easy. My favorite game was chess. My grandfather taught me how to play. I used to visit his house in the country. We would have chess tournaments. It was wonderful.
INTERVIEWER: What about a favorite place?
JERI: Hmm. My favorite place? I used to go to summer camp in Ireland. I loved that. I got to go horseback riding almost every day.
INTERVIEWER: Do you still go to Ireland?
JERI: No. Not very often.

3 Time for a change!

5 LISTENING [p. 18]

A Listen to Brad describe a "capsule hotel." Check the words that best describe it.

HOST: Welcome to the program *Your Home Is My Home*. Our guest tonight is Brad Philips from California. Brad, tell us a little bit about yourself. What do you do?
BRAD: Well, at the moment, I'm working as an English teacher in Tokyo, Japan. Tokyo is an exciting city, but it's also very spread out. It can sometimes take hours to go from one part of the city to another. When I don't feel like going all the way home, I sometimes stay in a capsule hotel.
HOST: A capsule hotel? Can you explain what that is?
BRAD: Yeah. It's a hotel with lots of small rooms. Actually, they're not really rooms. They're spaces that are two meters by one meter, and only a meter high. In other words, they're very cramped! But the hotel is cheap and very convenient.
HOST: And what's inside each little room, or should I say, each *space*?
BRAD: Well, inside every capsule there's a bed, a TV, a reading light, a radio, and an alarm clock. The hotel also has lockers, where you can keep your personal belongings.
HOST: That's great. And what kind of people stay in a capsule hotel?
BRAD: Well, probably people like me. People who miss the last train home or don't want to go all the way home only to turn around and come back to work again. So, it gets pretty busy, as you can imagine.
HOST: Finally, would you recommend a capsule hotel to other people?
BRAD: Sure! The rooms are small, but you get used to sleeping in a small space. I just wouldn't recommend a capsule hotel to people who can't relax in small, cramped spaces.

B Listen again. In addition to a bed, what else does the hotel provide? Write four things.

8 CONVERSATION [p. 19]

B Listen to the rest of the conversation. What changes would Brian like to make in his life?

BRIAN: Yeah! It's sometimes pretty hard to pay the rent. I'm thinking about changing jobs.
TERRY: What kind of job would you like to look for?
BRIAN: I'm not sure, but I wish I worked somewhere else. I'm sick of this place. I need to live somewhere more exciting.
TERRY: I know what you mean. Hey, maybe we could move to another city. We could even be roommates!
BRIAN: Yeah. Uhh. Maybe . . .

4 I've never heard of that!

2 CONVERSATION [p. 22]

B Listen to the rest of the conversation. How did Steve like the fried brains? What else did he order?

KATHY: Oh, good! Here comes the waiter now!
WAITER: Here are your snails. And for you, sir . . . the fried brains.
STEVE: Thank you.
KATHY: Mmm, these snails are delicious! How are the brains?
STEVE: Well, I think they're . . . yuck! Oh, sorry, I guess brains are too strange for me. Um, I think I'm going to order something else, if you don't mind.
KATHY: Oh, sure. Go ahead.
STEVE: Excuse me, waiter!
WAITER: Yes?
STEVE: Uh, I really don't care for this appetizer. Could you bring me something else?
WAITER: Yes, of course. What would you like instead?
KATHY: Try the snails.
STEVE: No, I don't think so. I'll tell you what. Just forget an appetizer for me, and bring me a nice, juicy hamburger . . . medium rare . . . with french fries and a large soda.

5 LISTENING [p. 23]

Listen to six people ask questions about food and drink in a restaurant. Check the item that each person is talking about.

1.
WOMAN: Have you finished with this?
MAN: No, I'm still drinking it. Thanks.

2.
MAN: Did you order this?
WOMAN: Yes, that's mine. Mmm, it looks great and smells delicious!

3.
MAN: Don't you like it?
WOMAN: I haven't tasted it yet. I'm waiting for the waitress to bring me a fork.

4.
MAN: Did you enjoy it?
WOMAN: Well, it was a little tough. I think it was cooked for too long.

5.
WOMAN: How is it?
MAN: Great. Just the way I like it: black and strong.

6.
MAN 1: Your turn or mine?
MAN 2: It's my treat this time. You paid last time. Remember?

11 LISTENING [p. 26]

A Listen to people explain how to make these snacks. Which snack are they talking about? Number the photos from 1 to 4.

1.
WOMAN: I love to eat this at the movies. Sometimes, I even make it myself at home. It's really easy. First, you put a little oil in a pan. Then heat the oil. When the oil's hot – but not too hot – put in the kernels. Next, when you see they're starting to pop, cover the pan. Shake the pan a little until the noise stops. After that, pour it into a bowl. Finally, sprinkle a little salt over it and enjoy!

2.
MAN: Let me tell you how to make my favorite snack. It takes some time, but it's worth it. First, you take an avocado and mash it. Next, you chop half a tomato and half an onion and add them to the avocado. After that, you chop a little cilantro – you know, Chinese parsley – and put that in, too. Then, squeeze a lemon or a lime on top. Finally, sprinkle the mixture with a little salt, pepper, and of course, hot sauce. Mmm, it's great with chips!

3.
WOMAN: A friend from New York City taught me how to make this. First, cut it in half. Then toast it. After that, let it cool a little and then spread cream cheese on it. It's really good for breakfast, but you can eat it any time.

4.
MAN: Some people buy the frozen kind at the supermarket, but I like to make my own. You need dough, olive oil, sauce, and cheese – lots of cheese. First, you roll out the dough into a circle and rub a little oil on it. Then put the dough into the oven and bake for a few minutes. Next, spoon a little sauce over the dough. After that, cover the sauce with grated cheese. Then put it back into the oven and bake for another ten minutes, or until the cheese melts. Finally, cut it into slices. You'll love it!

Units 3–4 Progress check

2 LISTENING [p. 28]

A Listen to three people talk about things they wish they could change. Check the topic each person is talking about.

1.
WOMAN: I get really bored on weekends. I wish I belonged to a club or sports team. If I belonged to a club, I'd have something to do. And I'd probably get to meet new people and make new friends.

2.
MAN: I wish I could type better. I should take a typing course this summer. I really need it for my schoolwork. And people say that if you can type really well, it's something you'll find useful later in life.

3.
WOMAN: Gosh, I really have to go on a diet. I've gained ten pounds since last year, and everyone tells me I look fat. If I don't lose weight now, I won't be able to get into any of my summer clothes. I wish I didn't like desserts so much!

B Listen again. Write one change each person would like to make.

5 Going places

2 CONVERSATION [p. 30]

B Listen to the rest of the conversation. Where are they going to stay? How will they get there?

JULIA: That's great! The more the merrier!
NANCY: By the way, where are we going to stay?
JULIA: Oh. We can stay at my aunt and uncle's beach house. They have plenty of room and I'm sure they'll be happy to have guests. I'll call them tonight to let them know what time we're going to arrive. I guess we'll leave pretty early. There's a direct bus every morning at 5:00 A.M.
NANCY: That's fine with me. I think I'll be too excited to sleep!
JULIA: I know! And the best thing is, we'll probably get there in time to spend a few hours at the beach after we get settled.

9 LISTENING [p. 34]

A Listen to an interview with a spokeswoman from the New York City Visitor's Center. Check the four topics she discusses.

INTERVIEWER: What should people do to make their visit to New York City safe and pleasant?
WOMAN: One important thing to remember is not to try to do too much in a short time. Ideally, you should start planning before you get here. You ought to decide in advance which sights you most want to see.
INTERVIEWER: Are there any good tours available?
WOMAN: Oh yes, lots. Several companies offer bus tours that stop at all the major tourist attractions. It's a good idea to buy a pass so you can get on and off wherever you like. You should visit our Web site to find out about the latest tours and special events.
INTERVIEWER: I see. And is New York a safe city for visitors?

WOMAN: It's safer than many cities in the world. But just like in any big city, you should still be careful. For example, don't go off on your own, especially at night. And don't be afraid to ask questions. Even American visitors have to ask for help when they come here. You'll find that New Yorkers are pretty friendly. They like welcoming visitors to their city and don't mind giving directions.

INTERVIEWER: One last thing – is it an expensive city to visit?

WOMAN: It can be, but there are plenty of cheap places in the city where you don't have to spend a fortune. If you're a student, you should bring your student ID card with you. That way, you can get a discount on entrance into museums and galleries. Oh! And never carry much money on you.

INTERVIEWER: Is there anything else you'd like to add?

WOMAN: Yeah, just that most people have a great time when they come to New York. And I'm sure you will, too!

B Listen again. For each topic, write one piece of advice she gives.

6 OK. No problem!

2 *CONVERSATION [p. 36]*

B Listen to the rest of the conversation. What complaints do Jason and Lisa have about their parents?

JASON: Have you noticed how forgetful Dad is getting? He's always forgetting where his car keys are. It drives me crazy.

LISA: And he can never find his glasses either.

JASON: I know.

LISA: You know what drives me crazy about Mom?

JASON: What?

LISA: Those awful talk shows she watches on TV. She just loves them.

JASON: Yeah, I think she watches them for hours every day.

LISA: Oh, well. I guess they're just getting old. I hope I never get like that.

JASON: Me, too. Hey, let's go and play a video game.

LISA: Great idea. By the way, have you seen my glasses anywhere?

6 *LISTENING [p. 38]*

A Listen to the results of a survey about family life. For each question, write men, women, boys, or girls.

JENNIFER: Welcome to this week's program, *Do Men Have it Easy?*, where we'll take a look at the roles and responsibilities of men and women in families. First, thanks to all of you who responded to our survey. John?

JOHN: Thanks, Jennifer. Later on in the program, we'll be taking your phone calls and talking to Dr. Walters, a family psychologist, who will answer your questions. And now for the results of the survey. Jennifer?

JENNIFER: Well, in response to the first question, "Who is the messiest person in the house?" the answer was boys! Ninety-two percent of you said that your sons or brothers don't help much around the house. They don't pick up their things, don't hang up their clothes, and leave their clothes lying around.

JOHN: Interesting. And what about the second question, Jennifer? That was, "Who does most of the work in the kitchen?"

JENNIFER: Well, 84 percent of you answered women. Many of you also explained that the boys and men usually take out the garbage. The girls and women tend to cook, do the dishes, and clean up.

JOHN: And what about the groceries, Jennifer?

JENNIFER: Well, according to our results, boys and girls usually put the groceries away.

JOHN: That's surprising. So what else do the women do?

JENNIFER: Ah, well, that's our next question, "Who worries most about expenses?" In the majority of homes, it seems that women worry most about household expenses. One young man wrote to us saying, "My mother always nags me and my sister. She tells us to get off the phone, to stop spending so long on the computer, to turn off the TV, well, everything really. I always thought she just liked to nag, but maybe she's really worried about money." I think that's probably true, don't you, John?

JOHN: Yes, very interesting. And now I'd like to introduce Dr. Walters. . . .

B Listen again. According to the survey, what specific chores do men, women, boys, and girls usually do? Take notes.

Units 5-6 Progress check

1 *LISTENING [p. 42]*

A Listen to Judy, Paul, and Brenda describe their summer plans. What is each person going to do?

1. Judy

MAN: So, what are you planning to do on your vacation, Judy?

JUDY: Oh, I'm going to do something different this year. I went to Hawaii last year and just relaxed on the beach for two weeks. This year, I'm going white-water rafting!

MAN: Ooh, that sounds fun. But what is that, exactly?

JUDY: Oh, well, they have these trips down the rapids. The water gets really rough, but I think it'll be really exciting. Oh, I'm doing some mountain climbing, too.

MAN: And you call that a vacation?

2. Paul

WOMAN: What are your plans for the summer, Paul?

PAUL: Oh, I'd love to go and lie on a beach somewhere, but I need to save some money for school. I think I'll stay home and get a job.

WOMAN: That doesn't sound like much fun.

PAUL: Oh, it won't be so bad. Some of my friends are going to work this summer, too, so we'll have a good time on the weekends.

3. Brenda

MAN: Have you planned anything for the summer, Brenda?

BRENDA: Yeah. I'm going to work the first month and save some money. Then I'm going to Mexico to visit my sister. She's working in Guadalajara. She says it's really interesting there, so I want to see what it's like. I'm really looking forward to it!

B Listen again. What is the reason for each person's choice?

7 What's this for?

6 *LISTENING* *[p. 46]*

A Guess the answers to the questions below. Then listen to a radio program about the Internet and check your answers.

HOST: We've all heard stories about how Internet use is growing. Today, however, we're talking with someone who has studied people who *don't* use the Internet. Let's welcome Dr. Tom Van Cleeve to the program.
DR. VAN CLEEVE: Thank you. It's nice to be here.
HOST: Thanks for coming. Now I understand that many people still don't use the Internet. Is that right? What can you tell us?
DR. VAN CLEEVE: That's right. My research has revealed that about 42 percent of the population never uses the Internet.
HOST: Forty-two percent! That's pretty high. And why is that?
DR. VAN CLEEVE: Well, they tend to be older people or people living in more rural areas. But there are also those who are worried about privacy, or who think that the Internet isn't necessary in their life. Some of these people are even proud to be independent from the online world.
HOST: Interesting.

B Listen to the rest of the program. Then answer these questions.

HOST: In your new book, you mention "net evaders." Can you explain what you mean by this?
DR. VAN CLEEVE: Well, lots of people live with someone who surfs the net, but they still don't log on themselves. I call this group the net evaders. What I found in talking to these people is that they sometimes ask a family member to send e-mails for them or to browse Web sites, but they don't want to do it themselves.
HOST: I know someone like that! [*laughs*]
DR. VAN CLEEVE: Yes, and then there's another group of people I call "Internet dropouts."
HOST: Internet dropouts. What exactly does it mean?
DR. VAN CLEEVE: It refers to people who once used the Internet, but have stopped using it for some reason. They may not have a computer anymore, may not have enough time, or simply may not be interested.
HOST: I see. Well, thanks very much for sharing that information with us, Dr. Van Cleeve.

7 *CONVERSATION* *[p. 47]*

B Listen to the rest of the conversation. Who does Jenny want to call next?

JENNY: That was fun! Let's call somebody else.
RICHARD: Is there anyone you need to call?
JENNY: Well, not really, but I'd like to see if there are any messages on my answering machine at home. Can you show me how to check?
RICHARD: I don't think I have that many minutes left.

9 *SPEAKING* *[p. 48]*

A Listen to people give advice about three of the things below. Write the name of each item in the chart.

1.
MAN: It's best to use a stand when you're filming with this. If you hold it by hand, the picture is often not very steady. Be careful when you put in the battery: If you push too hard, you can actually do some damage.

2.
WOMAN: Remember to wear protective gear whenever you use them. You can easily fall and hurt yourself. And make sure to skate on a flat surface, such as a parking lot, a tennis court, or a basketball court.

3.
MAN: Be sure to put it in correctly. Then punch in your secret code. Remember to press "enter." And don't forget to count your money before you walk away from the machine.

B Listen again. Complete the chart. Then compare with a partner.

8 Let's celebrate!

5 *LISTENING* *[p. 52]*

A Mike has just returned from Brazil. Listen to him talk about Carnaval. What did he enjoy most about it?

MIKE: Isn't that music fantastic? It's from a samba CD that I got when I was in Rio for Carnaval. Wow! Carnaval in Rio is really something! It's a party that lasts for four whole days. It's held in late February or early March, but you need to book a hotel room way in advance because hotels fill up really quickly. Carnaval is celebrated all over Brazil, but the most famous party is in Rio. The whole city is decorated with colored lights and streamers. It's really beautiful. Everyone is very friendly – especially to visitors from other countries. The best part about Carnaval is the big parade. The costumes are unbelievable – people work on them for months. It's really fantastic to watch. Everyone dances the samba in the streets. I'd really recommend you go to Rio for Carnaval if you ever have the chance.

B Listen again and answer these questions.

8 *CONVERSATION* *[p. 53]*

B Listen to the rest of the conversation. What did the bride and groom give each guest?

JILL: I'm curious. What did you and your husband give everyone?
EMIKO: Well, sugar is a symbol of happiness in Japan. So we gave each guest a ceramic box filled with sweets.
JILL: What a nice custom. It sounds like it was a wonderful day!
EMIKO: Oh, it really was . . .

Units 7–8 Progress check

4 *LISTENING* *[p. 57]*

A Listen to some information about unusual marriage customs. Check True or False for each statement.

1.
MAN: You know, this book about unusual marriage customs is really interesting.
WOMAN: Oh, yeah?
MAN: Yeah. Listen to this. It talks about this Indian tribe in Paraguay.
WOMAN: Uh-huh.
MAN: When two women in the tribe want to marry the same man, guess what they do.
WOMAN: I have no idea. What?
MAN: They have a boxing match and fight until one of them wins.

WOMAN: And the prize is the husband?
MAN: Of course!

2.
WOMAN: Huh. Does the book say anything about Malaysia?
MAN: Um. I don't know. Why?
WOMAN: Well, when people get married in Malaysia, they have to eat rice during the ceremony.
MAN: Yeah? What's so strange about that?
WOMAN: It's *uncooked* rice.
MAN: Hmm.

3.
MAN: Oh, here's another one. Don't laugh, but I think this is really romantic!
WOMAN: You think something is romantic? What is it?
MAN: In Italy, a friend or family member often brings a pair of white doves to the wedding. After the ceremony, the cage is opened and the doves fly into the air. The birds symbolize the couple's love and happiness.
WOMAN: You're right. That is romantic.

4.
MAN: And here's an interesting custom from India.
WOMAN: Let's hear it.
MAN: There's a special Hindu "water-pouring" ceremony during the wedding.
WOMAN: And what happens?
MAN: Well, when the Indian bride and groom are married, someone pours water all over both of them.
WOMAN: Why do they do that?
MAN: Uh, it says here that it brings the couple closer together.
WOMAN: Interesting.

B Listen again. Correct the statements that you marked false.

9 Back to the future

2 CONVERSATION [p. 58]

B Listen to the rest of the conversation. What else has changed in their neighborhood?

MATT: Well, what about that old bookstore? Do you know if it's still there?
TANYA: No, it's not. Now it's a pizzeria.
MATT: Really? Let's go check it out. All this talk about change is making me hungry!

5 LISTENING [p. 60]

A Listen to people discuss changes. Check the topic each person talks about.

1.
MAN: How long have you been living here?
WOMAN: Oh, for over 20 years.
MAN: And have you noticed a lot of changes during that time?
WOMAN: Oh, yes, quite a few. This is a much nicer place to live now than it used to be. It's much greener. When I first moved here, there weren't many trees around. But over the last few years, the city has planted trees everywhere. It's made such a difference.

2.
WOMAN: How do you like living here?
MAN: Well, it's an interesting city. But you really need a car here; otherwise, you can't go anywhere. There used to be a good bus system, but there isn't anymore.
WOMAN: Why is that?
MAN: Oh, I think they expect everyone to have a car, so they don't bother to provide decent bus service. It's getting worse and worse. These days, you have to wait for ages for a bus. And when one finally shows up, it's usually full!

3.
WOMAN 1: I can't believe how much this neighborhood has changed!
WOMAN 2: What do you mean?
WOMAN 1: Well, when Joe and I first bought this house – that was almost 20 years ago, of course – there were lots of young couples with children living on this street.
WOMAN 2: I don't see any kids out today.
WOMAN 1: That's because they've all grown up and moved out of their parents' houses. Just about the only young children we see around here these days are the grandchildren when they come to visit. It's a shame. I miss the sounds of kids playing. It's gotten way too quiet around here!

B Listen again. Write down the change and if things are better or worse now.

10 I don't like working on weekends!

2 CONVERSATION [p. 64]

B Listen to Brad call about the job. What else does the job require?

WOMAN: Holiday Cruise Lines.
BRAD: Hello. I'm calling about the assistant entertainment director job that's advertised online. Is it still available?
WOMAN: Yes, it is. There's just one thing we didn't mention in the advertisement. Do you speak any other languages?
BRAD: No, not really. . . .
WOMAN: Oh. We're really looking for someone who can speak at least one other language. We probably should have included that in the ad. I'm sorry.

5 LISTENING [p. 66]

A Listen to people talk about the kind of work they are looking for. Check the job that would be best for each person.

1. Bill
WOMAN: So what kind of job are you looking for?
BILL: Well, I haven't made up my mind. I love working with people, and I love traveling. I don't want a job where I'm stuck in an office all day. I want to get out and see the world.
WOMAN: Are you interested in working in business? That's where you can sometimes make good money.
BILL: I'm not really interested in making a lot of money at this point in my life. I'll worry about that later.

2. Shannon
WOMAN: What kind of career are you planning for yourself?
SHANNON: I don't know. I think I'd like to have a job where I can help people. Everybody else in my family is in law or business – you know, boring stuff like that. That's just not for me. I know I'd like to work overseas, though. Maybe in a children's hospital in a developing country. But that's a long way away. I have to get into medical school first, and that's not going to be easy!

3. Ben
BEN: What kind of job do I have in mind? Well, I don't want a regular nine-to-five job. Eventually, I'd like to get into acting – maybe even break into movies. But I guess that won't happen for a while.
WOMAN: So what are you doing in the meantime?
BEN: Well, I work out at the gym nearly every day. I need to be really fit. And I'm taking acting lessons as well so that I feel comfortable in front of the crowd. I just had some pictures taken to show to agents in the city. Would you like to see them?
WOMAN: Sure.

B Listen again. Answer these questions.

8 *WORD POWER* *[p. 67]*

C Listen to four conversations. Then check the adjective that best describes each person.

1. A boss
WOMAN: How do you like your new boss?
MAN: She's OK. I just wish she'd learn to lighten up a little.
WOMAN: What do you mean?
MAN: Oh, she never enjoys a joke. She never laughs. It's hard to even get a smile out of her.

2. A co-worker
MAN: Look what Mary gave me! Isn't this a great book?
WOMAN: Yeah, it is! Mary's so sweet – she's always giving her friends and co-workers presents. I wish there were more people like her in this world!

3. A teacher
WOMAN: What do you think of the new French teacher?
MAN: Well, she's kind of strange. She's in a good mood one minute and in a terrible mood the next.

4. A relative
MAN: Hey, what's wrong?
WOMAN: I'm fed up with my brother! It seems as if he's always angry at me about something.
MAN: Really?
WOMAN: Yeah. He gets upset so easily. I don't know what's the matter with him.

Units 9–10 Progress check

3 *LISTENING* *[p. 71]*

A Listen to Louisa and Tim discuss four jobs. Write down the jobs and check if they would be good or bad at them.

1. Louisa
TIM: I don't know what classes to take this semester. I can't decide what I want to do with my life. Have you thought about it, Louisa?
LOUISA: A little bit. My history professor says I should think about a career in politics. But I don't think I'd make a good politician.
TIM: Why not?
LOUISA: Oh, you know me. I'm not good at working with other people. I'm too moody. And politicians have to work with people all the time.
TIM: That's true. So what do you think you want to do?
LOUISA: Well, honestly. I think I'd make a good architect.
TIM: Oh, you would! You're so creative.
LOUISA: And I love drawing and, I don't know, making things. Plus, then I'd get to work alone a lot.

2. Tim
TIM: That reminds me of a problem I'm having.
LOUISA: What is it?
TIM: You know my parents have a restaurant, right? Well, my father wants me to be the manager.
LOUISA: And you don't want to?
TIM: No way. Restaurant managers have to manage other people. I'd be terrible. I'm too disorganized.
LOUISA: So, what do *you* want to do?
TIM: Well, I think I could be a good teacher. I like working with kids and I'm pretty patient.
LOUISA: That's true. And you're very hardworking.

B Listen again. What reasons do they give?

11 It's really worth seeing!

2 *PERSPECTIVES* *[p. 72]*

B Now listen and check your answers. What information is the most surprising?

WOMAN: The history of the Empire State Building is filled with many interesting facts and figures. It was designed by American architect William Lamb to become the tallest building in the world. Construction began in March 1930, and by October of that same year, 88 floors were already finished! In 1931, after 14 months and 25 million dollars, the building's 102 floors were officially opened by U.S. President Herbert Hoover. While it is no longer the world's tallest building, it is still recognized as a symbol of New York City and is visited by people from all over the world. It has even been featured in some of Hollywood's biggest films, including *King Kong* and *Sleepless in Seattle*.

6 *LISTENING* *[p. 74]*

Listen to three tour guides describe some very old monuments. Take notes to answer the questions below. Then compare with a partner.

1. The Pyramids. Who built them? Why were they built?
MAN: The Pyramids were built more than 4,000 years ago by the Egyptians. The most famous ones are on the west bank of the river Nile, outside of Cairo. They served as burial places for the Egyptian kings. After a king's death, his body was turned into what is called a "mummy." This preserved it. The king's mummy was placed inside the pyramid, together with treasures and the king's belongings.

2. Machu Picchu. How big is the city? When was it discovered?
WOMAN: Machu Picchu is an ancient Inca city in Peru. Construction of the city started in 1450. The ruins are about 2,400 meters above sea level – that's about 7,800 feet. The city covers about 13 square kilometers – that's about 5 square miles. For centuries, the city was buried in the jungle and wasn't discovered again until 1911. Today, Machu Picchu is one of the most famous tourist attractions in all of South America.

3. The Great Wall of China. Why was it built? How long is it?
MAN: The Great Wall of China is the longest man-made structure ever built. It was built to protect one of the Chinese kingdoms. Much of what exists of the wall today was built during the Ming Dynasty in the late 1400s, although parts of the wall are much older and go back to around 200 B.C. The wall is

about 35 feet high, or 11 meters, and a stone roadway runs along the top of it. The main part of the wall stretches for about 2,000 miles, that is, about 3,400 kilometers.

10 LISTENING [p. 76]

A Listen to a short talk about Colombia. Complete the chart.

MAN: Colombia is located in the northwestern part of South America and is the fourth-largest country in South America. It has coastlines on both the Atlantic and the Pacific oceans. It has a population of around 36 million and is a very beautiful country with snow-capped mountains as well as hot lowland plains. The capital city is Bogotá, which was founded by the Spaniards in 1538. Almost all Colombians speak Spanish, which is the country's official language. The religion of the majority of the population is Roman Catholic. Some of the most important industries are textiles and clothing. Other industries include mining and oil. Agriculture is the most important section of the economy, and Colombia's main agricultural products are coffee, flowers, sugar, bananas, rice, corn, and cotton. Colombia produces more coffee than any other country except Brazil.

B Listen again. Check the things the speaker mentions about Colombia.

12 It could happen to you!

4 LISTENING [p. 80]

A Listen to these stories about lucky breaks. What were the people doing before they got their lucky breaks? What was their lucky break?

1. Yang Zhifa

MAN: Thirty years ago, Yang Zhifa was just an ordinary Chinese farmer. He was living off the land and was very poor. Today he is recognized as the man who discovered a highly important archaeological site, sometimes called the "Eighth Wonder of the World." What happened?

One morning in March 1974, Zhifa and some other local farmers were looking for water. As they were drilling a well, they hit something hard. They found pieces of pottery and ancient weapons. Immediately, the head of the village reported the news to the local government, and in May 1976, the digging began. To everyone's surprise, there were over 8,000 soldiers made of terracotta lying underneath his land. The soldiers were over 2,000 years old, and had been buried along with the Emperor Qin, who wanted to take an army with him to his next life.

Today Yang Zhifa spends much of his time at the Terracotta Army museum. He sits, poses for pictures, and proudly signs autographs for the millions of tourists who visit from all over the world.

2. Gwyneth Paltrow

WOMAN: You could say that actress Gwyneth Paltrow was born lucky. After all, she is the daughter of two well-known talents. Her mother is an actress and her father was a writer, producer, and director. But like all people wanting to break into movies, she had to go to drama school and learn how to act. Today Gwyneth Paltrow is a successful international actress, and has even won an Oscar award. So how did it all begin?

According to Ms. Paltrow, her lucky break came when she was 18 years old. She was at a movie theater with her parents. While they were waiting in line to buy some popcorn, she noticed that Steven Spielberg was also in line. She was just about to order when he came over to her and said, "Hey, can I ask you a favor? Would you play Wendy in the movie *Hook*?" "Sure," she said, and so she got her first movie role.

B Listen again. How did the events change their lives?

7 CONVERSATION [p. 81]

B Listen to two other people at the party. What has happened since they last saw each other?

MAGGIE: Hey, Bob, how's it going?
BOB: Pretty good, thanks.
MAGGIE: I haven't seen you for a while. What have you been up to?
BOB: Well, I've been looking for a house to buy. I finally found one last month.
MAGGIE: That's terrific!
BOB: Yeah. I'm really tired of renting. So what have you been doing lately?
MAGGIE: Well, I just got back from a vacation in Italy.
BOB: Italy? Where in Italy?
MAGGIE: Mostly in the north, around Milan. I have a cousin there.
BOB: I see. Did you have a good time?
MAGGIE: Yeah. It was great. In fact, I just got engaged to a guy I met there.
BOB: You're kidding! Well, that must have been some vacation!

Units 11–12 Progress check

2 LISTENING [p. 84]

A Listen to people on a game show answer questions about Spain. What are the answers? Complete the chart.

HOST: Welcome to today's show! The rules of the game are simple: I will ask a question, and the first contestant to hit the buzzer gets to answer that question. Each correct answer is worth $100. Today's topic is "Spain." Are you ready, contestants? The first question, for $100, is: What currency is used in Spain? [*buzzer*] Contestant A!
WOMAN 1: The euro.
HOST: That's right, Contestant A. Spain used to use the *peseta*, but now they use the euro. And now for the next question: How many countries are next to Spain and what are they? [*buzzer*] Contestant A!
WOMAN 1: Spain is bordered by two countries: France and Portugal.
HOST: Correct! You're doing very well, Contestant A! Maybe our other contestants can catch up on our next question: What is the capital of Spain? [*buzzer*] Contestant B!
MAN: The capital is Madrid.
HOST: You're right, Contestant B. The capital is Madrid. Excellent. Let's see how you do with our next question: What is one of the most popular sports in Spain? [*buzzer*] Yes, Contestant C!
WOMAN 2: Um . . . um . . . hockey?
HOST: No, I'm sorry. Anyone else know the answer? [*buzzer*] Contestant A!
WOMAN 1: That would be bullfighting.
HOST: That's right. OK. There are only two questions left. Let's go, players! Next question: Spain is an

agricultural country. What are two of the main crops? [*buzzer*] Contestant C!

WOMAN 2: Olives and, uh, wheat?

HOST: Good for you! Olives and wheat are both grown in Spain. We only have one more question left, contestants. May I remind you that the winner of this round will be back here tomorrow for the championship playoff? And now for our last question: What are two of the main industries in Spain? [*buzzer*] Contestant B!

MAN: I think textiles and automobiles are made in Spain.

HOST: Yes! That's correct. Spain manufactures both textiles and automobiles. So, contestants, let's look at your scores. Contestant A, you answered . . .

B Listen again. Keep score. How much money does each contestant have?

13 Good book, terrible movie!

2 CONVERSATION [p. 86]

B Listen to the rest of the conversation. What happens next? What do they decide to do?

CAROL: Yeah. Her last movie was especially good. It's probably one of my favorites of all time.

ROGER: Actually, I didn't see that, but I heard it was just OK.

CAROL: Well, I'll call the theater and find out what time the movie starts. Hello. Could you tell me what time the new Halle Berry movie is playing tonight? Oh, really? Oh, OK. Thanks. You won't believe this. It's not showing anymore. It just finished playing last night!

ROGER: Oh, no!

CAROL: I guess we're back where we started! Why don't we just see what's on TV tonight?

ROGER: That's fine with me.

5 LISTENING [p. 88]

A Listen to people talk about books and movies. Do you think each person would recommend the book or movie?

1.

MAN: What did you think of the new Stephen King book?

WOMAN: Oh! Once I got started, I couldn't stop reading. I stayed up till 4:00 in the morning to finish it!

MAN: And wasn't the ending great?

WOMAN: Yeah, it really was! Such a surprise! And the whole story moved along so fast, too!

2.

WOMAN: How did you like the movie?

MAN: Well, I walked out after half an hour.

WOMAN: You did?

MAN: Yeah, it was so dull that I started falling asleep! And I've never seen such bad acting from Jim Carrey!

WOMAN: Oh, really? He's usually pretty good.

MAN: Well, not in this movie. I wish he'd choose better roles.

3.

MAN 1: What did you think of that documentary about Australia?

MAN 2: I learned so much! I didn't know they had so many different kinds of animals there. And the photography!

MAN 1: Yeah, it was something, wasn't it?

MAN 2: Uh-huh, it was pretty amazing. It made me really want to go there and see it for myself.

4.

WOMAN 1: Have you read that book that just came out about UFOs?

WOMAN 2: Yeah. What a waste of time! Just the same silly stuff about visitors to Earth from other planets.

WOMAN 1: Uh-huh. It said absolutely nothing new.

WOMAN 2: You know, I'm sick of hearing stories about little green creatures. If they're real, how come no one can ever take a picture of them?

B Listen again. Check the adjective that best describes what they say about each one.

8 PERSPECTIVES [p. 89]

B Now listen and check your answers.

WOMAN 1: Oh! Leonardo Di Caprio is also in it. He was the best part of the movie *Titanic*!

MAN: But I think my favorite Tom Hanks movie is probably *Castaway*. He really should have won another Oscar that year.

WOMAN 2: I remember laughing so hard the first time I saw *Home Alone*! I even went out and bought the DVD.

12 LISTENING [p. 90]

A Listen to two critics talk about a new movie. What do they like or not like about it? Rate each item in the chart from 1 to 3.

PAULINE: Welcome to *A Night at the Movies*! I'm Pauline Kahn. . . .

COLIN: And I'm Colin Hale. Good evening!

PAULINE: Tonight we're going to review the new James Bond film. Well, I really liked this new James Bond actor very, very much!

COLIN: Mm-hmm.

PAULINE: He's the best actor that's ever had the role – warm, human, even funny. A totally believable character.

COLIN: I have to agree, a perfect 007 type. Pauline, what did you think of the story?

PAULINE: It was a standard story for a Bond movie . . . uh, the usual beautiful women, the usual evil villain – nothing new.

COLIN: Well, I'm surprised. I have to say that I thought the story was unusually good. The racecar scenes were exciting, and the surprise ending was great.

PAULINE: Well, I can't agree with you there.

COLIN: Really? What did you think about the photography?

PAULINE: I wasn't very impressed at all by the photography. Everything looked fake, not real. I can't believe it was actually filmed in Africa, where the story took place.

COLIN: I can't believe you! I haven't seen such good photography in a long time, especially in the action scenes.

PAULINE: Now that brings up another weakness in the film: the special effects. Again, it's just the same old stuff . . . the car that flies, the pen that's really a gun. You get tired of that kind of thing.

COLIN: I'd hardly think you and I saw the same movie, Pauline. I have to say that the special effects were the best ever in a Bond film. For example, the scene where –

PAULINE: Excuse me, Colin. We're going to have to break for a commercial.

COLIN: You're right, Pauline. We'll be right back with our ratings.

B Look at the chart in part A. Guess how many stars each critic gave the movie. Then listen to the critics give their ratings.

PAULINE: So, Colin, how do you rate the new James Bond movie that we've reviewed this week?
COLIN: Well, Pauline, I'd have to say that I'm proud to give this movie my highest rating . . . four stars . . . and I would like to encourage everyone to go and see it soon! How about you, Pauline? You did like the new actor who plays James Bond.
PAULINE: That part's true, Colin; however, I have to give the movie only two stars . . . a rating of "fair."
COLIN: Hmm. Well, that's all from us tonight. See you next week.

14 So that's what it means!

3 CONVERSATION [p. 93]

B Now listen to Raj talk to his friend. What does he find unusual about the way people in North America communicate?

FREDDY: So how are things at school, Raj?
RAJ: Oh, pretty good, actually.
FREDDY: Do you find it easy to communicate with people?
RAJ: Most of the time – though there are some things I find a bit unusual – for example, the way that people end a conversation. You know, they'll say things like, "Hey, let's get together soon." At first, I thought that they were inviting me to do something, but then I realized it's just a way of saying good-bye. It's not really an invitation at all. It takes a bit of getting used to.

11 LISTENING [p. 96]

A Listen to three conversations about driving. Check True or False for each statement.

1.
MAN: Oh no. Not another parking ticket. That's the second one this week. Why did I get a ticket for parking here? I thought this was a free parking zone.
WOMAN: Maybe you can only park here after working hours. Is there a sign around anywhere?
MAN: Oh, you're right. There's one over there. I didn't even notice it. Looks like you can't park here till after 6:00 P.M.
WOMAN: How much is the fine?
MAN: Would you believe it! $60!

2.
WOMAN: I wonder why that traffic officer is signaling me?
MAN: Perhaps he means you're driving too fast.
WOMAN: No, I don't think so. The speed limit is 60 and I'm only going 55.
MAN: Hmm. I wonder why there are no other cars in this lane.
WOMAN: What do you mean?
MAN: Well, you see how the other cars are all in the lane next to us.
WOMAN: You're right. I think this one is just for buses and taxis. They really should put up better signs around here.

3.
MAN: That's weird. The last few cars driving toward us were flashing their lights.
WOMAN: I see what you mean. There's another one.
MAN: Maybe my lights are on or something. Let me check. No, they're off.
WOMAN: Do you think there's an accident up ahead? Maybe you'd better slow down.
MAN: Oh, now I see what's happening. There's a patrol car up ahead checking people's speed. How nice of those other drivers to let me know! Well, I'm within the speed limit – at least I am now!

B Listen again. Which drivers did something wrong?

Units 13-14 Progress check

3 LISTENING [p. 99]

A Listen to some people talking. Write what each person is talking about.

1.
MAN: Gee, that road sign looks kind of strange to me. I wonder what it means. Perhaps it means the road gets slippery when it's wet. Or it might mean that a lot of animals cross this road.

2.
WOMAN: Uh! That's the last time I'll watch one of his movies. It started out OK, but the ending was terrible! The last scene could mean they stay together. But it may also mean they never see each other again. I can't stand when directors leave the ending so open!

3.
MAN: Wow! That lecture really made me think. Everything the professor said makes sense. I could never understand Greek philosophy before, but he made it all so clear! Maybe this means I should change my major to philosophy!

4.
WOMAN: I can't believe how many rules they have at this pool. They look through all your bags to make sure you don't have any food or glass containers. I guess that probably means a lot of people try to bring those things in. All I wanted was to go for a swim! Uh!

B Listen again. What does each person mean? Check the best answer.

15 What would you do?

2 CONVERSATION [p. 100]

B Listen to the rest of the conversation. What would Phil do if he found $750,000?

PAT: So, what would you do if you found $750,000?
PHIL: Oh, you know me, Pat. I'm so honest, I scare myself sometimes. I'd take the money straight to the police.
PAT: I guess that wouldn't be such a bad idea. Maybe you'd be luckier than the guy in the article. Maybe the owner of the money would give you a big reward.
PHIL: Well, they say honesty pays. Right?

4 LISTENING [p. 101]

A Listen to three people talk about predicaments. Number them in the order they are discussed.

1.

JANE: I just got a postcard from my friend Kari. She lost all her money on vacation in Europe. Isn't that horrible?

BURT: Yeah, that's terrible.

SUSAN: Jane, what would you do if you were on vacation overseas and you lost all your money and credit cards?

JANE: I guess I'd call my parents and ask them to send me some money right away. What about you, Burt?

BURT: Yeah, I'd probably do the same thing . . . although maybe I'd try going to the American Express office to see if I could get a loan or something. What about you, Susan?

SUSAN: Well, I guess I'd probably sell my watch and camera . . . or I might get a job as a waitress somewhere till I made enough money to buy a plane ticket home.

2.

BURT: You know, I'm really worried about Carol.

SUSAN: Why?

BURT: Well, I think she has a serious shopping problem.

JANE: Really?

BURT: Yes, she keeps buying things and putting everything on her credit card. I don't think she realizes how hard it's going to be to pay all the money back. I don't know what to do. What would you do if you discovered a friend had major financial problems?

JANE: Oh, no question. I . . . I'd talk to her about it.

BURT: Oh, I don't think I would.

JANE: Why not?

BURT: Well, because it's really none of my business. I wouldn't tell a friend what to do in that type of situation . . . so I wouldn't say or do anything about it.

SUSAN: Well, I think I'd probably talk to her family about it. It's a personal problem, and they should try to help her first.

3.

SUSAN: You know, I was faced with a tough situation the other day. I was walking down the street and saw two people fighting. It looked pretty violent, but I didn't know what to do. So I just walked away. I figured it was none of my business. But now, I think I should have done something. What would you do if you saw two people fighting on the street?

JANE: I'm not really sure, but I know I'd have to do something. I guess I would call the police.

BURT: No, that takes too long. I'd try to break it up.

JANE: But you could get hurt if you did that.

BURT: Well, then I'd try to get someone to help me break it up. In the meantime, I'd shout for someone to call the police.

B Listen again. What suggestions do the people give for each predicament? Take notes. Which is the best suggestion?

10 *LISTENING [p. 104]*

A Listen to people calling Dr. Hilda, a counselor on a radio talk show. Complete the chart.

DR. HILDA: This is Dr. Hilda. Welcome to today's show. Now let's get started right away with our first caller. Hello!

CALLER 1: Hello, Dr. Hilda. I'm calling about my daughter. She's . . . she's dating an older man.

DR. HILDA: Oh. How old are these two people?

CALLER 1: My daughter's 18, and this man is 42.

DR. HILDA: Mm-hmm.

CALLER 1: I told her she had to stop seeing him, and . . . and now she won't speak to me. I feel terrible. Tell me, Dr. Hilda, what should I have done?

DR. HILDA: First, you should have spoken to this 42-year-old man. You should have asked him not to date your daughter for a couple of weeks – to give the situation some time to cool off. Then, if they still want to see each other and if the man seems like a nice person, you should let your daughter date him. You shouldn't worry so much about the age difference. OK, now let's go to our next caller. Hello, caller!

CALLER 2: Hello? Uh, I'm a first-time caller, and uh, well, my problem is that my father went away on a business trip, and I borrowed his brand-new car, and I had an accident.

DR. HILDA: Where is your mother?

CALLER 2: She's away, visiting some friends.

DR. HILDA: All right, go on.

CALLER 2: Well, I sent an e-mail to my father and I . . . I told him . . . well, I told him someone had stolen the car.

DR. HILDA: Oh! You should have told your father the truth! Your father would probably understand about a car accident, and he would be glad you weren't hurt.

CALLER 2: I'm not too sure about that!

DR. HILDA: Oh . . . give it a try, young man, because the truth is always better than a lie. OK, now let's hear from our next caller. This is Dr. Hilda. You're on the air.

CALLER 3: Hi, uh, I'm calling about a problem. Oh, it's kind of a personal problem . . . it concerns work.

DR. HILDA: Yes, go on.

CALLER 3: Well, uh, I invited some friends from the office to my house for a party a couple of weeks ago. Everything was fine until someone started talking about politics.

DR. HILDA: Oh! You shouldn't have let the subject of politics come up.

CALLER 3: Well, it came up, and, uh, well, I finally got really angry at one of my co-workers, and, uh, to prevent a fight, I asked him to leave.

DR. HILDA: And . . . what happened after that?

CALLER 3: Well, now it's caused a big problem in the office. Uh, he won't speak to me.

DR. HILDA: Again, you shouldn't have talked about politics at a party! It's not a safe topic.

CALLER 3: That's for sure.

DR. HILDA: And you shouldn't have gotten so angry either!

CALLER 3: That's true! But what should I do now?

DR. HILDA: You should apologize to your friend.

CALLER 3: Well, maybe that's a good idea. I'll give it a try.

DR. HILDA: Good! Well, folks, that's another show. I'm Dr. Hilda . . . until the next time.

B Listen again. According to Dr. Hilda, what should each caller have done?

16 What's your excuse?

7 *LISTENING [p. 109]*

A Listen to Albert inviting friends to his party on Saturday. What excuses do people give for not coming? Match the person to the excuse.

1. Scott

SCOTT: Hello?

ALBERT: Hi, Scott! This is Albert. How are things?
SCOTT: Oh, hi, Albert.
ALBERT: Um, you know, it's my birthday on Saturday, and I thought maybe you'd like to come to my party.
SCOTT: Oh, I really wish I could, but I won't be around this weekend. I'm leaving Friday night and won't get back till Sunday afternoon.
ALBERT: Oh.
SCOTT: I'm sorry, Albert. Uh, have a great party, though, and happy birthday.
ALBERT: Oh, thanks. And you have a great weekend, Scott.
SCOTT: Oh, thanks.
ALBERT: Well, bye.
SCOTT: See you around.

2. Fumiko
FUMIKO: Hello?
ALBERT: Fumiko? Hi, it's Albert. How are you?
FUMIKO: I'm fine. How are you?
ALBERT: Oh, I'm fine, too. Um, you know, Saturday is my birthday, and I was wondering if you'd like to come to my party.
FUMIKO: Oh. What time?
ALBERT: Say around 7:30?
FUMIKO: Oh, I'm sorry. I think I may already have plans . . . to go to the movies with my friends.
ALBERT: Oh, OK, Fumiko. I . . . I hope you have a good time.
FUMIKO: Thank you. And I hope your party's fun.
ALBERT: Yeah, well, I hope so, too. Uh, see you in class on Monday?
FUMIKO: Sure! Bye-bye!
ALBERT: Bye!

3. Manuel
MANUEL: Hello?
ALBERT: Hello, Manuel?
MANUEL: Hi, Albert. Hey! How are you doing?
ALBERT: I'm pretty good.
MANUEL: What's up?
ALBERT: Well, my birthday is Saturday and I'm having a little party with some friends, and I thought maybe you'd like to come.
MANUEL: Saturday?
ALBERT: Yeah.
MANUEL: Oh, you know, listen, I already promised my mother I'd take her to the new dance club downtown. She loves to dance, and she's really looking forward to it.
ALBERT: Oh, I didn't know your mom liked to dance, Manuel.
MANUEL: Oh, yeah, she loves it! And, well, Mom . . .
ALBERT: It's OK, Manuel. Don't worry about it.
MANUEL: I'm really sorry. OK, well –
ALBERT: See you soon.
MANUEL: Take care, Albert.
ALBERT: OK, bye, Manuel.
MANUEL: Bye.

4. Regina
REGINA: Hello?
ALBERT: Hello? Regina? This is Albert.
REGINA: Oh, hi, Albert. [*coughs*]
ALBERT: What's wrong?
REGINA: I . . . I've got the flu.
ALBERT: Oh, I'm sorry to hear that. I guess you won't be coming to my party on Saturday, huh?
REGINA: No, I guess not. I'm feeling pretty run-down.
ALBERT: Oh, I'm sorry. Well, hey, take care of yourself, Regina. I hope to see you next week.
REGINA: Yeah, me, too. [*coughs*] Bye.

B Listen. What happens on the night of Albert's birthday?

ALBERT: Happy birthday to me, happy birthday to me, happy birthday to me –

SCOTT, FUMIKO, MANUEL, REGINA: Surprise! Surprise! Happy birthday!

ALBERT: Oh, wow! Oh, no! Oh, my goodness! Scott, Fumiko . . . Wow, what a terrific surprise! Manuel, Regina! Well, you really fooled me! I can't believe it! Amanda, did you set this up? Gee!

11 *WRITING* *[p. 110]*

A Dan is out of town for the weekend. Listen to four voice mails he received. His roommate has written down the first message. Write down the three other messages.

DAN: Hi. This is Dan. Please leave your name, number, and a short message, and I'll call you back. Thanks! [*beep*]
BILL: Hi, Dan. This is Bill. It's about 9:00 on Friday evening. About our dinner plans: I'll meet you in front of Pizza House at 6:30 P.M. on Monday. OK? Bye! [*beep*]
MARIE: Hi, this is Marie. It's around 11:00 on Saturday morning. I'm just calling to let you know there's a French club meeting on Tuesday afternoon at two. See you then! Bye-bye! [*beep*]
PAULINE: Hello, Dan! This is your Aunt Pauline! I'm arriving on Wednesday, May 5th, late. I'll need you to pick me up at the airport at 11:30. By the way, I'm going to stay with you for three weeks. I hope that's all right. Good-bye, dear. [*beep*]
CARLA: Hi, Dan. This is Carla. Remember we planned to have dinner together on Monday? I'll meet you at 7:00 in front of the Seafood Grill on Water Street. OK? Hope your weekend was great! See you Monday! [*beep*]

Units 15–16 Progress check

3 *LISTENING* *[p. 113]*

A Listen to the conversations. Who would make these requests? Match conversations 1 to 6 to the correct person.

1.
WOMAN: Please pick up your things.
GIRL: In a minute. I'm on the phone.

2.
MAN: Excuse me. Can you move your car? You're blocking my driveway.
WOMAN: Oh, sure. I'm sorry, I didn't realize.

3.
WOMAN: How many of these should I take?
MAN: Don't take more than three a day.

4.
WOMAN: I missed English yesterday. Can I borrow your notes?
MAN: No problem. They're right here in my bag.

5.
MAN 1: Jake. Please come into my office.
MAN 2: Yes, sir. I'll be right in.

6.
GIRL: Can we leave now?
MAN: Please don't go until the bell rings.

B Listen again. Complete the requests.

Workbook answer key

1 A time to remember

Exercise 1

A

Verb	*Past tense*	*Verb*	*Past tense*
be	*was / were*	laugh	laughed
lose	lost	become	became
scream	screamed	move	moved
get	got	open	opened
write	wrote	have	had
hide	hid	do	did

B

My best friend in school *was* Miguel. He and I were in Mrs. Gilbert's third grade class, and we became friends then. We often did crazy things in class, but I don't think Mrs. Gilbert ever really got mad at us. For example, Miguel had a rat named Curly. Sometimes he hid it in Mrs. Gilbert's desk. Later, when she opened the drawer, she always screamed loudly and the class laughed. After two years, Miguel's family moved to another town. We wrote letters to each other for a few years, but then we lost contact. I often wonder what he's doing now.

Exercise 2

MARY: Are you from around here?
SÍLVIO: No, I'm from Brazil.
MARY: Oh, really? *Were you born* in Brazil?
SÍLVIO: No, I wasn't born there, actually. I'm originally from Portugal.
MARY: That's interesting. So, when did you move to Brazil?
SÍLVIO: I moved to Brazil when I was in elementary school. My parents immigrated there.
MARY: Did you grow up in Brazil?
SÍLVIO: Yes, I grew up in Brazil.
MARY: Where did you live?
SÍLVIO: We lived in Recife. It's a beautiful city in northeast Brazil. Then I went to college.
MARY: Did you go to school in Recife?
SÍLVIO: No, I went to school in São Paolo.
MARY: And when did you come to the United States?
SÍLVIO: I came here last week. I'm Sílvio Mendes. It's nice to meet you.
MARY: Nice to meet you, too. I'm Mary Burns.

Exercise 3

Answers will vary.

Exercise 4

A

Answers will vary.

C

1. False: She was born in Queens, New York.
2. False: She has a degree in Asian languages and cultures.
3. False: She played a waitress on *Beverly Hills 90210*.
4. True
5. True
6. False: She still has a lot of hobbies these days.

Exercise 5

2. My favorite pet was a cat called Felix.
3. We used to go to camp during summer vacations. It was really fun.
4. Our neighbors had a great tree house in their backyard. We used to sleep in it.

Exercise 6

Answers will vary. Possible answers:

2. They also used to go bicycling. Their dog Bruno always used to follow them.
3. And every year they used to play at the beach.
4. During the winter, Peter used to play the violin.
5. Kate and Peter both used to read.

Exercise 7

2. A: Did you use to collect shells?
   B: No, we didn't collect shells. We used to build sand castles.
3. A: Did you use to go swimming?
   B: Yes, we did. We used to go swimming for hours. Then we played all kinds of sports.
4. A: Really? What kinds of sports did you use to play? *or* What sports did you use to play?
   B: Well, we used to play beach volleyball with some other kids.
5. A: Did you use to lose?
   B: No, we didn't. We used to win!

Exercise 8

Answers will vary.

Exercise 9

MARIA: I'm an immigrant here. I was born in Chile and grew up there. I came here in 2001. I wasn't very happy at first. Things were difficult for me. I didn't speak English, so I went to a community college and studied English there. My English got better and I found this job. What about you?

Exercise 10

2. A: Tell me a little about yourself.
   B: What do you want to know?
3. A: How old were you when you moved here?
   B: About 16.
4. A: Did you learn English here?
   B: No, I studied it in Morocco.
5. A: By the way, I'm Lisa.
   B: Glad to meet you.

2 Caught in the rush

Exercise 1

2. bus stop
3. bicycle lane
4. traffic jam
5. news stand
6. taxi stand

Exercise 2

A

2. dark streets: install modern street lights
3. no parking spaces: build a public parking garage
4. crime: hire more police officers
5. car accidents: install more traffic lights
6. traffic jams: build a subway system

B

2. There is too much crime.
   The city should hire more police officers.
3. There are too many dark streets.
   The city should install modern street lights.
4. There are too many traffic jams.
   The city should build a subway system.
5. There are too many car accidents.
   The city should install more traffic lights.
6. There aren't enough parking spaces.
   The city should build a public parking garage.

C

2. There should be less crime.
3. There should be fewer dark streets.
4. There should be fewer traffic jams.
5. There should be fewer car accidents.
6. There should be more parking spaces.

Exercise 3

A

2. business district
3. parking garages
4. air pollution
5. police officers
6. train system

B

Dear Editor,

Life in this city needs to be improved. For one thing, there are too many cars, and there is too much smog, especially during rush hour. The *air pollution* is terrible. This problem is particularly bad downtown in the business district. Too many people drive their cars to work.

So what should we do about it? I think there should be more police officers at busy intersections. They could stop traffic jams. We also need fewer parking garages downtown. The city spends too much money building them. It's so easy to park that too many people drive to work. On the other hand, the city doesn't spend enough on public transportation. There aren't enough subway lines, and the train system needs a lot of improvement.

C

Answers will vary.

Exercise 4

A

Answers will vary.

B

1. rickshaw
2. ferry
3. subway
4. cable car

C

Answers will vary.

Exercise 5

2. A: Can you tell me where the buses are?
   B: Yes, there's a bus station just outside this building.
3. A: Oh, no. I don't have enough money.
   B: There's a cash machine right there.
4. A: Do you know what time the last bus leaves for downtown?
   B: No, but I can check the schedule for you.
5. A: Could you tell me where the taxi stand is?
   B: Sure. Just follow that sign.

Exercise 6

GUEST: Could you *tell me where the gym is*?
CLERK: Sure, the gym is on the nineteenth floor.
GUEST: OK. And can you tell me where the coffee shop is?
CLERK: Yes, the coffee shop is next to the gift shop.
GUEST: The gift shop? Hmm. I need to buy something for my wife. Do you know when the gift shop closes?
CLERK: It closes at 6:00 P.M. I'm sorry, but you'll have to wait until tomorrow. It's already 6:15.
GUEST: OK. Oh, I'm expecting a fax to arrive for me. Could you call me when it arrives?
CLERK: Don't worry. I'll call you when it arrives.
GUEST: Thanks. Just one more thing. Do you know how often the airport bus leaves?
CLERK: The airport bus leaves every half hour. Anything else?
GUEST: No, I don't think so. Thanks.

Exercise 7

2. We need less traffic downtown.
3. Could you tell me where the subway station is?
4. There aren't enough parking garages.
5. Do you know how often the bus comes?
6. Can you tell me what time the last train leaves?

Exercise 8

Answers will vary.

3 Time for a change!

Exercise 1

A

2. cramped/spacious
3. dangerous/safe
4. big/small
5. bright/dark
6. modern/old
7. quiet/noisy
8. reasonable/expensive

B

2. The rooms are too dark.
3. The living room is too cramped for the family. *or* The living room is too small for the family.
4. The bathroom isn't modern enough.
5. The yard is too small for our pets.
6. The street isn't quiet enough for us.
7. The neighborhood isn't safe enough.
8. The kitchen is too inconvenient.

Exercise 2

2. There aren't enough bedrooms.
3. It's not modern enough.
4. There aren't enough parking spaces.
5. The neighborhood doesn't have enough street lights.
6. There aren't enough closets.
7. It's not private enough.
8. The living room isn't spacious enough.

Exercise 3

REALTOR: How did you like the house on Twelfth Street?
CLIENT: Well, it's *not as convenient as* the apartment on Main Street.
REALTOR: That's true, the house is less convenient.
CLIENT: But the house is not as cramped as the apartment.
REALTOR: Yes, the house is more spacious.
CLIENT: I think there are just as many closets as in the apartment.
REALTOR: You're right. The closet space is the same.
CLIENT: The wallpaper in the apartment is not as shabby as in the house.
REALTOR: I know, but you could change the wallpaper in the house.
CLIENT: Mmm, the rent on the apartment is almost as expensive as (*or* not as expensive as) the house, but the house is much bigger. Oh, I can't decide. Can you show me something else?

Exercise 4

A

Answers will vary.

B

Answers will vary. Possible answer:

I live in a nice neighborhood. It's quiet and the people are friendly. There's a large park with a lake and lots of trees nearby. However, there aren't enough shops or restaurants.

My apartment is comfortable and bright, but it's cramped. The rooms are too small, and there isn't enough closet space. However, it's pretty convenient. For example, I have my own washing machine.

Exercise 5

A

be	***change***	***have***	***move***
healthier	my appearance	more free time	somewhere else
happier	my job	no homework	to a new place

B

2. I wish I could change my appearance.
3. I wish I had no homework.
4. I wish I had more free time.
5. I wish I could change my job.
6. I wish I could move somewhere else. *or* I wish I could move to a new place.

Exercise 6

A

Answers will vary. Possible answers:

2. He wishes he went out more often.
3. He wishes he went to the movies more often.
4. He wishes he visited his friends more often.
5. He wishes his weekends weren't boring.
6. He wishes he didn't spend his time cleaning the house and watching TV.

B

Answers will vary.

Exercise 7

2. A: I wish I could retire.
   B: I know what you mean.
3. A: Where do you want to move?
   B: Somewhere else.
4. A: I wish I could find a bigger apartment.
   B: It's very nice, though.

Exercise 8

2. The neighborhood isn't dangerous. *or* The neighborhood isn't too dangerous.
3. My apartment isn't private enough.
4. Our house has just as many bedrooms as yours.
5. I wish I had more closet space. *or* I wish I had enough closet space.
6. We wish we could move somewhere else.
7. The apartment isn't big enough.
8. I wish housework were not difficult.

4 I've never heard of that!

Exercise 1

ISABEL: I went to Sunrise Beach last week. *Have you ever been* to Sunrise Beach, Andy?
ANDY: Yes, I have. It's beautiful. Did you go there on the weekend?
ISABEL: Yeah, I did. I went on Sunday. I got up at 4:00 A.M.
ANDY: Wow! I've never woken up that early!
ISABEL: Oh, it wasn't so bad. I got to the beach early to see the sun rise. Have you ever seen a sunrise, Andy?
ANDY: No, I haven't. I prefer sunsets to sunrises.
ISABEL: Really? Then I went swimming around 6:00, but there were some strange dark shadows in the water. Have you ever heard of sharks at Sunrise Beach?
ANDY: Yes, I have. I heard a news report about sharks last summer.
ISABEL: Gee! Maybe I had a lucky escape on Sunday morning! Why don't you come with me next time?
ANDY: Are you kidding?

Exercise 2

A

Answers will vary.

B and C

Answers will vary. Possible answers:

2. Have you ever eaten raw fish?	Yes, I have. I ate some yesterday. I really liked it.
3. Have you ever tried Indian food?	Yes, I have. I tried some in an Indian restaurant last month. It was great.
4. Have you ever traveled abroad?	Yes, I have. I went to Russia last summer. I loved it.
5. Have you ever ridden a motorcycle?	Yes, I have. I rode my brother's motorcycle. It was scary.

Exercise 3

A

Answers will vary.

C

	Problem	*What didn't work*	*What worked*
Luis	headaches, stomachaches	taking medicine, not eating sweets	not eating fish
Sharon	sore mouth	not drinking milk, not eating cheese	not eating tomatoes
Fred	not able to hold his tools	taking medicine	not eating bread or pasta

Exercise 4

A

4 After that, pour the eggs into a frying pan. Add the mushrooms and cook.
2 Then beat the eggs in a bowl.
1 First, slice the mushrooms.
3 Next, add salt and pepper to the egg mixture.
5 Finally, fold the omelet in half. And enjoy! Your omelet is ready!

B

Answers will vary. Possible answer:
How to cook: scrambled eggs.
First, mix two eggs in a cup. Then heat some butter in a frying pan. Next, pour the egg mixture into the pan. After that, cook slowly for about three minutes and stir the egg mixture once or twice with a spoon. Finally, pour the scrambled eggs onto a plate.

Exercise 5

SYLVIA: I *went* to a Thai restaurant last night.
JASON: Really? I've never eaten Thai food.
SYLVIA: Oh, you should try it. It's delicious!
JASON: What did you order?
SYLVIA: First, I had soup with green curry and rice. Then I tried Pad Thai. It's noodles, shrimp, and vegetables in a spicy sauce.
JASON: I've never tasted Pad Thai. Was it very hot?
SYLVIA: No. It was just spicy enough. And after that, I ate bananas in coconut milk for dessert.
JASON: Mmm! That sounds good.
SYLVIA: It was.

Exercise 6

2. I had a huge lunch, so I skipped dinner.
3. What ingredients do you need to cook crispy fried noodles?
4. First, fry the beef in oil and curry powder and then pour the coconut milk over the beef.
5. We need to leave the restaurant now. Could we have the check, please?

Exercise 7

1. A: Have you ever tried barbecued chicken? You marinate the meat in barbecue sauce for about an hour and then cook it on the grill.
   B: Mmm! That sounds good.
2. A: Here's a recipe called Baked Eggplant Delight. I usually bake eggplant for an hour, but this says you bake it for only five minutes!
   B: That sounds strange.
3. A: Look at this dish – frog's legs with bananas! I've never seen that on a menu before.
   B: Yuck! That sounds awful.

Exercise 8

				1 b	e	e	n						
		2 b		o									
	3 b	r	o	u	g	h	t						4 m
		o		g									a
		k		h			5 s		6 f		7 d	i	d
		e		8 t	o	o	k		o		r		e
	9 t		10 h				i		r		i		
	r		a				p		11 g	i	v	e	n
12 r	i	d	d	e	n		p		o		e		
	e						13 e	a	t	e	n		
	14 d	e	c	i	d	e	d						

5 Going places

Exercise 1

A

take	*rent*	*go*
long walks	a camper	camping
sailing lessons	a car	swimming
a vacation	a condominium	on vacation
catch up on	***do***	
my studying	lots of hiking	
my reading	some fishing	
my e-mail	something exciting	

B

Answers will vary.

C

Answers will vary.

Exercise 2

DAVE: So, Stella, do you have any vacation plans?
STELLA: Well, *I'm going to paint my apartment* because the walls are a really ugly color. What about you? Are you going to do anything special?
DAVE: I'm going to rent a car and take a long drive.
STELLA: Where are you going to go?
DAVE: I'm not sure. I'll probably visit my sister Joanne. I haven't seen her in a long time.
STELLA: That sounds nice. I like to visit my family, too.
DAVE: Yes, and maybe I'll go to the mountains for a few days. I haven't been hiking in months. How about you? Are you going to do anything else on your vacation?
STELLA: I'll probably catch up on my studying. I have a lot of work to do before school starts.
DAVE: That doesn't sound like much fun.
STELLA: Oh, I am planning to have some fun. I'm going to relax on the beach. I love to swim in the ocean!

Exercise 3

A

2. A: How are you going to get there?
   B: I'm going to drive.
3. A: Where are you going to stay?
   B: I'm going to stay in a condominium. My friend has one near the beach.
4. A: Are you going to travel with anyone?
   B: No, I'm going to travel by myself.

B

2. Maybe I'll take the train.
3. I'm not going to stay in a hotel.
4. I think I'll ask a friend.

Exercise 4

A

Answers will vary.

C

1. True
2. False: Iguaçú Falls is bigger than Niagara Falls.
3. True
4. False: Rio de Janeiro has parks and beaches. Buenos Aires and Iguaçú Falls have parks.

Exercise 5

2. You should never leave cash in your hotel room.
3. You need to take your credit card with you.
4. You have to pay an airport tax.
5. You should let your family know where they can contact you.
6. You'd better not go out alone late at night.
7. You must get a vaccination if you go to some countries.
8. You don't have to get a visa for many countries nowadays.

Exercise 6

A

2. a windbreaker
3. a first-aid kit
4. suitable clothes

B

Answers will vary. Possible answers:

2. They'd better take windbreakers.
3. They need to take a first-aid kit.
4. He ought to take suitable clothes.

Exercise 7

Answers will vary. Possible answers:

2. You must buy good quality camping equipment.
3. You need to take a credit card.
4. You don't have to take a lot of cash.
5. You'd better bring cooking equipment.
6. You should remember to bring insect spray.
7. You shouldn't forget your passport or identification.
8. You ought to buy maps and travel guides.
9. You shouldn't pack a lot of luggage.
10. You don't have to remember to bring a jacket.
11. You'd better not forget a first-aid kit.

Exercise 8

1. I'm not going to go on vacation alone.
2. I want to travel by myself.
3. You should travel with a friend.
4. You must take warm clothes.

Exercise 9

A

Answers will vary. Possible answer:
First, I'm going to arrive in Lisbon, Portugal, on July 6th. I'm going to check in at the Tivoli Hotel. Then maybe I'll go shopping. I'm going to spend three days in Lisbon sightseeing. Then I'm going to take a tour bus across the border to Seville in Spain. Maybe I'll visit the cathedral. I'm going to see some flamenco dancing in the evening. Next, I'm going to rent a car and drive to Malaga on the Costa del Sol. I think I'll visit the old city center and spend time on the beach. I'm going to fly to Madrid on July 19th. I'll probably visit some museums. I'm going to take a tour of the city and see the sights. Finally, I'm going to go home on July 22nd.

B

Answers will vary. Possible answers:

2. I have to pack enough clothes.
3. I should get a passport.
4. I ought to get a vaccination.
5. I must make hotel reservations.

6 OK. No problem!

Exercise 1

2. Please put the dishes away.
   OK, I'll put them away.
3. Hang up the towels.
   OK, I'll hang them up.
4. Turn off the lights, please.
   Sure, I'll turn them off.
5. Turn on the radio.
   Sure, I'll turn it on.

Exercise 2

A

1. clean *up*
2. hang up
3. let out
4. pick up
5. put on *or* put away
6. take off
7. take out
8. throw out *or* throw away
9. turn down
10. turn up *or* turn off

B

Answers will vary. Possible answers:

2. Hang up your pants. They're on the floor.
3. Take out the trash. It smells bad.
4. Turn up the radio, please. I can't hear it.
5. Pick up those books. They shouldn't be on the floor.

Exercise 3

2. Take out the trash.
3. Turn down the TV.
4. Pick up your things.
5. Put away your clothes.
6. Turn on the radio.

Exercise 4

A

2. Please put the groceries away. The milk is getting warm.
3. Take your shoes off. They're dirty.
4. Clean up the kitchen, please. It's a mess.
5. Turn down the music. It's too loud.

B

Answers will vary. Possible answers:

2. In a few minutes. I'm busy right now.
3. I'm not staying long.
4. I'm doing my homework right now.
5. I don't think it's too loud.

Exercise 5

A

Answers will vary.

C

1. Strategy: soft
2. Strategy: hard
3. Strategy: fair

D

Answers will vary.

Exercise 6

2. Would you mind taking this form to the office?
3. Could you please turn the CD player down?
4. Would you mind not leaving the door open?
5. Would you let me share your book?
6. Can you pass me that book, please?

Exercise 7

2. A: Would you mind helping me?
   B: Sorry, I can't right now.
3. A: By the way, you're sitting in my seat.
   B: Excuse me. I didn't realize.
4. A: Would you like to come in?
   B: All right. Thanks.
5. A: Would you mind not taking all the coffee?
   B: I'm sorry, I'll make some more.
6. A: Can you turn the radio up?
   B: No problem.

Exercise 8

Answers will vary. Possible answers:

2. STEVEN: You're late! I've been waiting for you for half an hour!
   KATIE: I'm sorry. My watch stopped.
3. ROOMMATE 1: Could you turn the television down? I'm trying to study and the noise is bothering me.
   ROOMMATE 2: I'm sorry. I'll watch television later.
4. FATHER: You didn't mail the letters this morning.
   SON: Oh, sorry. I was in a hurry, and I forgot.
5. CUSTOMER: I brought this laptop in for repair last week, but it's still not working right.
   SALESPERSON: Oh, I'm sorry. I'll fix it for free this time.
6. NEIGHBOR 1: Could you do something about your dog? It barks all night and keeps me awake.
   NEIGHBOR 2: I didn't realize. It won't happen again.
7. RESIDENT: Would you mind moving your car? You're parked in my parking space.
   VISITOR: I'll move it right now.
8. TEACHER: Please put away your papers. You left them on your desk yesterday.
   STUDENT: Oh, I'm sorry! I forgot about them.

Exercise 9

1. Throw those empty bottles away. Put them in the recycling bin.
2. Would you mind picking up some groceries? We need coffee, milk, and rice.
3. Turn the faucet off. Water costs money!
4. My neighbor made a promise. He said, "I'll be sure to stop my dog from barking."

Exercise 10

A

2. not criticize my friends
3. mail these letters
4. not talk so loud
5. put away the DVDs
6. take off your sunglasses
7. turn down the oven
8. clean up your bedroom

B

Answers will vary. Possible answers:

2. Would you mind not criticizing my friends?
3. Can you mail these letters?
4. Would you please not talk so loud?
5. Could you put away the DVDs?
6. Can you take off your sunglasses?
7. Would you mind turning down the oven?
8. Would you mind cleaning up your bedroom?

Exercise 11

Answers will vary. Possible answers:

2. My roommates are often noisy late at night. I wish they would be quiet.
3. My roommate Lucy always opens the window in winter. I wish she wouldn't open it.
4. My friend Joe is always asking me for money. I wish he would ask someone else.
5. My cousin Carol never returns my phone calls. I wish she would return my calls.

7 What's this for?

Exercise 1

2. A computer is used for writing reports.
3. A robot is used for doing boring jobs.
4. A satellite is used for transmitting radio and TV programs.
5. A cell phone is used for talking to friends.

Exercise 2

2 ✓ CD-ROM ✓ data
A CD-ROM is used to store data.
3. ✓ satellites ✓ weather
Satellites are used to study the weather.
4. ✓ criminals ✓ DNA fingerprinting
DNA fingerprinting is used to identify criminals.
5. ✓ the Web ✓ information
The Web is used to find information.

Exercise 3

2. CD-ROMs are used for storing information on many subjects.
3. Police use DNA fingerprinting to identify criminals.
4. Computers are used to access the Internet.
5. Satellites are used for transmitting radio programs.
6. Home computers are used to pay bills.

Exercise 4

2. People used to write letters, but nowadays they usually send e-mails instead.
3. A cell phone is used to make calls from almost anywhere.
4. I used to have an electric typewriter, but now I own a laptop.
5. We just bought a new CD player. We used to have a cassette player, but it was terrible!
6. Modems are used to access the Internet.

Exercise 5

A

Answers will vary.

C

1. A, B, E
2. C
3. A, C
4. B, E
5. C, D

Exercise 6

A

Doing business	***Having fun***
cell phone	*CD player*
computer	camcorder
World Wide Web	computer
DNA fingerprinting	video game
	Internet chat room
	World Wide Web
	digital camera
	cell phone

B

Answers will vary. Possible answers:

2. I use a camcorder to record family celebrations.
3. I use the World Wide Web for researching school papers.
4. I use a cell phone to call for help when my car breaks down.

Exercise 7

3 Next, put it in a suitable place. Try not to expose it to direct sunlight.
1 First of all, make sure to open the box carefully. Don't drop it. It's fragile.
4 After that, remember to attach the wires from the speakers to the main unit.
5 Finally, plug it into an electrical outlet. Turn it on and enjoy your music!
2 Then take the stereo out of the box. Don't forget to remove the plastic bags around the speakers.

Exercise 8

Answers will vary. Possible answers:

2. Remember to keep it away from water.
3. Don't forget to get gas.

Exercise 9

My brother just bought *a* laptop. It's really great. It has a color screen; it is easier on the eyes than a black-and-white screen. The computer has a battery, so he can use it for up to eight hours without electricity. It also has an internal modem. If he wants to send a fax, he can do it electronically. He can also connect to the Internet. My brother always goes to a mountain climbing chat room. In fact, he plans to bring his laptop on his next hiking trip to chat with friends. It's an incredibly small computer, so he takes it everywhere.

Exercise 10

2. It's very fragile.
3. Unplug it.
4. Don't spill anything on it. *or* Don't spill drinks on it.
5. Try not to drop the package.

Exercise 11

A: What a day! First, my microwave didn't work.
B: What happened?
A: *It burned my lunch.*
Then I tried to use my computer, but that didn't work either.
B: Why not?
A: It didn't connect to the Internet.
After that I tried to use the vacuum cleaner.
B: Let me guess. It didn't pick up the dirt.
A: Worse! It spread dirt around the room.
B: Did you have your robot help?
A: Well, I tried to get it to clean the outside windows. But it refused.
B: I don't blame it! You live on the 50th floor!

8 Let's celebrate!

Exercise 1

Two of the most important national *holidays* in the United States are Independence Day and Thanksgiving Day. Independence Day, the Fourth of July, marks the United States' declaration of independence from Britain. Most towns, big and small, celebrate the Fourth of July with parades and fireworks. Families celebrate with barbecues or picnics. Thanksgiving Day is celebrated on the fourth Thursday in November. It is a day when people give thanks for the harvest. Most families have a large dinner with roast turkey.

Exercise 2

1. I hate April 15th! In the United States, it's the day when people pay taxes. I always owe the government money.
2. I don't like September. It's the month when school starts. I always miss summer vacation.
3. June is my least favorite month. It's the month when students in the United States take exams. I never study enough.
4. I have never liked winter. It's a season when I feel sad and depressed. The cold weather always affects my mood.

Exercise 3

										1 f					
										l				2 d	
		3 w			4 c	e	r	e	m	o	n	y		a	
		i								w				n	
		n		5 w		6 h	a	r	v	e	s	7 t		c	
		t		e						r		u		i	
		e		d						8 s	p	r	i	n	g
9 p	a	r	a	d	e							k		g	
u				i			10 j			11 p		e			12 p
n		13 a	n	n	i	v	e	r	s	a	r	y			r
c				g			w			r					e
h			14 c				e			15 t	r	i	c	k	s
			a				l			y					e
			k				r								n
16 c	e	m	e	t	e	r	y								t
			s						17 s	e	a	s	o	n	s

Exercise 4

A

Answers will vary.

C

	People give gifts on:	*The religious holidays are:*	*I celebrate:*
Easter		✓	Answers
Secretaries' Day	✓		will
Earth Day			vary.
Mother's Day	✓		
Father's Day	✓		
Labor Day			
Hanukkah	✓	✓	
Christmas	✓	✓	

Exercise 5

Answers will vary.

Exercise 6

Newly married couples often leave on their honeymoon before the wedding reception ends. When they go on their honeymoon, most couples like to be alone. After they come back from their honeymoon, many newlyweds have to live with relatives. They can only live in their own place when they have enough money to pay for it.

Exercise 7

2. The wedding ceremony is often held in a church.
3. The wedding reception is often held in a restaurant or hotel.
4. The couple's friends and family often give them a gift or money.
5. After the wedding reception, the couple usually goes on their honeymoon.

Exercise 8

Answers will vary. Possible answer:

In my country, before a man and woman get married, they usually get engaged. Sometimes the man gives his fiancée an engagement ring. After they get engaged, the couple plan their wedding.

Most couples get married in a church. The bride's family and friends sit on one side of the church and the groom's family and friends sit on the other side.

After the wedding ceremony ends, everyone goes to the reception. It's a time when people make speeches about the couple and give them gifts. Then the couple leave for their honeymoon.

Exercise 9

2. New Year's Eve is a night when many people have parties.
3. Everyone exchanges presents on Christmas.
4. After they leave the reception, many couples change into everyday clothes.
5. The bride and groom usually leave the reception before the guests do.

Exercise 10

Answers will vary. Possible answers:

2. What happens at midnight?
3. Do you serve any special food or drink?
4. Are we going to sing and dance?
5. What clothes should I wear?
6. Are there going to be any fireworks?

9 Back to the future

Exercise 1

Answers will vary. Possible answer:

In many cities nowadays, food shopping takes very little time. In the past, people *used to go* to a different shop for each item. For example, you bought meat at a butcher's shop and fish at a fish market. A fruit market used to sell fruit and vegetables. For dry foods like rice or beans, you had to go to grocery stores. Today, you get all these things at a supermarket. Many supermarkets make a lot of money these days. But times are changing. Before long, people will drive in their cars to huge superstores to buy everything. And who knows? Soon, everyone is going to have a computer at home. People already use them to purchase everything from food to furniture, from legal advice to medical help.

Exercise 2

1. A: When did people travel by horse and carriage?
   B: About 100 years ago.
2. A: When might doctors find a cure for the flu?
   B: In the next 50 years.
3. A: When did the first man go to the moon?
   B: About 35 years ago.
4. A: When is everyone going to have a computer at home?
   B: Soon.

Exercise 3

Answers will vary. Possible answers:

2. In the past, people used to collect records. Nowadays, they collect CDs.
3. A few years ago, people used typewriters. Today, they use computers.
4. About a hundred years ago, women wore long dresses. These days, they wear short skirts.
5. Nowadays, apartment buildings often have 20 floors. Sometime in the future, they might have 200 floors.

Exercise 4

A

Answers will vary.

C

	Advantage	*Disadvantage*
wind power	clean, lots of it	no energy without wind
waterpower	no pollution	expensive
geothermal power	cheap	not possible in most places
solar power	clean	no energy without sunlight

Exercise 5

1. A: What if I get in shape this summer?
   B: You might be able to come rock climbing with me.
2. A: What will happen if I stop exercising?
   B: Well, you might gain weight.
3. A: What if I get a better job?
   B: You'll be able to buy some new clothes.
4. A: What will happen if I don't get a summer job?
   B: You'll probably have to find a roommate when school starts.

Exercise 6

A

feel	*get*	*lose*	*quit*
energetic	married	touch	dieting
relaxed	a cold	weight	exercising

B

Answers will vary. Possible answers:

2. If I feel relaxed, I might sleep better.
3. If I get married, I'll have to save money.
4. If I lose touch with Linda, I'll be very sad.
5. If I lose weight, I'll be very happy.
6. If I quit dieting, I'll probably gain weight.

Exercise 7

Answers will vary. Possible answers:

2. I'll feel healthier if I eat better food.
3. If I get more exercise, I might have more energy.
4. If I don't get good grades in school, I won't be able to get a good job.
5. I might get more sleep if I go to bed earlier.
6. I'll be happy if I graduate this summer.

Exercise 8

A

Noun	*Adjective*	*Noun*	*Adjective*
energy	energetic	medicine	medical
environment	environmental	success	successful
health	healthy		

B

2. There are a lot of environmental problems in my country. There's too much air pollution and the rivers are dirty.
3. My health is not as good as it used to be. So I've decided to eat better food and go swimming every day.
4. My party was a great success. I think I might have another one soon!
5. If I start exercising more often, I might have more energy.

Exercise 9

2. In the future, few people will use cash to buy things.
3. People used to use bicycles more often than they do today. *or* In the past, people used to use bicycles more often than today.
4. If I get a better job, I'll be able to buy an apartment.
5. There's going to be a big new mall downtown.

Exercise 10

Answers will vary. Possible answer:

I used to live in a very quiet place. My parents' house was in a small village. There was only one store and very little traffic.

Now, I live in a big city. My job is pretty boring. I work in a small company. If my English improves, I may be able to get a job in an international company. I'd like to travel around the world.

Next year, I'm going to take a course in English. I might go on vacation in the United States and Canada. Then my English will be very good and I'll try and get a new job there.

10 I don't like working on weekends!

Exercise 1

1. A: I enjoy working in sales.
   B: So do I.
2. A: I like working night shifts.
   B: Gee, I don't.
3. A: I can't stand getting to work late.
   B: Neither can I.
4. A: I'm interested in using my language skills.
   B: So am I.

Exercise 2

2. Ichiro is a novelist, but he hates using a computer.
3. Gwen usually works alone all day, but she enjoys working with a team, too.
4. Ellen works for a large company, but she's interested in starting her own business.
5. Carlos has to use Portuguese and Japanese at work, but he's not very good at learning languages.
6. Cindy has to drive to work every day, but she doesn't like commuting.

Exercise 3

2. I'm not good at making decisions quickly.
3. I can't stand making mistakes.
4. I enjoy working with a team.

Exercise 4

Answers will vary. Possible answers:

2. I can't stand working late on Fridays.
3. I don't mind starting work early in the morning.
4. I'm interested in jogging and hiking.
5. I'm not interested in staying home.
6. I'm good at cooking delicious food for lots of people.
7. I'm not very good at making new friends.

Exercise 5

1. Sam doesn't smile or laugh a lot. He often looks worried about things. He's a very serious person.
2. You can trust Rosa. If she says she's going to do something, she'll do it. She's very reliable.
3. Joe isn't good at remembering things. Last week he missed another important business meeting. He's so forgetful.

Exercise 6

A

Answers will vary.

B

1. journalist
2. stock broker
3. truck driver
4. flight attendant

C

Answers will vary.

Exercise 7

2. Anita could be a good carpenter because she likes doing things with her hands and enjoys working with wood. She couldn't be a factory worker because she doesn't enjoy working in the same place everyday and hates being in noisy places.
3. Maria would make a good model because she's really interested in meeting people and enjoys wearing different clothes every day. She would make a bad accountant because she isn't good at organizing her time and she can't stand computers.
4. Larry could be a salesperson because he's really good at selling things and loves helping people. He wouldn't make a good detective because he isn't good at solving problems.

Exercise 8

1. Jerry could never be *a* nurse or teacher because he is very bad-tempered and impatient with people. On the other hand, he's an efficient and reliable person. So he would make a good bookkeeper or accountant.
2. Christine would make a terrible lawyer or executive. She isn't good at making decisions. On the other hand, she'd make an excellent actress or artist because she's very creative and funny.

Exercise 9

A

2. friendly/unfriendly
3. hardworking/lazy
4. interesting/ boring
5. level-headed/moody
6. patient/impatient
7. quiet/outgoing
8. reliable/forgetful

B

1. Su Yin is an outgoing person. She really enjoys meeting new people.
2. I can't stand working with forgetful people. I like having reliable co-workers.
3. Becky is very moody. One day she's happy and the next day she's sad.
4. Philip is an interesting person. I'm never bored when I talk to him.

Exercise 10

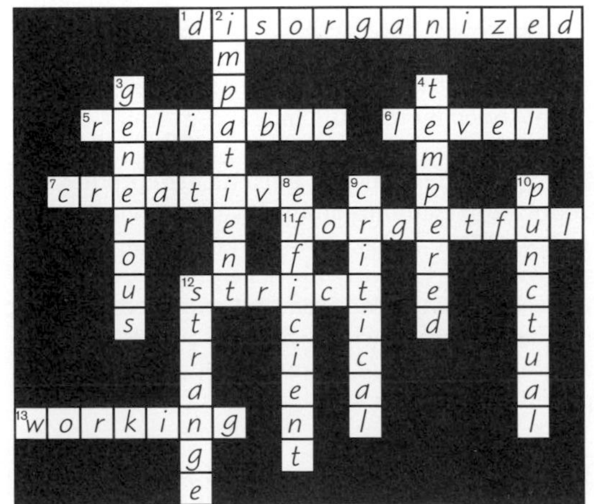

11 It's really worth seeing!

Exercise 1

2. The play *Romeo and Juliet* was written by William Shakespeare in the 1590s.
3. The telephone was invented by Alexander Graham Bell in 1876.
4. The picture *Sunflowers* was painted by Vincent van Gogh in 1888.
5. The antibiotic penicillin was discovered by Sir Alexander Fleming in 1929.
6. The music for the Disney movie *The Lion King* was composed by Sir Elton John in 1994.

Exercise 2

2. Many famous mysteries were written by Agatha Christie.
3. The first space satellite was launched by the Soviet Union in 1957.
4. The first human heart transplant was performed by Dr. Christiaan Barnard in 1967.
5. The Guggenheim Museum in New York City was designed by Frank Lloyd Wright.

Exercise 3

2. Big Ben was built by Sir Benjamin Hall in 1859.
3. The Eiffel Tower was designed by Gustave Eiffel in 1889.
4. Brasília was planned by Lucio Costa and Oscar Niemeyer in the late 1950s.
5. The Sydney Opera House was designed by Jorn Utzon in 1973.

Exercise 4

A

Rome, Italy
Mexico City, Mexico
Madrid, Spain
London, Great Britain
Manila, the Philippines
Ottawa, Canada

B

1. False: The name *Rome* may come from Ruma, the old name for the Tiber River.
2. True
3. True
4. False: The name *London* comes from Londinium, which may have been the name of a group of people.

Exercise 5

Ecuador *is* situated on the equator in the northwest of South America. It is made up of a coastal plain in the west and a tropical rain forest in the east. These two areas are separated by the Andes mountains in the center of the country.

The economy is based on oil and agricultural products. More oil is produced in Ecuador than any other South American country except Venezuela. Bananas, coffee, and cocoa are grown there. Many of these products are exported. Hardwood is also produced and exported.

Many people are of Incan origin. Several native languages are spoken there, for example, Quechua. Spanish is spoken in Ecuador, too.

Exercise 6

2. The peso is the currency that is used in Chile.
3. Millions of people visit Italy every year. Tourism is a very important industry there.
4. Gold mining is an important industry in South Africa.
5. Much of the world's wheat is grown in the Canadian prairies. It's used to make foods like bread and pasta.
6. A lot of meat, especially beef, is exported by Argentina.
7. The electronics industry was developed in many Asian countries in the 1980s. Now, a lot of computers and televisions are exported by countries like Korea.

Exercise 7

Answers will vary. Possible answer:

Every year, millions of tourists visit California. California *is known* for its beautiful scenery, warm climate, and excellent food. There are 20 national parks in California. They are visited by over 30 million people every year. Many world-famous museums are located there, including the Getty Center in Los Angeles and the San Francisco Museum of Modern Art.

The state is divided into two parts, called Northern California and Southern California. San Francisco and Yosemite National Park are located in Northern California. San Francisco is surrounded by water on three sides and is a city with a beautiful bay and several bridges. Its streets are always filled with tourists. On the north end of the bay is Napa Valley, where many excellent wines are produced. South of San Francisco, there is an area that is famous for its computer industries; it is called Silicon Valley. Many computer industries are located there. Los Angeles, Hollywood, and Disneyland are found in Southern California. Southern California is known for its desert areas, which are sometimes next to snowcapped mountains.

Exercise 8

1. The Experience Music Project in Seattle was designed by Frank Gehry.
2. The song *Mull of Kintyre* was written by Sir Paul McCartney.
3. German, French, and Italian are spoken in Switzerland.
4. Malaysia is governed by a prime minister.

Exercise 9

A

1. Who wrote *Beloved?*
2. What is grown in Thailand?
3. Where is Acapulco located?
4. When was Santiago, Chile, founded?

B

1. Do you know where the Golden Gate Bridge is located?
2. Can you tell me who *Don Quixote* was written by?
3. Do you know when antibiotics were first used?
4. Could you tell me who the tea bag was invented by?

Exercise 10

1804 The first steam locomotive *was built* in Britain.
1829 A speed record of 48 kph (35 mph) was established by a train in Britain.
1857 Steel rails were used for the first time in Britain.
1863 The world's first underground railway was opened in London.
1898 The first U.S. subway system was opened in Boston.
1964 "Bullet train" service was introduced in Japan.
1990 A speed of 512 kph (320 mph) was reached by the French high-speed train (called "TGV").
1995 Maglevs were tested in several countries. These trains use magnets to lift them above the ground.
1999 Two lines of Bangkok's "Skytrain" were completed.

12 It could happen to you!

Exercise 1

2. Mr. Yuen was cooking dinner.
3. The Hardings were watching television.
4. Andrew was sleeping.
5. Ann was reading the newspaper.
6. Jenny was using her computer.

Exercise 2

Answers will vary. Possible answers:
At 9:00 A.M., *I was with friends. We were having breakfast at a coffee shop before class.* At 11:00 in the morning, I was working. Around noon, I was having lunch. In the afternoon, I was taking English classes. About 10:00 last night, I was talking to a friend on the phone. At this time yesterday, I was doing my homework.

Exercise 3

CARL: How did you get your first job, Anita?
ANITA: Well, I *got* a summer job in a department store while I was studying at the university.
CARL: No, I mean your first *full-time* job.
ANITA: But that *is* how I got my first full-time job. I was working during the summer when the manager offered me a job after graduation.
CARL: Wow! That was lucky. Did you like the job?
ANITA: Well, I did at first, but then things changed. I was doing the same thing every day, but they didn't give me any new responsibilities. I was getting really bored when another company asked me to work for them.

Exercise 4

2. I met a really nice guy last week while I was jogging.
3. My car was giving me a lot of trouble, so I went to a mechanic.
4. Dinner arrived while I was talking on the phone.

Exercise 5

A

Answers will vary.

B

1. False: Richard Branson was born in England in 1950.
2. True
3. False: At 22, he had a record store and recording studio.
4. False: He owns Virgin Atlantic Airways.
5. False: He believes good employees make a business successful.

Exercise 6

A

2. Ruth and Peter have been going to graduate school since August.
3. Jim has been studying Chinese for a year.
4. Maria hasn't been teaching since she had a baby.
5. Cindy hasn't been living in Los Angeles for very long.
6. Felix and Anna have been traveling in South America for six weeks.

B

Answers will vary. Possible answers:

2. I've been studying architecture for 18 months.
3. I've been working here for a few weeks.
4. I've been playing chess since I was in high school.
5. I've been living in this city since 1996.
6. I haven't been swimming for ages.

Exercise 7

CHRIS: *What have you been doing lately?*
ALEX: I've been working a lot and trying to stay in shape.
CHRIS: Have you been jogging?
ALEX: No, I haven't been jogging. I've been playing tennis in the evenings with friends.
CHRIS: Really? Have you been winning?
ALEX: No, I've been losing most of the games. But it's fun. How about you? Have you been getting any exercise?
CHRIS: No, I haven't been getting any exercise. I've been working long hours every day.
ALEX: Have you been working on weekends?
CHRIS: Yes, I've even been working on weekends. I've been working Saturday mornings.
ALEX: Well, why don't we play a game of tennis on Saturday afternoon? It's great exercise!

Exercise 8

1. A: When I was a kid, I lived in New Zealand.
   B: Really? Tell me more.
2. A: I haven't been ice-skating for ages.
   B: Neither have I.
3. A: I was a teenager when I got my first job.
   B: Really? That's interesting.
4. A: I haven't seen you for a long time.
   B: Not since we graduated.

Exercise 9

2. A: Were you living in Europe before you moved here?
   B: No, I was living in Korea.
3. A: How long have you been studying English?
   B: I have been studying it for about a year.
4. A: What were you doing before you went back to school?
   B: I was selling real estate.
5. A: What have you been doing since I last saw you?
   B: I have been traveling around the country.

Exercise 10

2. He was a teenager when he started saving up for a world trip.
3. I was commuting to work when I lived in the suburbs.
4. I've had a part-time job for a year.
5. I haven't been saving enough money lately.
6. I haven't seen you for ages.

13 Good book, terrible movie!

Exercise 1

The President

Nathan Kane's movie *The President* is based on a true story about the life of a president. But don't watch this movie if you're interested in history. It isn't all true. However, Kane makes the film exciting, and the editing is outstanding. I was also amazed by the photography, which certainly deserves to win an Oscar.

The Patient

You will be surprised at how good *The Patient* is. It is one of the most fascinating films I've ever seen. It's a romantic story about four people during World War II. All the actors are fantastic. You won't be bored for one second. A must-see.

Exercise 2

2. I think the sequel to *Spider-Man* was just as good as the first movie. In fact, it was really terrific.
3. The animation was really great in *Finding Nemo.* I don't know how they made the fish do such fantastic things.
4. Uma Thurman is outstanding in *Kill Bill: Vol. 1.* I think she's a really great actress.

Exercise 3

2. A: His new movie is the dumbest movie I've ever seen.
   B: I didn't like it, either.
3. A: It's weird that they don't show more classic movies on TV. I really like them.
   B: I know. It's strange.
4. A: I think Sean Penn is a fabulous actor.
   B: Yeah, he's excellent.
5. A: The movie we saw last night was ridiculous.
   B: Well, I thought it was pretty good.

Exercise 4

Answers will vary.

Exercise 5

A

Answers will vary.

B

1 horror	2 musical
4 romance	3 science fiction

C

1. *The African Queen*
2. *The Wizard of Oz*
3. *Dr. Jekyll and Mr. Hyde*
4. *2001: A Space Odyssey*

Exercise 6

A

2. *A Beautiful Mind* is a movie which is based on a true story about a troubled genius.
3. Bill Murray is the actor who was nominated for his role in *Lost in Translation*.
4. Charlie Chaplin was an actor who was known for his roles in silent films.
5. *Crouching Tiger, Hidden Dragon* is a great movie which won a lot of awards.
6. Fred Astaire was an actor and dancer who made a lot of films about fifty years ago.

B

Answers will vary. Possible answers:

1. *The Phantom of the Opera* is a musical which has some terrific songs.
2. Denzel Washington is an actor who starred in *Glory* and *Training Day*.

Exercise 7

KAREN: Which one is Julia Roberts?

PEDRO: Oh, you know her. She's the one *who* starred in *Erin Brockovich*.

KAREN: Oh, I remember. That's one movie that was really interesting. We were glued to our seats.

PEDRO: Wasn't it based on the true story of a young mother who is working at a law firm?

KAREN: Right. Roberts plays a woman who discovers dangerous chemicals in the local water. Then she tries to defend the people who got sick.

PEDRO: What happens next? I've forgotten.

KAREN: Well, she decides to challenge the big company that polluted the water. She finally manages to win money for the residents who were affected.

PEDRO: I love movies that are about a real person.

KAREN: Especially when it's someone who fights the bad guy and wins!

Exercise 8

2. A romance is a movie that has a love story.
3. A comedy is a movie that makes you laugh.
4. A western is a movie that has cowboys in it.
5. A horror film is a movie that is scary.
6. A musical is a movie that has singing and dancing.
7. A nature film is a movie that tells you about animals or plants.

B

Answers will vary.

Exercise 9

1. I thought the special effects in *The Matrix* were terrific. They were very well made and exciting to watch.
2. I think the photography in *American Beauty* is marvelous. There are some scenes where very simple, everyday objects look strange and beautiful.
3. Nicole Kidman plays a main character in the movie *Cold Mountain*.
4. I've forgotten the name of the composer who wrote the music for the film *The Pianist*.

Exercise 10

Gangs of New York is a fascinating movie that (*or* which) was nominated for ten Academy awards. It's a drama that (*or* which) takes place in mid-nineteenth century New York City. It's the story of a gang of Irish immigrants who (*or* that) fight against a band of local anti-immigration citizens. The film tells the story of a young man who (*or* that) is seeking revenge against the powerful gang leader who killed his father. It's a fantastic movie that (*or* which) has something for everyone.

14 So that's what it means!

Exercise 1

A

B

Answers will vary. Possible answers:
2. It might mean he is angry.
3. It could mean they need help.
4. It must mean they need a taxi.
5. Perhaps it means she wants to turn.

Exercise 2

2. That sign is really <u>confusing</u>. What does it mean? It's not clear at all.
3. The food in that restaurant on the highway is <u>disgusting</u>. I'll never eat there again!
4. I drove for eight hours on a straight, flat road where the scenery never changed. I've never been so <u>bored</u>!
5. I couldn't get into the parking space and everyone was looking at me. It was pretty <u>embarrassing</u>.
6. I went bicycling all day. Now I'm so <u>exhausted</u> that I'm going to sleep for 12 hours!
7. I asked the taxi driver to turn off his radio because the loud music was very <u>annoying</u>.

Exercise 3

1. That sounds crazy!
2. Shh. Be quiet!
3. Come here.
4. Where's the bathroom?

Exercise 4

A

3	6
1	5
4	2

B

1. A: Oh, yuck. Those fried brains look disgusting.
   B: Try them. They're delicious.
   A: Really? Oh, they *are* good. I'm surprised!
   B: See. <u>The proof of the pudding is in the eating.</u>
2. A: Hey, what happened? You look so sad.
   B: I am. You know that guy I was dating. Well, last night he said he didn't want to see me anymore.
   A: Well, don't be too worried. You'll find someone else. <u>There are plenty of fish in the sea.</u>
   B: Thanks a lot. That really helps!
3. A: You know, the person who sits next to me in class gave me these flowers for my birthday. I'm amazed. I don't even know his name. What does that mean?
   B: <u>Don't look a gift horse in the mouth.</u> Just say thank you and don't worry.

C

Answers will vary. Possible answers:
1. It could mean <u>you shouldn't worry about past problems.</u>
2. Maybe it means you <u>should check something carefully before you decide if it is good or bad.</u>

Exercise 5

Answers will vary. Possible answers:
1. FATHER: Well, first you <u>*have to*</u> start the car.
   SON: Oh, yeah. I almost forgot.
2. FATHER: OK. Now remember, you <u>aren't allowed to</u> go above the speed limit.
   SON: I know.
3. SON: What does that sign mean?
   FATHER: That means you <u>can't</u> turn left.
   SON: OK.
4. FATHER: See that sign? It means you <u>can</u> turn left or you <u>are allowed to</u> go straight. Let's turn left, but be careful.
   SON: OK. This is great, Dad. It's easy.
5. FATHER: Hey, stop! Didn't you see that sign? It means you <u>must</u> come to a complete stop.
   SON: What sign? I don't see any sign.
   FATHER: Oh no! That's a problem!

Exercise 6

Answers may vary. Possible answers:
TONY: So, tell me what all these things mean, Tanya.
TANYA: Well, this one is the fan. <u>*You can use it*</u> to heat or cool your car.
TONY: And what about this one?
TANYA: That's your horn. You know, in the city, <u>you're not allowed to</u> use it after midnight.
TONY: OK. I'll try to remember that. And what does this one mean?
TANYA: I'm not sure. <u>It's probably</u> the hazard light. When your car breaks down, you turn it on.
TONY: What does this mean?
TANYA: Oh, that's your fuel light. <u>You have to</u> add gas when the light is on.
TONY: So, how do you like my new car?
TANYA: Like it? I love it! <u>You must</u> let me drive it.
TONY: Uh, I don't think so.

Exercise 7

1. It may mean you're not allowed to fish here.
2. You aren't allowed to light a fire here.
3. That sign might mean you're not allowed to swim here.
4. That sign probably means you can get food here.

Exercise 8

1. A: I fell asleep during class this afternoon. The teacher had to wake me up.
   B: Oh, that's <u>embarrassing!</u>
2. A: I went to the movies last night. The couple who sat behind me talked during the entire movie.
   B: That's <u>irritating!</u>
3. A: I drove all night to get there on time.
   B: Oh, that's <u>exhausting!</u>
4. A: I've met her, but I can't remember her name.
   B: That's <u>frustrating!</u>

Exercise 9

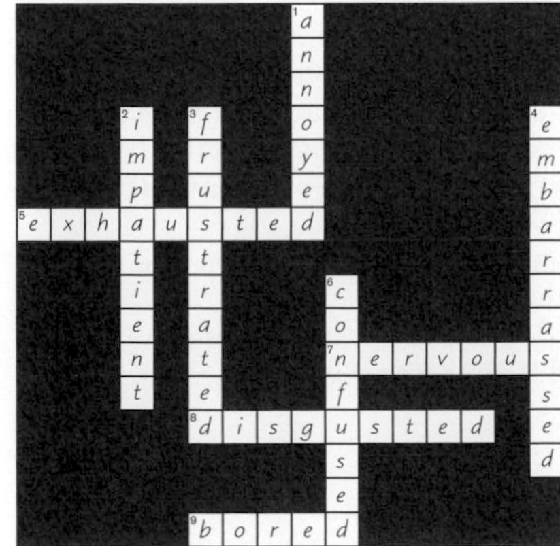

15 What would you do?

Exercise 1

A

Answers will vary.

B

Answers will vary. Possible answers.

2. If someone climbed through my neighbor's window, I think I'd call the police.
3. If my boss made things difficult for me at work, I guess I'd look for another job.
4. If a friend sounded unhappy on the phone, I'd invite him or her over.

Exercise 2

Answers will vary. Possible answers:

1. If a relative asked to borrow some money, I'd probably say no.
2. If I had three wishes, I wouldn't tell anyone about them.
3. If I could have any job I wanted, I'd be a movie star.
4. If I had a year of vacation time, I'd travel around the world.
5. If I could change one thing about myself, I'd be more patient.

Exercise 3

2. If I saw a friend cheating on an exam, I know exactly what I'd do. I'd go straight to the teacher.
3. I'm in a difficult predicament at work. I don't know whether to talk to my boss about it or just quit.
4. If I saw someone shoplifting in a store, I'd tell the store manager immediately.
5. I just won $20,000 in the lottery. I think I'll invest it.
6. I've just read a great novel. Would you like to borrow it?
7. I think Tom has financial problems, but he denies it. He says there's nothing wrong.
8. My aunt refused to lend me her car because she thinks I'm a terrible driver.

Exercise 4

A

Answers will vary.

B

6
3
5
4
2
1

C

Answers will vary.

Exercise 5

Answers will vary. Possible answers:

2. I wouldn't have asked her to speak more quietly. I would have moved to a different seat.
3. I wouldn't have told them to come back the next day. I would have suggested going to a restaurant.
4. I wouldn't have called the police. I would have asked them to turn their TV down.
5. I wouldn't have given her a bill for her room and board. I would have asked her to leave.
6. I wouldn't have decided not to say anything about it. I would have offered to buy a new vase.

Exercise 6

Answers will vary. Possible answers:

1. Last week I should have called my sister. I shouldn't have spent so much money.
2. Last month I should have studied harder. I shouldn't have been so lazy.
3. Last year I should have bought an apartment. I shouldn't have bought a new car.

Exercise 7

A

Dear Harriet,

I've never written to an advice columnist before, but I have a big problem. I'm going out with this really nice guy. He's very sweet to me, and I really want to *marry* him. In fact, we plan to have our wedding next summer. But he has a problem with money. He spends money like crazy! Sometimes he borrows money from me, but he never returns it. I want to save money because I want us to buy an apartment when we get married. However, if I tell him he has a problem with money, he denies it. He says, "I disagree with you. You worry too much. You just never want to go out and enjoy yourself." What can I do?

J. M., Seattle

Dear J. M.,

You and your boyfriend must *agree* on how you spend your money *before* you get married. If you both admit that there is a problem, you could probably find an answer. He should accept your idea of saving some money. And you shouldn't always refuse to go out and have fun. Don't forget that talking can really help. Good luck!

Harriet

B

Answers will vary.

Exercise 8

A

JUDY: Guess what, Tina! A university in New Zealand has offered me a scholarship.

TINA: Great! When are you going?

JUDY: That's just it. I may not go. What *would* you *do* if your boyfriend asked you not to go?

TINA: Well, I would invite him to come with me.

JUDY: I've tried that. He said he won't go. And he might break up with me.

TINA: That's ridiculous! If I were you, I would warn him not to try and control you. I was in a similar situation once, and I missed a big opportunity.

JUDY: Oh? What happened?

TINA: I was offered a job in Thailand, but my husband disliked the idea of moving, so we didn't go. I should have taken the job. I've always regretted my decision. In my situation, what would you have done?

JUDY: Oh, I would have accepted the offer.

TINA: Well, there's the answer to your predicament. Accept your scholarship!

B

Answers will vary.

Exercise 9

Answers will vary. Possible answers:

2. I wouldn't leave it where someone could see it.
3. I could never just leave it there.
4. I might try and sell it.
5. I might not tell any of my friends about it.

16 What's your excuse?

Exercise 1

Answers will vary. Possible answers:

2. Jenny asked James to type some letters.
3. Dave asked James to make copies of some disks.
4. Anita told James to file some documents.
5. Linda said not to forget to add paper to the copier.
6. Ricky told James to fax a report to New York.
7. Chuck told James to make coffee for him.
8. Katie said to make five copies of the agenda before the meeting.
9. Pete asked James to give him a ride home.
10. Olive said not to be late to work again.

Exercise 2

A

Noun	*Verb*	*Noun*	*Verb*
acceptance	accept	criticism	criticize
apology	apologize	excuse	excuse
complaint	complain	invitation	invite
compliment	compliment	sympathy	sympathize

B

2. I accepted an invitation to Terry and Anna's house for dinner.
3. I didn't want to go to Cindy's party, so I made up an excuse.
4. I was rude to my teacher. I must apologize to him.
5. My English teacher said my homework was excellent. I was really surprised by her compliment.
6. My parents criticize everything I do. I wish they weren't so negative.
7. I'm sorry you have the flu. I had it last week, so I really sympathize with you.
8. I received an invitation to Janet's party. I can't wait to go.

Exercise 3

2. Larry gave me an apology. He asked me to forgive him because he forgot about the party.
3. I couldn't go to the meeting, so I expressed my regrets.
4. Wendy told me she was graduating from college, so I offered her my congratulations.
5. Jill was very funny at the class party. As usual, she told lots of jokes.

Exercise 4

A

1. _b_ Thanks for your invitation. Unfortunately, I won't be able to make it. I have to work in the afternoon. I must say I'm really annoyed with my boss. She lives for her work and expects me to do the same. Anyway, enjoy yourselves!
2. _c_ I got your e-mail – thanks. I'd love to come, but I'll be out of town all weekend. I'm going hiking, too. I hope you have a great time and that the weather is good.
3. _a_ Thanks for your e-mail. I'm afraid I'm busy in the evening. It's my dad's 50th birthday, and I'm taking him and Mom out to dinner. But I might be able to come dancing later. Let's keep it open – OK?

B

_2_ be outdoors all weekend
_3_ go out on the weekend
_1_ work on the weekend

Exercise 5

A

2. Maria said her sister was having a baby.
3. Jim said he might have some houseguests on Saturday.
4. Keiko and Kenji said they were going camping this weekend.
5. Carlos said he was sorry, but he'd be busy on Saturday afternoon.

B

2. Tom and Nancy told her they'd be moving to their new apartment that day.
3. Franco told her he watched the football game on TV every Saturday.
4. Juliet told her she'd already made plans to do something else.

C

Answers will vary.

Exercise 6

A

2. a   3. e   4. b   5. d

B

2. William: "I'm sorry I'll be a little late to the party."
3. Robert: "I can't come for dinner on Friday. I have to work late."
4. Janice and Keith: "We're really sorry you have the flu. We hope you feel better soon."
5. Ben: "I'm going to ask Sarah to the party."

Exercise 7

1. A: We're going to go horseback riding. Do you want to join us?
   B: Sorry, I won't be able to.
2. A: I'm really sorry. We'll be out of town this weekend.
   B: No problem.
3. A: Meet us at 7:00. OK?
   B: Sounds like fun.
4. A: I'm sorry. I won't be able to make it.
   B: Well, never mind.

Exercise 8

A

	Accept	*Refuse*
2. Great.	✓	
3. Sounds like fun.	✓	
4. I've made other plans.		✓
5. I won't be able to make it.		✓
6. I'm busy.		✓
7. Thanks a lot.	✓	
8. I'd love to.	✓	

B

Answers will vary.

Appendix

Countries and nationalities

This is a partial list of countries, many of which are presented in this book.

Country	Nationality
Argentina	Argentine
Australia	Australian
Austria	Austrian
Bolivia	Bolivian
Brazil	Brazilian
Canada	Canadian
Chile	Chilean
China	Chinese
Colombia	Colombian
Costa Rica	Costa Rican
Czech Republic	Czech
Ecuador	Ecuadorian
Egypt	Egyptian
England	English
France	French
Germany	German
Greece	Greek
Hungary	Hungarian
India	Indian
Indonesia	Indonesian
Ireland	Irish
Italy	Italian
Japan	Japanese
Korea	Korean
Malaysia	Malaysian
Mexico	Mexican
Morocco	Moroccan
New Zealand	New Zealander
Paraguay	Paraguayan
Peru	Peruvian
the Philippines	Filipino
Portugal	Portuguese
Russia	Russian
Singapore	Singaporean
Spain	Spanish
Switzerland	Swiss
Thailand	Thai
Turkey	Turkish
the United Kingdom	British
the United States	American
Uruguay	Uruguayan
Vietnam	Vietnamese

Irregular verbs

Present	Past	Participle
(be) am/is, are	was, were	been
break	broke	broken
bring	brought	brought
build	built	built
buy	bought	bought
come	came	come
do	did	done
drink	drank	drunk
drive	drove	driven
eat	ate	eaten
fall	fell	fallen
feel	felt	felt
find	found	found
fly	flew	flown
forget	forgot	forgotten
give	gave	given
go	went	gone
grow	grew	grown
have	had	had
hear	heard	heard
keep	kept	kept
lose	lost	lost
meet	met	met
put	put	put
ride	rode	ridden
ring	rang	rung
run	ran	run
see	saw	seen
send	sent	sent
set	set	set
speak	spoke	spoken
stand	stood	stood
steal	stole	stolen
swim	swam	swum
take	took	taken
teach	taught	taught
tell	told	told
think	thought	thought
wear	wore	worn
write	wrote	written

Comparative and superlative adjectives

Adjectives with *-er* and *-est*

big
bright
busy
cheap
clean
dark
dingy
dirty
far
fast
heavy
huge
large
long
loud
messy
near
neat
new
nice
noisy
old
quiet
safe
shabby
short
slow
small
tall
young

Adjectives with *more* and *most*

average
beautiful
boring
comfortable
convenient
cramped
crowded
dangerous
delicious
difficult
exciting
expensive
famous
important
interesting
modern
patient
popular
private
serious
spacious
special
terrible
unusual

Irregular adjectives

good → better → best   bad → worse → the worst

Acknowledgments

Illustrations

Jessica Abel IA7
Rob De Bank 64, 75
Steve Cancel T-173
Tim Foley 43 (*top*)
Travis Foster 20, 39, 40, 48, 90, 97, IA3
Jeff Grunewald 48
Adam Hurwitz 24 (*bottom*), 37, 44, T-165, T-172
Randy Jones *v*, 2, 3, 16, 24 (*top*), 30, 31, 36 (*top*), 49, 62, 66, 67, 80, 81, 92 (*top*), 93 (*bottom*), 99, 100, 101, 106, 108, 109, IA1, IA6, IA14, IA15
Mark Kaufman 25
Scott Pollack IA9
Amy Saidens IA10
Dan Vasconcellos 15, 41, 68, 82, 110, 111, 112
Sam Whitehead 5, 6, 19, 33, 38, 43 (*bottom*), 47, 53, 54, 92 (*bottom*), 93 (*top*), IA4, IA13
Jeff Wong 9, 11, 22, 36 (*bottom*), 46, 58, 60, 79, 94, 102, 104, 107

Photo credits

2 (*left*) © Robert Daly/Getty Images; (*right*) © Peter Nicholson/Getty Images
5 © Ed Bock/Corbis
6 © Getty Images
7 © Reuters/Corbis
8 (*top row, left to right*) © Corbis; © Bob Rowan/Progressive Image/Corbis; (*bottom row, left to right*) © Paul A. Souders/Corbis; © Paul Harris/Getty Images; © age Fotostock
13 (*left to right*) Courtesy of Outrider; courtesy of PowerSki; courtesy of Trikke Inc.; courtesy of Wheelman Inc.
14 © SuperStock
17 (*left*) © Alamy; (*right*) © Jeremy Cockayne/Arcaid/Alamy
18 (*top*) © Roger Ressmeyer/Corbis; (*bottom*) Claudio Santini/Beateworks/Alamy
21 © Ghislain&Marie David de Lossy/Getty Images
22 (*left to right*) © Taesam Do/Getty Images; © Paulo Friedman/International Stock; © George Kerrigan; © Peter Johansky/Envision
23 © Bill Bachman/PhotoEdit
25 (*top*) © Corbis; (*middle row*) © George Kerrigan
26 (*top row, left to right*) © David Jeffrey/Getty Images; © Joel Glenn/Getty Images; © Ed Bock/Corbis; © Roy Morsch/Corbis; (*bottom*) © George Kerrigan
27 (*top*) © Alamy; (*bottom*) © Zefa/Masterfile
29 (*top*) © George Kerrigan; (*bottom*) © Shizuo Kimbayashi/AP/Wide World Photos
30 (*left to right*) © Ghislain&Marie David de Lossy/Getty Images; © Owen Franken/Corbis; © Joyce Choo/Corbis; © George Shelley/Corbis
34 (*top*) © Gavin Hellier/Jon Arnold Images/Alamy; (*bottom*) © age Fotostock
35 © Brad Wrobleski/Masterfile
38 © Getty Images
42 © Corbis
45 (*top*) © Pitchal Frederic/Corbis/Sygma; (*bottom*) © Roger Tulley/Getty Images
47 (*top to bottom*) © Michael Keller/Index Stock; © Jody Dole/Getty Images
48 (*left to right*) Courtesy of Rollerblade Inc.; courtesy of Yamaha Motor Corporation U.S.A.; courtesy of Long Island Savings Bank; courtesy of Sears Roebuck and Co.; courtesy of Kawasaki Motors Corp. U.S.A.
51 (*left to right*) © age Fotostock; © Jonathan Kirn/Getty Images; © Laurence Monneret/Getty Images
52 (*top*) © Ary Diesendruck/Getty Images; (*middle, left to right*) © Robert Frerck/Getty Images; © Martha Cooper/Viesti Associates; (*bottom*) © Henry Westheim
53 © Satoru Ohmori/Getty Images
55 (*top to bottom*) © Robert Frerck/Odyssey Productions/Chicago; courtesy of Korean Cultural Service; © AP/Wide World Photos
56 © Judith Collins/Alamy
57 © Paul Chesly/Getty Images
58 (*left to right*) © Austrian Archives/Corbis; © National Motor Museum/Motoring Picture Library/Alamy; © Ford Motor Co./AP/Wide World Photos
59 © Rick Gomez/Masterfile
63 © Ed Taylor Studio/Getty Images
65 © Gabe Palmer/Corbis
67 (*left to right*) © PBNJ Productions/Corbis; © George Shelley/Masterfile; © Larry Williams/Corbis
69 © Stewart Cohen/Getty Images
71 (*left to right*) © Syracuse Newspapers/Brian Phillips/The Image Works; © Tom Rosenthal/SuperStock; © Jeffrey Zaruba/Getty Images
72 © Peter Bennett/Ambient Images Inc./Alamy
73 (*left to right*) © Fotosearch; © George Kerrigan; © Amblin/Universal/The Kobal Collection; © George Kerrigan; © Robbie Jack/Corbis
74 (*left to right*) © Fergus O'Brien/Getty Images; © Dennis Hallinan/Getty Images; © Bob Higbee/Getty Images
76 (*top to bottom*) © Robert Frerck/Getty Images; © Sebastian Goll/Alamy; © Steve Raymer/Corbis
77 (*left to right*) © LifeinAsia.com; © Carl & Ann Purcell/Corbis; courtesy of the Stollwerk Museum
78 (*left to right*) © Neal Preston/Corbis; © Carlo Allegri/Getty Images; © Reuters/Corbis
80 © Juliet Coombe/Lonely Planet
83 (*left to right*) © ITAR-TASS/Yuri Belinsky/Newscom; © Mobile Press Register/Corbis; courtesy of Alexandra Nechita
84 © Warner Brothers/courtesy of Everett Collection
86 (*clockwise from top left*) © 20th Century Fox Film Corp./Everett Collection; © New Line/courtesy of Everett Collection; © Rufus F. Folkks/Corbis; © Columbia Pictures/courtesy of Everett Collection
87 © Damian Dovarganes/AP/Wide World Photos
89 © Universal/Marvel Entertainment/The Kobal Collection
90 © Fat Free Ltd./Miramax/The Kobal Collection/David Appleby
91 (*left to right*) © Reuters/Corbis; © George Kerrigan
105 © Ariel Skelly/Corbis
IA2 (*clockwise from top left*) © Corbis; © Tibor Bognar/Corbis; © age Fotostock; © James Marshall/Corbis
IA5A © Richard Price/Getty Images
IA5B © Liysa King/Getty Images
IA8 (*left to right*) © Corbis; © David Ball/Corbis; © Chuck Savage/Corbis
SS4 © George Kerrigan
SS11 © Getty Images
SS13 © George Kerrigan
T-201 courtesy of Segway